THE OXFORD HANDBOOK OF

COMPOUNDING

OXFORD HANDBOOKS IN LINGUISTICS

The Oxford Handbook of Comparative Syntax
Edited by Gugliemo Cinque and Richard S. Kayne
The Oxford Handbook of Cognitive Linguistics
Edited by Dirk Geeraerts
The Oxford Handbook of Applied Linguistics
Edited by Robert B. Kaplan
The Oxford Handbook of Computational Linguistics
Edited by Ruslan Mitkov
The Oxford Handbook of Linguistic Interfaces
Edited by Gillian Ramchand and Charles Reiss
[Published in Association with Oxford Studies in Theoretical Linguistics]
The Oxford Handbook of Case
Edited by Andrej Malchukov and Andrew Spencer

THE OXFORD HANDBOOK OF

COMPOUNDING

Edited by

ROCHELLE LIEBER

and

PAVOL ŠTEKAUER

OXFORD
UNIVERSITY PRESS

OXFORD

UNIVERSITY PRESS

Great Clarendon Street, Oxford OX2 6DP

Oxford University Press is a department of the University of Oxford.
It furthers the University's objective of excellence in research, scholarship,
and education by publishing worldwide in

Oxford New York

Auckland Cape Town Dar es Salaam Hong Kong Karachi
Kuala Lumpur Madrid Melbourne Mexico City Nairobi
New Delhi Shanghai Taipei Toronto

With offices in

Argentina Austria Brazil Chile Czech Republic France Greece
Guatemala Hungary Italy Japan Poland Portugal Singapore
South Korea Switzerland Thailand Turkey Ukraine Vietnam

Oxford is a registered trade mark of Oxford University Press
in the UK and in certain other countries

Published in the United States
by Oxford University Press Inc., New York

British Library Cataloguing in Publication Data

Data available

Library of Congress Cataloging in Publication Data

Data available

Typeset by SPI Publisher Services, Pondicherry, India
Printed in Great Britain
on acid-free paper by
CPI Antony Rowe, Chippenham, Wiltshire

ISBN 978–0–19–921987–2

1 3 5 7 9 10 8 6 4 2

Contents

PART I

PART II

Contributors

Mark C. Baker has been Professor of Linguistics and Cognitive Science at Rutgers, the State University of New Jersey, since 1998. He received his PhD from MIT in 1985, and also taught at McGill University in Montreal. He specializes in the morphology and syntax of less-studied languages, especially those of Africa and the Americas. He is the author of numerous articles and five books, including *The Polysynthesis Parameter* and *The Atoms of Language*.

Bianca Basciano is a PhD student in Linguistics at the University of Verona, Italy. Her main research interest lies in Chinese morphology, in particular compounding. She is involved in the Morbo/comp project based in Bologna and directed by Sergio Scalise. She co-authored with Antonella Ceccagno the article 'Compound headedness in Chinese: An analysis of neologisms', in *Morphology* (2007).

Laurie Bauer is Professor of Linguistics at Victoria University of Wellington, New Zealand. His PhD thesis, on compounds in English, Danish, and French, was published by Odense University Press in 1978, and since then he has written many works on morphology and word-formation including *English Word-formation* (Cambridge University Press, 1983), *Introducing Linguistic Morphology* (Edinburgh University Press, 1988, second edition 2003), and *Morphological Productivity* (Cambridge University Press, 2001). He is one of the editors of the new journal *Word Structure*.

Ruth Berman is Professor Emeritus, Linguistics Department, and Chair in Language across the Life Span of Tel Aviv University. Past president of the International Association for the Study of Child Language, she holds a BA in languages and literature from the University of Cape Town, an MA in linguistics and language teaching from Columbia University, and a PhD in Hebrew language and linguistics from Hebrew University, Jerusalem. Her research interests include Modern Hebrew, cross-linguistic study of language acquisition, later language development, and discourse analysis.

Antonietta Bisetto is Professor of Linguistics at the University of Bologna. She has worked on issues regarding Italian word formation (derivation and compounding) and the semantics–morphology interface on which she has published several articles.

Geert Booij is Professor of Linguistics at the University of Leiden, The Netherlands. He is the founder and one of the editors of the journal *Morphology* and its predecessor *Yearbook of Morphology*. His recent books are *The Morphology of Dutch* (2002) and *The Grammar of Words* (2005, 2007²), both published by Oxford University Press. He has published widely on the interaction of morphology and phonology, and more recently on morphology and Construction Grammar.

Hagit Borer is Professor of Linguistics at the University of Southern California. A syntactician, her research focuses on the interaction of the properties of words and the properties of phrases, taking into consideration results in syntax, morphology, semantics, and language acquisition.

Antonella Ceccagno is Associate Professor of Chinese Language and Chinese Sociology at the University of Bologna, Italy. In the linguistic field her research focuses on Chinese morphology, word formation and compounding in Chinese, gender in Chinese. She participates in the Morbo/Comp project. Her other fields of research are migration from China and the Chinese diaspora in Europe. She is a consultant to UN agencies on these issues.

Anna Maria Di Sciullo is the Principal Investigator of a major collaborative research initiative on Interface Asymmetries and the Cognitive System. Her work on asymmetry led her to be nominated Fellow of the Royal Society of Canada in 1999. She has published two MIT Press monographs on morphology. She has also published papers and edited books on configurations, UG and the external systems, projections and interface conditions, asymmetry in grammar, biolinguistic investigations, and the biolinguistic approach to language evolution and variation. Her work is supported in part by funding from the SSHRC to the MCRI on Interface Asymmetries and the Cognitive System, and by a grant from the FQRSC for research on Dynamic Interfaces at the University of Quebec at Montreal.

Jan Don is assistant professor at the University of Amsterdam. He graduated from Utrecht University in 1993 with a dissertation on conversion. Since then he has published on different aspects of the morphology of Dutch and the proper treatment of conversion in particular.

Carlos A. Fasola is currently a PhD student in Linguistics at Rutgers University. His research interests are in argument structure, phrase structure, the semantics of functional heads, and American Indian languages.

Bernard Fradin is a researcher at the *Laboratoire de Linguistique Formelle* (CNRS and University Paris 7 Diderot), Paris, France. His main current research interests centre on morphology and more specifically on the semantics of word-building morphology. Papers by him appeared in the proceedings of various international morphology meetings. He was in charge of the research group (GDR 2220)

'Description and modelisation in morphology' (2000–2007), which played a key role in the development of morphology in France in recent years. He published an essay *Nouvelles approches en morphologie* (Presses Universitaires de France, Paris) in 2003. He is the editor of *La raison morphologique* (John Benjamins) and co-editor of *Aperçu de morphologie du français* (Presses Universitaires de Vincennes, to appear), a book which offers new insights on several morphological and morpho-phonological phenomena of French.

Christina L. Gagné received her PhD in Cognitive Psychology at the University of Illinois at Urbana-Champaign in 1997 and is currently an Associate Professor at the University of Alberta, Canada. The aim of her research is to understand how conceptual knowledge affects the way people use and process language. In particular, her work focuses on the underlying conceptual structures that are involved in the interpretation of novel phrases and compounds. Her past work has shown that knowledge about the relations that are used to combine concepts plays an important role in the creation and comprehension of novel noun phrases as well as in the comprehension of compound words.

Heinz Giegerich is Professor of English Linguistics in the University of Edinburgh's School of Philosophy, Psychology and Language Sciences. His main research interests have been the phonology and the morphology of English; his contributions to linguistic theory fall mainly in the areas of Metrical Phonology, Lexical Phonology, and Morphology, and more generally the various interfaces of phonology, morphology, and syntax. He is the author of *Metrical Phonology and Phonological Structure* (Cambridge University Press, 1986), *English Phonology* (Cambridge University Press, 1992) and *Lexical Strata in English* (Cambridge University Press, 1999). He edits the *Edinburgh Textbooks on the English Language* and co-edits, with Laurie Bauer and Greg Stump, the international journal *Word Structure*.

Joachim Grzega, born 1971, studied English, French and German (specifically linguistics) at the universities of Eichstätt (Germany), Salt Lake City (USA), Paris–Sorbonne (France), and Graz (Austria). Since 1998 he has been teaching linguistics in Eichstätt, with interim professorships in Münster, Bayreuth, and Erfurt and Freiburg. His research fields are: historical lexicology and pragmatics, Eurolinguistics, intercultural communication, language teaching, academic teaching, linguistics and socio-economic issues. He is the editor-in-chief of *Onomasiology Online*.

Heidi Harley is Associate Professor of Linguistics at the University of Arizona. She has published on topics in lexical semantics, syntax, and morphology, often from the perspective of the Distributed Morphology framework. Languages on which she has worked include English, Japanese, Italian, Hiaki (Yaqui), Irish, and Icelandic.

Liesbet Heyvaert completed her PhD on English nominalizations at the University of Leuven (Belgium) in 2002. Since then she has been working as a postdoctoral researcher of the Fund for Scientific Research-Flanders (FWO). She has published mainly on nominalization (*-er, -ee, -ing*) and middle formation. She is the author of *A Cognitive-Functional Approach to Nominalization in English* (Mouton de Gruyter, 2003).

Ray Jackendoff is Seth Merrin Professor of Philosophy and Co-Director of the Center for Cognitive Studies at Tufts University. He is also a member of the External Faculty of the Santa Fe Institute. He is a past President of the Linguistic Society of America and was awarded the Jean Nicod Prize in Cognitive Philosophy in 2003. His most recent books are *Foundations of Language, Simpler Syntax* (with Peter Culicover), and *Language, Consciousness, Culture*.

Taro Kageyama is Professor of Linguistics at Kwansei Gakuin University, Japan. He received his PhD from the University of Southern California in 1977. His major books in Japanese include: *Lexical Structures* (1980; Ichikawa Award), *Grammar and Word Formation* (1993; Kindaichi Award), *Verb Semantics* (1996; Chinese translation, 2001). Edited books: *Verb Semantics and Syntactic Structure* (1997), *Voice and Grammatical Relations* (2006). Major articles in *Language, Lingua, Yearbook of Morphology, Journal of Japanese Linguistics, Japanese/Korean Linguistics, Gengo Kenkyu, English Linguistics*. He is editor of *Gengo Kenkyu* (Linguistic Society of Japan).

Dieter Kastovsky has been Professor of English Linguistics at the University of Vienna since 1981, and Director of the Department of Translation and Interpreting of the University of Vienna (1990–2006). His main research interests are English morphology and word-formation (synchronic and diachronic), semantics, history of linguistics, and language typology. His publications include *Studies in Morphology. Aspects of English and German verb inflection* (Tübingen, 1971), *Wortbildung und Semantik* (Tübingen/Düsseldorf, 1982), and more recently articles in *The Cambridge History of Linguistics* and *The Handbook of the History of English*.

Stanislav Kavka is Professor in Linguistics and the English Language at Ostrava University, Czech Republic, previously a guest lecturer at universities in Sweden, USA, and Germany, and presently working also at two English Departments in Poland and Slovakia. During his lifetime he has worked in the fields of phonology, ESP, comparative historical linguistics, and recently idiomatology. He is the author of a number of studies and textbooks and also of *Semantic Determinations Within the Noun Phrase of Modern English and Spanish* (Prague, 1980), *An Outline of Modern Czech Grammar* (Uppsala, Sweden, 1987), *A Book of Idiomatology* (Zilina, Slovakia, 2003).

Ferenc Kiefer holds a research professorship at the Research Institute for Linguistics, Hungarian Academy of Sciences. He was professor in general linguistics at

Budapest University until his retirement. Main fields of research: Hungarian and general linguistics, especially morphology, lexical semantics, and pragmatics. He has published more than two hundred articles and twenty books in English, Hungarian, French, and German. He was guest professor in Stockholm, Paris, Stuttgart, Vienna, Aarhus, and Antwerp.

Laura Malena Kornfeld teaches Spanish grammar and lexical theory at the University of Buenos Aires and the University of General Sarmiento, as well as different topics related to generative grammar in postgraduate programmes of other Argentinian universities; she is also assistant-researcher in the National Council of Scientific and Technical Research (CONICET). Her research interests include morphological and syntactic processes of word formation, inflection, grammaticalization, ellipsis, the relation between lexical and functional categories, as well as other phenomena that involve the syntax–morphology and syntax–lexicon interfaces, mainly in Spanish and its different varieties.

Rochelle Lieber is Professor of Linguistics at the University of New Hampshire. Her interests include morphological theory, especially concerning derivation and compounding, lexical semantics, and the morphology–syntax interface. She is the author of four books: *On the Organization of the Lexicon* (IULC, 1981), *An Integrated Theory of Autosegmental Processes* (State University of New York Press, 1987), *Deconstructing Morphology* (University of Chicago Press, 1992), and *Morphology and Lexical Semantics* (Cambridge University Press, 2004), as well as numerous articles and book chapters on all aspects of morphology. She is co-editor, with Pavol Štekauer, of *The Handbook of Word Formation* (Springer, 2005), and co-Editor-in-Chief of Wiley-Blackwell's *Language and Linguistics Compass*.

Marianne Mithun is Professor of Linguistics at the University of California, Santa Barbara. Her interests include morphology, syntax, discourse, intonation, and their interaction; processes of language change, particularly the development of grammatical systems; language contact; typology; relations between language and culture; and language documentation. She has worked with speakers of a variety of languages and their communities, among them Mohawk, Cayuga, Tuscarora, Oneida, Onondaga, Seneca, and Huron (Iroquoian); Central Pomo (Pomoan); Central Alaskan Yup'ik (Eskimo-Aleut); Navajo (Athabaskan); Cree (Algonquian); Lakhota, Dakota, and Tutelo (Siouan), Barbareño Chumash; and Kapampangan, Selayarese, and Waray (Austronesian).

Martin Neef is Professor of German linguistics at the University of Braunschweig (Germany). He has published in the fields of morphology, phonology, and written language, mostly on German. His major publications are *Wortdesign: Eine deklarative Analyse der deutschen Verbflexion* (Stauffenburg, 1996), *Die Graphematik des Deutschen* (Niemeyer, 2005), and *Eigennamen*: Special issue of *Zeitschrift für Sprachwissenschaft* (co-edited with Peter Gallmann, 2005). Currently, he is preparing a terminological dictionary on written language research (together with Rüdiger Weingarten).

Angela Ralli is Professor of General Linguistics and Chair of the Department of Philology at the University of Patras (Greece). She has studied Linguistics at the University of Montreal (BA, MA, PhD), speaks fluently four languages (Greek, English, French, and Italian), and is interested in morphology and dialectal morphological variation. She has several publications on morphology (compounding, derivation, and inflection), and is a permanent member on the scientific board of the *European Network for Linguistic Morphology*, and the *Mediterranean Morphology Meeting*.

Keren Rice is Professor and Canada Research Chair in Linguistics and Aboriginal Studies at the University of Toronto. In spring 2008 she was Cornell Visiting Professor at Swarthmore College. She has been involved in research on Athapaskan languages for many years, and is author of *A Grammar of Slave*, which won the Bloomfield Award from the Linguistic Society of America. She was the Director of Aboriginal Studies at the University of Toronto for many years, and serves as Director of the new Centre for Aboriginal Initiatives at the University of Toronto. She has published on Athapaskan languages and in phonological theory.

Sergio Scalise teaches General Linguistics at the University of Bologna. His main interest today is morphology and he has contributed to the development of the so-called 'Lexical Morphology' with several papers and books. He is the director of 'Lingue e Linguaggio', consulting editor of several international journals (such as *Morphology, Probus*), co-organizer of the Mediterranean Morphology Meetings. He is director of several national and international projects all related to morphology and linguistic theory. Among his books are *Generative Morphology* (Dordrecht: Foris, 1984), *Morfologia Lessicale* (Padua: Clesp, 1983), *Morfologia* (Bologna: il Mulino, 1994), and *Le lingue e il linguaggio* (Bologna: il Mulino, 2003, with G. Graffi).

Jane Simpson teaches linguistics at the University of Sydney. She studies Indigenous Australian languages (including Warlpiri, Warumungu, and Kaurna) and Australian English varieties, and has been involved in language maintenance and revitalization, language documentation, and digital archiving projects. She carries out research in morphosyntax, lexical semantics, and lexicography. She is currently involved in projects on child language acquisition in Aboriginal communities, and on a computational grammar of Indonesian in the Lexical-Functional Grammar framework.

Pavol Štekauer is Professor of English linguistics in the Department of British and US Studies, Šafárik University, Košice, Slovakia. His main research area has been an onomasiological approach to word-formation and word-interpretation. He also examines the typology and universals in word-formation. He is the author of *A Theory of Conversion in English* (Frankfurt am Main: Peter Lang, 1996), *An Onomasiological Theory of English Word-Formation* (Amsterdam/Philadelphia: John Benjamins, 1998), *English Word-Formation. A History of Research (1960–1995)* (Tübingen: Gunter Narr, 2000), and *Meaning Predictability in Word-Formation* (Amsterdam/Philadelphia: John Benjamins, 2005).

Bogdan Szymanek is Professor of English Linguistics, Head of the Department of Modern English, the John Paul II Catholic University of Lublin, Poland. His major research interests include morphology and its interfaces with other grammatical components, lexicology, English, and Slavic languages. He is the author of *Categories and Categorization in Morphology* (1988) and *Introduction to Morphological Analysis* (3rd edn., 1998).

Pius ten Hacken is senior lecturer at Swansea University. He is the author of *Defining Morphology* (Hildesheim: Olms, 1994) and a number of articles in the domains of theoretical and computational morphology. He is also the author of *Chomskyan Linguistics and its Competitors* (London: Equinox, 2007) and the editor of *Terminology, Computing and Translation* (Tübingen: Narr, 2006).

Raoul Zamponi is a contract professor of Anthropological Linguistics at the University of Siena (Italy). He has worked on little-known, extinct Amerindian languages and has written grammatical descriptions of Maipure (Arawakan) and of the isolates Betoi (Venezuela) and Waikuri (Mexico), in addition to other papers on the first two languages and Lule (Argentina). His work in progress includes, *inter alia*, a grammar of Fang (Bantu) and a complete documentation of Máku, a recently extinct Amazonian isolate.

ABBREVIATIONS

1	First Person
2	Second Person
3	Third Person
#P	Number Phrase
A	Adjective / Argument
AC	Appropriately Classificatory
ACC	Accusative
Adj	Adjective
ADJ	Adjectivizer
Adv	Adverb
AFF	Affect
AGEN	Agentive
Agr	Agreement
AGT	Grammatical Agent
AL	Alienable Possessor
ALL	Allative
AmE	American English
AmSp	American Spanish
AN	Adjectival Noun
AND	Andative
AP	Adjective Phrase
APPL	Applicative
AT	Asymmetry Theory
ATT	Attributive compound type
ATTR	Attributive
AUX	Auxiliary
B	Bounded
BEN	Benefactive
BPS	Bare Phrase Structure
BS	Bisetto–Scalise
BV	Basic Variety
C	Consonant
C³	Constraints on Conceptual Combination
CARIN	Competition Among Relations in Nominals

CAUS	Causative
Ch	Chinese
CI	Composed of Individuals / Conceptual-Intentional
CIS	Cislocative
CL	Classifier
ClP	Classifier Phrase
COLL	Collective
COM	Common Gender
COMP	Composed of
Compl	Complement
COORD	Coordinative
CRD	Coordinate compound type
CSC	Coordinate Structure Constraint
Cz	Czech
DAT	Dative
DEF	Definite
Det	Determiner
DET_{DEF}	Definite Determiner
DIM	Diminutive
DM	Distributed Morphology
D_M	Morphological workspace
DP	Determiner Phrase
D_S	Syntactic workspace
Du	Dutch
DU	Dual
DUP	Duplicative
D_Σ	Semantics workspace
D_Φ	Phonology workspace
E-Asp	External Aspect
EB	*Ekstra Bladet*
EMPH	Emphasis
En	English
ERG	Ergative
ERP	Evoked Response Potential
EUPH	Euphony (discourse marker)
EX	Exclusive
F	Function
FAC	Factual
FEM	Feminine
FI	Full Interpretation
FLB	Broad Language Faculty
FLN	Narrow Language Faculty

Fr	French
FS	Peter Høeg, *Frøken Smillas fornemmelse for sne*
FUT	Future / Irrealis
G	German
GB	Government-Binding
GEN	Genitive
Gk	Greek
Got	Gothic
H	Hungarian
HAB	Habitual Aspect
HPSG	Head-Driven Phrase Structure Grammar
i	Index
I	Instrument
I-Asp	Internal Aspect
IE	Indo-European
IEPS	Inferable Eventual Position or State
IG	Indo-Germanic
IMP	Imperative
IMPED	Impeditive
IMPF	Imperfective
INAL	Inalienable Possessor
IND	Indicative
INDEF	Indefinite
INF	Infinitive / Nominalizer
INFL	Inflection
INST	Instrumental
intr	Intransitive
INV	Inverse
IP	Inflection Phrase
It	Italian
Ja	Japanese
JR	Stem Joiner
L2	Second language
Lat	Latin
LCS	Lexical Conceptual Structure
LE	Linking element
LF	Logical Form
LOC	Local relation
LOC	Locative
LV	Linking vowel
MASC	Masculine gender
ME	Middle English

MEG	Magnetoencephalography
MG	Modern Greek
MHG	Middle High German
MID	Middle
MO	Morphological Object
ModE	Modern English
ModG	Modern German
MORBO	Morphology at Bologna Research Group
MSAP	Morpheme-to-Seme-Assignment Principle
N	Noun
NEG	Negative
NEUT	Neuter
NF	Non-Feminine
NOM	Nominative
NOM.PAST	Nominal Past
NOML	Nominalizer
NONPST	Non-past
NP	Noun Phrase
NPOSS	Non-possessed
NSUFF	Noun.suffix
Num	Numeral
O	Object / General Complement
OBJ	Object
OBL	Oblique
obs	Obsolete
OCC	Occupation
OE	Old English
OHG	Old High German
Op-domain	Operator domain
OPR	Objectified Predictability Rate
OPT	Optative
OS	Old Saxon
OSR	Onomasiological Structure Rules
OT	Onomasiological Type
P	Preposition
PAT	Grammatical Patient
PEJ	Pejorative
PF	Phonological Representation / Proper Function
Pg	Portuguese
PG	Proto-Germanic
PIE	Proto-Indo-European
PL	Astrid Lindgren, *Pippi Langstrømpe*

PL	Plural
PNS	Possessive Noun Suffix
Pol	Polish
POSS	Possessed / Possessive
PP	Prepositional Phrase
PR	Predictability Rate
Pred	Predicate
PRES	Present Tense
PRF	Perfective Aspect
PRG	Predictability Rate Gap
PRIV	Privative
Pro	Pronoun
PROG	Progressive
PROH	Prohibitive
PRON	Pronoun
PRSPT	Present Participle
PRT	Particle
PRTV	Partitive
PST	Past Tense
PSTPT	Past Participle
PTPL	Participle
PURP	Purposive
PV	Preverb
Q	Interrogative
Qu	Quantifier
RDP	Recoverably Deletable Predicate
RED	Reduplication
REFL	Reflexive
REL	Relative
REP	Repetitive
RES	Result
RHR	Right-hand Head Rule
Ru	Russian
S	Sentence
SBJ	Subject
SG	Singular
SHEL	Studies in the History of the English Language (Conference)
S-J	Sino-Japanese
Skr	Sanskrit
SLE	Societas Linguistica Europea
Slov	Slovak
SM	Sensorimotor system

Sp	Spanish
STA	Stative
SUB	Subordinate compound type
SUFF	Suffix
SVO	Subject Verb Object
sW	Semi-words
Temp	Temporal
TLOC	Translocative
TOP	Topic
tr	Transitive
UG	Universal Grammar
V	Verb / Vowel
VBLZ	Verbalizer
Ved	Vedic
VI	Vocabulary Item
VN	Verbal Noun
VP	Verb Phrase
W$^+$	Word Plus
WF	Word Formation
XP	Maximal phrase for arbitrary category
ZO	Zoic

PART I

PART 1

CHAPTER 1

....

INTRODUCTION: STATUS AND DEFINITION OF COMPOUNDING

....

ROCHELLE LIEBER AND
PAVOL ŠTEKAUER

MOST of us are familiar with the parable of the blind men and the elephant. Each of the men developed a theory of 'elephanthood' on the basis of a limited perception: one fellow's elephant was like a rope, another's like a broad leaf, a third's like a tree trunk, and so on. We conceived of this volume in the fear that our current picture of 'compoundhood' might be like the blind men's elephant, and in the hope that by putting together the disparate pieces of what we know, something like the whole elephant might appear. Each of us might have a limited perception, illuminating and interesting in its own way, but no one perspective gives the whole story. What we endeavour to do in this Handbook is to give a variety of pictures of compounding that both complicate and deepen our understanding of this important means of extending the lexicon of a language.

Our intention is to complicate our view both theoretically and descriptively. In terms of theory, we consider compounding from disparate frameworks, both generative and non-generative, and from different perspectives: synchronic, diachronic, psycholinguistic, and developmental. Descriptively, we hope to sharpen our understanding of what constitutes a compound by looking not only at familiar languages, but also at a range of typologically and areally diverse languages. The two views are complementary.

We will offer a brief overview of the volume in section 1.2, but first we try to take our own first pass at this distinctive species of word formation: do we really know what a compound is?

1.1 THE PROBLEM OF DEFINITION: WHAT'S A COMPOUND?

Compounding is a linguistic phenomenon that might at first glance seem straightforward: in his introductory text Bauer (2003: 40) defines a compound as 'the formation of a new lexeme by adjoining two or more lexemes'. But Marchand, in 'Expansion, transposition, and derivation' (1967), presents another view, in effect saying that compounds don't exist as a separate sort of word formation; indeed, he distinguishes only two basic categories of word formation: expansion and derivation. Whether a complex word belongs to one or the other category depends on whether what he calls the 'determinatum' – in effect, the head of the complex word – is an independent morpheme or not. For Marchand, an expansion is a complex word in which the determinatum is an independent morpheme. Expansions might have either a bound or a free morpheme as their 'determinant' – in current terms, their modifier or non-head element. This allows Marchand to class prefixed items like *reheat* or *outrun* as the same animal as compounds like *steamboat* or *colourblind*. Words in which the determinatum/head is bound are derivations; in effect, suffixed words constitute one category of word formation, compounds and prefixed words another.

The reader might ask why a handbook on compounding should begin by contrasting an apparently straightforward definition of compound with such a non-canonical view of compounds. The answer is precisely that there has always been much discussion of exactly what a compound is, and even of whether compounds exist as a distinct species of word formation. We can identify two main reasons why it is difficult to come up with a satisfying and universally applicable definition of 'compound'. On the one hand, the elements that make up compounds in some languages are not free-standing words, but rather stems or roots. On the other, we cannot always make a clean distinction between compound words on the one hand and derived words or phrases on the other. We might term these the 'micro question' and the 'macro question'.

Let us look at the 'micro question' first. In the 1960 edition of his magnum opus, Marchand, for example, assumes that "[w]hen two or more words are combined into a morphological unit, we speak of a compound' (1960: 11). But this definition of compound is rooted in the analytical features of English, in particular, its lack of inflectional morphemes. In inflectional languages like Czech, Slovak, or Russian, the individual constituents of syntactic phrases are inflected. Compounds result from the combination not of words, but stems – uninflected parts of independent words that do not themselves constitute independent words. It is the compound as a whole that is inflected. In Slovak, for example, we know that *rýchlovlak* 'express train' is a compound because the left-hand constituent (*rýchly*$_A$ 'fast') is devoid of an inflectional morpheme and displays a linking element *-o*. On the other hand, we know that *rýchly vlak* 'fast train' (any train that goes fast) is a syntactic phrase and not a compound because the adjective *rýchly* is inflected to agree with the noun. It is only the lack of inflectional morphemes in English that makes surface forms of English compounds and free syntactic groups identical in terms of their morphological forms (compare, for example, *blackboard* and *black board*).

In light of this issue, it would seem that defining a compound as a combination of two or more *lexemes*, as Bauer does, is the safer way to go: the term lexeme would seem specific enough to exclude affixes but broad enough to encompass the roots, stems, and free words that can make up compounds in typologically diverse languages. But with Bauer's definition we have to be clear about what we mean by 'lexeme'.

One problem hinges on how we distinguish bound roots from derivational affixes. One criterion that we might use is semantic: roots in some sense have more semantic substance than affixes. But there are languages in which items that have been formally identified as affixes have as much, or nearly as much, semantic substance as items that might be identified as roots in other languages. Mithun (1999: 48–50) argues, for example, for what she calls 'lexical affixes' in many Native American languages. Bearing meanings like 'clothes', 'floor', 'nape', 'knob' (in Spokane) or 'eat', 'say', 'fetch', 'hit' (in Yup'ik), they might look semantically like roots, but their distribution is different from that of roots, and they serve a discourse function rather different from that of roots (they serve to background information that has already been introduced in a discourse). So distinguishing lexemes from non-lexemes might not be possible in semantic terms.

Another criterion must therefore be formal: we might say that bound roots can be distinguished from affixes only by virtue of also occurring as free forms (inflected, of course, in languages that require inflection). But that means that words like *overfly* and *outrun* in English must be considered compounds, rather than prefixed forms (as Marchand would like). There are two problems with this conclusion. First, the status of verbal compounds in English is highly disputed, and these items are clearly verbal.[1] Second, even though *over* and *out* also occur as free morphemes in English, the form that attaches to the verbs *fly* and *run* behaves rather differently from the first element of a compound. Specifically, the first element of a compound in English is typically syntactically inert: it does not affect the syntactic distribution of the complex word. Yet *over-* and *out-* have clear effects on verbal diathesis:

(1)   a. *The plane flew the field ∼ The plane overflew the field.
       b. *Yitzl ran Bonki ∼ Yitzl outran Bonki.

In light of this, it's not clear that we should be any more satisfied with the formal criterion than with the semantic criterion.

Bauer's definition also runs afoul of what we have called the 'macro question': how do we distinguish compounds from phrasal forms? Recall that Bauer defines a compound as a 'new lexeme'. But how do we know when we have a 'new lexeme'? It is relatively clear that in English a *blackboard* is a different lexeme from a *black board*: the former is sufficiently lexicalized that it can refer to just about any object that one can write on with chalk, regardless of its colour. But does a form like *tomato bowl* constitute a new lexeme if I use that term in pointing to a bowl on the counter that just happens at this moment to be holding tomatoes? In other words, so-called deictic compounds (Downing 1977) seem no more like new lexemes than some syntactic phrases do, and yet they still show some of the characteristics that we attribute to compounds (stress pattern, for one). Even more fraught is the question of whether items like *a floor of a birdcage taste* or *a wouldn't you like to know sneer* are compounds. Certainly we would be hesitant to call items like these lexemes. And yet some theorists have argued that they are indeed compounds.

It would seem that the only way to answer such questions would be to come up with a list of criteria some number of which forms would have to satisfy in order to be considered compounds. But here too we run into problems. In spite of extensive research into compounds and compounding processes, there are hardly any universally accepted criteria for determining what a compound is. Donalies (2004: 76), for example, analyses Germanic, Romance, Slavic, Finno-Ugric, and Modern Greek constructions in terms of ten postulated criteria. Compounds:

- are complex
- are formed without word-formation affixes
- are spelled together
- have a specific stress pattern

[1] Kiparsky (1982), for example, makes no distinction between verbal compounds and other compounds in terms of their derivation, and Štekauer and Valera (2007) also suggest that the generation of verbal compounds in English is not always a matter of back-formation. Indeed, Bauer and Renouf (2001) cite a few new verbal compounds in their corpus-based studies. On the other hand a number of scholars, including Pennanen (1966) and Adams (1973), treat verbal compounds like *air condition* as a product of back-formation.

- include linking elements
- are right-headed
- are inflected as a whole
- are syntactically inseparable
- are syntactico-semantic islands/ ⁽?⁾
- are conceptual units

Some of these criteria deserve serious consideration, others are far less plausible, or at least have far less cross-linguistic applicability. For example, it goes without saying that compounds are complex, but this does not in and of itself distinguish them from derived words, which are also complex. Donalies' second criterion is also not very useful: apparently all it means is that compounding is different from derivation, but what that difference is is precisely what is at issue. Spelling and headedness differ from one language to the next, and even within a single language, as we will see, as does the presence or absence of linking elements. These criteria might have limited utility within a particular language or group of languages, but cross-linguistically they cannot be definitive. And we have already seen that it's not so easy to decide what constitutes a 'conceptual unit' if we take 'conceptual unit' to be similar to what Bauer calls a 'lexeme'. A potential criterion that Donalies does not mention is lexicalization or listedness. But it does not take long to dismiss that either as a criterion for compoundhood: the more productive the process of compounding in a language, the less chance that individual compounds will be lexicalized.

Spelling also cannot be taken as a plausible criterion for determining compoundhood. Spelling is generally rejected as a criterion of compoundhood in English because the spelling of compounds is so inconsistent.[2] Although there might seem to be a tendency for institutionalized compounds to be spelled as one word or hyphenated (cf. *blackboard* vs. *a black board*) this is hardly a hard-and-fast rule. As Szymanek has argued, '[o]rthography, i.e. spelling convention for compounds cannot be taken seriously... the orthography of English compounds is notoriously inconsistent: some compounds are written as single words (*postcard*, *football*), in others the constituents are hyphenated (*sound-wave*, *tennis-ball*), and in still others the constituent elements are spaced off, i.e. written as two separate words (*blood bank*, *game ball*)' (1998: 41). Some compounds occur in all three variants: *flowerpot*, *flower-pot*, *flower pot*. So spelling cannot be used to determine compoundhood in English. In Czech and Slovak, in contrast, spelling has sometimes been considered an important criterion because all compounds are spelled as one word, whereas syntactic phrases are spelled as separate words. But this puts the cart before the horse: if we acknowledge that the spoken language is primary, and the writing system only an artificial system designed to capture the spoken word, there must clearly be some criteria which lead writers to write a sequence as one

---

[2] For a different view, see, for example, Arnold (1966) and Achmanova (1958).

word rather than two (e.g. lack of inflection on the first item, see above). In other words, spelling cannot be taken as a criterion of compoundhood because it only secondarily reflects the situation in the spoken language.

That leaves us with the most important of the criteria for distinguishing compounds: (i) stress and other phonological means; (ii) syntactic impenetrability, inseparability, and unalterability; and (iii) the behaviour of the complex item with respect to inflection. We will start with the issue of stress, and then look more carefully at the other phonological and syntactic criteria mentioned above.

1.1.1 Phonological Criteria

1.1.1.1 *Stress in English*

Stress is a more relevant criterion for determining compoundhood, at least for English, and has been the focus of intensive research in recent decades. Nevertheless, we will see that it is still quite problematic. It is often said that English compounds bear stress on the left-hand constituent, whereas syntactic phrases carry a level stress or are stressed on the head, i.e. the right-hand constituent. But there are numerous problems with this generalization.

Some of these problems stem from factors that seem purely idiosyncratic. On the one hand, individual native speakers can vary in their pronunciation of particular forms, as can specific groups of speakers (Pennanen 1980). Kingdon (1966: 164), for example, claims that in American English 'there is a stronger tendency towards the simple-stressing of compounds', by which he means left-hand stress, although whether this is true or not is unclear to us. On the other hand, context and the pragmatic conditions under which a word is pronounced can influence the pronunciation of particular compounds. Kingdon (1958: 147), Roach (1983: 100), Bauer (1983: 103), and most recently Štekauer, Valera, and Diaz (2007) all point out that the position of stress in isolation may differ from that when such words are pronounced in sentence context. Spencer (2003) notes as well that stress can occasionally be used to distinguish between different readings of the same combination of constituents: for example ' toy factory is probably a factory where toys are made, but a toy ' factory is a factory which is also a toy. And as Bauer (1998b: 70–2) points out, even individual dictionaries can differ in the way they mark stress on particular compounds.

Nevertheless, theorists have repeatedly tried to find systematic explanations for why some English compounds bear left-hand stress and others do not. Some of these explanations take syntactic form as relevant. Marchand (1960: 15), for example, counts compounds with present or past participles as the second stem as a systematic exception to left-hand stress, giving examples like *easy-going, high-born, man-made*. We question the systematicity of this 'exception' though – of the three examples Marchand gives, two have left-hand stress for many speakers of American English, and it is easy to add other examples of compounds based on participles that follow the prevalent left-hand stress pattern of English compounds (*truck driving, hand held*). Indeed, Olsen (2000b) notes that synthetic compounds (including these participle-based forms) are systematically left-stressed.

Giegerich (2004, and this volume) also attempts to relate stress to the structural characteristics of N + N constructions. He argues that most attribute-head N + N constructions are phrases rather than compounds, and therefore bear stress on the right-hand constituent. For example in *steel bridge*, the noun *steel* modifies *bridge*, and therefore is a phrase and has right-hand stress. On the other hand, N + N combinations that exhibit complement-head structures (e.g. *battlefield, fruit market, hand cream*) are compounds, and therefore bear stress on the left-hand constituent, as do attribute-head collocations that are lexicalized. Plag (2006) shows experimentally that complement-head collocations generally do exhibit left-hand stress, but that attribute-head collocations do as well, albeit less frequently. This applies to novel compounds as well as to lexicalized ones, so left-hand stress in attribute-head collocations cannot be attributed to lexicalization, as Giegerich suggests. It therefore seems difficult to find a structural principle that explains the variability of stress in English compounds.

Other researchers have attempted to find semantic principles which influence the stress pattern of English compounds. For example, Jones (1969: 258) presents three semantic criteria conditioning the presence of a single main stress on the left-hand constituent:

(2)   a. The compound denotes a single new idea rather than the combination of two ideas suggested by the original words, i.e. the meaning of the compound is not a pure sum total of the meanings of its constituents.

   b. The meaning of the compound noun is the meaning of the second constituent restricted in some important way by the first element ('*birthday*, '*cart-horse*, '*sheepdog*). When the second compound constituent is felt to be especially important the compound is double stressed ('*bow* '*window*, '*eye* '*witness*) (Jones 1969: 259).

   c. The first element is either expressly or by implication contrasted with something ('*flute-player* – in contrast to, for example, *piano-player*).

But these criteria are highly problematic. Does *apple pie* with right-hand stress denote any less of a single new idea than *apple cake*, which has left-hand stress? And what exactly do we mean by 'new idea'?[3] Similarly, is *pie* any less importantly restricted by *apple* than *cake* is? Is *window* more important in *bow window* than in *replacement window*? Bauer (1983: 107) rightly calls in question the last criterion (as do Marchand 1960: 16–17 and Kingdon 1958: 151): if it were the case that left-hand

---

[3] A variation on this proposal can be found in Ladd (1984), who proposes that we find left-hand stress when the left-hand constituent designates a subcategory of the right-hand constituent. This, of course, still runs afoul of the *apple cake, apple pie* problem.

stress obtains when a contrast is intended, all compounds might be expected to be pronounced with left-hand stress. But this is certainly not the case: 'cherry 'brandy is contrasted with 'apricot 'brandy, 'peach 'brandy, and 'grape 'brandy, although all are double stressed.

Sampson (1980: 265–6) suggests that compounds in which the first stem describes what the second stem is made of receive right-hand stress, but only when the second stem denotes a solid and fixed artefact. So *iron saucepan* and *rubber band* are right-stressed, but *sand dune, wine stain, water droplet,* and *oil slick* are not, even though the first stem expresses what the second is made of. This would be a curious observation, if it were true, and we might ask why only this semantic class receives right-hand stress. But there are exceptions to this generalization, as even Sampson himself points out – for example, *rubber band* is typically left-stressed in American English. If composed foods constitute artefacts, *apple pie* is well-behaved, but *apple cake* is not.

Olsen (2000b) makes another attempt to find semantic criteria that distinguish right-stressed N + N collocations from left-stressed ones. In addition to the 'made of' criterion that Sampson proposes for right-hand stress, she adds compounds whose first stems express temporal or locational relations, citing examples such as *summer 'dress, summer 'night,* and *hotel 'kitchen.*[4] Left-hand stress, on the other hand, occurs in compounds 'where a relational notion is not overtly expressed by the head noun, but is inferable on the basis of the meaning of one of the constituents' (2000b: 60). So, for example, she argues that the compound *mucus cell* is left-stressed because 'we . . . know that *mucus* generally "lines" cells' (*ibid.*). There are a number of problems with her hypothesis, however. On the one hand, it is easy enough to find examples of left-stressed compounds whose first stems express temporal or locational meanings ('*restaurant kitchen,* '*winter coat,* '*summer school*[5]). And on the other, it is not entirely clear to us (knowing virtually nothing about biology!) that a *mucus cell* is so-called because it is lined with mucus, rather than made of mucus (in which case we would predict right-hand stress).[6]

Plag (2006b: 147–8) shows experimentally that stress assignment in novel compounds sometimes seems to depend on analogy to existing N + N constructions in the mental lexicon, with the head determining the analogical pattern. This effect has been observed in the literature for *street* and *avenue* compounds, where the former are left-stressed (*Fifth Street*) and the latter right stressed (*Fifth Avenue*) (Bauer 1983). But Plag's experimental data extend this result to compounds based

---

[4] The last of these is actually left-stressed for one of the present authors.

[5] The last of these examples is also cited by Plag (2006).

[6] Spencer (2003) provides a very useful appendix in which he lists particular semantic fields in which some compounds are left-stressed and others right-stressed, suggesting that semantic field can have nothing to do with the determination of stress. Spencer in fact argues that it is impossible to distinguish compounds from phrases in English on any basis, and indeed that within a theory like Chomsky's Bare Phrase Structure, there is no need to do so.

on musical terms such as *symphony* and *sonata*: the former are typically right-stressed, the latter left-stressed. Plag, however, leaves it as an open question 'how far such an analogical approach can reach' and what combination of factors can be held responsible for this kind of analogical behaviour.

What we are forced to conclude is that for English, at least, left-hand stress is often a mark of compoundhood, but certainly cannot be taken as either a necessary or a sufficient condition for distinguishing a compound from a phrase. As Spencer (2003: 331) so aptly puts it, 'there is a double dissociation between stress and structure'. There are phrases with left-hand stress and compounds with right-hand or double stress. We therefore need to look at other criteria that have been proposed for identifying compounds.

1.1.1.2 *Phonological criteria in other languages*

Languages other than English of course have other phonological means for distinguishing compounds from syntactic phrases, among them: distinctive tonal patterns (Bambara [Bauer, Chapter 17, this volume]; Hausa [Newman 2000: 190, 116]; Konni [Štekauer, Körtvélyessy, and Valera 2007: 66]); vowel harmony (Chuckchee [Bauer, Chapter 17, this volume]); stress patterns (German, Danish, modern Greek, Polish, Hebrew [see articles in this volume]; Ket [Štekauer, Körtvélyessy, and Valera 2007: 66]); segmental effects like fricative voicing (Slave [Rice, this volume]) or voicing (Japanese [Bauer, Chapter 17, this volume]); vowel deletion (Hebrew [Borer, this volume]) or vowel reduction (Maipure, Baniva [Zamponi, this volume]). In most cases, however, the literature does not allow us to tell how consistently these criteria distinguish compounding as a type of word formation. Much further research is needed to determine if in at least some languages compounding is phonologically distinctive in specific ways.

1.1.2 Syntactic criteria

Among the syntactic criteria that have been suggested for distinguishing compounds from phrases in English are inseparability, the inability to modify the first element of the compound, and the inability to replace the second noun of a nominal compound with a pro-form such as *one*.

Certainly the most reliable of these is the inseparability criterion: a complex form is a compound (as opposed to a phrase) if no other element can be inserted between the two constituents. While it is possible to insert another word into the phrase *a black bird*, e.g. *black ugly bird*, no such insertion is permitted with the compound *blackbird*. *Ugly* can only modify the compound as a whole: *ugly blackbird*. Although this criterion is almost foolproof, there are nevertheless cases that might call it into question. For example, if we were to consider phrasal verbs (i.e. verb plus particle combinations) as compounds of a sort (e.g. *he took his hat off*), this criterion would not hold for them. Of course, the solution here is easy: we need only decide that phrasal verbs are not compounds; Jackendoff (2002b), for example, considers them to be constructional idioms. Our second example is not so easily dismissed. In particular, it appears that the first constituents of items that we would otherwise have reason to call compounds can sometimes be coordinated, for example *wind and water mills* or *hypo- but not hyperglycaemic* (Spencer 2003). One might argue here, however, that these coordinated forms are really phrasal compounds, but of course that raises the issue of whether phrasal compounds really are compounds (see Lieber 1992a).

Yet another syntactic criterion of compoundhood might be modification of the first stem: the first stem of a compound does not admit modification, whereas in a syntactic construction modification is possible. With regard to adjective + noun complexes it appears that only phrases and not compounds can be modified by *very*. Therefore, we can say a *very black bird* if, say, we are pointing at a crow, but not **a very blackbird* if it is genus *agelaius* we are pointing out. But this test is not foolproof: relational adjectives can never be modified by *very* (**a very mortal disease*), so the test can only be used if the adjective in question is a qualitative one. Bauer (1998b: 73) considers a broader version of this criterion for noun + noun complexes, pointing out that it seems impossible to modify the first stem in *river-bed* with an adjective: **swollen river-bed* (where it is the river that is meant to be swollen). But in other cases, modification seems possible. He cites attested examples such as *Serious Fraud Office* and *instant noodle salad*.

Bauer (1998b: 77) also suggests as a test for compoundhood the inability to replace the second stem with a pro-form. In a phrase, it should be possible to replace the head noun with *one*, but not in a compound. So *a black one* can refer to our crow, but a *blackone* cannot be our *agelaius*. Nevertheless, Bauer shows that this criterion is also not foolproof. Although rare, examples like *He wanted a riding horse, as neither of the carriage ones would suffice* are attested, with *riding horse* and *carriage horse* otherwise having the appearance of compounds.

There are also language-specific syntactic criteria for distinguishing compounds from phrases. For example, Bauer (Chapter 21, this volume) notes that in Danish only a single N can take a postposed definite article. Therefore if a postposed definite article is possible, we have evidence that a sequence of two roots must be a compound. Fradin (this volume) points out that word order gives us evidence for compoundhood in French: if a sequence of lexemes displays an order that cannot be generated for syntactic phrases, we are likely dealing with a compound.[7]

---

[7] Marchand (1960) suggests this criterion for English as well, for compounds with present or past participle as the second constituent: *easy-going, high-born, man-made*. In these cases, Marchand (1960: 15) employs the following compoundhood criterion: the first constituent cannot syntactically function as a modifier of the right-hand constituent. The same principle is applied to the *grass-green* type characterized by two heavy stresses: an adjective cannot syntactically be modified by a preceding substantive (the corresponding syntactic phrase is 'green as grass').

1.1.3 Inflection and linking elements

A final criterion for compoundhood concerns inflection, in those languages in which nominal inflection figures prominently. In one scenario, we recognize a compound when the head of the compound bears inflection, but the non-head does not. In another possible scenario we know that we are dealing with a compound when the non-head bears a compound-specific inflection. The former situation holds in Dutch, as Don shows (this volume), where the non-head of the compound is uninflected, and the latter in Yimas, where the non-head is marked as Oblique (Bauer, Chapter 17, this volume, citing Foley 1991).

As has frequently been pointed out, however, there are many languages in which non-compound-specific inflection does sometimes occur on the non-head of a compound, and discussion centres on how to interpret such cases. In English the plural marker is not infrequently found inside a compound: *overseas investor, parks commissioner, programs coordinator, arms-conscious, sales-oriented, pants-loving* (Selkirk 1982: 52). Selkirk tries to explain some of these exceptions: 'it would seem that the actual use of the plural marker...might have the function (pragmatically speaking) of imposing the plural interpretation of the non-head, in the interest of avoiding ambiguity. This is probably the case with *programs coordinator* or *private schools catalogue*, for the corresponding *program coordinator* and *private school catalogue* are easily and perhaps preferentially understood as concerning only one program or private school' (1982: 52).[8] But surely this does not explain all cases. On the one hand, with respect to the initial stem of a compound like *dress manufacturer*, as Selkirk points out, it makes no sense to think of a manufacturer of one dress. On the other hand, a compound like *programmes list* doesn't seem to have any possible contrast: a *programme list* wouldn't be a list if it didn't involve more than one programme. It would seem that a plural is possible but not necessary in a compound to denote plurality of the first stem. Similarly, with possessive marking; it is not necessary to mark possessive on the initial element of a compound (for example, *gangster money*), but it is nevertheless possible (e.g. *children's hour*).

The issue of compound-internal inflection is inevitably bound up with that of so-called linking elements (also called interfixes or intermorphs in the literature). A linking element is a meaningless extension that occurs between the first and second elements of compounds. In some languages it is completely clear that this element is not an inflectional morpheme. For example, as Ralli (this volume) argues for modern Greek, the first element of a compound is always followed

---

[8] Allen (1978) tries to argue that the *s* in cases like *craftsman* is a linking element rather than a plural marker. She claims that the meaning of the first constituent in *craftsman, tradesman, oarsman, helmsman*, etc. is singular, and some of the first constituents of words of this class (*kinsman, deersman*) do not even have a plural. But it seems clear to us, as to Selkirk, that some of these forms indeed do denote plurals.

by -*o* which is semantically empty and is the historical remnant of a no-longer-existent theme vowel. For other languages, such as German and Dutch, there has been extensive discussion of whether the linking-elements can ever be construed as inflectional. The consensus is that while they may trace back historically to case or number markers, their status is quite different in the synchronic grammar: as mentioned above, they are meaningless, and often they do not correspond to any of the current inflectional forms of the nouns they occur on, although occasionally they may plausibly be interpreted as adding a plural flavour to the first element of the compound. See the chapters by Don and Neef in Part 2 of this volume for suggestions as to how linking elements in Dutch and German are to be handled.[9]

1.1.4 Summary

The picture that emerges here may seem a bit dispiriting: what are we to think if there are (almost) no reliable criteria for distinguishing compounds from phrases or from other sorts of derived words? One possible conclusion is that there is no such thing as a compound; Spencer (2003) argues this position for English. Another conclusion might be that there is simply a cline of more compound-like and less compound-like complexes, with no clear categorical distinction. As Bauer has put it (1998b: 78), 'none of the possible criteria give a reliable distinction between two types of construction. The implication is that any distinction drawn on the basis of just one of these criteria is simply a random division of noun + noun constructions, not a strongly motivated borderline between syntax and the lexicon.' A third conclusion is Olsen's (2000b): all noun + noun collocations are compounds for her. Plag (2006) simply remains agnostic on whether there is a distinction between noun + noun compounds and phrases.

So we return to the blind men and the elephant: not only are we not sure what the elephant looks like, but some of us are not even sure there's an elephant at all. There may be a single species, a range of related species, or the whole thing might be a delusion. Nevertheless, the majority of theorists – and us among them – seem to believe that it's worth looking further. We would not have been able to assemble so many interesting papers in this volume if this were not the case. Our approach is to broaden our focus and look for both theoretical perspectives that might bring new insight to the questions that compounds raise, and data from widely diverse languages that might be brought to bear on the issue of definition.

---

[9] See also Štekauer and Valera (2007) for examples of linking elements in other languages. Interestingly, they point out that the stem + stem type of compounds without any linking element is much more frequent than that with a linking element, but that in languages that have both types, the type with linking element is generally more productive.

1.2 PROSPECTUS

We have divided this handbook into two parts. In the first, we look at compounds from a broad range of perspectives, both methodological and theoretical. We consider the issue of compounds from both a synchronic and a diachronic point of view, and through the lenses of a number of contemporary theoretical frameworks. We have tried to be eclectic in our choice of theoretical perspectives, tapping both the more familiar traditions of Western Europe and North America, and the rather less visible (for Western readers, at least) traditions of Central European linguistics. And we have tried to bring in as well the views of specialists in psycholinguistics and language acquisition.

Chapters 2 and 3 continue our focus on issues of definition and classification. In his chapter on idiomatology, Kavka assesses the relationship between compounds and idioms, arguing that both exhibit a gradience from mildly to wildly idiosyncratic interpretation that begs us to consider them together. Scalise and Bisetto consider a wide range of systems that have been proposed for classifying different types of compounds and, finding them all inconsistent, propose a new scheme of classification that has better potential for cross-linguistic utility. They rightly suggest that having a broadly applicable schema for classifying compounds will inevitably help us to see typological and areal trends in compounding.

In Chapter 4, ten Hacken reviews the early history of the treatment of compounding in generative theory, starting with Lees's seminal monograph (1960) and tracing theoretical developments through the beginning of the Lexicalist movement in the late 1970s. His chapter sets the stage for Chapters 5–9, each of which approaches the analysis of compounding from a different theoretical perspective.

Several of these theories fit roughly into the generative tradition, but differ in where they locate compounding in the architecture of the grammar. Giegerich's view (Chapter 9) is an extension of the Lexicalist tradition. He explores a multi-level analysis in which he treats as compounds in English only those N + N combinations with initial stress, leaving all other N + N combinations to the syntax. Giegerich considers as well the extent to which the meanings of various types of N + N combination can be correlated with their stress behaviour. In their chapters Jackendoff (Chapter 6) and Di Sciullo (Chapter 8) propose frameworks that locate the analysis of compounds in the morphology. Both seek to derive compounds by mechanisms that are parallel (Jackendoff) or similar to (Di Sciullo) syntactic processes, but are not part of the syntax per se. Harley (Chapter 7), on the other hand, takes a purely syntactic approach to compounding, within the framework of Distributed Morphology, treating compounding as a species of syntactic incorporation.

In contrast to both the morphological and the syntactic approach, Lieber (Chapter 5) suggests that a perspicuous analysis of compounds is available within her framework of lexical semantic representation, and by inference, that the debate over whether to analyse compounding as morphology or as syntax is orthogonal to the most pressing issues in the analysis of compounds: what matters is not where compounds are derived, but how compound interpretation is to be arrived at. Booij (Chapter 10) approaches compounding from the perspective of Construction Grammar, another off-shoot of the generative tradition that has become prominent in the last decade or so, but which stresses the importance of hierarchically organized constructional schemas, along with the role of analogy for the generation of compounds.

Moving away from the generative tradition, in Chapter 11 Grzega maps various views of compounding from the 'onomasiological' perspective, a revived theoretical approach with a long tradition, especially in Central Europe and Germany. Heyvaert (Chapter 12) reviews analyses of compounding from the point of view of Cognitive Linguistics, which looks at language from the point of view of the cognitive abilities of the language user.

The next three chapters take a view towards the language user as well, looking at the perception, processing, and acquisition of compounds. In Chapter 13, Gagné reviews the copious psycholinguistic literature considering the nature of the mental representations in compounds, including such interrelated issues as the extent to which the individual lexemes of compounds or the whole compounds themselves are represented in the mental lexicon, the ways in which those representations are or are not linked, and the nature of lexical access in perception of compounds (for example, whether decomposition is involved or not). Štekauer, in Chapter 14, interrelates the word-formation and word-interpretation models in order to explain the predictability of the meanings of novel context-free compounds; his model explores the idea that there are always one or two dominant meanings 'winning' the competition among different potential meanings as a result of interplay between linguistic and extralinguistic factors. In Chapter 15, Berman looks at the acquisition of compounds, primarily in English and Hebrew, from the perspectives both of naturalistic and experimental data, and considers the extent to which the age and sequence of acquisition of compounds might be a matter of typological differences in languages.

Chapter 16 takes a diachronic view of compounding. There, Kastovsky looks both at the history of compounding in Indo-European, considering the origins of compounds, and at the treatment of compounding in the historical-comparative tradition.

The second part of this volume begins with the question of how to arrive at a typology of compounding given our present state of knowledge. Looking at a variety of languages, Bauer points out, perhaps surprisingly for some, that compounding is not a linguistic universal,[10] and moreover that at our present state of

---

[10] Indeed, in Štekauer, Körtvélyessy, and Valera's (2007) core sample of fifty-four languages, only forty-nine displayed compounding.

knowledge we know of no special correlations between aspects of compounding and other typological characteristics of languages cross-linguistically. In the remainder of this section, we look at the facts of compounding in a range of languages. Although we can make no claim to representative coverage of the languages of the world either in terms of typology or geographic area, we have nevertheless made an effort to represent both well-known and well-researched languages and lesser-known and under-documented languages. Our sample is heavily weighted towards Indo-European, where – as is often the case – the majority of published work has been done. Within Indo-European, the sample is again disproportionately represented by Germanic (English, Dutch, German, Danish) and Romance (French, Spanish), again partly because there has been long-standing and active debate about compounding in these subfamilies. Outside of Germanic and Romance in Indo-European, we cover Modern Greek and Polish. We have also attempted to sample a number of other language families, including Sino-Tibetan (Mandarin Chinese), Afro-Asiatic (Hebrew), Finno-Ugric (Hungarian), Athapaskan (Slave), Iroquoian (Mohawk), Arawakan (Maipure-Yavitero), Araucanian (Mapudungan), and Pama-Nyungan (Warlpiri), as well as one language isolate (Japanese). We might have wished for a wider range of languages, but we were limited both by issues of space in this volume, and by the dearth of research on compounding in many lesser-known and under-described languages. In spite of its limitations, this section nevertheless contains what we believe is the largest sample of descriptions of compounding in the languages of the world that has been brought together in a single volume, and we hope for that reason that it will be useful.

We have tried to arrange the volume so that each chapter is self-contained and can be read separately. We hardly expect our readers to plough through all the articles consecutively. But for those who are truly engrossed by the study of compounds and who have the stamina to do so, we hope that they will see that certain intriguing themes emerge time and time again, regardless of framework or language. Among those themes are the following:

- *The definitional problem*: Just about every article in this volume starts out by mentioning the difficulty in figuring out what constitutes a compound, either cross-linguistically or language-specifically. It seems almost impossible to draw a firm line between compounds on the one hand and phrases or derived words on the other, perhaps suggesting, as many in the tradition of Cognitive Linguistics have done, that compounding is a gradient, rather than a categorical phenomenon, with prototypical examples and fuzzy edges.
- *The problem of interpretation*: This is perhaps better stated as a range of problems, including the issues of distinguishing compounds from idioms, of how compounds are assigned their interpretations, and of the extent to which those interpretations may be predicted.

- *The component problem*: Given the difficulties above, what sorts of analyses are most appropriate for compounds, either cross-linguistically or language-specifically? What does the study of compounds tell us about what Jackendoff so aptly calls 'the architecture of grammar'? The study of compounds has the potential to illuminate large and long-standing (and perhaps ultimately unresolvable) issues about the relationship among major components of the grammar, especially of course morphology and syntax, and about the nature of 'wordhood'.

There are smaller leitmotifs that recur as well: issues of headedness, the nature of exocentricity, the relationship between compounding and other morphosyntactic phenomena such as incorporation, serial verbs, phrasal verbs, and the like.

We hope that ultimately this volume will serve as a resource for scholars and as a starting point and inspiration for those who wish to continue the work that still needs to be done on compounding. We suspect that we will never agree on what this particular elephant looks like, but if this volume accomplishes only one purpose, it should be to improve our certainty that there really is an elephant. We may still be blind, but we're pretty sure we're not delusional.

CHAPTER 2

COMPOUNDING
AND
IDIOMATOLOGY

STANISLAV KAVKA

2.1 INTRODUCING THE ISSUE

Were it an easy task to explain what 'a compound' is, this voluminous book would not have come into existence. Most linguistically untrained readers will take the term for granted, assuming that a compound is simply 'a composite word', the meaning of which can be sensed from the Latin *componere*. Nevertheless, this etymology, ubiquitous as it may be, exhibits many lacunae once the process of compounding is judged more closely by those who distinguish between composition and derivation, and – which is a crucial point to be mentioned here – once we deal with the phenomenon in different languages. In order to illustrate, in Czech, for instance, composition proper is subject to fairly rigid rules, which on the one hand make it necessary to separate out a specific category of 'compounded words', and on the other hand, to determine certain frequently used, recursive constituents as suffixes and prefixes rather than genuine compound elements.[1] As far as German

---

[1] Besides genuine compounds, 'složeniny', Czech grammar distinguishes also 'spřežky' (a term which cannot well be matched in English). Examples of compound-like suffixes and prefixes are *teploměr* (thermometer), *elektroměr* (electrometer); *zeměpis* (geography), *dějepis* (history), *pravopis* (orthography); *veletrh* (trade fair), *mimořádný* (extraordinary), *makroekonomika* (macroeconomics). Concise information and further references can be found in Havránek and Jedlička (1981: 93 ff.).

is concerned, composition is traditionally regarded as a subcategory of so-called 'extension' (Erweiterung), the other subcategory being derivation (Ableitung). And again, as in Czech compounds, certain fuzzy points which militate against establishing clear-cut boundaries cause linguists to recognize a transitional word-formation process referred to as Zusammenbildung. Finally, in Spanish it seems plausible to speak of lexical compounds (that is, genuine compounds), such as *pelirrojo* 'of red hair', and syntagmatic compounds, e.g. *fin de semana* 'weekend' – although, viewed semantically, one category borders on the other and even on what may be called a 'free combination' of words (i.e. syntactic phrases). It is not the intention of this chapter to deal with all these and similar peculiarities: Chapter 1 offers detailed information on definitions of compounds, and typological characteristics will be discussed too, in the following chapters. The nature of compound structure seems to be indefinable and therefore a serious object of (psycho-) linguistic research. Hence Aitchison (2003) may be right to claim that the knowledge of processes of compounding will help us to understand less obvious new word combinations, which appear in every language and very often enter concatenated expressions. I am convinced that idiomatology, too, will have a say in elucidating the issues involved.

2.2 PLACE AND SCOPE OF IDIOMATOLOGY

2.2.1 Defining the term

The term 'idiomatology' may not be familiar enough. Clearly, linguists employ specific terms in order to express their arguments and promote their own understanding of the given idea. However much they try to state precisely and unambiguously what they mean by the terms, their intention is not always crowned with success. In this context, readers will probably be more aware of such terms as *idiomaticity* or *phraseology*, or (if they are knowledgeable about Russian linguistics[2]) *idiomatics*. All these terms have been used to refer to one and the same area of interest, although they are not simply interchangeable. For example, phraseology may be fully acceptable for language teachers, who understand it as lists of 'useful phrases' for students to memorize. Idiomatic expressions, however, are based on semantic grounds rather than lexical ones. Moreover, 'phraseology', being derived from the base-term 'phrase', will have connotations of reference to grammatical structures. 'Idiomaticity', on the other hand, makes us think of the recursive

---

[2] See, for example, Anichkov (1992).

morpheme {-ity} (cf. *regularity < regular, priority < prior*) and hence explain the meaning of the term as 'a quality' derived, in turn, from an attribution of, say, 'constituting, or containing an idiom or idioms'. This is a definition of 'idiomaticity' offered and accepted generally by most linguists interested in the field. Let us notice one important fact, though. The term certainly refers to quality, but it does not always need to imply that what we wish to call 'idiomaticity of expression' depends on its containing an idiom: we say, for example, *a tall man* rather than *a high man*, without considering the expression as an idiom. As, for example, Reichstein (1984) suggests, the term itself can be used to point to the semantic and structural irregularity of phrasal idioms: suffice it to note illogical, semantically and / or grammatically anomalous forms such as *white lie, by and large, between two to five, it's me*, etc. In a broader sense of the term we can say that a given expression has 'proper idiomaticity' if it is judged intuitively by native speakers as natural, commonly acceptable. Hence the most concise definition of 'idiomaticity' will be one that renders it a 'function of familiarity and frequency of use' (Sonomura 1996). Finally, the term 'idiomatology', to my best knowledge first introduced by Grace (1981), was seen as more appropriate to be used by those who dealt with sociolinguistic and pragmatic aspects of language. It is true, however, that Grace himself used the term in a sense that is almost synonymous with the sense of 'idiomaticity': he compiled a list of unusual linguistic structures that deviate from expected ones, namely those violating grammatical rules, and he grouped them under the label 'idiomatology'. I claim that the term 'idiomatology' should be reserved for a truly linguistic discipline (a parallel to already traditional ones such as 'philology', 'phonology', 'morphology'), namely one that has its own goals to examine and its own methods of investigation. It is questionable (yet not impossible) whether we could even think of idiomatology as a kind of 'incorporating discipline' of all research in language use: indeed, idiomaticity, in both its broader and narrower senses, operates through and across all the levels of language analysis.

2.2.2 Understanding idiomatic expressions

2.2.2.1 *Lexical and grammatical variability*

Claiming (as the title of this chapter suggests) that compounds can be viewed and also studied as idiomatic expressions, or perhaps even as idioms proper, calls for an explanation of what we mean by these terms.

In speaking of 'idiomatic expressions' I have in mind multi-word chunks consisting of constituents which are bound together lexically and syntactically. These constituents need not necessarily be bound absolutely, although this kind of invariability is believed to be a significant feature of typical idioms, e.g. *red herring, cook one's goose*. However, there are combinations in which one constituent (called a 'collocate') can be replaced, cf. *chequered history/career; seize/grasp the nettle.*

Moreover, certain degrees of variance are permitted within grammatical categories, whereas syntactic variance (sometimes referred to as syntactic productivity) is hardly possible; *It speaks/spoke volumes – *volumes are/were spoken; He spilled the beans – *The beans were spilled* (unless we have in mind the literal meaning). For reasons of space, intricacies concerning possibilities of variance in genuine idioms cannot be commented upon;[3] fortunately, these will not affect the following discussion on compounds. Nevertheless, even if readers may judge the expression *spill the beans* as an idiom but *chequered history* as a collocation (due to the fact of the replaceable 'collocate' and the fixed 'base' in the latter case), it is still a delicate matter to determine the points at which a multi-word expression is called a 'collocation' rather than an 'idiom', to say nothing of a boundary between these two on the one hand, and so-called 'free combination' (practically 'syntactic string') on the other hand, for example *a small desk, open the door* (cf. *a writing desk; answer the door*). One reason is that we do not have any means of measuring the degrees on one or the other scale. The other reason is that the feature of variance, or variability, is by itself a complex phenomenon, involving both grammar and lexis. Therefore I prefer the idea of a continuum as displayed over multi-word (here: idiomatic) expressions, and I also take the point that semantic structure is a fundamental language component. Hence it follows that the first step to take when deciding on the appropriate status of idiomatic expressions is to ask about their variability as a lexical feature. Then the data must be verified against the background of grammatical variability, and also literalness (see section 2.2.2.2). I maintain that idioms proper will, in principle, be those multi-word expressions within which none of the components can be varied lexically.[4] The components simply cannot be varied because they are themselves semantically empty: for example, *pins and needles* or *spill the beans* cannot undergo any reasonable lexical variation. By contrast, *black coffee* allows for lexical variance (e.g. *delicious/sweet/ hot...black coffee*), which places it outside the domain of genuine idioms. The referent *black*, however, has much more to do with a type of coffee rather than with its colour, and this fact speaks in favour of its classification as a collocation rather than a free combination.

2.2.2.2 *The notion of literalness*

Degrees of variability are not the only criterion for classifying idioms and collocations; another relevant feature of multi-word expressions is 'literalness'. There exist expressions in which each constituent has its basic, fairly concrete, standard meaning, referred to as 'literal'. It is then expected that the total meaning of this

---

[3] Readers interested in the issue are referred to Kavka (2003: 47–93).

[4] By lexical variability (or lexical flexibility, as it is sometimes called) I understand all imaginable lexical processes, from those known in classical derivational morphology, via intensification, to determination.

expression as a cumulation of individual literal meanings will also be literal, e.g. *a beautiful woman*. However, things are not always as simple as that. The aforementioned example *black coffee* indicates a smooth transition toward another category of multi-word expressions in which at least one of the constituents does not show its literal meaning. Thus in *a blue film*, for instance, only the constituent 'film' carries its literal meaning, while 'blue' has apparently nothing to do with the colour it normally (i.e. in a standard way) denotes. And finally, we come across expressions in which no constituents are used in their literal meanings: the above-cited expression *spill the beans* will hardly be understood literally as {spill} 'let fall' + {beans} 'pulses'. We could say that its meaning is 'non-literal' – or perhaps 'figurative' (i.e. 'idiomatic'). A close inspection of examples will show that it may be useful to distinguish between the terms 'non-literal' and 'figurative', although they are synonymous. This is because there are expressions which can be interpreted both literally and non-literally, e.g. *grasp the nettle*, and there are expressions that can only be read non-literally, e.g. *white lie*. Then the interpretation 'grab/catch hold of the nettle [by hand]' will be literal, while 'deal decisively with an unpleasant matter' will be referred to as figurative.

2.2.3 Compositionality and predictability

Variability and literalness make up a highly complex phenomenon which is known as 'compositionality'. As shown above, variability (concerning lexical and grammatical features) is not viewed simply as present or absent; rather it represents a continuum encompassing three stages, namely, full variability, partial variability, and zero variability (i.e. invariability). The phenomenon of literalness likewise shows an ingenious texture of interrelations, which speaks in favour of its gradual character. Hence it follows that compositionality (as an interplay of variability and literalness) must be a scalar phenomenon: multi-word expressions are characterized as fully compositional (e.g. *shoot a bird*; *red ink*), semi-compositional (e.g. *shoot a film*; *red carpet*), or non-compositional (e.g. *shoot the breeze*; *blue blood*). It is clear that the situation as outlined here reflects the synchronic view; as time goes on, however, the originally literal multi-word expression can become fixed, showing lower and lower degrees of variability, which may result in it having a figurative or even a non-literal meaning. In other words, the expression moves along the scale of compositionality; from the historical perspective compositionality can be represented as a cline on which multi-word expressions are situated. Hence, expressions to be referred to as idiomatic must be those that are not compositional.[5]

---

[5] It is precisely this gradient character of compositionality that makes it rather difficult to draw a clear-cut dividing line between idioms and collocations (and free combinations). And yet these two categories are still widely used, mainly in applied linguistics, although their 'definitions' must seem to

It should be borne in mind that the concept of compositionality as presented here refers to the semantic unity of the given expression; therefore it would not be right to argue that compositionality is in a proportional relation to predictability. Even less could we say that 'compositional' is simply an equivalent term of 'predictable'. These two properties are not always interdependent: whereas compositional expressions can be claimed to be predictable, non-compositional ones are not automatically unpredictable. (Suffice it to compare the examples cited just above; or, for example, *describe a murder* vs. *commit murder – scream blue murder.*) In fact, my view of the concept of 'predictability' is basically in line with the one that defines it as (paraphrasing Štekauer 2005a) the degree of probability that a particular meaning of a naming unit (i.e. idiomatic expression) encountered for the first time by the interlocutor will be interpreted in preference to other possible (imaginable) meanings. Hence I believe, too, perhaps trying to extend the definition a little, that the issue of predictability, which concerns the process of comprehending, must be discussed from two perspectives, or, in other words, must be viewed as existing on two, yet interconnected, levels. On a more general level, there must be a device in people's minds which decides on the choice of either literal or figurative / non-literal meaning. Here we usually point to the role of context, which is believed to bias the interpretation. In my view the concept of context should be used in a broader sense, that is, it comprises not only 'verbal, linguistic context', or 'co-text', but also so-called 'context of situation', or 'co-situation', which involves phenomena connected with the cultural background, including speakers' current knowledge of the external world.[6] On another level we analyse the internal structure of the expression whose components add to the total meaning. Although this computation (to use the modern, rather fashionable term) is quite often difficult to describe (i.e. in idiomatic expressions generally), it is based, psycholinguistically speaking, on the process of cumulative association of the semantic roots of the respective components.[7] In idiomatic expressions this process presupposes the existence and, on the receiver's part, the 'decipherment' of metonymies, metaphors, even so-called underlying (or root) metaphors involved.[8] There are basically

be rather vague: only if we are familiar with the jargon of the field will we understand that 'relatively frozen expressions', 'loosely fixed expressions', and 'the least cohesive word combinations' (Bahns 1993, and others) are labels for what some of us would prefer to call, respectively, 'idioms', 'collocations', 'free combinations / syntactic groups'. Nevertheless, to be frank, these writers are aware of the relativity of the terms – although the effect of their use may be to create vagueness, for example when speaking of 'lexical items which occur with mutual expectancy greater than a chance, e.g. *rancid butter, curry favor*' (Nattinger and DeCarrico 1992) to refer to idiomatic expressions which others would very probably like to call collocations.

[6] Basic information on these terms can be found in Leech (1974: 360), Lyons (1983: 203, 216 ff., Fernando (1996: 250).

[7] I follow the terms and opinions promoted by Mitchell (1975). Also in Fernando (1996: 60).

[8] A good example cited in the literature is one that explains the underlying (conceptual) metaphors in the processing of the idiomatic expression *spill the beans*: these can be represented as 'the mind is a container' + 'ideas are physical entities'.

three hypotheses offering different ways of arriving at the proper interpretation of meaning: the Lexical Representation Hypothesis, the Configuration Hypothesis, and the Decomposition Hypothesis. The Lexical Representation Hypothesis regards idiomatic expressions as being stored in the mental lexicon in the form of morphologically compounded words, which are retrieved in the same way as any other 'simplex' word, so we might say there is in fact no decipherment. As the name suggests, the Configuration Hypothesis offers the idea that the meaning of the idiomatic expression is represented through a particular configuration of words treated as a lexical item. Speakers, or readers, are expected to recognize the configuration first, which is said to be possible after a certain amount of information has been accumulated. Although it is difficult to define this amount, it is true that some parts of the expression are more relevant than others, of which the most salient, called the 'key', is decisive in seeking a figurative interpretation. Finally, the Decomposition Hypothesis is based on the assumption that parts of idiomatic expressions are semantically empty and that their figurative meanings are obtained by accessing the idiomatic meanings of the expressions' components. It is my conviction that this hypothesis, although allowing for much subjectivity, works in favour of the idea of continua, which is my preferred way of viewing idiomatic expressions (see above, and also sections 2.2.2.1, 2.3.5).[9]

2.3 Compounds as idiomatic expressions

2.3.1 Compounds as a 'cross-cutting' class

Sonomura (1996) is one of those who regard idiomaticity of an expression in a broader sense of the term, maintaining that idiomaticity does not depend on whether or not the expression apparently involves an idiom. She is also one of those who reject the term 'phrase' (see section 2.2.1) and use the term 'phraseme' instead. The phraseme as a hyper-class is divided into three categories of multi-word expressions, namely, idioms, collocations, and formulas, categories which can then be further subdivided. Unlike Sonomura, whose approach is distinctly semantic, Fernando (1996) opts for a formal approach, distinguishing only two

---

[9] Comments upon the hypotheses are available in Swinney and Cutler (1979), Cacciari and Tabossi (1988), Nayak and Gibbs (1990), Tabossi and Zardon (1993), Van de Voort and Vonk (1995), to name but a few sources.

classes of further subcategorization, namely idioms and habitual collocations.[10] It
is worthy of note that neither of these authors mention compounds in their chief
classification or subclassification. Only Sonomura seems to be aware of the fact
that compounds cannot be simply ignored and she regards them as a specific
category of phraseme, together with binomials or trinomials (e.g. *tooth and nail; no
ifs, ands, or buts about it*) and phrasal, prepositional, and support verbs (e.g. *give in;
look up [a tree]; come home*). Indeed, compounds represent a specific category
because they are believed not to manifest all the characteristics attributed by
definition to idioms or kindred expressions. No wonder that Sonomura tried to
establish an independent class labelled 'cross-cutting'. Yet this heading is intended
to suggest something that is my conviction, too: namely, that there are many more
points of commonality than differences between compounds and idiomatic expressions, not excepting idioms proper, of course: compounds, like idioms, are
highly conventionalized, context-bound expressions. Suffice it to compare any one
of quite a few definitions of an idiom: put briefly and in my own words, an idiom
can be defined as a concatenation of more than one lexeme whose total meaning is
not easily arrived at from the meanings of its constituents. In the end, the
concatenation represents a new lexeme (a naming unit) of its own right and it
enters the lexicon. On reading this, one might be tempted to replace the term
'idiom' with 'compound' and then leave the definition untouched. And indeed,
this adapted definition of compound seems to be acceptable – except for one point:
namely, it is not always true that the total meaning of compounds can never be
derived from the meanings of their constituents. Specifically, if this were true, such
expressions as *wood-fire, Anglo-Saxon, dark-blue, bedroom, fellow-worker*, etc., quite
transparent as they are, could not very well be called compounds.[11] Hence it
follows that not all compounds are genuine idioms, in spite of the fact that many
'concatenated' expressions come to be highly lexicalized (e.g. *life boat, dog's ear,
redbreast, pickpocket, bluebell*) and might meet the above-cited definition of idiom.
The apparent problem can, of course, be solved satisfactorily once we accept the
idea of continuity, or 'fluidity', within the overlapping category of so-called idiomatic expressions (i.e. between collocations and idioms proper), allowing also for
fuzzy points where the domain of idiomatic expressions borders on free combin-

[10] The attribute 'habitual', as used by Fernando, refers to a quality which suggests the distinction
between collocations (conventionalized combinations of relatively high degree of variability) and the
remainder of truly variable combinations (in this treatise referred to as 'free').

[11] Examples that are presented in works by idiomatologists do not cover the whole scope of
complexes usually referred to as compounds. Such instances as *blackbird, afternoon, statesman* are
missing, and so also are those that border on derivation (including *Sunday, Frenchman, over-peopled*),
perhaps with the exception of N+N phrases, e.g. *fellow-worker, home nurse*. It is no wonder, because if
only 'multi-word chunks' consisting of a minimum of two words are discussed, then the *blackbird* type
of compounds must be ignored, to say nothing of expressions such as *gospel, daisy* (treated now as
monomorphemic), or *forecastle* (which resembles a compound in spelling only).

ations.[12] Hence I claim that the lexemes that we traditionally label 'compounds' could in fact be looked upon as idiomatic expressions in general, displaying all the characteristics as outlined here above (section 2.2.2) and exemplified here below (sections 2.3.3–5). In so doing, neither the concept of 'compound' nor the term itself (like that of 'word', for instance, and perhaps others) needs to be abandoned; for good measure, the concept and the term could be judged in the context of individual languages, both in synchronic and diachronic perspectives. That is, an expression referred to as 'compound' in one language will not always be ranked as a compound in another language,[13] although – and this is the point – we may have similar expressions (naming units) in mind. To this extent, namely from the functional point of view, compounds might represent a universal phenomenon.

2.3.2 English compounds as representatives of the category

There are thousands of idioms in current English, estimates running to over 4,500. Clearly, this figure is very rough because even if we could perhaps be in substantial agreement over the basic definition of an idiom, we would still be unable to capture the constant shifts in quantity due to the fact that some idioms fade out of use (and not only due to their triteness) while others come into existence, also extending or narrowing their meanings. It is even more difficult to give estimates of numbers of idiomatic expressions in general; and provided we accept the postulate that compounds can be treated as idiomatic expressions, we can only speak of there being a huge number of these expressions. Compounding has always been very productive throughout the history of English: those who are interested in the past of English will know of 'metaphorical' compounds (in Old English mostly of Germanic character, i.e. N+N type), their concatenations being referred to as 'kennings'; and later on, in Middle English, compounds – though perhaps less ornamental – did not decrease in number thanks to the influence of the typical Romance manner of compounding. It is necessary to add, however, that the present contribution does not deal specifically with the issue of productivity;[14] its aim is to give

---

[12] It is in this overlapping sphere that a qualitative change occurs, speaking in philosophical terms: as hopefully emerges from the present discussion, many frequently used and familiar free combinations can be viewed as candidates for compound status, awaiting, as it were, the general consensus in terms of conventionalization. See also section 2.3.5: it is possible that *blue hotel* might be read figuratively, in an appropriate context at least; likewise this has already occurred with, for example, *blue pencil, green thumb*, etc.

[13] For instance, the English *country house*, which I list as a prototype of (a class of) compounds, is matched with the Spanish *casa de campo*, which is described as a syntactic phrase (or syntactic group). See also footnote 1.

[14] Readers will find information on productivity in other chapters of this Handbook. Here I only mean to draw on the well-known fact that in some languages composition may be more productive than in others: suffice it to compare, for instance, Modern German, on the one hand, and Modern Czech, on the other.

evidence, by citing some prototypical examples, that (English) compounds are those naming units (or lexemes) that meet all the fundamental conditions allowing them to be ranked as idiomatic expressions.

2.3.3 Introducing the range of compounds

To start with, a few citations will be presented merely in order to show the range of compounds as idiomatic expressions. One extreme, if we agree on the definition of an idiom, can be illustrated by typically non-compositional units, such as *white lie*, and also *goldfish, redbreast, highbrow, common sense*, etc. The other extreme, however, is worthy of note. We will very probably come to an agreement that *front door*, for instance, forms a closer (semantic) unit than *green* (or *plastic*, etc.) *door* – perhaps because we sense that 'a front door' (and similarly, 'a front garden') is a typical notion for everyday life for the British (as is *front yard* for the Americans). If we now think of *black coffee*, the example cited and briefly commented upon above, I believe that this expression will be considered as a less compositional one on the scale than *front door*. These two, or three, examples (*plastic / front door, black coffee*) are listed in order to epitomize the fuzzy points within the area where idiomatic expressions border on free combinations. In this regard, it is proper to point out that the idea of the decisive role of context should be taken into consideration (see section 2.2.3), which is significant mainly in cases of metonymies (e.g. *the White House*), and other figures too (e.g. *stonewall*). Within these two 'extremes', some other prototypical examples (of commonly recognized or only potential compounds) will be discussed briefly below.

2.3.4 Compounds and compositionality

Briefly speaking, I regard 'compositionality' as the product of the continual complex interplay of variability and literalness, and as a complex phenomenon whose common denominator is the reference to semantic unity. In my view, idiomatic expressions should be considered to be non-compositional (see section 2.2.3); hence it follows that once we admit that compounds behave as idiomatic expressions, they must be defined as those lexemes which are basically non-compositional.

Compounds can be considered as non-compositional only because they are invariable: the sequence of constituents is fixed, and as for their lexical flexibility, attributive determinations (or modifications) are only external, that is, they will affect the whole compound rather than one or the other component. Appropriate examples are easy to find. Violation of the expected sequence of, for example, *sunrise, common sense, lazybones, forget-me-not*, etc. would result in nonsense words, or, in specific cases, a different meaning – then, of course, we cannot very well speak of 'violation'; further examples would be *red-white* vs. *white-red, or footbridge* vs. *bridge-foot*, where each of these has a status of compound. Moreover, quite often the fixed sequence is a matter of convention, as in *bitter-sweet* (*sweet-bitter), *deaf and dumb* (*dumb and deaf);[15] finally, needless to mention, the mere swapping-over of constituents will sometimes bring us into the domain of free combinations, e.g. *snow-cold / cold snow*. As with idiomatic expressions generally, certain morphological exponents can certainly occur, such as plural or tense morphemes, e.g. *playgrounds, dry-cleans/-ed*, with the exception of compounds of genuine non-literal meaning, e.g. *red tape*. The following two examples will serve well to illustrate attributive determinations, which are external: *a door-knob* can only be extended as, e.g. *a new [door-knob]*, not **a door [new] knob* or **a [new door] knob*, if these are to convey the same meaning as *a new [door-knob]*, namely 'a door-knob which is new'; and similarly, we would hardly accept as meaningful an expression such as **the snow-White House* when speaking of the US President's seat of office.

It is 'literalness' that co-creates the phenomenon of compositionality (see section 2.2.2.2). We will not have any doubts about the proper understanding of the labels 'literal' and 'non-literal' in the following examples: the expressions *door-knob, playground, Anglo-Saxon, colour-blind, dark-blue, green-painted* are literal in meaning, while *white lie, blue joke, lazybones* are typically non-literal. Yet there are many compounds whose meanings can be read both literally and figuratively (idiomatically); let us consider, for example, *flash+point, small+fish, deep+water, by+way*, etc. Here the problem is that the relation 'literal: figurative' tends to be judged on the basis of the relation 'concrete: abstract'. However, while expressions of literal interpretation will always be concrete, those of figurative (and non-literal) interpretation do not have to be abstract. It is beyond doubt that, for example, *the White House, lazybones, blackbird*, etc. would be considered as concrete enough, and yet, at least in my conception, they are not literal. The more we probe into the issue of literalness, the more we realize that the situation is far too complex, and complicated, to be projected into a box-like classification. In the end we have to accept the view that the decisive factor in distinguishing between literal and figurative interpretation of one and the same syntactic phrase is the weight of truly literal reference to the objective reality of both, one, or none of the constituents. Thus while the prototypes *door-knob* and *white lie* serve to illustrate exclusively literal and non-literal interpretations respectively, the following citations will document the situation between the two 'extremes': (a) *dark room; dark horse; dead duck, dead wood*; (b) *apple-tree, stone-fish, horse-fly, bulldog, lifeboat*. Let us note that the ones

---

[15] Here also the Latin-like 'multi-element expressions' belong, e.g. *kitchen-cum-scullery*. While allowing for discussion on their 'position between syntactic structures and "traditional" word-formations' (Stein 2000: 284), I am convinced that in my conception, these expressions can indeed be called compounds.

in (a) are either literal – then acting as free combinations – or they are figurative. The literalness of the respective referents determining a possible figurative reading differs too: we can imagine that 'a lab to process films' is both 'a room' and 'dark', but 'a person of unknown character' is not literally 'a horse of dark colour'. Yet I dare to speak of figurative meaning in both cases, simply because a truly literal meaning exists parallel to, and in fact also underlying the new figures (see also section 2.3.5). Further on, the examples in (b) are worthy of our attention because they partly draw on the 'figurative' type *dark room*, and yet their reading is not absolutely figurative or absolutely literal. That is, *tree, fish, fly*, etc. in the citations above are true literal referents, as is 'room' in *dark room*, but their other constituents do not refer to what they primarily mean. In other words, the fish called *stone-fish* (and similarly, e.g. *stone-fly, stone fox, stone marten, stone-fern*, etc.) has nothing to do with 'stone' as such – it is rather qualities of 'stone', or possibly the place where the fish live, that flash into our mind in this case. Similarly, *lifeboat* is not interpreted as 'living boat' but one used to save people's lives.

Various connotations of constituents add an extra layer of complexity to the description. For example, *blue carpet, blue joke*, and *blue pencil* are all English expressions, and their respective interpretations will differ, being only literal in *blue carpet*, only non-literal in *blue joke*, and both literal and figurative in *blue pencil*. In my conception, an acceptable solution is to think in relative terms, allowing for interpretation of some expressions as being more figurative (or less literal) than others. In the end, owing to the ingenious character of language, the concept of compositionality – a concept which also demonstrates 'fluidity' – will make it possible to treat compounds as idiomatic expressions and separate them from other concatenated sequences of expressions that I refer to as free combinations. Thus, for instance, if *a dark room* is to mean 'a photo lab', it will be labelled a compound – because even if we hesitate over its being literal or rather figurative in interpretation, we would hardly think of variability such as *a darker room* or *a small and dark room*; by this very token the expression is believed to be non-compositional, which is the essential characteristic of compounds as idiomatic expressions.

2.3.5 Compounds and predictability

In order to avoid misunderstanding, let me point out again (see section 2.2.3) that the compositionality of compounds does not depend on their predictability; or more precisely, the predictability of compounds is not directly proportional to their compositionality. What I mean to say is that compounds as non-compositional expressions are not necessarily non-predictable. Predictability will depend on other factors, too: from one side largely on context, from the other side on conventionality, the criteria of which are familiarity of the new meaning, frequency of its use, and its fixedness in the lexicon. Thus *red tape* in a context such as 'Preparing for the reconstruction of our house we had to cut through all sorts of red tape' will certainly not be interpreted literally;[16] and likewise, *blue film, bluestocking, [once in a] blue moon* are read figuratively (or downright non-literally, although their literal senses are imaginable) because their 'new' meanings have become familiar and accepted by all (or at least most) speakers.

Nevertheless, the issue is what makes (native) speakers think of either a literal or a figurative interpretation. Firstly, different theories work with hypotheses describing ways of arriving at a correct interpretation (see section 2.2.3). Here I will not argue about 'the best' procedure; yet my experience, based on an experiment (Kavka 2003: 94 ff.), speaks in favour of the fact that the figurative interpretation is the first to flash into our mind – and only if this appears inadequate do we revert to the literal reading. Certainly, what plays a significant role here is the 'force' of the context (i.e. its unambiguous range, its preciseness)[17] as well as the degree of lexicalization (i.e. awareness of the given figurative meaning among speakers, this meaning being subjectively obsolete, well-known, too progressive, or perhaps unfamiliar). Secondly, which may have a substantial bearing on the present topic, we should take one fact into account, namely that the process of building a compound is not a mirror-image of the process of comprehending a compound.[18] And yet my conviction is that during the process of comprehension we in fact try to decipher the process of building up the total meaning through the cumulative association of the semantic roots contained in the constituents. However, this cumulative association is not always straightforward enough to be viewed as a computation of the respective meanings of the constituents. Suffice it to compare, for instance, *playground – lifeboat – greybeard*. Their associative processes are not identical, reflecting their position on the scale of literalness (see section 2.3.4) and hence on the scale of compositionality: *playground* comes closer to the free-combination category – what it refers to is literally 'a ground to play on', whereas *lifeboat* does not mean, as has been pointed out above, 'a living boat' but 'a boat used to save lives'. (Similar are the above-cited *bulldog, stone-fish, horse-fly, apple tree*, and many others.) In any case, their meanings are easily predictable. Also predictable are the meanings of compounds represented by the prototype *greybeard*: these become non-compositional due to the figurative reference mostly to people (cf. *highbrow, blockhead, lazybones, pickpocket; bluebell*), and their meanings

---

[16] Compare with the following context, which it is hoped will bias the interpretation: 'Red tape rather than black tape would be better to insulate the wire.' (The omnipotence of context is sometimes overestimated; this issue, however, cannot be discussed here, for reasons of space.)

[17] Let us try to consider all possible extensions of (verbal) context 'It took me a long time before I *got the picture*': before this is done, the interpretation will, most probably, be 'before I understood'. Similarly with compounds, though less frequently, owing to their orthography and pronunciation: e.g., 'He got into *deep water*.' 'The lights went out, and the *dark room* made the girl scared.'

[18] Compare the metaphor used by Aitchison (1996: 197): 'we cannot automatically assume that going upstairs uses identical muscles to going down but in the reverse sequence'.

are based on underlying metaphorical or metonymical concepts – in our proto-type, 'grey beard' being a characteristic feature of an old man.

My final paragraphs revert to the complexity of the issue, stressing the phenom-enon of the gradient character of compound status as compared to free lexeme combinations. In the light of hypotheses describing and explaining the process of comprehension, mainly the Decomposition Hypothesis (see section 2.2.3), inter-pretation of the total meaning of a given compound is believed to depend largely also on the most probable reading of its constituents. Here, of course, a certain degree of subjectivity must be admitted, which on the speaker's part may often be welcomed as creativity and which on either part (both the speaker's and the receiver's) presupposes linguistic competence, including an awareness of sociocul-tural background. (As a matter of fact, the process of cumulative association is activated in the context understood in the broader sense.) I believe that the issue can be clearly illustrated by the prototype *country music / house / club*. These ex-amples remind us of free combinations, since we tend to understand their total meanings literally, in a very narrow sense of the word – therefore, they could very well be regarded as fully compositional. Nevertheless, the expected predictability encompasses in itself certain aspects of the interlocutors' knowledge, specifically of British interlocutors, which extends the conceptual (cognitive) meaning of *country* by adding certain 'associative-connotative' meanings. The constituent 'country' does not only refer to location: 'country music' means a specific genre typical of the south and west of the US; 'country house' is a large building, very often of historical value and partly open to the public; and 'country club' implies an exclusive membership of wealthy people. Seeing the expressions from this perspective, I do not see it as a problem to rank them as compounds.

2.4 CONCLUSION

In my view, compounds represent a larger range of lexemes than is commonly and traditionally believed. What I find important to point out is that they show quite a few features and properties that are characteristic of idiomatic expressions. As a matter of fact, they share with idiomatic expressions the ways in which they arise, their existence proper, and their interpretation.

Although perhaps taken for granted, we tend to use the term 'compound' to name an expression coming into existence through the combination of two or more simplex words (constituents), finally representing a unit syntactically and meaningfully invariable in the current context. The role of context should be stressed here: I believe that compounds cannot be treated strictly as isolated phenomena (of grammar or the lexicon). Their status will be understood more readily if they are viewed as parts of concrete, contextually defined utterances. Let me point out too that the aforementioned tentative definition of a compound also implies the idea of process: on the one hand, it makes it possible to look upon free combinations as potential candidates for compound status; and on the other hand, it allows for an analysis of the processing of meaning pragmatically viewed as a (very often creative) coinage of one specific meaning on the speaker's part and the choice from (usually more than one) possible interpretation(s) on the receiver's part. Put in psycholinguistic terms, the new meaning (i.e. the total meaning) is arrived at by computation of the meanings of the respective constituents, either directly or through figures of various types. What definitely sets compounds apart from free combinations is the complex phenomenon of compositionality: like idiomatic expressions, compounds are non-compositional, that is to say, they are restrained in their variability (flexibility) and/or literalness. It only remains to add one important thing: respecting the dynamic character of language, we must look upon compositionality as a scalar, gradient phenomenon.

CHAPTER 3

THE CLASSIFICATION OF COMPOUNDS

SERGIO SCALISE AND ANTONIETTA BISETTO

3.1 INTRODUCTION

Classification of compounds has been and still is a much-debated issue in the linguistic literature. From the beginning, almost every scholar dealing with composition has proposed his/her own view. There are several proposals in the current literature as well, as compounds have received much attention in recent years. Since compounds might be considered halfway between morphology and syntax, they pose a challenge in deciding what Jackendoff (1997) has called 'the architecture of the grammar'. As for the definition of what a compound is, the reader is referred to Chapter 1 in this book.

In our opinion all the existing proposals for classifying the huge variety of compounds of natural languages are – for one reason or another – unsatisfactory.

This work is part of a wider research programme on compounds that is made possible by the financial support of the University of Bologna (RFO 2004) and the Ministry of University (Prin 2005). We would like to thank the editors of this volume for their comments on a previous version of this chapter. Usual disclaimers apply.

Therefore, we intend to propose here a classification of compounds based on criteria that are as consistent as possible and, hopefully, universally valid.[1]

The paper is organized as follows: in section 3.2 and its subsections we point out and discuss the major problems arising from previous attempts at classifying compounds, be they contemporary or of years past; in section 3.3 and its subsections we analyse the classification proposed in Bisetto and Scalise (2005); in section 3.4 we propose amendments to the previous classification and discuss the basis for the amendments; finally, in section 3.5 we touch on a number of residual problems and propose our conclusions.

3.2 PROBLEMS IN THE CLASSIFICATION OF COMPOUNDS

The classifications of compounds that appear in current linguistic literature often lack interlinguistic homogeneity for the following reasons:

   (a) Terminology is often associated with a single language and thus not valid from an interlinguistic point of view (3.2.1);
   (b) Current research, but also less recent works, privilege the analysis of compounds formed by certain lexical categories and disregard a number of other types of compounds (3.2.2); and
   (c) Classifications have often been built upon inconsistent criteria (3.2.3) and therefore the different types of compounds are not easy to compare.

In the following sections we shall briefly discuss each of these points.

3.2.1 Terminology

Terminological problems can be ascribed to two separate causes: (a) diachronic changes in the meaning; and (b) the language-specific nature of a part of the adopted terminology that prevents the application of some specific labels to similar compounds in other languages.

---

[1] In this paper we use data from the CompoNet database, developed at the University of Bologna, Dipartimento di Lingue e Letterature Straniere Moderne. Our classification of compounds has been tested on the languages used in the MorboComp/CompoNet projects, i.e. Bulgarian, Catalan, Chinese, Czech, German, Dutch, English, Finnish, French, Modern Greek, Hungarian, Italian, Japanese, Korean, Latin, Norwegian, Polish, Portuguese, Russian, Serbo-Croatian, Spanish, Swedish, Turkish.

Problems identified under (a) can be exemplified by the term *bahuvrīhi*. This Sanskrit word, meaning (*having*) *much rice* (Whitney 1889: 502), has been used for identifying nominal compounds with possessive interpretation but ended up by indicating exocentric compounds *tout court*.[2] As shown by Bauer (2001b: 700), the term *bahuvrīhi* was finally applied 'to any compound which is not a hyponym of its own head element'.[3] The use of the term *bahuvrīhi* as a generic label for exocentric compounds is thus an incorrect extension; *bahuvrīhi* in fact refers to a specific subclass of exocentric compounds, namely possessive compounds.

The same applies to another Sanskrit term, *dvandva* 'couple', which originally indicated both the aggregate of two coordinated elements (*candrādityau* 'moon and sun') and a multiplicity of separate and coordinated elements (*rogaçokapar-ītāpabahanavyasanāni* 'disease, pain, grief, captivity, and misfortune') (Whitney 1889: 485–6). Currently the term is often used for indicating coordinate compounds as a whole (cf. e.g. Di Sciullo 2007b), without taking into account the fact that coordination in compounding has different outcomes. Coordination can in fact: (a) associate two individual elements without reference to any of them as a separate entity, as in true *dvandva* compounds (cf. the Sanskrit compound for 'father–mother = parents'); or else (b) express two 'properties' associated with an entity, as is the case in modern formations such as *poet-novelist* or *learner driver*.

One of the major problems with the analysis of compounds is that Anglo-Saxon linguistics has focused traditionally – and almost exclusively – on two types of formations: *root* (or primary) compounds and *synthetic* (or secondary) compounds. These two notions could not be adequately extended to languages such as Romance languages, in which terms like *root* or *synthetic* did not seem to apply conveniently. The notion of 'root compound' used for formations such as *steamboat* or *coffee cup* has not been extended to Romance languages because the lexemes in some of these languages (e.g. Italian and Spanish), when they are nouns, end in a vowel that bears 'grammatical information' and does not belong to the root (cf. Bisetto 2003).

In an Italian compound such as *capostazione* 'station master', the words *capo* and *stazione* are not 'roots' even though each of them can be described as being formed by a root (*cap-* and *stazion-*) plus a morpheme (*-o* and *-e*, respectively) indicating the inflectional class to which the lexemes belong (D'Achille and Thornton 2003).

As for the 'synthetic compound' label, used for constructions such as *taxi driver*, it long seemed inapplicable to Romance languages, because the type was thought to be non-existent there (cf. Bisetto 1994, 2001 and Guevara and Scalise 2004). Romance formations similar to synthetic compounds, the so-called VN compounds like *portalettere* (lit. 'carry letters') 'letter carrier', lack an overt derivational

---

[2] Sanskrit *bahuvrīhi* are nouns that acquire adjectival value as a consequence of the addition of *having* (Whitney 1889: 501).

[3] See, for example, Booij (2005a: 80) where it is maintained that *bahuvrīhi* compounds 'are sometimes considered to form a subset of the exocentric compounds'.

affix capable of making the structure of Italian – and more generally of Romance – formations identical to that of their Germanic counterparts (apart from the order of constituents, of course).

'Root compound' and 'synthetic compound' are therefore *language-specific* terms and, as such, can only refer to specific compounds of some but not all languages, unless the meaning of the terms be extended or modified.

Apart from the fact that these labels do not appear to be applicable across languages, one of the major problems of existing taxonomies is the variety of the criteria adopted for classification. The two labels mentioned in the preceding paragraphs, for example, can be considered as being based on a single criterion or on different criteria. Indeed, whereas *root* refers to the non-derivational nature of the relevant lexemes, in the definition of *synthetic* two different criteria were adopted (cf. Oshita 1995.)[4] The first criterion considers *synthetic* as equivalent to 'secondary' or 'deverbal', so that the distinction *root / synthetic* appears to be consistent. *Synthetic*, however, also means that the non-head constituent satisfies the argument structure requirements of the head;[5] in this second meaning, therefore, the *synthetic compound* label is based on a different criterion from the one used for defining *root compounds*.

A further example of inconsistency in the adoption of the defining criteria can be observed in labels such as 'phrasal' and 'neoclassical'. 'Phrasal' refers to the (phrasal) nature of the non-head constituent,[6] whereas 'neoclassical' refers to the (Greek or Latin) origin of one or both constituents. These two terms are descriptively apt for indicating these particular formations, but one cannot neglect the fact that the use of labels that refer to different kinds of information could well consign to the background, or indeed overlook, other fundamental data.

The multiplicity of criteria need not be excluded from the classification of compounds. However, we believe that all adopted criteria need to be consistent if we are to obtain a classification that is valid from an interlinguistic point of view.

3.2.2 Neglected categories

Coming to the second point, it is not too hard to observe that morphological research (and especially research on English) has generally privileged a few complex formations while neglecting others. The most analysed compounds are those with $[N+N]_N$ and $[A+N]_N$ or $[N+A]_N$ internal structure, whereas many other

---

[4] For a discussion of the issue, see Bisetto (2001).

[5] This is, specifically, the position adopted by Marchand (1969), where these compounds are defined as *verbal-nexus*. Actually, though, *verbal-nexus* compounds are superordinate with respect to synthetic compounds because, as can be seen in the representation in (1c) below, the latter are but a part of *verbal-nexus* compounds.

[6] Ackema and Neeleman (2004) argue that the head constituent can also be phrasal.

structural types have been almost ignored. Little attention has been paid to a variety of formations, such as:

(a) compound adjectives of the [A+A]$_A$ (*bitter-sweet*), [A+N]$_A$ (It. *giallo limone* 'lemon yellow'), [V+A]$_A$ (Du. *druipnat* 'drip-wet') and [N+A]$_A$ (*girl crazy*) type;

(b) compounds containing words that are not nouns, such as (i) adverbs (It. *sottosopra* 'upside down'); (ii) prepositions (Fr. *sans papiers* lit. 'without documents'); (iii) pronouns (*self-determination*); (iv) particles (*make up*); and (v) verbs (*portacenere* 'ash tray').

Actually, in addition to the aforementioned structures ([N+N]$_N$ and [A+N]$_N$ or [N+A]$_N$), other compound structures can be found, as is the case with [V+V]$_V$, [V+V]$_N$, [A+V]$_V$, [N+V]$_N$, [N+V]$_V$, [V+N]$_N$, [V+N]$_V$, [Pro+N]$_N$, [Pro+V]$_V$, [P+A]$_A$, [Adv+V]$_V$, etc.

The properties of these formations have been studied only on an occasional basis, although in some instances they represent highly productive patterns as is the case with Italian [V+N]$_N$ compounds.[7]

3.2.3 Criteria for classification

As noted above, one of the most prominent problems in compound taxonomy is the heterogeneity of the adopted criteria. In this section we will deal precisely with this issue.

Let us consider the notions of endocentricity / exocentricity and the notion of coordination. The first two notions define compounds on the basis of the presence (endocentric) vs. absence (exocentric) of a head constituent. The notion of coordination is, conversely, based on the relation between the two constituents of the compound. If we do not want to be forced to say that coordination bears no relation whatsoever with endocentricity / exocentricity, then we need to allow these two notions to intersect. As we shall see later, the intersection of the defining criteria is of the essence for obtaining a classification that is adequate from a descriptive point of view.

3.2.3.1 *Current and previous classifications*

In order to illustrate the above-mentioned issue, we now present a significant, though not comprehensive review of classifications proposed in research works on compounds, illustrated in (1) by means of tree diagrams:[8]

---

[7] There are of course exceptions. VN formations, for instance, have been analysed by many, among these Zwanenburg (1992), Di Sciullo (1992a) and Villoing (2003) for French and Bisetto (1994, 1999) for Italian.

[8] The representations in (1a–i) are not to be found in this form in the reference works, but are rather the result of our own interpretation, which in some cases can be partial and schematic: the tree diagram representation appeared however useful for a more immediate comparison between the various proposals.

(1) a.

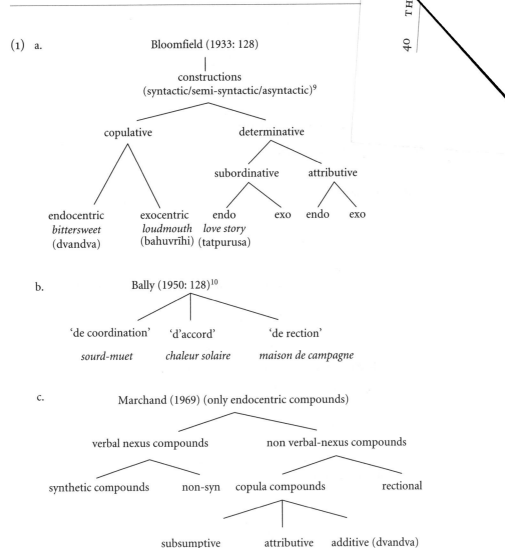

Bloomfield (1933: 128)

constructions
(syntactic/semi-syntactic/asyntactic)[9]

copulative   determinative

                    subordinative   attributive

endocentric   exocentric   endo   exo   endo   exo
bittersweet   *loudmouth* *love story*
(dvandva)   (bahuvrīhi) (tatpurusa)

b.   Bally (1950: 128)[10]

    'de coordination'   'd'accord'   'de rection'

    sourd-muet   *chaleur solaire*   *maison de campagne*

c.   Marchand (1969) (only endocentric compounds)

        verbal nexus compounds   non verbal-nexus compounds

    synthetic compounds   non-syn   copula compounds   rectional

        subsumptive   attributive   additive (dvandva)
        oak tree   *girlfriend*   *fighter-bomber* *steamboat*
                          blackboard   *Austria-Hungary*

[9] The constituents of a syntactic compound 'stand to each other in the same grammatical relation as words in a phrase' (e.g. *blackbird* and *a black bird*). In semi-syntactic compounds, the compound 'shows more than the minimum deviation from the phrase' (cf. *to housekeep* vs. *keep house*); 'Asyntactic compounds have members that do not combine in syntactic constructions of their language' (cf. *door-knob*).

[10] Bally uses a sort of Lexical Integrity Principle for separating phrases and compounds. In fact he contrasts *chaleur vraiment tropicale* 'really tropical heat' with **chaleur vraiment solaire* 'sunheat'. It should be noted though that Bally's proposal is difficult to assess since – as a general rule – his distinction between compounds and phrases is far from clear (for instance, apparently Bally deems the expression *forme et valeur* 'form and value' to be a compound, cf. § 146, p. 128).

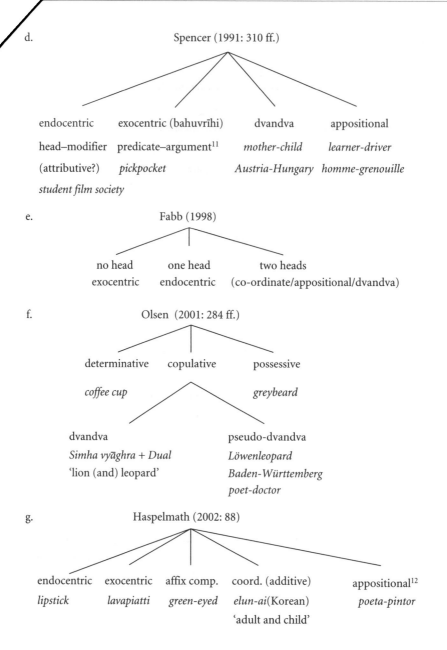

d.   Spencer (1991: 310 ff.)

endocentric	exocentric (bahuvrīhi)	dvandva	appositional
head–modifier	predicate–argument[11]	*mother-child*	*learner-driver*
(attributive?)	*pickpocket*	*Austria-Hungary*	*homme-grenouille*
student film society			

e.   Fabb (1998)

no head	one head	two heads
exocentric	endocentric	(co-ordinate/appositional/dvandva)

f.   Olsen (2001: 284 ff.)

determinative	copulative	possessive
coffee cup		*greybeard*

dvandva	pseudo-dvandva
Simha vyāghra + Dual	*Löwenleopard*
'lion (and) leopard'	*Baden-Württemberg*
	poet-doctor

g.   Haspelmath (2002: 88)

endocentric	exocentric	affix comp.	coord. (additive)	appositional[12]
lipstick	*lavapiatti*	*green-eyed*	*elun-ai*(Korean)	*poeta-pintor*
			'adult and child'	

---

[11] According to Spencer 'Predicate–argument relations can be observed in endocentric compounds', too (e.g. *taxi driver*).

[12] Haspelmath adds yet another type: 'The last type of compound to be mentioned here is again exocentric..., but it shares with coordinative compounds the feature of semantic equality of both compound members: classic Tibetan *rgan-gžon* 'old-young = age'.

h.

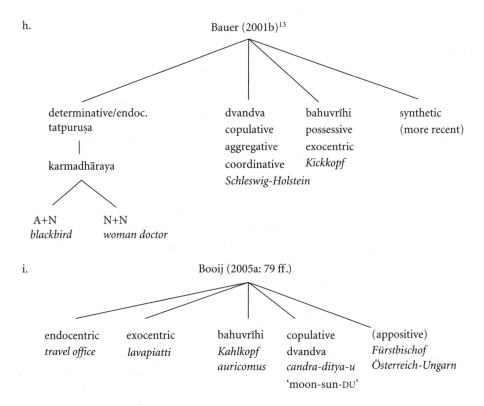

Bauer (2001b)[13]

determinative/endoc.
tatpuruṣa

karmadhāraya

A+N   N+N
blackbird   *woman doctor*

dvandva
copulative
aggregative
coordinative
Schleswig-Holstein

bahuvrīhi
possessive
exocentric
Kickkopf

synthetic
(more recent)

i.

Booij (2005a: 79 ff.)

endocentric
travel office

exocentric
lavapiatti

bahuvrīhi
Kahlkopf
auricomus

copulative
dvandva
candra-ditya-u
'moon-sun-DU'

(appositive)
Fürstbischof
Österreich-Ungarn

As a start, let us examine four rather similar proposals: Spencer, Haspelmath, Booij, and Bauer.

These classifications are based on a single criterion, the presence/absence of the head. This criterion is on the same level as the criterion that ascertains, for example, whether a formation is copulative (Booij and Bauer), *dvandva* (Spencer), coordinate, or appositional (Haspelmath). In other terms, these scholars seem to consider endocentricity and exocentricity as having the same nature as the other notions; therefore they do not allow them to 'intersect' the other classes. Spencer, for instance, proposes a three-pronged approach: (a) head–modifier endocentric constructions – which can possibly also include attributive compounds; (b) verb–argument exocentric formations (*bahuvrīhi*); and (c) *dvandva* compounds – a group that possibly also includes appositional constructions. However, separating endocentric and exocentric compounds from *dvandva* implies the unfortunate consequence that one might assume that the latter cannot be analysed for endo/

---

[13] Bauer's essay is a typical example of what was said in note 8. Bauer acknowledges the fact that existing classifications are problematic (for example, in his own view, a compound like *woman doctor* should be seen as a coordinate and not as a *karmadhāraya*). On the other hand, Bauer's goals were typological and not classificatory.

exocentricity. The fact is, though, that *dvandvas* and (Spencer's) appositional compounds differ precisely in that the former are exocentric and the latter endocentric. In other words, head–modifier compounds are not the only possible endocentric compounds, just as verb–argument compounds are not the only possible exocentric ones.

Also, Haspelmath's classification (endocentric, exocentric, appositional, coordinate, and affixed) seems to overlook the fact that affixed compounds, as also (additive) coordinates like *adult-child*, are exocentric, whereas appositives are endocentric.

In Booij's arrangement, although Sanskrit-type *dvandvas* (with dual or plural inflection) are accurately distinct from copulatives (which are singular in number), the distinction between endocentric and exocentric compounds and *bahuvrīhi* and copulatives is a source of redundancy given that the notion of exocentricity applies to *dvandva* copulatives whereas endocentricity applies to appositive copulatives.

Similar observations also apply to the classification arising from Bauer's work. In Bauer's taxonomy, the notion of head is not properly extended to all types of compounds. By separating *dvandvas* and *bahuvrīhis*, for example, the fact that (also) *dvandvas* can be exocentric (just like *bahuvrīhis*) does not come to the fore. Furthermore, by making 'synthetic compounds' distinct from other groups, the author seems to exclude the possibility of applying the endo/exocentricity criterion to them.

In addition to the problems so far discussed, all stemming from having considered notions such as exocentric and endocentric as being equivalent to other notions such as *dvandva* and synthetic, these classifications also suffer from an inconsistency of criteria. Let us consider, for example, Haspelmath's proposal. His classification is based upon various criteria: (a) presence/absence of the head (giving rise to the distinction between endocentric and exocentric compounds); (b) formal structure (achieved by introducing a class of 'affixed compounds'); and (c) syntactico-semantic relation between constituents (determining the class of appositional compounds). Thus it is by no means easy to understand whether criterion (a), relating to the presence/absence of the head, would actually apply to compounds grouped on the basis of criterion (b), i.e. formal structure, and whether there can exist a possible relation between affixed and appositional compounds.

Different observations can be made as regards the solutions proposed by Olsen and Fabb. Although coherent, by virtue of the use of a single criterion (the number of heads), Fabb's classification is too restrictive when confronted with the variety of recognized compounds.

Olsen's classification presents two advantages: first of all, it uses the notion of determinative as opposed to coordinate compound; and secondly, building upon previous work by Fanselow (1981, 1985), it underlines the differences between true Sanskrit *dvandas* and Germanic copulatives. In contrast to the former, the latter do not carry a dual reference but rather a single one and should thus be dubbed 'pseudo-*dvandvas*', as originally suggested by Fanselow. However, besides the two

classes of 'determinatives' and 'copulatives', Olsen also introduces a class of possessive (exocentric) compounds, whose designation is based on a different criterion. Determinatives, like *dvandas* and pseudo-*dvandvas*, are identified on the basis
of the relation between constituents (subordination vs. coordination)[14] whereas
possessives are defined on the basis of the relation between the complex construction and its 'missing' head. An undesirable consequence of this mixture of criteria
is that it is unclear whether the notion of exocentric/endocentric applies to
determinative and copulative compounds.

While on this subject, one should note that all existing classifications show an
inconsistent use of labels; in other words, the same label is not always used for
identifying the same type of compounds (although admittedly this is quite normal
in every scientific taxonomy). For instance, what Olsen defines as copulative (e.g.
dottore-poeta 'poet-doctor') is appositional according to Haspelmath and Spencer
(e.g. *poeta-pintor* 'painter-poet' and *learner-driver*).

Let us now briefly touch upon other classifications which could be seen as
'traditional'. Bloomfield consistently used the notions of 'subordinative' and 'copulative', which apply to both endocentric and exocentric compounds. In his opinion,
subordinative and copulative 'constructions' can belong to both classes. It follows
that this classification is based upon two different criteria (i.e. the relation between
constituents and the presence of a head) but at different levels of application.

Likewise Marchand's proposed taxonomy, which is both articulate and rich, is
based upon consistent criteria, both when dealing with endocentric formations
(the only ones represented under 1c) and when dealing with exocentric compounds.[15] Marchand's three different levels of classification are actually each
based on a single criterion: 'verbal/non verbal nexus' considers the presence (or
absence) of a verb in the head constituent; 'synthetic/non-synthetic' and '*copula/
rectional*', are based on the grammatical relation between the constituents, as is the
case with the further subdivision between 'subsumptive', 'attributive', and 'additive'
(*dvandva*) that applies to copula compounds.

Lastly, Bally's proposed classification, based on the single criterion of the grammatical relation between the head and the non-head constituent and enabling him
to identify the 'de coordination', 'd'accord' and, 'de rection' types, is also insufficient as it does not take into account the notion of head. One could say that the
proposals from Bally and Fabb appear, so to speak, complementary. Another
problem associated with Bally's proposal is that his domain of compounds includes

---

[14] Actually *dvandva* and pseudo-*dvandva* copulatives are defined also by means of a second
criterion: denotation.

[15] In this work we have not represented the taxonomy of exocentric constructions because,
according to Marchand, exocentrics belong to the domain of derivation. As a matter of fact, these
formations receive their syntactic category by means of a (zero) affixation process and therefore
cannot be considered as true compounds.

forms that at present would be clearly considered as phrases (*nos parents et amis* 'our parents and friends').

In order to show the persistence of terminological problems, let us briefly consider a recent proposal by Di Sciullo (2007b). Classification of compounds is not among the goals of Di Sciullo's work; however, in it she does use a classification scheme with three types of compounds: 'root', 'deverbal', and '*dvandva*'. The three types of formations are considered as being equivalent to three different types of 'relations', namely modification, verb–argument relation, and apposition. Let us now illustrate Di Sciullo's classification of compounds as we did before, by means of a tree diagram:

(2)

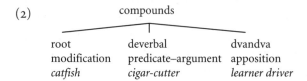

root	deverbal	dvandva
modification	predicate–argument	apposition
catfish	*cigar-cutter*	*learner driver*

According to Di Sciullo, root compounds instantiate a modification relation, deverbal compounds include a predicate–argument relation, and *dvandva* compounds are formed by the apposition of two constituents. But, again, the terminology seems not to be adequate since 'root' refers to the non-derivational nature of the head constituent; 'deverbal' refers to the derived nature of the head; and '*dvandva*' refers to the grammatical relation between the two constituents. Further, the term *dvandva* is used as a pure synonym of coordinate while we saw how it is appropriate to make a distinction between *dvandva* in its Sanskrit meaning (indicating exocentric forms) and pseudo-*dvandva*, in Fanselow/Olsen's terminology, indicating endocentric formations.

3.3 BISETTO AND SCALISE (2005)

In an attempt at overcoming the problems illustrated above, Bisetto and Scalise (2005) proposed a classification based on a very simple assumption. Given that the peculiarity of compounds lies in their being word forms whose constituents are connected by a grammatical relation that is not overtly expressed (see *apron string* vs. *string of the apron*), we suggested that the classification, at the first level, be based solely and consistently upon this criterion.[16]

---

[16] This position is not new. Marchand (1969: 18), for instance, observed that all compounds can be explained on the basis of the syntactic relations that underlie the corresponding sentences. For a similar position, see also Tollemache (1945). Bloomfield (1933: 233) in his time had also observed that one of the two lines of classification of compounds concerned the 'relation between members'.

Basically, the grammatical relations that are possible between the two constituents of a compound are those existing in syntactic constructions: subordination,
coordination, and attribution. We thus proposed the following classification:

(3)

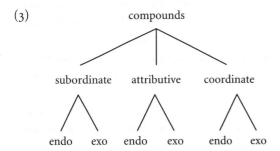

Compounds are to be defined as 'subordinate' when the two components share a
head–complement relation. For example, in a compound like *taxi driver*, *taxi* is
clearly the 'complement' of the deverbal head. The situation is identical in compounds like *apron string*, where *apron* and *string* have a strong 'of relation' that could
well be defined as a head–complement relation. As a matter of fact, *apron string* can
be construed in different ways: 'string of an apron', 'string resting on an apron',
'string threaded into an apron', etc. This notwithstanding, the relation between its
two constituents is always a head–complement relation, i.e. one of subordination.

It should be noted that a clear subordinate relation comes into place also when
the head is missing, as in *cutthroat* or *lavapiatti* ('wash + dishes = dishwasher'), and
not only when the compound is endocentric, as is the case with the synthetic
formations of Germanic languages of the *taxi driver* type. Even in these cases the
head–complement relation is determined by the presence of the verb. Although it is
not the head of the formation, it is nonetheless the verb that selects the other
constituent. Actually, this type of formation is not possible if the noun cannot be a
complement of the verb (from a semantic point of view). For example, formations
like the Italian **contaluce / *contaacqua / *contagas* lit. 'count-light, count-water,
count-gas' are not possible because nouns like *luce*, *acqua*, and *gas* are uncountable,
and as such cannot be the object of the verb *contare* (cf. Bisetto 1999). In other
words, these constructions are impossible because the verb cannot select the
relevant noun.[17]

Attributive compounds are made up of different formations. These consist in a
noun-head that can be modified by an adjective, as in *blue cheese*, where *blue*
conveys a property of *cheese*, or else by a noun or a verb. In this second case also, the
non-head conveys a property of the head. In particular when the non-head is a
noun, its attributive value is associated with a metaphorical interpretation, as in
snail mail and *key word*.

---

[17] Cf. on the contrary, the grammatical compounds *contagocce* 'dropper' and *contachilometri*
'milometer'.

Coordinate compounds are formations whose constituents are connected by the conjunction 'and'. They are potentially recursive even in Romance languages (cf. It. *poeta pittore regista*, 'director-painter-poet'), where recursiveness in compounding is not common. From a semantic point of view, these compounds can be considered to be characterized by two heads (*painter-poet* is both a 'poet' and a 'painter') even though, as claimed by Bloomfield (1933), only one of the nouns can act as the head. As a general rule, only one of the nouns can be pluralized, and, in those languages where gender is relevant, it is precisely that noun that confers the gender on the compound formation.[18]

The compounds of these three classes can be both endocentric and exocentric, and therefore some of the compounds quoted in the various proposals grouped under (1) can be grouped into six classes, as follows:

(4)

SUBORDINATE		ATTRIBUTIVE		COORDINATE	
endo	exo	endo	exo	endo	exo
love story	lavapiatti	blackboard	greybeard	bittersweet	Austria-Hungary
steamboat	pickpocket	girlfriend	Kickkopf	oak tree	mother-child
coffee cup		green-eyed	Kahlkopf	fighter-bomber	elun-ai
lipstick		blackbird	auricomus	learner-driver	Schleswig-Hol.
			loudmouth	poet-doctor	candra-ditya-u
				poeta-pintor	
				woman doctor	
				Fürstbischof	

Given that compounds in (4) did not represent all possible types (note that, for example, in the 'attributive/endocentric' column there are no compounds with a non-head noun) new examples have been added to the list:

(5)

SUBORDINATE		ATTRIBUTIVE		COORDINATE	
endo	exo[19]	endo	exo	endo	exo
apple cake	killjoy	blue cheese	white collar	actor-author	mind-brain
brain death	cut-throat	atomic bomb	greenhouse	priest-hermit	north-east
fingerprint		backyard	paleface	singer-bassist	
mailman		French kiss	long-legs	dancer-singer	

[18] Pluralization can actually apply to both constituents. This is what generally happens in Romance languages, where formations like the Italian *cantanti-attori* lit. 'singers actors' are perfectly acceptable. In coordinate endocentric compounds whose two constituents have varying gender, as in the name of the Italian region *Friuli-Venezia Giulia*, the gender of the compound as a whole is given by the masculine gender of the component in head position *Friuli*.

[19] The reduced number of exocentric compounds shows that in Germanic languages exocentricity is not as common as in Romance languages. This is probably due to the fact that Germanic languages are head-final languages. In a Romance language like Italian, the most productive type of compound are exocentric [V+N] nouns, as in *scacciapensieri* 'pastime'.

sun glasses	ape man	freelance	artist-designer
water pipe	ghost writer		king-emperor
taxi driver	keyword		merchant tailor
stonecutter	public opinion		
arm control	swordfish		
babycare			
agoraphobia			

In such a theoretical framework, neoclassical compounds – which concern those particular entities called 'semiwords' (sW) (Scalise 1984) – are generally encompassed in the subordinate class, albeit with some exceptions. The use of the neoclassical label therefore is only a means for describing the kind of constituent that is used. The relation that binds the two constituents of the greater part[20] of neoclassical formations is, indeed, subordination, as the examples in (6) illustrate:

(6) NEOCLASSICAL COMPOUNDS

sW+sW	sW+N	N+sW
anthropology	floriculture	mineralogy
hydrology	hydrophobia	insecticide
philosophy	anthropocentrism	musicology

Hydrology is the 'science of water', *hydrophobia* is the 'fear of water', and so on. Also the so-called phrasal compounds have been placed within one of the three proposed classes. Let us observe the following examples:

(7) PHRASAL COMPOUNDS
[floor of a birdcage] taste
[punch in the stomach] effect
[pipe and slipper] husband

According to the classification in (3), these formations have been placed among attributives: the non-head phrases involved in the constructions actually act as properties that characterize the head-nouns (*a terrible taste, a painful effect, a boring husband*).

In *phrasals*, therefore, the non-head has a metaphorical interpretation: saying that something caused a 'punch in the stomach effect' is not the same as saying that we received a punch in the stomach – rather that we are feeling exactly as if we had received one. If we maintain that a husband is of the 'pipe and slippers' type rather than of the 'newspapers and TV' type, the metaphorical and modifying function of the phrasal expression does not change.

---

[20] The relation can also be different, as in *calligrafia* 'calligraphy' which is attributive.

3.3.1 Selection in compounding

The categorization into subordinate, coordinate, and attributive compounds is confirmed by the manner in which the head selects the non-head in each of the three groups (cf. Scalise, Bisetto, and Guevara 2005).

If we are to represent compounds according to (a slightly modified version of) the theory of representation in terms of lexical semantics by Lieber (2004),[21] we can lay down the following scenario, in which the arrows indicate the related features and the heads are in small capitals:

(8)   SELECTION IN COMPOUNDING

    a. COORDINATE COMPOUNDS

	ACTOR		DIRECTOR
skeleton			
	[+ material, dynamic ($[_i]$)]		[+ material, dynamic ($[_i]$)]
body			
	\<human, professional\>	↔	\<human, professional\>
	\<show business\>	↔	\<show business\>
	\<works in theatres, films, etc.\>	↔	\<works in theatres, films, etc.\>
	\<receives directions\>		\<gives directions\>
	\<...\>		\<...\>

    b. N+N SUBORDINATE COMPOUNDS

	apple		CAKE
skeleton			
	[+material ($[_i]$)]		[+material ($[_i]$)]
body			
	\<physical\>		\<physical\>
	\<shape\>		\<shape\>
	\<edible\>	↔	\<edible\>
	\<can be an ingredient\>	↔	\<made with ingredients\>
	\<...\>		\<baked\>
			\<made for parties\>

    c. ATTRIBUTIVE COMPOUNDS

	snail		MAIL
skeleton			
	[+material ($[_i]$)]		[+material ($[_i]$)]
body			
	\<gastropod\>		\<institution\>
	\<secretes slime\>		\<means of communication\>
	\<*very* slow\>	↔	\<takes time\>
	\<...\>		\<...\>

---

[21] In Lieber's theoretical model, every lexeme is represented in terms of *skeleton* and *body*. The former carries grammatical information that is relevant for syntax, the latter carries semantic information of an encyclopedic nature.

The coordinate compounds in (8a) are virtually identical in the two levels of representation: the two constituents show a perfect matching of the *skeletons* and a high level of matching in the features of the encyclopedic *body*.

To the contrary, as far as selection is concerned, in subordinate compounds as in (8b), both endocentric and exocentric, the skeleton plays no significant role: what really matters is the full set of encyclopedic features of the respective bodies. At least one of the features of the body of the head constituent is to match the encyclopedic features that characterize the non-head (as in 'edible' and 'made with ingredients' in the given example).

In attributive compounds with a noun as the non-head, the skeleton does not play any significant role, just as in subordinate compounds. What matters is that the non-head fulfils at least one of the encyclopedic features of the head. The matching feature is the only relevant piece of information brought by the non-head of the compound; the rest of the information is simply ignored (for example, the facts that a snail is a gastropod and that it secretes slime play no role at all in the *snail-mail* compound). The non-head has the sole function of specifying a trait of the *body* of the head (in this case, 'slow' specifies the information 'takes time'). In other words, the non-head has an 'adjectival' function; in terms of Lexical Conceptual Structure (LCS) the non-head constituent is construed as a Property and no longer as a Thing (cf. Jackendoff 1990: 43–58). The attributive relation is of course highly evident when the non-head is an adjective (as in *blackbird*).

The grouping of compounds in three major classes is thus supported by the fact that the mechanisms by which the head selects the non-head are consistently different in each of the three classes.

3.4 A NEW PROPOSAL

Our proposed classification has been tested on a wide sample of languages with good results. But, as research has progressed and more and more data have been analysed, as predicted in Kuhn's vision of the evolution of science, the need has arisen to add further levels of analysis to the classification.

The classification we propose therefore has an extra level of analysis with respect to our previous proposal.[22] Subordination, attribution, and coordination are but the macro-level of discrimination of compounds. A second classification level is

---

[22] This elaboration is not completely new. It is actually a sort of return to the past, in the sense that there is a reclamation of Bloomfield's and Marchand's classifications, obviously with the refinements and modifications that our contemporary point of view calls for.

needed in order to account for the different semantic/interpretative relations that come into place between the constituents of the compounds in each class.

(9)

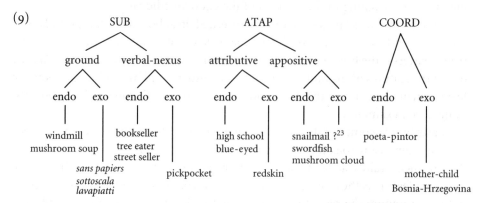

Indeed, subordinate compounds need to be grouped into subclasses capable of highlighting the nature of the constituent that determines the semantic relation between members – and, therefore, the interpretation of the compound. Previous literature on compounds, as we have seen, traditionally separated subordinates into *root/primary* and *verbal–nexus/secondary/syntactic* based on the deverbal or non-deverbal derivational nature of the non-head constituent. The first class was subject to a semantic relation called the *R-relation* (Allen 1978), whereas in the second class the relation between the two constituents was wholly attributed to the presence of the underlying verb in the deverbal head. The *R-relation* was thus determined by the aggregate of the semantico-encyclopedic information associated with the two constituents, the *body* according to the terminology in Lieber (2004). According to Pustejovsky (1995), one can say that the interpretation of *root compounds* depends on the possibility of associating the different semantic pieces of information in the *qualia structure* of the two constituents. The different interpretations allowed by these compounds depend on the possibility of varying the association between the features of the respective qualia structures: these features are elicited from the context in which the compound formations are to be found.[24] These compounds are defined as *ground*, a term that we agree to adopt because in our view it appears more neutral and more general as opposed to the traditional definition of *root*.[25]

The interpretation of *verbal-nexus* compounds is, conversely, determined by the presence of the base verb of the derivative acting as the head. The term – as we have

---

[23] Please note that in our database exocentric appositive compounds are not easy to track, with possible exceptions like the Norwegian *kryssord* 'crossword = crossword puzzle' and the Chinese *rén shé* 'people snake = illegal immigrant'.

[24] On the interpretation of new compounds by speakers, see e.g. the works by Wisniewski (1996) and Wisniewski and Love (1998).

[25] Baroni, Pirrelli, and Guevara (2007) use the term 'grounding'.

seen above – has a long tradition but, contrary to what has traditionally been proposed, in our opinion this class includes not only those compounds that show a head–argument relation but also those showing a head–complement/adjunct relation. In other words, in disagreement with Selkirk (1982), we deem that compounds like *tree eater*, in its 'someone eating on a tree' interpretation, should be seen as verbal-nexus compounds. It is the semantic information associated with the verb *to eat* that enables us to construe *tree* as the place where someone can eat; therefore, even in this case, it is the presence of the verb that determines both the relation between the head and the non-head and the interpretation of the compound. As a matter of fact, *tree* can be seen as a semantic argument of the verb *to eat* (cf. Lieber 1983), in syntactic terms as an adjunct of the verb.

Compared with our 2005 classification, the ATAP class of compounds is a redesignation of attributive compounds. The creation of this new label enables separation, at a lower level, of attributive and appositive formations. In our tree diagram, this class stands between subordinates and coordinates so as to indicate a special feature of these formations, namely that they have properties that may draw them nearer to the one or the other class. The two ATAP classes are meant to include formations featuring a differently expressed attribution relation. Attributive compounds can actually be defined as formations whose head is modified by a non-head expressing a 'property' of the head, be it an adjective or a verb: actually, the role of the non-head categorial element should be that of expressing a 'quality' of the head constituent. Appositives, to the contrary, are compounds in which the non-head element expresses a property of the head constituent by means of a noun, an apposition, acting as an attribute.

Having said that, a few observations are due. Our claim is that the first level of classification (subordinate, coordinate, attributive/appositive) is to express the 'hidden' relation between the two constituents. The second-tier classes introduced by us are a specification of this first level. The grammatical relation is not modified; it is rather complemented with some semantic-interpretative information that is not unconnected with the categorial nature of the constituents. Subordinate compounds can thus be divided into *ground* compounds, corresponding to those formations that are traditionally defined as *root*, i.e. lexemes that can be both simple and complex. In the latter case, when they include a verb, this is incapable of influencing the interpretation of the compound. The semantic relation between the two constituents is actually determined, as seen above, by the semantico-encyclopedic information associated with the component lexemes. In particular (cf. section 3.3.1), it is the information of the head constituent that selects a piece of information of the non-head, thus determining the interpretation of the compound.

Conversely, the interpretation of *verbal-nexus* compounds – an extremely productive class in Romance languages – is heavily dependent on the presence of a verb. It is the verb that selects 'semantically' the non-head to combine with, be it an argument or an adjunct (cf. *bookseller* vs. *street seller*).

In appositives that, together with attributives, make up the ATAP class, the noun plays an attributive role and is often to be interpreted metaphorically. Metaphoricity is the factor that enables us to make a distinction between, e.g., *mushroom soup* (a subordinate *ground* compound) and *mushroom cloud*, where *mushroom* is not interpreted in its literal sense but is rather construed as a 'representation of the mushroom entity' (cf. Wisniewski 1996 and Scalise, Bisetto, and Guevara 2005) whose relevant feature in the compound under observation is shape. In appositives the non-head can also be a verb, as in the Dutch *druip nat* 'wet through' (Guevara and Scalise 2004) where the verbal form *druip* acts as a modifier of *nat*. In attributives, to the contrary, the non-head is an adjective.

In coordinate compounds, which can feature different structures like N+N, A+A, V+V, and also Adv+Adv plus other more peripheral types of structures, there appears to be no need for making further distinctions that call into action the subtype of grammatical relation between the two constituents. Specific discriminations can be made if we are to look at the semantics of the two constituents: coordinates can actually be synonyms (Ch. *liănmiàn* 'face face = face'), antonyms (It. *saliscendi* 'go up go down = elevator') and reduplicates (It. *lecca-lecca* 'lollypop'). In analysing their meaning, it could be said that they are additive (e.g. *Baden-Württemberg*) or redundant as is the case with, e.g., *palm tree*, a formation that Marchand defined as 'subsumptive'.

Other distinctions are possible in respect of other classes of compounds, for example Italian VN nominal compounds. These formations can be analysed as agentive (*portalettere* 'mailman'), instrumental (*spremiagrumi* 'citrus-fruit squeezer'), eventive (*alzabandiera* '(ceremony of) hoisting the flag'), or locative (*puntaspilli* 'pin-cushion'); these distinctions are however based on different criteria from those informing the proposed classification and could well call for further investigations into the classificatory framework.

3.5 SOME RESIDUAL PROBLEMS AND SOME CONCLUSIONS

The proposed classification (which could be seen as a sort of 'return to the past') presents the advantage of being based on explicit criteria, and in general it seems to work satisfactorily. Obviously, there do exist borderline cases in respect of which the analysis is less clear-cut and leaves room for different interpretation. Let us consider, by way of example, the compounds *greybeard* and *green-eyed*. They are both attributives according to the proposed classification, since the relation between *grey* and *beard* and between *green* and *eye* is in both cases attributive. From the semantic point of view they are both possessives because their interpretation is, respectively, 'whose beard is grey' and 'whose eyes are green'. However they differ in that the first is a *bahuvrīhi* compound in the Sanskrit meaning of the term, i.e. it is exocentric, whereas the second is not because it carries a derivational affix that makes it endocentric. Thus, the two formations are not particularly problematic from a taxonomic point of view and can be placed in the same ATAP macro-class, then in the same attributives sub-class and finally separated depending on the presence or absence of the head. The main problem, however, is deciding whether formations like *green-eyed* are to be considered at all as compounds. Actually their structure is of the parasynthetic type,[26] that is, they are not A+A structures (**green+eyed*) because *eyed* does not exist as a stand-alone adjective,[27] nor can they be considered derivational compounds (*green eye+ed*) given that *green eye* is not a compound.

The same remarks apply to formations such as *greybeard*. As observed by Whitney (1889), these constructions can be viewed as compounds since they are construed as having a zero morpheme conveying the meaning of 'having'. In today's terminology, we would say that they are nominalized by means of a zero suffix expressing the relation of possession (*he who has*). In both cases we therefore have the same type of parasynthetic formation, the difference lying in the *overt* presence (in affixal position) of the head element in one case and its absence in the other. Still, in both cases, it is the presence of the *overt* or *covert* element that makes them compounds.

Summing up and concluding, the core of the proposed classification is the grammatical relation between the constituents of the compound. *Taxi driver*, *high school*, and *poet-doctor* are prototypical compounds representing the three possible grammatical relations: subordination, attribution, and coordination. We believe this first stepping-stone to be essential and it should always be seen as the first level of classification. We also believe that this first tier should be kept separate from all other criteria, such as internal structure or the semantic relation between constituents or their categorial status. These criteria, so to speak, should come into play only 'after' the grammatical classification.

For example, ATAP compounds do not form a homogeneous class because the non-head can be either an adjective (*blackbird*), a noun (*swordfish*), or a verb (*playground*). This entails that the classification can probably be enriched with a further discrimination based on the category of the non-head constituent.

By no means can our proposed classification be deemed to be final, but anyone wanting to follow up on this issue will necessarily have to come to grips – just as we did – with the diverse compound formations that populate the languages of the world.

---

[26] Parasynthetic compounds are formed by a non-compound complex base and a derivational affix. On this type of compounds, cf. most recently Melloni and Bisetto (2007).

[27] In this respect see Booij (2005b).

CHAPTER 4

....

EARLY GENERATIVE APPROACHES

....

PIUS TEN HACKEN

THE Chomskyan revolution had an almost immediate impact on the study of compounding, because one of the first works devoted primarily to applying, rather than developing, the theoretical framework addressed the issue of the analysis of compounding quite prominently. This work (Lees 1960) also set the agenda for generative research on compounding for more or less two decades. It is this period that is the focus of the present chapter.

The chapter starts by presenting Lees's seminal work, setting out the main points of its analysis as well as its theoretical context and the immediate reactions it provoked (section 4.1). In the late 1960s and early 1970s, research in generative linguistics was determined by the conflict between generative semantics and the Chomskyan response to it. The field of compounding was not exempt. The two opposing viewpoints and their consequences for compounding are discussed in sections 4.2 and 4.3, respectively. In the late 1970s and early 1980s we can observe a gradual reorientation, resulting in a change of research questions. This process and the legacy of the preceding period are described in section 4.4.

4.1 A TRANSFORMATIONAL ACCOUNT
OF COMPOUNDING

When Lees (1960) proposed his transformational account of compounding, it was a highly innovative approach. For about two decades, research on compounding in generative linguistics was determined by criticism of this approach and attempts to adapt and improve it. In this section, I will first consider the main elements of Lees's treatment of compounding (section 4.1.1), then look at the context from which it emerged and the initial criticism it provoked (section 4.1.2), and finally describe how the ideas were received in Germany, where they became highly influential (section 4.1.3).

4.1.1 Lees's foundational work

Lees (1960) presents a transformational account of what he calls 'English Nominalizations'. Two appendices (1960: 186–201) compare the resulting analysis for English with the corresponding data in German and Turkish. Nominals, the subject of Lees's work, are characterized by the fact that they 'are not themselves sentences, but rather they are noun-like versions of sentences' (1960: 54). They are divided into two classes, one of which includes, for instance, the italicized subject clause in (1), the other one compounds.

(1)   *That he came* was obvious.

The division into two classes is not a crucial part of the analysis. In fact, 'There is no a priori reason to separate the analysis of nominal compounds from that of other nominalizations' (1960: 124). In Lees's analysis, all nominalizations are derived from sentences by means of a sequence of transformations. Many of the transformations used in the derivation of compounds are not specific to compounds. The rule that distinguishes compounds from other constructions is the NPN-transformation (1960: 174–5), which has the general pattern in (2).

(2)   NPN-TRANSFORMATION
       $X_1 - X_2 - X_3 - X_4 - X_5 - X_6 \Rightarrow X_1 - X_4 - X_2 - X_6$

The six elements to the left of the arrow in (2) indicate that the input string is divided into six parts, some of which may be zero. The full version of the rule states constraints on some of these numbered elements. Lees gives a number of alternative specifications for X_2, X_3, X_4, and X_5, corresponding to different types of compound. X_1 and X_6 only serve to cover any context not affected by the transformation. Whenever one type of specification applies to a string, (2) deletes the parts matching X_3 and X_5 and reverses the order of the parts matching X_2 and X_4.

Two examples will illustrate the general pattern of derivations in which (2) is used. The first is *population growth*, discussed by Lees (1960: 138). Three stages in the derivation are given in (3).

(3) a. The population grows.
  b. ...growth of the population...
  c. ...population growth...

The starting point for the compound is a deep structure corresponding to the sentence (3a). A number of transformations shared with other nominalizations produce a structure corresponding to (3b). By the application of (2), (3b) is turned into the compound (3c). Here X_1 and X_6 match the initial and final ..., respectively, X_2 matches *growth*, X_3 *of the*, X_4 *population*, and X_5 is empty. The effect of (2) is therefore to reverse the order of the two components of the compound and to delete any material between them. An example in which X_5 is not empty is *grindstone*. Lees (1960: 160–1) gives a sequence of seven applications of different transformations, but the crucial stages are given in (4).

(4) a. The stone is for N_a.
  b. John grinds knives on the stone.
  c. ...stone to grind knives on...
  d. ...grindstone...

In Lees's analysis, the deep structure corresponding to the two sentences in (4a) and (4b), the former with an underspecified constituent N_a, jointly constitute the starting point for the derivation. This is because in early generative grammar, phrase structure rules only generate structures for simple sentences, without any embedding. *Kernel* sentences are sentences in which only obligatory transformations have applied to a deep structure, e.g. (3a), (4a), and (4b). Embedding is the result of *generalized transformations* taking two phrase structures as their input and producing a structure that combines the two. By the application of a generalized transformation and a number of other transformations, (4c) is produced. This is the stage when (2) applies, producing (4d). The matching of most components is analogous to the one for (3b), but in (4c), X_5 matches *knives on*.

Lees's derivation of compounding links compounds to underlying sentences. He proposes a classification of compounds on the basis of the roles of the two components (i.e. X_2 and X_4 in (2)) in the underlying sentence (1960: 125). The main classes are listed in (5), each with an example used by Lees.

(5) a. Subject–Predicate   *girlfriend*
  b. Subject–'Middle Object'   *arrowhead*
  c. Subject–Verb   *population growth*
  d. Subject–Object   *steamboat*
  e. Verb–Object   *book review*

   f. Subject–Prepositional Object   *garden party*
   g. Verb–Prepositional Object   *grindstone*
   h. Object–Prepositional Object   *bull ring*

In the interpretation of the labels in (5), the order of the components is not essential. Thus, (5e) covers both *book review* and *chewing gum*. The scope of the classification and of the derivation mechanism is not restricted to endocentric compounding. Exocentric compounds of the type *redskin* are included in (5a), *pickpocket* in (5e), and *egghead* in (5f). Copulative compounds are argued to be unproductive (1960: 178). In a short final section, Lees (1960: 172–3) treats compounds with a proper name as the first component, e.g. *Marshall plan*.

An issue not mentioned here so far is the stress pattern. Compounds have stress on X_4 in (2). Lees states that he will use the stress pattern as 'a useful method of cutting down the wealth of data to be explained' (1960: 120). The stress pattern for compounds is introduced by the full version of (2) as a side effect of the other operations it carries out. In an appendix, he gives extensive lists of nominal phrases, expressions which do not have the stress pattern of compounds but that are semantically and otherwise parallel to compounds (1960: 182–5). Lees shows that what he calls the 'traditional view', i.e. that these nominal phrases are not compounds, 'has certain consequences which to us seem rather awkward' (1960: 180). As an example, this criterion makes *Madison Street* a compound and *Madison Avenue* a phrase.

4.1.2 Context and evaluation of Lees (1960)

The impact of Lees (1960), in particular in American linguistics, can be seen by the fact that it was extensively reviewed in *Language, Word*, and the *International Journal of American Linguistics*. These reviews do not concentrate on compounding, however. The main property that made the book innovative was the fact that it proposed an analysis of a substantial fragment of English in the new framework proposed by Chomsky (1957). Therefore, much of the discussion in Hill (1962), Householder (1962), Schachter (1962), as well as Matthews (1961) is devoted to presenting and evaluating the theory of transformational-generative grammar in general. There is also good internal motivation for this, because the first two chapters of Lees's book describe the base rules, the lexical rules, and the major transformational rules of English as a background to the analysis of nominalizations.

As Lees (1960: v) describes in the acknowledgement, the book is a revised version of his PhD dissertation, which was supervised by Morris Halle and completed in 1959. It appeared as part 2 of Vol. 26, No. 3 of the *International Journal of American Linguistics*. In 1963 it was reissued by Mouton and reprinted four times with additional prefaces by 1968.

As Lees states in his preface to the second printing, the book 'was originally inspired by my research on nominal compounding' (1960: xxviii). Accordingly, the original preface mainly serves to place the book in the context of compounding research. The novelty of the approach was certainly not the idea of devising a classification of compounds. The classification proposed in (5) could easily be interpreted as a modified version of Jespersen's (1942) influential treatment. Motsch (1970: 209) traces the idea that compounds are reduced sentences back to Brugmann (1900), an article Lees (1960: xix) discusses in his preface. Brekle (1970) refers to even earlier sources. What is new in Lees's approach, however, is the correlation of the relationship between compounds and sentences with the classification by means of a set of rules generating the compounds.

In the preface to the third edition (1960: xxix–xlv), dated January 1964, Lees reacts to criticism ('Some Criticisms Answered'). There are hardly any references for this criticism, but it can be deduced from his reaction to it that it must have been directed primarily against transformational-generative grammar as such. In any case, the reviews of Lees (1960) are not the source of this criticism. In general they work from within the framework adopted by Lees. The only point which clearly reflects the opposition between Post-Bloomfieldian and Chomskyan linguistics in the reviews is the question of the native speaker competence as the object of linguistic research.[1] Both Hill (1962: 437) and Householder (1962: 344) refer to the problem of disagreement about the data in describing idiolects. Otherwise, reviewers seem happy to discuss elements of the mechanism on the basis of the general framework adopted by Lees (1960).

In the mechanism for the treatment of compounding, three elements attracted criticism in the reviews. The first is the distinction between kernel sentences and transforms. This is an element of the general formalism that is used in compounding as illustrated in (3) and (4). Matthews (1961: 199–204) and Hill (1962: 442–3) discuss where the boundary between kernel sentences and transformed sentences should be drawn. Schachter suggests 'that the distinction made between kernel and derived sentences [...] is not really a fundamental one after all' (1962: 142). This suggestion prevailed and Chomsky (1965: 17–18) only mentions kernel sentences as an intuitive notion without theoretical significance. He replaced generalized transformations of the type that would combine (4a–b) by the recursive application of rewrite rules.

A second point of criticism concerns the lexical rewrite rules. Before the introduction of the lexicon, subclasses of verbs had to be introduced by rules such as $V \rightarrow V_i$ for every class i of verbs. The problem is that classes overlap, as Matthews (1961: 204–5) notes, and cross-classify, as shown by Schachter (1962: 138–40).

---

[1] Ten Hacken (2007) gives an account of the Chomskyan revolution highlighting the role of this issue. As this analysis shows, Householder's (1962) fundamental criticism of Chomskyan linguistics is based on a radically different view of the status of linguistic data. In the light of this, it is remarkable how constructive Householder's (1962) criticism of Lees (1960) is.

Chomsky (1965: 79–88) recognized the problem and introduced the lexicon as a solution.

The introduction of recursive phrase structure rules and of the lexicon change the underlying theoretical framework. Their main significance is that by broadening the range of possibilities, they make some of Lees's choices in the domain of compounding less compelling. It is for this reason that the third issue, the power of the compounding rules, grew in importance.

The issue of the power of the rules used by Lees (1960) appears in different forms. One is that the rules generate impossible compounds. Householder (1962: 352–3) observes that the process generating *peanut butter* on the basis of 'butter is made of peanuts' cannot be applied to 'steel is made of iron'. In his words, 'if the word *all* can be prefixed to the subject', no compound is possible. He notes that the same restriction does not apply in syntax, so that, for instance, *black charcoal* is grammatical. Lees's (1960: 121) defence in such cases is that the compounds are at least in principle possible. As Schachter (1962: 145) remarks, however, this does not take into account the difference in grammaticality between the morphological and the syntactic formations.

Another form in which the problem of the power of the rules emerges is the question of the ambiguity of compounds. The existence of *flour mill* ('mill producing flour') and *windmill* ('mill powered by wind') predicts that *flour mill* can also mean 'mill powered by flour'. Matthews (1961: 208) claims that this meaning is too far-fetched to be available to speakers of English. Householder (1962: 342–3) questions whether this is a grammatical difference. This is related to Schachter's observation that in cases such as *grapefruit* 'the compound cannot be replaced by its putative source without a change in the meaning' (1962: 145–6). He argues that in such cases the rule is rather an etymological formula than an actual formation rule. Matthews (1961: 207) points out that for some compounds, e.g. *cranberry*, no source exists at all.

The examples of *flour mill*, *grapefruit*, and *cranberry* can be seen as three points on the cline from regular to lexicalized compounds. The introduction of the lexicon in the mid-1960s provided another place to account for these effects, not available to Lees in 1960. Rohrer's (1966) review of the second printing gives additional arguments for using the lexicon. He points out that if Lees's rules generate *doctor's office* and *newspaper clipping*, they also produce *doctor office* and *newspaper's clipping* (1966: 164). Rohrer observes that the former 'sounds unusual' and the latter 'is ungrammatical'.[2]

Perhaps the most serious form of the problem of excessive power of the rules is exemplified by the discussion of *pontoon bridge* by Lees (1960: 123). He proposes the alternative bases in (6):

---

[2] '*Dóctor òffice* klingt ungewöhnlich, *néwspaper's clìpping* ist ungrammatisch.' My translation.

(6)   a. bridge supported by pontoons (cf. *steamboat*)
       b. bridge floating on pontoons (cf. *seaplane*)
       c. bridge made of pontoons (cf. *blockhouse*)
       d. pontoons in the form of a bridge (cf. *cell block*)

The different analyses in (6) correspond to different classes in (5). The examples in brackets are given by Lees to show this parallelism. The examples in (6a–b) correspond to (5d), (6c) corresponds to (5h), and (6d) to (5f). As he notes, 'it is not even obvious which interpretation *is* the most commonly used' (1960: 123), because their predicted different meanings in (6) can in fact not be distinguished semantically.

At the same time as the lexicon introduced an alternative way to treat idiosyncrasies in compounding, Chomsky (1965: 144–5) proposed the condition of recoverability of deleted material in transformations. This proposal restricted deletion to dummy elements, lexically specified elements (e.g. *you* in imperatives), designated representatives of a category (e.g. indefinite pronouns for NPs), or elements repeated in the structure (erasure under identity). Under such a constraint, the ambiguity in (6) is excluded in principle. No transformation can derive *pontoon bridge* from any of (6a–d), because it would delete lexical material that cannot be recovered.

As opposed to the introduction of recursive phrase structure and of the lexicon, the constraint on the recoverability of deleted material directly affects Lees's (1960) account of compounding. Recursive phrase structure and the lexicon modify and extend the descriptive potential. Minor changes in the statement of rules can adapt the original account to these theoretical modifications. The constraint on deletion makes transformations such as (2) unstatable, thus striking at the heart of the account. This did not mark the end of transformational approaches to compounding, however. In fact, Rohrer (1966: 170) ends his review with an unambiguously positive answer to the question whether it is worth continuing Lees's effort to account for word formation on a transformational basis.

4.1.3 Lees and Marchand

Lees (1960) can be seen at the same time as a contribution to transformational grammar and as a contribution to the research on compounding. In North America, it was primarily perceived in the former perspective. Discussion concentrated on the mechanisms proposed much more than on the analysis of compound types. In Europe, however, Lees's work became known primarily as one of the sources of inspiration of Marchand's (1969) handbook of English word formation.

In the first edition of his handbook, published in 1960, Marchand had taken Charles Bally's 'syntagma principle' as a basis for linking word formation with syntax. According to Kastovsky (2005: 104), who was Marchand's assistant at Tübingen, Marchand never adopted transformational-generative grammar. The discussion between Marchand and Lees is marked by incommensurability effects. As described in more detail in ten Hacken (2007), incommensurability effects are visible as overt declarations of mutual non-understanding and by disagreement on the status of evidence. They can be explained by the fact that the two sides of the discussion adopt different sets of criteria to evaluate theories. This can make an argument that is very strong in the perception of one side entirely irrelevant to the other side.

Marchand's (1965a, b) criticism of Lees (1960) is embedded in two articles in which he presents his new approach to compounding. As he makes explicit from the start, 'the grammatical analysis attempted here is not intended to replace the treatment given in [the first edition of] my book, but to supplement the description of morphological and semantic patterns given there' (1965b: 118). Of the two articles, (1965a) is devoted to compounds with a verbal or deverbal component and (1965b) to other compounds. Lees (1966), while published after the second, reacted to the first only. Kastovsky (1974a: 16–18) and Kürschner (1977) summarize the debate and react to Lees (1966).

A clear indication of the incommensurability of Lees's and Marchand's theories is that both sides state that the other side misunderstands them. According to Lees, 'Marchand is quite mistaken in his assessment of the transformational description of expressions' (1966: 1), whereas Kastovsky states that 'Lees' reaction* to Hans Marchand's criticisms and own suggestions, however, showed that he had misunderstood many of Marchand's arguments' (1974: 17, footnote at * deleted).

Among the specific points of Marchand's criticism, the three listed in (7) are the most interesting.

(7) a. Lees does not explain how one underlying sentence pattern can lead to radically different compound patterns;
     b. he covers only grammatical aspects of compounds and neglects morphological and semantic aspects; and
     c. he does not motivate the individual transformations used to derive a compound from a sentence.

As an example of (7a), Marchand (1965a: 59–60) contrasts the derivation of *population growth* in (3) with the derivation of *wading bird* from 'the bird wades'. Both deep structures have a subject and a verb, but they end up in different parts of the compound. Lees (1966) obviously struggles to understand this objection. In the framework he works from, the choice of a particular derivational path in a particular context simply does not belong to the domain of linguistics. It would be tantamount to explaining why speakers decide to use an active or a passive version of a sentence, both of which are derived from the same deep structure. At the same time, the opposite derivations are equally possible for Lees, but they have different properties. Thus, *growth population* is countable like *wading bird* and *bird wading* is non-countable like *population growth*. Marchand (1965a: 61–2) suggests treating this phenomenon by means of what would later be called 'topicalization rules' and elaborated by Brekle (1970). Such rules determine which element of the underlying sentence is taken as which part of the resulting compound. It is worth noting that Kürschner (1977: 134–5) considers such a mechanism superfluous.

The problem in (7b) is mentioned by Marchand (1965b) in various places, but not in Marchand (1965a), so that Lees (1966) does not react to it. An example of the problem is *whetstone*, as discussed by Marchand (1965b: 123–4). The derivation of this word is parallel to *grindstone* in (4). Marchand objects to Lees's derivation because it fails to represent the semantic element of 'purpose', which he considers essential for such words. The issue is arguably at least in part a matter of the theoretical framework. Lees (1960) assumes a framework in which it is sufficient to generate a deep structure and derive a surface structure. As long as the notion of 'purpose' is represented in (4a), the semantic component will be able to deal with it appropriately. For Marchand this is not sufficient. In his words (1965b: 122), 'That this whole *for*-group is based on the concept of purpose does not escape Lees, but he fails to see that this is a semantic, not a grammatical matter.'

The problem in (7c) is perhaps of the most general interest. Marchand states his objection to Lees's way of linking compounds to underlying sentences as follows:

The fact of the relationship is stated, the remaining difficulty then being that of finding out by which way we arrive at the compound. We have the sentence as a point of departure, we also have the end of the journey, which is the compound. The route consists of the transforms which are made to fit our purpose.

(Marchand 1965b: 120)

This objection is very much in line with criticism from within generative grammar. There are too many possible ways to relate the deep structure and the surface structure. To some extent, transformations can be motivated by their use in other constructions. This is not sufficient, however, to demonstrate that intermediate structures such as (3b) and (4c) have to be part of the derivation. The problem this raises for explanation was one of the reasons why Chomsky (1965) constrained the form and operations of transformations.

In view of the objections in (7), Marchand (1969) did not take over the idea of transformations as proposed by Lees (1960). However, he did adopt Lees's idea to relate compounds to underlying sentences in a consistent way. In Marchand's words, 'The basic assumption is that a compound is explainable from a sentence'

(1969: 44). More specifically, compounds are related to 'an underlying sentence whose syntactic relations they mirror' (1969: 55).

4.2 DEVELOPMENT OF TRANSFORMATIONAL APPROACHES

From the mid 1960s onwards, the community of generative linguistics became polarized about the position of semantics in a theory of language. This polarization is described by Newmeyer (1986) as an opposition between generative semantics and interpretive semantics. As section 4.2.1 shows, generative semantics is more transformationally oriented and therefore closer to Lees (1960). However, from the late 1960s, it was generally agreed that the compounding theory of Lees (1960) had to be revised. Section 4.2.2 outlines attempts by Lees (1970) and Levi (1978) to do so. Section 4.2.3 describes the main theoretical development in Germany, inspired both by Lees (1960) and by Marchand's work.

4.2.1 The emergence of generative semantics

In the earliest versions of generative theory, transformations were the only mechanism for expressing the relationship between different sentences or constituents. Two related sentences were derived from the same deep structure by applying different transformations to it. The three changes to the theory discussed in section 4.1.2 reduced the role and the power of transformations. The introduction of recursion in the rewrite rules generating deep structure led to the abolition of generalized transformations. The introduction of the lexicon created an alternative way to relate items. The condition of recoverability of deleted material excluded many transformations proposed earlier, in particular the ones proposed by Lees (1960) for compounds.

In the mid 1960s, the tendency to make syntax more inclusive gained ground. More and more aspects of meaning and use of a sentence were included in its deep structure representation until deep structure had become identical to semantic representation. For the lexicon, this meant that semantic primitives would be inserted at deep structure and manipulated by transformations afterwards. McCawley (1968) famously proposed that *kill* was the surface form of a structure with the four elements *cause, become, not,* and *alive.* The position of complex words in generative semantics was often that of providing guidance for the analysis of morphologically simple words with similar meaning components. Thus, the analysis of *driver* into two components, *drive* and *-er*, was paralleled by the analysis of *thief* into primitives corresponding to *steal* and *-er*.

4.2.2 Constraints on deleted predicates

Building on his earlier theory of compounding, Lees (1970) proposes a direction for the development of an improved theory. As stated in the editor's preface, Bierwisch and Heidolph (1970: 5), the volume in which this article appeared, is a selection of papers from the Tenth International Congress of Linguists, Bucharest 1967. Lees (1970) proposes a solution to some of the problems observed by Rohrer's (1966) review of Lees (1960). At least one of the solutions is clearly inspired by the early stages of generative semantics.

One problem Lees (1970) addresses is related to the use of the labels in (5). Rohrer (1966: 167) observes that the use of generalized transformations with two kernel sentences makes a term such as *object* ambiguous. It can refer to the object of the embedded sentence or of the matrix sentence. As Lees (1970: 177) shows, the introduction of recursion in the base solves this problem.

Another problem Rohrer (1966: 164–6) raises is the question of the ambiguity of the deleted predicate in compounds of, for instance, the (5d) type. According to Rohrer, if the constraint on the recoverability of deleted material is to be observed, Lees would need to specify the predicate to be deleted in the transformation, which requires individual transformations for each deleted predicate. This is all the more problematic because of the spurious ambiguity illustrated in (6).

The solution Lees (1970) proposes is entirely in line with the general tendency in generative semantics. One component of the solution is to replace the labels in (5) by more semantically oriented ones, such as agent, location, instrument. Only his 'general complement' corresponds fairly directly to 'object'. The next component is the semantic analysis of nouns such as *thief*. Compounds such as *car thief* 'require no special assumptions about the underlying verb since the latter is reconstructable from the meaning of the head-noun' (1970: 182). As a final component, for compounds without such an underlying verb, he proposes that their underlying structure involves a 'generalized verb'. This concept can be illustrated by the general transformational sequence in (8).

(8)   V   O   I $\rightarrow$ N$_2$ V-s N$_1$ $\rightarrow$ N$_2$+N$_1$
          | |
          N$_1$ N$_2$

In the formalism used in (8), different stages in the derivation of a compound are separated by arrows. These stages can be compared to the informal representations in (3) and (4). In the underlying structure, O stands for general complement and I for instrument. Lees claims that the compounds derived according to the pattern in (8) 'all fall into two subsets in such a way that the V of each member of one subset may be viewed as a variant of the verbs *impel, energize, activate, power, propel*, etc., while the V of each of the others is a variant of *cause, engender, produce, yield*, etc.' (1970: 181–2). An example of the former is *steamboat* and of the latter *hay fever*. These two subsets then correspond to two generalized verbs. A generalized verb is 'the minimal set of semantic features which characterize all variants in the sets [of verbs]' (1970: 182). After an overview of a number of classes designated by patterns such as (8) and subdivided where appropriate on the basis of generalized verbs, Lees draws the following conclusion:

More sophisticated analysis in the study of compounding provides some evidence for the view that the deepest syntactic structure of expressions is itself a more or less direct picture of their semantic descriptions!

(Lees 1970: 185)

Whereas Lees (1970) only suggests some avenues to explore in revising his earlier theory, Levi (1978) presents a full-fledged new account of what she calls 'complex nominals'. The scope of her theory includes expressions such as:

(9)   a. apple cake
      b. film producer
      c. presidential refusal
      d. musical clock

Levi (1978: 1–2) calls (10a) a compound, (10b–c) nominalizations, and (10d) a noun phrase with a non-predicating adjective. Compared to Lees (1960), she excludes from the scope of her theory nominalizations such as (1) and exocentric compounds, which have a different syntactic structure. The use of a lexicon allows her to concentrate on the productive, regular formation of complex nominals, delegating to the lexicon any idiosyncratic meaning component of lexicalized expressions, e.g. *soap opera*, and proper nouns, e.g. *Madison Street*. She considers metaphor a separate phenomenon, interacting with compounding in (10):

(10) a. bottleneck
      b. hairpin turn

In (10a) the metaphor applies to the result of compounding and in (11b) to the input of the (highest-level) compound.

   Complex nominals include adjectival constructions such as (9c–d). Levi (1978: 15–17) argues that such adjectives are nouns at deep structure.[3] At the stage where compounding operates, pairs such as *atomic bomb* and *atom bomb* have the same representation.

---

[3] Levi (1978) generally uses the term *Logical Structure* for the representation that historically evolved from deep structure in the emergence of generative semantics.

A major concern in Levi's work is to avoid the excessive power of transformations assumed by Lees (1960). In particular, the derivation of complex nominals
should not involve the deletion of material that is not recoverable. In cases such as
(9b–c), this is not so difficult, because the predicate of the underlying sentential
representation is still overtly recognizable in the output. The process at work here is
nominalization. As noted above, in generative semantics there is no underlying
difference in this respect between (9b) and *car thief*, because *steal* is part of the deep
structure representation of *thief*. Levi (1978: 167–72) assumes four nominalization
rules corresponding to act, product, agent, and patient. There is no simple correspondence between these nominalization types and the resulting form, which leads
to systematic ambiguity.

For cases such as (9a, d), in which the right-hand element of the compound does
not contain a verb, Levi assumes that the predicate is deleted in the course of the
derivation. In order to maintain recoverability, she assumes that there is a finite
number of *recoverably deletable predicates* (RDPs). The idea of RDPs is related to
that of Lees's (1970) generalized verbs, but Levi (1978: 76–7) proposes a closed set
of nine RDPs, illustrated in (11).

(11) a. CAUSE₁   *accident weather, mortal blow*
      b. CAUSE₂   *air pressure, genetic disease*
      c. HAVE₁   *picture book, musical comedy*
      d. HAVE₂   *city wall, feminine intuition*
      e. MAKE₁   *honey bee, musical clock*
      f. MAKE₂   *snowball, stellar configuration*
      g. USE   *windmill, vocal music*
      h. BE   *pine tree, reptilian pets*
      i. IN   *desert rat, nocturnal flight*
      j. FOR   *doghouse, juvenile court*
      k. FROM   *olive oil, rural visitors*
      l. ABOUT   *tax law, social satire*

At deep structure, an embedded clause with the RDP as its predicate is attached as a
modifier to the head noun. The first three predicates can be active or passive in this
embedded clause, as illustrated in (11a–f). In the detailed discussion of each RDP,
Levi (1978: 86–106) emphasizes that they do not have the same range of meanings as
the corresponding English words. The examples in (11) are all from Levi's (1978)
lists and give a suggestion of the semantic interpretation of each RDP. Levi (1978:
121–8) gives a step-by-step account of the derivation of a number of complex
nominals and also gives detailed specifications of the crucial transformations.

One of the properties of Levi's account is that each complex nominal is inherently and multiply ambiguous. A complex nominal with a non-verbal head that is
not lexicalized in a particular interpretation has exactly twelve different meanings,
corresponding to (11a–l). If the complex nominal has a deverbal head, the four

nominalization readings are available in addition to these. According to Levi, this ambiguity is reduced in practice by 'judicious exploitation of semantic clues, lexicalization, and pragmatic or extralinguistic (encyclopaedic) knowledge' (1978: 158). As an example of a semantic clue, IN requires a locative noun (concrete, abstract, or temporal), so that it is unlikely to apply to *musical clock*. Lexicalization is special, because it depends on direct storage after earlier use, whereas the other strategies are based on inference and apply also to entirely new formations. However, pragmatic considerations may also override lexicalization. Thus, *snow-ball* may be used to refer to the coloured ball used in a football game when snow on the field makes a white ball difficult to see.

By the introduction of a specific set of RDPs, ambiguity of the type illustrated in (6) is significantly reduced. Whether the approach conforms to the letter and the spirit of Chomsky's (1965: 144–5) condition on the recoverability of deleted material is debatable. The examples he gives refer to classes of one or two specified elements, rather than nine. In addition, the twelve readings in (11) have a potential for overlap. Thus, Levi (1978: 281–2) notes that the subclass of (11f) with mass-noun modifiers, e.g. *snowball*, can also be analysed as a subclass of (11h) when BE is taken to express composition. Van Santen (1979) mentions as another problem the vagueness of the RDPs. Thus, the difference in meaning between *fertility pills* and *headache pills* cannot be expressed in terms of the RDP, because both involve FOR.

4.2.3 Developments in Germany

In Germany, compounding was much more prominent on the linguistic agenda than in America in the late 1960s and early 1970s. This may well reflect a difference in scientific culture. In America, there is a strong tendency to select a limited amount of interesting data as a basis for a proposal to modify or extend an existing theory. As a consequence, it is rather the theory than the data which takes centre ground. Thus, McCawley (1978: xi), in his preface to Levi (1978) expresses his regret that 'recent linguistic publications' are so much more concerned with 'talk[ing] about linguistics' than with 'do[ing] linguistics'. This makes comprehensive over-views of large data sets, such as compounding, uncommon. Lees (1960) and Levi (1978) represent rare exceptions. By contrast, in Germany, large-scale application of a theory is much more common. As a typical example of this, Marchand's (1969) discussion of word formation takes the form of a theoretically informed inventory rather than a theory with examples. The two further works on compounding discussed here, Brekle (1970) and Kürschner (1974), have a somewhat stronger theoretical orientation than Marchand (1969), but both also propose an overview of compounding processes that can be considered comprehensive rather than eclectic.

Brekle (1970) is a study of English nominal compounding. This study was carried out in Tübingen as a basis for the *Habilitation*, a degree above PhD, and was completed in 1968. The preface clearly identifies Marchand ('meinem verehrten Lehrer')[4] as the central influence:

> Die vorliegende Arbeit baut auf die Ergebnisse der jüngsten Arbeiten Hans Marchands zur Theorie der Syntax und Wortbildung* auf, entwickelt diese zum Teil weiter und versucht den speziell hier behandelten Bereich der englischen Nominalkomposition mittels eines expliziten grammatischen Modells in einem theoretischen Rahmen darzustellen.[5]
>
> (Brekle 1970: 9; footnote at * deleted)

Apart from Marchand, two other influences can be recognized in Brekle's work, those of Lees and of generative semantics. Brekle (1970: 54) represents the theoretical framework referred to in the above quotation as one in which deep structure corresponds to *content* and surface structure to *expression*, and rejects Chomsky's conception of deep structure explicitly (1970: 49–50). By adopting a generative framework, Brekle diverges from Marchand's orientation. The influence of Lees, however, seems to be largely filtered through the perception of his theory by Marchand. Brekle's research agenda is determined by Marchand's criticisms of Lees's approach, as listed in (7). Thus, he develops a mechanism of *topicalization* to solve the problem in (7a).

Brekle takes predicate logic as the basis for his deep structure formalism. This choice is in line with mainstream generative semantics. He sets up this formalism with rigorous precision, providing formal definitions of all components of the formulae he uses. The discussion of the formulae in (12) will give a sense of the approach he takes.

(12) a. AFF[LOC(R, y), w]
      b. LOC[AFF(F, w), z]
      c. λy\{AFF[LOC(R, y), SOTH]\}
      d. λR\{AFF[LOC(R, y), SOTH]\}
      e. Q_y^1, Q_R^2
      f. Q_R^1, Q_y^2

The formulae in (12) belong to three different classes, which Brekle calls 'Satzbegriffstypen' (12a–b), 'satzsemantische Strukturformeln' (12c–d), and 'Topikalisierungen' (12e–f). Brekle (1970: 149–52) discusses the derivations from the two underlying sentence structures in (12a–b), in which AFF ('affect') and LOC ('local relation') are predicate constants. Whereas (12a) represents phrasal expressions such as '(some) mouse living in a hole', with location as an argument, (12b) is

---

[4] 'my adored teacher'.

[5] 'The present work builds on the results of the latest works by Hans Marchand on the theory of syntax and word formation, develops these further and attempts to represent the focus of this study, the area of English nominal compounding, by means of an explicit grammatical model in a theoretical framework.' (my translation)

illustrated by 'wood drifting on a river', where the location is an optional modifier. Brekle distinguishes twenty-five such types.

In (12c–d), the λ operator isolates different variables corresponding to (12a). They represent more specific information about the realization of (12a). In (12c), the location is selected as the central concept, as in *living room*, in (13d) the locative predicate, as in *country life*. The variable *w* in (12a) is replaced by 'SOTH' in both cases, a pronominal constant. An example where the corresponding structure has λw is *fieldmouse*. In this way, each compound type is divided into a number of subtypes.

In (12e–f), the topic-comment structures corresponding to (12c–d) are given. Pronominal constants are not represented. Variables are ranked by a Q with a subscript indicating the variable and a superscript indicating the rank. Given that each formula of the type illustrated in (12c–d) has exactly one topic-comment structure, in which the first-ranked variable is the one under the λ and the others are ranked from left to right, we can understand Kürschner's (1977) claim that topic-comment structure is dispensable.

Kürschner (1974) presents a study of German nominal compounding, originally carried out as a PhD in Tübingen. He identifies Lees (1960), Brekle (1970), and Marchand (1969) as the 'three studies' that 'have been most influential on my work' (Kürschner 1974: 197). He discusses the problems of a transformational account of compounding in much detail and arrives at an account that is quite different from any of these sources of inspiration. Instead of a sentential origin of compounds, Kürschner adopts a structure [$_{NP}$ N S], in which S is a relative clause modifying N. He uses the German examples in (14) to illustrate his analysis.

(13)   a. Holzhaus   ('timber house')
           b. Putzfrau   ('cleaning woman')

In (13a), the deep structure [$_{NP}$ N S] has *Haus* as N and a relative clause as S in which *Haus* and *Holz* occur and a relation between the two is expressed. The standard account of relative clauses at this stage of transformational grammar, as presented by Jacobs and Rosenbaum (1968: 199–212), involved deletion under identity of the modified noun, here *Haus*, in the relative clause. The problem Kürschner (1974: 80–1) identifies in the derivation of (13a) along these lines is the large amount of deleted material, including the tense and the predicate of the relative clause.

If it is assumed that only deep structure is taken into account in semantic interpretation, as Chomsky (1965) proposed, and that the relative clause and the compound have the same deep structure, they should have the same meaning. However, Kürschner (1974: 90–4) argues that the class of compounds exemplified by (13b) makes this impossible. Whereas the relative clause implies actual activity, the compound implies habitual or professional activity. These meanings overlap but are not identical.

In order to solve these problems, Kürschner (1974: 103–5) first of all rejects the idea that the same deep structure should underlie the relative clause and the compound. Instead, they have different but related deep structures. The deep structure of the compound (13a) does not specify the tense and the exact relationship in the S of [$_{NP}$ N S], whereas the one for the relative clause does. In a similar way, the habituality of the action is specified in the deep structure of the compound (13b), whereas the one for the corresponding relative clause has tense specification.

In his detailed elaboration of German compound classes, Kürschner uses Fillmore's (1968) Deep Case labels and predicates that are similar to Lees's (1970) generalized verbs. Thus, one of his classes, exemplified by *Zeitungsjunge* ('newspaper boy') has a deep structure with an Agent, an Object, and a generalized verb *transfer* (Kürschner 1974: 168–9).

4.3 LEXICALIST APPROACHES

Although generative semantics was highly popular, Chomsky continued to assume a model in which deep structure was part of syntax and the meaning of an expression was derived from syntactic representations by means of interpretive rules. The introduction of the lexicon made a new type of mechanism available. Botha (1968) discusses the position of compounding in relation to the lexicon, arguing against Lees's (1960) analysis without however proposing an alternative. Chomsky (1970) discusses first of all nominalizations of the type in (14b).

(14)   a. John has refused the offer.
       b. John's refusal of the offer

Chomsky argues that (14b) is not transformationally derived from the deep structure underlying (14a). The relationship between the items in (14) should be covered in the lexicon instead. Chomsky (1970: 188) refers to this hypothesis as the *lexicalist hypothesis*, without however formulating it explicitly. Chomsky (1970) does not discuss compounding directly, and leaves many issues concerning the structure of the lexicon unresolved. In section 4.3.1 we will consider some proposals to elaborate the structure of the lexicon and in section 4.3.2 a proposal for compounding rules compatible with the lexicalist hypothesis.

4.3.1 Compounds in the lexicon

Two questions arise immediately when it is accepted that the grammar has a lexicon and that word formation is treated in the lexicon rather than in the transformational component of the grammar. They are listed in (15):

(15)   a. How is the regularity of word formation accounted for?
   b. How is the non-existence of predicted words accounted for?

In a sense, the question in (15a) is the reverse of a well-known issue raised by the transformational approach. In a transformational approach, the question was how to account for the difference in meaning between *fertility pills* and *headache pills*. In a lexicalist approach, this difference can be encoded trivially in the lexical entries for these compounds. The relationship with the component words, however, which was automatically expressed in the transformational account, becomes an issue in the lexicalist approach.

The question in (15b) refers to so-called 'possible words'. The set of possible words includes all results of word formation processes, independently of whether they are actually used. Given the recursive nature of compounding, the set of possible words is infinite.

Halle (1973) proposes a model for solving the issues in (15) in which the lexicon is a system of four components. The first is a list of morphemes, the second a set of word formation rules, the third a filter, and the last one a dictionary. Word formation rules produce the set of possible words on the basis of the list of morphemes. The filter marks all non-existing words such that they are not available to the syntax at the stage of lexical insertion. It also adds any idiosyncratic properties that cannot be predicted by the word formation rules. The resulting list constitutes the dictionary, to which syntactic rules have access.

It is noteworthy that Halle (1973) does not discuss compounding, because it is immediately obvious that Halle's model is not attractive as a solution for the representation of compounds. The recursive nature of compounding implies that the filter, which has to exclude each individual non-occurring word, is not only far too powerful, but not even a finite device, so that it fails to meet one of the most basic conditions of a grammar. Scalise (1984: 23–34) discusses Halle's model in more detail.

In his Full Entry Model, Jackendoff (1975) reverses some of the assumptions made by Halle (1973). His starting point is not a list of morphemes, but what Halle calls the *dictionary*, that is, a list of lexical entries ready for insertion in the appropriate contexts. The form, meaning, and syntactic constraints for the insertion are fully specified in the entries. This makes the solution of (15b) trivial, but complicates (15a). Jackendoff proposes an original solution to this problem. Instead of treating word formation rules as generative rules, he considers them as redundancy rules. The perspective changes from the formation of entries to calculating the amount of information they contain. According to Jackendoff (1975: 643), the information cost of a lexical entry W consists of the three components listed in (16):

(16)   a. the information that W exists
   b. the information about W that cannot be predicted by a rule R
   c. the cost of referring to R

Jackendoff (1975: 655–8) addresses the problem of compounding explicitly and I will illustrate the application of (16) with one of his examples, *garbage man*. The fact that this word exists and is listed in the lexicon, as opposed to, for instance, *tissue man*, is counted in (16a). There are many aspects of the word that are regular. The lexicon has an entry for *garbage* and one for *man* and much of the information of these entries applies to *garbage man*. This can be used by (16b) if we assume that there is a redundancy rule specifying that two nouns can be concatenated and that the properties of the two nouns are used to determine (many) properties of the result. One can also imagine more specific rules giving increasingly specific information about how the result relates to the two nouns. The cost referred to in (16c) gives us a tool to find the optimal balance between generality and specificity of these rules. The more generally a rule R is applicable, the less the cost of referring to R.

4.3.2 Lexicalist compounding rules

The first detailed study of the rules characterizing compounds in a lexicalist framework is Allen's (1978) unpublished PhD dissertation. She proposes two rules for compounds, paraphrased in (17) and (18).

(17)   IS A CONDITION
       In the compound [X Y]$_Z$, Z 'IS A' Y.

(18)   VARIABLE R CONDITION
       In the primary compound [X Y]$_Z$, the meaning of X fills any one of the feature slots of Y that can be appropriately filled by X.

Allen's (1978: 105) condition in (17) is 'purposefully ambiguous between syntactic and semantic interpretations' of IS A. A *water mill* is a type of *mill* but the compound is also a countable noun like *mill*. (17) is of course not an entirely new insight. Similar observations, though in different frameworks, were made by Bloomfield (1933: 235) and Marchand (1969: 11). The use as a constraint in the lexicon is new, however. As such, (17) is the forerunner of Williams's (1981) Right-hand Head Rule.

   The condition in (18) is originally expressed in terms of operations on feature matrices (Allen 1978: 93–4). Allen (1978: 92) argues that if we consider *water mill* in its non-lexicalized form, it may have a range of possible meanings including the ones in (19), but not the ones in (20).

(19)   Possible meanings of *water mill*
       a. 'mill powered by water'
       b. 'mill producing water'
       c. 'mill located near the water'

      d. 'mill for analysing the content of water'
      e. 'mill where the employees drink water', etc.

(20)   Impossible meanings for *water mill*
      a. 'mill which lives near the water'
      b. 'mill which grinds water'
      c. 'mill which drinks water'
      d. 'mill made out of water'
      e. 'mill which searches for water', etc.

The fact that *water mill* is lexicalized in sense (19a) does not mean that (19b–e) are impossible meanings. In a context in which any *mill* in the discourse universe is a *windmill*, *water mill* can well be used in the sense (19c). However, the effect illustrated in (19) is stronger in compounds for which no meaning has been lexicalized. The point of (20) is that each of the proposed relationships between the two nouns is possible if we replace *mill* or *water* or both by other nouns. Thus, the relationships in (20a), (20c), and (20e) are possible for *water rat* instead of *water mill*, although for *water rat* only the one in (20a) is lexicalized. In the case of *water mill*, the semantics of *mill* excludes them. (20b) and (20d) are impossible because *water* is not an appropriate filler of the relevant slot of *mill*. However, the most common reading of *coffee mill* is parallel to (20b) and of *chocolate bar* to (20d).

It is interesting to compare Allen's (1978) approach to the ones of Lees (1960) and Levi (1978). Allen and Levi agree that Lees's approach involves transformations that are too powerful. They describe the relationships between the two elements of a compound but they delete content words that cannot be recovered. Levi (1978) proposes to constrain the number of predicates associated with the compounding rule. Allen (1978) does not link the predicates to the rule of compounding but to the components of the compound. This is possible because she does not assume that deep structure contains explicit representations of the predicates, but that semantic interpretation rules infer the predicates from the semantic structure of the component words.

4.4 TOWARDS A NEW SET OF RESEARCH QUESTIONS

In the late 1970s a major shift in research questions can be observed in the area of compounding. This change is documented in sections 4.4.1 and 4.4.2. In section 4.4.3, the legacy of the early approaches is briefly summarized.

4.4.1 Rewrite rules and feature percolation

Lees (1960) links the formation and the classification of compounds and the work we have considered all elaborates, modifies, or argues against his approach. After Levi (1978) no further prominent studies of compounding in generative semantics were published. In the lexicalist approach, after Allen (1978) attention turned to the formation of compounds rather than the relationship between the components. In reaction to the earlier transformational accounts, it was the use of rewrite rules that became prominent.

The idea that rewrite rules could be used to generate compounds is by no means new. In his review of Lees (1960), Householder (1962) starts the discussion of the compounding chapter as follows:

> The first question, of course, is this: why cannot most of these compounds (and relatively few non-compounds) be generated by a recursive rule of the form N→N+N with no restrictions on form and no linking with phrases or kernel sentences?
>
> (Householder 1962: 342)

Before the introduction of the lexicon, Householder's suggestion can only be taken to illustrate his poor understanding of the aims of generative linguistics (cf. ten Hacken 2007: 167–74). Until the lexicon extended the expressive potential, transformations were the only mechanism to account for relationships between expressions. Therefore only transformations could lead to an account with more than observational adequacy. Only the emergence of lexicalism allowed for the meaning of compounds to be accounted for without transformations.

Even after Chomsky's (1970) seminal paper, it took a long time for rewrite rules to be proposed for compounding. Jackendoff (1977: xi) invokes the 'misplaced bias against phrase structure' inherited 'from the early work in generative grammar' as a reason why X-bar theory remained without proper elaboration for a long time. Selkirk (1982), however, extends the domain of X-bar theory to the internal structure of words. In the coverage of bound morphemes (affixes and neoclassical stems in English), she also uses the bar level−1. Lieber (1981: 44) traces this idea back to an unpublished manuscript by Selkirk from 1978. Selkirk's (1982) account of compounding is based on three components. The first is a set of rewrite rules, given here in (21).

(21)   a. N → {N/A/V/P} N
        b. A → {N/A/P} A
        c. V → P V

Following Selkirk (1982: 16), curly brackets are used in (21a–b) to indicate alternatives. The second component is the Right-hand Head Rule (RHR), similar to (17), of which Selkirk (1982: 20) proposes a new, refined version. The purpose of this rule is to determine which element of a word is its head. The final component is the well-formedness condition in (22) (1982: 21).

(22)   PERCOLATION

If a constituent α is the head of a constituent β, α and β are associated with an identical set of features (syntactic and diacritic).

Selkirk (1982: 76) proposes a more refined version of (22), without changing the general idea. Compared to the accounts of compounding inspired by Lees (1960), Selkirk's account is striking not only by its use of rewrite rules instead of transformations, but also by its scope. She describes the semantics of compounding as follows:

The notion 'head' is crucial in characterizing the semantics of compounds. This emerges quite clearly when we consider $_N$[N N]$_N$ compounds, for example. The compound *apron string* designates a string that is somehow related to an apron, by being attached to one, in the form of one, or whatever.

(Selkirk 1982: 22)

If we consider a compound [X Y]$_Z$, Selkirk does not attempt to characterize the relationship between X and Y, but only the one between Z and the head, which the RHR identifies as Y in English.

Rules such as (21) are typical of the interpretation of X-bar theory in Jackendoff (1977), in which the X-bar formalism is used to organize rewrite rules. The transition to a Principles and Parameters framework as presented by Chomsky (1981), however, interprets X-bar theory as a replacement of idiosyncratic rewrite rules. In line with this approach, Lieber (1981) develops an alternative in which the labels in the word structure tree are not determined by rewrite rules such as (21) but only by the categories of the morphemes in the lexicon and a set of feature percolation rules replacing (22). Lieber (1981: 47) proposes generic rewrite rules generating unlabelled trees. For English compounding, she proposes a feature percolation convention that is similar to the RHR (1981: 54). Compared to Selkirk (1982), Lieber (1981) addresses the same questions and proposes a solution on the basis of a large number of shared assumptions.

4.4.2 Verbal compounds

The increased interest in headedness and feature percolation coincided with a concentration of research effort on a particular subclass of compounds, usually called *verbal compounds*. The first publication specifically devoted to this area is Roeper and Siegel (1978). They describe their nature as follows:

Many recent analyses* have failed to distinguish verbal compounds (such as *coffee-maker*) from a class of compounds we shall call *root* compounds (such as *bedbug*). There are two distinctions to be made: verbal compounds are marked by *-ed*, *-ing*, and *-er*, while root compounds need not show any morphological marking; and verbal compounds have a verb base word, while root compounds may combine many syntactic categories

(Roeper and Siegel 1978: 206: footnote at * deleted)

In earlier accounts, verbal compounds are not recognized as a separate class. Lees (1960) integrates verbal compounds into the domain of his rules without treating them in any special way. In terms of the classification in (5), we find *coffee maker* in (5e) and *baby sitting* in (5g), but these classes also include, for instance, *asking price* and *bowling ball*, respectively, which are root compounds according to Roeper and Siegel. Marchand (1965a: 57) distinguishes 'verbal nexus substantives', but they also include both *crybaby* and *housekeeping*. Levi (1978) distinguishes two classes, one derived by means of RDPs and one by means of nominalization, but the latter is much wider than Roeper and Siegel's verbal compounds, because it also includes items such as *car thief*, in which the verb is only visible in a type of analysis not adopted outside generative semantics.

It is not difficult to explain why verbal compounds were recognized as a separate class at precisely this point in time. Whereas for root compounds an account consisting of (21) and (22) or equivalent mechanisms may be sufficient, much more can be said about verbal compounds. In a verbal compound the subcategorization properties of the verb embedded in Y will determine the role of X in relation to Y. This explains the interpretation of *coffee maker*.

Roeper and Siegel's (1978) article was seminal in a way similar to Lees (1960) in the sense that it determined a highly productive research field. In the framework of Jackendoff's full-entry theory, they propose an account in terms of what they call 'lexical transformations'. This aspect of their proposal was generally criticized in subsequent literature. Another point of general criticism was the delimitation of the domain. Thus, Allen (1978: 156–8) argues that Roeper and Siegel restrict it arbitrarily by listing only three suffixes. She proposes to generalize it to all compounds with deverbal nouns as the right-hand component, including, for instance, *mail delivery*, *snow removal*, and *population growth*. The fact that the delimitation of the domain becomes an issue illustrates the increased importance of verbal compounds as a class.

An issue on which opinion was divided was which of the two structures in (24) is the correct one.

(23)   a. [coffee [make-er]$_\alpha$]
      b. [[coffee make]$_\beta$-er]

In applying her general framework to verbal compounding, Selkirk (1982: 28–43) argues for (23a). This structure can be generated by (21a), because α is a noun. It is not possible to generate (23b), because β is not a possible word. By contrast, Lieber (1983: 267) argues for structure (23b). She argues that (23a) is only appropriate for compounds such as *apprentice welder*, where the first element is not interpreted as an object of the verb.

In subsequent years, many different proposals for the treatment of verbal compounds were made and no general theory of morphology could be presented without one. Spencer (1991: 324–43) gives an overview of the different proposals.

The length of this overview (nineteen pages as against five devoted to root compounds) further illustrates the relative prominence of this type of compounding in the field.

4.4.3 The legacy

Although any cut-off point is to some extent arbitrary, the fact that in the same year Levi's book and Roeper and Siegel's article appeared and Allen's PhD dissertation was accepted makes 1978 a good candidate for the end of the 'early period' in the generative research of compounding. The starting point is surely marked by Lees (1960). This period was dominated by the research questions in (24).

(24) a. How are compounds related to underlying sentences?
      b. How can compound formation and classification be linked?

A certain degree of consensus was reached within the dominating framework at the end of this period. This framework was determined by Chomsky's (1970) lexicalist hypothesis. The consensus was largely negative. In response to (24a), it was found that no relation could be specified. The transformational accounts proposed by Lees (1960) and successors were generally rejected. In response to (24b), the idea that the syntactic or semantic classification could be linked in an interesting way to the formation of compounds was given up. To the extent that classifications of this type were an important part of most traditional accounts of compounding, e.g. Jespersen (1942), this result marked a more significant break with earlier work. Although not much work has been done on the semantics of root compounds in lexicalist varieties of generative grammar, Allen's (1978) insight that it is not the construction but the components of the compound that determine its semantics was largely adopted. This insight was based on earlier work such as Gleitman and Gleitman (1970) and Downing (1977).

In the wake of the negative responses to (24) a number of new research questions emerged. Because of the results achieved in the period 1960–1978, the study of these questions could be undertaken without the burden of having to address these in hindsight rather unrewarding issues.

....

CHAPTER 5

A LEXICAL
SEMANTIC
APPROACH TO
COMPOUNDING

....

ROCHELLE LIEBER

In this chapter I will explore the interpretation of compounds in terms of the framework of lexical semantic analysis developed in Lieber (2004). In that work, I offered an analysis of typical English root compounds like *dog bed*, synthetic compounds such as *truck driver*, and coordinative compounds such as *producer-director*, all of which arguably are endocentric. Here I will adopt the classification of compounds argued for in Bisetto and Scalise (2005) and use it to extend the analysis of compounds beyond that of Lieber (2004), both in terms of its empirical coverage of English compounding processes, and in terms of its applicability to forms of compounding that are little attested in English. What will emerge from this analysis, I believe, will be not only a deeper understanding of the full range of compounding in English (and other languages), but also a deeper understanding of the nature of exocentricity. In effect, I will argue that exocentricity does not constitute a single phenomenon, but encompasses a number of different situations. In this, I am in agreement with the preliminary results of Scalise et al.'s extensive typological study of compounding (Scalise and Guevara 2007).

In section 5.1 I will give a brief overview of the system of lexical semantic representation developed in Lieber (2004). Section 5.2 will extend the treatment of the semantic body of lexical items beyond that given in Lieber (2004) and consider the relationship between the skeleton and the body on a cross-linguistic basis; as we will see, the nature of the semantic body is critical to the range of interpretation available to any given compound. I will argue there that the semantic body is not completely unsystematic as I suggested in Lieber (2004), but rather has some order: in addition to purely encyclopedic facets of meaning that probably are unsystematic, and that perhaps differ in detail from speaker to speaker, the body is also a repository of those universal features of meaning that are not syntactically active in a particular language. These features do, I will argue, figure prominently in restricting the possible meanings of compounds. In section 5.3, I will adopt the system of classification for compounds developed in Bisetto and Scalise (2005, and this volume), and show how it can be applied in terms of the current system. Then, section 5.4 will offer specific analyses of several different types of compounds, from which will emerge my conclusion in section 5.5 that exocentricity cannot be treated as a single unified phenomenon. In section 5.6 I will turn my attention to a kind of compounding that is nearly unattested in English, but is quite productive in Chinese, Japanese, and a number of other languages, namely verb–verb compounds.

5.1 THE FRAMEWORK: SKELETONS

In Lieber (2004) I developed a system of lexical semantic representation that allows us to answer a fundamental question about the semantics of complex words, specifically why the relationship between form and meaning is frequently not one-to-one in languages. I argued that the starting point for answering this question is to develop a system of representation that allows us to characterize the meanings both of simple lexemes and affixes, and to show how such meanings can be integrated in the derivation of complex words. The semantic representation of morphemes consists of what I call the semantic/grammatical skeleton and the semantic/pragmatic body. The skeleton is comprised of all and only features that are of relevance to the syntax in a given language. Such features act as functions that in turn are organized hierarchically along with their arguments, much as the Lexical Conceptual Structures of Jackendoff (1990) are. The difference between Jackendoff's semantic functions and the ones I proposed in Lieber (2004) lies in their grain size: my semantic functions represent smaller atoms of meaning than Jackendoff's and, as I argued there, are more suitable for characterizing the sorts of meanings that are encoded in affixes. In Lieber (2004) I proposed and motivated six semantic features, and in Lieber (2007) I added a seventh:

(1)   SEMANTIC FEATURES

[± **material**]: The presence of this feature defines the conceptual category of SUBSTANCES/THINGS/ESSENCES, the notional correspondent of the syntactic category Noun. The positive value denotes the presence of materiality, characterizing concrete nouns. Correspondingly, the negative value denotes the absence of materiality; it defines abstract nouns.

[± **dynamic**]: The presence of this feature signals an eventive or situational meaning, and by itself signals the conceptual category of SITUATIONS. The positive value corresponds to an EVENT or Process, the negative value to a STATE.

[± **IEPS**]: This feature stands for 'Inferable Eventual Position or State'. Informally, we might say that the addition of [IEPS] to a skeleton signals the addition of a path. The positive value implies a directed path, and the negative value a random or undirected path.[1]

[± **Loc**]: Lexical items that bear the feature [Loc] for 'Location' are those for which position or place in time or space is relevant. For those items which lack the feature [Loc], the notion of position or place is irrelevant. Further, those which bear the feature [+Loc] will pertain to position or place. [−Loc] items will be those for which the explicit lack of position or place is asserted.

[± **B**]: This feature stands for 'Bounded'. It signals the relevance of intrinsic spatial or temporal boundaries in a SITUATION or SUBSTANCE/THING/ESSENCE. If the feature [B] is absent, the item may be ontologically bounded or not, but its boundaries are conceptually and/or linguistically irrelevant. If the item bears the feature [+B], it is limited spatially or temporally. If it is [−B], it is without intrinsic limits in time or space.

[± **CI**]: This feature stands for 'Composed of Individuals'. The feature [CI] signals the relevance of spatial or temporal units implied in the meaning of a lexical item. If an item is [+CI], it is conceived of as being composed of separable similar internal units. If an item is [−CI], then it denotes something which is spatially or temporally homogeneous or internally undifferentiated.

[± **scalar**]: This feature signals the relevance of a range of values to a conceptual category. With respect to [−dynamic] SITUATIONS it signals the relevance of gradability. Those SITUATIONS for which a scale is conceptually possible will have the feature [+scalar]. Those SITUATIONS for which a scale is impossible will be [−scalar]. With respect to SUBSTANCES/THINGS/ESSENCES the feature [scalar] will signal the relevance of size or evaluation (i.e. this will be the feature which characterizes augmentative/diminutive morphology in those languages which display such morphology).

---

[1] See Lieber and Baayen (1997) and Lieber (2004) for a more formal definition of this feature.

These features define functions that take arguments. Functions and their arguments are organized hierarchically, as shown in (2):

(2)   a.   [F$_1$ ([argument])]
      b.   [F$_2$ ([argument], [F$_1$ ([argument])])]

Both lexical bases and affixes have skeletons that consist of features that take one or more arguments. In this system SUBSTANCES/THINGS/ESSENCES are the notional equivalent of nouns, and are characterized by at least the feature [material] and possibly also the feature [dynamic], if they are processual in nature. (3) gives the skeletons of some typical SUBSTANCES/THINGS/ESSENCES:

(3)   a.   truck   [+material ([ ])]
      b.   time   [−material ([ ])]
      c.   chef   [+material, dynamic ([ ])]
      d.   war   [−material, dynamic ([ ])]

The first argument of SUBSTANCES/THINGS/ESSENCES is the so-called 'R' argument (Higginbotham 1985) which establishes referentiality in this class of lexemes. SUBSTANCES/THINGS/ESSENCES may of course have more than one argument:

(4)   author [+material, dynamic ([ ], [ ])]

The presence of the feature [dynamic] without [material] defines the class of SITUATIONS, the notional equivalent of both verbs and adjectives. Both adjectives and stative verbs are characterized by the negative value of this feature; adjectives are differentiated from verbs by the presence of the feature [scalar], which encodes gradability in adjectives:

(5)   a.   love   [−dynamic ([ ], [ ])]
      b.   red   [−dynamic, +scalar ([ ])]
      c.   pregnant   [−dynamic, −scalar ([ ])]

Eventive verbs may be characterized by the feature [+dynamic] alone, when they are simple activity verbs. Coupled with some value of the feature [IEPS], [+dynamic] signals verbal meanings that involve change of state or change of path, either directed (with the [+IEPS] value) or random (with the [−IEPS] value).

(6)   a.   simple activity verb: kiss   [+dynamic ([ ], [ ])]
      b.   change of state: grow   [+dynamic, +IEPS ([ ])]^2
      c.   change of place: descend   [+dynamic, +IEPS ([ ], [ ])]
      d.   manner of change: walk   [+dynamic, −IEPS ([ ])]

In this system, affixes are assumed to have skeletons, just as simplex lexemes do, and to fall into the lexical semantic classes defined by the system of skeletal features.

---

[2] See Lieber (2004) for a treatment of the causative version of *grow*. Briefly, causatives are claimed to have bipartite skeletons, of which the inchoative/unaccusative version of the verb shown here forms a part.

For example, in Lieber (2004) I argued that the suffixes *-er* and *-ee* are both characterized by the semantic features [+material, dynamic]; they differ in the semantic restrictions placed on the R argument of *-ee*:

(7) a. -er   [+material, dynamic ([ ], <base>)]

    b. -ee   [+material, dynamic ([sentient, nonvolitional], <base>)]

Affixes are integrated with their bases to form a single referential unit. This integration is effected by the Principle of Coindexation, which matches an affixal argument to a base argument as follows:

(8)   PRINCIPLE OF COINDEXATION
        In a configuration in which semantic skeletons are composed, coindex the highest non-head argument with the highest (preferably unindexed) head argument. Indexing must be consistent with semantic conditions on the head argument, if any.

Semantic headedness is assumed to follow from syntactic headedness. The coindexation of the complex words *writer* and *employee* are shown in (9):

(9) a. [+material, dynamic ([$_i$], [+dynamic ([$_i$], [ ])])]
          -er   *write*

    b. [+material, dynamic ([sentient, nonvolitional-i], [+dynamic ([ ], [$_i$])])]
          -ee   *employ*

The suffix *-er* has no special requirements on the semantics of its coindexed argument, and therefore is coindexed with the highest argument of its base; from this follows that the complex word is generally interpreted as bearing one of the thematic relations associated with external arguments (agent, instrument, experiencer, etc.). The suffix *-ee*, however, must be coindexed with a base argument that can be interpreted as sentient but also non-volitional; since the highest argument of the verb *employ* must be volitional, the affix therefore coindexes its argument with the internal argument of *employ*, giving rise to the patient or theme interpretation.[3]

5.2 THE FRAMEWORK: THE RELATIONSHIP BETWEEN SKELETON AND BODY

In Lieber (2004) I devote only passing attention to the semantic body. I suggest there that the body encodes various perceptual, cultural, and otherwise encyclopedic aspects of meaning including shape, size or dimension, colour, orientation, origin,

---

[3] See Lieber (2004) for a full account of the complex polysemy displayed by these two affixes.

use, and so on, and that the precise contents of the semantic body can differ from one speaker to another. Here I would like to explore in more detail what the semantic body might look like and what the relationship is between skeleton and body. Lieber (2004) was focused exclusively on word formation in English. In that work I made no claims as to how the system should work cross-linguistically. As my aim here is to talk about compounding in general, I must therefore devote some attention to cross-linguistic matters. My tentative proposal here will be that the seven features defined above are both syntactically relevant in English and also necessary for accounting for word formation in English, but that they may be neither necessary nor sufficient in accounting for word formation in languages other than English. Rather, they form a subset of universal semantic features from which each language chooses. In other words, I will assume that the set of semantic features that may be syntactically active in any given language is larger than the set that is active in any single language. Syntactically inactive features may, however, be semantically active in a particular language and such semantic activity can be visible in the interpretation of compounds.[4] I will argue that this is the case in English.

My proposal is that the semantic body is not a completely random selection of bits of encyclopedic knowledge, but rather has at least some systematicity and structure. In some respects, my proposal will be reminiscent of Pustejovsky's (1995) 'qualia structures', but its structure and the motivation for that structure will be quite different. I propose that the semantic body contains at least two layers. Let us hypothesize that one layer of meaning is relatively systematic, consisting of those universal semantic features that are not syntactically active in the language in question. This layer of meaning should be relatively stable from speaker to speaker. The second layer of meaning is purely encyclopedic, consisting of assorted bits of information: colour, precise shape contours, precise manners of motion, special functions or origins, and so on. This part of the meaning is probably the locus of specialized user knowledge and may be more or less elaborate from one speaker to another. To extend my physical metaphor a bit, one could think of the systematic part of the body as its muscular structure, and the unsystematic part as a layer of fat; for humans at least the former is relatively uniform from one individual to the next, whereas the latter may vary widely.

What, then, would the muscular part of the body look like? Its precise nature would depend on two things: first, what the universal set of features is that could be active cross-linguistically, and second, what the set of features is that is syntactically active in the language in question. With regard to the first, my suggestion is inevitably partial and programmatic. I cannot, of course, determine definitively what the full range of cross-linguistic features should be in this chapter. What I will therefore do

---

[4] My proposal is perhaps a bit reminiscent of Whorf's (1956) distinction between overt and covert categories. By overt categories, Whorf meant categories with overt morphological or syntactic marking. Covert categories were those that had some visible semantic effects (say, affecting selection of certain prefixes), but which were not morphologically marked as a class.

here is to propose a number of features that seem to be likely candidates, by looking at features that seem to be syntactically active in languages other than English. Then we will see what work they can do if we assume that they form part of the semantic body in English. My test grounds will be the facts of English compounding.

As one way of adding to this small list, I have chosen to look at languages that manifest noun classes or noun classifiers that have some semantic basis, and to see what distinctions can be relevant in those languages.[5] Cross-linguistic research has revealed a number of semantic distinctions that frequently play a role in noun-class and noun-classifier languages. Allan (1977: 298) characterizes those distinctions as follows:

It is no coincidence that the existing categories of classification closely correspond to what Locke 1689 called the 'primary qualities of bodies': these he identified as SOLIDITY (my 'consistency'), EXTENSION (my 'shape' and 'size'), MOTION or REST (included in my 'material'), NUMBER (my 'quanta', and perhaps even the 'non-discrete' subcategory of 'consistency') and FIGURE (my 'shape').

Payne (1986: 114–15) elaborates on Allan's categories:

It is common for objects to be classified by several features at once. MATERIAL refers to the essential 'essence of the entities referred to by nouns' and subsumes the categories of animate, inanimate, and abstract. SHAPE can be grossly broken down into saliently one dimensional (long) objects, saliently two dimensional (flat) objects, and saliently three dimensional (round) objects. In addition, there are the non-dimensional subcategories of 'prominent curved exterior', 'hollow', and 'annular' which indicates holes and entrances of various kinds. CONSISTENCY may be either flexible, hard, or non-discrete. The non-discrete category applies to tacky, liquid and aggregate (mass) nouns. SIZE has to do with relative smallness or largeness. ARRANGEMENT has three subcategories. First, it identifies objects in some specific, but non-inherent configuration, such as coils (of rope) or packets (of matches). Secondly, arrangement can intersect with LOCATION to indicate specific position such as extended horizontal, extended vertical, objects in parallel, objects in a row. Thirdly, arrangement can intersect with QUANTA to identify configurations such as 'heap' or 'clump'. Quanta itself has to do with number such as 'singular', 'dual', 'plural', 'bunch', 'heap', 'basketful', or 'yards'.

---

[5] According to Dixon (1986: 105), the distinction between a language with noun classes and one with noun classifiers is the following:

Noun classes constitute an obligatory grammatical system, where each noun chooses one from a small number of possibilities. Ways of marking noun class include a prefix to the noun (and usually also to other constituents in the noun phrase, or in the sentence, that show concord with it), as in Bantu languages; an obligatory article, as in French and German; or an inflectional suffix that shows a portmanteau of case and noun class, as in Latin.

Noun classifiers are always separate lexemes, which may be included with a noun in certain syntactic environments; there is usually a largish set of classifiers (perhaps not clearly delimited in scope), but not every specific noun may be able to occur with one.

For our purposes, we can treat the two phenomena together because they share the two characteristics that are relevant to our discussion of the relationship between the skeleton and the body, namely that the distinctions made by both noun class and noun classifier systems are syntactically active, and that these distinctions have a semantic basis.

Grinevald adds to Allan's categories a category of social interaction ('categorizing humans by social status, sex, age, and distinguishing them sometimes from deities and other entities endowed with special powers') and functional interaction (2000: 51–2) ('categorizing items by their use, such as food or transportation for instance').

If such semantic categories can be syntactically active in noun-class/classifier languages, we might guess that they might still play a semantic role in languages in which they do not play a syntactic role. This is, of course, not an exhaustive list of possible semantic features. For one thing, many of these features are specific to nominal semantics, and we might expect to add features relevant more specifically to prepositions, adjectives, and verbs. For example, in the analysis of the semantics of spatial prepositions in Lieber (2004) I in fact proposed several distinctions that might be counted as part of the 'muscular' structure of the body. I argued there that semantic distinctions like <orientation> and <dimensionality> were necessary to describe the distinctions among such prepositions in English. To those I added <direction of focus>, which was intended to capture whether a preposition was oriented towards or away from a fixed focal point (e.g. the distinction between *from* and *to*), and <contact>, which conveyed whether the preposition implied contact or not (e.g. *to* versus *toward*).

For the sake of argument, let's assume that the following features are part of the universal inventory. I will represent those features that are syntactically active in English by enclosing them in square brackets. Syntactically (but not semantically) inactive features in English will be presented in angle brackets:

(10) FEATURES
        [material]
        [dynamic]
        [IEPS]
        [CI]
        [B]
        [Loc]
        [scalar]
        <animate>
        <human>
        <female>
        <age>
        <artefact>
        <n dimension>
        <orientation>
        <consistency>
        <function>
        <contact>
        <motion with respect to focal point>

The interpretation of the features <animate>, <human>, and <female> is the obvious one, the first distinguishing between animate and inanimate entities, the second distinguishing between humans and non-human animates, and the third distinguishing male from female. The feature <age> might be conceived of as binary, with the positive value counting as 'adult' and the negative value as 'child', or the feature might be conceived as multi-valued; nothing in what follows hinges on this choice. The feature <n dimension> will be a multi-valued feature, with n ranging between 1 and 3. The feature <orientation> might be binary, with values of <horizontal> and <vertical>, or in its place we might conceive of more than one feature denoting more complex orientations. Similarly, the features <consistency> and <function> might have to be multi-valued (or perhaps broken down into more than one feature). For the moment, I will treat the feature <function> as relevant to denoting not only what a thing might be used for (e.g. a knife cuts) but also what a person might do (an author writes). As nothing hinges on the precise definitions of these features we will leave their definitions a bit vague at the moment.

Some of these features clearly stand in a hierarchical relationship to others. For example, only entities that are [+material] can bear a value of the feature <animate>, and only entities that are <+animate> can bear the feature <human> or the feature <female>. Features that denote dimensionality and orientation are similarly restricted to [+material] entities. Interestingly, although it is logically possible to make distinctions between different types of [−material] (i.e. abstract) entities – for example, those that denote mental states (e.g. *love, courage, fear*) versus those that denote non-psychological abstractions (e.g. culturally defined abstractions like *law* or *omen*) – these distinctions are not to my knowledge made in noun-class/classifier languages. I will therefore leave open the question of whether distinctions such as these should be encoded in the universal system of features, for example in a binary feature like <psychological>.

Let us assume then that features such as these will either be syntactically active or part of the semantic body. For any given lexical item in a language, individual features may also be present or absent; in other words, as in Lieber (2004), we will assume that individual features may be present or absent, and if present may have whatever range of values is relevant (typically the range will be binary). See Lieber (2004) for defence of using features in both a binary and a privative fashion in lexical semantic theory. And again, these features are certainly not exhaustive; they should be sufficient, however, to see how the semantic features of the body can help to explain the semantic interpretation of compounds.

In what follows, I will now add bodily features to the skeletal representations discussed in section 5.1. (11) gives the lexical semantic representations of the simplex nouns *author* and *bed*:

(11)   a. author   [+material, dynamic ([ ], [ ])]
                        <+animate>
                        <+human>
                        <function>
                        {writes for publication, . . . }

        b. bed   [+material ([ ])]
                        <−animate>
                        <+artefact>
                        <3 dimension>
                        <horizontal>
                        <function>
                        {for sleeping, contains comfortable surface, . . . }

The lexical entries in (11) have three parts: skeleton, relevant features comprising the systematic part of the body, and encyclopedic elements; the latter are given between curly brackets.

5.3 THE CLASSIFICATION OF COMPOUNDS

Here I will adopt the classification of compounds argued for in Bisetto and Scalise (2005, and this volume). Their classification first distinguishes compounds on the basis of the grammatical relationship between the compounded elements: these elements can be in a relationship of coordination, subordination, or attribution. Once compounds have been divided on the basis of the grammatical relation between their elements, they are further divided on the basis of a semantic criterion – endocentricity vs. exocentricity:

(12)   Classification of compounds (Bisetto and Scalise 2005)

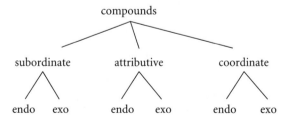

Subordinate compounds consist of two elements, one of which bears an argu-mental[6] relation to the second. Argumental relations include not only the familiar ones between an event and its participants (for example, as in the English com-pound *truck driver*, see below), but also the sort of relationship we find in N+N compounds like *table leg* or *tea merchant*. In each of these latter compounds, the head (right-hand) element has two arguments, the typical 'R' argument of a noun, and a second one (e.g. *leg of a table*). In subordinate compounds of this sort, the non-head satisfies the 'non-R' argument of the head.[7] In the scholarly literature devoted to compounding in English, the quintessential subordinate compounds are 'synthetic' compounds like *truck driver* and *cost containment*, where the non-head bears a complement relation to the head. As I've argued elsewhere (Lieber 2004), there are also compounds like *city employee* in which the first stem seems to have a subject interpretation rather than a complement one. Here I will add other examples of subordinate compounds with subject interpretation, namely 'revers-ible' compounds (see Jackendoff, this volume) like *dog attack* and *attack dog*. Among the subordinate compounds should also be classed those like *cut-throat* in English or *lavapiatti* 'dishwasher' (lit. 'wash dishes') in Italian.

The second group contains what Bisetto and Scalise call 'attributive' com-pounds. In these, one element stands in the relation of attribute or modifier to another. In this class we find many of the compounds that have been called in the literature on English compounding the root or primary compounds, for example *file cabinet, dog bed, greenhouse, hard hat*, etc. Also classed as attributive would be compounds like *Sunday driver* in which the head has an eventive argument structure, but the non-head nevertheless bears a modifier relation to it.

In the final grammatical class are so-called copulative compounds like *blue-green, producer-director*, or *mother-child* (e.g. a *mother-child relationship*); in this type of compound the two elements may be simultaneously predicated of a single referent (e.g. *producer-director*), or they may denote a relationship between the two elements (e.g. *mother-child*), or they may be combined into a third referent (e.g. Georgian *dá-dzma* 'sister-brother = siblings' [Wälchli 2005: 3]).

---

[6] Bisetto and Scalise (2005, this volume) actually limit the argumental relation displayed in subordinate compounds to complements and adjuncts. I believe that the classification needs to be expanded to include compounds in which the argumental relation is subject-oriented.

[7] Although I am in general agreement with Bisetto and Scalise about the nature of subordinate compounds, there are examples on whose classification we disagree. In addition to the subordinate compounds I've indicated here, Bisetto and Scalise count as subordinate also any NN compound in which the relation between the two nouns can be paraphrased by 'of'. For them, compounds like *apple cake* and *apron string* are subordinate rather than attributive. In contrast the only NN compounds that should be counted as attributive are those that cannot be paraphrased with 'of', for example, *snail mail* or *cake apple*. I am reluctant to count *apron string* and *apple cake* as subordinate, however, because their heads have no argument structure other than the single 'R' argument. I will not pursue further here the question of which compounds fall into which class, although this is certainly an interesting question.

Bisetto and Scalise also argue that within each of these types of compounds can be found both endocentric and exocentric exemplars. Endocentric compounds are, of course, those in which the compound as a whole is a hyponym of its head element. Exocentric compounds are those in which the compound as a whole is not a hyponym of its head. In (13) I give examples of each subclass of compounds.

(13)   a. SUBORDINATE
           endocentric: dishwasher, city employee, table leg, attack dog
           exocentric: pickpocket, lavapiatti

       b. ATTRIBUTIVE
           endocentric: dog bed, sky blue, blackboard
           exocentric: air head, blue blood

       c. COORDINATE
           endocentric: producer-director, bitter-sweet
           exocentric: mother-child, dá-dzma 'sister-brother = siblings'
                                          (Georgian example from Wälchli 2005: 3)

In what follows we will look systematically at each subclass of compounds to see how they may be analysed using the framework outlined above.

5.4 THE ANALYSIS OF COMPOUNDS

In this section I will go systematically through the six compound types in the Bisetto-Scalise taxonomy, for the most part illustrating my analysis with examples from English. Rather than starting with the most common types of compounds in English, however, I will start with some types that are poorly attested in English (but which occur with some frequency in other languages). It will emerge from the analysis that attributive compounds serve as a sort of default compound type.

5.4.1 Coordinate compounds

Coordinate compounds can manifest at least four possible semantic patterns, only three of which occur in English (for the fourth, we will use the Georgian example above):

(14)   a. Endocentric simultaneous interpretation: *producer-director*
       b. Endocentric mixture interpretation: *blue-green*
       c. Exocentric relationship interpretation: *mother-child*
       d. Exocentric collective interpretation: *dá-dzma* 'sister-brother = siblings'

I will consider the endocentric and the exocentric interpretations in turn.

5.4.1.1 *Endocentric coordinate*

The endocentric simultaneous reading occurs when both the skeleton and the formal body features of the two compounding elements are identical, the two elements differing only in encyclopedic aspects of meaning. Consider the representation for *scholar-athlete* in (15):

(15)   *scholar*   *athlete*
        [+material, dynamic ([$_i$])]   [+material, dynamic ([$_i$])]
                 <animate>   <animate>
                 <human>   <human>
                 <function>   <function>
                 {studies...}   {plays sport...}

The coindexation in (15) is straightforward: as both nouns have only the single R argument, they are coindexed. The nouns *scholar* and *athlete* are both concrete processual, and both denote humans who do something (denoted here by the feature <function>). The specific things that they do are in the encyclopedic part of the lexical representation. Given the close match between the skeletons and formal parts of the bodies of the two compounding elements, encyclopedic features may be added together to result in the simultaneous reading.

Endocentric coordinative compounds may receive the 'mixture' reading if the skeletons and body features of the two elements being compounded are identical, and if one of the skeletal features in question is [+scalar], which allows for intermediate states for the denotations of the compounded elements. Consider the representation for *blue-green* in (16):

(16)   *blue-green*
                 blue   *green*
        [−dynamic, +scalar ([$_i$])]   [−dynamic, +scalar ([$_i$])]
                 <colour>[8]   <colour>
        {sky, wavelength xyz,...}   {grass, wavelength pqr,...}

Here, there is only one possible way in which the single arguments of the adjectives can be coindexed. Given that colours are scalar qualities, we actually have two ways of interpreting such compounds. In English, the typical way is to assume a blend of the colours – something intermediate between green and blue. We should note, however, that there is nothing necessary about this reading. Although it seems not to happen in English, other languages have colour compounds that denote not a

---

[8] Here, I'm fudging a bit. Determining the body features of adjectives would require a cross-linguistic study of those aspects of adjectival semantics that can be syntactically active in the languages of the world. I leave this as a future project. It seems safe to say that whatever those features are, colours like *blue* and *green* will have the same ones.

mixture of the two colours but a simultaneity of them: take, for example, the nicknames of two Italian soccer teams the *rossoneri* 'red-black-PL' (for the Milan team) and *bianconeri* 'white-black-PL' (for the Turin team).[9] The team names refer to the shirts worn by players, in the first case, shirts with both red and black, and in the second, shirts with both white and black.

5.4.1.2 *Exocentric coordinate*

The two possible endocentric coordinate interpretations thus result from near-identity of lexical semantic representations, with differences occurring only at the level of encyclopedic elements. Exocentric coordinate interpretations, on the other hand, result when there is identity only up to a point – at least of skeletons and perhaps of some bodily features – along with direct incompatibility of at least one body feature. There are two ways in which the direct incompatibility can be resolved.

Consider first the representation of the Georgian example *dá-dzma* 'sister-brother = siblings' in (17):

(17)   *dá-dzma* 'sister-brother = siblings'

dá	*dzma*
[+material, dynamic ([$_i$],[ ])]	[+material, dynamic ([$_i$],[ ])]
\<animate\>	\<animate\>
\<+gender\>	\<+gender\>
\<+female\>	\<−female\>
{…}	{…}

As is obvious from the representation in (17), the representations are identical up to the feature \<± female\>, which has conflicting values. Given that there is nothing which can be simultaneously a brother and a sister, and nothing which stands midway between a brother and a sister, other interpretations are forced. One path that can be taken in the interpretation of such a conflict is to assume a set or collective reading of the compounded elements. This is the route taken in Georgian, where *dá-dzma* is the set of brothers and sisters, namely siblings. In effect, with such an interpretation the compound is forced to be semantically exocentric, where 'brother-sister' is neither a brother nor a sister but a collectivity of both.

The other route in interpreting such conflicting lexical semantic representations is to opt for syntactic rather than semantic exocentricity. This is the route that English prefers to take. Consider the representation in (18):

---

[9] Many thanks to Sergio Scalise for these examples.

(18)   *mother-child (relation, party)*

mother	*child*
[+material, dynamic ([$_i$],[$_j$])]	[+material, dynamic ([$_j$],[$_i$])]
<animate>	<animate>
<gender>	<gender>
<+adult>	<−adult>
<+female>	
{...}	{...}

First, I should explain the unusual cross-indexing in (18). Both *mother* and *child* are relational nouns, which in Lieber (2004) are treated as two-place processual nouns. Although one can clearly be both a *mother* of someone and a *child* of someone else, if we were to coindex the highest arguments of the two nouns in the compound, we would be identifying *mother* and *child* as referring to the same individual, just as we did in the case of *scholar-athlete* above. This, however, is an ontological impossibility: at least in a world in which human cloning is as yet impossible, one cannot be the child or the mother of oneself. The only plausible coindexing is the crossing one in (18).

We can now return to the interpretation of such compounds. Syntactic exocentricity is a possibility if compounds such as these are predicated of a third noun; since the semantic mismatch disallows a simultaneous or mixture reading, other readings can be forced, but only by virtue of further predication. Indeed, what the third noun is determines what kind of interpretation the compound as a whole is given. One possibility is for the compound to be interpreted as a collectivity (just as it is in Georgian); this is the case if the compound is predicated of a noun like *party* or *dance* (*a mother-child party* would be a party with mothers and children). If, on the other hand, the head of the phrase is something like *relationship, interaction,* or *discussion,* we can interpret *mother-child* as denoting a 'between' relationship. In other words, the precise relationship between the compounded elements is coerced by the head they are predicated of.[10]

Note that it is still possible to get compounds of this sort in English if the bodily features and even the skeletal features of the compounded elements don't match perfectly. But the more different the two nouns, the less plausible the compound seems. (19) illustrates compounds with increasingly disparate nouns:

---

[10] Note that it is not necessary to assume that in being predicated of a noun, compounds like *mother-child* must become adjectives. It is well known in English that nouns can modify other nouns, as for example is the case in collocations like *leather jacket* or *stone wall*. It is also orthogonal to my point whether such collocations are treated as compounds or phrases.

(19) a. mother-child
          cat-dog
      b. veterinarian-dog
      c. doctor-scalpel   } relationship
          gardener-tree
      d. mother-truth
          idea-researcher

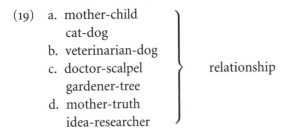

My general impression is that the compounds in (19a) are perfectly plausible; in each case the two compounded elements differ only in a single bodily feature and/or in encyclopedic bits of meaning. Those in (19b) differ a bit more: *veterinarian* is a concrete processual noun, and *dog* just a concrete noun. They therefore differ in the presence of the feature [dynamic] in the former and its absence in the latter; the skeletal features, in other words, are overlapping. The two differ as well in the body feature <± human>. This compound is a bit iffy to my ears, but not implausible. The compounds in (19c) seem less plausible, however: here the compounded elements differ both in the skeletal feature [dynamic] that *doctor* and *gardener* possess and *scalpel* and *tree* respectively lack; they are also quite different in body features. Finally the compounds in (19d) are to my ear quite a stretch: the compounded nouns here differ in the skeletal feature [material], *truth* and *idea* being [−material] and *mother* and *researcher* being [+material, dynamic]. This is not to say that such compounds are ruled out – only that they are less likely.

5.4.2 Subordinate compounds

As mentioned above, I reserve the term 'subordinate' for compounds that exhibit an argumental relation between the two compounded elements. As with coordinate compounds, subordinate compounds come in endocentric and exocentric varieties. We begin here with endocentric ones, as they receive a relatively straightforward analysis within the framework of Lieber (2004).

5.4.2.1 *Endocentric subordinate*

Endocentric subordinate compounds include N+N compounds like *tea merchant* or *table leg*, as well as compounds like *truck driver* or *city employee* that have traditionally been referred to in the English tradition as synthetic or deverbal compounds. Cross-linguistically, such compounds are among the most widely attested of compound types (Sergio Scalise, p.c.). Consider the representation in (20):

(20)   *truck driver*
          truck   -er   drive
       [+material ([$_j$])]   [+material, dynamic ([$_i$], [+dynamic ([$_i$], [$_j$])])]

In (20), the complex word *driver* is first created, with the affix *-er* subordinating its verbal base and coindexing the highest verbal argument. As argued in Lieber (2004), *-er* has no special semantic requirements for its R argument, and therefore is free to link with the highest verbal argument whatever its semantic nature (volitional or non-volitional, sentient or non-sentient, etc.). The Principle of Coindexation then indexes the highest non-head argument with the highest unindexed head argument, which in this case is the second argument of *drive*. The first element of the compound must then be interpreted as the internal argument of *drive*.

As argued in Lieber (2004), this indexing of endocentric subordinate compounds is the typical one, but not the only one. Consider the representation of the compound *city employee* in (21):

(21)   *city employee*
       city   *-ee*
       [+material ([ⱼ])] [+material, dynamic ([sentient, nonvolitional-i]),
       employ
       [+dynamic ([ⱼ],[ᵢ])])]

The affix *-ee* in English preferentially links its R argument to the verbal argument that matches its semantic requirements most closely. With a verb like *employ* that has a clearly volitional first argument, the second argument is the best match. When *city* is then compounded with *employee* the highest verbal argument is still unindexed, and may be coindexed with *city*'s R argument. This noun gets an argumental interpretation, but in this case it is the external argument interpretation.

The careful reader will note that I have left out any indication of body features in (20) and (21). In the cases above the interpretation of the compound seems to depend entirely on the pattern of indexing between the two stems, and the interpretation of the verbal argument that gets coindexed with the non-head. There are cases, however, where body features arguably play some role.[11] Consider, for example, the compound *cookbook author*:

(22)   *cookbook author*
           cookbook   *author*
       [+material ([ᵢ])] [+material, dynamic ([ ],[ᵢ])]
           <−animate>   <+animate>
           <+artefact>   <+human>
                                   <function>
       {contains recipes,...}   {writes things,...}

---

[11] Body features clearly also play a role in the likelihood that a compound will be coined. For example, given the choice between the nouns *van* and *peanutbutter* as the first element in a compound in which the second element is the noun *driver*, clearly the features of *van* are more compatible with *driver* than are the features of *peanutbutter*.

Given the Principle of Coindexation, as we have set it out, the highest (and only) argument of the non-head *cookbook* would be coindexed with the highest argument of the head, which is the R argument. However, the two nouns identified would then have incompatible body features; I assume, in other words, that the body features of a noun are part of its referential nature, and that they do not apply to extra arguments of the noun, should there be any. The second argument of *author*, however, is free in interpretation, and therefore can be felicitously coindexed with the R argument of *cookbook*.

Also among the subordinate compounds would be what Jackendoff (this volume) calls 'reversible' compounds like *kick ball* and *ball kick*. As Jackendoff points out, although the head of the two compounds 'profiles' different stems (so a *kickball* is a kind of *ball* and a *ball kick* is a kind of *kick*), the relation between the stems is identical: each has something to do with balls being kicked. The reversible nature of these compounds is easily handled within the present framework:

(23) a. *kick*   *ball*
          $[-\text{material} ([_i\ ], [+\text{dynamic} ([_i\ ], [_j\ ])])]\ [+\text{material} ([_j\ ])]$
      b. *ball*   *kick*
          $[+\text{material} ([_j\ ])]\ [-\text{material} ([_i\ ], [+\text{dynamic} ([_i\ ], [_j\ ])])]$

In the examples in (23), we can see that although the head of the compound is different in the two cases, the Principle of Coindexation gives us the same indexing for both compounds. Hence, what Jackendoff calls 'reversibility'.[12]

5.4.2.2 *Exocentric subordinate*

This is a type of compound that is very poorly attested in English; the few examples include items like *pickpocket* and *cutpurse*, the latter archaic if not obsolete. However, this form of compounding is quite productive in Romance languages like French, Spanish, and Italian. Consider the representation in (24):

(24) *pick pocket*
          pick[13]   *pocket*
      $[+\text{dynamic} ([\ ],[\ ])]$ $[+\text{material} ([\ ])]$
          <manner>   <−animate>
                                        <+artefact>
                              {contains stuff, on article of clothing, ... }

The Principle of Coindexation once again tells us to coindex the highest non-head argument with the highest unindexed head argument. It is, however, not entirely

---

[12] Note as well that such reversible compounds may have a 'subject' orientation as well as a 'complement' orientation, as seen for example in compounds like *dog attack* and *attack dog*.
[13] As with adjectives, I have paid insufficient attention to what the body features of English verbs should be. But again, I leave this issue open, as the analysis of these compounds does not hinge on it.

clear which element is the head in such compounds, or if they even have a head.[14] Let us assume first, for the sake of argument, that since compounds are typically right-headed in English, the head argument would be the R argument of *pocket*. If so, then the first argument of *pick* would be coindexed with the sole argument of *pocket*. However, this indexing would result in a serious semantic mismatch: the highest argument of *pick* must be interpreted as sentient and volitional, but the R argument of *pocket* is inconsistent with that interpretation. Rather, the R argument of *pocket* is consistent with the interpretation that is required by the second argument of *pick*, which must be non-volitional (sentience seems not to matter for this verb – one can pick apples or people). This case would seem to require a slight modification of the Principle of Coindexation, as follows:

(25) PRINCIPLE OF COINDEXATION (revised-*a*)
In a configuration in which semantic skeletons are composed, coindex the highest non-head argument with the highest (preferably unindexed) head argument. Indexing must be consistent with semantic conditions on arguments, if any.

In (25), I have generalized the requirement of consistency of indexed arguments such that semantic requirements on either a head argument (as in -*ee*) or a non-head argument can drive non-standard indexings. Given the modification in (25), the representation of *pick pocket* will be (26):

(26) *pick pocket*

$$\begin{array}{cc} pick & pocket \end{array}$$

$$[+\text{dynamic} \,([_{\text{sentient, volitional}}], [_i\;])] \quad [+\text{material} \,([_i\;])]$$

$$\begin{array}{cc} <\text{manner}> & <-\text{animate}> \\ & <+\text{artefact}> \\ & \{\text{contains stuff, on article of clothing}, \dots \} \end{array}$$

The first argument of *pick* fails to be indexed in the compound because to index it with the only available argument, the R argument of *pocket*, would result in a serious semantic mismatch. But the second argument of *pick* is quite consistent with the semantics of *pocket*, so that indexing is preferred. *Pocket* is therefore interpreted correctly as the internal argument of *pick*. Suppose on the other hand that compounds like *pickpocket* are headless. Such a scenario would require a different restatement of the Principle of Coindexation, to determine how the parts of a complex word would be integrated in the absence of a head. One possible restatement of the Principle of Coindexation might be (27):

---

[14] Scalise (1992) argues that the Italian equivalents of these compounds are indeed headless.

(27)   PRINCIPLE OF COINDEXATION (revised-*b*)
        In a configuration in which semantic skeletons are composed, coindex the
        highest non-head argument with the highest (preferably unindexed) head
        argument. Indexing must be consistent with semantic conditions on the
        head argument, if any. In the case of a headless structure, coindex seman-
        tically compatible arguments.

This statement of the Principle of Coindexation is obviously clumsier than the
one in (25), but it would give us the same indexing. I will leave open which
solution is the preferable one, as English gives us little reason to choose
between the two.

   We can now ask the most important question: why do such compounds receive
exocentric interpretations? My hypothesis is that the unlinked verbal argument,
which remains unlinked in the compound, is still interpretable as an implicit
argument of the left-hand element of the compound. Note that such compounds
are typically either agentive (as with *pickpocket* or *cutpurse*) or instrumental (e.g.
lavapiatti 'dishwasher' in Italian or *sacacorcho* 'corkscrew' in Spanish). If the
argument of the initial verbal element remains as an active albeit implicit argument
we might expect it to have any of the range of interpretations consistent with
external arguments, but not the interpretation consistent with internal arguments
(e.g. themes, locations); this would account for the implicit reference of such
compounds to agents or instruments.

5.4.3 Attributive compounds

Generally analyses of compounding in English start with attributive compounds, as
they are among the most frequently attested in the languages of the world. I have
saved them for last here because I will argue that they constitute a kind of default
semantic type: they are what occurs when the skeletons and bodies of compounding elements are too disparate to be interpreted as coordinates and lack the sort of
argument structure that gives rise to subordinates.

5.4.3.1 *Endocentric attributive*

This type of compound is extraordinarily productive in English and the other
Germanic languages. As is well known, endocentric attributive compounds can be
formed from any combination of adjective and noun in English, although N+N
compounds are by far the most productive:

(28)   ENDOCENTRIC ATTRIBUTIVES IN ENGLISH
        N+N   file cabinet, dog bed, book case, phone book
        N+A   sky blue, rock hard, ice cold

A+N   hard hat, blackboard, poorhouse
A+A   red hot, wide awake

I will confine my discussion here to N+N compounds, as the analysis generalizes easily to the other types.

Consider the representation of the compound *dog bed* in (29):

(29) *dog bed*

dog	*bed*
[+material ([$_i$])]	[+material ([$_i$])]
<+animate>	<−animate>
<−human>	<+artefact>
	<function>
{four legs, wags tail,...}	{for sleeping,...}

The Principle of Coindexation gives us only one option for integrating the compounding elements together: since each has only a single argument, they must be coindexed. In this case, although their skeletons are arguably the same, their body features are completely incommensurate, thus ruling out any sort of coordinate interpretation. Further, there is no verbal element here, so a subordinate interpretation is ruled out. The indexing requires that both nouns be predicated of the same referent, with the second determining both the syntactic and the semantic type of the whole (again, this follows from morphosyntactic headedness). The first element must therefore be related to the second in some way other than coordination or subordination – but how it is related is otherwise left open. In other words, as has been pointed out frequently in the literature on compounding, the relationship between the head and the non-head of an N+N compound is free to be fixed by context. Although individual endocentric attributive compounds may be lexicalized with specific meanings and although specific combinations of nouns may be predisposed pragmatically towards particular interpretations (for example, a *dog bed* is much likelier to be interpreted as a bed for a dog than as a bed made of dog; cf. Štekauer 2005a, this volume; Jackendoff, this volume), the relationship between the compounding elements is not fixed by formal rules. The attributive interpretation is in fact the interpretation that arises in the absence of any formally fixed relation between the compounding elements.

5.4.3.2 *Exocentric attributive*

This brings us finally to our last type of compound, the exocentric attributive ones, exemplified by compounds like *birdbrain*, *whitecap*, and *ponytail* in English. In terms of representation, they work exactly as endocentric attributive compounds do. For example, the compound *birdbrain* would have the representation in (30):

(30) *bird brain*

bird	brain
[+material ([$_i$])]	[+material ([$_i$])]
<+animate>	<−animate>
<−human>	<−artefact>
{flies, lays eggs, ...}	{body part, part of nervous system}

A comment first on the body characteristics of the word *brain*. I am assuming that a body part is not by itself an animate entity: science fiction notwithstanding, brains without bodies cannot be sentient or act volitionally, the hallmarks of animate entities. As inanimate entities, however, brains are clearly natural rather than man-made, hence the specification <−artefact>. Again, given this representation, only one pattern of indexing is possible. As in the endocentric example above, bodily features are completely disparate, thus ruling out a coordinate interpretation. Lacking a verbal element, the compound is not interpretable as subordinative either. What remains is the default attributive interpretation.

What is different in the exocentric cases is that, as argued by Booij (1992: 39), such compounds are interpreted metonymically. Whatever process of semantic inferencing allows us to refer to a customer in a restaurant as 'the ham sandwich', if she/he is eating a ham sandwich, allows us to refer to a person as a *birdbrain* or a *redhead* if they act foolishly or have red hair. In terms of representations and indexing, there is no difference between endocentric and exocentric compounds. Indeed, it is possible for the same compound to have both an endocentric and an exocentric reading. For example, the compound *hard hat* in English can refer at the same time to a kind of helmet worn by construction workers and metonymically to the construction workers themselves.

This analysis in fact makes an interesting prediction, namely that there should be a subtle difference between this sort of metonymic exocentricity and the exocentricity of *pickpocket* and the like. In the exocentric subordinate cases, the compounds should be able to refer to agents (*pickpocket, cutpurse*), instruments (Italian *lavapiatti* 'dishwasher'), or any of the thematic roles typical of external arguments, but nothing else. In contrast, the exocentric attributive compounds should have fewer limitations in interpretation; specifically, they need not be restricted to particular kinds of participants in an event. Indeed this seems to be the case, as exocentric attributive compounds can refer to people and to things of various sorts (for example a *whitecap* is a wave, *ponytail* is a hair style), and are not limited to agentive or instrumental readings. In other words, what I referred to as the implicit argument in the exocentric subordinative compounds limits the interpretation imposed by the coindexed first argument of the verbal element; the exocentric attributive compound has no such restriction when interpreted metonymically.

5.5 THE NATURE OF EXOCENTRICITY

The analysis of compounds within the present lexical semantic framework shows clearly that exocentricity is not a unified phenomenon, but rather arises in a number of ways. This is not, of course, a novel claim – the recent work of Scalise and collaborators suggests the same conclusion. What emerges from this analysis clearly, however, are the various mechanisms by which exocentricity can be established. In the case of coordinate compounds, exocentricity occurs when representations are largely overlapping down to a particular countervalued body feature. For subordinate compounds exocentricity results from an unindexed verbal external argument that is free to receive an implicit (but determinate) interpretation. Finally, in the case of attributive compounds, exocentricity is a function of a metonymic interpretation; such cases are predictably freer in interpretation than subordinate cases.

5.6 A NOTE ON V + V COMPOUNDS

It is beyond the scope of this chapter to give a full treatment of verbal compounds. For one thing, an enormous literature has accumulated on the subject, with lively argument as to whether various classes of compounds are to be treated lexically or syntactically (see, for example, Li 1990, 1993, 1995; Lin 1996; Nishiyama 1998; Chang 1998; Packard 1998; Naumann and Gamerschlag 2003; Ke 2003; Tai 2003; Fukushima 2005). Nevertheless, here I will try to show briefly that at least the sort of V + V compound that is common in Japanese is amenable to analysis within the system developed here with no added machinery.[15] My analysis will rely heavily on that of Fukushima (2005); although Fukushima is working within a rather different framework his analysis is quite compatible with my own.

Fukushima (2005) distinguishes three kinds of V + V compounds that are arguably lexical (as opposed to syntactic) in nature. I will concentrate on these types here. Examples are from Fukushima (2005: 570–85):

(31)   JAPANESE LEXICAL VV COMPOUNDS
    a. COORDINATE: *naki-saken*
        Taroo-ga   *naki-saken-da*
        Taroo-SBJ   cry-scream-PST
        'Taroo cried and screamed'

---

[15] I will not attempt here to provide an analysis of V + V resultative compounds in Chinese, as the data are complex and raise issues about the mapping between lexical semantic representations and hierarchical syntactic structure that are well beyond the scope of this chapter. (See Ceccagno and Basciano, this volume).

   b. CAUSE: *odori-tukare; ki-kuzure*

     Hanako-ga   *odori-tukare-ta*

     Hanako-SBJ   dance-get.tired-PST

     'Hanako got tired from dancing'

     sebiro-ga   *ki-kuzure-ta*

     suit.jacket-SBJ   wear-get.out.of.shape-PST

     'The suit jacket got out of shape from wearing'

   c. MANNER: *tobi-oki; ture-sat*

     Ziroo-ga   *tobi-oki-ta*

     Ziroo-SBJ   jump-get.up-PST

     'Ziroo got up with a jumping motion'

     Taroo-GA   *kodomo-o*   *ture-sat-ta*

     Taroo-SBJ   child-OBJ   take-leave-PST

     'Taroo left taking the child.'

Fukushima, in his detailed and careful analysis, makes the following assumptions:

- grammatical relations are hierarchically organized, with the highest argument being the argument that is least oblique. In terms of Japanese case marking, the (subject) *ga* argument is highest, (object) *o* next highest, and (oblique) *ni* the lowest.
- arguments can be characterized in terms of Dowty's (1991) proto-roles.
- argument synthesis (i.e. the integration of argument structures of the compounded verbs) is head-driven, in the sense that arguments of the head are matched with arguments of the non-head.

It is clear from Fukushima's analysis that coordinate compounds are considered double-headed, but his assumptions about the headedness of the other types of compounds are less clear to me. In any case, integration of the argument structures of component verbs proceeds by starting with the highest (least oblique) argument of the head verb and matching it with the highest argument of the non-head, making sure that matched arguments are compatible in terms of proto-role characteristics. If the highest argument of the head does not match the highest argument of the non-head, the latter is skipped over, and the next highest argument of the non-head is considered. This procedure is followed until all arguments of the head have been exhausted. Matched arguments are coindexed.

    I have left out a few details here, but it should be obvious from the description of Fukushima's analysis above that his argument-matching procedure is rather close in nature to the Principle of Coindexation argued for in Lieber (2004) and slightly revised here. Indeed, I believe it is a straightforward matter to replicate Fukushima's analysis within the present framework. The advantage of doing so, of course, is that it then becomes easy to see how this form of compounding fits within an overall analysis of the lexical semantic properties of word formation.

I will start here with Fukushima's example of a coordinate compound *naki-saken* 'cry-scream':

(32) *naki-saken* 'cry-scream'

cry	*scream*
[+dynamic ([$_i$])]	[+dynamic ([$_i$])]
\<personal\>	\<personal\>
\<sound emission\>	\<sound emission\>
{noise caused by pain, sorrow, etc.}	{noise – loud, piercing}

The two verbs comprising the compound have identical skeletons, and arguably bodies that are very similar. My representation of the body features of these verbs is meant merely to be an approximation, as I have not developed a picture of the body in verbs in any coherent way yet. We might guess, for example, that body features for verbs might include indications of whether the relevant event were visual, auditory, or tactile, or whether it involved bodily posture, spatial orientation, or contact of a particular sort. Whatever the specific features are, it is likely that they will be identical in verbs such as this, at least down to the specific nature of the noise emitted. Given that each verb has only one argument, and that these arguments are semantically compatible, the two sole arguments of the compounded verbs will be coindexed; with skeletons and bodily features so similar, the overall interpretation of the compound will be additive.

The second kind of compound in Japanese is what Fukushima calls 'cause'. The interpretation of such compounds appears to be like resultatives with the result being the head verb in this case.[16] The analyses of two such compounds, *odori-tukare* 'dance-get.tired' ('get tired from dancing') and *ki-kuzure* 'wear-get.out.of. shape' ('get out of shape from wearing'), are shown in (33):

(33) a. *odori-tukare* 'dance-get.tired'

odori	*tukare*
[+dynamic, −IEPS ([$_i$])]	[+dynamic, +IEPS ([$_i$])]
\<personal\>	\<personal\>
\<posture\>	\<...\>

   b. *ki-kuzure* 'wear-get.out.of.shape'

ki	*kuzure*
[−dynamic ([$_{sentient}$], [$_{nonsentient-i}$])]	[+dynamic, +IEPS ([$_{nonsentient-i}$])]
\<...\>	\<...\>

---

[16] Fukushima does not say this explicitly, but it appears to be the case based on the interpretation of the compounds.

Regardless of what we assume about headedness, in (33a) the sole argument of 'dance' will get coindexed with the sole argument of 'get tired'. As the skeletons of the two verbs are quite different (the former being a verb of manner of motion, the latter a change-of-state-verb), the compound will not get a coordinate interpretation. Instead, the argument of 'get tired' is identified with the argument of 'dance'. If the right-hand verb is indeed the head, we arrive at the interpretation 'get tired by dancing'. The interpretation of (33b) is only slightly more complex. Again, we have two incompatible skeletons: 'wear' is an activity verb, and 'get out of shape' a change-of-state verb. No coordinate interpretation is therefore possible. Further, since the verb 'wear' has two arguments, the first of which must be sentient, it will be impossible to coindex this argument with the sole argument of 'get out of shape', which is non-sentient. The only possible indexing then identifies the second argument of 'wear' with the argument of 'get out of shape'. The interpretation, again assuming the headedness of the right-hand verb, then is something like 'get out of shape by wearing'. The first argument of 'wear' remains unlinked, and therefore is interpreted as an implicit argument, much as was the case in English compounds like *pickpocket*.

Finally we turn to the V+V compounds that Fukushima calls 'manner' compounds. The analysis of two of these, *tobi-oki* 'jump-get.up' ('get up by jumping') and *ture-sat* 'take-leave' ('x leave taking y') are given in (34):

(34)   a. *tobi-oki* 'jump-get.up' ('get up by jumping')

       tobi   *oki*

     $[+\text{dynamic}, -\text{IEPS} ([_i \ ])]$ $[+\text{dynamic}, +\text{IEPS} ([_i \ ])]$

     <orientation>   <orientation>

     <...>   <...>

   b. *ture-sat* 'take-leave' ('x leave, taking y')

       ture   *sat*

     $[+\text{dynamic} ([_i \ ], [\ ])$ $[+\text{dynamic}, +\text{IEPS} ([_i \ ])]$

     <contact>   <directed away from focal point>

In both cases the dissimilarities between the skeletons of the component verbs preclude a coordinate interpretation. But in both cases, it is also possible to coindex the highest arguments of the two verbs, as they are in both cases semantically compatible. In (34a), as each verb has only a single argument, the interpretation will be something like 'get up by jumping'. In (34b), where the left-hand non-head verb has a second (unindexed) argument, this argument is free to be satisfied syntactically: the resulting compounded verb therefore has an interpretation something like 'x leave taking y', with x being the shared argument and y being a second argument realized in the syntax.

5.7 CONCLUSION AND PROSPECTUS

Making use of Bisetto and Scalise's (2005) classification of compounds and my own framework of lexical semantic analysis, I have tried in this chapter to show how a wide range of compound types might be analysed. I have given specific attention to types of compounding that – at least in the literature on compounding in English – tend to be less discussed: coordinative compounds, exocentric compounds of various sorts, reversible compounds. Two main claims have resulted from this study: first, exocentricity is not a unitary phenomenon, and second, endocentric attributive compounds – the kind that have received by far the most attention in the literature on English – are a sort of semantic default, appearing when more constrained types of semantic relation are not sanctioned by the skeletons and bodies of the constituent parts of the compound. Further work, of course, remains to be done. First, as section 5.6 suggests, in order to extend the analysis fully to V+V compounds it will be important to further develop the universal semantic features necessary for verbs. Second, further work on headedness in both coordinative and exocentric compounds will allow us to decide among possible versions of the Principle of Coindexation.

CHAPTER 6

COMPOUNDING IN THE PARALLEL ARCHITECTURE AND CONCEPTUAL SEMANTICS

RAY JACKENDOFF

6.1 THE PARALLEL ARCHITECTURE

The basic premise of the Parallel Architecture (Jackendoff 1997, 2002a) is that phonology, syntax, and semantics are independent generative components in language, each with its own primitives and principles of combination. The theory builds on insights about linguistic structure that emerged in the 1970s. First,

This study is based on a corpus of approximately 2,500 compounds. About half of these were collected by students in my Semantics course at Brandeis University in spring 1997. I wish to thank Erica Goldman, Joy Budewig, and Kristen Lauer for their help in organizing of this material. The corpus also includes many examples from the literature, in particular Lees's (1960) corpus, as well as about 400 examples from random issues of the *Boston Globe* and *The Nation*. I am grateful to James Pustejovsky for much useful discussion; to him and Joan Maling, Federica Busa, Hildy Dvorak, and Dan Dvorak for further examples; and to Nigel Love, Herbert Brekle, Christian Bassac, Geert Booij, Peter Culicover, Susan Olsen, Biljana Mišić Ilić, and Shelly Lieber for comments on earlier versions of this article.

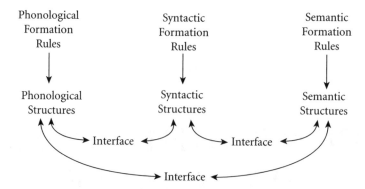

Figure 6.1. The Parallel Architecture

phonology was demonstrated to have highly articulated structure that cannot be derived directly from syntax: structured units such as syllables and prosodic constituents do not correspond one-to-one with syntactic units. Moreover, phonological structure includes several independent substructures or *tiers*, each with its own type of generative structure: segmental-syllabic structure, the metrical grid, intonation contour, and (in tone languages) the tone tier. The tiers are correlated with each other by *interface rules*: principles that establish optimal correspondence between structures of two independent types. Such rules are not derivational. Since these phonological structures cannot be derived from syntactic structures, the connection between syntax and phonology must also be mediated not by derivations, but by a component of interface rules.

The 1970s also witnessed the development of various approaches to semantics, as different as formal semantics and Cognitive Grammar. What they have in common is that although they see semantic structures as combinatorial and potentially unlimited in complexity, these structures are not built out of syntactic units such as NPs and VPs (as they were in Generative Semantics). Rather, they are built of characteristic semantic units such as conceptualized objects, events, times, properties, and quantifiers, which do not correspond one-to-one with syntactic categories. This argues that semantics too is a generative component of language, and that therefore it cannot be derived from syntax either. Rather, it must be correlated with syntax by a component of interface rules. Moreover, semantic structure, like phonology, demonstrably has an articulation into tiers, including at least propositional structure (who did what to whom) and an orthogonal dimension of information structure (topic/focus/common ground; old vs. new information).

The result is an architecture of the form in Figure 6.1. Phonology and semantics have further internal articulation of a similar sort. Syntax too may be articulated into tiers: LFG is well-known for proposing an articulation of syntax into constituent structure (the standard tree) and functional structure (grammatical functions); a stripped-down version of the latter is the grammatical function tier of

Culicover and Jackendoff (2005). Autolexical Syntax (Sadock 1991) and Role and Reference Grammar (Van Valin and LaPolla 1997) propose an articulation into phrasal and morphosyntactic tiers, essentially principles that operate above and below the word level respectively.

Figure 6.1 offers a model in terms of which various other theories can be compared. For instance, in mainstream generative grammar (Chomsky 1965, 1981, 1995a), the combinatorial properties of phonology and semantics are derived from syntax; hence there are no independent formation rules for phonology and semantics, only derivational interfaces from syntax into these two components. By contrast, Cognitive Grammar (e.g. Langacker 1987) claims that all (or at least most) syntactic structure is semantically motivated, so it eliminates or minimizes the syntactic formation rules. Within the Parallel Architecture, the empirical issue is the proper balance between these two extremes.

An important constraint on the balance comes from the fact that semantic structure ultimately has to be rich enough to support inference. In the mainstream architecture, all this richness has to come from syntax, which puts syntactic theory under constant pressure for greater articulation and complexity. This pressure has come to fruition twice, first in Generative Semantics, and again in late GB and the Minimalist Program. By contrast, the Parallel Architecture grants semantics its own generative capacity, and therefore syntax has to be only rich enough to modulate the mapping between semantics and phonology – a Simpler Syntax (Culicover and Jackendoff 2005).

In the Parallel Architecture, a well-formed sentence is a triplet consisting of well-formed phonological, syntactic, and semantic structures, plus links between corresponding constituents of the three, established by the interface components. A word therefore is to be thought of not as a passive unit to be pushed around in a derivation, but as a part of the interface components. It is a long-term memory linkage of a piece of phonology, a piece of syntax, and a piece of semantics, stipulating that these three pieces can be correlated as part of a well-formed sentence.

This leaves the way open for including in the lexicon all manner of units larger than single words, such as the lexical VPs *kick the bucket* and *bite the dust*. Syntactically these are identical to the phrasally composed VPs *throw the shovel* and *chew the gum*. But semantically they differ, because their meanings are introduced as a whole from the lexicon rather than being composed online from the individual parts. In addition, the lexicon contains *meaningful constructions* (the stock-in-trade of Construction Grammar), such as the sound+motion construction illustrated in (1a). The verbs describe sound emission, and therefore do not license the path PPs; moreover there is no word that expresses the understood motion of the subject. The meaning is instead provided by a construction that imposes an idiomatic interpretation on the VP and takes both the verb and the PP as arguments. (1b) states it informally.

(1)   a. The trolley squealed around the corner.
           The bullet whizzed by my ear.

       b. [$_{VP}$ V PP] = 'go PP while V[produce sound]-ing'

Construction (1b) can be thought of as a lexical item, though this time without phonology. It is more 'rule-like' than words and idioms, because it consists entirely of variables that must be filled by other items. In turn, regular VPs, idiomatic VPs, and sound+motion VPs are all instantiations of the more general piece of structure (2), which therefore can also be thought of as a lexical item, this time consisting only of syntactic structure.

(2)   [$_{VP}$ V (NP) (PP)]

Thus we arrive at the position that words, idioms, and rules of grammar are all stated in a common format, namely as pieces of stored structure. This continuum between idiosyncrasy and regularity is a feature of Cognitive Grammar, HPSG, and Construction Grammar as well as the Parallel Architecture. Such a treatment goes strongly against the traditional assumption, preserved in mainstream generative grammar, that a language can be partitioned cleanly into a lexicon and a grammar. Rather, words are in one corner of a multidimensional continuum of stored structures, maximally general rules are in another corner, and there are all sorts of phenomena of varying degrees of regularity in between.

6.2 COMPOUNDS: ON THE CUSP BETWEEN GRAMMAR AND LEXICON

In a theory with a strict division between lexicon and grammar, compounds are problematic. On one hand, a speaker must store thousands of lexicalized compounds with semi-idiosyncratic meanings. One knows not just that *peanut butter* is a buttery substance made from peanuts, but exactly what peanut butter *is* and what it tastes like. On the other hand, new compounds can be built on the fly, so they can't all be stored in the lexicon. Among the several hundred compounds in my corpus from the *Boston Globe*, at least several dozen were novel to me, including *cotinin* [sic] *level, politician tycoon, aid inflow, locality pay,* and *spring seepage.* Downing (1977) stresses the frequent coining of compounds in particular discourse situations, citing for instance *bike girl* for a girl who left her bike in the vestibule. Brekle (1986) and Sadock (1998) make similar observations. There is also evidence from acquisition: Clark, Gelman, and Lane (1985) observe that children begin understanding novel compounds and coining their own between about 2½ and 3½.

Moreover, compounding is recursive, often in novel fashion. Downing cites *apple juice seat* having been used to denote a seat at which apple juice was set on the table. Some years ago, my daughter left something for our cats, accompanied by the note 'Maggie and Peanut's *heat wave present*'. And the *Boston Globe* corpus has examples like *campaign finance indictment, winter weather skin troubles,* and *health management cost containment services.*

Compounds can show evidence of a little internal syntactic structure, whether completely or partially lexicalized, or totally novel.

(3)   a.   CONJUNCTION
          [health and welfare] fund
          [media, retail, and property] empire
          [relaxation and [focus concentration]] techniques
          [Fresh Pond Parkway] [sewer separation and surface enhancement] project

      b.   ADJECTIVE–NOUN
          [foreign exchange] flow
          [smoked pork shoulder][boiled dinner]

      c.   PAIRED ARGUMENTS
          [Port-cornstarch] mixture
          [town-gown] tensions

      d.   NUMERAL–NOUN
          [two-car] garage
          [2,300-word] corpus]
          (note *car garage, *word corpus)

The frequency of novelty demonstrates that compounding cannot just consist of a list, but rather must include a productive rule system.

The difficulty with a productive rule system, though, is that it suggests relatively exceptionless regularity. How is it possible to reconcile the productivity of compounds with their rampant idiosyncrasy? From a morphosyntactic point of view, listed compounds look exactly like productive ones.

The situation with VPs offers some perspective. VPs are certainly generated by a productive rule system. At the same time there are hundreds of idioms consisting of whole or partial VPs, and these too must be stored in the lexicon. Of course, the syntactic variety of VPs, especially freely generated ones, is far greater than that of compounds. But qualitatively the problem of reconciling productivity with lexical listing is exactly the same. So compounds do not present a unique problem in this respect.

The Parallel Architecture's approach to the lexicon, illustrated above for VPs, generalizes nicely to compounding: it requires no principled line between freely generated compounds and morphosyntactically complex listed items with the same structure. For example, *soccer ball*, like *peanut butter*, is listed in my lexicon:

I can connect it to particular physical objects. But if I were to encounter the term *backgammon ball*, which I have never heard before, I would still know what the term purports to denote (even though I know there is no such thing). Yet in terms of the linguistic system, both receive similar analyses – just by different routes.

The productivity of compounds means that language users must have a set of principles that enables them to interpret new compounds. Lexicalized compounds are for the most part specialized instantiations of these principles. Of course, the lexicon being what it is, we also expect some proportion of lexicalized compounds to exhibit inexplicable irregularity due to historical drift and capricious coinages.

The task for the language learner, then, is to learn the lexicalized compounds and to acquire the principles for interpreting novel compounds. These two processes are obviously interdependent. At the outset, *all* compounds are novel, and children somehow list some of them in their lexicon. The child's evidence for the general principles, insofar as they are not innate, must come from generalizing over the learned compounds (see Jackendoff 2002a, section 6.9 for more on this view of acquisition).

Do speakers really have general principles for compounding? Gleitman and Gleitman (1970) and Ryder (1994) asked subjects to give putative definitions of constructed novel compounds. In both experiments, subjects were far from reliable in giving answers that conformed to linguists' intuitions, for example giving definitions like these:

(4)   a. Ryder (1994: 137)
          willow forest: 'a willow that grows in the forest'
          giraffe land: 'a giraffe on land'

      b. Gleitman and Gleitman (1970: 156–7, 167)
          house-bird wash: 'a bird that washed the house'
          bird-house glass: 'a birdhouse made of glass'

These definitions are reminiscent of the performance of agrammatic aphasics on reversible passives and object relatives: the subjects seem to be driven by a need to create maximal semantic plausibility, grammatical principles be damned. Such results lead us to ask whether there is any grammatical competence at all involved in interpreting novel compounds.

I believe there is, but it is not of the sort we are led to expect from standard syntax. Standard syntax pretty well determines the meaning of a novel phrase from the meanings of the words and the principles for mapping syntactic structure into combinatorial relations among constituent meanings. In the case of a novel compound, though, the general principles yield only a vast range of possible meanings. The language user must home in on the intended meaning of a novel compound by making use of (a) the semantic details of the constituent words and (b) the discourse and extralinguistic context. In the experimental situations presented by the Gleitmans and Ryder, the compounds are presented in isolation with no contextual support. And the semantic details of the constituent words press for a meaning relation at odds with that demanded by the grammar, in particular right-headedness. Evidently the grammatical principles are sufficiently unstable (for some speakers) that they can be overwhelmed by semantic plausibility in such situations.

My conclusion is that, although compounding is indeed productive, the productivity is rather fragile by the usual syntactic standards. When I teach compounding in Introductory Linguistics, students enjoy building up a compound like (5a) piece by piece, in such a way that everyone understands it at the end. But if I were to present it as a whole to a naive class, few would get it. By contrast, the syntactic paraphrase (5b), while unwieldy, is nevertheless easier to comprehend.

(5) a. an inflectional morphology instruction manual software programming course

   b. a course in programming the software that accompanies manuals that teach inflectional morphology

Similarly, example (6a), from the *New York Times* (3 June 2007), is initially hard to understand, because one's tendency is to parse it pairwise, like (6b). There is no grammatical support for the proper parsing (6c).

(6) a. child camel jockey slavery
   b. [[child camel] [jockey slavery]]
   c. [[child [camel jockey]] slavery]
      i.e. 'slavery of [children serving as camel jockeys]'

The upshot is that the fragility of productive compounding also has to be part of the account.

6.3 COMPOUNDS AS A RELIC OF PROTOLANGUAGE

Bickerton (1990) proposes that the language capacity evolved in two stages, 'protolanguage' and modern language; he conceives of the former as having had a vocabulary and pragmatics, but no syntax or morphology as such. This stage for him is not just hypothetical: in the standard manner of evolution, it was not thrown away when modern language evolved. Rather, modern language was built on top of it, as a refinement. Moreover, in situations where the complexity of modern language is disrupted or impaired, elements of protolanguage still emerge.

The sorts of situations Bickerton has in mind include pidgin languages, the two-word stage of language learning, agrammatic aphasia, the language acquired by late first-language learners such as Genie (Curtiss 1977), and what apes instructed in sign language can learn. In each of these cases, vocabulary is acquired and words are concatenated into larger utterances. However, inflectional morphology is at best highly defective, functional categories are rarely used, and syntax does not go much beyond simple basic clauses. Subordination is largely absent, replaced by parataxis (jamming two independent clauses together); and many of the connections between words and between clauses are left up to the hearer's understanding of context.

These situations of course differ in many respects, due to their different genesis (in particular, the apes appear to string words together rather randomly, if we are to believe Terrace [1979]). What is interesting is that when less than full language is in evidence, the parts that appear (or remain) are remarkably similar. Bickerton argues that these are all instances of the re-emergence of protolanguage, which is in some sense more resilient in the brain than the refinements of modern language.

Three further cases can be added to this collection. One is the degree of language competence achieved by the right hemisphere (Baynes and Gazzaniga 2005). Another is the 'home sign' created by deaf children of non-signing parents (Goldin-Meadow 2003). The third comes from a massive longitudinal study of immigrant second-language learners by Klein and Perdue (1997). All of them turn out to pass through a stage of second-language competence that Klein and Perdue call the Basic Variety (BV) – and some fail to progress beyond this point despite years of exposure.

Klein and Perdue say (1997: 333) that although 'the BV is a highly efficient system of communication,...it lacks some of the structural characteristics which we typically find in fully fledged languages'. Speakers of BV acquire vocabulary, but there is hardly any morphology or closed-class vocabulary, and no syntactic subordination – only parataxis. Word order in BV is determined in terms of rudimentary functional principles, primarily Agent First and Focus Last[1] – principles that also apply broadly in pidgins and function as strong defaults in modern language as well. However, these principles do not require full principles of syntax: they can be regarded as mappings directly between semantic roles and linear order of words in phonology. In short, BV too has the telltale symptoms of protolanguage.

Jackendoff (2002a: chapter 8) suggests that protolanguage is a cognitive 'scaffolding' on which modern language is built, both in evolution and in development. Under this view, various 'modern' aspects of language can be added or lost

---

[1] As pointed out by some of the commentators on Klein and Perdue's paper in the same issue of *Second Language Research*, some of the word-order effects may be artefacts of the range of target languages studied by Klein and Perdue. I leave this question open, as it is not too important to the point at hand.

piecemeal in different situations, revealing different amounts or aspects of the 'scaffolding'. The surprise is how robust this protolinguistic scaffolding is, emerging over and over again under different conditions.

In terms of the Parallel Architecture, protolanguage is a subsystem of modern language: it consists of Figure 6.1 with the syntactic component omitted, and with a direct interface between phonology and semantics. By contrast, mainstream generative grammar has to consider protolanguage a completely unrelated system, since it claims that phonological and semantic combinatoriality – and a correspondence between them – cannot exist without the generative capacity of syntax.

This view of modern language as 'laid over' a protolinguistic substrate leads to the intriguing possibility that the coverage is incomplete: that relics of earlier stages of the language capacity remain as pockets within modern language. These relics would have only rudimentary grammatical structure, and such grammatical structure as there is would not do much to shape semantic interpretation. Rather, we would expect semantic interpretation to be highly dependent on the pragmatics of the words being combined and on the contextual specifics of use. I suggest that compounding fills the bill completely.

This view of compounding explains the properties that make it not look like the rest of morphology (differences stressed by Sadock 1998): compounding is actually not a *grammatical* phenomenon, but a *proto*grammatical one. Even the right-headedness of (English) compounds, their most grammatical feature, really only relies on a language-specific correlation of linear order with semantic headedness, not on X-bar head–argument structure. In this respect it resembles the Agent-First and Focus-Last principles of BV.[2]

Pushing this point further, the syntax of English compounding is to some extent even blind to syntactic category. Nominal compounds need not be constructed from two nouns (*doghouse*): there are also compounds like *[long$_A$bow$_N$]$_N$*, *[watch$_V$-dog$_N$]$_N$*, *[under$_P$current$_N$]$_N$*, *[blow$_V$up$_P$]$_N$*, *[over$_P$kill$_V$]$_N$*, *[skin$_N$deep$_A$]$_A$*, and *[worm$_N$eaten$_V$]$_A$*; all of which have the characteristic left-hand stress of compounds.[3] Moreover, there are pairs of semantically indistinguishable N+N and A/P+N compounds, such as *atom bomb* vs. *atomic bomb*, *sea life* vs. *marine life*, and *topcoat* vs. *overcoat*, suggesting that syntactic category hardly makes a difference. And for some compounds such as *guard dog*, there is no fact of the matter as

---

[2] Notice, by the way, that the standard Head Parameter in syntax is also a correlation of linear order with headedness. So perhaps it is no surprise that compounds often generalize with X-bar structures in their headedness, as Lieber (1992a) suggests.

[3] Lieber (2004) argues out that V+P compounds such as *blowup* are simple zero-nominalizations of verb–particle combinations. I find this plausible for many cases, but not for exocentric V+P compounds such as *pullover* (a sweater), *pushover* (a person), and *turnover* (a pastry). Lieber also suggests that P+V compounds such as *overkill* are actually prefixed nominalizations. Here I am less convinced, as there are many examples that are semantically idiosyncratic, such as *undertow*, *outlook*, *downdrift*, *outcast*. In any event, the main point about categorial unselectivity stands, even if less robustly.

to whether they are V+N ('a dog that guards') or N+N ('a dog that serves as a guard'). In short, compounding is only barely syntactic. It has right-headedness and the recursive properties illustrated in (3)–(4), but that's about all.

Klein and Perdue observe that although BV lacks morphology of the usual sort, one kind of morphology does appear (in the target languages that permit it): compounding. This exception – along with the early appearance of compounding in language acquisition – follows from the view urged here. The argument is that (a) BV is an 'advanced' protolanguage rather than a full modern language, (b) compounding is (relatively) protolinguistic, but (c) the rest of morphology is a feature of modern language. Therefore we should expect compounding but not other morphology to appear in BV, and we should expect compounding to be in many respects different from other morphology.

Under this hypothesis, compounding takes on an unexpected status in grammatical theory. It is not some odd peripheral aspect of morphology; it is a system that reveals some of the evolutionary roots of modern language, as it were a coelacanth of grammar. Such a conclusion should not be taken as too radical. After all, the semantic relations that link discourse together are not marked syntactically either. Rather, hearers use the meanings of the sentences plus understanding of the context – including social context – to create the semantic linkages from sentence to sentence, whether spoken by the same or different speakers. Compounding is just the same sort of phenomenon writ small. (Jackendoff 2002a suggests some other possible phenomena in the corners of modern grammar where earlier evolutionary stages might be showing through.)

6.4 PRELIMINARIES TO SEMANTIC ANALYSIS OF ENGLISH N+N COMPOUNDS

In principle, the Parallel Architecture is compatible with a variety of semantic theories, but it has been developed specifically in terms of Conceptual Semantics (Jackendoff 1983, 1990, 2002a, 2007). The goal of Conceptual Semantics is a formal account of linguistic meaning that connects meaning with human conceptualization, with inference, and with perception and action. Its motivating questions are: What is the formal structure of our knowledge of the world? How is this structure expressed linguistically? How much of it do we share with non-linguistic organisms such as babies and apes? How do we reason (i.e. connect new meanings to old)? How do we talk about what we see (i.e. connect perception to meaning)?

In particular, Conceptual Semantics is concerned with the totality of meaning, not just the part composed directly from syntactic structure, so-called linguistic semantics. It is deeply concerned with details of word meaning and how these interact with composition of phrase meanings. At the same time, it incorporates a great deal of what is usually called pragmatics: aspects of meaning that are not encoded in word meanings or in relations conveyed directly by syntactic structure.

This outlook impacts on the approach to compounding: the goal is an account of compound meaning that is as rich as the account of word meaning. The basic intuition, as in other approaches, is that the meaning of a compound is a function of the meanings of its constituents. Thus the problem is: given two nouns N_1 and N_2 meaning X_1 and Y_2 respectively, what is the function $F(X_1, Y_2)$ that yields the meaning of the compound $[N_1N_2]$?

Of course, it is important to recognize the limits of compositionality in compounds. For novel compounds (such as *backgammon ball*), compositionality should be all that is available. But lexicalized compounds usually also incorporate idiosyncratic information. For instance, nothing principled predicts the difference in shape between stereotypical *soup bowls* and *fish bowls*, or that a *boxcar* is a kind of railroad car but a *kiddy car* is a kind of toy. And general principles cannot account for cranberry morphemes (*cranberry, bassethorn, bogeyman, iceberg, fig newton*) or 'strawberry' morphemes (real words within compounds that play no role in the compound's meaning, e.g. *strawberry, cottage cheese, polka dot, tea cozy, hillbilly, sheepfold*). So sometimes lexicalized meaning has to ignore the semantics of one noun or the other, just as it ignores *bucket* in *kick the bucket*. Still, on the whole there is significant compositionality.

A common technique for analysing compounds has been to establish a phrasal paraphrase and to assign the meaning of the paraphrase to the compound. However, it has often been noticed that it is sometimes impossible to establish a single best paraphrase for a compound. Lees (1960: 123), for instance, discusses the example *pontoon bridge*:

...it is not even obvious which interpretation *is* the most commonly used, but the following might occur to us:

(7)   bridge supported by pontoons   (like *steamboat*)
      bridge floating on pontoons   (like *seaplane*)
      bridge made of pontoons   (like *blockhouse*)
      pontoons in the form of a bridge   (like *cell block*)

Gleitman and Gleitman (1970: 95) make similar remarks: 'We suspect that the person who says *lion-house* would consider it rather odd if someone asked him: "Did you mean *a house for a lion, a house suitable for lions*, or *a house lions can live in*?" Obviously the speaker meant any of these indifferently.' Levi (1978) also discusses this issue at length.

This problem presents two different cases. First, the paraphrases may be pure semantic variants, as in Gleitman and Gleitman's 'house for a lion' and 'house suitable for a lion', or *felafel ball* = 'ball made of/created from felafel'. Here, a proper semantic analysis should abstract $F(X_1, Y_2)$ from the particular way it happens to be expressed in the paraphrase.

Slightly more complex multiple paraphrases arise in cases like (8).

(8)   a. ticket window = 'a window at which tickets are bought/at which tickets are sold'

b. toll booth = 'a booth at which tolls are paid/at which tolls are collected'

c. movie theater = 'a theater where movies are seen/at which movies are shown'

d. grammar school = 'a school where grammar is taught/at which grammar is learned or studied'

Here the multiplicity arises from different ways of orienting the same connection between N_1 and N_2. *Buy* places the initiative with the recipient of goods, *sell* with the original owner; in a real transaction of course both must play an active role. Similarly with the payment and collection of tolls, the seeing and showing of movies, and the teaching and the learning of grammar. The solution, then, is that $F(X_1, Y_2)$ likely consists of the simple event schema, bereft of perspective or focus. The paraphrases, however, create alternative perspectives, because the overt use of a verb forces us to choose a particular frame of thematic roles.

The following examples, like *pontoon bridge*, present a different situation.

(9)   a. box car = 'car that carries boxes/that resembles a box/that serves as a box'

b. refrigerator car = 'car that has a refrigerator as significant part/that serves as a refrigerator'

c. elevator shaft = 'shaft that an elevator travels in/that is part of an elevator'

d. file folder = 'folder in which one places a file/that forms part of a file'

Unlike (8), these cases are not lexical or perspectival variants of the same relation. *Resembling* a box and *serving as* a box are quite distinct relations.[4]

Lees, Levi, and the Gleitmans suggest that there is no fact of the matter about which paraphrase is correct. Someone learning these words is typically given no evidence (e.g. 'This is called a box car because it looks like a box'): the relation is normally taken to be self-evident and without need of explanation ('That one is called a boxcar'). This being the case, what can the learner do? *Boxcar* is not ambiguous: it picks out the same objects no matter which reading is assigned to

---

[4]   Some of these examples play on an ambiguity in one of the constituent nouns. In *elevator shaft*, is the elevator the box that one rides in, or is it the whole piece of machinery including motor, cables, pulleys, controls, *and* the shaft? *File folder* plays on an ambiguity in *file*: in the first reading, the file is an individual piece in a collection of information; in the second, the file is the physical instantiation of the entire collection.

it. It is not like *football* (the game) vs. *football* (the ball). Nor is *boxcar* vague: it does not leave open a continuous range of possibilities on a scale, the way, say, *cold* does.

I propose that there is another way that *boxcar* can have multiple meanings besides being ambiguous or vague: it can have all the meanings in (9a) simultaneously. We might call such a word *promiscuous* (by contrast with *ambiguous*). If such a solution seems like giving up, one must remember that a word meaning is an entity in a brain, not in a logical system. It is altogether in the style of the brain to arrive at multiple solutions to the same result, and for a result so obtained to be more stable in perception and memory. A standard example of this is the system for depth perception, where a single perceptual feature relies on partially redundant evidence from sensory cues (e.g. lens accommodation), perceptual cues – both monocular (e.g. occlusion) and binocular (e.g. stereopsis) – and cognitive cues (e.g. knowing what size familiar objects should be).

The claim, then, is that *pontoon bridge* and *boxcar* are promiscuous rather than ambiguous. A learner attempts all possible strategies for combining N_1 and N_2 (presumably in parallel), and since there are multiple satisfactory strategies that do not conflict, *all* such semantic combinations are stored in memory as part of the meaning of the compound. (Of course, if asked to define the compound, speakers will likely give only one of the combinations and be satisfied with that.) A linguist seeking to analyse these compounds faces the same problem as the learner. The insistence on a single best solution is only a prejudice, which, I admit, is well grounded in scientific and common-sense practice. But in dealing with brain processes it is, I believe, sometimes counterproductive and should be judiciously abandoned when inappropriate.

6.5 ASPECTS OF COMPOUND MEANING THAT COME FROM SEMANTICS OF NOMINALS

The semantics of compounding involves a number of distinct components. This section sketches three components implicated in the combinatorial semantics of nouns in general; the next two sections add components that are specifically involved in compounding.

6.5.1 Profiling

The first general component might be called *profiling* (roughly following the usage of Langacker 1987; Brekle 1976 calls it *topicalization*): picking out a character in an event and designating this character as the one being referred to. For instance, the action of *driving* involves an agent directing the motion of a vehicle; the nominal *driver* picks out the agent. A standard way to notate this is through lambda-abstraction, which binds an argument within an expression to a variable outside (10b).

(10)   a. DRIVE (A, B) = 'A drives B'
        b. λx[DRIVE (x, INDEF)] = 'individual who drives something'

For my purposes a slightly different notation for profiling proves useful. In (11), the head of the expression is *PERSON* and the expression after the semicolon is a modifier. What makes the expression a well-formed modifier is that it contains a variable α which is bound by the superscript on *PERSON*. Profiling an argument of a function, then, consists in binding it to something outside the function; this is the semantic counterpart of a relative clause in syntax.

(11) $PERSON^{\alpha}$; [DRIVE (α, INDEF)] = 'a person α such that α drives something'

Any argument can be profiled; for instance the distinction between *employer* and *employee* is shown in (12).

(12)   employer: $PERSON^{\alpha}$; [EMPLOY (α, INDEF)]
        employee: $PERSON^{\alpha}$; [EMPLOY (INDEF, α)]

The Parallel Architecture notates the relation between syntactic and semantic constituency in terms of coindexing. Thus (10a) and (11) can be notated more precisely as (13a) and (13b) respectively, and the productive use of the -*er* suffix can be encoded as the schemas (13c, d), where *F* is a variable function of some unspecified number of variables.[5] '=' now stands for the interface relation between syntax and semantics.

(13)   a. A_1 drives$_2$ B_3 = DRIVE$_2$ (A_1, B_3)
        b. drive$_1$-er$_2$ = PERSON$_2$$^{\alpha}$; [DRIVE$_1$ (α, INDEF)]
        c. V_1-er$_2$ = PERSON$_2$$^{\alpha}$; [$F_1$ (α, ...)]   (agentive -*er*)
        d. V_1-er$_2$ = OBJECT$_2$$^{\alpha}$; [$F_1$ (INDEF, ... WITH α)]   (instrumental -*er*)

The semantic structure of (13b) also appears in morphologically different nominals such as (14a), as well as in compounds such as (14b). The differences among them show up in the coindexation between the morphosyntax and the semantic structure.

---

[5] This formalization is not too different from many others in the literature, for example Rappaport Hovav and Levin (1992), Lieber (2004), and Booij (2007). I omit the details for specifying that the first argument of *F* is an agent. See Jackendoff (1990). I have oversimplified the rest of the semantics of -*er* and -*ee* nominals, as not especially relevant to the present discussion.

(14) a. $violin_1\text{-}ist_2 = PERSON_2{}^{\alpha}; [PLAY\ (\alpha, VIOLIN_1)]$

     b. $violin_1\ play_2\text{-}er_3 = PERSON_3{}^{\alpha}; [PLAY_2\ (\alpha, VIOLIN_1)]$

6.5.2 Action modality

Busa (1997) develops an analysis of *agentive nominals* – nouns that denote characters individuated by their actions. For example, although *violinist* denotes someone who plays the violin, it is actually ambiguous between an occupation (15a), a habitual activity (15b), or an ability (15c). It can even be used in a case where playing the violin is a specific activity on a specific occasion (i.e. a stage-level predicate); (15d) might be used in a situation in which all the players in the orchestra switched instruments as a joke or are rank beginners. All this is unchanged, of course, if we substitute the compound *violin player*.

(15) a. She's a violinist in the Pittsburgh Symphony but hasn't played since they went on strike.

     b. She's an occasional violinist.

     c. She's a good violinist, but hasn't played since she sold her violin ten years ago.

     d. None of the violinists can play the violin!

These variant interpretations will be called the *action modalities* under which a nominal can be understood.

It might appear from (15) that the choice of action modality is just a matter of pragmatics. But there are action nominals whose action modality is an essential part of the lexical meaning (and this is Busa's main concern). For instance, *pedestrian* is a stage-level predicate: someone on foot on a particular occasion. I don't remain a pedestrian when I'm driving my car. Similarly, when one counts *passengers* carried by American Airlines, I count as a different passenger on each trip. Conversely, someone who only happens to discuss economics on a particular occasion is unlikely to be called an *economist* (except perhaps sarcastically); someone is an economist by occupation. A *customer* may be either current (stage-level) or habitual; for the occupation, the term is *buyer*. And the difference between a *whore* and a *slut* is whether the action in question is an occupation or a habit.

Among compounds, some (e.g. *milkman*, *garbage man*, *mailman*) lexically denote occupations; others (*fisherman*, *bartender*, *violin player*) are more open in their action modality. Novel coinages in particular may often be understood as stage-level, with specific function and specific action. For instance, Downing's (1977) *bike girl*, 'girl who left her bike in the hallway on this particular occasion', is of this sort, parallel to *pedestrian*. In the context of a recipe, *starch bowl*,

'bowl currently containing starch', has this same action modality, which I'll call 'current'.

An important action modality is Ruth Millikan's (1984) notion of *proper func-tion*.[6] Roughly, '[h]aving a proper function is a matter of having been "designed to" or of being "supposed to" (impersonal) perform a certain function' (Millikan 1984: 17). Crucially, an object need not *actually* ever perform its proper function. Millikan's striking example is a sperm: only one of millions ever performs its proper function of fertilizing an egg.

Three major classes of things can have proper functions. The first class is *artefacts*: concrete objects constructed by people[7] who have some function in mind for them, or who benefit from their functioning. The second class is *parts*. For parts of artefacts, such as the back of a chair, the proper function is clear: the part serves part of the proper function of the artefact. But parts of organisms also have proper functions: the heart is to pump blood, the leaves of a plant are to perform photosynthesis, and so on. A third class of objects with proper functions is objects that are 'destined' to become something: the proper function of a seed is to become a plant, of an egg to become an animal, and of a fiancée to become a wife – whether or not these situations actually come to pass.

Action modality will be formalized as an operator on a profiled action. So, for instance, the occupation reading of *violinist* can be notated as (16a), and the 'current' reading of *starch bowl* as (16b). For a noun that denotes an artefact such as *book*, the proper function is part of its lexical entry, as in (16c).

(16)   a. $violin_1ist_2 = PERSON_2{}^{\alpha}; [OCC\ (PLAY\ (\alpha, VIOLIN_1))]$
       b. $starch_1\ bowl_2 = BOWL_2{}^{\alpha}; [CURRENT\ (CONTAIN\ (\alpha, STARCH_1))]$
       c. $book_1 = [BOOK^{\alpha}; [PF\ (READ\ (PERSON, \alpha))]]_1$

It is an interesting empirical question what the full range of action modalities is.

6.5.3 Cocomposition

An important way in which natural language semantic composition goes beyond simple Fregean compositionality is *cocomposition*, first explored extensively by Pustejovsky (1995). The best-known example involves the complement of verbs

---

[6] Millikan develops the notion of proper function in the context of a theory of language that I find difficult to endorse in general. Nevertheless this notion, extracted from her overall approach, is of great utility in a mentalistic analysis of concepts.
   [7] Or other intention-having beings, since it makes sense to include beaver dams among artefacts.

such as *finish*, which semantically must be an activity. *We finished singing* and *We finished the job* undergo ordinary composition, as their complements are activities. However, the complements in *we finished the book* and *we finished the beer* do not denote activities. Nevertheless, their interpretations *do* incorporate an activity, most probably 'reading the book' and 'drinking the beer' (other possibilities depend on context). Crucially, the default activity is dependent on the choice of noun. Where does this extra piece of meaning come from? The obvious source is the internal structure of the noun's meaning, in particular from the noun's proper function.

Let me formalize just enough of this to make it useful in the analysis of compounds. (17a) is what would result from composing *finish* and *book* in simple Fregean fashion; it is ill-formed because a book is not a kind of activity. (17b) is a slightly more complex but well-formed expression; the unspecified function F serves as a sort of 'adapter plug', 'coerced' into the interpretation, so that all selectional restrictions can be met (Jackendoff 1997: chapter 3). The first argument of F, the actor, is bound to *BILL* by the αs; this is the semantic expression of control (Culicover and Jackendoff 2005: chapter 12), so that it is Bill who is performing the action F.

(17) a. Bill$_1$ finished$_2$ the book$_3$ = *FINISH$_2$ (BILL$_1$, BOOK$_3$)
  b. Bill$_1$ finished$_2$ the book$_3$ = FINISH$_2$ (BILL$_1^\alpha$, F (α, BOOK$_3$))
     'Bill finished doing something with the book'

The content of the coerced function F is filled out by incorporating material from the proper function of *book*. (18a) makes this proper function explicit, following the analysis of *book* in (16c). This makes it possible to treat F as a copy of *READ*, as in (18b).

(18) a. FINISH$_2$ (BILL$_1^\alpha$, F (α, [BOOK$^\beta$; PF (READ (PERSON, β))]$_3$))
  b. FINISH$_2$ (BILL$_1$, READ (α, [BOOK$^\beta$; PF (READ (PERSON, β))]$_3$))

A fancier way of notating this is (19), where the binding indicated by the two γs makes it explicit that F is filled out by copying *READ*. An approximate paraphrase would be 'Bill finished doing with the book what one is supposed to do with books, namely reading it.'

(19)   FINISH$_2$ (BILL$_1^\alpha$, F$^\gamma$ (α, [BOOK$^\beta$; PF (READ$^\gamma$ (PERSON, β))]$_3$))

One can imagine other formal ways of working this out; Pustejovsky's own formalization is quite different. But the general idea is clear. First, when pieces of meaning that are expressed cannot link up semantically, it is sometimes possible to add unspoken functions in order to create well-formed semantic connections (coercion). Second, it is possible to fill out these functions by binding them (or profiling them) from inside the meanings of nouns (cocomposition).

6.6 THE COMPOUNDING SCHEMATA, THE BASIC RELATIONS, AND COCOMPOSITION WITH THE NOUNS

Establishing the semantic structure of a compound N_1N_2 involves two factors: designating a head – in English, N_2 – and determining the semantic relation between N_1 and N_2. There are two routes for connecting things semantically to N_2. First, N_1 can be an argument of N_2, as in *violin player*. These are so-called synthetic compounds; the general schema appears in (20a). Second, N_1 can be part of a modifier of N_2. The rest of the modifier must be established by coercion, as in (20b). (The coerced function is notated as F.)

(20)   N+N COMPOUND SCHEMAS (or CONSTRUCTIONS)
      a. Argument schema: $[N_1\ N_2] = [Y_2\ (\ldots, X_1, \ldots)]$
                         'an N_2 by/of/ ... N_1'
      b. Modifier schema: $[N_1\ N_2] = [Y_2^{\alpha}; [F\ (\ldots, X_1, \ldots, \alpha, \ldots)]]$
                         'an N_2 such that F is true of N_1 and N_2'

What is the range of possibilities for *F*? Many accounts in the literature, for instance Downing (1977), Selkirk (1982), Ryder (1994), and Lieber (2004), have despaired at finding a systematic account of the possibilities. Jespersen (1942: 137–8) says: 'Compounds... say nothing of the way in which the relation is to be understood. That must be inferred from the context or otherwise... The analysis of the possible sense-relations can never be exhaustive.' Other accounts such as Lees (1960) and Levi (1978), noting that *F* is not entirely arbitrary, have attempted to enumerate a set of functions that accounts for all compounds, either in semantic or syntactic terms (e.g. for Lees, in terms of a set of deletable verbs in the underlying forms of compounds).

In the present account there is a generative system that creates an unlimited set of possibilities for *F*. This generative system includes:

- a family of basic functions or relations, many of which can be profiled on either variable
- the set of action modalities, which are applied to the function *F* to provide further possibilities
- cocomposition of aspects of noun meaning with the function *F*
- a set of structural principles that can be combined to build structurally more complex realizations of *F*.

Section 6.5.2 dealt with action modalities; this section deals with the basic functions and cocomposition; section 6.7 deals with the structural principles.

First I must discuss the reversibility of the basic functions, which has not to my knowledge been discussed in the literature. Consider the pair *helicopter attack* and *attack helicopter*. In semantic structure, they both must encode that the helicopter is attacking. In the former case, *attack* takes an argument. Hence the meaning of the compound (21a) is an instance of schema (20a). In the latter, *helicopter* serves as N_2. Since it does not take an argument, schema (20b) must be applied. Within (20b), the argument–head relation can be instantiated by cocomposing *ATTACK* with *F*, resulting in (21b). ((21b) also says the modifier is a proper function.)

(21)   a.   helicopter$_1$ attack$_2$ = ATTACK$_2$ (HELICOPTER$_1$, INDEF)
            'an attack on something by helicopter(s)'

      b.   attack$_1$ helicopter$_2$ = HELICOPTER$_2$$^\alpha$; [PF (ATTACK$_1$ (α, INDEF))]
            'a helicopter whose proper function is to attack things'

If neither of the nouns takes an argument, then schema (20b) is required for either order of the nouns. Example doublets are *lunch bag*, 'a bag whose proper function is to hold/carry a lunch', vs. *bag lunch*, 'a lunch meant to be held/carried in a bag'; and *beef stew*, 'stew made out of beef', vs. *stew beef*, 'beef meant to be made into stew': the relation between the two nouns is the same, just differently profiled and sometimes with different action modality.

Here is a list of the (most prominent) basic functions for English compounds, with examples. This list is not far off others that have been proposed in the literature. With one exception, these seem rather plausible as functions that are readily available pragmatically. (Reminder: X_1 is the meaning of N_1, Y_2 is the meaning of N_2, except in the last two cases.)

- CLASSIFY (X_1, Y_2), 'N_1 classifies N_2': *beta cell, X-ray*. This is the loosest possible relation, in which the meaning of N_1 plays only a classificatory role.
- $Y_2(X_1)$, '(a/the) N_2 of/by N_1': *sea level, union member, wavelength, hairstyle, helicopter attack, tooth decay*. This is the argument schema. It is sometimes reversible, with the extra coercion shown in (21b): $X_1(Y_2)$, 'an N_2 that N_1's things': *attack helicopter, curling iron, guard dog*; also 'an N_2 that people N_1': *chewing gum, drinking water*.
- BOTH (X_1, Y_2), 'both N_1 and N_2': *boy king, politician-tycoon*. (*Dvandva* compounds)
- SAME/SIMILAR (X_1, Y_2), 'N_1 and N_2 are the same/similar': *zebrafish, piggy bank, string bean, sunflower*. This is not reversible, because the function is symmetric; asymmetry arises only through profiling.
- KIND (X_1, Y_2), 'N_1 is a kind of N_2': *puppy dog, ferryboat, limestone*. Reversible: *seal pup, bear cub* (there are other possible analyses as well, perhaps promiscuously).
- SERVES-AS (Y_2, X_1), 'N_2 that serves as N_1': *handlebar, extension cord, farmland, retainer fee, buffer state*.
- LOC (X_1, Y_2), 'N_2 is located at/in/on N_1': *sunspot, window seat, tree house, background music, nose hair, doughnut hole*. Reversible: 'N_1 located at/in/on N_2',

or, reprofiled, 'N_2 with N_1 at/in/on it': *raincloud, garlic bread, inkpad, stairwell, icewater, water bed.*[8]

- LOC_{temp} (X_1, Y_2), 'N_2 takes place at time N_1': *spring rain, morning swim, 3 a.m. blues*. A special case of LOC (X_1, Y_2).
- CAUSE (X_1, Y_2), 'N_2 caused by N_1': *sunburn, diaper rash, knife wound, surface drag.*
- COMP (Y_2, X_1), 'N_2 is composed of N_1': *felafel ball, rubber band, rag doll, tinfoil, brass instrument*. Reversible: 'N_1 is composed of N_2', or, reprofiled, 'N_2 that N_1 is composed of': *wallboard, bathwater, brick cheese, sheet metal.*
- PART (X_1, Y_2), 'N_2 is part of N_1': *apple core, doorknob, fingertip, stovetop, mould cavity*. Reversible: 'N_2 with N_1 as a part': *snare drum, lungfish, string instrument, ham sandwich, wheelchair*. If N_1 is a mass noun, this relation paraphrases better as 'N_2 is composed in part of N_1': *gingerbread, cinnamon bun, cheesecake, noodle soup*. Reversible: 'N_2 that forms part of N_1': *stew beef, cake flour, lunch meat.*[9]
- MAKE (X, Y, FROM Z), 'X makes Y from Z.' This creates two families of compounds, depending on which two arguments are mapped to N_1 and N_2.
    a. 'N_2 made by N_1': *moonbeam, anthill, footprint, horse shit*. Reversible: 'N_2 that makes N_1': *honeybee, lightbulb, musk deer, textile mill*
    b. 'N_2 made from N_1': *apple juice, olive oil, grain alcohol, cane sugar, cornstarch*. Reversible: 'N_2 that N_1 is made from': *sugar beet, rubber tree.*[10]
- PROTECT (X, Y, FROM Z), 'X protects Y from Z.' This is the one function in the group that does not seem especially 'basic'. It too creates two families of compounds:
    a. 'N_2 protects N_1': *chastity belt, lifeboat, safety pin*
    b. 'N_2 protects from N_1': *mothball, flea collar, cough drop, mosquito net, sun hat.*

The basic functions can fill in *F* in (20b) to build compound meanings, as in (22).

(22)   window$_1$ seat$_2$ = SEAT$_2^{\alpha}$; [LOC (α, AT WINDOW$_1$)]
        felafel$_1$ ball$_2$ = BALL$_2^{\alpha}$; [COMP (α, FELAFEL$_1$)]

Another way that *F* can be filled in is through cocomposition with the internal semantic structure of N_2. For example, the basic locative relation LOC seems to invoke only locations paraphrasable by *at, in,* or *on,* perhaps the least marked spatial relations. However, if part of the meaning of one of the nouns is another spatial relation, this relation may be used to fill in *F*. (23a) shows the internal

---

[8] These cases verge closely on 'N_2 with N_1 as a part', below. It is not clear to me whether they are distinct.

[9] The difference between COMP and PART can be illustrated by the ambiguity of *clarinet quartet*. On the COMP reading it means 'quartet of four clarinets'; on the PART reading it means 'quartet of which a clarinet is a distinctive member', e.g. a clarinet and three strings.

[10] This relation differs from PART in that Z is no longer identifiable as such in Y. However, the distinction is slippery.

structure of *fountain*. Its proper function, 'liquid flows out of', cocomposes with F to produce the semantic structure (23b) for *water fountain*.[11]

(23)   a. $fountain_1 = FOUNDAIN_1^\alpha$; [PF (FLOW (LIQUID, OUT-OF α))]

      b. $water_1\ fountain_2 = FOUNTAIN_2^\alpha$; [PF (FLOW ($WATER_1$, OUT-OF α))]

Similar cases are *coal mine* ('dug out of'), *gas pipe* ('flows through'), *staple gun* ('shot out of'), *Charles River bridge* ('crosses over'), and Downing's (1977) *toe-web* ('extends between'). In all these cases, N_2 has a proper function, and N_1 is an argument of the proper function. This approach accounts for large families of compounds such as those in (24).

(24)   a. N_2 is a container (*photo album, carbarn, coffee cup, soapdish, fishtank*):

      $coffee_1\ cup_2 = CUP_2^\alpha$; [PF (HOLD ($COFFEE_1$, IN α))]

      b. N_2 is a vehicle (*cattle car, baby carriage, garbage/ice-cream/oil truck*):

      $cattle_1\ car_2 = CAR_2^\alpha$; [PF (CARRY ($CATTLE_1$, IN α))].

      c. N_2 is an article of clothing (*pinky ring, face mask, necktie*):

      $pinky_1\ ring_2 = RING_2^\alpha$; [PF (WEAR ($\alpha$, ON $PINKY_1$))]

      d. N_2 is an incipient stage of something else (*rosebud, chick embryo, grass seed*)

      $rose_1bud_2 = BUD_2^\alpha$; [PF (BECOME ($\alpha$, $ROSE_1$))]

      e. N_2 is agent of an action (*silk merchant, eye doctor, bus driver, pork butcher*)

      $silk_1\ merchant_2 = MERCHANT_2^\alpha$; [OCC (SELL ($\alpha$, $SILK_1$))]

      f. N_2 is an artefact (*hair dryer, fire extinguisher, stomach pump*)

      $hair_1\ dry_2\text{-}er_3 = X_3^\alpha$; [PF ($DRY_2$ (PERSON, $HAIR_1$, WITH α))]

6.7 GENERATIVE SCHEMAS FOR F

In *attack helicopter* (21b), N_1 serves as one of the functions making up F, and N_2 serves as its argument (and is then profiled). In *window seat* (22), N_1 serves as an argument of one of the basic functions, which in turn is a modifier of N_2. In *water fountain, coffee cup*, and so on (23)–(24), N_1 serves as an argument of the proper function of N_2. Suppose N_1 cannot sensibly serve any of these roles. Then further options have to come into play, in which the relation is more distant.

One possibility is that F, the modifier of N_2, is further modified by a function G, and N_1 is an argument of G. In order for G to serve as a modifier of F, it must also have another argument that is bound to F. Thus formally this schema is (25).

[11] Brekle (1986) calls this kind of cocomposition a *stereotype compound*. Bassac (2006) analyses this process – correctly, in my opinion – in terms of Pustejovsky's (1995) *qualia structure* internal to noun meanings, most prominently the telic quale, which specifies proper function of an object.

(25) $[N_1 N_2] = [Y_2^\alpha; [F^\beta (\ldots, \alpha, \ldots; [G(\ldots X_1, \ldots, \beta, \ldots)])]]$

An example is (26), *steamboat*. Here *F* is filled in from the lexical semantics of *boat*, 'something whose proper function is to move in water', and *G* is the basic function *CAUSE*, encoding the means by which the boat moves.

(26) $steam_1 boat_2 = [BOAT_2^\alpha; [PF(MOVE^\beta (\alpha); CAUSE (STEAM_1, \beta))]]$
              $\lfloor F \rfloor$ $\lfloor G \rfloor$
             'a boat that moves   by steam causing it to do so'

Another way to fit N_1 in is for one of the arguments of *F* to be a function *G*, and N_1 serves as one of *G*'s arguments. Formally this schema is (27).

(27) $[N_1 N_2] = [Y_2^\alpha; [F (G(\ldots X_1 \ldots), \ldots, \alpha, \ldots)]]$

An example is (28), *barber shop*. As in previous cases, *F* is filled in from the proper function of *shop*: 'place whose function is for people to buy goods or services'. *G* is the service being paid for, and it comes from profiling the proper function of *barber*, 'person who cuts hair', in the fashion illustrated for *finish (reading) the book* in section 6.5.3.

(28) $barber_1 shop_2 =$
$[SHOP_2^\alpha; [PF (LOC (BUY (PERSON, [G^\beta ([BARBER_1^\gamma; OCC (CUT^\beta (\gamma, HAIR)])]); IN \alpha))]]$
      $\lfloor \quad F \quad \rfloor$ G - - - - - - - - - - $\rightarrow$ (G bound to CUT)
       'a shop whose proper function is that in it people buy what barbers do, namely cut hair' (more concisely, 'a shop where people buy (the service of) barbers cutting hair')

For a more complex case, consider *piano bench*, 'bench on which one sits while playing the piano'. Sitting comes from the proper function of *bench*, and playing comes from the proper function of *piano*. These two functions are connected by the basic function of temporal location, 'while'. Formally, 'sitting' is *F*, from the lexical semantics of *bench*; it has a temporal modifier whose function is LOC_{temp}. One argument of LOC_{temp} is bound to *F*, and the other is bound to *G*, 'playing', which is profiled from the proper function of *piano*. The formal structure is (29), and the structure of this example is (30).

(29) $[N_1 N_2] = [Y_2^\alpha; [F^\beta (\ldots, \alpha, \ldots; [G (\beta, H(X_1))])]]$

(30) $piano_1 bench_2 = BENCH_2^\alpha; [PF (SIT^\beta (PERSON^\gamma, ON \alpha));$
                            $\lfloor F \rfloor$
                'a bench on which one sits,
          $[LOC_{temp} (\beta, H^\delta (\gamma PIANO_1^\varepsilon; [PF (PLAY^\delta (PERSON, \varepsilon))])])]]$
         $\lfloor G \rfloor$ H - - - - - - - - - $\rightarrow$ (H bound to PLAY)
     such sitting being while doing what one does to a piano, namely play it' (more concisely, 'a bench on which one sits while playing the piano')

Other compounds of this type are *bass stool, bike helmet, lobster bib, dessert wine,* and *coffee cake.*

Many of the analyses above have introduced unexpressed arguments, for instance the person sitting on a piano bench while playing the piano. Another type of unexpressed argument sneaks in in compounds like *birdbrain* 'someone with a brain like a bird's'. This is a case of the general schema (31), where N_1 and N_2 are both arguments of a modifying function F. This is the schema for exocentric compounds, a special case of the schema for metonymy.

(31) Exocentric compound schema: $[N_1 \, N_2] = [Z; [F(\ldots, X_1, \ldots, Y_2, \ldots)]]$
      'something such that F is true of N_1 and N_2'

Here are four cases, each slightly different in how the constituent nouns are incorporated. Since these are exocentric compounds, sometimes the head has to be lexically stipulated. Aside from that, the composition of schemas is of the same character as in other compounds.

(32) a. $\text{bird}_1\text{brain}_2$ = $\text{PERSON}^{\alpha}; [\text{SIMILAR (BRAIN}^{\beta} (\alpha), F^{\beta} (\text{BIRD}_1))]$
      'person whose brain is similar to that of a bird'

      b. $\text{sea}_1 \text{ horse}_2$ = $Z^{\alpha}; [\text{SIMILAR} (\alpha, \text{HORSE}_2)]; [\text{HABITUAL (LOC} (\alpha, \text{IN SEA}_1))]$
      'something similar to a horse that is habitually in the sea'[12]

      c. $\text{canvas}_1\text{back}_2$ = $\text{DUCK}^{\alpha}; [\text{BACK}_2{}^{\beta} (\alpha); \text{SIMILAR} (\beta, \text{CANVAS}_1)]$
      'duck whose back resembles canvas'

      d. $\text{coat}_1\text{tail}_2$ = $Z^{\alpha}; [\text{SIMILAR} (\alpha, \text{TAIL}_2)]; [\text{PART (COAT}_p, \alpha)]$
      'something similar to a tail that is part of a coat'

6.8 CLOSING REMARKS

By the time we get to (28), (30), and (32), a large proportion of the meaning is connective tissue: unexpressed basic functions, lambda-abstracted functions, and bound variables. Nevertheless, the overall result should be clear. The semantic relation between N_1 and N_2 arises by adding coercing functions either in argument or in modifier positions, and by cocomposing these either with the basic functions or with internal semantic structure from N_1 and N_2. This is fairly straightforward when there is only one coercing function, but complexity increases quickly with

---

[12] I can imagine a better action modality here for 'lives', but it is not crucial to the present point.

multiple coercions. The resulting number of options for the semantic relation between N_1 and N_2 also increases quickly, which seems consistent with the literature's limited success at enumerating them. In the present approach, the repertoire of possible relations is created by a generative system which, aside from the rudimentary linking of N_1 and N_2 into the structure, is entirely within the semantics. So in a sense Jespersen (1942: 138) is correct in saying 'The analysis of the possible sense-relations can never be exhaustive' – and yet it is systematic.

One might object that *piano bench* does not *feel* as complex as (30). I offer two replies to such an objection. First, for decades we have been accustomed to vaunting the covert complexity of language beneath its intuitive transparency. The covert complexity for Conceptual Semantics should not be any less than for other formal theories of syntax and semantics, particularly given its aspiration to semantic explicitness. In fact, by virtue of the Parallel Architecture, it has been possible to keep *all* complexity out of the syntactic component – it is only the *meaning* that is complex. Second, for those who find *any* sort of formalism objectionable, the challenge is to find a notation that (a) is more perspicuous, (b) still retains all the necessary semantic distinctions, and (c) does so with a constrained set of basic relations and schemata.

The questions raised by this account are the same ones that have persisted in the literature, but they can perhaps be couched more precisely. Here are four; other researchers will surely have more.

- What is the full set of basic functions, and how uniform are they cross-linguistically?
- To what extent are these functions generally available for pragmatics and non-linguistic conceptualization, and to what extent are they special to language – or to English?
- How extensive can coerced and cocomposed functions be in compounds, and to what extent does the answer differ between lexicalized and novel compounds?
- What other basic morphosyntactic patterns must be added to the simple N_1N_2 structure in (20) in order to account for the quasi-syntactic elaborations in (3) (e.g. *health and welfare fund*), and what is their status vis-à-vis morphology, syntax, and protolanguage?

Other traditional questions have been answered by the present account, for example why the possible relations between N_1 and N_2 are so varied yet not altogether wild; and precisely how the meanings of the two nouns contribute to the meaning of the compound. Above all, because the Parallel Architecture liberates the generative capacity of semantics from that of syntax, it has been possible to give a semantically based account of compounds that is sufficiently formal to see what is going on, while keeping the syntax as absolutely simple as it looks.

CHAPTER 7

COMPOUNDING IN DISTRIBUTED MORPHOLOGY

HEIDI HARLEY

7.1 INTRODUCTION

The Distributed Morphology framework attemps to present a fully explicit, completely syntactic theory of word formation. Compounding, prima facie, presents a seemingly paradigm case of morphology-as-syntax. It is productive, and manipulates items which are canonically themselves free morphemes and clearly independent terminal nodes. As shown by Lieber (1992a), nominal compounding in English and other Germanic languages can even include syntactically complex phrases, as in the following four examples from *Tucson Weekly* film reviews by James DiGiovanna:

(1) a. These aren't your standard *stuff-blowing-up effects*.   3 June 2004

  b. When he's not in that mode, though, he does an excellent job with the *bikini-girls-in-trouble genre*.   30 November 2006

  c. I've always found it odd that the people who complain most about realism are *comic-book and science-fiction fans*.   23 December 2004

  d. There's the aforementioned *bestiality and drooling-stroke-victim jokes*.   29 March 2001

Despite the apparently tailor-made empirical phenomena, there have been very few Distributed Morphology proposals concerning compounding, beyond the unspoken assumption of a standard syntactic treatment for noun-incorporation cases like that proposed in Baker (1988), which predates the DM framework itself. Consequently, the following discussion is more an exploration of the consequences of the DM network of assumptions for various types of compounding, rather than a survey of extant proposals.

The key to understanding compounding in DM is understanding the nature of Roots within the theory. For the purposes of this paper, I will assume that a compound is a morphologically complex form that is identified as word-sized by its syntactic and phonological behaviour and contains two or more Roots:

(2)   **Compound**: A word-sized unit containing two or more Roots.

First, I will briefly review the structure of the DM framework, with attention to the status of inflectional, derivational, and Root morphemes within it. Then I will consider the implications of the theory for various familiar forms of English compounding, including synthetic argument compounds, synthetic modifier compounds, primary ('root') compounds, and phrasal compounds.

7.2 BACKGROUND: DISTRIBUTED MORPHOLOGY IN 2008

In Distributed Morphology, all identifiable morphemes are the realizations of terminal nodes of a hierarchical (morpho)syntactic structure. Abstract feature bundles are manipulated by syntactic operations (Merge, Move, Agree, etc.) into an appropriate tree structure, along the lines proposed by Minimalist syntactic theory (Chomsky 1995a). The derivation of this tree structure at some point splits into two subderivations, one of which fine-tunes the structure further to create a semantically interpretable object (LF), and the other of which adjusts it to create a well-formed phonological representation (PF).

Distributed Morphology holds that the subderivation on the way to PF contains various parameterizable operations with which languages manipulate terminal nodes before they are 'realized' by the addition of phonological material. These operations can adjust feature content, fuse two terminal nodes into one, split one terminal node into two, and even, within a limited domain, reorder terminal nodes or insert extra ones. These adjustments are postulated to account for the many and varied empirical situations in which observed morphological structure is not isomorphic to syntactic structure. Nonetheless, there is a clear foundational principle at work: where there is a morpheme, there is a terminal node of which that morpheme is the realization.

Terminal nodes come in two varieties: feature bundles and Roots, called in some earlier work 'f-morphemes' and 'l-morphemes' (Harley and Noyer 2000). An agreement morpheme is a typical example of a realization of the feature-bundle type of terminal node. An Agr terminal node may be composed, depending on the language, of person, number, gender/class, and case features. Its phonological realization, a 'Vocabulary Item', is specified for a subset of the features of the terminal node which it will realize. In this way, a Vocabulary Item which is under-specified, containing just a few features, may be compatible with several different terminal nodes, allowing for underspecification-driven syncretism without requiring underspecification in the syntactico-semantic representation. Vocabulary Item insertion occurs in a competition model, to capture the effects of the Elsewhere Principle (Kiparsky 1973).

It is important to note that the features of feature-bundle terminal nodes are in general semantically contentful, as they are subject to interpretation at the LF interface. For example, the [+past] feature which may occupy a Tense terminal node is interpreted as an ordering relation between two events at LF (Zagona 1988, Demirdache and Uribe-Etxebarria 1997). On the PF branch, this same feature typically conditions the insertion of the Vocabulary Item *-ed* (which happens to be a suffix) into the T° terminal node in English. Similarly, the [+Definite] feature which may ocupy a D° terminal node conditions the insertion of the Vocabulary Item *the* into the D° terminal node in English at PF, and has a particular unique-ness-presupposition interpretation at LF.

The other type of terminal node is 'Root'.[1] Roots carry the non-grammatical, encyclopedic semantic content of a given message. It is perhaps easiest to think of them as the lexicalization of a pure concept, though their interpretations can vary depending on the syntactic contexts in which they find themselves, as in, for example, idioms. It is thus more precise to understand them as instructions to access certain kinds of semantic information, which may vary depending on the morphosyntactic context of the Root in question.

Root Vocabulary Items are also subject to competition, though much less obviously so than feature bundles. For the most part, a single abstract Root is realized deterministically by a single Vocabulary Item — $\sqrt{CAT}$ is realized by 'cat', $\sqrt{WALK}$ is realized by 'walk', etc. However, certain Roots are realized by different Vocabulary Items in different circumstances, for example, in cases of suppletion.[2]

---

[1] In tree and bracket notation, the 'Root' category is symbolized by $\sqrt{}$.

[2] Because of the tendency for a learner to behave in accordance with the Mutual Exclusivity principle when learning content words (Markman, Wasow, and Hansen 2003) – that is, they assume that different sounds have distinct meanings – suppletion in Root Vocabulary Items is usually limited to highly frequent items for which the learner will get a lot of evidence. Suppletion in feature-bundle Vocabulary Items, on the other hand, is much more common, since their content is partially given by UG and they are all highly frequent in any case.

√GO is realized as 'go' in one morphosyntactic context, and as 'went' (or 'wen-', according to Halle and Marantz 1993) in another – that is, when √GO is c-commanded by a [+past] T°. Siddiqi (2006) also proposes that word-internal alternations like 'ran/run' are instances of Vocabulary Item competition for a single Root terminal node √RUN, rather than produced by post-insertion, phonological Readjustment Rules of the kind proposed by Halle and Marantz.

Roots are acategorical, needing to be Merged in the syntax with a category-creating feature bundle, n°, a°, or v° (Marantz 2001). These category-creating terminal nodes may be null (as in 'cat', composed of [[√CAT]√ n°]$_{nP}$) or overt (as in 'visible', composed of [[√VIS]√ a°]$_{aP}$). Not only that, they come in different 'flavours', i.e. contribute different semantic information, just as, for example, different Tense heads do. The most well-studied head of this type is the verb-creating v°, which has varieties that mean CAUSE, as in *clarify* (tr), 'cause to be clear'; BE, as in *fear*, 'be afraid of'; BECOME, as in *grow*, 'become grown'; and DO, as in *dance*, 'do a dance'. However, it is clear that other types of category-forming heads may have different semantic features too. The a° head can mean at least 'characterized by' as in *care-ful*, *comfort-able*; 'able to be', as in *ed-ible*, or 'like', as in *yellow-ish*, *box-y*. The n° head has varieties that mean 'the event or result of', as in *concord-ance*, *congratulat-ion*, *mix-ing*; 'the agent or instrument of', *mix-er*, *discuss-ant*; or 'the property of', as in *happi-ness*, *elastic-ity*.

These derivational feature-bundle nodes are, like all terminal nodes, subject to competition in Vocabulary Insertion, so in English, for example, n$_{PROP}$ can be realized by the VI *-ness* or the VI *-ity*, with the winning VI depending on which Root the n° has Merged with, just as, for example, the Num$_{PL}$ terminal node can be realized as *-s* or *-i* depending on whether it has merged with the nP 'cat' or the (bound) nP 'alumn-'. These constraints on realization are part of the licensing conditions attached to individual Vocabulary Items – morphologically conditioned allomorphy, also called 'secondary exponence', and central to accounting for morphologically based selection effects in the framework.

Category-forming feature bundles can, of course, be stacked: a Root can be merged first with an n°, then an a°, then an n° again, if desired, as in *pennilessness*, [[[[*penni*]√-Ø]$_n$-less]$_a$ness]$_n$. Each subsequent merger affects the particular inflectional terminal nodes with which the structure can be combined, since such terminal nodes have their own morphosyntactic and semantic restrictions; Degree nodes, for example, are compatible only with adjectives (aPs); T° nodes with verbs (vPs), and Num nodes with nouns (nPs).

In the theory, there is no hard-and-fast distinction between inflectional terminal nodes and derivational terminal nodes: they are simply feature bundles containing different kinds of features, subject to morphosyntactic and semantic well-formedness conditions as the derivation manipulates them. The fundamental distinction is between Roots and all other terminal nodes; only Roots refer to encyclopedic semantic content.

A final key point: no feature-bundle terminal node is necessarily realized by affixal phonological material, or necessarily realized by non-affixal phonological material. The 'derivational' feature bundles can be realized by Vocabulary Items (VIs) that are bound (v_{CAUSE} as -*ify*) or free (v_{CAUSE} as *get*), and the 'inflectional' feature bundles can realized by VIs that are bound (T_{PAST} as -*ed*) or free (T_{FUT} as *will*). Similarly, the Vocabulary Items (VIs) which realize Roots can be free ($\sqrt{SEE}$) or bound ($\sqrt{VIS}$); they always occur in construction with a category-creating node, but that node need not be realized by an overt affix.

7.3 COMPOUNDING AS SYNTAX

As noted above, compounding appears to represent an ideal case of morphology-as-syntax. The phrasal compounds listed above, for example, contain apparently syntactically formed phrases, such as *drooling stroke victim* ([A [N]]$_{NP}$) or *bikini girls in trouble* ([[N] [P N]$_{PP}$]$_{NP}$). The central puzzle of compounding for DM, then, is why these complex elements behave as apparently X° units in the phrasal syntax, inaccessible for, e.g., phrasal movement, and unavailable as a discourse antecedent for pronominal reference? Why are they subject to special phonological rules?

The answer given by Baker for noun-incorporation cases – syntactic head-to-head movement – forms one key part of the answer. Compounds are formed when Root(-containing) heads incorporate. I will follow Baker in assuming that this accounts for their behaviour as syntactic X°s (indivisibility, etc.), as well as the impossibility of phrasal movement out of them, and I will argue that this also (indirectly) accounts for the impossibility of discourse antecedence from within a compound.

The other key part of the answer, provided by the DM framework, lies in the idea that compounds are constructed when phrasal elements merge with a Root before that Root is itself merged with a categorizing terminal node. To motivate this idea I will first present a quick analysis of *one*-replacement effects, and then explore the consequences of that proposal for synthetic compounds.

7.3.1 *One*-replacement, Roots, and internal arguments

In Harley (2005), I proposed to use the concept of a categorizing nP to capture the standard English *one*-replacement paradigm, in which arguments and adjuncts behave differently with respect to their inclusion in the antecedent of anaphoric *one*. Given a nominal which can take an argument, such as *student* (*of chemistry*), the argument of that nominal must be included in the interpretation of anaphoric *one*, while superficially similar adjuncts may be excluded, as illustrated in (3).

(3)   a. ?*That student of chemistry and this one of physics sit together.
      b. That student with short hair and this one with long hair sit together.

In fact, it seems reasonable to claim that the argument PP *of chemistry* is not an argument of *student* per se, but rather an argument of the Root, √STUD, considering that it is also an argument of the verb:

(4)   She studies chemistry, and he studies physics.

The notion that (internal) argument selection is a property of Roots makes intuitive sense, since it is Roots which contain the encyclopedic semantic information that would differentiate a type of event which necessarily entails an internal argument from one which does not.

If the Root selects for an internal argument, then the Root must merge with that argument before it merges with its category-determining feature bundle. The structure of *student of chemistry* in (3a) is thus that shown in (5a). The Root √STUD first merges with its DP argument *chemistry*. The √P (Root phrase) structure then merges with n°, ultimately realized as -*ent*. The Root head-moves to attach to n°.[3] I assume that the *of* heads a 'dissociated morpheme' inserted into the structure as a Last Resort operation to realize the inherent case of the argument DP, as a DM implementation of the 'inherent case' proposal of Chomsky (1986). The structure of *study chemistry* is given in (5b) for good measure.

(5)   a.

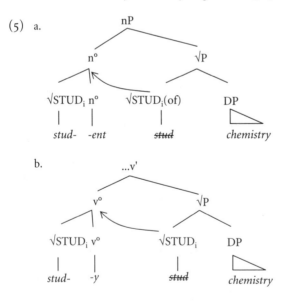

      b.

---

[3]   The mechanism of head movement could be either the conflation mechanism adopted in Harley (2004) or the phrasal-adjunction-plus-morphological-merger mechanism proposed in Matushansky

In contrast, the modifer *with short hair* in *student with short hair* in (3b) above does not modify the root √STUD; rather it modifies the nP *student*. The structure of *student with short hair* is thus that in (6), below. The Root √STUD first merges with n° and then head-moves to incorporate into it.[4]

(6)

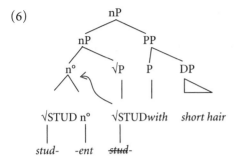

Given these structures, all that needs to be asserted about anaphoric *one* is that it necessarily takes an nP as its antecedent, not a √ or √P. Given that *chemistry* merges as part of √P before the nP superstructure is added on, *chemistry* must necessarily be included in the interpretation of *one* in (3a). Since the adjunct *with long hair* is merely adjoined to nP, however, it can be included in the interpretation of *one* or not, as the discourse demands; in (3b), the pragmatics of the situation suggest that *with long hair* is not included in the interpretation of *one*, which is understood merely as the simplex nP *student*.

I therefore conclude that the arguments of Roots are merged with the Root before the categorizing terminal node is added. Let us now turn to the consequences of this assumption for synthetic compounds.

7.3.2 Synthetic compounds

Canonical synthetic compounds are formed when a nominalized or adjectivalized verb and its internal argument appear in an N+N or N+A compound together, as in *truck-driver, drug-pusher, car-chasing (dog)*, or *grass-clipping (machine)*. Given the conclusions from *one*-replacement above, it must be the case that the complement noun composes with its Root before the Root is merged with the categorizing n° head. The complement noun is of course itself a noun, so it has its own n° head within; as should be clear by now, 'noun' = nP in the present framework. The structure of *truck-driver*, then, is given in (7):

(2006). For the purposes of the present paper, it doesn't matter what technical implementation of head movement is adopted, so long as it behaves in accordance with the standard assumptions about the process.

[4] In fact, under Bare Phrase Structure assumptions, the merger and incorporation of √STUD could happen in a single step; for the purposes of the proposal here, it doesn't matter whether incorporation follows merger or is simultaneous with it.

(7)

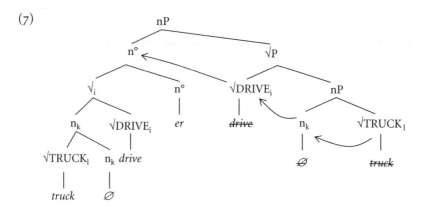

The complement of $\sqrt{}$DRIVE is first created by merging $\sqrt{}$TRUCK and a nominalizing n° head; I assume head-movement into n° from its complement. Subsequently this structure merges as the argument of $\sqrt{}$DRIVE, and then incorporates into it. This incorporation, being syntactic, must be feature-driven. Since incorporated elements satisfy their Case needs by incorporation in Baker's system, let us assume that this feature is Case-related.[5] Finally, the complex head [[[$\sqrt{}$TRUCK]$_\sqrt{}$ n]$_{nP}$ $\sqrt{}$DRIVE]$_{\sqrt{}P}$ merges with the categorizing agent-flavoured n°, and head-moves into that, creating the complex head [[[[$\sqrt{}$TRUCK]$_\sqrt{}$n]$_{nP}$ $\sqrt{}$DRIVE]$_{\sqrt{}P}$ n]$_{nP}$, which is then realized by Vocabulary Insertion as *truck-driver.*

If, rather than the nP *truck,* the argument of $\sqrt{}$DRIVE had been a DP, e.g. *the truck,* or *trucks,* the step of incorporation into the Root $\sqrt{}$DRIVE would not have occurred and the argument would be stranded to the right of the head, giving *driver of the truck,* or *driver of trucks,* rather than [*the-truck*]-*driver* or *trucks-driver.* One important question, within a syntactically based word-formation framework, is what blocks such DP incorporation, while allowing nP incorporation.[6] We will defer an answer to this question until the discussion of phrasal compounds in section 7.4.1 below.

The evidence of argumental synthetic compounds, then, suggests that compounding occurs when the $\sqrt{}$-containing constituents of a phrasal $\sqrt{}$P incorporate first within themselves and then into a category-creating head such as n° or a°. Note that *-er/-or* nominals may be formed on bound Roots, as in *groc-er, tract-or* or

---

[5] If incorporation did not occur, some kind of case-licenser would be needed, such as Last-Resort *of* (*driver of trucks*), or some other P° head. See Larson and Yamakido (2006) for a related proposal.

[6] Conjoined NPs in synthetic compounds, like *car- and truck-driver,* do not, I think, represent the incorporation of a phrasal element. Conjunction by *and* in English is subject to linearity effects, and can operate on non-constituents, like SBJ+V sequences in Right-Node Raising cases, and on sub-word constituents, like *pre-* and *post-colonial,* etc. It would be possible to treat these as a kind of conjunction reduction case – *car-driver and truck-driver* – or to search for a way to incorporate them within Phillips' (2003) parser-based account of such constituency-defying coordinations.

brok-er; they need not be formed on free verbs, even when in synthetic compounds, as in *stockbroker*.

It is useful to note that the division within DM into Root and category-creating heads allows us to avoid the most pressing problem associated with this type of structure for these cases of synthetic compounds, namely, the prediction that English verbs should also permit noun-incorporation-style compounding (see e.g. Lieber 2005: 380–1). The claim here is that English Roots allow incorporation into them. They are not yet of any category. In order to become nominal or verbal, they have to incorporate further into a category-creating head, n°, a°, or v°. These heads can have their own restrictions on what may or may not incorporate into them; see discussion below in section 7.4.1.

7.3.3 Modificational synthetic compounds

Another subtype of synthetic compounds, which I will call 'modificational', makes it clear that the incorporated element can be something other than an argument of the root. In these (adjectival) compounds, composed of a deverbal adjective plus an incorporated adjective, the incorporated element is a modifier of the verb contained within the deverbal adjective. Roeper and Siegel (1978) show that this kind of compound can only be formed from verb+modifier pairs where, in the corresponding verb phrase, the modifier would be the 'first sister' of the verb – that is, no internal argument of the verb may intervene. Consider the examples in (8):

(8) a. quick-acting baking powder   (It acts quick(ly))
     b. fast-falling snow   (It falls fast)
     c. snappy-looking suit   (It looks snappy)
     d. light-stepping horse   (It steps lightly)
     e. odd-seeming sentence   (It seems odd)

When the verb has an internal argument, as with transitive *grow* in (9a) below, a compound adjective can only incorporate the internal argument, as in (9b); incorporating the adverb (which is not the 'first sister') is impossible (9c). However, when no overt internal argument intervenes between the verb and the adverbial element, as with intransitive *grow* in (9d), the adverb may incorporate (9e).[7]

(9) a. The farmer grows wheat quickly.
     b. a wheat-growing farmer

---

[7] Note that while the Unaccusativity Hypothesis entails that single arguments of intransitive unaccusative verbs are base-generated in the same position as the object arguments of their transitive counterpart, that position might not be sister to the Root. In the argument structure framework of Hale and Keyser (1993), the internal arguments of change-of-state verbs like *grow* are in a vP-internal specifier position, rather than in 'first sister' position.

c. *a quick-growing farmer
   (bad where it's the things he's growing that grow quickly)
e. The wheat grows quickly.
f. quick-growing wheat

The 'first sister' constraint is extremely suggestive given the usual understanding of syntactic constraints on incorporation (i.e. that only governed items may incorporate), in conjunction with the assumptions of the Bare Phrase Structure (BPS) theory of Chomsky (1995b). Under BPS, there are no vacuous projections: projections and bar-level distinctions are only created epiphenomenally, by Merge. Arguments must be introduced by 'first merge', attaching to the Roots which select them, so modifying adjuncts will be introduced second, adjoining to a projection of the Root. However, in cases where no internal argument is introduced, the modifier will be the first thing merged to the Root. In this circumstance, in which Root and modifier are sisters, the Root will govern the modifier, just the same as it would govern its internal argument. In these circumstances, I propose, the modifier may incorporate, creating a compound; the analysis is a variant of that proposed in Roeper (1988).[8] The basic structure proposed is illustrated in (10):

(10)

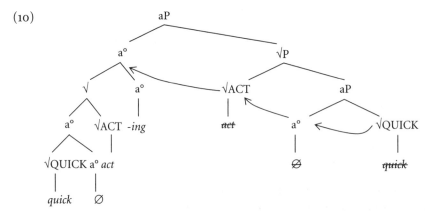

A problem arises, here, however. The -ing suffix may affix only to actual verbs, never to bound Roots. In this way, -ing is different from -er/-or nominals, which may be formed on bound Roots (grocer, etc.). To account for this, we should posit a licensing restriction on -ing such that it can only be inserted in the context of structures headed by the category-creating head v^o. In that case, the structure in (10) perhaps should also contain a null v^o head above √ACT. However, such an intermediate verb-creating category head would produce the problematic

---

[8] The feature which drives movement in this case is unlikely to be a Case feature, however, suggesting that perhaps a more general property should be appealed to in naming it. In Harley (2004) I named the feature a [± affix] feature; this would do here as well, of course.

prediction of verb-incorporation in English, described at the end of the previous section. The complex head $[[[\sqrt{\text{QUICK}}]_{\sqrt{}}a]_a \sqrt{\text{ACT}}]_{\sqrt{}}$ would be categorized as v^o by movement into a v^o head prior to moving into the a^o head realized by -ing, entailing that *to quick-act should then be a possible English verb. Above, this very problem in argumental compounds was obviated by the Root-incorporation treatment at the end of the last section. Carrying this analysis over to the structure in (10), here, means that we are assuming that -ing may attach to Roots as well as vPs. This correctly rules out *to quick-act, but comes at the cost of predicting that forms like *tract-ing (from the root of tract-or) should be well-formed. See below for an approach to this problem.

7.3.4 Primary ('root') compounds

The recognition that modifiers can incorporate so long as they are the first things merged with the Root of the head of the compound points the way to a treatment of regular primary compounds.[9] The relationship between the head noun and the compounded nouns in primary compounds is different from that in argumental synthetic compounds. In the latter case, the compounded noun is an internal argument of the Root of the head noun, and the interpretation of the compound is unambiguous. In the former, a sort of interpretive free-for-all obtains, where encylopedic and pragmatic information combine to determine the understood relationship beween the two nominal roots, as in, for example, nurse shoes vs. alligator shoes. Broadly speaking, the relationship is again modificational, with the proviso that the nature of the modification is determined pragmatically: nurse shoes are [shoes [(for) nurses]] while alligator shoes are [shoes [(of) alligator (skin)]]. One could imagine a proposal where a null phrase-head selected the modifying nominal prior to incorporation ($[[\sqrt{\text{SHOE}}]_{\sqrt{}}$ [P [n $[\sqrt{\text{NURSE}}]_{\sqrt{}}]_{nP}]_{PP}]_{\sqrt{}P}$), providing a locus for the underspecified semantic relationship between the two nouns; in the interests of structural parsimony, however, I will assume that no such relational head is necessary, and that the head noun's Root and the modifying noun are in a direct sisterhood relationship. As long as the head noun's Root is not itself multivalent, no argumental interpretation for the sister noun will be available, and consequently it is up to the interpretive component to construct some plausible relationship between the incorporated noun and the head noun. The nature of that constructed interpretation has been addressed much more thoroughly elsewhere (see e.g. the discussion in Kastovsky 2005, among many others), and will not be pursued here. The crucial thing for the proposal under

---

[9] These are usually called 'root' compounds, but since that could create confusion given the use of 'Root' within DM, I will use the term 'primary' here instead.

discussion is that the modifying nominal be introduced as sister to the Root of the head noun before it is categorized by its own n° head, as illustrated below:

(11)

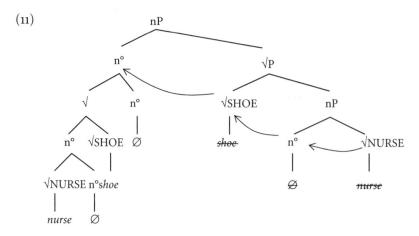

Having sketched a general incorporation-style treatment within DM of these three types of compounds, we must now address some of the thorny questions raised by syntactic treatments of X°-internal phenomena. In particular, why can't elements larger than nP generally be included in English nominal compounds? And, given that it is usually impossible for such elements to appear within compounds, how come they sometimes *can* appear? That is, how can the phrasal compounds exemplified in (1) above be accounted for in a principled way? Let us consider these problems in turn.

7.4 FAILURE OF INCORPORATION

There are two major ways in which compounding can be non-productive which raise issues for the syntactic approach. First, certain syntactically derived constituents refuse to participate in compounding on the non-head side – they cannot incorporate into a Root. This is the case for full DPs, in cases like *[drugs]-pusher* or *[that-novel]-writer*. Second, certain syntactic categories refuse to *host* compounding, on the head side: they can't be heads of compounds, that is, they do not allow incorporation of a compounded Root. This is the case for v° in English, since there are no productively incorporated verbs like *to quick-act* or *to truck-drive*.

What rules out compounding of phrasal elements larger than nP, like [drugs]-pusher or [that-novel]-writer? In the proposal here, such compounding would entail incorporation of the complex $[[\sqrt{DRUG}]_\sqrt{} n°]_{nP}$ ('drug') up through the higher functional complex, into Num° ('-s') and D°. Two possible approaches to the ill-formedness of such incorporation spring to mind. First, it might be the case that in English, elements other than n° or a° simply cannot host incorporation. This constraint could be syntactic in nature – the requisite features for driving head-to-head movement do not appear in feature bundles like D° or Num° in English. Alternatively, the constraint might be morphophonological in nature: there might be, for example, prosodic requirements on the realizaton of D° terminal nodes or other 'inflectional' feature bundles that forbid the inclusion of more than one independent stress-bearing Root in their phonological makeup (see e.g. Hale 2003 for a proposal exploiting the notion of a morphophonological template attached to verbal terminal nodes in Navajo).

For the failure of incorporation of DPs in cases like *trucks-driver or *[the-truck]-driver, an account of the first type seems appropriate. Above, it was proposed that the feature which drives incorporation of nP is Case-related. If an nP is merged with Num° or D° material, that Case-related nP feature must be checked DP-internally; the feature is no longer accessible for checking via incorporation into a Root. Consequently, *trucks-driver is not possible.[10]

However, the prohibition on noun-incorporation into verbs in English seems more amenable to an explanation of the second kind. Whatever the nature of the prohibition, it must be parameterizable, since, in some languages (e.g. Mohawk), v° can host incorporation, in contrast to the English situation in which n° and a° may host incorporation, but v° may not (*to truck-drive). A parameter attachable to particular categories of terminal node seems more appropriate.

As noted above, Hale (2003) proposed that Navajo verbs are subject to a prosodic morphophonological constraint – a prosodic template – which determines their morphological behaviour with respect to incorporation.

Similarly, let us assume that English v° is subject to a constraint such that it cannot host internally complex heads containing more than one Root element. This will prevent incorporation of complex heads containing multiple Roots into Engish verbs: *to quick-act or *to truck-drive will be ruled out because the v° in which the final verb is realized contains more than one Root.

Recall, however, that we ended section 7.3.3 with something of a conundrum. Since -ing attaches only to verbs (i.e. to items that have merged with v°), formations like quick-acting seem as though they must contain a v° head. This v° head would intervene between the topmost a° head, realized by -ing, and the Root √ACT. But if that is so, then the incorporated Root [quick-act]√ has moved into v°, resulting in a constituent which would, if pronounced, end up as the incorporated verb *to quick-act. (The same remarks apply, of course, to truck-driving, etc.)

---

[10] If, in accordance with Siddiqi's (2006) proposal, the plural VI mice is a Root VI in its own right, competing for insertion into √MOUSE, rather than a phonologically readjusted version of mouse in a+PL context, it explains why mice can occur in compounds but rats cannot: √MOUSE in a compound structure might be realized by 'mice', while √RAT could never be realized by 'rats'; the -s morpheme is an independent VI that realizes Num°. See Siddiqi (2006) for discussion.

The problem can be resolved, however, when we consider that in *quick-acting*, the head which actually ends up having two Root Vocabulary Items realized in it at Spell-Out is a°. We can assume that the prohibition prohibits Roots being realized in a v° *in its base position*. If they move through v° on up into another head, such as a°, the original v° will not contain the offending extra Roots at Spell-Out, and the prohibition on multiple Roots in v° will not be violated. *Quick-acting* will be well-formed, while *to quick-act* will not.[11]

We have, then, technical proposals to implement the ban on incorporation by DPs and the ban on incorporation into v°. How, then, can phrasal compounds be formed? They certainly include both DPs and vPs, to say nothing of CPs and PPs (though they cannot themselves *be* a DP; Lieber 1992a:12). What allows the formation of compounds like *stuff-blowing-up effects*?

7.4.1 Phrasal compounds

We have proposed that compounding is characterized by incorporation, which in English produces right-headed structures, as is clear from the contrast between incorporated *truck-driver* and non-incorporated *driver of trucks*. Phrasal compounds, however, do not exhibit that inverted order within the modifying phrase: we have *bikini-girls-in-trouble genre*, not *trouble-in-girls-bikini genre*. Consequently, it is clear that the phrase itself is not subject to internal syntactic incorporation. Indeed, given our assumption above that DPs may not incorporate, such phrases could not incorporate internally, since it would involve the DP *trouble* head-moving into the P *in*.

Rather, the phrase seems to be frozen as an expression evoking a particular abstract conceptualization of the compositional meaning determined by the internal phrasal syntax. In some cases, as has often been remarked, these compounds have a quotative flavour, as in this example from DiGiovanna:

(12)   'And frankly, DMX is a pretty compelling action hero in the Arnold Schwarzenegger "why bother acting when I've got this scowl perfected?" school of drama.' 6 March 2003

These quotative phrasal compounds evoke a particular attitude that might be attributed to a putative utterer of the phrase in question. Intuitively, the phrase has been fully interpreted, and an associated concept extracted from it – an attitude, in the case of quotatives, or an abstraction from an existing conceptual category, in the case of complex nP phrases as in *stuff-blowing-up effects* or *bikini-girls-in-trouble genre*.

---

[11] This view of the prohibition on incorporation into verbs in English is particularly compatible with the treatment of head-movement as phonological conflation of Harley (2004).

Further, these phrases needn't be part of a compound. They can be directly attached to derivational morphemes like -*ish*, -*y*, or -*ness* (e.g. *feeling a bit rainy-day-ish /a bit 'don't bother'-y /the general 'bikini-girls-in-trouble'-ness of it all*). This suggests that these phrases have undergone a derivational process into an appropriate category prior to affixation.

I will follow Sato (2007) in treating such phrasal elements as having undergone zero-derivation to a nominal category (see Ackema and Neeleman 2004: chapter 4 for a related approach; the analysis also is Lieber-and-Scalise-ish; Lieber and Scalise 2006: 28). In DM, this entails that the complex phrase is affixed by a zero n° head, in a schema like this:

(13) $[[XP]\ n^\circ]_{nP}$

The semantic contribution of this n° head will be to 'reify' the content of the XP-phrase: it will denote a concept evoked by the phrasal syntax, though not compositionally determined by it.

The resulting nominal is then expected to be able to participate in nominal affixation (e.g. with -*ish*), like any other nominal. Further, it should then be able to participate in primary compounding like any other nominal.

This still raises significant puzzles in the current framework. The incorporation of the nominalizing n° into the Root of the primary compound clearly brings along the complex XP, since the XP ends up in prenominal position in the right-headed compound. This means that the complex XP must have incorporated into the n° head during the nominalization process – but, according to what we have said so far, the DPs, vPs, etc. contained within the XP should prevent such incorporation. How can the XP incorporate?[12]

Descriptively, the entire XP is behaving syntactically like a Root, rather than like an internally complex XP. I suggest that this is a necessary part of the reification operation: in order for the XP's denotation to compose with the reifying n° head, it must be interpreted *as if uttered*. That is, the LF of the XP has to be accessed by the Conceptual-Intentional system, and fully interpreted. The XP itself is then not able to enter into further computation *as itself*; rather, it becomes a symbol, a Saussurean sign, for the concept which it evokes. Technically, we could propose that the XP is created in a separate derivational workspace from a separate numeration, sent off to LF for interpretation, and then 'renumerated' as a Root, in the derivation of the matrix clause – a Root denoting the abstract concept that was evoked by the previous computation of the XP's compositional meaning. (For the concept of 'renumeration' see Johnson 2002).

---

[12] Carnie (2000) proposes to allow phrases to incorporate into head positions so long as they are assigned the correct features, in an account of Irish nominal-predicate constructions. The account here adds the step of semantic interpretation and renumeration to the derivations of these head-like phrases in an attempt to account for their particular interpretive properties.

This is really just speculative, but it has the right consequences in the framework. In DM, Saussurean signs are necessarily Roots – only Roots can contribute non-grammatical semantic content. Hence the XP behaves like a Root, morphosyntactically speaking.

7.5 CONCLUSIONS

In the above, I have envisaged compounding as incorporation into an acategorial Root, in a framework in which word formation is treated purely syntactically. The distinction between Root and category-forming functional head within the Distributed Morphology framework enables this approach to treat the syntax of verbal argument structure and the syntax of argument structure in synthetic compounds in an entirely parallel way without making incorrect predictions about the availability of incorporation into V in English.

A simple extension allows the approach to apply to modificational synthetic compounds and to primary compounding in English as well. The difference between these three types of compounding resides in the semantic relationships between the Roots which are the target of incorporation and the elements which are generated as their first sister. Some roots (especially those that can become verbs) have argument structure, and the first-sister element, if appropriate, can be interpreted as satisfying that argument structure, generating an argumental synthetic compound. Other such Roots, especially those with event structure, can be modified in the same way as their corresponding verb can; in such cases, an incorporated first-sister modifier results in a modificational synthetic compound. Primary compounds are formed when either the Root is semantically purely 'nominal' in character – having no argument or event structure – or when the incorporated element does not form an appropriate argument or event-structure modifier. In such cases, the incorporated element is interpreted as being in some kind of relationship with the head noun, where the particular relationship involved is determined via a complex inference involving the semantics and pragmatics of the two items involved.

Finally, I sketched a possible approach to phrasal compounds within the framework, one which, however, still leaves many questions unanswered. Nonetheless, I hope to have shown that compounding is certainly tractable within the Distributed Morphology framework, and that perhaps certain insights the framework makes available allow for a perspicacious treatment of some of the well-known questions associated with the phenomenon.

CHAPTER 8

....

WHY ARE COMPOUNDS A PART OF HUMAN LANGUAGE? A VIEW FROM ASYMMETRY THEORY

....

ANNA MARIA DI SCIULLO

COMPOUNDS are a part of human language. They may include functional elements, such as case markers and prepositions, as well as phrases, and the order of their constituents, while being rigid within a given language, differs cross-linguistically, as the examples in (1) illustrate. Notwithstanding their diversity, compounds share some basic properties. They include more than one constituent. They are opaque syntactic domains. Their semantics is not necessarily compositional, and their stress pattern does not generally coincide with those of words or phrases.

I thank the editors of this volume for their comments. This work is supported in part by funding from the Social Sciences and Humanities Research Council of Canada to the Interface Project, grant number 214–2003–1003, as well as by a grant to the Dynamic Interfaces Project from FQRSC, grant number 103690.

(1)   a. spell-checker
          paper bag
          redneck

      b. *homme-de-paille* (French)
          man-of-straw
          'strawman'

      c. *aam khaanaa acchaa lagtaa hai*
          mango eat-INF good seems is
          'It feels good to eat mangoes.' (Hindi)

      d. *awoko-busi* (Yoruba)
          driver-bus
          'bus driver'

      e. *pijen-o-erx(ome)* (MG)
          come-LV-go
          'come (and) go'

      f. *bou-dati* (Japanese)
          stick-stand
          'stand straight'

Recent developments in evolutionary psychology (Hauser, Barner, and O'Don-nell 2007) indicate that compounds are not a part of the language of non-human primates, and a natural question that comes to mind is why they are a part of human language.

According to Hauser, Chomsky, and Fitch (2002), recursivity is a distinctive aspect of the language faculty (i.e. the biological basis of language). The language faculty must be the generative engine enabling the production and the compre-hension of compounds, since recursivity can be observed in compounds. Further-more, new compounds can be coined in any language. Children produce these forms quite early, around age 2 or 3 (see Clark and Barron 1988, Hiramatsu et al. 2000, Nicoladis 2007), sometimes with meanings that they are unlikely to have heard before, and always without any formal instruction. The identification of the operations generating these constructs will contribute to our knowledge of the language faculty. Compounds also have properties that differentiate them from phrases and sentences, and the identification of these properties will contribute to our understanding of how the language engine operates within the overall archi-tecture of the language faculty. Compounds also have interface properties that make them interpretable by the external systems. Special cues accessible to the sensorimotor system (SM) contribute to making compounds tractable by humans, even though their structure may include unpronounced constituents accessible only to the human conceptual-intentional (CI) system, as discussed in this chapter. The identification of these overt and covert cues will contribute to our under-standing of the contact between linguistic expressions and the external systems.

This chapter raises the following theoretical questions:

- Why are compounds a part of human language?
- How do their properties follow from the human computational system (C_{HL})?
- How do they satisfy the interface legibility conditions?

I address these questions from the viewpoint of Asymmetry Theory (Di Sciullo 2003a, b, 2005a, and related works). I argue that compounds are a part of human language because they are derived by the operations of C_{HL} while they satisfy the interface interpretability condition in ways that phrases and sentences do not.

Their properties, including strict linear precedence relations, strict scope, and opacity, follow from the C_{HL} without requiring additional operations or conditions besides those that are needed independently for the derivation of other sorts of linguistic expressions.

I focus on the properties of English compounds, which I take to be derived in the morphological workspace (D_M) of the grammar, and follow Di Sciullo (2005b) in taking French compounds to be derived in the syntactic workspace (D_S) of the grammar, and transferred to D_M. Both sorts of derivations generate domains of asymmetric relations (phases), and they differ with respect to the preservation of asymmetry. Given Asymmetry Theory, compounds have a unifying property, namely, they include a functional projection asymmetrically relating their parts. The simplified representations in (2) capture the unity and the differences in the linear order of the constituents of these constructs.

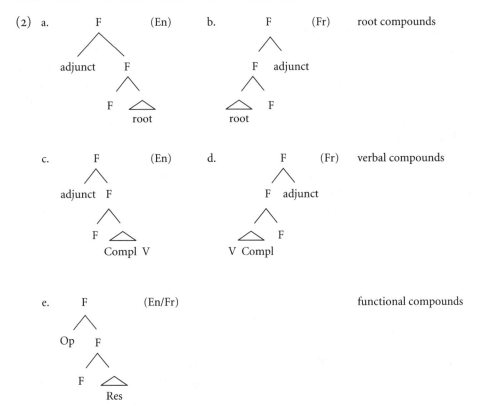

Compounds are domains of the computation, the locus of independently motivated (uninterpretable) active feature-checking. Like the syntactic domains, they are subject to the Interpretability Condition (Full Interpretation) requiring that only interpretable elements survive at the interfaces.

In Asymmetry Theory, compounds are derived in the morphological workspace by the recursive operations of the morphology (Di Sciullo 2005a, b; Di Sciullo and

Landman 2007; Di Sciullo and Tomioka 2007; Di Sciullo and Banksira, in press). The lexicon has no generative role in this model, as is the case in Chomsky (1970), and Di Sciullo and Williams (1987). The lexicon is a repertoire of items, including affixes, stems, roots, compounds, and idioms, with their underivable properties, which must be learned. Asymmetry Theory shares properties with the lexicalist approach to compounds (see Levin and Rappaport Hovav 1999, Lieber 2004), where fine-grained descriptions of affixes and roots are provided (see Di Sciullo 1992b, 2007a). It also shares properties with Distributed Morphology (Halle and Marantz 1993; Marantz 1997, 2000, and related works), which offers a more con-strained approach to derivation and compounding. Borer (2003, 2005) proposes an intermediate view where argument structure is either determined by the compu-tation or specified in a minimalist lexicon. Limits of the lexicalist and the distrib-uted approaches are discussed in Borer (2003, 2005a, b), and in Reinhart and Siloni (2005). If compounds were purely lexical-semantic objects, I would not expect compound-internal object/adjunct asymmetries to be observed, contrary to facts. If compounds were pure syntactic objects, I would not expect syntactic opacity to be observed cross-linguistically; neither would it be possible to account for their morphological compositionality, as discussed in section 8.3. Given Asymmetry Theory, the restrictions on the derivation of English compounds follow from the application of the operations of the grammar in different workspaces.

The organization of this chapter is as follows. First, I discuss the asymmetries observed in the domain of English compounds and relate them to the ones observed in the domain of affixed forms. Second, I show how compounds are derived in Asymmetry Theory. Finally, I consider how they satisfy the *Interface Interpret-ability Condition* and bring to the fore recent experimental results on compound processing.

8.1 ASYMMETRY

According to Asymmetry Theory (AT), asymmetric (i.e. directional) relations are the core relations of the language faculty.[1] Asymmetry is hard-coded in the morphology, since the configurational primitive of D_M is the minimal tree, that

---

[1] Asymmetry, as a formal property of the relations derived by the grammar, has been discussed in various works. It has been shown to be a property of syntactic relations (Reinhart 1983, Kayne 1994, Moro 2000, Chomsky 2000), phonological relations (Raimy 2000, van der Hulst and Ritter 2003), and morphological relations (Roeper 1999; Hale and Keyser 2002; Di Sciullo 2003a, b, 2005a). See Di Sciullo (2003a, b) for discussion.

is, a tree with only one complement and only one specifier, with the hierarchical structure in (3). The operations of D_M apply to minimal trees, the elements of which cannot be extracted in the course of the morphological derivation.[2]

(11)

If English compounds are derived in D_M, asymmetries that are not typical of phrases and sentences are expected to be observed in compounds. This is effectively the case, as further evidenced below, and is an instance of the *Strict Asymmetry of Morphology*.

(4) STRICT ASYMMETRY OF MORPHOLOGY
     Asymmetry is the characteristic property of morphological relations.

According to AT, there is a basic property of relations that differentiates morphological from syntactic derivations: morphological relations are strictly asymmetrical. In other words, morphology is blind to symmetrical, bidirectional relations. This is not the case for syntactic derivations if Moro (2000) is correct in assuming that points of symmetry can be generated in the course of a syntactic derivation, for instance in the case of the derivation of copular and inverse copular constructions. According to Dynamic Antisymmetry, movement must destroy the points of symmetry by moving one or the other constituent in a symmetrical relation, e.g. *the reason for his success is his great determination, his great determination is the reason for his success*. Interestingly, points of symmetry are never created in morphological derivations. If it were the case, similar situations would be expected in syntactic derivations, contrary to facts. As evidenced in Di Sciullo (2005a), on the basis of the ordering of affixes with respect to roots, morphological derivations are strikingly distinct from syntactic derivations. The fact that the parts of a morphological expression cannot be inversed (5) without giving a difference in semantic interpretation (6) provides evidence that morphological relations are asymmetric only. This also holds for compounds, such as the ones in (7), where those in (7b) are excluded, and those in (7c) have a different interpretation from (7a), provided that there is a world of interpretation where they can be interpreted.

(5) a. bio-logic-al
     b. *bio-al-logic, *al-bio-logic, *logic-bio-al, *logic-al-bio, *al-logic-bio

---

[2] The minimal tree is a primitive of D_M; it is not a primitive of D_S, since the operations of D_S may apply to objects which do not have an internal structure, as is the case for Chomsky's (2001) definition of Merge.

(6) a. *enlight* (tr.) to illumine, to enlighten (archaic)
     b. *lighten* (intr.) to become lighter; brighten, to be luminous; shine, to give
        off flashes of lightning

(7) a. human primate, non human primate
     b. *human primate non, *primate human non, *non primate human
     c. #primate non human, ##human non primate

Furthermore, the fact that no scope ambiguity is observed in morphological
objects including two scope-taking affixes provides additional evidence that morphological relations are asymmetrical only. For example, *undeniable* includes
negation, spelled out as the affix *un-*, and a modal, spelled out by the affix *-able*,
and negation scopes over the modal, but the inverse scope interpretation, where the
modal scopes over the negation, is not available. Thus if *x is undeniable*, then *it is
not possible to deny x*, and it is not the case that *it is possible not to deny x*. Likewise,
scope ambiguity is not observed in compounds including scope-taking elements,
such as quantifiers, which brings further support to the asymmetry of morphological relations. Thus, if *x saw no one*, then *x saw nobody*, and it is not the case that
there is somebody that x did not see. See Di Sciullo (2005a) for discussion.

Compounds are formed of strictly asymmetric relations.[3] This is evidenced by
the fact that the constituents of a compound cannot be reordered without giving
rise to morphological gibberish or to a difference in interpretation, as further
illustrated in (8)–(9).[4,5] Different orders, if interpretable in a given world, yield
different interpretations, which indicates that compounds with the inverse order of
constituents are not derivationally related.

(8) a. a huge [hard disk] /*a huge [disk hard]
     b. a [football] team /* a [ballfoot] team
     c. a [four-star] hotel /* a [star-four] hotel

(9) a. a big [paper bag] /≠ a big [bag paper]
     b. a [blue-grey] sky /≠ a [grey blue] sky
     c. a spectacular [hit-and-run] /≠ a spectacular [run and hit]

---

[3] Asymmetric relations are directional. Thus, if A precedes B, then B does not precede A. If
A dominates B, then B does not dominate A. If A asymmetrically c-commands B, then B does not
asymmetrically c-command A. Asymmetric relations have been shown to play a central role through the
derivations and the interfaces between the grammar and the external systems. Binding relations between
pronouns and their antecedents have also been couched in terms of the asymmetric c-command relation
(see Chomsky 1981, and related works). Conditions on extraction from embedded contexts (islands)
have also been widely discussed since Ross's (1968) seminal work.

[4] Compounds are asymmetrical in terms of formal properties of relations (precedence dominance,
asymmetrical c-command), as defined in note 3.

[5] Our point differs from Bisetto and Scalise's claim (in this volume) that some compounds, e.g.
producer-director, blue-green, pass-fail, mother-child (relations) are symmetrical with respect to their
lexical semantic interpretation. For example, a *producer-director* is someone who is both a producer
and a director. However, there is little empirical evidence for treating conjunction in natural languages
as a symmetrical relation.

Given Asymmetry Theory, the recursive operation of the grammar applying in the morphological workspace combines structures with inherently asymmetric properties. Furthermore, the parts of a compound cannot be reordered in the course of its derivation to the SM interface because in AT, there is no rule that displaces the parts of morphological constituents. Given the recursive operation that combines minimal trees, it follows that asymmetric c-command holds between the parts of a compound. In Kayne's (1994) Antisymmetry framework, this would be a consequence of the Linear Correspondence Axiom, according to which the precedence relation between the terminal elements of a linguistic expression is a function of the asymmetric c-command between the pre-terminal elements of this expression. Thus, the structural relations in compounds cannot be reduced to sisterhood, even though most compounds include two pronounced constituents only.

8.1.1 The medial F-tree

Di Sciullo (2005b) provided empirical evidence for the hypothesis in (10) according to which functional (F) projections asymmetrically relate the parts of compounds.

(10)   F-TREE HYPOTHESIS
        All compounds include an F-tree.

The F-tree is an instance of the minimal tree, which is a primitive of the D_M, and finds its root in the basic asymmetry of morphological relations. The other constituents of a compound may take the whole F-tree as a complement, or may be located in the complement of the F-tree. The head of the functional projection may be legible at the phonetic interface, whereas it is necessarily legible at the semantic interface.

(11)

A first argument in favour of this hypothesis comes from the fact that a root compound (12) instantiates a modification relation, which by standard assumptions maps onto a functional relation (see Cinque 1999, Carlson 2003). Thus, the first constituent of a root compound in English, whether an adjective (A) or a noun (N), occupies the specifier of an F-tree; the second constituent is located in the complement position of the F-tree (13).

(12)   a. floppy disk, pink orange, dark villain
       b. rubber band, ash tray, golf ball, kitchen towel
       c. jet black, ruby red, lily white, steel blue, powder blue

(13)

A second argument in favour of the F-tree hypothesis is that a functional head must be part of the structure of compounds for interface interpretability considerations. Functional heads are part of the closed set of functional elements. Thus, a connective must be SM-legible in compounds such as the ones in (14a), which are not well formed otherwise (14b). Given that a pronounced F-head is part of (14a), an unpronounced F-head is required for the interpretation of compounds such as the ones in (14c). Other unpronounced functional heads than AND and OR may fill the F-head, including WITH (15 a), TO (15b), and IN (15c). Thus, we have the F-heads in (16).

(14)   a. bed-and-breakfast, hit-and-run, truth-or-dare
       b. *bed-breakfast, *hit-run, *truth-dare
       c. learner-driver, student-worker, assistant-teacher

(15)   a. martini soda, gin (and) tonic, vodka soda
       b. Montreal-Boston train, New York-Dubai flight
       c. Paris, Texas; Venice, California; Tucson, Arizona

(16) a.

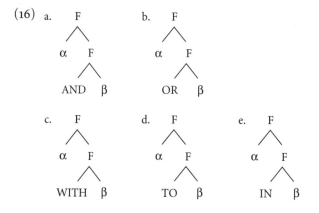

Since there is no modification relation between the members of these compounds, the specifier position of the F-tree cannot be the locus of one of the constituents of the compounds. The only option available is that the first constituent takes the F-tree as its complement and the second constituent occupies the complement position of the F-tree. The F-tree is required at the semantic interface for interpretation. Conjunctions, disjunctions, and prepositions are F-heads providing the semantic relations between the constituents of compounds, whether they are legible at SM (e.g. *hit-and-run, truth-or-dare, martini-with-soda*) or not (e.g. *a win-win situation, a mother-child conversation, martini-soda*). The presence of unpronounced F-heads in compounds brings further support to the analysis of these constructs in terms of asymmetric relations.[6] The F-head bears the semantic features relating the parts of compounds whether or not the F-head is legible at the SM interface.

A third argument for the F-tree hypothesis is that it is also required for SM interpretation. The linking vowel (LV) -o- is found in English and in Romance languages (17–18) in a restricted set of compounds where the first member is a stem. In Modern Greek (MG), LVs are generalized in compounds, provided that there is the proper morphophonological context (19). Compounds with medial LVs are found in many languages, including those in the Hellenic, Germanic, Romance, and Slavic families, as illustrated in (20) with Polish and Russian.

(17) lexico-semantic, syntactico-pragmatic, Judeo-Spanish pronunciation

(18) italo-américain,   judéo-chrétien,   sado-masochiste (Fr)
      'Italo-American',   Judaeo-christian',   'sadomasochist'

(19) a. *pagovuno* (MG)
         pag-o-vun-o
         ice-LV-mountain-NEUT.NOM.SG
         'ice-berg'

      b. *kapnokalierjia*
         kapn-o-kalierg-i-a
         tobacco-LV-cultivat(e)-ion-FEM. NOM.SG
         'tobacco cultivation'

      c. *aspromavro*
         aspr-o-mavr-o
         white-LV-black-NEUT.NOM.SG
         'white and black'

(20) a. *cheboopiekacz* (Polish)
         cheb-o-opiek-acz
         bread-LV-toast-er.NOM
         'toaster'

      b. *vinodelie* (Russian)
         vin-o-delie
         wine-LV-making
         'wine producing'

According to the F-tree hypothesis, an F-head is part of the morphological structure before it is transferred to the phonology workspace (D$_\Phi$). Thus no additional morphophonological operation for the insertion of a linking vowel is

---

[6] See Munn (1992), Thiersch (1993), and Kayne (1994) for discussion on the asymmetric properties of coordination structures. See Sportiche (1999) and Kayne (2004) for the analysis of prepositions as categories generated in the functional field.

needed. The F-head is spelled out by the LV. While the presence of the LV is constrained by the morphophonology, its position in D_Φ is provided by the F-tree, which is transferred from D_M to D_Φ.

Thus, the motivation for the medial F-tree hypothesis is threefold. First, a compound with a modification relation includes the F-tree, since modifiers occupy the specifier of functional projections. Second, the F-tree must be a part of compounds for semantic interface legibility. Third, it must also be a part of compounds for phonetic interface legibility. Since it must be legible at the CI interface, the F-tree is a part of the derivation of compounds even in the cases where it is not legible at the SM interface.

8.1.2 Configurational asymmetries

Configurational asymmetries are observed in compounds. This is predicted by AT, since according to this theory, asymmetric relations are the core relations of morphology.

Given the architecture of AT, morphological and syntactic derivations share the generic properties of the grammar and differ with respect to the instantiation of these properties. Morphology and syntax share the object/adjunct (internal argument/modifier) asymmetry, which maps onto a hierarchical structure where an adjunct (modifier) is higher in the functional projection than the logical object (internal argument), as minimally represented in (21).[7]

(21) a.   b.

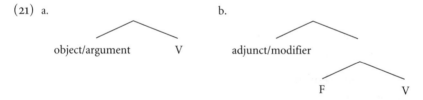

object/argument   V   adjunct/modifier

                                            F   V

As seen in the previous section, the derivation of compounds includes an F-tree contributing to compound-internal asymmetry. One consequence of the minimal F-tree is that it derives the configurational basis of the object/adjunct asymmetry.

The asymmetry between objects and adjuncts has received much attention in works on compound formation (e.g. Baker 1988, Rosen 1989, Rivero 1992, Spencer 1995, Kuiper 1999). A major puzzle concerning compounds is that even though

---

[7] It is generally assumed that modifiers are generated in the extended projection of a head. Thus, they sister-contain the element they modify. The difference between internal arguments and modifiers is a major consideration in syntactic theories that follow Montague's insight of strict compositionality (Montague 1973). Modifiers exhibit different patterns of combinatorial properties from arguments such as objects both in syntax and semantics (see Davidson 1967, Higginbotham 1985, Heim and Kratzer 1998, Cinque 1999). One of the consequences of these studies is the general consensus that syntactic modifiers and arguments must be represented in structurally distinct manners.

Head-movement captures the compound formation of object-verb type (Baker 1988), it cannot account for the presence of adjunct-verb compounds. The derivation of compounds, be they object-verb or adjunct-verb compounds, follows from the application of the operations of AT, as discussed in section 8.2.

English verbal compounds provide direct empirical evidence of the object/adjunct compound-internal asymmetry. In English verbal compounds, the dependent of the verb is either its logical object (22a) or an adjunct (22b) or both (22c). Interestingly, in the latter case, the adjunct must precede the object, cf. (22d).

(22)   a. blood testing
         b. clinical testing
         c. clinical blood testing
         d. *blood clinical testing

Here again, in AT the strict ordering of the constituents of a compound follows from the properties of the operations of the grammar, which apply under asymmetric Agree, as defined in section 8.2. Consequently, modifiers are generated higher than the predicates and their arguments. Given that there is no displacement operation in D_M, asymmetries in dominance relations, such as the one illustrated in (23), are preserved through the derivations.[8]

(23)   [$_F$ clinical F [$_N$ blood testing]]

Assuming, as Chomsky does (various works from 1995 on), that subjects (external arguments) are not adjuncts (contra Kayne 1994), the fact that subjects do not generally merge with verbs in the derivation of compounds brings additional support to the view that the object/adjunct asymmetry, and not another sort of asymmetry, such as the syntactic complement/non-complement asymmetry (Huang 1982; Rizzi 1980; Chomsky 1981, 1995a, 2001), is the crucial asymmetry in the derivation of compounds.

Interestingly, finer-grained linear precedence asymmetries between different sorts of adjuncts are observed in English compounds, suggesting further that asymmetric relations are hard-wired in morphology. The examples in (24) show that an agentive adjunct must follow a spatial-locational adjunct. The examples in (25) illustrate that a sequential/temporal modifier must precede a spatial-locational modifier. Thus we have the morphological configurations in (26). Syntactic adjuncts do not show the restrictions on linear precedence relations observed in compounds: compare (24)–(25) to (27). This also indicates that morphological asymmetries cannot be equated to syntactic asymmetries.

---

[8] Syntactic complement/non-complement asymmetries have been extensively discussed in the literature (Huang 1982, Chomsky 1981, Rizzi 1990, Chomsky 1995a), and different conditions have been proposed to account for the fact that in embedded contexts extractions from complements are more natural than extractions from adjuncts. The complement/non-complement asymmetry cannot be attested on the basis of extraction, since compounds are morphological expressions, and thus, their constituents are not subject to internal Merge (movement), as discussed in Di Sciullo (2005a).

(24) a. expert-tested drug
      b. hospital-expert-tested drug
      c. *expert-hospital-tested drug

(25) a. hospital expert tested drug
      b. bi-annual hospital expert tested drug.
      c. *hospital bi-annual expert tested drug

(26) a. [$_F$ hospital F [$_F$ expert F [$_A$ tested]]]
      b. [$_F$ bi-annual F [$_F$ hospital F [$_F$ expert F [$_A$ tested]]]]

(27) a. This drug has been tested by experts in a hospital.
      b. This drug has been tested in a hospital by experts.
      c. Since 1984, this drug has been tested by experts in a hospital twice a year.
      d. Since 1984, this drug has been tested by experts twice a year in a hospital.

Furthermore, the fact that the direct object, but not the indirect object, may be part of a verbal compound (28) also follows from the theory without further stipulations, such as the First Sister Principle (Roeper and Siegel 1978). If we assume that functional heads including prepositions are generated outside of the verbal projection V (Kayne 2001, Sportiche 1999), and that they are generated higher than the verbal projection, it follows that the indirect object of such verbs cannot be part of a compound. Thus, we have:

(28) a. assignment giving (to students) /*student giving (of assignments)
      b. letter sending (to relatives) /*relative sending (of letters)
      c. book arranging (on shelves) /*shelf arranging (of books)

Given that the recursive operations of the grammar apply under asymmetric Agree, as defined below in (51), to two minimal trees, it follows that a verb may only combine with its direct object. In effect, only the features of the direct object are properly included in the features of the verb, and the indirect object may only combine with a preposition, which is indirectly related to the verb.

Thus, the restrictions on linear precedence and dominance relations between the parts of compounds are predicted by AT, according to which morphological relations are strictly asymmetric.

8.1.3 Compounding and derivation

The asymmetries observed in English compounds correlate with the asymmetries observed in derivational morphology.

According to the morphological types of affixes defined in Di Sciullo (2005a, c), affixes distribute in three morphological types, operator affixes, modifier affixes, and predicate affixes (29). Operator affixes, both internal-bound and external-bound, scope over the other types of affixes, and modifier affixes scope over (sister-containing) predicate affixes, as expressed in the hierarchy in (30). A sample of the affix types is provided in (31)–(33).

(29)   TYPOLOGY OF AFFIXES

Affix type	Determines	Subtypes	
Predicate affix	argument structure	primary	secondary
Modifier affix	aspectual modification	external	internal
Operator affix	operator-variable binding	internal-bound (specifier)	external-bound (head)

(30) $[_{Op}$Op-af $[_{Op}$ Opx $[_{Mod}$ Mod $[_{Mod}$ F $[_{Pred}$ Spec $[_{Pred}$ Pred-af$]]]]]]$

(31)   SAMPLE OF ENGLISH PREDICATE AFFIXES

	AFFIX TYPE	PART OF		EXAMPLES
a.	PRIMARY	Lower-order predicates	N	-er (writer), -ee (advisee), -ion (production)
			V	-ize (vaporize), -ate (alienate), -ify (codify)
b.	SECONDARY	Higher-order predicates	A	-able (readable), -ive (instructive)
			A	-ous (dangerous), -ic (symbolic), -al (accidental)
			ADV	-ly (happily)

(32)   SAMPLE OF ENGLISH MODIFIER AFFIXES

	AFFIX TYPE	PART OF	EXAMPLES
a.	POSITIONAL	N	pre- (pre-university), post- (postgraduate), fore- (forecast), ex- (ex-cop), mid- (midnight)
b.	DIRECTIONAL	N	pro- (pro-rata), anti- (anti-body), counter- (counteroffer), self- (self-respect)
c.	SEQUENTIAL	V	re- (rewind), dis- (discharge), un- (unload)
d.	SPATIAL	V	en- (enthrone), a- (await)
e.	NUMERAL	A	semi- (semi-annual), bi- (bipolar), di- (disyllabic), tri- (tridimensional), quadri- (quadrilateral)
f.	PRIVATIVE	A	un- (unclear), non- (non-permanent), in- (incomprehensible), a- (asocial)

(33)   SAMPLE OF ENGLISH OPERATOR AFFIXES

	AFFIX TYPE	POSITION	PART OF	EXAMPLES
a.	INTERNAL–BOUND	Specifier	D	*th*-words (*the, this, that, those, . . .*)
				wh-words (*who, what, where, when, . . .*)
				pronouns (*him, her*)
			C	complementizers (*th-at*)
b.	EXTERNAL–BOUND	Head	V	*-ed* (*washed*), *-s* (*drives*)
			N	*-s* (*cats, dogs*)
			A	*-most* (*leftmost*)

The configurational asymmetries observed in compounds pattern with the ones observed in affixed forms.

First, the argument/modifier asymmetry attested in compounds follows from the fact that elements in the domain of secondary predicates (adjectival and adverbial modification) asymmetrically c-command the elements in the domain of the primary predicates (primary predicates and their arguments). The facts in (22) illustrate that in a compound, a modifier must precede an argument.

(34)

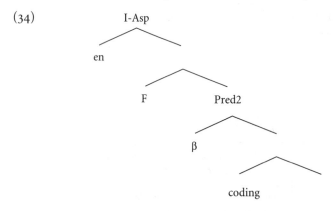

(35)

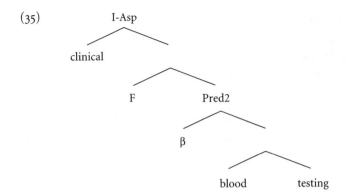

Second, I have shown in Di Sciullo (1997, 1999, 2005a) that derivational affixes present asymmetries in dominance relations. In particular, affixes modifying the aspectual features of the verbal root to which they apply, such as spatial prefixes, are generated lower in the verbal projection tree than affixes modifying aspectual features, without affecting the argument structure of the verbal root, such as the sequential affixes.

French verbs including sequential (iterative and inverse) and spatial (directional and locational) prefixes present asymmetries in linear order, as schematized in (36a), recursivity (36b), and locality effects (36c). Taking af_1 to be external aspect affixes, and af_2 to be internal aspect affixes, the facts in (37)–(40) illustrate the asymmetries. E-prefix must precede I-prefix (37); E-prefix can be iterated, I-prefix cannot (38); I-prefix must be spelled out if E-affix is, when the root does not have I-Asp features (39); I-prefix affects the structure of the v, E-prefix does not (40).

(36)   a. $af_1 > af_2 >$ root /*$af_2 > af_1 >$ root
        b. $af_1^n > af_2 >$ root /* $af_1 > af_2^n >$ root
        c. $af_1 > af_2 >$ root /* $af_1 > af_2 >$ root

(37)   a. *Julie a réemporté/*enréporté les livres.* (Fr)
        'Julie brought the books back again.'

        b. *Lucie a réenfermé/*enrefermé le chat dans la cave.*
        'Lucie locked the cat in the basement again.'

(38)   a. *Marie a rerefait / redéfait le puzzle.*
        'Mary redid/undid the puzzle again.'

        b. **Jane a aa/enemporté/aem/emapporté les livres à Paul.*
        'Jane brought the books to Paul.'

(39)   a. *Il a réembouteillé/*rebouteillé le vin.*
        'He rebottled the wine.'

        b. *Il a réembarqué/*rebarqué sur le bateau.*
        'He embarked on the boat again.'

(40)   a. *Il a (re)dormi pendant des heures.*
           'He slept again for hours.'
        b. *Il a (r)endormi Jean immédiatement.*
           'He made Jean sleep again immediately.'

Given Asymmetry Theory, E-Asp asymmetrically c-commands I-Asp affixes in the aspectual modification domain (41), and the asymmetry illustrated in (25) follows without requiring movement (42).

(41)

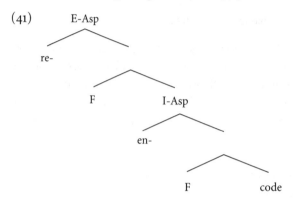

(42)

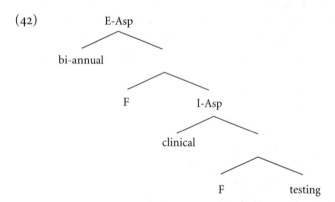

If compounding and derivation in English share basic architectural properties of the language faculty, we expect asymmetries to be found in compounds. The examples above, where the sequential modifier must precede the spatial modifier, show that this prediction is also borne out.

Third, we correctly predict that compounds including elements with operator features are a part of natural languages. Quantifiers such as *somebody* and *everybody* provide the empirical content for this prediction. They are bipartite constituents. They include a functional head, a quantifier, and a complement of the head, namely, a restrictor to the variable internally bound by the quantifier (operator):

(43)

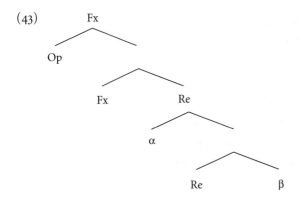

(44)

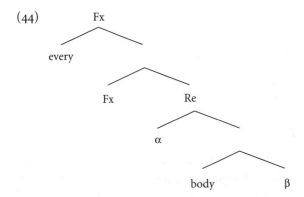

Quantifier structures are impenetrable: their parts cannot be separated by other material, including adjectives. This is not the case for their phrasal counterparts, as illustrated in (45) and (46). Furthermore, their parts cannot be separated by other material, including adjectives, whereas this is not so for DPs. Furthermore, their semantic interpretation is the result of the composition of a small set of semantic features, including [+human] and [+thing]. Thus, in (47), *someone* may only refer to a set of humans, whereas this is not the case for the syntactic counterpart in (48), which can refer to a set of humans as well as to a set of things. See Di Sciullo and Landman (2007) for discussion.

(45) a. [Everybody] left.
      b. [Everybody] nice left.
      c. *[Every nice body] left.

(46) a. [Every student] left.
      b. *[Every student] nice left.
      c. Every [nice student] left.

(47) a. I saw someone.
      b. He discovered someone nice.
      c. Here is somebody important.

(48) a. I saw some nice ones.
      b. He discovered some nice ones.
      c. Here is some important (body of) work.

To summarize, in this section I have provided additional evidence that compounds are domains where strict asymmetric relations hold. In the next section, I provide the derivation of compounds, given the operations of Asymmetry Theory.

8.2 Deriving compounds with Asymmetry Theory

8.2.1 The operations of D_M

Asymmetry Theory extends the Derivation-by-Phase model (Chomsky 2001, 2004) to a fully parallel model, where the derivation of linguistic expressions takes place in parallel workspaces, each one being an instantiation of the generic properties of the grammar.[9]

Deriving compounds in a different workspace from phrases provides an architectural account for the fact that these expressions have different derivational properties, as well as different interface properties, including linear order, stress assignment, and compositionality. For example, in English, the Nuclear Stress Rule (Chomsky and Halle 1968) places main stress on the rightmost constituent of a syntactic phrase, whereas the Compound Stress Rule stresses the left member of

---

[9] The generic properties include the distinction between interpretable and uninterpretable features, and a set of generic operations, applying under Agree (46), as well as an Interface Interpretability Condition requiring that only interpretable elements in an asymmetric relation are legible at the interfaces. The generic operations are the following:

(i) Shift (α, β): Given two objects α and β, Shift (α, β) derives a new object δ projected from α.
(ii) Link (α, β): Given two objects α and β, α sister-containing β, Link (α, β) derives the object (α, β), where α and β are featurally related.
(iii) Flip (T): Given α Minimal tree α in D_1, Flip (T) derives a mirror image of α at PF.

The operation in (i) is the generic form of the essential operation of recursive systems. This operation is asymmetric since only one object may project its label. The operation in (ii) is the generic operation deriving dependencies between features. This operation is directional, thus asymmetric, contrary to the coindexing operation, which is bidirectional (see Higginbotham 1985 on the directional properties of dependencies). The operation in (iii) contributes to the linearization of the constituents and applies in the phonological workspace D_Φ. Independent evidence in favour of this operation is provided in Williams (1994) and in Wurmbrand (2003b). The operations in (i)–(iii) have different instantiations in D_S and D_M.

a compound. Compounds also generally exhibit opacity with respect to syntactic and semantic operations, as discussed in various works including Di Sciullo and Williams (1987), Di Sciullo (1992b, 2005a). Their parts cannot be questioned or passivized, and the antecedent of a pronominal anaphor cannot be a nominal element included in a compound.[10]

The operations of D_M, (49) and (50), apply to minimal trees under Agree (51) and recursively derive morphological domains legible at the interfaces. The operations of D_Φ, including (52), derive morphophonological domains legible at the SM interface. The morpho-semantic properties of morphological objects are legible at the CI interface, whereas their morphophonological properties are legible at the SM interface.

(49) M-Shift (T_1, T_2): Given two trees T_1 and T_2, M-Shift (T_1, T_2) is the tree obtained by attaching T_2 to the complement of T_1.

(50) M-Link (T): Given a tree T containing a position $\delta 1$ and a position $\delta 2$, such that $\delta 1$ sister-contains $\delta 2$ and $\delta 1$ agrees with $\delta 2$, M-Link (T) is the tree obtained by creating a featural relation between $\delta 1$ and $\delta 2$.

(51) Agree ($\varphi 1$, $\varphi 2$): Given two sets of features $\varphi 1$ and $\varphi 2$, Agree holds between $\varphi 1$ and $\varphi 2$, iff $\varphi 1$ properly includes $\varphi 2$.

(52) M-Flip (T): Given a minimal tree T such that the Spec of T has no PF features, M-Flip (T) is the tree obtained by creating the mirror image of T.

Given Asymmetry Theory, the morphological scope relations are derived in D_M and are legible at the CI interface. The ordering of the morphological constituents is derived in D_Φ by the operation in (52). This operation derives the effect of Head movement, which can thus be dispensed with.[11]

English compounds are not derived by Merge, as defined in (53), the generalized transformation that builds syntactic structure bottom-up by combining two autonomous subtrees as daughters of a single node. This operation applies only in the derivation of syntactic objects. It does not apply in the derivation of morphological objects.

---

[10] See also Kastovsky (1981) and Lieber (1992a) on anaphoric islands.

[11] Compounds have been argued to be X^0 domains derived in the syntax by Head-movement (Baker 1988; Lieber 1992a; Roeper, Snyder, and Hiramatsu 2002, among other works). A major puzzle concerning compounds is that even though Head-movement derives object-verb compounds (Baker 1988), it cannot account for adjunct-verb compounds. The derivation of compounds, be they object-verb or adjunct-verb, follows from the application of the same recursive structure-building operation along the lines of Asymmetry Theory. If compounds form a natural class, it is unlikely that they are derived by different operations, e.g., external merge and internal merge for object-verb compounds, and external merge only for adjunct-verb compounds. Furthermore, Head-movement is not a possible operation in the Minimalist Program. One reason is that it violates Chomsky's (2000) Extension Condition, according to which operations may only expand trees upwards. Another reason is that while it is assumed that XP traces/copies are interpreted as semantic categories of type <e> (Portner and Partee 2002), it is not clear how the trace/copy left by Head-movement is interpreted at the CI interface (LF). Furthermore, Head-movement cannot derive compounds including XP structure, and such compounds are found cross-linguistically. Thus, this operation faces theoretical and empirical problems. According to AT, Head-movement does not apply in the derivation of compounds because it is not a possible operation of the grammar.

(53) Merge: Target two syntactic objects α and β, form a new object Γ {α,β}, the
      label LB of Γ(LB(Γ)) = LB(α) or LB(β).   [(Chomsky 1995a)]

In Chomsky (2004), Merge subdivides into external and internal Merge. External
Merge (53) applies to two syntactic objects and forms a new object; internal Merge
(Move) displaces an already merged syntactic object. While external Merge is the
indispensable operation of recursive systems, Move (54) implements the displace-
ment property of natural languages. Uninterpretable features are checked under
Agree (55), which plays a central role in both external Merge and internal Merge.

(54) Move: Select a target α, select a category β that is moved, β must have
      uninterpretable features, α must be phi-complete to delete the uninterpret-
      able feature of the pied-piped matching element β, merge β in Spec-LB(α),
      delete the uninterpretable feature of β.

(55) Agree

      α > β
      └──┘

      Agree (α, β), where α is a probe and β is a matching goal, and '>' is a
      c-command relation. Matching is feature identity. The probe seeks a matching
      goal within the domain XP, generated by the probe. Matching of probe and
      goal induces Agree.

As defined above, Move (internal Merge) and Agree cannot apply in the derivation of compounds because compounds are not syntactic XP domains.

According to Asymmetry Theory, both syntactic and morphological domains
are derived by the recursive operations of the grammar. The primitives and the
implementation of these operations differ, depending on whether the derivation
takes place in the syntactic or in the morphological workspace. In the syntactic
derivation, the recursive operation combines two autonomous subtrees as daughters of a single node, whereas in the morphological derivation, it combines two
subtrees by substituting one tree to the complement position of the other.

In Asymmetry Theory, the properties of morphological expressions including
compounds, such as strict precedence, strict scope, and atomicity, are not the
consequence of construction-specific rules or conditions, but follow from the
properties of the computational system. The model does not reduce morphology
to syntax, while it allows similarities between the two subsystems to follow from
their parallel architecture. The crucial difference between D_M and D_S is that D_M
manipulates asymmetric relations only.

From the operations of Asymmetry Theory, it follows that compounds are
virtually infinite expressions. In fact, recursive compounds are found cross-
linguistically. For example, recursive compounds are found in French as well
as in English, e.g. *acides aminés, acides aminés alpha* (Fr), cf. *amino-acids, alpha-
amino-acids* (but see Roeper, Snyder, and Hiramatsu 2002 for a different view).

Moreover, since the recursive operations of D_M apply to minimal or derived trees, and a tree has a head by definition, it follows that headedness is a property of all compounds. The head of a morphological object with respect to a feature F is the highest sister-containing head M marked for F features.[12, 13]

8.2.2 Morphological phases

The notion of 'phase' was introduced in Chomsky (2001) as a way to account for the cyclicity of syntactic operations, which is required for optimal computation. It is a local domain where uninterpretable features are checked and deleted in order to meet the Interface Interpretability Condition. The phase has an F-XP configuration, it is impenetrable, and it is isolable at the interfaces. The syntactic phase is propositional (vP, CP), and it is a complete functional complex.

In the Derivation-by-phase model, a constructed syntactic object is sent to the two interfaces by the operation Transfer, and what is transferred is no longer accessible to later mappings to the interfaces. The phase is part of the principles of efficient computation, since it reduces the computational load in the derivations. The complement of a phase is sent to Spell-Out and thus is no longer accessible for further computation – only the head and the edge (the specifier and the adjuncts) of a phase are.

I argued in Di Sciullo (2004, 2007a) that morphological derivations also proceed by phase, which contributes to reducing the computational complexity arising in the morphological derivation.[14]

---

[12] According to (i), a morphological object has more than one head. According to (ii), the head$_F$ is determined derivationally. Given (ii), the head of a compound may in some cases be legible only by the CI system, but not by the SM system.

(i) DEFINITION OF 'head$_F$' (read: head with respect to the feature F)
    The head$_F$ of a word is the rightmost element of the word marked for the feature F.
                                                         (Di Sciullo and Williams 1987: 26)
(ii) DEFINITION OF *head$_F$* OF A MORPHOLOGICAL DOMAIN
    The head$_F$ of a morphological domain D_i is the highest sister-containing head of D_i marked for the feature F.

                                                         (Di Sciullo 2005a: 42)

Thus, in *postage stamp*, *stamp* is the Head$_{category}$ because it is the highest sister-containing head with categorial features. In *paper cutter*, the Head$_{category}$ is the affix *-er*, and in French *coupe-papier*, the Head$_{category}$ occupies the same position as in the equivalent English construction, but does not have legible features at the SM interface.

[13] Given the poverty of the stimulus in language acquisition, the child develops a grammar on the basis of his genetic endowment. Headedness might very well be a property of all compounds, even though there is no direct evidence of headedness in some compounds. If this is the case, then the traditional distinction between endocentric and exocentric compounds can be dispensed with.

[14] See Di Sciullo and Fong (2005) for the computational implementation of the model, and for an example of the reduction of the derivational complexity with cases such as *computerizable*.

Morphological and syntactic phases are parallel.[15] Similar to a syntactic phase, a morphological phase includes an F-XP configuration (see Di Sciullo 1996). Second, the Head$_F$ of a morphological domain is the highest sister-containing head marked for the feature F (see Di Sciullo 2005a). Third, an affix asymmetrically selects the head of its complement (see Di Sciullo 1997, 2005a, and also Collins 2002 for syntactic selection).

Like a syntactic phase, a morphological phase is subject to the Interpretability Condition. According to Chomsky (2001), vP is a strong phase and thus opaque to extraction at the CP level. The only position from which extraction can take place is from the head and the edge (the specifier and the adjoined positions) of the phase. However, the morphological phase is subject to a stronger impenetrability condition than the syntactic phase. The edge of a morphological phase is accessible to the next phase up for uninterpretable feature-checking without leading to movement. Furthermore, a morphological phase is isolable at the interfaces, whereas its parts are not.

The locality restrictions on active feature checking, such as the ones illustrated in (56), follow from a morphological derivation by local domains. The operations of D_M derive morphological domains, where active features must be checked (deleted/valued) before the domains reach the interfaces in order to satisfy the Interface Interpretability Condition, which requires that each element be interpretable at the interfaces.

(56) a. [$_{Asp-Ph}$ un- Asp [$_{Pred-Ph}$ [α] -able [[β] deny [[δ]]]]]

    b. [$_{Op-Ph}$ [γ] -s [$_{Pred-Ph}$ [α] -er [β] produce [δ]]]]

    c. Ph1 Spell-Out → [[β] produce [δ]]
       Ph2 Spell-Out → [$_{Pred-Ph}$ [α] -er [[β] produce [δ]]]
       Ph3 Spell-Out → [$_{Op-Ph}$ [γ] -s [$_{Pred-Ph}$ [α] -er [[β] produce [δ]]]]

---

[15] The notion of cyclic domain has been recently discussed in terms of Chomsky's (2001) notion of phase, Uriagereka's (1999, 2003) notion of Multiple Spell-Out, and Collins's (2002) notion of phase as a saturated constituent. See Adger (2003) and Holmberg (2001) for phonology, and Chierchia (2001) and Nissenbaum (2000) for semantics. A phase has the following properties: it is an F-XP configuration, it is subject to Impenetrability, and it is isolable at the interfaces (Chomsky 2001, Legate 2003, Adger 2003, Matushansky 2003). According to Chomsky (2001), a phase is a propositional category (vP, CP). Chomsky (2000) provides evidence that syntactic phases are propositional on the basis of examples such as

[John [t thinks [Tom will [t win the prize]]]]
and
[which article is there some hope [α that John will read t$_{wh}$]]

in which the lower propositional domain constitutes a domain of cyclic interpretation and spell-out. It has been shown that other categories besides propositions are syntactic phases; see Adger (2003) for DPs and Legate (2003) for VPs.

For example, in (56a), the head of a Pred-domain is accessible to checking by an element in the Asp-domain, namely by the privative affix *un-*, but the complement of the Pred-domain is not.[16] The derived expression is correctly interpreted as a derived adjective, and not as a derived verb. In (56b), the flectional affix *-s* has two values: the plural inflection of nominal categories, and the third person singular present tense inflection of verbal categories. The head of a Pred-affix is accessible to operations from the next domain up, i.e. the Op-domain, but its complement is not. The derived morphological expression is correctly interpreted as a plural derived nominal, and not as the nominalization of a tensed verb.

Assuming that the material in the sister position of the head of a phase is spelled out and transferred to the interfaces, roots with their feature structures would be transferred to the interfaces first, independently from the full inflected expressions of which they are a part, spelled out subsequently, and no longer accessible to the computation (56c). Derivational complexity may also arise in the derivation of compounds, and morphological phases contribute to the efficiency of the computation. Recursive compounds are also derived by phases, where active (uninterpretable) features are deleted locally within and across phases. A feature of the complement of the lower phase, Ph_1, cannot enter into an Agree relation with a feature of the higher phase, Ph_2. Likewise, the parts of compounds are transferred to the interfaces independently (57).

(57)   a. $[_{Pred-Ph}$ alpha F $[_{Pred-Ph}$ hydroxi F $[\alpha$ acid $\beta]]]$

   b. Ph1 Spell-Out → $[\alpha$ acid $\beta]$
       Ph2 Spell-Out → $[_{Pred-Ph}$ hydroxi F $[\alpha$ acid $\beta]]$
       Ph3 Spell-Out → $[_{Pred-Ph}$ alpha F $[_{Pred-Ph}$ hydroxi F $[\alpha$ acid $\beta]]]$

According to Asymmetry Theory, the morphological phases are not determined categorically, but they are determined derivationally. A minimal morphological domain is the result of the application of first Merge, defined as in (53). A maximal morphological domain is a domain where the operation in (50), checking active features and relating interpretable features, may no longer apply. The morphological phases are defined within the limits of the Pred-domain, the Asp-domain, and the Op-domain, and uninterpretable feature-checking/elimination and feature-sharing take place within and across adjacent morphological phases.[17]

---

[16] Given the featural definitions in (58), in (56a) the aspectual feature $[-F_1]$ of the modifier affix *un-* is checked by the aspectual feature $[+F_1]$ of the secondary predicate affix *-able*, and in (56b), the $[-Re]$ feature of the inflection operator *-s* is checked by the $[+Re]$ feature of the *-er* affix.

[17] See also Marantz (2003), where abstract functional categories, including small v and small n, head the nominal and verbal phases, where each functional complex is a morphological phase.

In AT, feature-checking applies to pairs of contra-valued features and results in the deletion/valuing of an active feature, that is, the negative value of a feature.[18] The morphological features, including the Argument $[\pm A]$ and Predicate $[\pm \text{Pred}]$ features, occupy the head and the dependents (specifier and complement positions) of the morphological trees, and are independently needed in the grammar. The combination of these features defines the morphological categories as follows:

(58)   a. Pred-domain: argument: $[+A, -\text{Pred}]$, primary predicate: $[-A, +\text{Pred}]$, secondary predicate: $[+A, +\text{Pred}]$, expletive: $[-A, -\text{Pred}]$

   b. Asp-domain: external modifier: $[+F_E, -F_I]$, internal modifier: $[-F_E, +F_I]$, bare event: $[+Ev, -F_I]$, participant: $[-Ev, -F_I]$

   c. Op-domain: operator: $[-X, -\text{Re}]$, variable: $[+X, -\text{Re}]$, restrictor: $[-X, +\text{Re}]$, dependents: $[-X, -\text{Re}]$

Interpretable features are also part of the morphological derivations. These features are the positive values of the features above, the referential $[+R]$ feature for nominal categories of Di Sciullo and Williams (1987), the terminus $[+T]$ and the subinterval features $[+S]$ for event- delimiting categories, as defined in Di Sciullo (1997), and the small set of substantive features, namely $[+\text{human}]$, $[+\text{thing}]$, $[+\text{manner}]$, $[+\text{time}]$, $[+\text{place}]$, $[+\text{reason}]$, entering in the semantics for functional words, as defined in Di Sciullo (2005a).

The converging derivations yield interpretable morphological expressions, whereas derivations that do not converge, e.g. interface expressions with surviving active features, yield morphological gibberish. In the next section, I illustrate the active feature-checking in the derivations of compounds instantiating a modification relation (root compounds), a predicate–argument relation (verbal compounds), and an operator–restrictor relation (functional words).

I thus take a morphological phase to be a unit of morphological computation that starts with a morphological numeration and ends with Spell-Out. A morphological phase is a domain for cyclic interpretation and Spell-Out. It is a subsection of a morphological derivation.

8.2.3 Derivations

8.2.3.1 *Root compounds*

Root compounds, such as *blueprint, paper bag,* and *dark blue*, instantiate a modification relation. Given AT, the non-head is a modifier (secondary predicate) of the head and thus occupies the specifier of a minimal tree headed by the functional head F:

---

[18] Morphological and syntactic checking applies to different features and has different effects. While active syntactic features are associated with syntactic categories, such as Tense and Complementizer, active morphological features are associated with morphological categories such as argument (A) and predicate (Pred). Furthermore, syntactic checking may lead to overt movement, whereas this is not the case for morphological checking.

(59)   [$_{Mod}$ Root$_2$ F [$_{Pred}$ Root$_1$]]

(60)

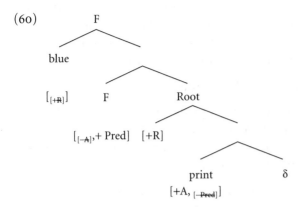

The root (primary predicate) merges with the modifier by the operation in M-Shift. This operation applies under Agree, defined in terms of the proper subset relation. Thus the features of the modifier must be a superset of the features of the modified root for a convergent derivation. Checking takes place, and the uninter-pretable [−A] and [−Pred] features are deleted. Furthermore, M-Link creates a link between the two [+R] features, thereby directionally identifying the referen-tial [+R] feature of the modifier *blue* to the referential feature of the head$_{category}$ of the construct, which is *print*, since it is the highest head with categorical features. The modifier *blue* has categorical features, but it is not a head (likewise for the modifier *paper* in *paper bag* and the modifier *dark* in *dark blue*). Thus, a root compound has only one referent even though it includes two [+R] roots.

(61) Numeration: < [blue [F $_{[−A, +Pred]}$ [χ]], [[+R] [print$_{[+A, −Pred]}$ δ]]] >
                            [+R]

(62) D$_M$: 1. [blue [F$_{[−A, +Pred]}$ [χ]]]
                     [+R]

        2. [[+R] [print $_{[+A, −Pred]}$ [δ]]]

        3. [blue [F$_{[−A, +Pred]}$ [[+R] print$_{[+A, −Pred]}$ [δ]]]]   by M-Shift
                     [+R]

        4. [blue [F$_{[−A̶, +Pred]}$ [[+R] print$_{[+A, −Pred]}$ [δ]]]]   by M-Link
                     [+R]

        5. [[blue [F$_{[−A̶, +Pred]}$ [[+R̶] print$_{[+A, −Pred]}$ [δ]]]]   by M-Link
                     [+R̶]

        6. [[blue [F$_{[−A̶, +Pred]}$ [[+R̶] print$_{[+A, −Pred̶]}$ [δ]]]]   by M-Link
                     [+R̶]

The result of the derivation in D$_M$ (i.e. step 6 in (62)) qualifies as a morphological phase and thus can be transferred to D$_Σ$, where it is interpreted by the semantic rules as a predicate, a category of semantic type $<e, t>$, and to D_Φ, where M-Flip does not apply, since the edge of the phase (the specifier of the F-tree) has SM-features, that is, *blue* occupies this position. The transferred phase in (63) has no formal or semantic features, but only phonetic features interpretable at the SM interface, where only phonetic, but not formal or semantic features are interpreted.

(63) D_Φ: 1. [[] [blue [F [] print []]]]   by Transfer from D_M to D_Φ

Given the feature matrices in (58a), we correctly predict that expletives, such as *it* or *there*, cannot be part of compounds because uninterpretable [−Pred] features will be left unchecked (see (64)) as they reach the CI interface, and the expression will fail to satisfy the Interface Interpretability Condition.

(64)   a. I saw a nice blueprint of the Venice conference poster.
       b. *I saw a nice it-print of the Venice conference poster.
       c. *I saw a nice there-print of the Venice conference poster.

(65)   a. $[_F it\ F_{[-A,\ -Pred]}\ [_{Pred}\ print_{[+A,\ -Pred]}]]$
       b. $[_F there\ F_{[-A,\ -Pred]}\ [_{Pred}\ print_{[+A,\ -Pred]}]]$

The derivation of English root compounds brings additional evidence to the hypothesis that active feature-checking applies in morphological domains.

8.2.3.2 *Verbal compounds*

Verbal compounds, such as *chess player*, instantiate a predicate–argument relation, and they may also instantiate a modification relation, as in *dirty player* (i.e. someone who plays dirty). I focus on the first subtype.

Given AT, in a deverbal compound the bare noun occupies the complement position of the tree headed by the base verb, and the affix occupies the head of the functional projection containing the verbal structure, (66), (67).

(66) $[_F\ \alpha\ af\ [_{Pred}\ \beta\ [root\ \delta]]]$

(67)

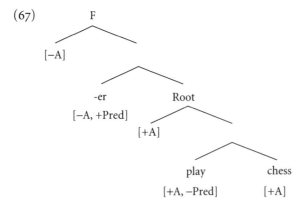

We illustrate the derivation of verbal compounds with the derivation of *chess player* in (69), concentrating on the uninterpretable [−A] feature located in the non-head position of the nominal affix. Given the numeration in (68), the first step in the derivation is the transfer of the minimal tree headed by the verb *play* from the numeration to the morphological workspace. The second step is the transfer of the minimal tree headed by the noun *chess*. Given that the features of *play* properly include the features of *chess*, M-Shift applies and yields the representation in step 3. The next step is the transfer of the minimal tree headed by the primary (Pred₁) affix *-er* to the workspace. M-Shift applies at step 5, attaching the structure obtained at step 3 to the complement position of the nominal affix. Agree is satisfied since a primary affix may take a root as its argument. In the last step of the derivation, M-Link applies to the structure obtained at step 5, and the uninterpretable [−A] feature of the nominal affix is deleted by the closest [+A] feature.[19] At Step 6, M-Link applies again, given that the Pred₁ affix *-er* is lexically determined to saturate the external argument of the verbal root with which it merges. This can be seen by the fact that an adjunct *by*-phrase may not be interpreted as an agent (70).

(68)   Numeration: $< [[-A] \text{ [-er } [+A]]], [[+A] \text{ play } [+A]], [\alpha \text{ [chess } \beta]] >$

(69) D_M: 1. $[[+A] \text{ play } [+A]]$
             2. $[\alpha \text{ [chess } \beta]]$
             3. $[[+A] \text{ play } [\alpha \text{ [chess } \beta]]]$ by M-Shift
             4. $[[-A] \text{ [-er } [+A]]]$
             5. $[[-A] \text{ [-er } [[+A] \text{ play } [[\alpha \text{ [chess } \beta]]]]]]$ by M-Shift
             6. $[[-\cancel{A}] \text{ [-er } [[+A] \text{ play } [[\alpha \text{ [chess } \beta]]]]]]$ by M-Link
             7. $[[-\cancel{A}] \text{ [-er } [[+\cancel{A}] \text{ play } [[\alpha \text{ [chess } \beta]]]]]]$ by M-Link

(70)   a. A chess player came in.
       b. The chess player by John.
       c. John's chess player.

The linear order of the constituents is derived in the D_Φ workspace by the transfer of the result of the derivation that took place in D_M, namely step 1 in (71), and by the application of M-Flip, namely step 2 in (71). M-Flip applies in this derivation since there are no SM-legible features at the edge of the phase (i.e. in the specifier of the affixal head).

(71) D_Φ: 1. $[[] \text{ -er } [[] \text{ play } [\text{chess}]]]$ by Transfer from D_M to D_Φ
             2. $[[\text{chess}] \text{ play } [\text{-er}]]$ by M-Flip

The derivation of English verbal compounds is based on the same operations as the ones applying in the derivation of deverbal nouns, such as *player* ((72)–(74)).

---

[19] A [−A] feature occupies the edge of the phase, since *-er*, unlike a causative affix, does not have a [+A] feature in this position.

The argument feature of the root can be saturated in the morphological derivation. The examples in (75) show that it can be saturated in the derivation of a compound, but it cannot be saturated naturally (see (75c), which is not fully acceptable to my informants) in the derivation of a syntactic phrase. This is not the case for event nominals however, such as *destruction*, e.g. *the destruction of the city.*

(72)   Numeration: $< [[-A] [-er [A]]], [[+A] [play [+A]]] >$

(73) D_M: 1. $[[+A] \text{ play } [+A]]$
              2. $[[-A] [-er [+A]]]$
              3. $[[-A] [-er [[+A] \text{ play } [+A]]]]$ by M-Shift
              4. $[[-\mathrm{A}] [-er [[+\mathrm{A}] \text{ play } [+A]]]]$ by M-Link

(74) D_Φ: 1. $[[] -er [[] \text{ play } []]]$ by Transfer from D_M to D_Φ
              2. $[\text{play } [] [-er]]$ by M-Flip

(75)   a. John plays chess.
       b. John is a chess player.
       c. (?)John is a player of chess.

Given the feature matrices in (58a), we correctly predict that expletive pronouns, such as *it* or *there* (76), cannot be part of verbal compounds either because uninterpretable $[-A]$ features will be left unchecked, see (77), as they reach the CI interface, and the expression will fail to satisfy the Interface Interpretability Condition.

(76)   a. *John is a great it-player.
       b. *Mary enjoys there-players a lot.
       c. *It-players are hermits.

(77)   a. $[_F \text{ it } F_{[-A, \ -\mathrm{Pred}]} [\text{Pred } \text{-er } _{[-A, \ +\mathrm{Pred}]} \cdots]]$
       b. $[_F \text{ there } F_{[-A, \ -\mathrm{Pred}]} [\text{Pred } \text{-er } _{[-A, \ +\mathrm{Pred}]} \cdots]]$

The restrictions imposed by the nominal affix -*er* on the head of its complement are met in the derivation in (73), and asymmetric Agree holds between the selector and the selectee. The active $[-A]$ feature occupies the specifier position of the affix -*er*, and it is checked/deleted by the $[+A]$ feature of the specifier of the root *play*. However, in the derivation in (79), the active $[-A]$ feature of -*er* cannot be checked by the $[+A]$ feature of the root, since *arrive* has a $[-A]$ feature in its specifier position.[20] Thus M-Link does not apply in the derivation. Thus, the derivation in (79) yields morphological gibberish (#*arriver*). This expression fails to satisfy FI at the interface, since it includes active features.

(78)   Numeration: $< [[-A] [-er [A]]], [[-A] \text{ arrive } [+A]] >$

---

[20] Unaccusative verbs such as *arrive* have one argument feature only, and it is located in the complement of their minimal tree.

(79) D_M: 1. $[[-A]$ arrive $[+A]]$
            2. $[[-A]$ $[-er$ $[+A]]]$
            3. $[[-A]$ $[-er$ $[[-A]$ arrive $[+A]]]]$ by M-Shift

(80) D_Φ: 1. $[[]$ -er $[[]$ arrive $[]]]$ by Transfer from D_M to D_Φ
            2. $[[arrive$ $[]][-er]]$ by M-Flip

As discussed in Di Sciullo (2005a), *arriver* is possible within verbal compounds including a modification relation, as is the case in the examples in (81), resulting from a Google search. This fact suggests that compounding interacts with derivation in the derivation of morphological domains. Furthermore, it indicates that in compounds including modification relations, the modifier is higher than the secondary and the primary predicate domains; see (82), including examples with *depart* and *fall*, which are also unaccusative.

(81) a. Are you an early arriver or late arriver Movie Forum?
      b. The late arriver definitely needs counselling, but not on class time.
      c. The late arriver is perceived as less sociable and less competent than early or on-time arrivers.

(82) [early F $[[-A]$ -er $[[-A]$ arrive $[+A]]]]$
      [late F $[[-A]$ -er $[[-A]$ depart $[+A]]]]$
      [easy F $[[-A]$ -er $[[-A]$ fall $[+A]]]]$

In Di Sciullo (2005a) I provided an analysis of these structures in terms of argument structure type-shifting. Argument structure type-shifting is the structural face of semantic type-shifting. M-Link applies in (83) and relates the features of the F-head to the features of the verb, bringing about a change in the argument structure of the verbal head, which shifts from an unaccusative to an unergative argument structure (83), thus satisfying the requirements imposed by the nominal affix -*er* on its complement. The uninterpretable $[-A]$ feature in the specifier of this affix is deleted by entering into an Agree relation with its new closest $[+A]$ feature.

(83) [early F $[[-A]$ -er $[[+A]$ arrive $[-A]]]]$
      [late F $[[-A]$ -er $[[+A]$ depart $[-A]]]]$
      [easy F $[[-A]$ -er $[[+A]$ fall $[-A]]]]$

The derivation of verbal compounds brings additional evidence to the hypothesis that active feature-checking applies in morphological domains. See Di Sciullo (2007a) for evidence from deverbal nouns and adjectives in Italian.

8.2.3.3 *Functional compounds*

Functional words, such as determiners and quantifiers, instantiate an operator–restrictor relation, where the operator occupies the edge of the morphological phase, the variable occupies the head of the F-tree, and the restrictor occupies the head of the complement of that phase, as illustrated in (84), (85), with *everybody.*

(84)   [$_{Fx}$ Root$_2$ F [$_{Re}$ Root$_1$]]

(85)

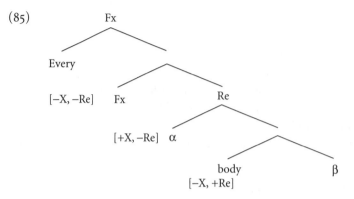

According to AT, quantifiers, as well as other functional words, have an internal morphological structure, derived in D$_M$, as can be seen in the derivation in (87)–(88), given the numeration in (86). M-Flip does not apply at D$_\Phi$ (87), since *every* occupies the edge of the phase.

(86)   Numeration: $<$ [every [F [χ]]], [[β] body [δ]] $>$

(87)   D$_M$:   1. [every$_{[-X, -Re]}$ [F$_{[+X, -Re]}$ [χ]]]
            2. [[α] [[body$_{[-X, +Re]}$ [δ]]]]
            3. [every$_{[-X, -Re]}$ [F$_{[+X, -Re]}$ [[β] body$_{[-X, +Re]}$ [δ]]]]
              by M-Shift
            4. [every$_{[-\cancel{X}, -\cancel{Re}]}$ [F$_{[+X, -\cancel{Re}]}$ [[β] body$_{[-\cancel{X}, +Re]}$ [δ]]]]   by M-Link

(88)   D$_\Phi$:   1. [every F [body []]]   by Transfer from D$_M$ to D$_\Phi$

We correctly predict that operators cannot merge with predicates or arguments in the morphological derivation; they may only merge with restrictors, cf. (89a) vs. (89b). Thus, *every house* and *every print* are not morphological domains, they are syntactic domains, whereas *everyone* and *everybody* are morphological domains. They qualify as morphological phases, they have an F-XP structure, and they are strongly impenetrable. For example, an adjective cannot occupy an intermediate position. Their stress pattern is typical of compound stress, and their interpretation is fixed, as illustrated above in (45)–(48).

(89)   a. [$_{Op}$ every$_{[-X, -Re]}$ [F $_{[+X, -Re]}$ [$_{Res}$ body$_{[-X, +Re]}$]]]
      b. [$_{Op}$ every$_{[-X, -Re]}$ [F $_{[+X, -Re]}$ [$_{Pred}$ house$_{[-A, +Pred]}$]]]

The derivation of functional compounds also provides evidence in support of the hypothesis that active feature-checking applies in morphological domains.

8.2.4 Summary

Morphological phases are the local domains of morphological computation. The locality of active morphological feature-checking makes morphological domains parallel to syntactic domains. The strong impenetrability of morphological phases, and the fact that they are not of the same semantic types (e.g. <e, t> vs. < t >), make them different semantic objects. Furthermore, as mentioned earlier, syntactic and morphological phases are not the same type of phonological object, considering the fact that they are subject to different stress rules, which, according to Asymmetry Theory, have parallel derivations.

8.3 Interpretability

Recent works on the language faculty (Hauser, Chomsky, and Fitch 2002; Chomsky 2004) suggest that the narrow syntactic component of the language faculty (FLN) satisfies conditions of highly efficient computation, and could be close to an optimal solution to the problem of linking the sensorimotor (SM) and the conceptual-intentional (CI) systems.[21] In other words, the language system would provide a near-optimal solution that satisfies the Interface Interpretability Condition given the central role of asymmetry in the derivations.

(90) INTERFACE INTERPRETABILITY CONDITION
      Only interpretable elements in asymmetric relations are legible at the
      interfaces.   (Di Sciullo 2005a: 34)

According to Asymmetry Theory, language is the best solution to the interface legibility conditions because the asymmetry of linguistic expressions matches with the asymmetry of the external systems. The Interface Interpretability Condition relates to work in physics and biology/genetics (Thompson 1992, Hornos and Hornos 1993, among others), according to which asymmetry breaks the symmetry of natural laws, and brings about stability in an otherwise unstable system. In this perspective, Jenkins (2000) suggests that word order is an expression of the symmetry-breaking phenomenon. I developed a model of the language faculty where asymmetric relations are hard-wired, the operations of the morphology apply to objects that are already asymmetric, and their asymmetry is preserved through the derivation. It

---

[21] The FLN corresponds to overt syntax and differs from the language faculty in a broad sense (FLB), which includes the external systems, CI and SM.

is likely that, at the interfaces, the asymmetric relations between the interpretable elements of linguistic expressions enable contact with the external systems.

Fiorentino and Poeppel (2007) investigate morphophonological decomposition in compounds using visual lexical decision with simultaneous magnetoencephalography (MEG), comparing compounds, single words, and pseudo-morphemic foils. According to Fiorentino and Poeppel, the behavioural differences suggest internally structural representations for compound words, and the early effects of constituents in the electrophysiological signal support the hypothesis of early morphological parsing. These results accord with the ones reported in Di Sciullo and Tomioka (2007), which provide behavioural support for Asymmetry Theory, according to which compounds are formed of elements in asymmetrical relations. The results of the semantic priming with Japanese object–verb and adjunct–verb compounds indicate that adjunct–verb compounds take longer to process than object–verb compounds. This suggests that human perception is sensitive to the difference in the underlying structures. More structure is processed in the case of the adjunct–verb compounds, such as *ni-zukuri* (Ja), lit. 'stick stand'='stand straight', than in the case of object–verb compounds, such as *bou-dati* (Ja), lit. 'parcel make'='parcel-making'.

In N+V compounds in languages such as Japanese, there is no overt element indicating the sort of relations between the constituents. In some cases the noun is an object of the verb, and in other cases it is an adjunct. Yet, these compounds are efficiently processed. The question is then: what enables this processing? Given Asymmetry Theory, compound processing is enabled by the presence of unpronounced functional heads with interpretable features. On the one hand, these functional heads ensure that compounds have an asymmetric structure cross-linguistically. On the other hand, they enable morphological compositionality (91)

(91) MORPHOLOGICAL COMPOSITIONALITY
       The interpretation of a morphological object (MO) is a function of the interpretation of its morphological feature structure.

According to (91), the interpretation of a compound is more abstract than the interpretation of its pronounced constituents. Given (91), a unified account can be given to the interpretation of the different sorts of compounds. Thus a *mousetrap* is a trap to catch mice, and a *hairbrush* is an instrument to brush hair, but a *redneck* is not a neck, it is a person who lives in the American south with certain political views. The substantive semantic properties relating the parts of compounds fall into the realm of encyclopedic knowledge. The properties of these features are not part of the genetic endowment of FLN. They are the result of the interaction between FLB and knowledge of the world.

Morphological compositionality abstracts away from the standard definition of semantic compositionality, according to which the interpretation of a constituent is a function of the interpretation of its audible parts and the way the parts are syntactically related. The substantive features of the parts of a morphological object are not sufficient in the interpretation of the whole object. Independent evidence comes from *cran*-morphemes, which do not have independent substantive semantic features outside of the *berry* paradigm, as well as forms that have different denotations outside of compounds, such as *step* in *stepsister*, and the like. The abstract morphological features and the way they enter into agreement and linking are determinant in the interpretation of these constructs. The morphological compositionality of compounds also crucially relies on the presence of unpronounced heads, with constant meaning. The substantive content of the parts of compounds is provided ultimately by the CI systems, interfacing with encyclopedic knowledge, a topic we leave for further research.

8.4 SUMMARY

Thus, compounds are a part of natural languages because they are derived by the recursive operations of the language faculty. The fact that compounds may include recursive structure follows as a direct consequence. Moreover, the recursive operation deriving compounds is limited to a structure-building operation. Head movement or Internal Merge (Move) may not apply in the derivation of compounds. In other words, the derivation of compounds does not require more generative power than a context-free grammar, whereas the derivation of phrases and sentences requires the generative power of a context-sensitive grammar.

On the one hand, I argued that compounds can be a part of languages because their properties, and in particular their asymmetric properties, are derived by the recursive operation of the language faculty. On the other hand, I argued that compounds are a part of human language in addition to phrases and sentences because they meet the interface legibility conditions in a different way from phrases and sentences. Specifically, morphological compositionality ensures the interpretability of these constructs, which may override the substantive features of their SM-legible parts.

The rationale offered by Asymmetry Theory for the presence of compounds in human language targets fundamental properties of the language faculty instead of external factors, such as the principles of semantic transparency, simplicity, conventionality, and productivity (Clark and Berman 1984, Clark, Hecht, and Mulford 1986).

CHAPTER 9

COMPOUNDING AND LEXICALISM

HEINZ GIEGERICH

9.1 INTRODUCTION

9.1.1 Some history

The term 'Lexicalism' refers to a stage in the evolution of Generative Grammar which began in the early 1970s and succeeded the period usually referred to as that of the 'Aspects model' (Chomsky 1965) or, at the time, the 'Standard model'. Lexicalism proposed a return to the traditional modularization of the grammar whereby the morphology and the syntax are held to be distinct not only regarding the nature and 'size' of the units which they concatenate but also regarding the characteristics of the outcomes of such concatenation. The morphology – in Lexicalism integrated in the lexicon, hence the term – produces members of lexical categories (words) while the outcomes of the syntax are members of phrasal categories.

The *Aspects* model had recognized no fundamental distinction between the morphology – derivational or inflectional – and the syntax. The lexicon was an inactive repository of morphemes, which would be concatenated in the transformational component of the syntax. *Destruction* would be derived from *destroy* by means of a transformation which differed merely in detail, not in principle, from the familiar passive transformation (*the men destroyed the house – the house was destroyed by the men*). Lees (1960) and Marchand (1965a, b) pioneered the same approach for compounds, such that for example *sunrise, watchmaker* would derive from the underlying sentences *the sun rises, s/he makes watches* respectively. Given also that allomorphy – associated for example with the vowel shift alternation: *serene–serenity, weep–wept* – was held to be non-distinct from the phonology, and part of the grammar's phonological component (Chomsky and Halle 1968), morphology had no separate, identifiable place in the *Aspects* model; and the word had no systematic status in the grammar.

Chomsky's 'Remarks on Nominalization' (1970), initiating the Lexicalist model, presented an analysis now considered classic of the difference in behaviour between gerund – (1b) below – and non-gerund nominalizations (1c), under an *Aspects* account all derived from sentences as given in (1a). The summary given here draws on Scalise (1984: 17 ff.) and Spencer (1991: 69 ff.).

(1)   a. Tom amused the children with his stories.
        Fred severely criticized the book.
        John doubted the proposal.

      b. Tom's amusing the children with his stories
        Fred's severely criticizing the book
        John's doubting the proposal

      c. *Tom's amusement of the children with his stories
        Fred's severe criticism of the book
        John's doubt about the proposal

Gerund inherit subcategorization and other syntactic properties from the base verb: those in (1b) are transitive, and like verbs they are modified by adverbs. In contrast, nominalizations such as those in (1c) do not inherit the syntactic behaviour associated with their base verbs: they cannot take objects and are modified by adjectives. Also, gerund formation is fully productive while for the formation of non-gerund nominalizations, a wide range of different morphological processes is available of which only a small sample (including conversion) is given in (1c). Nominalizations moreover tend to have a range of meanings well beyond the meaning 'act of' characterizing gerunds: *retirement, marriage,* and indeed *nominalization* can denote both act and state, a *construction* may be an act or an object, *revolution* may have little to do semantically with the base verb *revolve*.

Chomsky (1970) concluded that unlike gerunds, nominalizations such as those in (1c) cannot be derived transformationally without granting uncontrollable power to transformations. And given the wide range of semantic relationships available among the elements of compounds (discussed further below, and elsewhere in this volume) the same is true for the derivation of compounds from underlying sentences developed by Lees (1960) and Marchand (1965a, b), and for the derivational morphology in general. Instead, Chomsky (1970) called for a separate, 'lexical' derivation of morphologically complex words, governed by principles different from those of the syntax and subsequently to be explored in programmatic publications such as Halle (1973), Aronoff (1976), and others.

The reinstatement of the word level in the grammar thus promised to account for fundamental differences between syntactic and morphological constructions. Phrases and sentences are held to be fully transparent, and the mechanisms producing them assumed to be fully productive. While sentences are uttered and then forgotten, words have a more permanent existence. Words are 'coined' and then often retained; and once retained in a speech community their meanings and often also their forms are prone to change through time, possibly losing the structural transparency they may initially have had. In the Lexicalist model, the lexicon therefore has a dual function in that it is both a repository of words, which may or may not have internal structure, and an active component of the grammar (the 'morphology'), in which words are assembled from the familiar morphological building-blocks by means of operations which may or may not be fully productive in the synchronic grammar. Lexicalism led to the recognition of morphology as a self-contained subdiscipline of Generative Grammar, to the emergence of the lexicon as a separate, active component of the grammar, and eventually to substantial progress in the understanding of the morphological, phonological, and semantic structure of words.

9.1.2 Structure and scope of the lexicon

Lexicalism assumes a sharp divide between the lexicon and the syntax. Given that all and only members of lexical categories originate in the lexicon, the divide between the two modules must be as sharp as is the distinction between lexical and phrasal categories in the grammar. Given also that the lexicon is both an active morphological component that assembles words and a repository of irregular, 'listed' words both morphologically complex and simple, further modularization within the lexicon has been proposed. I first deal briefly with the latter modularization – the subtheory of 'lexical stratification' or 'level-ordering' – before turning to the theory's expression of the lexicon–syntax divide.

Lexical stratification, as part of a theory of morphology–phonology interaction, originated with Siegel (1974) and Allen (1978). Early on, development of the phonological side of the theory clearly outpaced research into the stratification of the morphology, so that the label 'Lexical Phonology' misleadingly came to be applied to the whole of the theory – see e.g. Halle and Mohanan (1985), Kiparsky (1985), Mohanan (1986), Booij and Rubach (1987), Borowsky (1990). Particular progress on the phonological side of the theory was initially made in two related areas. Firstly, the theory succeeded in reining in the excessive abstractness of phonological derivations which had beset the Generative Phonology of Chomsky and Halle (1968): Kiparsky (1982); see also Giegerich (1999: Chapter 4). Secondly, and particularly relevant below in this chapter, in distinguishing between 'lexical' and 'postlexical' phonological phenomena, the theory rediscovered the fact, lost in the Chomsky–Halle era, that morphophonological phenomena of the type *serene– serenity* have rather different characteristics from phonological phenomena which occur in and are often confined to connected speech: while the former are categorial in output, sensitive to morphological structure, and often notable for exceptions and idiosyncrasies (compare for example *serenity* and *obesity*), the latter are typically gradient, free of lexical exceptions, driven by speech style, tempo, etc., and applicable across the entire domain (Mohanan 1986). Indeed, a given phonological phenomenon may occur in a lexical and a postlexical version. The palatalization of certain spirants, for example, is categorial as a lexical phenomenon in English (*confess–confession, confuse–confusion*), but gradient and optional postlexically, as a connected-speech phenomenon (in *bless you, I advise you*, etc.). The applicability of a given process, phonological or morphological, not on a single stratum but on contiguous strata is in fact to be expected (Mohanan 1986: 47; Giegerich 1999: 99). The process's particular application characteristics are then predicted by its stratal siting: the differences between the lexical and postlexical versions of palatalization are predicted by the general characteristics of the lexical and postlexical phonology respectively.

A stratified lexicon comprises an ordered sequence of two or more morphological domains. In English, stratum 1 (of two) is root-based; its outputs are listed and often formally and/or semantically irregular (compare the meanings of *fraternal, fraternize*, and *fraternity*); bases are prone to stress shifts (*solemn–solemnity*) and other phonological distortions (*serene–serenity*). The Structure Preservation Condition (Borowsky 1990) ensures that all stratum-1 outputs conform with the phonotactic constraints also holding morpheme-internally: essentially, stratum-1 forms 'look like' morphologically simple words – compare *solemnity* and *omnibus, serenity* and *America.*

Stratum 2 in English is word-based, housing the regular, rule-driven morphology including fully productive derivational processes, regular inflection, and compounding. Note that consonant clusters may occur across the morphological boundaries in such forms which would be ill-formed in morphologically simple words – *goodness, keenly, watchmaker*, etc. – and that affixation is stress-neutral, giving rise to stress patterns alien to morphologically simple forms: *driverlessness.*

A central role in the architecture of the stratified lexicon, and indeed in defining the role of the lexicon vis-à-vis the syntax, is played by the Elsewhere Condition (Kiparsky 1982, Giegerich 2000). This condition essentially stipulates that of two rival forms competing for example for the same meaning, the 'listed', irregular form will take precedence over its regular, rule-driven rival. This principle ensures the ordering of strata – in particular the disjunctive order of all irregular morphology before the regular morphology, as well as of course the ordering of 'lexical' processes before 'syntactic' processes where those are in competition. Such ordering of modules, from the specific to the general, in turn accounts for synonymy blocking – for example, stratum-1 *wept, fifth* block the formation of regular, stratum-2 **weeped, *fiveth*. Similarly expressed are certain ordering generalizations among affixes, such that for example a stratum-2 form cannot receive a stress-shifting (stratum-1) affix, or more generally that Latinate affixes do not attach to Germanic bases: **homelessity* (Selkirk 1982; see Giegerich 1999: Chapter 3, for discussion).

Lexical strata are self-contained components insulated from each other through the Bracket Erasure Convention (Kiparsky 1982). This convention, originating in Chomsky and Halle's (1968) phonology and somewhat paralleled on the morphological side by the Adjacency Condition (Allen 1978), ensures that at the end of each stratum, all internal morphological brackets are deleted, so that morphological complexity arising on one stratum is visible only to the morphological and phonological operations of that stratum, and invisible to those of the next stratum. A stratum-2 phonological rule simplifying morpheme-final /mn/ clusters, for example, would affect the stratum-2 form [[*damn*]*ing*] as well as the simple form [*damn*], and would distinguish on that stratum between the configurations '*mn*]' and '*m*]*n*' (leaving the latter intact: *calmness*). But Bracket Erasure at the end of stratum 1 will ensure, given the rule's sensitivity to morphological bracketing, that forms coming through from stratum 1 and containing morpheme-final /mn/ are unaffected (*damnation, solemnity*), just as morphologically simple forms with medial /mn/ are (*omnibus*).

9.1.3 The lexicon–syntax divide

Given that in Lexicalism the lexicon produces members of lexical categories and the syntax members of phrasal categories – for example, constructions labelled N and NP respectively – there must be a divide between the two modules despite the fact that both modules concatenate morphemes into complex linguistic forms. The lexicon–syntax divide must be as sharp as is the distinction between N and NP, or between V and VP for example. It is less clear, however, whether all of what is traditionally known as the 'morphology' takes place in the lexicon; nor has the precise formal nature of the lexicon–syntax divide been beyond dispute.

Forms of Lexicalism weaker than the original version put forward by Chomsky (1970) and Halle (1973) have argued that the inflectional morphology (Anderson 1982), or at least some of it (Booij 1996), applies in interaction with the syntax and hence within that module rather than in the lexicon. In these models the distribution of the morphology across grammatical modules thus resembles the well-known distinction between lexical and postlexical phenomena drawn on the phonological side, as discussed above (Kiparsky 1982; Booij and Rubach 1987; Mohanan 1986). The recognition of some postlexical morphology weakens the basic modular distinction somewhat, but it endangers it no more fundamentally than does the recognition of a lexical/postlexical distinction in the phonology. As was noted above, applicability of a process in contiguous modules should not be surprising. And the distinction between the derivational morphology of the lexicon's final stratum and the syntax – notably that between compounds and phrases, at issue in this chapter – is unaffected. But how is it to be expressed in the grammar?

Botha (1984) proposed the 'No Phrase Constraint', whereby syntactic phrases cannot be embedded in compound words. This constraint, ruling out for example *expensive watch maker* ('maker of expensive watches') has many, apparently obvious counterexamples to be discussed below (*severe weather warning, affordable housing policy*). Leaving such problems aside for the moment, we can in any case subsume the No Phrase Constraint under the more general 'Lexical Integrity Principle' (Lapointe 1980; Di Sciullo and Williams 1987; Scalise and Guevara 2005), whereby syntactic processes can manipulate members of lexical categories ('words') but not their morphological elements. Such manipulation would include the attachment of modifiers: if *watchmaker* is a compound noun then its elements cannot be individually modified; and the impossibility of both *expensive watchmaker* and *watch skilled maker* is predicted by the Lexical Integrity Principle. Independent modification, as well as other syntactic operations such as the replacement of the head by the pro-form *one* (Stirling and Huddleston 2002: 1511 ff.) – *a watchmaker and a clock one* – may then serve as syntactic tests for the compound or phrasal status of a given form.

Further questions regarding lexical integrity may be raised here but not discussed. It is an issue for the theory, for example, whether the Lexical Integrity Principle has independent formal status in the grammar (as has usually been assumed), and what its exact form actually is. It may well be the case either that its effects are nothing but the manifestation of the Bracket Erasure Convention at the end of the lexicon's final stratum, or alternatively that, as Ackema (1999: Chapter 4) has argued, observed lexical-integrity effects derive from other principles of syntactic architecture. Whatever it is that causes such effects, independent principle or not, the notion of lexical integrity in some way defines the lexicon–syntax divide, expressing the traditional view whereby words are the atoms of syntactic structure. No syntactic operation can affect the elements of words.

I shall in what follows discuss the question of what Lexicalism has to contribute to our understanding of compounds – and indeed whether our knowledge about compounds is consistent with the assumptions of Lexicalism. As much of this discussion will focus on the distinction between compounds and phrases – on the lexicon–syntax divide, therefore – it is appropriate that the compounding phenomenon's manifestation in English, and involving in particular English nouns, should dominate the discussion.

9.2 THE PROBLEM OF ENGLISH COMPOUNDS

English is of course not unusual in its ability to concatenate lexemes so as to form not only phrases (*black bird*) but also complex lexemes (*blackbird*). What is fairly unusual, though, is the fact that the two construction types are not morphosyntactically distinct. Given the paucity of the English inflectional system, neither the phrase nor the compound will have an inflectional ending on an adjectival first element. Compare German *schwarze Drossel* ('black thrush') vs. *Schwarzdrossel* ('blackbird'), where the distinction is clear.

Moreover, and again unlike in languages such as German, it is possible in English not only for adjectives but also for nouns to function as attributes in noun phrases. A noun-plus-noun construction is not necessarily a compound, as some grammars claim (e.g. Burton-Roberts 1997: 163). Payne and Huddleston (2002: 448 ff.) take the view endorsed here that constructions such as *London college* are phrases, for reasons which will be set out in detail below. In some such cases, apparent nouns in the attribute position may in fact be adjectives. This seems especially to be so where the attribute noun denotes 'material', as in *steel bridge*. As there is no productive derivational suffix to make available denominal adjectives of the appropriate denotation – *-en* is unproductive beyond *wooden, woollen* (Marchand 1969: 270) – *steel* is arguably a noun-to-adjective conversion for those speakers who also accept it in the predicate position (*this bridge is steel*) and simply a noun (like *London* in *London college*) for those speakers for whom the predicate is ungrammatical.

The distinction between phrase and compound implies a structural ambiguity in the language, then, such that identical concatenations straddle the lexicon–syntax divide: they can be either phrase or compound. This fact about English has loomed large in research on English word formation. Anglists of many generations have attempted (and ultimately failed) to draw a sharp distinction between compound and phrase: Koziol (1937), Jespersen (1942), Marchand (1969), Faiß (1981), Liberman and Sproat (1992), Bauer (1998), Olsen (2000b, 2001), Giegerich (2004) – to name just a few.

One criterion invoked for drawing the phrase–compound distinction has been stress, such that compounds stress the first element (*wátchmaker*) while phrases stress the second (*blue bóok*). Indeed there are independent reasons to associate fore-stress in two-element compounds, as well as the stress patterns found in larger compound constructions (*làbour party fínance committee*) with lexical status: Liberman and Prince (1977) strikingly demonstrated that the metrical structure of such constructions is governed by principles identical to those found in non-compound nouns (*aróma, ìntrodúction*).

Nonetheless the difference in stress is known to be of limited use in drawing the compound–phrase distinction. If, like Marchand (1969: 20 ff.) and more recently

Liberman and Sproat (1992), we assume fore-stress to be a robust diagnostic such that all and only compounds have fore-stress, then an apparently spurious category distinction arises for pairs of semantically very similar constructions: there are well-documented, random stress differences between *Madison Ávenue* and *Mádison Street*, *Christmas púdding* and *Chrístmas cake* (Lees 1960, Schmerling 1976), *apple píe* and *ápple cake*, and *olive óil* (end-stressed for many British speakers) and *córn oil*. *Ice cream*, discussed by Bloomfield (1933) for displaying a variable stress pattern like *olive oil*, must then be a phrase for some and a compound for other speakers 'although there is no denotative difference of meaning' (Bloomfield 1933: 228). The reality seems to be that phrases invariably have end-stress while both stress patterns are available to compounds. Given that some of the pairs given above denote names for streets and traditional dishes, and not for example streets or avenues located in Madison, we may assume on separate, semantic grounds that they are compound nouns.

Jespersen (1942), in early recognition of the problems regarding stress as the defining criterion of compound status, argues that the compound–phrase distinction is essentially semantic: 'We may perhaps say that we have a compound if the meaning of the whole cannot be logically deduced from the meaning of the elements separately' (Jespersen 1942: 137). But as it stands, this criterion seems similarly to fail in defining compound status, for two reasons. Firstly, while it is the case that many complex lexemes, including many compounds, are semantically opaque to a greater or lesser extent (*opportunity, comparable; greenhouse, silver-fish*, etc.), there is no true generalization in English whereby all complex lexemes are semantically opaque: non-compound examples such as *kindness, sincerity, uneven*, and many other complex lexemes are perfectly transparent (Di Sciullo and Williams 1987; Bauer 1998). There is then no principled reason why compounds should be opaque when other lexemes may not be; indeed, while for example the semantics of the highly productive 'synthetic compound' construction (*watchmaker, birdwatcher, coach driver*) is different from that of a phrase such as *nice driver*, it is not exactly opaque. Secondly, it is not at all clear in Jespersen's argument how the meaning of a phrasal construction is 'deduced logically from the meaning of the elements separately'. I will discuss this in the following section and demonstrate that Jespersen does indeed have a point. Compounds often, though not always, fail to conform with the compositional semantics typically associated with the attribute–head relationship in noun phrases. Again the reality seems to be that phrases invariably have a particular, default semantic structure while both the default and various kinds of non-default semantics are available to compounds.

It would appear, then, that neither the phonology nor the semantics provide criteria for compound status that are not also present in at least some phrases. This is the problem which a wealth of research, listed above, has failed to solve. It remains to be seen whether Lexicalism provides a better answer – in particular, whether the syntactic criteria associated with the Lexical Integrity Principle correlate with the predictions, however few, made by the phonology and the semantics regarding lexical status.

9.3 THE SYNTAX–LEXICON CONTINUUM OF ATTRIBUTION

Morphological and phonological processes are known often to straddle the stratal divide in the lexicon; and when they do then their stratum-specific characteristics will derive from properties more generally associated with that stratum. The same is true for phenomena occurring on both sides of the lexicon–syntax divide: recall for example that end-stress, obligatory in syntactic phrases (*blue book*) may also occur in lexical constructions (*Christmas pudding*), where it competes apparently randomly with fore-stress (*Christmas cake*). While, as we have seen, such at least partial continuity across modular divides is to be expected, one contribution Lexicalism has made is the recognition that the properties of individual phenomena or processes may in reality be associated more generally with the module in which the process takes place. Lexical end-stress may thus be expected to have lexical exceptions, while in the syntax it must apply across the board.

I want to show in what follows that nominal compounding is the lexical reflex of the attribute–head relationship found in the syntax of the English noun phrase, and that the differences between the lexical and syntactic versions of the phenomenon are consistent with the general properties of the lexicon and the syntax respectively. In particular I will show that the two dichotomies of ascriptive vs. associative and (to a lesser extent) intersective vs. subsective attribution not only characterize the phenomenon of attribution in the syntax but also serve to set up the basic categorization needed for the understanding of compounding.

9.3.1 Ascriptive attribution

It is a probably uncontroversial assumption about formal grammar that all constructions originating in the syntax are semantically transparent and the outcomes of fully productive processes; non-transparent or non-productive constructions (*red herring, court martial*) are by definition lexical. The semantic interpretation of a phrase is the product of the lexical semantics of the words involved and of the semantics associated with the particular construction of that phrase. Thus in linguistic forms such as the noun phrases in (2) below, the lexical semantics of the adjectives and nouns involved is amalgamated in such a way that the noun is the head and the adjective its dependent functioning as an attribute.

(2)   beautiful picture
      white board
      black bird
      small elephant

Prototypical adjectives such as those in (2) bring to the attributive position their ascriptive – sometimes called 'qualitative' – nature (Siegel 1980; Beard 1981; Ferris 1993; Payne and Huddleston 2002), such that the adjective denotes 'a property which is valid for the entity instantiated by the noun' (Ferris 1993: 24): *beautiful* expresses a property of the picture. The fact that ascriptive adjectives normally have a second, predicative usage (*the picture is beautiful*) follows from the semantics of ascription, characterized by the relationship 'is' between the head and its dependent.

   Given that properties are prototypically denoted by adjectives (Ferris 1993), and also that adjectives clearly constitute the default category in the attributive position (Payne and Huddleston 2002: 444 ff.), it stands to reason that the ascriptive adjective should be the default attribute, whose behaviour strongly informs the semantics of attribution in general. This implies, however, that this position may also be occupied by members of a lexical category other than adjective, or that attributes may be non-ascriptive. I deal with these two further possibilities in turn.

   Ascriptive attribution can be performed by nouns. In (3a) I list examples of appositional, and in some cases copulative (*dvandva*) constructions (Marchand 1969: 24). The examples in (3b) mostly denote 'material'.

(3)   a. boy actor   b. luxury flat
         gentleman farmer   metal bridge
         rogue trader   paper bag
         singer-songwriter   olive oil
         actor-director   corn oil
         manservant   avocado oil
         fighter-bomber   thistle oil

These lists exemplify the kind of construction within which the compound–phrase distinction is most difficult to draw (Giegerich 2004). *Dvandva* constructions are usually treated as compounds (Olsen 2001); and indeed some of them tend to have fore-stress (*manservant*). Among the culinary oils listed in (3b) *olive oil* may have end-stress, the others probably fore-stress, despite the fact that thistle oil is comparatively new on the scene. This points towards lexicalization – a poorly defined but intuitively appealing notion to which I return below.

   Any stress variation found in such cases is either random or dialect-specific (Giegerich 2004), like Bloomfield's (1933) example of *ice cream* cited earlier. In contrast, the forms listed in (4) below are stress doublets, where the different stress patterns signal clear-cut semantic differences:

(4)   toy factory
       woman doctor
       metal separator
       steel warehouse
       glass case
       driving instructor
       dancing girl

Given the apparent unreliability of both the stress criterion and the semantic criterion, noted in section 9.2 above, the robustness of the stress–meaning relationship in these examples is striking. Under end-stress, attribution is ascriptive: 'factory which is a toy', 'doctor who is a woman'; under fore-stress, semantic relations are apparently more complex. This non-ascriptive form of attribution will be discussed in the following section; here we note that the end-stressed versions of such doublets are probably all amenable to a phrasal analysis. Again, the possible insights contributed by Lexicalism to such analysis will be considered further below.

9.3.2 Associative attribution

Non-ascriptive adjectives in English, exemplified in (5a) below, are associative (Ferris 1993; Payne and Huddleston 2002), at times called 'relational' (Beard 1981; Leitzke 1989). Such adjectives, represented for the moment by *dental* in *dental decay*, do not express a property of the nominal head but an entity associated with it (Ferris 1993: 24; Pullum and Huddleston 2002: 556; Giegerich 2005a). Thus, *dental* does not describe the nature of the decay (as e.g. ascriptive *slow* or *unexpected* would) but identifies what is decaying.

In that respect, the semantics of associative adjectives is noun-like to the extent that such adjectives constitute a category mismatch of adjectival morphosyntactic behaviour paired with nominal semantics. Denoting entities rather than properties, adjectives of this kind always stand in a recurrent semantic relationship, though not necessarily in a transparent morphological relationship, to a noun, such that the meaning of the attribute is 'associated with', 'pertaining to'. *Dental*, for example, partners the noun *tooth* in that the adjectival attribute means 'pertaining to teeth'. Similarly, *avian* means 'pertaining to birds'. Unsurprisingly then, the phrases in (5a) have the synonyms listed in (5b).

(5)   a. dental decay   b. tooth decay
          avian influenza   bird 'flu
          rural policeman   country policeman
          vernal equinox   spring equinox
          tropical fish   warm-water fish

The distribution of associative adjectives is restricted in several ways. For example, they cannot occur in the predicative position (*this decay is dental) – a fact that follows from the semantics of 'pertaining to'. Moreover, such adjectives are often restricted to specific heads (*vernal cabbage). These deficiencies – and there are more: associative adjectives are neither gradable nor modifiable, for example (Giegerich 2005a) – clearly suggest that associative adjectives constitute within the category 'Adjective' a non-default (or atypical) subclass, whose associativeness is specified in the individual adjective's lexical semantics. If that is so then it is not surprising that some members of this subclass should also have default, ascriptive senses which should then give rise to the syntactic behaviour typical of ascriptive adjectives: modifiability, predicate occurrence, etc. This is notably the case for items such as feline, equine, bovine, etc. (her face is rather feline), where metaphorical ascriptive usages are possible. Note also the second, ascriptive sense of dental in dental fricative, the ambiguity of criminal lawyer and many similar forms, as well as the unusual associative sense of friendly in the notorious collocation friendly fire ('gunfire associated with one's own side').

While the semantics of the examples in (5a) above is fairly straightforward ('associated with'), those in (6) (mostly from Levi 1978) display more complex semantic structures:

(6)   a. papal motorcade – papal murder – papal visit
          presidential plane – presidential election – presidential lie
          professorial salary – professorial appointment – professorial comment

      b. symphonic overture – operatic overture
          electrical clock – electrical generator
          musical clock – musical comedy

In (6a), papal murder and papal visit display argument–predicate relationships; yet what exactly those are, agent or patient, depends on real-world expectations and encyclopedic knowledge. The Pope is more likely to be victim than culprit, but he does go visiting. The same goes for the other two sets of three: in each case the first example is simply 'associated with', the other two have (possibly opposite) argument structures. Similarly, the interpretation of the examples in (6b) depends entirely on encyclopedic knowledge – a symphonic overture has the internal structure of a symphony while an operatic overture is part of an opera.

Such observations suggest that at least some associative-adjective constructions may be lexical. Semantic complexity such as that shown in (6) is not otherwise known to characterize attribution in the syntax. Such an analysis is consistent with the defective behaviour of associative adjectives noted above – with arbitrary distribution restrictions, non-predicative usage, failure to undergo modification. Moreover, such constructions very often have fore-stress:

(7) ́polar bear   medical profession   mental institution
     ́solar system   medical building   mental hospital
     solar panel   Medical Faculty   mental disease
     tidal wave   electrical worker   dental care
     postal service   legal work   dental treatment

If fore-stress is unavailable in the syntax, as we assume here, then the examples in (7) must be lexical like those in (6), if for different reasons. That does not mean, however, that all associative-adjective constructions must be lexical: there are no compelling reasons why those in (5a) should be, for example. Again, we will see below whether the analytical tools provided by Lexicalism serve to settle the issue.

I noted above that associative adjectives have the semantics of nouns, and that the constructions under discussion here tend to have noun-plus-noun synonyms as in (5b) above. It follows that such compounds, 'root compounds' or 'primary compounds' in traditional terminology, also display the 'associated with' relationship among their elements. So, then, do all of these:

(8) a. mountain railway   b. milk bottle
        school dinner   milkman
        village shop   milk-float
        summer fruit   milk-fever
        university exam   milk-tooth
        garden path   milkweed

The difference between the two sets, significantly, is twofold. Firstly, the examples in (8a) will have end-stress for most speakers while those in (8b) have fore-stress. Secondly, the examples in (8a) are fairly transparent while most of those in (8b) are not. It follows from the lexical semantics of *mountain* – 'place', among other things – that a mountain railway is a railway located in the mountains. In all those examples, the precise sense of 'associated with' can be inferred from the lexical semantics of the first element (Fanselow 1981: 156 ff.; Olsen 2000b). This is not the case in (8b) – in particular there is no way in which the precise nature of fever's, teeth's, and weed's association with milk can be inferred from either element. Like (6) above, the interpretation of these items depends heavily on encyclopedic knowledge.

Similarly, we can now pin down the semantic difference that accompanies the stress difference in the doublets in (4) above – *toy factory*, etc.: the stress contrast in fact correlates with the contrast between ascriptive and associative attribution, where the semantic interpretations of the latter, like the examples in (6), display argument structures and/or encyclopedic information not expected of attribution in the syntax.

Such constructions must be lexical – lexicalized perhaps for specific senses, of which the 'associated with' relationship allows many. Associativeness is more versatile than ascription. It is not surprising, therefore, that mainstream primary compounding follows the associative pattern which, as we have yet to demonstrate, occurs in its most basic form also in the syntax, alongside ascription.

9.3.3 Intersective and subsective attribution

A further aspect of attribution which nicely illustrates the syntax–lexicon continuum is the distinction between intersective and subsective attribution, found within the category of ascriptive attribution. In its basic form, ascriptive attribution is intersective. *Beautiful picture*, for example, denotes the intersection of the set of pictures and the set of beautiful objects. Contrast the examples given in (9):

(9)   beautiful dancer
      heavy smoker
      big eater
      old friend
      good chef

These phrases are ambiguous. They allow not only intersective readings (for example 'dancer who is a beautiful person') but also subsective readings whereby a beautiful dancer may be someone who dances beautifully without being beautiful. *Beautiful* may modify *dancer* or the semantic element 'dance' embedded in *dancer*. Similarly, a heavy smoker may not be a heavy person but someone who smokes heavily. *Heavy smoker* does not then represent the intersection of the set of heavy objects (or people) and the set of smokers. Corresponding predicate constructions (*this dancer is beautiful, this smoker is heavy,* etc.) tend to be unambiguous: they correspond to the intersective reading of the attribute. Indeed there seems generally to be a tendency for the predicate construction to be available only to adjectives with intersective interpretations, or to enforce such interpretations.

Subsective attribution has received much attention in recent research, after Siegel's (1980) influential dissertation (see e.g. Pustejovsky 1995, Jackendoff 1997, Bouchard 2002). The details of the analysis are not as relevant here as is the consensus regarding the general approach. Firstly, the site of the semantic complexity giving rise to intersective/subsective ambiguity is the head rather than the attribute. Subsectiveness is not encoded in the lexical semantics of the adjective. Secondly, subsectiveness does not depend on morphological structure: *beautiful* subsectively modifies the semantic element 'dance', not the verb *dance* contained in *dancer*. This must be so because *old friend* and *good chef*, whose heads are not morphologically complex, allow subsective interpretations; and it is important for present purposes because if morphological structure were relevant here then under the Lexical Integrity Principle such constructions would have to be lexical, which probably they are not.

I return to this issue in the following section, noting here for the moment that we have no reason to believe subsective attribution to have lexical status. However, subsectiveness is also found in 'synthetic compounds', one of the most productive forms of compounding:

(10)   watchmaker
        train-spotter
        coach-driver
        bird-watcher

Synthetic compounds are characterized by a subsective argument–predicate relationship between their elements. As we just saw, subsective interpretations are possible, if not by default, among phrasal constructions; but the argument–predicate relationship is probably confined to lexical constructions – recall the discussion of (6a) above, to be concluded in the next section.

9.4 ATTRIBUTION AND THE SYNTAX–LEXICON DIVIDE

I showed in the preceding section that the semantics of attribution can be ascriptive or associative. We have reason to believe that the former constitutes the default – ascriptiveness occurs freely both in attributes and in predicates while associativeness is possible for attributes only. Moreover, associative adjectives often default into ascriptive senses. Within ascription two subtypes are possible: intersective and subsective ascription. Intersectiveness is possible both for attributes and for predicates; ambiguous interpretations default to intersectiveness in the predicate position: *beautiful dancer – the dancer is beautiful*. Intersectiveness again seems to be the default.

If we take the reasonable view, in line with the Elsewhere Condition, that in the syntax–lexicon continuum, default patterns belong in the syntax while non-defaults are more likely to be lexical, then a picture emerges where the attribute–head relationship straddles the modular divide. Students of English compounding will not be surprised to hear this, given the difficulty in systematically distinguishing compounds and phrases. I will in this section attempt to correlate the phonological and semantic criteria which are already known in the Anglist literature with those provided by Lexicalism. In particular the Lexical Integrity Principle, discussed in section 9.1.3 above, will furnish us with syntactic diagnostics for lexical status, such that the elements of constructions originating in the lexicon – compounds – are not individually available to syntactic operations.

There appear to be three syntactic operations that might serve as diagnostics here: firstly, coordination within either the dependent or the head (*red and blue books, wooden bridges and fences*); secondly, independent modification of either element of the construction (*a very tall man, a tall old man*); thirdly, the use of the pro-form *one* (*a red book and a blue one*). All three are discussed in some detail by Bauer (1998); and all three have their problems.

The most problematic of the three is the coordination phenomenon, which seems to reach deep into the lexicon rather than stopping at the border: Wiese (1996b: 69 ff.) observes examples in German where coordination (or the deletion of the first occurrence of two identical heads) occurs freely among the elements of forms which involve prefixes and suffixes, and which therefore must be lexical: *be- und entladen* ('to load and unload'), *ess- und trinkbar* ('edible and drinkable'), *mütter- und väterlich* ('motherly and fatherly'). With Booij (1985), Wiese argues that the relevant deletion operation of repeated heads affects phonological words: **winz- oder riesig* ('tiny or huge'), where vowel-initial *-ig* does not have phonological word status, is impossible. This phenomenon is therefore irrelevant to the Lexical Integrity Principle as the units affected by it are phonological rather than syntactic. Comparable cases in English, involving forms which must be compounds on account of their fore-stress alone, need not worry us then: *wind- and water-mills* (Bauer 1998: 75), *clock- and watchmaker, timber and pallet merchants, pallet makers and suppliers*, etc.

Independent modification is clearly a more reliable diagnostic for the lexicon–syntax divide: not only are forms such as **un-very large, *harm-totally-less* absolutely ungrammatical, the test also distinguishes nicely between phrases and compounds in many cases where the distinction is already clear on independent – for example stress – grounds: compare *a brilliantly white board* and **a brilliantly whiteboard, a white wall-mounted board* and **a white-wall-mounted board*. Similar examples involving synthetic compounds (**expensive watchmaker, *watch- skilled maker*) were noted earlier.

The test's limitations are that, firstly, some adjectives – for example associative adjectives – are not modifiable: **obviously dental decay*. It remains to be seen whether this means that associative adjectives can only occur in lexical constructions, such that *dental decay* is lexical. I return to this question below.

Secondly, recall the examples first given in (3) and (4) above where nouns function as ascriptive attributes – *boy actor, gentleman farmer, rogue trader*, as well as the ascriptive (end-stressed) versions of *toy factory, metal separator, woman doctor*. Given the nature of the intersective ascription present in all such examples, forms such as *young boy actor, educational toy factory, elderly woman dóctor* are structurally ambiguous: it is unclear whether in such cases the adjective modifies the entire noun-plus-noun construction or merely its first noun. Note, in contrast, that in noun-plus-noun constructions displaying associative modification – (8) above – no ambiguity arises: in *tall mountain railway, remote village shop, hot summer fruit,* the adjectives *tall, remote,* and *hot* must modify the entire compound despite the fact that *tall mountain, remote village,* etc. would be semantically straightforward. In such cases, adjectival modification is a possible diagnostic, then, for the distinction between ascriptive and associative noun-plus-noun constructions; and it appears to confirm the lexical status of the latter type; but it fails to tell us whether *boy actor* is a compound or a phrase.

The third test to be invoked here is 'pro-*one*' – the replacement of the head of a noun phrase by the pro-form *one,* as in *a red book and a blue one.* There is no doubt that this is a credible syntactic operation (Hornstein and Lightfoot 1981; Stirling and Huddleston 2002) which, under the Lexical Integrity Principle, should therefore be able to distinguish between compounds and phrases in that it should be unable to affect the head of a compound. Indeed, to begin again with straightforward synthetic compounds, **a watchmaker and a clock one,* **a bird-watcher and a deer one,* etc. are ill-formed.

Consider now once more the examples of ascriptive attribution listed in (3) above. Pro-*one* is straightforwardly possible in most cases – *an adult actor and a boy one, a genuine trader and a rogue one, a basic flat and a luxury one.* Pro-*one* requires countability and is hence unavailable in *olive oil,* etc. The oddness of forms such as *a full-time director and an actor one, a full-time songwriter and a singer one* is probably connected with having an agent noun as an attribute. *Boy* and *rogue* are 'better' attributes than *actor* and *singer.* If that is so then the lexicon–syntax divide runs somewhere through the set of ascriptive noun-plus-noun forms (of which some will in any case be lexical on account of their fore-stress: *manservant*). And the same probably goes for the examples of associative attribution by nouns, listed in (8) above. While there is likely to be variation among speakers among the end-stressed, semantically transparent examples in (8a), those in (8b) are clearly more likely to resist pro-*one.* (See Bauer 1998: 77 for more discussion of similar examples.)

Similarly, pro-*one* serves to draw the lexicon–syntax line through the set of associative-adjective constructions discussed in section 9.3.2 above. Recall that I informally distinguished three subsets of such constructions: those where the relationship between adjective and noun is straightforwardly 'associated with' – *dental decay, avian influenza,* etc. in (5a); those where an argument–predicate relationship is present – *papal visit, presidential election,* etc. (6a); and those whose interpretation requires significant, encyclopedic information not available from the adjective's lexical semantics: *symphonic overture, electrical clock,* etc. (6b). While all such constructions in principle qualify for lexical status – and recall from (7) that many of them have fore-stress – I showed in Giegerich (2005a) that examples from the first subset will typically yield to pro-*one* while those of the other two subsets won't; and when for example those in (11c) do then they will often enforce an ascriptive, default interpretation as discussed above. Here are some examples:

---

(11) a. Is this a feline disease or a bovine one?
Is he a rural policeman or an urban one?
Is this a cold-water fish or a tropical one?

b. *Do you mean the presidential murder or the papal one?
*Do you mean the parliamentary election or the presidential one?
*Have they made a junior appointment or a professorial one?

c. *Is this the Home Office or the Foreign one?
*Is he a constitutional lawyer or a criminal one?
*Is he a theatrical critic or a musical one?
*Is he an electronic engineer or an electrical one?

For more detailed analysis, as well as for discussion of the data, the reader is referred to Giegerich (2005a). We note here merely that pro-*one* rather impressively appears to confirm a lexicon–syntax divide rather speculatively drawn on semantic grounds above: cases where the full interpretation of the 'associated with' relationship involves argument structure or significant encyclopedic information, rather than being able to be inferred, do not belong in the syntax but are lexical. Such findings exemplify, and indeed make sense of, Jespersen's (1942: 137) claim 'that we have a compound if the meaning of the whole cannot be logically deduced from the meaning of the elements separately'.

There are, then, at least two syntactic 'tests' which under the Lexical Integrity Principle should, and apparently do, draw a clear distinction between compounds and phrases, thereby demarcating the lexicon from the syntax. Both produce encouraging results, as we have just seen. However, to produce a sharp lexicon–syntax divide, as the Lexical Integrity Principle suggests there is, such tests have to correlate with each other as well as with the other, non-syntactic criteria known to be applicable to the compound–phrase distinction. Recall from section 9.2 that there are two such criteria. Noun phrases have end-stress while compounds have end-stress or fore-stress – the phonological criterion. And noun phrases have transparent attributive semantics while in compounds, semantic relations may be opaque or at least more complex – the semantic criterion. A theory which draws a modular distinction between the lexicon and the syntax and which includes the Lexical Integrity Principle will then make the predictions stated in (12) below. Readers should prepare for disappointment.

(12) a. The elements of a fore-stressed construction do not allow pro-*one* or individual modification.

b. The elements of a semantically opaque construction do not allow pro-*one* or individual modification.

c. The elements of a construction allowing pro-*one* are amenable to individual modification, and vice versa.

9.5 MISMATCHES

Before setting out to test the predictions spelt out in (12), we should note that the phonological and the semantic criteria alone cannot give rise to mismatches. Fore-stressed constructions may or may not be fully transparent, as may end-stressed constructions. Fore-stressed, transparent *corn oil* (compare *olive oil*, end-stressed for many) and end-stressed *country house*, somewhat opaque due to connotations of grandness, extensive grounds, etc. (and again compare fore-stressed *town house*), do not in themselves constitute a problem for Lexicalism: for different reasons these must be lexical. The theory and, as we have seen, the data require lexical-integrity effects to draw the lexicon–syntax line.

9.5.1 Mismatches involving stress

There does continue to be dispute in the literature as to whether or not end-stress is confined to phrasal constructions, but the literature agrees that fore-stress is confined to compounds (Marchand 1969; Liberman and Sproat 1992; Bauer 1998; Olsen 2000b; Giegerich 2004). In line with the Lexical Integrity Principle it follows that no speaker should allow the pro-*one* operation for fore-stressed associative-adjective constructions. This prediction is as safe as are the two assumptions that it is based on: that regarding the pro-*one* construction and that regarding fore-stress. Interestingly, the prediction is not borne out by speaker behaviour.

Fore-stress is not uncommon among such forms – see (7) above, as well as Olsen (2000b) and Giegerich (2005a) – including *dental building, dental appointment, mental hospital, Medical Faculty*. For those, speakers will readily accept pro-*one*, as in (13):

(13) ˋ Is this the medical building or the dental one?
Do you have a medical appointment or a dental one?
Is this the general hospital or the mental one?
Is this the Arts Faculty or the Medical one?

Forms such as these are compound nouns in regard of their phonological behaviour; but the pro-*one* operation can nevertheless identify, and replace, their heads. The lexicon–syntax divisions referred to by the phonology and by pro-*one* are clearly not quite identical.

Neither are those, apparently, referred to by the phonology and the modifiability of constituents. Again, the modification test works well for some clear-cut cases – recall **expensive watchmaker* ('maker of expensive watches') first discussed in sections 9.1.3 and 9.4 above. However, apparent or real counterexamples are well-attested (Sproat 1985; Lieber 1992a; Wiese 1996b; Carstairs-McCarthy 2002, 2005) – consider those in (14):

(14)   a. Charles and Di syndrome   b. open door policy
           pipe and slipper husband   cold weather payment
           floor of a birdcage taste   severe weather warning
           off the rack dress   sexually transmitted disease clinic

All such constructions must be noun compounds rather than phrases because, firstly, they may have the main stress on their first constituents (for example on *Di*); secondly, they do not conform with the pre-head modification patterns known for NPs; and thirdly, their second elements are not amenable to modification – *a floor of a birdcage salty taste*. Assuming that the first constituents of these compounds are syntactic phrases, Lieber (1992a: 14) concludes that '[r]ules of word formation must at least be allowed to refer to phrasal categories which are presumably generated as part of the syntax'.

It has been shown, however, that the assumption whereby the first constituents in such constructions are generated in the syntax, rather than in the lexicon, is not really safe. Wiese (1996b) has argued that the embedded 'phrases' in (14a) have the status of quotations, which may suggest some sort of lexical storage. And cases such as those in (14b) may be lexicalized phrases (or clichés: Carstairs-McCarthy 2002: 82) – perhaps displaying figurative senses (*open door policy* – compare *wooden door policy*), perhaps being subject to jargon-specific technical definition (such that, for the purpose of benefit payment, *cold weather* denotes a specific average temperature lasting for a specific number of days). Under such an analysis, constructions such as *open door policy* and *cold weather payment* – and indeed *Lexical Integrity Principle* and *No Phrase Constraint*, both terms apparent counterexamples to what they denote! – are amenable to the same lexical treatment as Spencer (1988) proposed for apparent bracketing paradoxes such as *Baroque flautist* (vs. *wooden flautist*, where *Baroque flute* is lexical and *wooden flute* phrasal).

But a formal model of such constructions, distinguishing sharply between NP and N, faces the problem here of where to draw the line: clearly, lexicalization is a gradient phenomenon. On the empirical side, the restrictions on the nature of the first constituents in such constructions remain an open question. How absolute is the ungrammaticality of *wooden door policy*, for example in *hapaxes* or in newspaper headlines? (*It is our policy not to fit wooden doors in areas liable to flooding. This wooden-door policy... HOUSEBUILDERS ASSOCIATION SLAMS WOODEN DOOR POLICY.*) It would appear, then, that at least some cases of the form exemplified in (14) above constitute counterexamples to Lexical Integrity as long as Lexicalism does not address the phenomenon – itself poorly understood – of lexicalization (Hohenhaus 2005; Lipka 2005). Research in this area is overdue.

9.5.2 Mismatches involving semantic opacity

I turn finally to phrasal names – adjective-plus-noun constructions commonly
used as names for bird (or plant) species. Such forms, exemplified in (15a) below,
usually have end-stress although some of the more common species names of this
form have fore-stress (*Blackbird, Blue-Tit*). (15b) gives examples of the competing,
noun-plus-noun formula for bird names, which seems always to have fore-stress.
Standard ornithological handbooks such as Hume (2002) give hundreds of similar
examples.

(15)   a. Green Woodpecker   b. Eagle Owl
          Grey-headed Woodpecker   Sand Martin
          Snowy Owl   Tree Sparrow
          Arctic Tern   House Sparrow
          Common Tern   Sandwich Tern
          Little Tern   Song Thrush

Forms such as those in (15b) are clearly compound words on both formal and
semantic grounds. And those in (15a) must be of the same lexical status despite
their phrasal appearance: given their naming function, their semantics is indistinguishable from that of noun-plus-noun forms and indeed from that of monomorphemic bird names (*Swallow, Osprey*, etc.). Note also that such constructions
are rather less transparent than they may appear: there are green woodpeckers
other than those that bear the species name; and in Britain, Arctic Terns are more
common than Common Terns.

As we would expect of lexical constructions, names such as those in (15a) can
only be modified in their entirety: *a juvenile Green Woodpecker*, etc. Their elements
cannot be modified: **a grass-Green Woodpecker*, **a Common juvenile Tern*. Such
forms would be possible in a phrasal sense only: 'a woodpecker which is grass-
green', 'a tern which is both common and juvenile'. This modification failure is
consistent with the lexical status of (15a).

However, once again the pro-*one* construction reaches parts that modification
cannot reach: *He logged five Arctic Terns and two Common ones. Grey-headed
Woodpeckers are hard to distinguish from Green ones.* Such statements are well-
formed and attested, unlike, for example, **a Snowy Owl and an Eagle one*.

It would appear, then, that not only the stress criterion and the syntax produce
occasional mismatches but that the semantic criterion of opacity faces similar
problems. Moreover, as we just saw, the syntactic tests themselves – pro-*one* and
modifiability – fail to exactly correlate. The form *Common Tern* is more phrase-like
than *Eagle Owl* is, and sufficiently so to count as a phrase for the purposes of pro-
one, but not sufficiently so to allow individual modification.

9.6 COMPOUNDING AND LEXICAL
STRATIFICATION

I showed in the preceding section that Lexical Integrity, and the lexicon–syntax divide stipulated by that principle, is not as robust as has been claimed. While it is true that in many compelling cases, the criteria invoked by scholars of word formation for the definition of compounds coincide with the syntactic criteria brought to the debate by Lexicalism, there are other cases which show that the phonological, semantic, and syntactic dividing lines between the modules are not quite congruent, however close they may be.

In this section I return, finally, to another aspect of Lexicalism relevant to the study of compounding: the sub-theory of lexical stratification. Lexical strata have their own characteristics – on stratum 1, for example, morphologically complex forms are irregular, opaque, and therefore listed in specific ways (Kiparsky 1982; Giegerich 1999: Chapter 3), while stratum 2 has productive rules giving rise to transparent and regular forms. There has been dispute over the number of lexical strata, in English and elsewhere; but it is uncontroversial that at least in English, compounding should be part of the final stratum: see Giegerich (1999: Chapters 1 and 2) for a summary of that particular research history. Compounding, viewed as a single phenomenon of word formation, is hugely productive and indeed also in other ways the most syntax-like of all word formation.

However, not all forms of compounding in English are equally productive (Bauer and Huddleston 2002). Notably, even among nominal compounds there are some subtypes which in English are not the outcomes of productive processes, of synchronic 'rules' in the sense of the stratum-2 morphology. Among these are left-headed constructions – *Princess Royal, court martial, Procurator Fiscal*, etc. – as well as exocentric (*bahuvrīhi*) compounds of the type *hatch-back, red-neck, shit-head*, etc. The former type are old loans from French, the latter deliberately, and often facetiously, coined. All must therefore be stratum-1 forms. This diagnosis is consistent with the fact that such constructions can be part of regular, stratum-2 compounds – *hatch-back driver, red-neck fan* – while they cannot have regular compounds or stratum-2 affixations as constituents: **rearhatch-back, *reddish-neck, *law-court martial.* Left-headed and exocentric compounding is simply not productive.

That a productive, stratum-2 phenomenon such as compounding should have sporadic and irregular stratum-1 counterparts is not surprising: in Giegerich (1999: Chapter 2) I discuss numerous such cases in the suffix morphology of English. As I noted above, attestation of a given process, phonological or morphological, not on a single stratum but on contiguous strata is only to be expected (Mohanan 1986: 47; Giegerich 1999: 99).

The inability of a stratum-1 form's components to undergo stratum-2 processes is of course strongly reminiscent of the lexical-integrity effects discussed above. *Reddish-neck* is entirely comparable to *expensive watchmaker*. And this is only one example showing that the lexicon–syntax divide is probably no more significant in the grammar than the divide between the two lexical strata of English. In Giegerich (2005b) I give more examples.

But we have also seen above that the lexicon–syntax divide is not robust. Notably, we came across cases in section 9.5 where fore-stressed constructions lacked on the syntactic side the lexical integrity predicted for them by the theory. The phonological and syntactic lexicon–syntax divides are not congruent. On closer inspection, irregular compounds such as *Princess Royal, court martial, hatch-back, red-neck* exemplify the very same phenomenon on the lexicon-internal divide between strata. It is an essential feature of stratum 1 on the phonological side that forms produced there should conform with the phonotactics of morphologically simple items: Structure Preservation is central to the architecture of the stratum-1 phonology (Kiparsky 1982, 1985; Borowsky 1990). But stratum-1 compounds – in particular the consonant sequences at the internal juncture – freely violate this condition.

This is, then, another example of a modular divide which is expected by the theory to affect congruently the phonology, the semantics, and the morphosyntax. Claimed to express a major generalization about the organization of the grammar, the reality of the modular divide is such that there are some, apparently insignificant cases where the phonological divide is not quite the same as the morphosyntactic divide. As a formal theory of grammar, this is exactly the kind of problem that we ought to expect Lexicalism to have to confront. Modules will overlap; it is a matter of one's meta-theoretical persuasions whether such overlap is itself amenable to formalization.

CHAPTER 10

COMPOUNDING AND CONSTRUCTION MORPHOLOGY

GEERT BOOIJ

10.1 INTRODUCTION

Word-formation patterns can be seen as abstract schemas that generalize over sets of existing complex words with a systematic correlation between form and meaning. These schemas also specify how new complex words can be created. For instance, the word-formation process for endocentric compounds in English and Dutch can be represented as follows:

(1) $[[a]_X [b]_{Yi}]_Y$ 'Y$_i$ with relation R to X'

(The lower-case variables a and b in this template stand for arbitrary sound sequences.) Schema (1) can be interpreted as the formal representation of a construction, that is, a particular structural configuration with a specific meaning correlate. The fact that the right constituent and the structure as a whole are dominated by the same syntactic-category variable Y is the formal expression of the generalization that the syntactic category of the compound is determined by its right constituent. For instance, if Y_i has the value N, the compound as a whole is also an N. The relevant meaning correlate is that the right constituent functions as the semantic head of the compound, and that a semantic relation between the two constituents is invoked. The specific nature of that relation, however, is left unspecified in the schema, since it is not predictable on structural grounds.

The traditional notion of construction and its importance for theories of linguistic structure have recently received renewed attention within the theoretical framework of Construction Grammar (cf. Goldberg 2006 and the literature mentioned there). The basic idea of Construction Grammar can be summarized as follows:

In Construction Grammar, the grammar represents an inventory of form-meaning-function complexes, in which words are distinguished from grammatical constructions only with regard to their internal complexity. The inventory of constructions is not unstructured; it is more like a map than a shopping list. Elements in this inventory are related through inheritance hierarchies, containing more or less general patterns.

(Michaelis and Lambrecht 1996: 216)

As suggested by this quotation, both syntactic patterns and word-formation patterns might be seen as constructions. This idea of morphological patterns as constructions has been developed in a number of publications (cf. Riehemann 1998; Koenig 1999; Jackendoff 2002a: Chapter 6; Booij 2002a, b, 2005b).

In this chapter I will present a constructional theory of compounding that makes use of some basic ideas of Construction Grammar, in particular constructional schemas, and the idea of a hierarchical lexicon (with multiple linking between words, and intermediate nodes between the most abstract schemas and the individual lexical items in order to express intermediate levels of generalization). Similar ideas have been developed in the framework of Cognitive Grammar (Langacker 1988, 1998a, b; Croft and Cruse 2003). More specifically, the purpose of this chapter is to provide morphological argumentation in support of such a view of morphology and the lexicon, a view that will be referred to as Construction Morphology. The empirical domain that I will focus on is, for obvious reasons, that of compounding. In section 10.2, some basic assumptions concerning the role of word-formation schemas in the lexicon will be spelled out, and it will be shown how they can be applied in the analysis of endocentric compounds. In section 10.3, the issue of headedness will be discussed in relation to various categories of compounds. Section 10.4 focuses on synthetic compounds, and in section 10.5 I will show how Construction Grammar enables us to give an insightful account of compound-like phrases. Section 10.6 presents a summary of my findings.

10.2 WORD-FORMATION TEMPLATES
AND THE HIERARCHICAL LEXICON

The idea of word-formation templates in a hierarchical lexicon can be illustrated quite nicely by means of compounding. In many languages, compounding is a productive word-formation process, and the notion of 'rules' has therefore played an important role in accounting for this type of word formation. In Dutch, for instance, we find right-headed nominal, adjectival, and verbal compounds, and hence we might assume the following morphological rule for Dutch compounding:

(2) $X + Y \rightarrow [XY]_Y$

In this rule, X and Y stand for the syntactic categories N, A, and V, and the label Y of the resulting compound expresses the generalization that the right constituent of a Dutch compound functions as its head, and thus determines the syntactic category of the word as a whole. In other words, the generalization about the position of the head in endocentric compounds in Germanic languages such as English and Dutch expressed by the so-called Right-hand Head Rule (RHR: Williams 1981) can be expressed directly in the output form of this rule, without making use of an additional rule or principle.

Word-formation rules such as (2) have two functions: they function as redundancy rules with respect to existing complex words, and specify how new complex words can be made (Jackendoff 1975). Note, however, that rule (2) in its present form does not say anything about the semantic regularities in the interpretation of such compounds.

Instead of speaking about word-formation rules, we might also speak about word-formation templates (or schemas). We then replace rule (2) with a word-formation template for Dutch that generalizes about the structure of existing compounds, and that can be used for making new compounds as well. This is schema (1), repeated here for convenience:

(3) $[[a]_X [b]_{Yi}]_Y$ 'Y$_i$ with relation R to X'

The use of phonological variables (a and b) indicates that phonological information does not play a restrictive role in this type of word formation. In (3) the general meaning contribution of the compound schema is also specified, since morphology is about form–meaning pairs. The nature of R is not specified, but is determined for each individual compound on the basis of the meaning of the compound constituents, and encyclopedic and contextual knowledge (Downing 1977).

Template (3) does not yet express that it is not only the syntactic category of the head that is identical to that of the whole compound, but that the two Y-nodes are also identical with respect to properties such as gender and declension class for nouns, and conjugation class for verbs. Hence, we elaborate template (3) as template (3)' in which [αF] stands for the set of relevant subclass features:

(3)' $[[a]_X [b]_{Yi}$ $]_Y$ 'Y$_i$ with relation R to X'

$$\mid \quad \mid$$

    [αF] [αF]

Template (3)' thus specifies the category of right-headed endocentric compounds of Dutch.

The format of (3') implies that compounding is a construction at the morphological level with a systematic pairing of form and meaning. It specifies that the head Y is not only the formal head, but also the semantic head: a Dutch compound denotes a certain Y, not a certain X. By specifying both the form and the meaning of this class of words, we are reminded of the fact that morphology is not a module of the grammar on a par with the syntactic or the phonological component. Instead, morphology is word grammar. Hence, it deals with three different and systematically related aspects of complex words: phonological form, formal structure, and meaning (cf. Jackendoff 2002a). That is, we assume a tripartite parallel architecture of the grammar.

Template (3') is to be seen as the node in the hierarchical lexicon of Dutch that dominates all existing compounds of Dutch. The individual compounds of Dutch inherit their non-unique (formal and semantic) properties from this dominating node, and from their constituent lexemes. For instance, the following substructure of the Dutch lexicon may be assumed for the adjectival compound *sneeuwwit* 'snow-white':

(4)

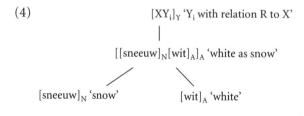

$[XY_i]_Y$ 'Y$_i$ with relation R to X'

$[[sneeuw]_N[wit]_A]_A$ 'white as snow'

$[sneeuw]_N$ 'snow' $[wit]_A$ 'white'

This tree is a 'multiple inheritance tree' with two types of relations: 'instantiation', and 'part of'. The word *sneeuwwit* is an instantiation of the general template at the top of the tree, and the lexemes *sneeuw* and *wit* form part of that adjectival compound (cf. Krieger and Nerbonne 1993). In this example, the relation R is interpreted as 'as' since the word means 'white as snow'.

A graph like (4) makes it clear that a complex word bears several kinds of relations. It is not only an instance of an abstract word-formation schema, but it is also linked to other words in the lexicon. The compound *sneeuwwit*, for example, is linked to *wit* and to *sneeuw*. The lexemes *wit* and *sneeuw* will be linked to other complex words as well. Thus, we get the word families {*wit, sneeuwwit*, etc.} and {*sneeuw, sneeuwwit*, etc.}. The existence of such word families manifests itself in the family-size effect: the larger the size of the family of a word, the faster that word can be retrieved in a lexical decision task (de Jong et al. 2000). The existence of the abstract word-formation schema, on the other hand, manifests itself in the productive coining of new compounds by the language user.

This word-formation schema itself is obviously based on a set of existing compounds. It is knowledge of existing compounds that is a precondition for the language user to develop the abstract schema. That is, both the instantiation relation and the part-of relation are based on paradigmatic relationships between words in the lexicon. The morphological structure assigned to the word *sneeuwwit* is a projection of such paradigmatic relationships on the syntagmatic axis of word structure.

One advantage of this approach to word formation is that generalizations about sub-patterns can be expressed in a straightforward way. The following generalization holds for the set of Dutch endocentric compounds (cf. Booij 2002a: Chapter 4 for the relevant data): only N+N compounding (and under certain conditions to be discussed below, V+N compounding as well) is recursive, both in the head position and the non-head position, that is, their constituents can be compounds themselves. Other types of endocentric compounds do not allow for recursivity. For instance, an adjectival compound such as *muislichtgrijs* 'mouse light grey' is felt as odd, although both *muisgrijs* 'mouse grey' and *lichtgrijs* 'light grey' are existing adjectival compounds of Dutch. Recursive N+N compounding is illustrated in (5):

(5) a. LEFT CONSTITUENT RECURSIVE
     $[[[[ziekte]_N[verzuim]_N]_N[bestrijdings]_N]_N[programma]_N]_N$
     illness absence fight programme
     'programme for reducing absence due to illness'
     $[[[aardappel]_N [schil]_V]_V[mesje]_N]_N$
     potato peel knife
     'knife for peeling potatoes'

   b. RIGHT CONSTITUENT RECURSIVE
     $[[zomer]_N [[broed]_V[gebied]_N]_N]_N$
     summer breed area
     'breeding area for the summer'

   c. BOTH CONSTITUENTS RECURSIVE
     $[[[grond]_N[water]_N]_N[[over]_P[last]_N]_N]_N$
     ground water over burden
     'groundwater problems'

Another example of a specific property of a subset of the Dutch endocentric compounds is that compounds with a nominal head allow certain types of phrases to function as the non-head constituent whereas other compounds do not. For instance, whereas *oudemannenhuis* 'old men's home' is well-formed, an adjectival compound such as *oudemannenzwak* (lit. 'old men weak') 'weak as old men' is odd. In short, we must be able to state generalizations about subclasses of compounds without obliterating the commonalities of all Dutch endocentric compounds.

Generalizations about subsets of words can be expressed in a hierarchical lexicon, by assuming intermediate levels of abstraction in between the most general template and the individual existing compounds. That is, the following structure of the compounding part of the Dutch lexicon may be assumed:

(6)

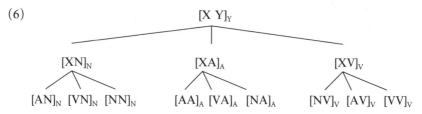

Each of the lowest nodes in (6) will dominate a subset of the Dutch compounds with the relevant structural property. The second and the third of these nodes, $[VN]_N$ and $[NN]_N$, will be without restrictions on the internal complexity of their constituent lexemes, whereas to all other nodes, the condition 'X and Y $\neq$ compound' will have to be added. This accounts for the first observation made above as to the larger range of structures that nominal compounding in Dutch allows for. Thus, we can make generalizations about subsets of compounds, while at the same time expressing the common properties of the whole set of Dutch compounds. The possibility of generalizations at different levels of abstraction is a clear advantage of this representation of word-formation patterns, as we will also see below.

In the hierarchical-lexicon approach, exceptions to generalizations are dealt with by assuming default inheritance: properties of higher nodes are percolated to lower nodes, unless the lower node bears a contradictory specification for the relevant property. As pointed out by Krieger and Nerbonne (1993: 91), '[t]he key advantage of default specifications is that they allow the description of sub-regularities, classes of items whose properties are largely, but not perfectly regular'. The use of inheritance trees is a prominent feature of Network Morphology (cf. Corbett and Fraser 1993, Hippisley 2001), Construction Grammar (cf. Taylor 2002, Croft and Cruse 2003, Goldberg 2006), and Typed and Construction-based Constituent Structure Morphology (Koenig 1999). Examples of the use of inheritance trees in the domain of derivational morphology can be found in Riehemann (1998), and Hippisley (2001).

A basic feature of this approach to word formation is that abstract schemas and individual instances of those schemas coexist. Once the abstract schemas have been discovered, the individual items on which they are based will not necessarily be lost from lexical memory (Langacker 1998a, Tomasello 2003). Thus, we avoid the rule/

list fallacy: the fact that there is a productive rule for the formation of a certain linguistic construct does not imply that the outputs of that rule should not be listed in the lexicon. It is obvious that we need this option for compounds. We have to specify the existing (or established) set of compounds of a language, while we also want to express that most of them have been formed according to a regular and productive schema that gives rise to novel compounds as well.

The idea of a hierarchical lexicon is also in line with the consideration mentioned above that people acquire the morphological system of a language, that is, the abstract morphological schemas, on the basis of their knowledge of a set of words that instantiate these patterns. Once they have come across a sufficient number of words of a certain type, they can infer an abstract schema, and will be able to expand the relevant class of words. The endpoint of language acquisition is therefore to be defined 'in terms of linguistic constructions of varying degrees of complexity, abstraction, and systematicity' (Tomasello 2000: 238).

This view of word formation is in line with Vallès's (2003: 141) position that 'word formation patterns emerge from paradigmatic relations and the function of rule-learning might be to help organize the lexicon, to give it structure; its role is to express generalizations about what is part of the lexicon'. This means that the native speaker's competence to create new compounds and derived words is based on abstractions over sets of existing complex words and the words that are paradigmatically related to them.

The need for intermediate generalizations for subclasses of compounds is particularly clear from the phenomenon of the blurred boundary between compounding and derivation (Booij 2005b). The Dutch lexicon contains a number of compounds of the form $[[hoofd]_N[x]_N]_N$, with the meaning 'main $[x]_N$' (hoofd means 'head').

(7)   *hoofdingang* 'main entrance'
      hoofdgebouw 'main building
      hoofdbezwaar 'main objection'
      hoofdverdachte 'main suspect'
      hoofdbureau 'main office'

Therefore, the language user may assume a schema that generalizes over this set of complex words:

(8) $[[hoofd]_N[x]_N]_N$ 'main $[x]_N$'

In this schema, one of the positions is filled by a specific lexical item. Hence, it is a constructional idiom in the sense of Jackendoff (2002a): a productive idiomatic pattern, with both variable and lexically fixed positions (cf. also Pitt and Katz 2000).

This schema will be dominated by the general schema for N+N compounding, which in its turn will be dominated by the general schema (3'). The semantic generalization for this schema is that the constituent *hoofd* 'head' in these words carries the specific meaning 'main'. This specific meaning of *hoofd* 'head' when embedded in these compounds is quite clear from the fact that in the English glosses we cannot use the English translation of *hoofd* 'head', but have to use *main* instead. Since this meaning 'main' is strictly dependent on the occurrence of *hoofd* within compounds, this lexical morpheme becomes similar to affixes, whose meaning is also dependent on their occurrence in complex words: outside complex words affixes do not have meaning.

Another example of this situation is the productive use of the adjective *oud* 'old' in complex words, as in *oud-burgemeester* 'ex-mayor'. The meaning of *oud* in its bound use is 'former, ex-', and the literal meaning 'old, of high age' does not apply at all. This bound use of the morpheme *oud* is productive, and we can add this morpheme to all sorts of nouns.

These facts have raised the question whether we have to assume prefixes *hoofd-* and *oud-* respectively for Dutch. In De Haas and Trommelen (1993: 51), for instance, the morpheme *oud* with the meaning 'ex-, former' is indeed qualified as a prefix. This problem pops up repeatedly in the analysis of Dutch word-formation patterns (cf. Booij 2005b).

The terms 'affixoid' and 'semi-affix' have been introduced to denote morphemes which look like parts of compounds, and do occur as lexemes, but have a specific and more restricted meaning when used as part of a compound. The following Dutch words also illustrate this phenomenon (data taken from Booij 2005b):

(9) a. *boer* 'farmer'   *groente-boer* (lit. 'vegetables-farmer') 'greengrocer'
     kolen-boer (lit. 'coal-farmer') 'coal trader'
     les-boer (lit. 'lesson-farmer') 'teacher'
     melk-boer (lit. 'milk-farmer') 'milkman'
     patat-boer (lit. 'chips-farmer') 'chips seller'
     sigaren-boer (lit. 'cigar-farmer') 'cigar seller'
     vis-boer 'fishmonger, fish dealer'

    b. *man* 'man'   *bladen-man* (lit. 'magazines-man') 'magazine seller'
     kranten-man (lit. 'newspapers-man') 'newspaper seller'
     ijsco-man (lit. 'ice cream-man') 'ice cream seller'
     melk-man 'milkman, milk seller'

The heads of the complex words have a specific and recurrent meaning when used in that context, just as was the case for the word *hoofd* above. The morpheme *boer* 'farmer' (etymologically related to the English morpheme *bour* in *neighbour*), when part of a complex word, has the meaning 'trader in', and no longer means 'farmer'. Crucially for a classification as semi-affix, the 'bound' use of these morphemes is productive (T. Becker 1994), as is illustrated here for *boer*. This morpheme is used in combination with nouns that do not denote agricultural products, and words with this morpheme form a series of words with a shared meaning component. A similar observation can be used for the lexeme *man* 'man' when used in compounds.

The observation of morphologically incorporated lexemes having specific meanings and being used productively with that specific meaning also applies to lexemes in the non-head position of compounds (data again from Booij 2005b):

(10) a. NOUNS USED AS PEJORATIVE PREFIXOIDS
           kanker 'cancer'   *kanker-school* 'bloody school'
           kut 'cunt'   *kut-ding* 'worthless thing'
           kloot 'testicle'   *klote-houding* 'bad attitude'

      b. NOUNS USED AS PREFIXOIDS OF POSITIVE EVALUATION
           meester 'master' *meesterwerk* 'very good piece of work'
           wereld 'world'   *wereld-vrouw* 'fantastic woman'

      c. NOUNS USED AS PREFIXOIDS WITH INTENSIFYING MEANING
           steen 'stone'   *steen-koud* 'very cold', *steen-goed* 'very good', *steen-rijk* 'very rich'
           beer 'bear'   *bere-sterk* 'very strong', *bere-koud* 'very cold', *bere-leuk* 'very nice'

In the last example, the prefixoid *bere-* derives from the noun *beer* 'bear', followed by the linking phoneme -*e* (schwa).

The analytical problem that there is no sharp boundary between compounding and affixal derivation is not solved by postulating a category of semi-affixes or affixoids. That is just a convenient description of the fact that the boundary between compounding and derivation is blurred, but does not in itself provide an explanation of why this is the case. What we need is a model of morphological knowledge that will enable us to explain these facts. It will be clear by now that the model of the hierarchical lexicon proposed above will be adequate for this purpose, when we combine it with the idea of constructional idioms, partially lexically specified productive patterns. For instance, the use of *man* with the specific meaning 'trader' exemplified in (10) will be accounted for by the following constructional idiom of Dutch:

(11) $[[x]_N[man]_N]_N$ 'trader in X'

This template will be dominated by the general schema for N+N compounding, and most of its properties derive from this general schema. It will also be linked to the noun *man*. The only specific property is that of the recurrent conventionalized interpretation of *man* as 'trader', which is a semantically richer specification than the meaning of *man*.

10.3 HEADEDNESS ISSUES

Since Williams (1981) the importance of the notion of 'head' for the analysis of
morphological constructs has received new recognition and attention. It is clear
that Williams' Right-hand Head Rule cannot be a rule in the sense of a universal
since many languages have left-headed compounds. Hence, one might consider the
position of the head as a morphological parameter. For instance, Germanic languages may be qualified as right-headed, and Romance languages such as Italian as
left-headed (Scalise 1984; 1992). The problem for such a parameter approach is that
Italian and Spanish also have sets of right-headed compounds. Examples of such
compounds in Spanish are the following:

(12)   *auto-escuela* 'car school', *cine-club* 'cinema club', *eco-sonda* 'echo sounder',
        tele-novela 'television novel', *video-arte* 'video art'

Rainer and Varela (1992: 121) make the following remark with respect to these types
of compound:

Such right-headed n-n compounds would have to be limited to a fixed number of first
elements... which is quite atypical since compound types can generally be defined at the
categorical level.... Another property which they share with prefixes is their form: they are
typically bisyllabic and end in a vowel.

Therefore, they consider *auto-* etc. as prefixes. 'The alternative would consist in
setting up an independent sub-type of word formation characterized by right-
headedness, a purely pragmatically driven rule of interpretation, and severe restrictions on the number and form of elements that can serve as left constituents.'
(Rainer and Varela 1992: 121–2).

However, in the framework of construction morphology we can still analyse
these words as compounds. We then assume a list of constructional idioms such as

(13)   [auto [x]$_N$]$_N$ '[x]$_N$ with relation R to car'

instead of a general abstract template for right-headed compounds. By lexically
specifying the left constituent of these compound schemas we state that the class of
right-headed compounds in Spanish is restricted to compounds that begin with a word
that is a member of a restricted and definable set of words. Moreover, these compounds
will be specified as right-headed, and therefore, these constructional idioms will not be
linked to the node for left-headed N+N compounds in the lexicon of Spanish.

The same observation can be made for Italian. As pointed out by Schwarze
(2005: 149), a restricted set of nouns can occur in right-headed compounds. The
best example is that of compounds beginning with *auto* 'car', as in:

(14)   *autocentro* 'car centre', *autoconvoglio* 'convoy', *autodromo* 'motor-racing cir-
        cuit', *autolinea* 'bus route', *autoservizio* 'car service', *autostop* 'hitch-hiking'

They contrast with the regular left-headed N+N compounds such as *autoambu-lanza* 'ambulance', *autobotte* 'tank truck', *autocisterna* 'tank truck', and *autopompa* 'fire truck'. Other types of right-headed compounds in Italian begin with words or roots such as *foto-*, *radio-*, and *tele-*.

Schwarze uses these data to argue that we must distinguish between rules and pattern-imitation:

Constructed words arise from a generative system which may be described in terms of rules. These rules operate on morphological segments and their semantic representations in such a way that the forms and meanings of possible words are defined. . . . Complex, non-constructed words, on the other hand, are brought about by 'paragrammatical procedures' [such as univerbation and pattern-based word formation]

(Schwarze 2005: 137)

In the framework presented here these data receive a straightforward interpret-ation: these subsets of right-headed compounds can be accounted for by means of constructional idioms such as:

(15)   [[auto]$_N$[x]$_N$]$_N$ 'car with relation R to [x]$_N$ '

The same mechanism can be used to account for root compounds. In Italian, for instance, the root *tele* can be used in compounds such as *telespettatore* 'television watcher'. The morpheme *tele* is not a word by itself, but only occurs as part of complex words, hence it is to be qualified as a root. It also lacks a syntactic category. The fact that *tele* is a root can be expressed by assuming a constructional idiom [*tele* [x]$_Y$]$_Y$ which states that *tele* can only occur as part of a complex word, and does not determine the syntactic category of the compound in which it occurs.

The next category to be discussed is that of exocentric compounds. A famous class is that of Italian V+N compounds such as

(16)   *porta-lettere* (lit. 'carry letters') 'post man',
       lava-piatti (lit. 'wash dishes') 'dish washer'

Neither of the constituents of these compounds is the head. A *lava-piatti* is neither a 'wash' nor a 'dishes'. Hence, the formal structure of these words is as follows:

(17)   [[a]$_V$ [b]$_{Nx}$]$_{Ny}$ 'entity that performs action V on N$_x$'

The different indices x and y indicate that there is no identity between the category of the right constituent and the category of the whole compound.

In sum, by analysing 'wrong-headed' and exocentric compounds in terms of specific morphological constructions, we can maintain the generalization that most Italian compounds are left-headed without obliterating the existence of productive patterns of compounding that do not conform to this general-ization.

10.4 SYNTHETIC COMPOUNDS AND EMBEDDED PRODUCTIVITY

The productivity of a certain word-formation pattern may be dependent on its being embedded in another morphological pattern. I refer to this phenomenon as embedded productivity. This is the case for verbal compounding in Dutch. That is, verbal compounds may be qualified as 'bound compounds'. Let us first focus on N+V compounding. This type of compounding appears to be non-productive in Dutch. What we do find for Dutch are the following classes of verbal compounds:

(i) conversions of nominal compounds such as $[[[voet]_N[bal]_N]_N]_V$, 'to play football';

(ii) isolated cases of back formation: $[[beeld]_N [houw]_V]_V$ derived from *beeld-houwer* (lit. 'statue-cutter') 'sculptor'; $[[woord]_N[speel]_V]_V$ 'to play with words' from *woordspeling* 'word-play, pun';

(iii) separable complex verbs such as *piano-spelen* 'piano-play, to play the piano'. Such verbs are not verbal compounds, but phrasal verbs (cf. Booij 1990); the two parts are separated in main clauses, as in *Jan speelt heel goed piano* 'John plays the piano well';

(iv) defective N+V verbs that mainly occur in the infinitival form, such as $[worst]_N[happ-en]_V$ 'to sausage-eat'; some of these verbs have finite forms but only in embedded clauses where the two parts are linearly adjacent (. . . *dat Jan worsthapte* 'that John sausage ate').

Embedded in nominal compounds, however, N+V compounds appear to be quite productive as observed in Booij (2002a: 150); the following examples illustrate this pattern:

(18) $[[[aardappel]_N[schil]_V]_V[mesje]_N]_N$ (lit. 'potato peel knife') 'potato peeler'
$[[[brand]_N[blus]_V]_V[installatie]_N]_N$ (lit. 'fire extinguish installation') 'fire extinguisher'
$[[[koffie]_N[zet]_V]_V[apparaat]_N]_N$ (lit. 'coffee make machine') 'coffee maker'

In these nominal compounds the left constituent is an N+V compound in which the N functions as the Patient of the verb. Remember that, as mentioned in section 10.2, only compounding with nominal heads is recursive. Note, however, that Dutch does not have the corresponding compound verbs *aardappelschil* 'to potato-peel', *brandblus* 'to fire-extinguish', and *koffiezet* 'to coffee-make' as N+V compounds (*koffiezet* does occur, however, but as a phrasal, separable verb). That is, this N+V pattern is only productive when morphologically embedded.

$[NV]_V$ compounding in Dutch is not only triggered by V+N compounding (the N+V compound feeds the non-head V position of these V+N compounds), but also by suffixation with the deverbal suffixes *-er, -ster, -ing,* and *-erij:*

(19)   *aandacht-trekk-er* 'attention drawer'
       brand-bluss-er 'fire extinguisher'
       gif-meng-er 'poison mixer, poisoner'
       grappen-mak-er (lit. 'jokes maker') 'comedian'
       kinder-verzorg-ster 'children's care worker (FEM.)'
       kranten-bezorg-ster 'newspaper deliverer (FEM.)'
       rokkenn-naai-ster 'skirts sewer (FEM.)'
       vee-hoed-ster 'cattle herd (FEM.)'
       evangelie-verkondig-ing 'gospel preaching'
       hand-oplegg-ing 'laying-on of hands'
       kinder-verzorg-ing 'child care'
       tempel-reinig-ing 'temple cleansing'
       bijen-houd-erij 'bee keeping'
       bloem-kwek-erij 'flower nursery'
       vlaggen-mak-erij 'flag making'
       wijn-zuip-erij 'excessive wine-drinking'

These types of complex words are usually referred to as synthetic compounds since both compounding and derivation seem to be involved in these word-formation processes.

The proper account of complex words of the type [NV-*er*]$_N$ has evoked a lot of discussion in the morphological literature on English and Dutch (cf. Lieber 1983, Booij 1988). The main objection raised against assuming N+V compounds as bases for these kinds of derivation (the hypothesis put forward by Lieber 1983 for English) is that, both in English and Dutch, N+V compounding is not productive (Booij 1988; Lieber 2004: 48). On the other hand, from a semantic point of view the assumption of N+V bases is attractive because the N in these examples functions as the Patient of the V. Therefore, another analytical option has been proposed: in Booij (1988), a word such as *brandblusser* 'fire extinguisher' is analysed as a case of N+N compounding in which the head noun is a deverbal N. That is, the semantic unit corresponding with N+V is not reflected by a structural unit N+V. Instead, the notion 'inheritance of argument structure' is invoked: the deverbal noun inherits the Patient argument of the verb, and the left constituent receives this Patient role.

Once we accept the idea that productivity of a certain word-formation pattern may be linked to its occurrence in certain morphological constructions, another attractive analytical option is offered: these words have been derived by means of the conflation of N+V compounding and the suffixation of -*er* to these N+V compounds. The resulting structure gives direct expression to the generalization that the noun and the verb belong together from the semantic point of view. The Dutch word *grappenmaker* 'comedian', for instance, refers to someone who makes jokes, and an *aandachttrekker* (lit. 'attention drawer') is someone who draws attention. This analytical option provides a way of overcoming the problem that N+V compounding is at first sight unproductive. Thus, the structural analysis is the same as that proposed by Lieber (1983), but combines this with template conflation. Through unification of the templates $[NV]_V$ and $[V\ er]_N$ we get the template $[[NV]_V\ er]_N$. This latter, unified template can be qualified as productive, unlike the N+V template in isolation. More generally, the observed productivity boost of N+V compounding in deverbal word formation can be expressed by unification of the relevant templates. Hence, the following productive unified templates can be postulated for Dutch:

(20) $[[[N][V]]_V\ er]_N$
        $[[[N][V]]_V\ ster]_N$
        $[[[N][V]]_V\ ing]_N$
        $[[[N][V]]_V\ erij]_N$

These templates will be dominated by two different word-formation templates, one for N+V compounding, and one for deverbal nouns in -*er*, -*ster*, -*ing*, and -*erij*. The templates will be instantiated by complex words such as those listed in (19).

The words in (19) are referred to as synthetic compounds since they seem to be cases of compounding and derivation at the same time. The account outlined above makes this notion of simultaneity more precise: structurally there is a hierarchy in that the compound is the base of a derived word, and the systematic co-occurrence of the two word-formation processes is expressed by template unification. In order to use the notion of conflation, we need templates or schemas for the specification of these recurrent combinations of word-formation patterns. Such templates, in which both variable and lexically specified positions occur, are in fact constructional idioms at the word level, and thus provide additional evidence for a constructional approach to morphology.

10.5 COMPOUND-LIKE PHRASES

In many languages certain types of phrases perform similar functions to words (Jackendoff 1997, 2002a; Booij 2002a, b). For instance, the following Dutch A+N phrases function as terms to refer to (classes of) objects:

(21)   *dikk-e darm* 'large intestine'
        hog-e hoed (lit. 'high hat') 'top hat'
        vrij-e trap 'free kick'
        zwart-e doos 'black box'

We know for sure that the A+N combinations are phrases, since the adjectives are inflected: the final -*e* is an inflectional ending (a schwa). The specific property of these A+N phrases is that the A position cannot project into a full AP with modifiers. For instance, in the phrase *hele zwarte doos* 'very black box' the specific meaning of 'black box' as used for the registration device in airplanes gets lost. Similarly, Giegerich (2005a) presents ample evidence from English that certain classes of A+N combinations such as *polar bear* and *mental institution* must be considered lexical even though they are phrasal in nature.

Ralli and Stavrou (1998) discuss similar data from Modern Greek. They argue for a distinction between A+N compounds and A+N constructs for this language. For instance, the A+N combination *psixros polemos* 'cold war' is qualified as a construct rather than a compound since there is inflection of the adjective, and agreement of the adjective with the noun. On the other hand, the A+N combination *aghri-o-ghatos* 'wild cat' is a real compound consisting of the non-inflected adjectival root *aghri* followed by a linking element -*o*- and the noun *ghatos* 'cat'. What we therefore need to account for these A+N-constructs is a constructional schema [AN]$_N$ that is dominated by the more general constructional schema for Greek NPs, and generalizes over the set of 'non-projecting' A+N combinations that function as conventionalized terms rather than as descriptions.

In Hoekstra (2002), a study of Frisian N+N combinations, a distinction is proposed between two classes of N+N compounds: the regular, garden variety ones, and a specific class of genitive compounds. In the latter type of N+N compounds, the first noun is inflected and bears genitive case. That is, such compounds have phrasal characteristics because case-marking of a word-internal constituent by another constituent of the same complex word should be ruled out. Hoekstra therefore concludes that such genitive compounds must be analysed as lexical phrases, and he points out that we should use the idea of the constructional idiom for this purpose. That is, these N+N combinations have phrasal status, which explains why the head noun can impose genitive case-marking on the other noun. Yet, they are lexical, since they form a set of established expressions.

Similar syntactic, yet lexical constructions can be found for modern Hebrew (Borer 1988). The difference between Frisian and Hebrew is that in Frisian it is the modifier that is case-marked (with the genitive ending -*s*), whereas in modern Hebrew it is the head noun that is marked as having a relation with another noun. Hence, the head noun appears in the construct state form (*beyt* is the construct state form of *bayit* 'house'):

(22) Frisian: *kening-s-dichter* 'king's daughter'
       Hebrew: *beyt xolim* (lit. 'house sicks') 'hospital'

Another class of compound-like complex expressions is that of the particle verbs in Germanic languages such as Dutch, Frisian, and German. As has been shown in a number of publications (cf. Booij 1990, Blom 2005, and the references mentioned there), these particle verbs cannot be considered verbal compounds of the type [Particle V]$_V$. They are phrasal in nature because the particle and the verb are split, with other words intervening, in root clauses. Yet they require lexical specification. Construction Grammar provides a natural account for these 'lexical phrases': they can be accounted for in terms of constructional idioms. For instance, the Dutch particle *door*, which corresponds with the polysemous preposition *door* 'through, by', evokes a specific meaning of continuation when combined with verbs. Examples are *dooreten* 'to continue eating' and *doorwerken* 'to continue working'. Hence, the following phrasal constructional idiom has to be assumed in the lexicon of Dutch:

(23)   [[door [x]$_V$]$_V$' 'to continue V-ing'

The framework of Construction Grammar thus provides the means to do justice to both the phrasal and the lexical nature of such word combinations. More generally, by making use of the notion of 'construction' in morphology and in syntax alike, we are able to give an adequate treatment of both morphological and syntactic word combinations that function as terms and to account for both their similarities and their differences (complex word vs. phrase) in a model of the grammar in which there is no separation of syntax and the lexicon (cf. Jackendoff 2002a: Chapter 6). We thus get rid of hybrid concepts such as 'syntactic compound'.

10.6 CONCLUSIONS

In this chapter I have showed how some basic insights of Construction Grammar can be applied to the domain of compounding, and how compounding provides empirical support for this grammatical model.

First of all, we saw how (semantic or formal) generalizations about subsets of compounds can be made while at the same time the common or default properties can still be expressed.

We also saw that the regularities concerning the position of the head in compounds are more complicated than can be handled with a simple left-right parameter. The notion of 'constructional idiom' appears to be the key to a proper account of the relevant complications, as well as for dealing with prefix-like constituents of compounds.

The possibility of conflation of word-formation schemas was seen to provide a formal account for the co-occurrence of word-formation patterns, in particular in the domain of synthetic compounding.

Finally, we note that the difference between compounds that are words in the morphological sense and lexical phrases receives a straightforward representation in such a model of the grammar.

CHAPTER 11

COMPOUNDING FROM AN ONOMASIOLOGICAL PERSPECTIVE

JOACHIM GRZEGA

11.1 BASIC DEFINITIONS: ONOMASIOLOGY, COMPOUNDING

In word-formation studies, approaches have always been rather analytical. The first synthetical approaches are those by Dokulil (1962), Jackendoff (1975), and Aronoff (1976). The two latter stem from generative linguistics and therefore more or less exclude the extralinguistic aspects. An onomasiological approach,[1] though, takes an extralinguistic entity and the need of a speaker to denote an extralinguistic entity as a starting point and also as the central point that the word-finding process must be linked to. The cognitive and conceptual sides of word formation thus play a more prominent role than formal aspects. Dokulil's approach can be termed the first onomasiological one and will be presented in more detail below. Again, an onomasiological perspective departs from an extralinguistic entity (a concept) and

[1] The term *onomasiology* was coined by Adolf Zauner in 1902, but the onomasiological approach had already been carried out, notably by Friedrich Diez (1875).

looks for forms that denote or may denote this concept, for example 'What are English names for long thin pieces of fried potato, eaten hot?' (answer: *French fries* in the US and *chips* in Britain) or 'What could be a (new) name for long thin pieces of fried potato, eaten hot?' (potential answer: *freedom fries*). The onomasiological perspective may be purely synchronic, or static, or it may include diachronic, procedural aspects. If procedural aspects are included, the coinages of designations can be grouped into (a) already existing names used in a new way (also referred to as semantic change), (b) borrowings, (c) new coinages based on indigenous linguistic material. This latter is referred to as word formation.[2]

The second term that we need to define is *compound*. The term is not used unequivocally. The only feature that all definitions share is that the term refers to the sticking together of elements. This means that, in onomasiology, where the cognitive aspects are more important than formal ones, there are also approaches where derivation and compounding are not kept apart; the boundary that separates a *compound* from other word-formation processes differs from model to model. As we have said, in many classical works compounding is juxtaposed with derivation. But the differentiation between the notions of compounding and derivation is indeed far from being natural (see already Koziol 1937: 42 and *passim*, and Hansen et al. 1982: 49, 65).[3] Marchand, for instance, says that '[t]he coining of new words proceeds by way of combining linguistic elements on the basis of a determinant/determinatum relationship called syntagma. When two or more words are combined into a morphological unit on the basis just stated, we speak of a compound' (1969: 11). Derivation, in contrast, is '[t]he transposition of a word to the role of determinant in a syntagma where the determinatum is a dependent morpheme' for Marchand (1969: 11). However, what do we do with a case like *beautiful* = {beauty}+{full}, traditionally seen as a derivation, and cases like *chairman* ['tʃermən] (not [-mæn]), traditionally seen as a compound? This definition is not unanimous among onomasiologists either. A definition of compound must therefore be presented separately for every model.

The following chapter will be structured in a historical order. In each section, a linguist and his overall model will be presented, then the definition and subtypes of compound according to the respective model will be given. The linguists whose models are presented are Miloš Dokulil, Ján Horecký, Pavol Štekauer, Andreas Blank, Peter Koch, and Joachim Grzega.[4] The chapter will also briefly discuss a

---

[2] The forces influencing the decision when a new word is coined and what type of process is used are manifold. A complete catalogue of such forces has been suggested by Grzega (2002b, 2004). An experiment on the preferred word-formation patterns for new words was carried out by Štekauer et al. (2005).

[3] More recently, Ungerer (2002) tried to juxtapose prefixation, suffixation, and composition from a cognitive perspective, not ignoring that there are overlapping areas. Since his approach is not onomasiological, however, this is not further commented on.

[4] Although the title of Gorog's (1981) article suggests that his contribution will have to do with something central to word formation, his article just highlights the affinity of some word-formation patterns with certain concepts.

number of phenomena related to compounds and will illustrate the various theoretical works with examples from the original works and some additional examples from English. At the end of the chapter there will be a brief summary juxtaposing the various models.

11.2 COMPOUNDING IN ONOMASIOLOGICAL MODELS

11.2.1 Miloš Dokulil

As already mentioned the first comprehensive onomasiological theory of word formation was developed by the Czech linguist Miloš Dokulil (1962, 1968, 1997). Though not triggering a fundamental change in linguistics, Dokulil's model had impact particularly on linguists from Slavic countries – the Slovaks Buzássyová (e.g. 1974), Horecký (e.g. 1983, 1994, 1999), Furdík (e.g. 1993), and Štekauer (e.g. 1996, 1997a, 1998, 2001, 2005a, 2005b), the Poles Puzynina (1969), Grzegorczykowa (1979), Szymanek (1988), and Waszakowa (1994), and the Russian Neščimenko (1963, 1968) – but also on the German linguists Fleischer (1969), Polenz (1973), and Huke (1977).

11.2.1.1 *The overall model*

The core idea of Dokulil's onomasiological theory of word formation is the idea of 'onomasiological category'. Since any act of naming a concept rests on its reflection and processing in the human mind, Dokulil introduces the notion of onomasiological category, defined as different ways of structuring the concept in terms of its expression in a language, i.e. the basic conceptual structures underlying the naming process. In principle, they include two elements. The concept to be designated is first classed as a member of a certain conceptual group in an 'onomasiological base' or 'onomasiolo- gical basis' (Cz. *onomasiologická báze*). Then, within the limits of this group, the basis is specified by an 'onomasiological mark', or 'onomasiological feature' (Cz. *onoma- siologický příznak*).[5] The onomasiological categories are thus based on traditional logic: classifying something into a class of objects first and then finding its specific properties that differentiate this object from other members of this class. For example, the onomasiological base of Cz. *černice* 'black earth' is -*ice* 'something', that of Cz. *černozem* 'black earth' is -*zem* 'earth', and that of En. *black earth* is *earth*. Its

---

[5] The terms *basis* and *feature* are the translations used by Horecký, *base* and *mark* are the translations used by Štekauer and Grzega.

onomasiological mark is *black*. While looking similar to Marchand's determinant/ determinatum distinction, Dokulil's terms, in contrast to Marchand's, focus on the level of conceptual processing. The base is always simple, the mark may be simple or complex. A simple mark within the conceptual category of SUBSTANCE is Quality (e.g. Cz. *černice* 'black earth' or En. *blackberry*) or Action conceived without regard to its Object (e.g. Cz. *soudce* 'judge' or En. *singer*). An example with complex marks is Cz. *hráč na housle* 'violin player' (lit. 'play + agent [suffix] + on violin'), where the Object of Action (the violin) is specified in addition. The examples also show that the two elements of the mark, that is, the determining and the determined components, may or may not be explicitly given. In Dokulil's view, the basic types of onomasiological structure can be determined according to the categorial nature (SUBSTANCE, ACTION, QUALITY, CIRCUMSTANCE) of the base and the determining element of mark, called *motive*. For example, a concept of the category of SUBSTANCE is determined by its relation to a concept of the category of (a) SUBSTANCE (e.g. Cz. *straník* 'member of a political party' < *strana* 'political party'+-*(n)ík* 'thing or person related to X'); (b) QUALITY (e.g. Cz. *černice* 'black earth'); (c) ACTION (e.g. Cz. *soudce* 'judge$_N$' < *soud-* 'judge$_V$' + -*ce* 'person having to do with X'); (d) CONCOMITANT CIRCUMSTANCE (e.g. Cz. *večerník* 'evening paper'<*večer* 'evening'+-*(n)ík* 'thing or person related to X'). Other onomasiological structure types are determined in a parallel way. These types can represent the multiplicity of semantic relations, including the bearer of Quality, Agent, Instrument of Action, Patient, Result of Action, etc.[6] A given structure may be realized by several naming units, emphasising its different aspects (AmE. *French fries* vs. *freedom fries*).

Dokulil differentiates between three onomasiological categories:

(a) the 'mutational type' (Cz. *mutační typ*): an object of one conceptual category is characterized (and named) according to its direct or indirect relation to an object of the same or some other conceptual category (e.g. Cz. *černice* 'black earth')

(b) the 'transpositional type' (Cz. *transpoziční typ*): the phenomenon, usually conceived as a mark, dependent on a SUBSTANCE, is abstracted from all the phenomena upon which it objectively depends, and is viewed as an independent phenomenon, for example, the objectification of Quality (e.g. Cz. *rychlý* 'rapid' – *rychlost* 'rapidity' or En. *rapid – rapidity*) and the objectification of Action (e.g. Cz. *pád* 'fall, falling' – *padání* 'to fall (imperfective)' or En. *fall$_V$* – *fall$_N$*)

(c) the 'modificational type' (Cz. *modifikační typ*): this type is based on adding a 'modifying' feature, for example, diminutives and augmentatives (e.g. En. *dog – doggy* or Cz. *pes* 'dog' – *psisko* 'big dog'), change of gender (e.g. Cz. *lev* 'lion' – *lvice* 'lioness' or En. *lion – lioness*), names of the young (e.g. Cz. *had* 'snake' – *hádě* 'young snake' or En. *pig – piglet*), collectivity (e.g. Cz. *kámen* 'a stone' – *kamení* 'stone [collective entity]' or E. *man – mankind*).

---

[6] Dokulil (1962) gives a very fine-grained classification of these relations.

After the selection of an onomasiological base and an onomasiological mark on the semantic level of the word-formation process, the speaker selects a word-formation base and a formans from an inventory of productive word-formation categories, classes, and subtypes on the formal level.

11.2.1.2 *Compounds according to this model*

Compounds are listed as one possible type of word formation (beside suffixation, prefixation, suffixation-prefixation, regressive derivation, conversion, and special word-formation processes such as abbreviation and contamination), but the phenomenon is not further commented on in Dokulil's theory, since this word-formation type is marginal in Standard Modern Czech. As a matter of fact, Dokulil's ideas would be well applicable also to compounds: examples from English are *blackberry* for the mutational type, *beautiful* for the transpositional type, and *she-goat*, *bear cub*, *mankind* for the modificational type.

11.2.2 Jan Horecký

11.2.2.1 *The overall model*

Departing from Dokulil's 1962 work, Horecký claims that Dokulil's concept of onomasiological structure deserves more than just marginal treatment (cf. Horecký 1994: 43). Horecký's (1983) model of word formation is a multi-level model that encompasses:

(1) an object of extralinguistic reality or an ideal object
(2) the pre-semantic level of concepts (logical predicates, noemes)
(3) the level of semantic features
(4) the level of onomasiological relations
(5) the level of onomatological structures
(6) the phonological level

Some of the logical predicates of the pre-semantic level are realized as semantic markers. Horecký's semantic level is very fine-grained. He provides an inventory of thirty-nine distinctive semantic features for Slovak, their relations, and their hierarchical organization. At the top of the hierarchy, there are very broad categorial markers (e.g., Substance, Quality, Agent names, names of Relations), which are part of the formal level represented as the onomasiological base. Further down the hierarchy, the semantic markers represent the generic level. They reflect a feature common to all of the meanings of a particular naming unit. The next level represents the specific, or differentiating, level. The formal side of the linguistic sign is composed of the onomasiological, the onomatological, and the phonological structures. The onomasiological structure includes a base and a mark. The base also unites relevant grammatical categories, including a word-class. On the

onomatological level, both the inventory of morphemes and the expression of base
and mark are located. Finally, the phonological level determines the specific form
of morphemes and other phonological features.

11.2.2.2 *Compounds according to this model*

Due to the structure of the Slovak language, Horecký distinguishes subtypes of
prefixations and suffixations. However, occasionally he uses the terms *compound
words* and *derived compound words* (e.g. Horecký 1994: 44f., 49), by which he
obviously simply refers to words that consist of a compound and a derivational
affix. For instance, he explains that in the Slovak word *delostrelec* 'artilleryman' (i.e.
delo-strel-ec, lit. 'cannon-shoot-er'), from the point of view of the onomasiological
structure, the suffix *-ec* has to be taken for the base because this suffix puts the word
in the large set of nouns denoting the Agent of Action; the onomasiological mark of
such compounds is complex.

Horecký (1994: 44f.) casts particular light on what he calls *derived possessive
compounds* like Slov. *ostrochvost* 'sharp-tail' (< *ostrý* 'sharp' + *chvost* 'tail'). According to him in a word like *ostrochvost* the whole complex 'sharp tail' serves as the
onomasiological mark. The onomasiological base is not present here in the form of
a formally realized constituent. Horecký says that we cannot use either the term
zero-derivative-morpheme or that of zero-suffix, since the notion of zero-morpheme makes sense only in the frame of a closed system.

11.2.3 Pavol Štekauer

Despite the works by Dokulil, Horecký, and Szymanek,[7] it was only in 1998 that
Pavol Štekauer rang in a truly new interpretation of word formation – on a

---

[7] Szymanek has added some interesting ideas adopted by Štekauer, but was not interested in
compounding, only in derivational morphology (affixation) in Polish and English (in contrast to
inflectional morphology). Szymanek (like Beard 1995) is a staunch supporter of the 'Separation
Hypothesis' in word formation, assuming a strict separation of form and meaning. Szymanek's
model includes three levels of representation: (a) the level of cognitive categories (concepts), (b) the
level of derivational categories (functions/meanings), (c) the level of derivational exponents (formatives). Like Dokulil (1962), Szymanek distinguishes between derivational category, defined as 'a
class of lexemes characterized by a single derivational function', and derivational type, defined as
'a group of complex lexemes characterized by a singleness of derivational function and of its formal
exponence (e.g. all English agent nouns ending in *-er*) (1988: 60). Szymanek says (1988: 93): 'The basic
set of lexical derivational categories is rooted in the fundamental concepts of conception' (the
'Cognitive Grounding Condition') and proposes twenty-five fundamental and prototypically arranged cognitive categories such as OBJECT, SUBSTANCE, EVENT, ACTION, STATE, PROCESS, NUMBER,
PERSON, AGENT, INSTRUMENT, POSSESSION, NEGATION, CAUSATION, SIMILARITY, PLACE. A derivational category may be rooted in more than one cognitive category. The derivational category of,
for example, privative verbs is rooted in three cognitive categories: CAUSATION+NEGATION+POSSES-
SION (*flea – deflea*). On the other hand, a single cognitive category may underlie more than one
derivational category. For instance, the cognitive category INSTRUMENT underlies the derivational
category of instrumental nouns and instrumental verbs (*open – opener* and *hammer – to hammer*).

cognitive and onomasiological basis.[8] Štekauer sees his model as a reaction to the formalism of many generative morphologists and thus emphasizes the interrelation of the cognitive abilities of a speech community with both extralinguistic and linguistic phenomena.

11.2.3.1 *The overall model*

Štekauer's model represents a word-finding process that is initiated by an individual speaker's concrete need for producing new naming units and that consists of five levels:

(1) the conceptual level, where the concept to be named is analysed and conceptually categorized in the most general way, as 'SUBSTANCE, ACTION (with internal subdivision into ACTION PROPER, PROCESS, and STATE), QUALITY, and CONCOMITANT CIRCUMSTANCE (for example, that of Place, Time, Manner, etc.)' (Štekauer 2001: 11)

(2) the semantic level, where the semantic markers or semantic components are structured

(3) the onomasiological level, where one of the semantic components is selected as the onomasiological base (representing a class like Agent, Object, Instrument, etc.) and another as the so-called onomasiological mark of this base (the mark can further be divided into a determining constituent – sometimes distinguishing between a specifying and a specified element – and a determined constituent) (= naming in a more abstract sense)

(4) the onomatological level (with the Morpheme-to-Seme-Assignment Principle [MSAP]), where the concrete morphemes are selected (= naming in a more concrete sense) and where the name-coiner demonstrates creativity, but within productivity constraints (cf. Štekauer et al. 2005)

(5) the phonological level, where the forms are actually combined, respecting morphological and suprasegmental rules.

Štekauer recognizes five onomasiological types:

(a) Onomasiological Type 1, which formally shows all three constituents – onomasiological base, determining constituent, determined constituent – e.g. *[[piano] [play]]-[er]*

(b) Onomasiological Type 2, where the determining constituent is not expressed formally, e.g. *[lock] [pin]*, *[play]-[er]*

(c) Onomasiological Type 3, where the determined (actional) constituent is not represented in the form, e.g. *[pian(o)][ist]*, *[piano][man]*

(d) Onomasiological Type 4, where the onomasiological mark cannot be split into a determining and a determined part, e.g. *[un][happy]* and *[extra][large]*

(e) Onomasiological Type 5, traditionally known as 'conversion'.

---

[8] Cf. also the preliminary works by Štekauer (1992, 1996). A concise illustration of his onomasiological theory is presented in Štekauer (2001) and Štekauer (2000: 1–28).

11.2.3.2 *Compounds according to this model*

Štekauer explicitly abstains from the traditional distinction between compounds and derivations[9] and claims that on the onomasiological level certain salient aspects and relations are selected and are then expressed on the onomatological level through the combination of morphemes (either free or bound). Thus the relation of 'Agent of an Action' can be expressed in English by the morphemes (-)*man, -er, -ist, -ant*, and others. So various types traditionally called 'compounds' fit various onomasiological types.

As regards the compounds traditionally termed 'exocentric', 'bahuvrīhi', or 'pseudo'-compounds Štekauer writes (e.g. 2001: 3; his emphasis):

I propose to explain 'exocentric compounds' by a two-step process in which only the first has word-formation relevance. The first step consists in the formation of an **auxiliary, onomasiologically complete** (i.e. with both the base and the mark included), *naming unit*. The second step is based on mere **elliptical shortening**. . . . Therefore, this type of naming units can be analysed on a par with the underlying 'full', auxiliary, version, although the latter has not come to be used (institutionalised).

Štekauer constitutes his view by arguing that the plural of *sabertooth* is not **saberteeth*, but *sabertooths*; therefore, one should assume a shortened onomasiological base (e.g. *animal* or *tiger*).

11.2.4 Andreas Blank

Andreas Blank has become known for his cognitive approach on semantic change, which he elaborated in his landmark book from 1997 (Blank 1997a), but he also tried to apply his theory to the issue of word formation (Blank 1997b), classifying particularly Romance examples.

11.2.4.1 *The overall model*

In Blank's model, too, speakers first analyse a concept to be named into various salient sub-concepts. The most salient sub-concept that already has a designation will then serve as a semantic basis for a coinage. The semantic difference between the basic concept and the concept to be named will then be filled by adding an affix or a second sub-concept ('co-basis'). These relations between basis, co-basis, and the new concept are based on the same associative principles as with semantic change: these principles, first suggested by Roudet (1921), are contiguity (i.e. the co-occurrence of things or concepts in a given context), contrast, and similarity.

---

[9] This was already done by Coseriu (1973). Bauer too admits the difficulty of distinguishing clearly between composition and derivation: 'the forms *ism* and *ology*. These are now used, especially in the plural, as lexemes in their own right' (Bauer 1983: 35). He also points at the cases of *burger* from *hamburger* or the development from *wise* of a suffix, or 'suffixoid', *-wise*.

11.2.4.2 *Compounds according to this model*

In Section 5 of his paper Blank focuses on composition, within which he contrasts five different types:

(1) Type 'similarity/contrast within a category+conceptual contiguity': Blank (1997b) explains this type as follows: 'Traditionally speaking, we could say that one part determines the other, but I will plead here for a different interpretation: a double conceptual relation between the new concept expressed by the compound and the two concepts that form the compound. [...]this type of compounding is characterized by the similarity between a prototype and a peripheral member as well as by conceptual contiguity.' As examples Blank lists, among other words: Fr. *wagon-lit* 'sleeping car' (lit. 'car-bed'), It. *autostrada* 'freeway' (lit. 'auto-street'), Pg. *máquina de escrever* 'typewriter' (lit. 'machine for writing').

(2) Type 'similarity/contrast within a category' and 'metaphorical similarity': here the determinatum can be viewed as in type 1, but the determinant originates in a metaphor; Blank's example: ModE. *frogman.*

(3) Type 'double similarity/contrast (coordinated compounds)': Blank describes this type as follows: 'This type is characterized by the absence of determination. The concept to be expressed shows particular deviation from the prototype of two (or even more) categories, but doesn't really fit into any of them' (Blank 1997b), e.g. ModE. *deaf-mute*, Fr. *moissoneuse-batteuse-lieuse* 'combine harvester' (lit. 'mower-beater-harvester') or It. *portafinestra* 'French window' (lit. 'door-window').

(4) Type 'integral metonymies and metaphors (called exocentric compounds)': Among Blank's examples are Fr. *chasse-neige* 'snowplough', It. *cavatappi* 'cork-screw', Sp. *limpiabotas* 'shoeshine boy'

(5) Type 'double contiguity': This type seems to go particularly with words consisting of a verbal element and a following noun like Fr. *chasse-neige* 'snowplough'.

11.2.5 Peter Koch

Koch does not specifically deal with word formation, but has established an overall scheme of word-finding processes.

11.2.5.1 *The overall model*

Peter Koch's model (2001: 19, 2002: 1159ff.) consists of three dimensions, or axes:

(a) the morphological axis (including 'zero' [= semantic change], conversion, suffixation, prefixation, composition, and others)

(b) the cognitive-associative, or semantic, axis (including various forms of contiguity, similarity, and contrast)

(c) the stratification axis (differentiating between foreign models and autochthonous models)

According to Koch not only semantic shifts, but also all sorts of word formations can be triggered off by any of his eight cognitive-associative relations.

11.2.5.2 *Compounds according to this model*

Apart from the simple entry 'composition', Koch's makes no further refinements. As can be seen from the rest of the list, where prefixation and suffixation occur, Koch uses a traditional definition of compounds as the connection of two stems. However, it should be noted that Koch's model allows the integration of compound types effected by foreign influences, namely loan translations, loan renditions, and pseudo-loans (including 'neoclassical compounds').

Loan translations are a mixture of word formation and borrowing: it seems that on the onomatological level the single elements of a foreign coinage have been translated, e.g. OE *an·horn* < Lat. *uni·corn*, OE *hæl·end* < Lat. *salva·tor*, OE *god·spel* < Gk. *eu·angelion*, ModE *super·man* < G. *Über·mensch*, Fr. *gratte-ciel* < En. *sky·scraper*.

Loan renditions are another mixture of word formation and borrowing: it seems that on the onomasiological level a foreign coinage comes into play in the form of its underlying motives, or iconemes.[10] This means that the image behind the foreign coinage is now rendered with indigenous material, e.g. G. *Wolken·kratzer* < En. *sky·scraper*, ModE *brother·hood* < Lat. *fratern·itas*, OE *leorning·cniht* < Lat. *discip·ulus*.[11] In other words, the name-giver seems to resort to the semantic level, looks at a foreign language on the way to the onomatological level, and comes back to the native language on the onomatological level.

Lexical *pseudo-loans* are the third mixed type of word formation and borrowing: words that consist of foreign material, but never existed in this form in the 'donor language'. The already mentioned 'neoclassical compounds' are one form of pseudo-loans. Also of note, the prestige of English attracts many nations to form pseudo-Anglicisms. It seems as if here the name-giver reaches the onomatological level and there takes material from a foreign language, which then undergoes the usual adaptation changes on the morphophonological level. However, with calques we have the problem that we cannot always decide whether the coinage was really modelled on a foreign term or whether it represents an independent, albeit parallel construction.

---

[10] Alinei (1995, 1997) uses the term *iconym*.

[11] The terminology used here is an extended and revised version of Betz's classification (1949).

11.2.6 Joachim Grzega

In Grzega (2004), I established an overall model of processes and forces of lexical change. This model of naming processes tries to connect and further elaborate the models by Štekauer, Blank, and Koch.[12]

11.2.6.1 *The overall model*

In Grzega (2004)[13] I first presented a linguistic sign model that includes the ideas of the previously presented onomasiological models as well as psycholinguistic observations (Figure 11.1). This scheme is to be read as follows: When a speaker has to designate a particular Referent in context (by *context* I mean speaker–hearer situation, type of discourse, communicative goal, syntactical co-text), the speaker first tries to categorize the referent by perceiving its global and local features[14] (i.e. a referent-to-concept classification is produced). If the speaker can categorize the Referent as an element of a familiar Concept, the speaker makes a cost–benefit analysis (conversational maxims: motoric and cognitive effort on the cost side vs. persuasion, representation, image, relationship, and aesthetics on the benefit side) and decides, more or less consciously, either to take an already existing word (provided that there was no misclassification of the Referent or in the choice of the word, which would trigger lexemic change) or to create a new designation. Then the concept is first analysed and categorized. Several (salient) aspects and

---

[12] The model also integrates approaches by Dirven and Verspoor (1998). Although Dirven and Verspoor's work is only an introductory book, it offers a number of valuable points for word formation. In the section on compounds Dirven and Verspoor (1998: 57) – following Bauer (1983: 188; cf. above) – write that people's interpretation is rooted in their cultural knowledge. It can be added that due to this it is possible to express such prototypical relations between two sub-concepts or sub-aspects by simply connecting two stems with each other. Dirven and Verspoor also note (1998: 58): 'In *tennis shoes* the purpose relation is clear. In *horse shoes* and *snow shoes* the purpose relation is self-imposing, too, but the notion of "shoes" has now been extended to that of "a protecting or supporting structure for the feet"'. This shows that several processes of onomasiological/lexical creation can be combined, in this instance metaphor and composition. The multitude of associations and relations that can be expressed by merely sticking two word(stem)s together was already illustrated by Whitney (1875: 121) – however, in a way that rather resembles the generative approach. Dirven and Verspoor (1998: 60) also illustrate the relevance of compounds in the creation of taxonomies: 'If we invented a new simple form for each conceptual subcategory, we would overburden our memory capacity and no longer have a clearly hierarchically structured lexicon.' The author's examples are convincing: *motorway* as a subtype of *way*, *miniskirt* as a subtype of *skirt*, *sportscar* as a subtype of *car*, and *electronic mail* as a subtype of *mail*. However, it can be asked why there is a compound *motorway* as a subtype of *way*, whereas other subtypes are the non-derived *avenue*, *alley*, and *street*. And why is there a compound *sportscar*, but also *van*, which is formally independent of *car*.

[13] For the following description of Grzega's (2004) overall model see also the concise English version in Grzega and Schöner (2007: 53ff.), on which this summary is based.

[14] There are studies that suggest that both the more general, 'global' features and the more specific, 'local' features of a concept are processed simultaneously (see e.g. Mangold-Allwinn et al. 1995: 133ff., Kolb/Wishaw 1990), even though there are signs that 'global' features are processed more *rapidly* than 'local' features (cf. Dietrich 2002: 124).

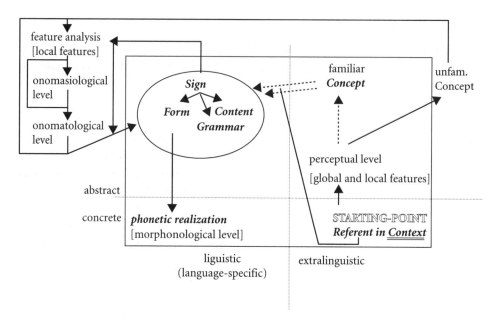

Figure 11.1. Linguistic sign model (from Grzega 2004)

associations (similarity, contrast, contiguity, partiality) are activated in the speaker's mind. Then the speaker passes the onomasiological level (where the semantic components for the naming units are selected) and the onomatological level (where the concrete morphemes are selected). The level of feature analysis (and possibly the onomasiological level) can be skipped if a speaker simply borrows a form from a foreign language or variety; it is also skipped if the speaker simply takes an already existing word and shortens it.

In sum, there is a choice of several types of processes, including

(1) adoption of either (a) an already existing word of the speaker's own idiom (semantic change) or (b) a word from a foreign idiom (loanword)
(2) syntactical recategorization (i.e. conversion)
(3) composition (in the broad sense, i.e. compounds and derivations, which are, very consciously, not further subclassified)
(4) clarifying compounds (i.e. tautological compounds) and others.

The coinages may be based on a model from the speaker's own idiom, on a model from a foreign idiom, or, in the case of root creations, on no model at all.

The process is completed with the actual phonetic realization on the morpho-phonological level (which may possibly be influenced by a foreign sound model).

In order to create a new word on the onomatological level, the speaker first highlights one or two physically and psychologically salient aspects on the ono-masiological level (respecting the situational context, i.e. the conversational maxims and the motives for innovating). The search for the motivations (ico-nemes) is based on one or several cognitive–associative relations. These relations include, amongst others, (a) identity (e.g. with loans); (b) 'figurative', i.e. indi-vidually felt, similarity of the concepts (e.g. with metaphor), partially in connec-tion with contiguity of concepts; (c) contiguity of concepts (e.g. with metonymy), partially in connection with 'figurative' similarity of the concepts. The concrete associations may or may not be incited by a model, which may be from the speaker's own idiom or a foreign idiom.

The differentiation between models from the speaker's own language and foreign models within both the cognitive–associative aspect and the formal aspect shows that foreign influences cannot easily be included as a separate unique process in an overall scheme. Foreign influence can become effective on various levels. For instance, foreign influence triggers off loan rendering and loan translation on the onomasiological level (and, as to loan translation, also on the onomatological level). Formal foreign influence comes up on the perceptual level in the form of full, true loans, morphological pseudo-loans, or folk-etymological adaptions; on the onomatological level in the form of pseudo-loans and coinages with assumed foreignized material that accidentally also exists in the foreign language (for the correct classification of assumed pseudo-loans knowledge of the chronological development is vital!); and on the morphophonological level in the form of phonetic loans. (Loan creations and the so-called substituting loan-meanings are not linguistic but cultural loans and therefore have to be excluded as ghost phenomena in a linguistic terminology.)

11.2.6.2 *Compounds according to this model*

Like Štekauer, I abstain from the traditional compound/derivation distinction and simply speak of composite forms. While my overall model does not distinguish between any subtypes of compounds, or composite forms, I have done so in specific chapters on word formation (Grzega 2002a, 2004: 113f.), where the follow-ing types are introduced as revised and extended versions of Štekauer's termin-ology (including the encompassment of 'metaphorical' expressions):

(1) the 'simplex structure' (simplex composites), e.g. *blackberry, vice chair*
(2) the 'complete complex structure' (complex composites), e.g. *piano player, skyscraper*
(3) the 'incomplete complex structure 1' (composites with absence of determin-ing component of the mark), e.g. *pianist, pianoman*
(4) the 'incomplete complex structure 2' (composites with absence of deter-mined component of the mark), e.g. *player*

(5) the 'incomplete complex structure B' (composites with absence of the base), e.g. *redbreast*[15]

(6) the 'copulative structure' (copulatives, or determination-absence, composites), e.g. *actor-singer, deaf-mute*

This model integrates what are traditionally called 'exocentric compounds' (e.g. *redbreast*) as base-absence composites or 'incomplete complex structure B'. In addition to this, the model incorporates a type called *copulative composites*: two hierarchically equal morphemes, i.e. lacking a determination pattern, known from the types sometimes called 'copulative compounds' (e.g. *German-French [couple]*) and 'additive compounds' (e.g. *deaf-mute*).

Like Koch's, my model enables the inclusion of compound types effected by foreign influences, namely loan translation, loan renditions, and pseudo-loans (including 'neoclassical compounds'[16]). In addition to this, the model includes the composite phenomenon of folk-etymologies. These are forms like *sparrow-grass* (from Lat. *asparagus*), *bridegroom* (from OE *brydguma* lit. 'bride-man'), and *nick name* (from ME *eke name* lit. 'additional name'). Definitions of *folk-etymology* vary from author to author, but it seems largely accepted (cf. Olschansky 1996) that each folk-etymological change is motivated by a similarity (maybe even a homonymy) of expressions (for a more thorough discussion of the problem see Grzega (2004: 130f. and 233f.). The levels of the word-finding process do not seem to be relevant; what the speaker does is to assume a wrong selection on the onomatological and onomasiological level with the consequence that even the elements on the semantic level (connotation and some of the semantic markers) are reordered, or reinterpreted. Although this happens subconsciously, folk-etymology is nonetheless some type of word formation, and unless we want to see the phenomenon of remotivation as a separate word-coining process aside from 'borrowing', 'semantic change', and 'word formation proper', we should in fact include it here.

Apart from this, the model also includes, unlike Štekauer's, cases like *peacock, reindeer*, or *hound dog*. But these are remarkable, as the meaning of the second element is already encompassed in the first, as is especially visible in the compound *hound dog*, which exists beside the simplex *hound*. Here the speaker has not gone through the word-finding process in the usual way. At the beginning of the process is an unmotivated word, e.g. *pea, rein, hound*. On the onomasiological level, the speaker selected a base, but not a mark, since the mark was already represented by the unmotivated word. Therefore, on the onomatological level, only the morpheme for the base had to be selected. On the phonological level, the original word is then treated like a mark, which is why it appears in first position in English, for example (*hound dog*, not **dog hound*).

---

[15] We may also speak of 'incomplete complex structure and metonymy' or 'word-formation metonymy' or 'metonymy composition'.

[16] On this specific type of word formation cf. Bauer (1998).

11.3 SUMMARY

To sum up, there are two cognitive-onomasiological approaches to the name-finding process, Dokulil/Horecký/Štekauer on the one hand and Blank/Koch on the other, that are merged in the model presented in Grzega (2004). In the first approach the main point is the differentiation between a step in the name-finding process that can be termed naming in a more abstract sense, where an onomasiological base and an onomasiological mark are selected, and a step that can be termed naming in a more concrete sense, where the concrete morphemes are selected. In the second approach the associations related to extralinguistic, formal, and mental types of similarity, contrast, and contiguity are focused on.

While Dokulil, Horecký, Blank, and Koch understand *compounding* – a little unfortunately – in its traditional formal definition and not in a definition that derives from the overall model and thus view this process differently from affixation, Štekauer's word-formation model abstains from making this distinction at all (the model only knows *onomasiological types*, excluding any sort of non-regular name-giving processes, such as blends, semantic changes, and loans). The overall model in Grzega (2004) does not distinguish between the traditional forms of compounding and affixation either, but it uses the term *composites* in order to distinguish the junction of morphemes from other types of name-giving processes (such as blending, clipping, semantic change, borrowing).

The different views shall be juxtaposed in a nutshell with the help of a few examples:

(1) En. *strawberry* would be a traditional compound, although the motivation as 'berry having to do with straw' is not quite transparent. Blank and Koch define it as a compound based on similarity within a category plus conceptual category. For Dokulil (and Horecký) this word would be considered a compound falling into the onomasiological category of the mutational type. I would term it a composite with absence of determining component of the mark. Štekauer would put the word into his onomasiological type 3. The same classification holds true for the German equivalent *Erdbeere* (lit. 'earth-berry').

(2) AmSp. *frutilla* 'strawberry', lit. 'fruit+diminutive suffix', and Ru. *zemlyanika* 'strawberry', lit. 'earth+diminutive suffix', would not be seen as compounds in the terminologies of Dokulil, Horecký, Štekauer, Blank, and Koch. In my model, I would still term it a composite with absence of the determining component of the mark.

(3) En. *raspberry* and En. *gooseberry* are compounds in the traditional definitions (although *rasp-* would be special, because it is a cranberry morpheme). Since such formations are not regular and productive, they would not fall in the realm of word formation in Štekauer's model; they are not mentioned in the models by Dokulil, Horecký, Blank, and Koch. In my model, En. *raspberry* would fall into the group of

clarifying, or tautological, compounds, since the original *rasp* was supplemented by a synonym *raspberry*, which caused the first to fall more and more into desuetude; En. *gooseberry*, in my model, would fall into the category of subconscious blending (folk-etymology), since this compound was triggered by an opaque form *groser*, from Fr. *groseille* 'gooseberry'.

(4) En. *skyscraper* and its equivalents Fr. *gratte-ciel* (lit. 'scrape-sky'), Sp. *rasca-cielos* (literally 'scrape+skies'), G. *Wolkenkratzer* (lit. 'clouds'+'scrape'+agent suffix) are quite tricky. According to Štekauer's model, the word *scrape* would first have passed what he calls the Lexical Component of the mind, where its usage would be changed in a metaphorical way (as the building doesn't scrape literally), before it can be used in the Word-Formation Component to coin a word of onomasiological type 1 (complete complex structure). The status of *skyscraper* etc. in Dokulil and Horecký doesn't seem clear. In Blank's (and Koch's) model these words would be included as compounds based on integral metonymy and metaphoricity. In my model, such forms would be classified in the formal group of complex composites, without any further auxiliary constructions, since similarity relations are on a par with contiguity relations.

(5) Words traditionally termed *exocentric compounds*, e.g. En. *redbreast* ∼ Fr. *gorgerouge*, would be seen as compounds based on integral metonymy and metaphoricity in Blank's model. Their status in Dokulil's model is unclear. Štekauer postulates an auxiliary onomasiological type 1. Horecký speaks of a formally unexpressed onomasiological base, which seems to conform with my group of base-absence composites.

(6) Du. *roodborstje* (lit. 'red'+'breast'+diminutive suffix) and G. *Rotkehlchen* (literally 'red'+'throat'+diminutive suffix) would of course be suffixations in the models by Dokulil, Horecký, Blank, and Koch. In the model presented in Grzega (2004) they would be put into the category of complex composites.

(7) Finally, again, a word like *unhappy* is not a compound in the traditional sense, but would be seen as one in the model presented in Grzega (2004) and would then fall into the category of simplex structures.

CHAPTER 12

....

COMPOUNDING IN COGNITIVE LINGUISTICS

....

LIESBET HEYVAERT

COGNITIVE Linguistics constitutes 'a cluster of many partially overlapping approaches' (Geeraerts and Cuyckens 2007: 3). Before looking into what the Cognitive Linguistic approach has thus far contributed to the analysis of compounding, I will therefore make explicit the assumptions and claims behind the overall cognitive framework and point to its potential with respect to the modelling of compounding (section 12.1). In section 12.2, I will give a thematic overview of the existing cognitive analyses of particular compound types: in 12.2.1, I will discuss the cognitive analyses to do with the compositionality of compounding and the head–modifier analysis that lies behind the distinction between exocentric and endocentric compounds; in 12.2.2, I will describe Ryder's (1994) schematic analysis of noun+noun compounds and her description of the language user in the production and understanding of compounding; in 12.2.3, I will present an overview of the cognitive analyses that view compounding from the perspective of ongoing language processing. In section 12.3, finally, I will recapitulate and sketch some possible avenues for further research.

12.1 COGNITIVE LINGUISTICS: FUNDAMENTALS

Without doubt the basic tenet of Cognitive Linguistics is that the language system, in its synchronic formal properties as well as in the diachronic changes it goes through, is fundamentally determined by the language user's cognitive abilities. The most basic psychological abilities that are claimed to be crucial for language use are the abilities of *symbolization, composition, comparison/categorization,* and *schematization.* Crucially, because all of these cognitive processes are claimed to be involved in language use, they are also reflected, it is argued, in the *language system* itself and the terminology used to describe the cognitive abilities applies to the (description of the) language system as well. Put differently, to cognitive linguists, any analysis of linguistic structure has to articulate what we know of cognitive processing, i.e. it must have 'psychological reality' (Langacker 1987: 42). In what follows, I will briefly consider the cognitive abilities that figure most prominently in Cognitive Linguistics, identify how they are reflected in linguistic structure, and point to issues to do with them that have particular reference to the analysis of compounding.

12.1.1 Cognitive abilities

12.1.1.1 *Symbolization*

Symbolization, Langacker (1999: 94) argues, builds on the general psychological ability of *association*, whereby 'one kind of experience is able to evoke another'. In language, symbolization concerns the relation between a structure in phonological space and the structure in semantic space that it is able to evoke. When such a symbolic relationship becomes automatized, it acquires 'unit' status and forms a symbolic unit (e.g. [[OPENER]/[opener]], whereby the semantic unit [OPENER] is associated with the phonological unit [opener]; see, for instance, Langacker 1987: 77). The simplest kind of symbolic unit is the morpheme, 'in which a semantic and a phonological structure participate as unanalysable wholes in a symbolic relationship' (Langacker 1987: 58). The syntagmatic integration of basic symbolic units leads to the formation of a composite symbolic structure or a 'grammatical construction', the latter term being used to denote the relationship of integration between the component structures and the resulting composite structure (Langacker 1987: 277).

The language system (viewed as a massive network) consists of three types of units: first, phonological (e.g. [m]), semantic (e.g. [MOTHER]), and symbolic units, i.e. units associating a semantic with a phonological unit (e.g. [[MOTHER]/[mother]]);

second, schematic symbolic units or grammatical patterns (e.g. for -*ee* nominalizations: [[V/...]-[[-EE]/[-ee]]]); and, third, the categorizing relationships of
elaboration/instantiation, extension, and mutual similarity (see below, and Langacker
1987: 62).

Within the domain of compounding, novel symbolic units, including 'creative'
formations, are common. It is not surprising therefore that among the issues that
keep on resurfacing in research into compounding (including cognitive research) is
the identification of the rules and constraints that can explain the productivity of
compounds and the issue of lexicalization (see, for instance, Bauer 1983, 2001a;
Ungerer 2007: 651). In Cognitive Grammar, the productivity of a structure (defined
as the likelihood that a structure is activated and leads to the construal of novel
units) as well as the issue of lexicalization are fundamentally tied up with what is
called the 'degree of entrenchment' of a unit. The notion of 'entrenchment'
captures the idea that a lot of what speakers say is based on prepackaged, ready-
made units that are so deeply 'entrenched' in our memory that 'their activation has
become a highly automated routine' (Schmid 2007: 118). Units come to be entrenched and their activation automated to the extent that they have been used
before, and constructions thus fall 'along a continuous scale of entrenchment in
cognitive organization' (Langacker 1987: 59; see also Schmid 2007: 118).

It has been pointed out in Cognitive Linguistics that the *productivity* of a unit
correlates positively with both entrenchment and specificity (Langacker 1991: 48):
the more deeply entrenched and specific (or non-schematic) a unit is, the more
likely it will be activated to create novel units. And if based on schematic rather
than specific units, Langacker (1991: 48) points out, low-level schemas are more
likely to be invoked by the language user than more abstract schemas. Evidence in
favour of this claim comes from the fact that instantiations of a schema are not
'distributed randomly through the space of possibilities defined by the highest-
level schema' (Langacker 1991: 48) but concentrated in certain regions which
correspond to low-level schemas. The low-level nature of productivity which
Langacker describes can be clearly observed among -*er* nominalizations: both the
agentive and the non-agentive types of -*er* derivations are characterized by certain
'regions' of productivity or low-level schemas which give rise to instantiations that
are sufficiently entrenched to be established as units. Agentive regions of productivity are, for instance, those of agent-like instrumental nouns (such as *computer,
printer, parser*); non-agentive regions of productivity are especially those that
designate non-agentive instruments (e.g. *front-loader, stroller, stepper, walker*) and
items of food (e.g. *broiler* 'chicken suitable for broiling'; *cooker* 'apple for cooking').
In traditional approaches, this low-level-driven production of novel expressions is
referred to as 'analogy' or the direct modelling of new formations on specific,
familiar ones. The cognitive approach differs from analogy, however, in its
emphasis on the role of schematization: as Langacker (1999: 144) remarks, 'even
the learning of specific expressions (required as the basis for analogy) involves

abstraction and schematization from actual usage events'. Or, as Tuggy (2007: 101–102) puts it,

the very notion of analogy implies that the ways in which the new structure is analogous, or similar, to the old are crucial to the new formation. That is, there must be some basis for the analogy; and that basis will constitute an incipiently established schema.... To the extent that such schemas become entrenched and begin to participate directly in sanctioning the formation of new structures, the mechanism of rule-based creativity is active.

He gives the example of *deskjet*, which was coined on the analogy of *inkjet*, as an extension that was sufficiently sanctioned by the schema of *inkjet* to be acceptable, but which entailed the activation of a new schema containing the specifications common to both *inkjet* and *deskjet*. The compound *laserjet* then activated yet another new schema, [[[NOUN]/[...]]-[JET]/[jet]], which now sanctions formations such as *OfficeJet*, *PaintJet*, and *DesignJet*. As long as such partially schematic relationships as those from *deskjet* or *laserjet* to *PaintJet* and *OfficeJet* are also important for establishing the latter, however, the mechanism of analogy is also at work.

As far as **lexicalization** is concerned, then, the parameters of specificity and entrenchment are equally determining: structures are lexicalized or come to form part of the 'set of fixed expressions in a language' (Langacker 1991: 45) if, firstly, they are high in specificity and represent individual expressions rather than schemas, and, secondly, if they are highly entrenched, that is, they have achieved the status of conventional units (Langacker 1991: 45). Note that symbolic complexity is not considered to be relevant to lexicalization: lexical items can take the form of morphemes, words, phrases, or even longer sequences (Langacker 1991: 45). It is an important aspect of the cognitive network model of language that it thus includes both abstract, schematic constructions and specific structural units that are sufficiently entrenched to have become lexicalized. Langacker (1987: 35) calls the latter 'conventional expressions' and includes formulaic sequences (e.g. *take it for granted that*), collocations (e.g. *great idea*), and even more elaborate, clause-like units (e.g. *kill two birds with one stone*; *I'll do the best I can*). Similarly, established compounds are assumed to be part of the language system themselves, as conventional, lexicalized expressions, each of them instantiating their own schematic unit. In addition, there are non-lexicalized instances of compounding, or compounds that are not sufficiently entrenched to become themselves part of the language system as specific structural units but which the language user creates and understands as instantiations of structural schemas that do belong to the language system.

12.1.1.2 *Composition*

The notion of **composition** is used to refer to the language user's ability to integrate two or more *component* structures to form a *composite* structure (Langacker 1999:

94). In language, the psychological ability of composition involves the creation of relationships on the so-called syntagmatic plane (Langacker 1987: 75) or relationships of 'valency'. An example of a composite structure is the compound *can opener*, which combines the symbolic units [[CAN]/[can]] and [[OPENER]/[opener]], which in turn has two components, namely [[OPEN]/[open]] and [[ER]/[er]]. The integration of two or more components into a composite structure is argued to depend on (semantic and phonological) 'correspondences' established between substructures within the component elements.

In the case of a compound such as *can opener*, these correspondences are quite prominent (a *can* being an object that is designed in such a way that it requires an instrument which is generally described as an *opener* to open it). Often, however, 'valence relations depend crucially on properties that are too marginal or too context-dependent to figure in any plausible dictionary-type characterization of a component' (Langacker 1987: 156). Noun compounds furnish many striking examples here. Langacker gives the example of *buggy whip*, where 'Only a fairly inclusive characterization of *buggy* (one incorporating the notion of a driver and the means he uses to encourage the horse pulling the buggy) brings into the picture an entity that can be placed in correspondence with the referent of *whip* (or conversely), thereby permitting the integration of the two component structures to form a coherent composite scene' (Langacker 1987: 157).

Notice that Langacker describes composite structures as consisting of *components* rather than *constituents*. The use of an alternative term for the notion of constituents reflects a fundamental aspect of the Cognitive perspective on composite structures, which rejects the typical 'building-block' view of compositionality. As also pointed out by Taylor (2002: 100), 'strict compositionality...turns out to be the exceptional condition'.

A fully compositional expression would be the phrase *black bird*, because the composite structure inherits the profile of *bird* and its content is exhausted by that of its components. The compound *blackbird*, designating a specific type of black bird, however, is more precise in content than anything that can be deduced from *black* and *bird* alone. Even further removed from full compositionality is the compound *blackboard*, which 'is not a board in the usual sense, and is not necessarily black' (Langacker 1987: 450).

Importantly, compositionality is in Cognitive Grammar distinguished from *analysability*, which pertains to 'the extent to which speakers are cognizant (at some level of processing) of the contribution that individual component structures make to the composite whole' (Langacker 1987: 457). And while the regularity of composition obviously has its impact on the potential for such recognition, analysability is to be distinguished from compositionality because speakers 'can be quite aware of individual components within a structure that manifests only partial compositionality'. They may also be relatively unaware of the components within an expression they are familiar with and that is fully compositional

(Langacker 1987: 457). (It can be pointed out here that Cognitive Linguistics does not view this as an argument in favour of seeing compounding as a morphological rather than syntactic phenomenon.) Or one component may be intuitively more salient than another, as in the compound *screwdriver*, where the unit *screw* seems much more prominent than the second element *driver* (Langacker 1987: 465).

12.1.1.3 *Comparison, categorization, and schematization*

In addition to symbolization and composition, language use is also claimed to involve the psychological abilities of **comparison** and **categorization**. The language user, Langacker (1987: 65–73) argues, solves the problem of coding a detailed, context-dependent conceptualization linguistically by continually making comparisons or *categorizing judgements*, thus trying to assess whether a specific expression can be categorized as a member of the category defined by a conventional linguistic unit (or a unit that is widely shared by the language users of a speech community).

The cognitive ability of categorization through which the language user gives structure to the world around him results in many different types of categories, lexical and grammatical. These categories themselves are also conceptually grouped into larger groupings of categories, such as type-of groupings or taxonomies (e.g. 'car' is a member of the category 'means of transport'); part–whole groupings (e.g. 'wheels' are parts of the category 'car'); and conceptualization groupings, such as *domains* or 'aspects of an experience that are conceptualized as associated', such as the domain of 'combustion' (Cienki 2007: 181). Within taxonomies, the cognitive model further distinguishes what it calls 'basic-level items' or 'types of category that come to our mind most readily in our daily interaction with the world' (Radden and Dirven 2007: 9), such as 'car', 'train', and 'plane'. Such basic-level terms are more salient than their superordinate category 'means of transport' or any of their subordinate categories, they are simple in form, are used frequently, and learned early by young children (Radden and Dirven 2007: 9).

When the language user is comparing or making categorizing judgements, structures which at first sight appear very different may be quite comparable from a more coarse-grained perspective (Langacker 1999: 93). The ability of categorization therefore also necessarily involves the ability of **schematization**: to determine whether a usage event *elaborates/instantiates* or *extends* the properties of specific conventional units, the language user may have to abstract away from certain points of difference and portray the distinct structures involved in his/her categorizing judgement with lesser precision and specificity (Langacker 1999: 93). An elaborative or instantiating novel usage is conventional, or, in more traditional terminology, *grammatical*: it conforms to the linguistic convention that is embodied by the linguistic unit and is thus fully sanctioned by it. The language user can, however, also opt for a usage event that shows a discrepancy with the conventional linguistic unit and thus extends the category. The usage event is then either ill-formed or merely non-conventional.

A construction in the system network of language is not only situated on the syntagmatic plane of composition, but also on a *schematic* plane, which is orthogonal to that of the syntagm and includes both *schemas* (e.g. [[V/...]-[[-EE]/ [-ee]]]) and *specific instantiations* of schemas (e.g. [[ATTEND/attend]-[[-EE]/ [-ee]]]). Importantly, because in the cognitive approach to language the relation between usage events and the more abstract representations in the speaker's grammar is essential and much more direct than traditionally assumed, the linguistic system is conceived of as containing both:

The linguistic system is built up from such lexically specific instances [or usage events, L.H.], only gradually abstracting more general representations, such as phonemes, morphemes, and syntactic patterns, from the repetition of similar instances of use...This means that any general representations that emerge from the operation of the system necessarily are tied to, i.e. activated in concert with, specific instances of those patterns. Abstract utterances without any phonetic or lexical content do not exist.

(Kemmer and Barlow 1999: ix)

Notice that the cognitive notions of 'schema' and 'instance' apply not only to symbolic units but also to phonological and semantic units. Semantic units linked through schematic relationships are thus, for instance, the concepts [ANIMAL] and [DOG], [COLOUR] and [RED], [GREEN] and [BLUE].

As pointed out by Ungerer (2007: 655), the cognitive notion of 'schema', broadly defined as a 'superordinate concept, one which specifies the basic outline common to several, or many, more specific concepts' (Tuggy 2007: 83) offers 'a flexible way of generalization that is not understood as a fixed a priori rule, but takes account of salience based on frequency of use' (see also Schmid 2007). Importantly, the notion of schema underlies Langacker's (1987) view of composition and valence relations: in Cognitive Linguistics, the components within a composite structure are viewed as elaborations of the schematic specifications of the composite head or 'profile determinant'. Take, for instance, the head *ate* in the sentence *he ate the apple*: the process *ate/eat* has a schematically characterized *eater* implied, which is elaborated in the sentence by *he*, as well as schematically characterized *food*, elaborated by *the apple*.

In clear cases, Tuggy (2007: 107) suggests, the schematic specifications implied in the head of a composite structure 'sanction...the formation of the composite structure'. In linguistic structure in general, and compounding in particular, however, the meaning of a composite structure will often be different from that of its head or profile determinant together with its schematically characterized substructures. In the compound *French toast*, for instance, *toast* is the head or profile determinant, but it differs in meaning from the non-compound use of *toast*, and its relation to the composite meaning is one of 'partial' rather than 'full' schematicity: *toast* is a slice of bread that has been toasted (held close to a source of radiant heat); *French toast* has first been dipped into a milk-and-egg batter, and

has then been fried rather than toasted. The component *French* does not correspond clearly to anything salient in the composite structure (Tuggy 2007: 108). The
schematic interpretation of valency relations in compounds, I will show below,
underlies Ryder's (1994) analysis of noun+noun compounds.

12.1.1.4 *Metaphor, metonymy, and blending*

In addition to these general cognitive abilities, which underlie the Cognitive
Grammar model of language (Langacker 1987 and 1991), a major strand within
Cognitive Linguistics has emphasized the centrality of **metaphor** and **metonymy**
to our linguistic conceptualization of the world (cf. Lakoff and Johnson 1980).
Rather than being mere figures of rhetoric, it has been argued, metaphor and
metonymy are basic cognitive abilities that enable the language user to extend the
conceptual categories associated with existing linguistic categories. Metaphor
involves the language user mapping the structure of one conceptual domain (or
very general area of conceptualization, e.g. madness) onto another domain (e.g.
love), as in *I'm crazy about her.* In metonymy, on the other hand, one conceptual
category (e.g. crown) is mapped onto another one (e.g. monarch) within the
same general conceptual domain or within the same more specific knowledge
structure or frame (monarchy) (see Radden and Dirven 2007: 14). The notions
of 'conceptual metaphor' and 'conceptual metonymy' are used to designate
the general systematic cross-domain correspondences such as CONTAINER FOR
CONTENTS (metonymy) and A CONCLUSION IS A DESTINATION (metaphor). The
relation with specific metonymical and metaphorical expressions (e.g. *The kettle
is boiling* and *We arrived at the conclusion*) is like that between a schema and its
instances, as distinguished within the cognitive network model of language in
general.

   Within Blending theory (Fauconnier and Turner 2002), which was originally
developed as a complement to metaphor theory but has gradually come to cover a
wider range of data, communication is considered from an *online* perspective, and
the language user's ability to evoke short-term memory packages of knowledge
('mental spaces') while producing or interpreting language is given central place.
Because they are constructed as we think and talk, mental spaces are partial,
ad hoc assemblies, be it linked up with long-term *schematic* knowledge (e.g. the
frame of 'walking') and with long-term *specific* knowledge (e.g. a memory of the
time you climbed Mount Rainier in 2001) (Fauconnier 2007: 351). The mental
space that includes you, Mount Rainier, the year 2001, and your climbing the
mountain, for instance, can then be activated on many different occasions. By
involving conceptualizations by the individual in a specific context and for a
specific purpose, mental spaces differ from 'domains', which are broader and
'encompass many aspects of an experience that are conceptualized as associated'
(Cienki 2007: 181). (For more examples of (types of) mental spaces, see Fauconnier 2007.) The integration of two or more mental spaces within a construction is

called 'conceptual blending'. Blending research tries to reconstrue the mental work that is required from the language user to grasp the meaning of a construction. It differs from the standard metaphorical/metonymical approach in its attention to *emergent signification*, that is, the fact that the blending of mental spaces gives rise to emergent new meanings that could not be inferred from either of the mapped domains. In 'conceptual blending' at least four 'mental spaces' are involved (see Taylor 2002: 530):

- at least two input spaces, I_1 and I_2;
- at least one generic space, G, which captures the commonalities between the input spaces, and facilitates the establishment of correspondences between elements of the input spaces;
- a blended space, which inherits selected elements from the input spaces, as well as having emergent meaning of its own.

The theory can be illustrated by means of the following example adapted from Fauconnier (1990) and described in Taylor (2002: 530–1):

(1)   In France, Bill Clinton wouldn't have been harmed by his relationship with Monica Lewinski.

This sentence invites us to set up two mental spaces: one involving the reality of recent US politics (I_1), with the President and Lewinski, the President's relationship with Lewinski, the scandal, the denials, the attempt at impeachment, and the revelation of all the sordid details in the press. The second input space (I_2) is invited by the phrase *In France* and is populated by entities which correspond to the entities in I_1. This is possible because there exist two generic spaces, or spaces which are schematic for both I_1 and I_2. The first could be called 'Western democracies' and includes entities such as an elected Head of State, the media, public opinion, and so on. The second generic space, which we could call 'personal relations' contains such entities as marriage, middle-aged men, and their sexual encounters with younger females. In order to interpret example (1) correctly, we need to establish a blend of the two input spaces. This blend is hypothetical, as indicated by the use of *would*, and incorporates elements from both input spaces. In the counterfactual blended space, Bill Clinton is seen as the President of France and had a sexual affair which, however, was evaluated as harmless. As a result of this blending, the actions in the two spaces undergo what Fauconnier and Turner (2002: 92f., 312–25) call *compression* and the conceptual complexity of the inputs is reduced considerably. A newly integrated and unified conceptual structure emerges that is cognitively manageable.

The theory of conceptual blending can be applied to both non-metaphorical examples such as (1) and metaphorical ones as in (2) (based on Taylor 2002: 532).

(2)   She's imprisoned in her marriage.

When used to account for metaphor, the two input spaces are the source and target domain of the metaphor (prison and marriage); the generic space captures the cross-domain commonalities between both (any involuntary, unpleasant, confining, un-rewarding situation); and the blend consists of items selected from input spaces. The metaphorical blend, however, also acquires a number of specific characteristics of its own: for example, if a woman is 'imprisoned in her marriage', she has the option of 'escaping' from her marriage, but the manner of escaping (in the blend) is quite different from the manner of escaping implied in the input space 'prison'.

Like the cognitive abilities of *symbolization, composition, comparison/categoriza-tion*, and *schematization*, the abilities of metaphorical and metonymical mapping as well as blending find their expression in the language itself. Blending is thereby not only a conceptual phenomenon, but may also be at work at the structural levels of sentence and word: a sentence such as *They prayed the boys home again* can be analysed as a blend of the caused-motion construction and the specific semantics of *praying* and *hoping that the boys would return home*. Within traditional morph-ology, the notion of 'blend' has been used to refer to forms created by combining elements of input forms, such as *motel* ('motor'+'hotel') and *brunch* ('breakfast' and 'lunch') (Taylor 2002: 533).

As I will show below, the majority of cognitive linguistic research into com-pounding is to be situated in the domain of metaphorical/metonymical and blending research. Research into the metaphorical/metonymical properties of compounding has sought to map the various ways in which the language user extends the conceptual categories associated with the linguistic categories of which compounds are made up. Blending research approaches compounds as conceptual blends of two or more mental spaces that are integrated into a new blended space that contains information projected from both input spaces, as well as showing a new, emergent conceptual structure in its own right, whose set-up differs from those of the two input spaces.

12.1.2 A usage-based approach

That our language system is shaped by the cognition of the language user is one of the reasons why cognitive linguists have systematically emphasized the importance of a **usage-based** approach to language analysis: a better understanding of the language user's psychological processing is crucial to a better understanding of language itself. More particularly, actual language use is viewed as 'a problem-solving activity that demands a constructive effort and occurs when linguistic convention is put to use in specific circumstances' (Langacker 1987: 65). Ultimately, it is emphasized in Cognitive Linguistics, it is the language user who 'enters into dialogue' with the language system and can 'exploit it in a fashion that responds to all the varied constraints inherent in the situation' (Langacker 1987: 66). Usage events thus play a double role: they result from, but also themselves shape the linguistic system 'in a kind of feedback loop' (Kemmer and Barlow 1999: ix). This systematic interaction between the language system (or the conventionalized language units in human cognition) and language usage (i.e. the constructive effort of the language user) forms the 'crucible of linguistic structure' and the 'source of language change' (Langacker 1987: 70). To understand specific language structures and the diachronic changes they show, therefore, we must consider them from a truly *usage-based* perspective, that is, we must attach substantial import-ance to their actual instantiations in real language use.

In line with its usage-based perspective, Cognitive Linguistics situates the cre-ation of new compounds (or the extension of existing compound schemas) in the language user rather than in the language system. To explain creativity in com-pounding one consequently has to consider the general cognitive abilities of the language user: 'Creating a novel expression is not necessarily different in funda-mental character from problem-solving activity in general' (Langacker 1987: 65). As will be shown in section 12.2, cognitive approaches to the analysis of specific compounding systems typically pay explicit attention to the issue of creativity and to the 'problem-solving' role of the language user and the listener in the production and understanding of novel compounds.

12.2 COGNITIVE ANALYSES
OF COMPOUNDING

Plag (2003: 132) starts his chapter on compounding by forewarning readers seeking clear answers to their questions 'that compounding is a field of study where intricate problems abound, numerous issues remain unresolved, and convincing solutions are generally not so easy to find'. Cognitive Linguistics cannot explain all the intricate problems involved in compounding. One of its assets, however, is that it can offer a comprehensive model of language, in which many issues relevant to the analysis of compounding can be coherently inte-grated. I have in what follows opted for a thematic approach. That is, I have grouped together the cognitive analyses of compounding that have thus far been published with respect to the following topics: the 'compositionality' of com-pounds and their typical modifier–head analysis (12.2.1); creativity in compound-ing (12.2.2); and, finally, the 'live' or 'online' processing of compounds by speaker and hearer (12.2.3).

12.2.1 Compositionality and the modifier–head analysis of compounding

Among the issues most frequently discussed with respect to compounding are the analysability of compounds as composite structures, and the distinction between endocentric and exocentric compounding and the notion of 'head' underlying it. The distinction between endocentric and exocentric compounds has figured prominently in the cognitive literature on compounding. In general, we could say that the cognitive standpoint on this issue has been to reject the dual distinction between endocentric and exocentric compounds and argue for a continuum or cline of compounding instead (see, for instance, Dirven and Verspoor 1998). Importantly, moreover, within Cognitive Linguistics, the non-compositionality of many constructions has never been regarded as something problematic, 'to be dealt with outside the confines of grammatically based linguistic semantics (as a matter of lexicon, pragmatics or performance)' (Langacker 1987: 452).

In Dirven and Verspoor (1998) a cline of transparency/analysability is argued for ('analysability' pertaining to 'the extent to which speakers are cognizant (at some level of processing) of the contribution that individual component structures make to the composite whole', Langacker 1987: 457). This cline is associated with different degrees of productivity: at the fully productive (or transparent) end of this cline are those compounds whose component meanings are 'unequivocally analysable and hence immediately transparent', such as the compound *apple tree* (Dirven and Verspoor 1998: 60); at the other end of the transparency continuum lie what Dirven and Verspoor call 'darkened compounds', or compounds which are no longer analysable, where the semantic link between the components is non-transparent. All those compounds that involve metaphorical or metonymical processes, such as *red tape* ('long, irritating bureaucratic procedure'), are to be situated here. In between the two extremes of the continuum, then, are those compounds that are partially analysable and transparent, where the components may still be analysable but the semantic link between them has become less apparent. The example which Dirven and Verspoor give of this type is *blackbird*, which does not so much denote a type of black bird as a bird species.

Benczes (2006) takes issue with Dirven and Verspoor's analysis of metaphorical and metonymical noun+noun compounds as 'darkened' or 'non-analysable' (in the cognitive sense) and hence semantically opaque. She shows that what have traditionally been labelled 'exocentric' compounds can be coherently accounted for within a cognitive-linguistic framework combining the notions of metaphor, metonymy, blending, profile determinacy, and schema theory (see also Booij 1992 for a semantic interpretation of exocentric compounds in terms of metonymy). The systematicity that can be found in metaphorical and metonymical compounds has, more particularly, to do with the part of the compound that is activated by conceptual metaphor and/or metonymy: this can be the modifier;

the profile determinant (or head); the relationship between the modifier and the profile determinant; or the compound as a whole. In addition, the metaphors and metonymies that participate in the meaning of noun+noun compounds are mostly established ones that are found in all sorts of linguistic phenomena; and the semantic relations between the constituents of the compounds are the same as those that exist between the constituents of endocentric compounds (e.g. part–whole as in *fingertip*; cause–effect as in *hay fever*; location–located as in *pocketbook*, etc.).

Following Downing (1977), Warren (1978), and Geeraerts (2002), Benczes distinguishes three major types of compounds: metaphor-based compounds, metonymy-based compounds, and metaphor- and metonymy-based compounds.[1] Crucially, within these general types, Benczes (2006) distinguishes further sub-types depending on precisely *which* component unit is metaphorical/metonym-ical. In the metaphor-based compound *hen party* ('a party to which only women are invited'), for instance, it is the modifier which is metaphorical; in *belly button* ('navel'), it is the profile determinant or head; in *flame sandwich* ('a note consist-ing of a negative statement surrounded by two positive statements') both modifier and head are metaphorical. And, finally, there are those metaphorical compounds where it is the relationship between modifier and head that is metaphorical (e.g., *sandwich generation* 'people who must care for both their children and parents').[2]

Benczes (2006: 184) concludes that 'the main difference between endocentric compounds such as *apple tree* and exocentric compounds such as *hammerhead* is not transparency of meaning, but creativity: the latter represent a type of nominal construction that has been coined by a more imaginative, associative and creative word formation process, based on conceptual metaphor and metonymy'. Benczes thus shows that if the linguistic analysis of their metaphorical/metonymical prop-erties is not restricted to the head noun only, but includes other parts of the compound (the modifier, the relation between the two constituent nouns of the compound, and the compound as a whole), they do show semantic transpar-ency. Benczes therefore proposes to use the term 'creative compound' for meta-phorical and metonymical compounds, deliberately blurring the distinction between endocentric and exocentric compounds and classifying also traditionally endocentric compounds such as *armchair* and *handwriting* as 'creative': 'the former has a metaphorical modifier, while the latter exhibits a metonymical profile

---

[1] For a complementary cognitive description of the interaction between metaphor and metonymy in compounding, see Geeraerts (2002), who in his discussion of Dutch compounds distinguishes between cases in which metaphor and metonymy occur consecutively, cases in which they occur in parallel, and cases in which they occur interchangeably.

[2] As was pointed out to me by one of the referees, the first constituent *sandwich* is also metaphor-ical here.

determinant' (Benczes 2006: 187).[3] Notice that the analysis of these compounds as requiring some degree of creativity is in accordance with Langacker's analysis of them in terms of compositionality: even the most transparent noun+noun combinations require some processing from the listener to access the composite meaning of the compound. The main difference according to Benczes, then, between traditionally endocentric constructions such as *armchair* and *handwriting* and traditionally exocentric ones such as *hammerhead* is a difference in degree of creativity: a compound such as *hammerhead* can be considered to be more creative 'in the sense that a greater effort is required from the listener to understand its meaning: we need to employ both conceptual metaphor and metonymy consecutively' (Benczes 2006: 188).

Interestingly, Benczes explicitly links up her view of the traditional distinction between exocentric and endocentric compounds with Langacker's network model of language. Both types of compounding, she argues, are based upon the same, high-order constructional schema [N+N]. The constructional subschemas of metaphorical and metonymical compounds, however, represent extensions of this higher-order schema, which range from being only mildly creative (*armchair*, *handwriting*) to being more creative (*hammerhead*): 'The notion of degree of extension therefore is synonymous with the concept of degree of creativity among creative compounds: the more extended a compound, the more imaginative, associative thinking is required from the listener to arrive at the compound's meaning' (Benczes 2006: 189). Creative extension can also be correlated with transparency of meaning. In particular, it depends on the component that is affected by metaphor or metonymy whether a compound is perceived as being more or less semantically transparent (see also Libben et al. 2003). As shown in Libben et al. (2003), the processing of a compound with a non-transparent head component (e.g. *jailbird*, *fleabag*) takes longer than the processing of compounds with a non-transparent modifier (as in *godchild*).

In the cognitive literature on compounding, we find a number of other interesting observations with respect to the idea that the semantic value of an endocentric compound is typically predictable from the value of its parts (compositionality) and that the individual contribution of its components is analysable (analysability). An attribute-listing experiment reported on in Ungerer and Schmid (1998) reveals that many compounds attract attributes which cannot be traced back to their source categories (i.e. to the categories of their component units). A compound such as *wheelchair*, for instance, was also assigned attributes to do with the categories of INVALID, HOSPITAL, ENGINE. Ungerer and Schmid (2006:

---

[3] The compound *handwriting* 'the style of someone's writing' is analysed by Benczes (2006: 154–5) as an example of an ACTION FOR RESULT conceptual metonymy whereby through the head or profile determinant *writing* the domain of writing, and more precisely the *result* of the action of writing, i.e. 'the style of writing that is produced on a sheet of paper', is accessed.

97) suggest that if more and more attributes are no longer felt to be related to the source categories but are linked only with the compound category WHEELCHAIR, the compound itself might in the end acquire basic-level status, as has happened in the case of NEWSPAPER and AIRPLANE. As a linguistic reflection of this change to basic-level category, the latter 'tend to drop the first element, thus assimilating to the simple form of basic level categories as *paper* and *plane*'. This process, Ungerer and Schmid (2006: 98) argue, can be studied in its various stages starting with items like *apple juice* and *wheelchair* and finishing with *(motor)car* and *(air)plane*, giving 'a tangible view of what has traditionally been called lexicalization'.

In Ungerer and Schmid (2006: 92–5), it is also argued that the existence of both type-of and part–whole relationships in our conceptualization of the world and its categories should set us thinking about the traditional, type-of-oriented or modifier–head analysis of certain endocentric noun+noun compounds: the standard view which posits a basic head item and a strictly specifying modifier element is far too rigid. With many compounds, the modifier category supplies more than just the specifying attribute. Ungerer and Schmid give the example of the compound *apple juice*, which has typically been analysed as a modifier–head compound designating a type of juice. In an attribute-listing experiment reported on in Ungerer and Schmid (1998), however, they managed to show that in categorizing APPLE JUICE the language user makes much wider use of the first basic-level category, i.e. that of APPLE, than is assumed by traditional analyses: while most of the attributes which their informants listed for the compound were also named for the head category JUICE (e.g. 'liquid', 'supplied in bottle or carton', 'served in glasses'), a significant number of informants also listed attributes from the category of APPLE (e.g. 'yellow or similar colour', 'fruity'). The compound APPLE JUICE, they conclude (2006: 93), while still denoting a type-of relationship (i.e. a type of JUICE), 'should throw first doubts on the rigidity of the modifier–head arrangement' because its modifier category supplies more than just the specifying attribute. The attribute-listing results for compounds like *coat collar, shoelace, shirtsleeve, lampshade* only reinforce these doubts, since most attributes assigned to these compounds are related to the first basic-level item, i.e. the so-called 'modifier', rather than to the 'head'. As Ungerer and Schmid (2006: 94) point out, 'Here the point is reached where the traditionally assumed parallelism between type-of relationships and modifier–head structure is no longer maintained.' From a cognitive perspective, they are no longer type-of compounds but *part–whole* compounds, conceived as parts or accessories of the wholes represented by the first element of the compound (e.g. COAT, SHOE, SHIRT). This conceptual overriding effect of the first element, Ungerer and Schmid (2006: 95) go on to argue, can in attribute-listing experiments also be observed with compounds which we all classify as 'type-of' compounds. When informants were asked to name attributes for RAIN, COAT, and RAINCOAT, for instance, it turned out that RAINCOAT has more in common with RAIN than with COAT. If we accept the cognitive view that category descriptions include attributes, the idea that for the ordinary language user certain noun+noun compounds that have traditionally been analysed as type-of compounds are in fact more closely related to the comprehensive cognitive category of their first element cannot be dismissed. A comparable claim has been put forward in Benczes (2006): the view of semantic transparency underlying her study – i.e. as a property of individual constituents rather than of the entire multimorphemic expression – supports Libben et al.'s (2003) study of compounding which showed that *both* constituents of noun+noun compounds show priming effects, regardless of the degree of transparency involved, or the status of the component unit in question (Benczes 2006: 184).

12.2.2 Creativity from a schematic and usage-based perspective

There have been many attempts at classifying the semantics of the relationship expressed by especially nominal compounds (e.g. Lees 1960 and 1970; Brekle 1970; Downing 1977; Levi 1978) and a wide range of semantic categories have thus far been proposed for them (see Adams 2001 for an overview). However, as pointed out by Plag (2003: 148), 'such semantically based taxonomies appear somewhat futile' because of the 'arbitrariness' with which they arise. More promising, Plag argues, 'is to ask what kinds of interpretations are in principle possible, given a certain compound' (2003: 149).[4] One area in which Cognitive Linguistics has contributed to the analysis of compounding is that of the description of the semantic relations that can hold between the component units of noun+noun compounds. In particular, the notion of 'schema' has proved to be a useful instrument here. As I pointed out earlier (section 12.1.1.3), in Cognitive Linguistics, the components within a composite structure are viewed as elaborations of the schematic specifications of the composite head or 'profile determinant' (see the example of *He ate the apple*). It was Ryder (1994) who first applied the 'schematic' perspective on valency (or syntagmatic relationships within composite expressions in general) to the analysis of the semantics of (endocentric) noun+noun compounds. She (1994: 72) hypothesizes that to create and understand a compound, it must be possible to 'establish a correspondence between a schema connected with each of the two structures'. Ideally, as in sentential valency relations, the components of a compound have a common or identical schema as part of their semantics: consider the sentence *The boy walked*, where the central schema for *walk* includes a slot for an entity to do the walking, and the noun *boy* is connected to the schema *walk*, among many other schemas. If it is not easy to find such an identical schema, Ryder (1994: 72) suggests, the language user will for each component look for a

---

[4] This is exactly the question that is examined in Štekauer (2005a).

schema that is similar to the schema for the other component, thereby 'altering the values in one or both of the schemas to create a common composite structure'. The example which Ryder gives here is that of the sentence *The fish is walking*, where the word *walk* does not have any event schemas that allow the entity doing the walking to be a fish. Viewed from the perspective of the *fish*, there is no connection to a schema that involves *walking*. To be able to interpret the sentence *The fish is walking* the language user will consequently have to accommodate the existing schemas associated with its components. Either the *walking* schema is adapted to the idea of, for instance, forward movement at a moderate pace for which no legs are required; or the schema of *fish* is accommodated into that of a mutant fish with legs.

The same thing, Ryder suggests, can be expected to happen in the creation and interpretation of compounds, even though valence relations between nouns are much more complex than are those between predicates and nouns. She hypothesizes that, in order to interpret a non-lexicalized compound, language users follow a specific series of processes: they first select a linguistic template from their own stock of established compounds or templates that is perceived to have characteristics similar to that of the new compound to use as an analogy. If many templates are possible, the listener will check what information the context can give about the compound's meaning. The listener then checks the information provided by the template against what he or she knows about the real world, that is, he or she searches for a 'semantic information schema' that is common to the two element nouns that can be used to instantiate the template. If a problem is encountered in these first two processes, the language user will opt for one of the following strategies: he or she will look for or create a new semantic information schema that the two nouns can share; accommodate one or both of the nouns' meanings (preferably the meaning of the profile determinant) so that a common semantic information schema can be found; or use the linguistic template or a semantic information schema from one of the nouns without attempting to instantiate it, creating what Ryder calls a 'semantic skeleton'.

These hypotheses are confirmed by two psycholinguistic experiments that Ryder reports on in which she confronted people with made-up noun+noun compounds. Her subjects were asked to give a definition of the semantics of the compounds, which Ryder then analysed into a set of schematic relations. She was thus able to show that, when confronted with a combination of units that does not seem to be related, the language user will look for a schema that is common to both of the constituents. If necessary, she shows, that will involve adjusting one or both of the compound's schemas to make them compatible. Because nouns are typically connected to a large number of schemas, in the case of compounds the language user usually has several schemas available, and, consequently, several possible interpretations of the non-lexicalized compound. When the language user finds no immediate schema that fits both components, he or she will adjust an existing schema or even create a new one. Ryder concludes that the semantic relationships embodied in creative noun+noun compounds may appear to be chaotic because they cannot be explained by means of a single, general level of semantic relationships. However, through her analysis she shows that the boundaries of that chaos can be identified if one starts from the hearer and his/her attempts to link up specific lexical compounds to a range of templates. Building on Ryder's schematic analysis, Oster (2004) uses the cognitive notion of 'schema' to develop a methodology which can serve as a tool for the creation and interpretation of compounds from specific technical fields.

12.2.3 Compounding from the perspective of ongoing language processing

Cognitive Linguistics not only looks at linguistic and conceptual (e.g. metaphor and metonymy) categories that are tacitly assumed to be stored in long-term memory. Through the notion of 'blending', it also includes aspects of ongoing language processing, traditionally studied by psycholinguists using experimental methods (Ungerer and Schmid 2006: 257).

As pointed out in Ungerer (2007: 655–6), 'Most word-formation processes involve semantic combination or fusion, and this qualifies them for an analysis in terms of conceptual blending as proposed by Fauconnier and Turner.' A compositional compound such as *apple juice* could thus be explained as a set-up of two input spaces ('apple space' and 'juice space'). The emergent structure in the blended space can then be said to be characterized by the integration of the core information of the first input space into the second (Ungerer and Schmid 2006: 271). The theory of conceptual blending seems particularly suited to elucidating ad hoc compounds and processes like lexicalization (Ungerer 2007: 656). The large majority of blending analyses of compounding thus far available in the literature are meticulous discussions of specific compounds and their semantics. Let us have a look at a number of them.

In Ungerer and Schmid (2006: 271), for instance, the example of the compound *wheelchair* is given, which, as discussed earlier, is less compositional than *apple juice*, having acquired a number of attributes that go beyond the meanings inherent in the constituents *wheel* and *chair*. To account for these extra attributes, one could assume an additional input space 'hospital' or 'invalid' or both. Or the extra meaning could be argued to arise from the blending process as newly emergent conceptual structure. 'Yet no matter how a more detailed blending analysis will explain these compounds, the compression in these blends has long led to deeply entrenched structures in the blended space – or firmly lexicalized items in more traditional terminology – so the blending process will not be repeated every time these items are used' (Ungerer and Schmid 2006: 271). As pointed out by Coulson (2001: 142–4) the online quality of the blend only comes to the fore when the entrenched interpretation does not fit a specific context, as with her example *pet fish*, which normally calls up the context of a fish tank, but might be used by a biologist investigating shark behaviour for her favourite specimen of shark. Such ad hoc uses of compounding showing discrepancies with entrenched or lexicalized meanings, Ungerer and Schmid (2006: 271) observe, are 'particularly frequent with compounds created in family discourse or in conversation with close friends'. They give the example of *cherry jeans*, for which a relatively conventionalized meaning is probably 'jeans of a cherry-like colour'. Yet in specific contexts the blending of the input spaces 'jeans' and 'cherry' may lead to quite different emergent structures in the blended space, such as 'garment soiled by stains of cherry juice' or 'jeans used for cherry picking'. Such an emergent structure will, however, very much depend on specific knowledge about the fact that an accident has happened and has resulted in a stain, or about the context of cherry-picking and about the fact that the person referring to *cherry jeans* has worn or intends to wear a certain pair of dungaree jeans for cherry picking. As Ungerer and Schmid (2006: 271) point out, 'An emergent structure dependent on such a constellation has little or no chance of achieving wider currency, let alone permanence: it is a typical product of context-dependent online conceptualization.'

Fauconnier and Turner (2002: 354) give the examples of *dolphin-safe* 'tuna that has been harvested without harming dolphins', *child-safe* 'room that is free of the typical dangers for children', and *shark-safe* 'beach that is protected from shark attacks'. All of these compounds, they argue, require the listener to construct elaborate integration networks that differ from compound to compound.

In a number of recent cognitive publications (Bundgaard, Ostergaard, and Stjernfelt 2006, Benczes 2006), the influence of conceptual blending theory and/ or its applicability to compounding in general is questioned. While in her account of 'creative' compounds, Benczes (2006: 58) suggests that 'blending theory is the way forward in accounting for the semantics of creative compounds', she also points out that it cannot in itself be sufficient to explain the semantics of compounds and that blending theory, which necessarily builds on a great amount of intuition on the part of the linguist in constructing blend networks, at times leave substantial leeway for the linguist to include data based on subjective criteria. Bundgaard et al. (2006) argue that blending theory is not always the best way to approach non-compositional compounds and their meaning. According to them, blending theory tends to focus too much on the identification of the mental spaces that might be involved, rather than on the description of the actual compound and of the cognitive operations involved in it. The language user, they argue, does not always construe compounds as blends or mappings of two *different* conceptual frames: in a large majority of English compounds, XY compounds are instead *asymmetric* constructions in which one element (Y) evokes the schematic frame and the other element (X) serves to specify it in greater detail: that is, the 'mental spaces' which blending theory posits for compounding do not have the same

weight and do not assume the same function. Compounds are therefore constructions, and their form itself has a meaning independent of the terms that instantiate
it (Bundgaard et al. 2006: 372). The online construal of compounds is considerably
facilitated by this: the language user knows beforehand what the schematic structural relation is between X and Y and does not need to recruit two full-fledged
frames for X and Y and then make his way by trial and error through the many
mappings that are possible between these mental spaces (Bundgaard et al. 2006:
381–2).

Importantly, this view does not constitute a return to the building block view of
compounding, the authors argue, because the frame evoked by Y is fluid and
dynamic: 'it may comport several qualitative dimensions and it may be dependent,
often in a complicated way, on entrenched schemata, ongoing discourse, contextual meaning, and implied information' (Bundgaard et al. 2006: 372). It is the
different types of cognitive operations effectuated on the frames which is interesting. Describing compounds then consists in unfolding the frame of the Y-element
(its default frame or the one it has been endowed with in a specific speech
situation), and showing what 'zone', 'slot', or 'element' of it that X specifies. It is
the authors' guess that this description 'is coextensive with a classification of how
frame structure is expressed by language in general (hence the difficulties of the
classificatory approach)' (Bundgaard et al. 2006: 382). At least a considerable
number of compounds elaborate on an event frame (characterized by, for instance,
an agent, an act, a possible patient, a result). The different roles that *dolphin, child,*
and *shark* play in the compounds *dolphin-safe, child-safe,* and *shark-safe* are thus
not due to the fact that they bring their own respective frames to the compound
structure, but to the fact that they elaborate or activate different positions in the
schema or frame of *safe.*

12.3 CONCLUSIONS AND POSSIBLE AVENUES FOR FURTHER RESEARCH

Compounds range from being relatively straightforward structures which are
(almost) fully compositional, such as *heartbeat, police dog,* and *nightfall,* to less
compositional but still literal cases (e.g. *blackboard*), to metaphorical or metonymical structures (such as *heartland, armchair, redskin*). There are many interesting
issues related to their formal and semantic properties, their use, and their creation:
issues that have thus far figured in the literature on compounding concern productivity and creativity, analysability, the semantics of compounds and their formal
status as composite expressions, the use of metaphor and metonymy in com-

pounding, etc. In this chapter, I have argued that the general framework of Cognitive Linguistics has a number of interesting assets for the description and theoretical modelling of these issues. I pointed to the fact that it can offer a coherent and systematic account of compounding that is sufficiently rich and complex to deal with a number of fundamental issues that are not all-or-nothing categories, such as lexicalization (entrenchment), creativity/extension and its link with schematization, compositionality, the blurring of word- and sentence-level categories (morphology and syntax). Importantly, I also argued, Cognitive Linguistics thereby not only pays attention to the general cognitive abilities of the language user in construing and understanding compounds, it also models how these abilities find their expression in language structure, and it moreover brings the online processing of compounding into the picture.

The cognitive research agenda with respect to compounding thus far shows a strong bias towards the semantic analysis of compounds, as metaphorical or metonymical expressions, or as the integration of distinct mental spaces into one conceptual blend. In his paper on word formation in Cognitive Linguistics, Ungerer (2007: 651) remarks: 'Cognitive Linguistics has the potential to stimulate word formation research. Indeed, it can provide both the theoretical background and the empirical tools to complete a process that had already been set going: the semanticization of word-formation analysis.' At the same time, however, several authors have in recent publications called for a broadening of the cognitive approach to compounding to also include other, more formal aspects of the cognitive model. Bundgaard et al. (2006: 370) point out that 'Blending theory on its own merely diagrams the dynamic, cognitive process of meaning construal; it does not describe compounding as a linguistic phenomenon and therefore has only limited descriptive import' (Bundgaard et al. 2006: 370). Sweetser (1999) argues that the analysis of compounding requires the full 'regalia' of Cognitive Linguistics: not merely blending theory, but also the cognitive perspective on 'construal' or the linguistic conceptualization of a particular situation, involving possible variation in terms of selection, perspective, and abstraction. I fully agree with Bundgaard et al. and Sweetser.

In addition, it seems to me, Cognitive Linguistics should move beyond the ad hoc inclusion of compound examples in discussions of basically other, more abstract phenomena (such as compositionality or schematicity) and strive for elaborate and coherent descriptions of *systems* of compounding (along the lines of Benczes 2006). Secondly, it would be interesting to try to write out the abstract system network that can account for the distinct subtypes of compounding and the categories and intricacies which they encompass. Finally, it might also be interesting to reconsider a number of strictly 'formal' analyses (e.g. Lees 1960; Levi 1978) as well as the linguistic templates which Ryder (1994) posits for compounding, from the symbolic perspective characteristic of Cognitive Grammar, systematically looking at how the formal features of constructions encode their semantics. As has been argued in Heyvaert (2003), the analysis of word-formation patterns can benefit greatly from identifying systematic relationships between constructions which appear to instantiate distinct schemas but in fact show a number of systematic resemblances in terms of the semantic/structural categories that they embody. Gleason (1965: 202) first pointed to the descriptive relevance of such relationships and termed a 'regular and systematic' relationship between two grammatical structures which have the same lexical items but are different in structure (e.g. *The dog bit the man – The man was bitten by the dog*) 'agnation'. Relationships of agnation have always figured prominently in the description of nominalizations, and played a central role in Lees's transformational-generative approach to them. However, these systematic resemblances between word-formation patterns and clausal agnates have often been restricted to purely formal features, and have failed to be linked up with the semantics of the constructions (for a more elaborate discussion, see Heyvaert 2003). It would be interesting to see whether the symbolic Cognitive Grammar approach to constructions and their semantics can shed new light on existing purely formal treatments of certain compound types.

CHAPTER 13

....

PSYCHOLINGUISTIC PERSPECTIVES

....

CHRISTINA L. GAGNÉ

13.1 INTRODUCTION

....

Psycholinguistic research is concerned not just with the structure of language, but also with how such structure is represented and used (see Fillenbaum 1971 for an overview of the early history of psycholinguistic research). In short, psycholinguists study how language is acquired, represented, and used by the human mind. Compound words offer an interesting test case for psycholinguistic theories because even though they represent a unified concept, like simple words, they also embody an underlying structure, like phrases and sentences. The study of compounds by researchers taking a psycholinguistic approach has greatly increased in the last twenty years; a search using Google Scholar reveals that the percentage of all books, articles, journals, and citations returned from the search term *psycholinguistic(s)* that also include the term *compound* has risen from 5.6 per cent (127 hits out of 2,240 hits for the term *psycholinguistic(s)*) in 1980–1986 to 11.4 per cent (1,390 hits out of 12,100) in 2000–2006.

Although an in-depth discussion of compound research is beyond the scope of this chapter, my aim is to provide an overview of experimental psycholinguistics (see Semenza and Mondini 2006 for an overview of neuropsychological research of compounds). In particular, I will discuss theoretical approaches taken concerning the representation and processing of compounds, and factors that influence compound processing. In addition, I will discuss current directions and issues in psycholinguistic research.

13.2 THEORETICAL ISSUES
AND APPROACHES

Although early psycholinguistic research has suggested that there is underlying structure to words (Murrell and Morton 1974), questions still remain about the nature of that structure as well as about how morphologically complex words are processed. Indeed, many of the theoretical controversies that arose in the early 1960s and 1970s are still being debated (see Frost, Grainger, and Rastle 2005a for a recent overview of issues in morphological processing). Much of this debate centres around three main issues: the nature of the representations (whole words vs. constituents), the point at which the constituent representations are accessed (if at all), and whether morphologically based representations exist as independent structures.

13.2.1 How are complex words represented?

For over thirty years, researchers have been debating whether the mental representation of a word is accessed on the basis of the entire form of the word, or on the basis of the components of the word (see Wheeler 1970 for an early discussion of this issue). Various theoretical approaches have emerged and they contrast both in terms of the nature of the representation used to access a compound word (whole words vs. constituents), and in terms of the point at which information about the constituents becomes available. At one extreme are theories proposing that there is an independent mental representation for each word and that words are accessed via these whole-word representations (see e.g. Manelis & Tharp 1977, Bradley 1980, Lukatela, Gligorijevic, Kostic, and Turvey 1980, Butterworth 1983, Henderson 1985, Monsell 1985, Bybee 1995). This claim extends even to words that can be formed via compositional rules; 'even where a composition rule exists, the lexicon preserves the redundant entry' (Henderson 1985: 68).

At the other extreme of this issue are theories that claim that morphologically complex words are decomposed and accessed via their constituents. For example, Taft and Forster (1976) conducted some of the earliest psycholinguistic research addressing the question of whether compound words are decomposed. They proposed that the primary code for access is the first constituent, although the second might provide a secondary access route. They argued that a lexical search is conducted for all of the letter combinations (from left to right) until an appropriate lexical representation (also called a lexical entry) is accessed. To illustrate, during the processing of an item such as *henchman*, a lexical search will be conducted for *h, he, hen, henc, hench,* and so on until one of these combinations matches a lexical entry. If no entry is found, the item would be classified as a non-word. If an entry is found, then the content of this entry is examined to determine whether the remaining letter of the stimulus item could be combined with this recovered lexical entry to form a valid word. In the case of *henchman*, several entries (*he, hen,* and *hench*) will be encountered and evaluated. This original model has been replaced with one based on an interactive-activation framework in which aspects of words are represented at different levels (representing, for example, graphemes, morphemes, words, and concepts) and the levels are connected to each other via links which either activate related entries or inhibit unrelated entries (see Taft 1994 for a critique of the earlier Taft and Forster model and for a description of the new framework). Like its predecessor, the new model is based on the principle that words are accessed via their constituents (see also Taft 1985, Libben, Derwing, and de Almeida 1999, Taft 2004, Fiorentino and Poeppel 2007 for other decomposition-based approaches).

In between these two endpoints of this debate are partial-decomposition theories that posit that some words are decomposed and some are not (e.g. Stanners et al. 1979; Caramazza, Laudanna, and Romani 1988; Pollatsek, Hyönä, and Bertram 2000). For example, derived words are accessed as whole-word representations, whereas inflected words are activated via their stems (Stanners et al. 1979). I will consider these theories in more detail in the following section.

13.2.2 When (if at all) does decomposition occur?

The second major issue that is relevant for psycholinguistic theories of compound words concerns the point at which representations of the constituents become available. For example, at what point do the representations of *tea* and *cup* become available during the interpretation of *teacup*? Some theories maintain that decomposition is obligatory and precedes access to the lexical representation of a complex word (Taft and Forster 1975, 1976; Taft 1979, 1994, 2004). However, there is debate about whether decomposition is active or passive. In some views (such as Taft and Forster 1975; Taft 1979), a multimorphemic word is actively parsed by a decomposition process. In other views (such as Taft 1994), representations of a compound's constituents are activated whenever they match the orthographic information contained within the stimulus. Because constituents are connected to the representations of the whole word, activating the constituents' representations also activates the whole-word representation. Thus, in this approach, the input is not actively decomposed by a special mechanism that parses the input stimulus, but nonetheless the word is still accessed via the activation of its constituents.

In contrast to this pre-lexical approach to decomposition, other theories argue that the activation of a compound's constituents (if it occurs) either accompanies or follows the lexical access of the compound (Butterworth 1983; Giraudo and Grainger 2000, 2001). In another variation of this view, decomposition of a word into its constituents only occurs as a kind of 'back-up' process to be used when whole-word access is unsuccessful (van Jaarsveld and Rattink 1988).

A third approach to the question of when decomposition occurs is represented by dual-route theories that assume that both whole-word representations and constituent representations might be activated during word recognition and that words can be recognized either by activating the whole-word form or by activating constituents of the word (Burani and Caramazza 1987; Schreuder and Baayen 1995; Pollatsek et al. 2000; Juhasz, Inhoff, and Rayner 2005).

One specific example of this approach is the Morphological Race model (Schreuder and Baayen 1995, 1997; Baayen, Dijkstra, and Schreuder 1997). According to this model, the ease of recognizing a word depends on several factors including the frequency of the entire word and the frequency of the constituents, as well as the number of words sharing the same constituent. This framework proposes that only complex words with specific linguistic characteristics (for instance with a low frequency) are decomposed into their constituents. If complex words are frequently encountered in the language, then full-form representations corresponding to these words will be established in the system and used during processing. However, if complex words are not frequently encountered, then they will be more likely to be processed via segmentation into their constituents. A key component of this model is that two independent access processes operate in parallel: one that looks up the whole-word representation and one that decomposes the incoming stimulus into constituents. Ease of processing is determined by which process first activates the correct meaning representation.

Another example of a model which assumes that both whole-word forms and constituent representations are activated during word recognition is the Augmented Addressed Morphology model proposed by Caramazza and colleagues (Caramazza et al. 1985; Burani and Caramazza 1987; Caramazza et al. 1988). Unlike the Schreuder and Baayen model, this model assumes that familiar complex words are always accessed via their whole-word representation and that only novel complex words are accessed via segmentation. A second difference is that Caramazza's model proposes that frequently occurring complex words have their own lexical representation and that the activation of the whole word occurs more quickly than does activation of its constituents, whereas Schreuder and Baayen's model proposes that semantic transparency and frequency of use will influence whether a complex word is processed by activating its lexical representation or by a rule-based composition process of its constituents.

13.2.3 Is morphology explicitly represented?

Nagy and Anderson (1984) report that more than 60 per cent of the new words that readers encounter contain morphological structures with sufficient information to allow the reader to make a reasonable guess about the meaning of the whole word. This suggests that morphological information might be useful for interpreting complex words. However, because words that share morphemes also share phonology, orthography, and meaning, it is difficult to isolate a morphological effect. Indeed, there appears to be an interaction among morphological, phonological, semantic, and orthographic information (Zhou, Marslen-Wilson, Taft, and Shu 1999). Nonetheless, there has been some indication of a morphological effect that is distinct from effects such as the semantic effect and phonological effect (Bentin and Feldman 1990; Sandra 1994; Zwitserlood, Bölte, and Dohmes 2000; Roelofs and Baayen 2002; Assink and Sandra 2003; Baayen and Schreuder 2003; Frost et al. 2005b; Gumnior, Bölte, and Zwitserlood 2006). The issue of morphological structure as it relates to compounding has not yet been fully examined because although there has been much research on inflected words, derived words, and verbs (Napps, 1989; Feldman 1991; Marslen-Wilson et al. 1994; Zwitserlood, Bolwiender, and Drews 2005), there has been relatively little research conducted with compounds. Still, thus far, the evidence gained from studies involving compounds suggests an influence of morphemic structure (see e.g. Dohmes, Zwitserlood, and Bölte 2004).

Although there has been some empirical evidence that morphology plays a role in the processing of complex words, the question of whether morphology is explicitly represented in the system, or whether morphological structure emerges from representations of form and meaning remains unanswered. Some researchers argue in favour of explicitly including information about a word's morphological structure in the mental lexicon. For example, Sandra (1994) argues that the morpheme should be considered the basic unit of representation in the lexical system. He points out that much of psycholinguistic research has focused on the access representations that mediate between the perceptual system and the mental lexicon; he argues that researchers should also focus on linguistic representations within the mental lexicon and that these representations contain linguistically relevant information (such as semantic and syntactic information). Roelofs and Baayen (2002) also support the inclusion of morphological information in psycholinguistic theories of word-processing, and suggest that morphemes might act as planning units during the production of complex words rather than acting as units that convey semantic information; that is, the morphological rules that govern a complex word's structure might not influence a word's semantic interpretation (see also Aronoff 1994). Theories such as the *supralexical* model of morphological representation (Giraudo and Grainger 2000, 2001) assume that related forms are linked through higher (more abstract) morphemic representations that form an interface between word form and word meaning, but that these abstract morphological units are independent of word-form representation, and are accessed only after form-specific representations (such as phonology and orthography) have been activated.

Not all researchers agree that morphology is explicitly represented. For example, Taft and Kougious (2004) suggest that the correlation between form and meaning might be based on a systematically structured orthographic form such that the initial consonant–vowel–consonant unit of a word (excluding prefixes) might be associated with a word's meaning. If so, morphological information need not be explicitly represented. By this view, morphology is represented in terms of these orthographically-related clusters of words, rather than as separate, independent morphological representations. Others, such as Bybee (1995), suggest that morphology is best represented in terms of links between whole-word representations of morphologically related words.

13.3 FACTORS THAT INFLUENCE THE EASE OF PROCESSING OF A COMPOUND WORD

13.3.1 Overview of psycholinguistic methods

Psycholinguistic research frequently draws on techniques and experimental procedures common to cognitive psychology as well as to neuropsychology. In general, the researcher manipulates a factor (or factors) that he/she thinks might influence processing and then examines whether there is an observable change in a dependent variable. The particular procedure and dependent variable differs across studies. The most common procedure is the use of response time: participants perform a task (such as deciding whether a stimulus item is a real word) and the time to make a decision is recorded by a computer. During a lexical decision task, for example, participants see letter strings and decide, as quickly as possible, whether the string corresponds to a real word (e.g. *apple*) or to a non-word (e.g. *fleg*). Another procedure that has been used is eye-tracking: eye-movements are recorded while participants read compound words (alone or, more typically, in context) and the time spent on various parts of the stimulus is calculated. Of particular interest are first-fixation durations (time spent on a word or part of a word before moving to a new location) and gaze durations (total time spent on a word or part of a word). More recently, electrophysiological brain-recording measures, such as EEG and MEG, have been used. These methods provide measures of neural activity in various parts of the brain (see e.g. Fiorentino and Poeppel 2007). By using these methods and procedures, researchers have identified several factors that influence the processing of compounds. In the following sections, I will discuss some of the factors that seem particularly robust in terms of their effect on compound processing.

13.3.2 Whole-word and constituent frequency

Word frequency refers to how often a word has been encountered in either printed or spoken language. For example, in the CELEX database (Baayen, Piepenbrock, and van Rijn 1993), the word *cat* has a frequency of about 25 in a million words. Numerous studies have found that high frequency words are responded to more quickly than are low-frequency words (Rubenstein and Pollack 1963; Scarborough, Cortese, and Scarborough 1977; Gernsbacher 1984; Gardner et al. 1987).

The frequency of a compound's constituents also influences processing. Overall, responses to multimorphemic words are faster when the words contain high-frequency constituents than when they contain low-frequency constituents (e.g. Burani, Salmaso, and Caramazza 1984; Andrews 1986). However, the various studies differ in terms of which constituent produces a frequency effect. Some studies have found influence of only the first constituent (e.g. Taft and Forster 1976; van Jaarsveld and Rattink 1988). Others have found an influence of the second constituent. Juhasz et al. (2003), for example, note that the influence of the frequency of the first constituent is stronger for compounds that have low-frequency second constituents. Finally, Zwitserlood (1994) found that the frequency of both the first and second constituents were correlated with response time in a lexical-decision task.

Part of this discrepancy about which constituent influences processing might be due to lexical-decision times being unable to provide information about early and late stages of processing: lexical-decision times reflect the time required to process both constituents as well as the time required to make a decision on the entire letter-string. Therefore, to get a better sense about the influence of the various constituents at different stages of processing, some researchers have used eye-movement data (Inhoff, Briihl, and Schwarts 1996; Pollatsek et al. 2000; Bertram and Hyönä 2003; Juhasz et al. 2003; Andrews, Miller, and Rayner 2004). During this procedure the time that is spent looking at various regions of the stimulus is recorded. Several eye-tracking experiments have found an influence of one constituent when the frequency of the other constituent was held constant: for example, Pollatsek and Hyönä (2005) showed an effect of the first constituent and Pollatsek et al. (2000) found an influence of the second constituent. Other studies have varied the frequency of both constituents in the same experiment: Andrews et al. (2004) recorded eye-movements while participants read compounds that were embedded in sentences and found that the first constituent's frequency influenced first-fixation times, whereas both the first and second constituent's frequency influenced gaze duration and total looking time. Although the size of the effects were small and marginally significant in both experiments, they do provide some indication that the early stages (as indicated by first-fixation duration) are affected by the first constituent whereas later stages of processing (as indicated by gaze duration) are influenced by the second constituent. Data reported by Juhasz et al. (2003) reveal a similar pattern. In sum, the relative influence of the first and second constituents does not appear to be constant across all stages of processing; instead, the first constituent, in particular, is more influential at very early stages of compound processing than at later stages.

13.3.3 Family size

Nagy et al. (1989) examined whether the ease of processing a word depended on the frequency of related words. For example, they examined whether the time required to recognize *stair* was influenced by the frequency of *stairs*, which is an inflectional relative. To do so, they selected words that varied in terms of the frequency of the inflectional, derivational, and non-morphological relatives. For example, *slow* and *loud* have identical frequencies, yet the frequency of *slowly* (a derivational relative of *slow*) is three times larger than the frequency of *loudly* (a derivational relative of *loud*). Non-morphological relatives are words which share the same letter sequence but different morphemes (e.g. the words *feel* and *feet* are non-morphological relatives of the word *fee*). Thus, unlike previous research which focused on whether the speed with which a person recognizes a complex word (e.g. *quietness*) depends on the frequency of its stem (e.g. *quiet*), Nagy et al.'s research focused on whether processing a complex word depends on the frequency of its relatives (e.g. *quietness*, and *quietly*). If the processing of a monomorphemic word (e.g. *quiet*) is influenced by the frequency of morphologically related words, then this result would indicate that experience with a complex word increases the ease with which its stem (*quiet*) can be processed. This finding would suggest that morphologically complex words (such as *quietness*, *quietly*, and *quieter*) are either stored in a decomposed form rather than as a whole-word form, or that the representations of words with related stems are linked together such that accessing one increases the ease of accessing morphologically related words. An advantage of this approach is that they did not need to include any morphologically complex words in the stimuli set. In doing so, they avoid the concern raised by researchers, such as Andrews (1986) and Rubin, Becker, and Freeman (1979), that the morphological decomposition is the result of a special strategy adopted by participants when the stimulus set contains many morphologically complex words.

Nagy et al. (1989) found that frequency of inflectional and derivational relatives influenced speed of processing: it took less time to respond to words with high-frequency relatives than to words with low-frequency relatives. This finding suggests that the morphological relations between words (not just simple overlap of word parts, such as letter sequences) are represented in the lexicon. Nagy et al. (1989) introduced the concept of a *word family* and proposed that the lexicon might be organized such that entries for related words are linked or, perhaps, grouped together under the same entry. If so, then accessing an entry would result in the partial activation of related entries. For example, accessing *join* would also access *joins* and *joint*.

Although the notion that properties of a word's morphological family influences ease of processing did not receive much attention when originally introduced, it has started to receive considerable attention in recent years as researchers have regained an interest in the question of whether experience with a compound's constituents in other lexical constructions plays a role in compound processing. In particular, current researchers have been exploring the influence of family size. Family size reflects the productivity of a particular morpheme and refers to the number of derived and compound words that are formed from a base morpheme. Family size appears to have a facilitatory effect: for example, response times to a simplex noun are faster when it appears as a constituent in a large number of derived words and compounds than when it appears as a constituent in a small number of words in the language (Schreuder and Baayen 1997). The processing of complex words (i.e. derived and inflected words) in Dutch are similarly affected (Bertram, Baayen, and Schreuder 2000). In addition, family size influences subjective frequency ratings (Baayen, Tweedie, and Schreuder, 2002; de Jong et al. 2002). The existence of the family-size effect suggests that the mental lexicon might consist of networks of morphological relations. In other words, complex words share aspects of form and meaning and this information influences the ease with which a word can be processed.

13.3.4 Influence of recent exposure to related items

To examine more closely the extent to which the representations of a compound and its constituents are interconnected, psycholinguists have examined whether exposure to a compound influences the ease of processing one of its constituents, and vice versa. Several studies have found that processing a compound facilitates the subsequent processing of one of its constituents. For example, Weldon (1991) found that the identification of the word *black* was facilitated by prior exposure to either *blackbird* or *blackmail*. Likewise, Masson and MacLeod (1992) demonstrated that a constituent (e.g. *break*) is more accurately identified when it has been seen as part of a noun phrase (e.g. *coffee break*) than when it has not been previously studied. Osgood and Hoosain (1974) found that prior exposure to either a noun phrase (e.g. *copper block*) or a nonsense phrase (e.g. *sympathy block*) facilitated the subsequent processing of a single word from that phrase (e.g. *block*).

Findings such as these suggest that identifying a compound word involves activating the lexical representation of the constituent words. However, an alternative explanation is that the speed-up in processing the constituent is due to orthographic overlap. That is, the processing of *black* might be faster following *blackbird* due to some form of activation of the lexical detector for the letter-string *black*, rather than due to morphological analysis. Research by Zwitserlood (1994) explicitly tested this explanation. In her study, participants viewed a Dutch compound followed (300 ms later) by either the first or second constituent. Viewing the compound reduced the time needed to respond to its constituent: for example, viewing *kerkorgel* (church organ) speeded responses to *orgel*. Likewise, viewing *kerkorgel* speeded responses to *kerk*. This occurred even for opaque compounds: viewing *klokhuis* (apple core, but literally clock-house) speeded responses to *huis* as well as to *klok*. However, she did not find any evidence of priming when there was only orthographic overlap, but no morphological constituency, between the prime and target: *kerstfeest* (Christmas) did not facilitate the processing of *kers* (cherry). This finding suggests that it is not the case that responses were faster because it was easier to identify the individual letters (see also Flores d'Arcais and Saito 1993 for an examination of this issue using a non-alphabetic language).

Just as processing a compound can speed the subsequent processing of its constituents, so does processing of a constituent speed the subsequent processing of a compound with that constituent (Lima and Pollatsek 1983; Inhoff et al. 1996; Jarema et al. 1999; Libben et al. 2003). For example, prior exposure to *tea* facilitated the processing of *teaspoon*, which suggests that processing a compound word results in the accessing of the lexical representation of the constituent words.

A related question concerns whether the semantic representations of the constituents are also accessed as a result of processing a compound. If so, then one would expect processing to be easier if the item is preceded by a word that is semantically related to one of the constituents. Sandra (1990) found that lexical-decision times were faster for transparent Dutch compounds when they were preceded by a word that was semantically related to one of the compound's constituents (e.g. *milkman* was aided by exposure to *woman*), but opaque compounds were not so aided (e.g. *butterfly* was not aided by prior exposure to the word *bread*). Likewise, no priming was observed for pseudo-compounds (e.g. *girl* did not influence time required to respond to *boycott*). Based on these findings, Sandra concluded that semantically opaque compounds are not automatically decomposed during word recognition. In his 1990 paper, Sandra was less committed about whether transparent compounds require their own unified representation in the lexicon. However, in a later paper, Sandra (1994) suggested that morphemic-based representations are used, but that a single representation for the entire compound is still required because a representation containing just the morphemes and the relation is not sufficient for providing a full meaning of the phrase.

Zwitserlood (1994) also examined whether exposure to compound words affects the ease of processing semantic associates of either the first or second constituents for Dutch compounds. In her studies, participants made lexical-decision judgements on target words that were semantically related to either the first or second

the languages varied in terms of the effects of word-structure variables (such as length, word frequency, and syllables). Surprisingly, they found strong cross-linguistic correlations. For example, Chinese word frequencies predicted response times in Spanish. These cross-linguistic correlations suggest that length and frequency effects might reflect differences in familiarity and accessibility at the conceptual level, rather than differences in accessing the lexical representation for a word. Related to this issue, Bates et al. found that word frequency was not only associated with response times to the target word, but also with response times to alternative words (such as synonyms and morphological variants of the target) which suggests that frequency effects were not at the level of word selection (because a high-frequency target should have suppressed, and hence slowed down response times to competitors) but at a point at which recognition of the picture was being used to narrow down the selection of possible lexical items.

The locus of family-size effect also appears to be at the semantic/conceptual level rather than at the word-form level (see del Prado Martin et al. 2005 for a discussion; also de Jong et al. 2002). If so, then family size might reflect familiarity with the usage of the constituent in linguistic constructions; this information is especially relevant for compounding because the more experience someone has with a particular constituent, the easier it is to use that constituent in a compound (Gagné and Spalding 2004, 2007).

13.4.2 Increased focus on processing issues

Earlier work in the field often interpreted the data in terms of differences in representation. However, more recent views have considered the possibility that the data might reflect differences in terms of processing. For example, Andrews et al. (2004) suggest that the first constituent might play a dominant role in processing (especially of long words) because this is where people tend to look at a word, rather than due to the first constituent having a special role in the retrieval process (as suggested by Taft 1991). If so, then one would expect the first and second constituents to exert an influence at different time intervals (see Juhasz et al. 2003 for a similar claim). This explanation is consistent with a recent view put forth by Dunabeitia, Perea, and Carreiras (2007). They suggest that during early processing, the lexeme corresponding to the first constituent becomes activated and also activates (to some extent) the compound. For example, upon reading *teacup*, the lexemes *tea* and *teacup* might be retrieved. However, recognition of the entire word cannot occur until the second constituent is processed (i.e. until *cup* is processed). Processing the second part of the compound activates both *cup* and *teacup* which then allows for a verification process during which the orthographic, morphological, lexical, syntactic, and semantic retrieval of the word is completed. According to this view, the second constituent (or, more generally, the ending constituent) plays a larger role in the later stages because it is the constituent that is used to complete the activation–verification procedure.

An increased focus on the role of processing, rather than purely representation, is also seen in discussions concerning the influence of semantic transparency on compound processing. In particular, there has been the suggestion that the influence of semantic transparency might reflect differences in processing, rather than differences in representation. Processing opaque compounds, like transparent compounds, might automatically activate the conceptual representations of their constituents, but these representations must then be deactivated because their meanings conflict with the meaning of the compound (Libben 2005). Indeed, compound processing appears to activate all possible interpretations for a given compound. To test this, Libben et al. (1999) used ambiguous novel compounds that could be parsed in two ways. (For example, *clamprod* could be parsed as *clam+prod* or as *clamp+rod*.) These items were used as primes in a recall task. Presentation of the ambiguous compound aided the recall of semantic associates of all four possible constituents (*sea*, *hold*, *push*, and *stick*, which, in order, are related to *clam*, *clamp*, *prod*, and *rod*). This indicates that during the processing of *clamprod*, the lexical and conceptual representations of the constituents of both morphemes were accessed.

13.4.3 Interest in integration and meaning construction

Although much of the work on compounds has been concerned with the extent to which compounds are decomposed into their constituents, more recently there has started to be greater discussion about the question of how the constituents become integrated. Inhoff et al. (2000) examined the effect of spacing on eye-fixations for German compounds (which are typically written without a space) and found that final fixation times were longer for spaced compounds than for non-spaced compounds. They concluded that the insertion of a space facilitated the participants' ability to access the constituent word forms, whereas the lack of a space benefited the integration of the constituents to form a unified representation of the compound. Juhasz et al. (2005) found that these results extend to English compounds.

More recently, Koester, Gunter, and Wagner (2007) have reported evidence of a semantic composition process, which refers to the integration of the constituent's meanings. They observed that slow negative shift in ERP signal (which is thought to be affected by ease of semantic composition) is larger for items that are judged to be more difficult to integrate and is larger for transparent compounds, which can be processed using a semantic composition process, than for opaque compounds. Although Koester et al.'s data suggest that the interpretation of transparent compounds involves semantic integration, and that integration occurs after the presentation of the head constituent, it is not yet clear what occurs during the integration process. Indeed, there has been recent speculation about what the composition process might entail. For example, is it the case that composition entails the simple conjunction of the two constituents, or is it a more interpretive process (see Fiorentino and Poeppel 2007; Taft 2004 for brief discussions of this issue)?

The issue of integration and composition during compound processing leads to the larger question of how the meaning of a compound word is determined. The production and use of compound words has often been provided as an example of linguistic productivity (Libben and Jarema 2006). Thus, psycholinguistic theories must ultimately be able to explain not just how known compounds are processed but also how new compounds are created. As yet, this is a relatively undeveloped area of the research within the field of psycholinguistics because more emphasis has been placed on the representation and structure of existing compounds.

Determining the meaning of a novel compound is not straightforward because the constituents can be related in multiple ways. It also seems to be the case that the meaning of a compound goes beyond just the meaning of the individual compounds. Thus, researchers are faced with a challenging paradox: Namely, how can compounds be both productive yet not purely compositional?

An added piece of complexity to this puzzle is that even compounds and noun phrases that have an established (some might say 'lexicalized') interpretation can take on an alternative meaning. That is, the meaning of even established compounds is not static. For example, Gerrig (1989) found that the existence of a lexicalized meaning for a familiar phrase (e.g. *foot race*) interfered with the derivation of an innovative meaning (e.g. *a race that is one foot long*). More recently, Gagné, Spalding, and Gorrie (2005) found that the reverse is also true: the recent creation of an innovative meaning for a familiar phrase (e.g. *bug spray*) decreased the ability of participants to view the normal, established meaning as being acceptable. This finding suggests that the established meaning was competing with the innovative meaning constructed in the previous sentence and this competition decreased the availability of the established meaning. This raises the question of what drives meaning construction.

Part of the solution might come from taking a broader perspective on compound processing. In particular, examining how the conceptual system interacts with the linguistic system might prove to be helpful. There have already been several psycholinguistic theories that suggest that the lexical representations of semantically transparent compounds are linked to their constituents at the conceptual level (Zwitserlood 1994, Libben 1998, Taft 2004). For the most part, however, the conceptual level of such theories is not envisioned in the same way that cognitive psychologists envision concepts. The conceptual level of current psycholinguistic theories primarily equates concepts with word meaning, which only encompasses part of the knowledge in the conceptual system. In contrast, cognitive theories view concepts as playing an important role in human understanding and explanation. For example, identifying something as a bear allows one to take action to avoid being attacked by it. Concepts are also used for reasoning: if one knows that all mammals have spleens and that bears are mammals, one could reason that bears are also likely to have spleens. In short, cognitive theories of concepts view the conceptual system as a highly complex and interrelated system of knowledge and posit that this system performs many functions in addition to communication.

Although there are cases where the full meaning of a word is not entirely derivable from its parts (e.g. *snowman* is not a real man), the parts are not unrelated to the meaning of the word (see Sandra 1994 for a discussion of this issue). The conceptual system might be able to provide some of the extra information needed to interpret a compound because it contains knowledge about how objects interact in the world. In short, the conceptual system contains extralinguistic knowledge that is obtained via experience with the world, and language users might use this knowledge when interpreting both novel and familiar compounds.

One aspect of the conceptual system that might be particularly relevant is knowledge about how concepts relate to other concepts. It appears that people draw on knowledge about how concepts can be combined with other concepts and that availability of a particular relation affects the ease with which novel compounds and phrases can be interpreted: the more highly available a relation is, the easier it is to interpret the phrase (Gagné and Shoben 1997; Gagné 2001, 2002; Gagné and Shoben 2002; Gagné and Spalding 2006a). In this way, relation availability provides an important constraint on what conceptual knowledge is used during the interpretation of familiar and novel compounds. This research suggests that a compound's constituents are not just conjointly activated but are bound together in a particular way, and the availability of a particular relational structure influences ease of processing. This finding entails that people possess and use knowledge not only about how words relate to each other, but also about how the internal components of a word (and their associated concepts) are related. This process of selecting a relation and constructing a unified representation is obligatory for novel compounds and phrases because they lack a whole-word representation. Recently, Gagné and Spalding (2004, 2007) have argued that this relation-selection process also occurs for familiar compounds.

13.5 FINAL THOUGHTS

Psycholinguistic research has focused on determining the underlying psychological representations and processes that are required to use both simple and complex words. The data reinforce the claim that the mental lexicon is highly structured, with multiple levels of representation. This structure is most readily apparent in the case of compound words: compound words appear to be stored such that their representations share aspects of form and meaning with other words (both simplex and complex). The conceptual system is also highly structured and consists of a highly interconnected network of relations among concepts. Compound processing appears to take advantage of the highly structured nature of both systems, although the exact nature of the interconnectivity and coordination of these systems remains to be discovered.

CHAPTER 14

MEANING PREDICTABILITY OF NOVEL CONTEXT-FREE COMPOUNDS

PAVOL ŠTEKAUER

14.1 INTRODUCTION

This chapter aims to deal with the predictability of meanings of novel context-free compounds. While this topic has not yet been addressed by the mainstream morphological and psycholinguistic research, it is closely related to extensively discussed topics of compound interpretation.

The basic difference between compound-interpretation theories and a meaning-predictability theory outlined below can be best illustrated by the different focus of these accounts. While the basic question of compound interpretation is 'How is a novel compound interpreted?' or 'What is the mechanism involved in the interpretation of novel compounds?', the basic question of the meaning-predictability theory is 'Which of the usually numerous possible meanings is the most predictable one?' or 'Why is it that a language user who comes across a novel compound selects its one particular reading in preference to all the other possible readings?' From this it follows that the crucial factor of a meaning-predictability theory is competition among potential readings, and the identification of a large number of factors that affect the meaning-prediction process, also including the evaluation of their role in this process. Thus, while a meaning-predictability theory does not avoid dealing with the interpretation mechanism (thus sharing significant part of its scope with the word-interpretation theories), its main focus is on the identification of the numerous factors that condition each novel compound-interpretation act and decide on the 'winner' of the 'meaning competition'.[1]

14.2 RELATED THEORIES

14.2.1 Dokulil and his concept of 'meaning predictability'

The first to speak about the 'meaning predictability' of novel context-free naming units (complex words) was, to my knowledge, the Czech linguist Miloš Dokulil. In his short but seminal (1978) paper he examines the position of a speaker of a language who encounters a new naming unit outside context for the first time. Dokulil derives meaning predictability from the relation between the structural, word-formation meaning and the specific lexical meaning. The word-formation meaning can be of various degrees of abstraction, ranging over specific naming units, word-formation types and subtypes, and categories. The word-formation meaning of a particular naming unit cannot be inferred from it itself; it can only be identified in relation to its next higher class, in particular word-formation type or rule. So, for example, the type underlying words like Cz. *učitel* 'teacher', *žadatel* 'applicant', *spisovatel* 'novelist' makes it possible to identify the word-formation meaning of any word formed according to this type as 'a person performing the activity identified by the verbal element'.

From the point of view of meaning predictability the most advantageous situation is if the word-formation and the lexical meanings are identical (like the above-mentioned Czech deverbal agent nouns).

---

[1] It is important to stress that there is no place for the term 'correct' reading in a theory of meaning predictability. This assumption derives from the concept of word formation as creativity within productivity constraints. When coining a new naming unit, a language user can usually select from a range of options available to him at the individual naming-act levels. As a result, while the coiner produces a new naming unit with one and only one meaning in mind, his/her naming strategy need not coincide with an interpreter's expectations. The most predictable reading need not correspond to the meaning with which the naming unit was coined by a language user, that is, its meaning need not correspond to what Murphy (1988: 539) calls the *best fitting slot* in the head noun's schema. All readings are 'correct' if they are interpretable, that is to say, if they are *acceptable to a speech community as meaningful representatives of a particular novel naming unit*.

There are, however, many cases when one cannot infer the lexical meaning from the word-formation meaning. One of Dokulil's examples concerns nouns derived from colour adjectives–the lexical meaning is too specialized in regard to the word-formation meaning: Cz. *zelenina* 'vegetables', derived from Adj. *zelený* 'green', vs. *modřina* 'bruise', derived from *modrý* 'blue' vs. *šedina* 'grey hair' from *šedý* 'grey'.

On the other hand, the lexical meaning may also be more general than the corresponding word-formation meaning, a situation which also hampers predictability. Cz. *truhlář* 'cabinet-maker' derived from *truhla* 'coffin' denotes an Agent who, in addition to coffins, also produces all sorts of furniture; *sedlář* 'saddle maker' from *sedlo* 'saddle' produces – apart from saddles – harnesses in general and other leather products.

Meaning predictability is significantly influenced by the *onomasiological category*.[2] Naming units of the *modificational* and the *transpositional* types feature a high level of agreement between the word-formation and the lexical meanings, and therefore a very good predictability (diminutives such as Cz. *strom* 'tree' – *stromek* 'little tree'; frequentatives such as Cz. *psát* 'write' – *psávat* 'write frequently'; feminine names derived from masculines; objectified action – Cz. *hoření* 'burning'$_N$ derived from *hořet* 'burn'$_V$ – or quality: Cz. *chytrost* 'ingenuity' derived from *chytrý* 'ingenious'). In contrast to them, the *mutational* type is usually (but not always) difficult to predict, mainly (but not exclusively) substantives denoting inanimate objects because, as suggested by Dokulil, 'rather than by one mark, substances are usually determined by a large set of marks which resist any reduction to a single mark as a motive of a naming unit' (1978: 248; my translation). Therefore, it is here that word-formation and lexical meanings may deviate from each other, which reduces the overall meaning predictability. For illustration, one and the same word-formation type 'colour adjective + suffix *-ka*' has given rise to a series of words of unpredictable meanings: Cz. *růžovka* 'rose$_A$-suffix' denotes a sort of mushroom; *červenka* 'red-suffix' denotes a species of bird; *hnědka* 'brown-suffix' denotes a brown horse; *zlatka* 'gold-suffix' denotes a sort of coin; and *bělka* 'white-suffix' denotes a white animal (cow, horse, dog, hen), white flour, a sort of light cherry, or even soil rich in lime. Important exceptions to this tendency towards unpredict-

---

[2] Dokulil's classical onomasiological model distinguishes three types of onomasiological category: mutational, modificational, and transpositional. The commonest type is the mutational category. It consists of two basic constituents, the onomasiological mark (Marchand's 'determinant') and the onomasiological base (conceptual class; Marchand's 'determinatum'), representing an onomasiological structure. It is based on the relation between the concepts standing for the mark and the base. There are four basic concepts, SUBSTANCE, ACTION, QUALITY, and CIRCUMSTANCE. For example, *evening paper* relates the categories CIRCUMSTANCE and SUBSTANCE, *to redden* the categories QUALITY and ACTION. Within this general structure, more specific relations can be distinguished, based on semantic categories like Agent, Patient, Bearer of Quality, Result, Possession, Origin, etc.

The transpositional type of onomasiological category is based on hypostatization of QUALITY or ACTION (*rapid* → *rapidity*, *fall*$_V$ → *fall*$_N$). The modificational type includes various modifications of a concept, such as the formation of diminutives, augmentatives, change of gender, the young of animals, collectivity.

ability are, for instance, names of different types of population, such as Cz. *venkovan* 'countryman', *měšťák* 'townsman', *cizinec* 'foreigner'; adherents of movements *komunista* 'communist', *husita* 'Hussite'; or names of locations, for example, *včelín* 'bee-house', *ředitelna* 'headmaster's study'.

In general, Dokulil maintains, more specific (and therefore, richer in constituting features) objects to be named increase the tension between the relatively simple word-formation meaning and the relatively rich lexical meaning.

Other important factors conditioning meaning predictability are according to Dokulil the degree of explicitness/implicitness of a naming unit (compounds tend to express the content more explicitly than affixed words – compare, for example, Cz.*rychlovlak* 'fast-train' vs. *rychlík* 'fast-suffix', or *černozem* 'black-soil' vs. *černice* 'black-suffix') word-class of the motivated and the motivating words; semantic class of the motivating word(s); the monosemy vs. polysemy of the word-formation structure, of its constituents, and of the word-formation type; and last but not least, the productivity of the word-formation type.

14.2.2 Gagné and Shoben and their concept of 'competition'

Christina Gagné, first with Shoben (1997), then alone (2002), and later with Spalding (2006a, 2006b, 2007, n.d.), introduced in the field of meaning interpretation the idea of *competition*.[3] This competition is examined at the level of semantic relations existing between the modifier and the head of a combined concept realized in a language as a Noun+Noun compound. The general concentration of psycholinguistic and cognitive research on concepts follows from the postulation that '[t]o interpret a novel compound (e.g. *chocolate twig*), one must access the concepts denoted by the words and select a relation that links them together' (Gagné 2002: 723). The principle of competition is discussed within the CARIN theory (CARIN = Competition Among Relations In Nominals). According to this theory, the representation of the modifier concept includes knowledge about the thematic relations with which the modifier is usually used in conceptual combinations. This information, labelled as the *availability of the relation*, influences the interpretation of novel context-free compounds. Gagné and Shoben (1997: 74) assume that 'the availability of a specific thematic relation varies from constituent to constituent and that this difference in availability affects the ease with which two constituents are combined'. A compound with a more frequently used thematic relation is easier to interpret than a compound based on a relation that is not used frequently. For example, the main thematic relation of *mountain* is 'Locative' (*mountain cabin, mountain stream, mountain resort*). On the other hand,

---

[3] In the same year, Štekauer (1997a) also used this term to discuss the meaning predictability of converted naming units.

there are only few 'Made of' relations for *mountain* (*mountain range*). Consequently, language users tend to interpret its combinations as ones based on the
Locative relation. By implication, the ease of interpretation of compounds is
proportional to the degree of probability of a particular thematic relation. Gagné
(2001: 237) labels the knowledge about the probability of individual semantic
relations for a given concept as *relational distribution* reflecting a person's experience with the language and with combined concepts in particular. The *frequency of
the selected relation* appears to be an important factor for the interpretation of
novel combined concepts. A speaker's previous experience with similar combinations affects the *lexical availability* of one or more constituents in the subsequent
combination and/or the *relation availability* that is used to link the modifier and
the head noun. In other words, our former experience may influence the meaning
that is assigned to the individual constituents and the selection of the semantic
relation between the modifier and the head.

According to the CARIN model, the modifier and head noun are not equally
involved in assessing relation information. It is assumed – unlike the majority of
other psycholinguistic works in the field – that the crucial role in the interpretation
of novel combined concepts is played by the *modifier*, not by the head:[4] the
selection of a particular relation is facilitated when a modifier used in this particular conceptual combination is previously frequently used in the same relation as the
current combination. In addition, the selection of a particular semantic relation
may also be affected by previously encountered combinations with a *similar
modifier*. For example, recent exposure to *scholar accusation* should facilitate the
interpretation of *student vote* because both combinations require the same general
relation (Noun by Modifier according to Gagné).[5]

To sum up, during the interpretation of a modifier–noun combination, various
relations *compete* for selection. The more often a relation has been used with a
modifier, the more available it is and the more likely it is to be selected. The
modifier 'suggests' relations and these choices are evaluated in light of the head
noun. The *availability* is determined by the *strength of the competing relations*. The
competition among semantic relations is expressed by the *strength ratio* and the
index of relation availability is called the *competition index*. Relations with strong
competitors are less available than relations with weak competitors. Gagné and
Spalding's experiments (2006a, 2007) show that 'the *number of competitors* does
make an independent contribution above and beyond the contribution of the
selected relation's frequency' (n.d.: 9), and that '[o]nly the most highly available
relations for a particular modifier compete and affect ease of processing' (ibid.).

---

[4] For an opposite view stressing the decisive role of the head concept, see, for example, Wisniewski
(1996).
[5] R. Lieber (personal communication) notes that Gagné's example is ambiguous because for her the
first one means 'accusation pointed at a scholar' and the second 'vote by students'.

Moreover, Gagné and Spalding conclude that 'having no competitors seems to be more important than the selected relation's frequency' (2006a: 18).[6]

14.2.3 Costello and Keane and their concept of 'constraints' upon interpretation

Costello and Keane's C^3 *model* (Costello 1996; Costello and Keane 1997, 2000, 2001) reflects a large number of possible meanings inherent in any conceptual combination. The C^3 model (Constraints on Conceptual Combination) uses three basic constraints to identify the best interpretation: the 'diagnosticity', the 'plausibility', and the 'informativeness' constraints. 'Diagnostic properties of a concept are those which occur often in instances of that concept and rarely in instances of other concepts...' (Costello and Keane 2001: 257). According to this principle, the compound *cactus fish*, for example, is preferably interpreted as 'a prickly fish' rather than 'a green fish' because PRICKLY is more diagnostic of 'cactus' than GREEN. The plausibility constraint requires a plausible interpretation on the basis of past experience. Consequently, a plausible interpretation of *angel pig* is 'a pig with wings on its torso' rather than 'a pig with wings on its tail'. Finally, according to the informativeness constraint the interpretation of a novel conceptual combination should convey some new information.

14.2.4 Other sources

The meaning predictability theory is related to a large number of other works of morphologists, cognitive linguists, and psycholinguists. It is especially within the psycholinguistic framework that the interpretation of (mainly) N+N compounds has been paid systematic attention in recent decades.

Morphologists have mostly concentrated on the identification of general semantic relations between compound constituents. No doubt, the most influential among them has been Levi's (1978) set of *Recoverably Deletable Predicates*, including the predicates CAUSE, HAVE, MAKE, BE, USE, FOR, IN, ABOUT, and FROM. Even though Levi's closed set failed to overcome the main defect of Lees's (1960) approach, namely the vagueness and ambiguity of the predicates, it became the basis for a number of psycholinguistic experiments.

Zimmer (1971, 1972) should be credited for, *inter alia*, his notions of *classificatory relevance* and *appropriately classificatory* (AC) relationship. An important impetus

---

[6] For a discussion concerning the methodology of sampling and the data evaluation within the CARIN framework, see Wisniewski and Murphy (2005) who point out the important role of 'familiarity' and 'plausibility', and the subsequent response by Gagné and Spalding (2006a).

for experimental research in the field of context-free interpretation of novel N+N compounds was Downing (1977), thanks to her experimental research and her discussion of 'habitual' vs. 'temporary' relations, as well as semantic redundancy.

Allen's (1978) *Variable R Condition* is a morphological predecessor of what came to be one of the strongest models within psycholinguistic research, the *slot-filling model* (also labelled as feature model or schema model) (e.g. Cohen and Murphy 1984; Smith and Osherson 1984; Hampton 1987; Smith et al. 1988; Murphy 1988, 1990), which stresses the role of the head concept functioning as a *schema* with a certain number of *slots* that are filled by the modifier values. According to this approach, differences in the interpretability of context-free N+N compounds are related to the *relative salience* of particular meaning aspects (slots in a schema-based model, attributes in the feature-based model).

The *relation model* (Gagné and Shoben 1997; Gagné 2001, 2002; Gagné and Spalding 2006a, b, in press) emphasizes the central role of *thematic relations* between compound constituents and the language speaker's *linguistic knowledge* of the relative strength of the individual thematic relations bound to a particular *modifier concept*. This knowledge facilitates the interpretation of compounds by preferring the interpretation based on a thematic relation which is more readily available to the modifier concept.

The *analogy-based model* (Derwing and Skousen 1989, Skousen 1989, Ryder 1994) accounts for the interpretation of novel, context-free compounds primarily by lexicalized (i.e. established, institutionalized) compounds that serve as certain *interpretation patterns* or *schemas*.

Some psycholinguists combine these two basic approaches. Wisniewski (1996), for example, distinguishes two fundamental interpretation strategies: *relation linking* and *property mapping* from one compound constituent to the other, with *hybridization* representing an extreme case of property mapping, i.e. the combination of properties of the constituents.

An important inspiration for a meaning-predictability theory also comes from those authors who point out that individual features of objects/their semantic representations are not of equal value, and represent a hierarchy. In other words, not all semantic features of the motivating words (features of concepts) are equally significant for a coinage interpretation. These prototypical features are discussed in the literature under different labels: 'predominant features' (Clark and Clark 1979), 'natural function' (Beard 1995), '(proto)typical features' (or 'prototypes') (Hampton 1983, 1987; Murphy 1988; Smith et al. 1988), or 'diagnostic properties' (Costello 1996; Costello and Keane 1997, 2000, 2001).[7]

---

[7] For a much more detailed overview of the various approaches to compound-meaning interpretation see Murphy (2002), Štekauer (2005a), and Gagné (this volume).

14.3 MEANING PREDICTABILITY OF NOVEL CONTEXT-FREE COMPOUNDS

14.3.1 General

My first discussion of meaning predictability is given in Štekauer (1996) and concerns the predictability of conversions. Two predictability rules were proposed, one for the number of possible conversion processes and another for the number of possible meanings. The present discussion is primarily based on Štekauer (2005a) which represents an attempt to outline a comprehensive theory of meaning predictability covering the products of all word-formation processes, that is to say, it is not restricted to N+N or A+N compounds. A theoretical framework is provided by:

- an onomasiological theory of word formation (mainly Štekauer 1996, 1998, 2001, 2002, 2005b); and
- the concept of word formation as creativity within productivity limits (Štekauer et al. 2005; Körtvélyessy 2008);

and the following theoretical principles and postulates:

- a theory of meaning predictability should be related to a theory of word-formation;
- meaning predictability is a cline;
- most predictable readings are motivated by the semantic components representing prototypical features of the motivating objects;
- predictability of any novel naming unit relies heavily on the conceptual-level analysis and the knowledge of listeners/readers. Therefore, experimental results for native speakers should not significantly differ from those for non-native speakers;
- predictability of the individual readings of novel context-free naming units can be calculated; and
- there are a large number of linguistic and extralinguistic factors which affect the meaning predictability for each novel naming unit.

14.3.2 Interrelation of meaning predictability and word formation

A point of departure for a general theory of meaning predictability has been the *onomasiological theory of word formation* complemented by the principles of *word formation as creativity within productivity limits*. Since various aspects of this theory have been presented in a number of publications (see above),[8] it will suffice to note

---

[8] See Štekauer (2005b) for a summary of the basic tenets.

that its focus is on the *triadic relations* in any word-formation act, that is, the relations between extralinguistic reality (object to be named), speech community (coiner), and the word-formation component; in this way, it emphasizes the *active role* and *cognitive activity* of a *coiner*. At the same time, it establishes a framework for the treatment of the individual word-formation processes on a common basis. It assumes that naming units do not come into existence in isolation from factors such as human *knowledge, cognitive abilities* and *experiences; discoveries* of new things, processes, and qualities; human *imagination*, etc. An object to be named is envisaged and construed in relation to other objects. Thus, the structural relationships in the lexicon are preceded (or dominated) by a network of *objective relationships* which, by implication, should be taken into consideration in the process of naming. The advantage of an onomasiological model of word formation for the theory of meaning predictability is that the model lays emphasis on an *active role* of language users in the process of giving names to objects instead of presenting word formation as an impersonal system of rules detached from the objects named and language users; the active role of a language user is crucial also in the process of meaning interpretation as both word formation and word interpretation are *cognitive acts*.

Since each word-formation act is a highly individual act it is at the same time a highly *creative act*, because a potential coiner is usually aware of a number of options available to him/her both at the level of selecting some of the (usually) prototypical features of an object to be named as the motivating features and at the level of morphematic expression of these features by selecting from the options available in the lexicon (MSAP: *Morpheme-to-Seme-Assignment Principle*). Consequently, this creative nature of word formation affects meaning predictability as the interpreter cannot be sure which of the naming strategies and routes has been preferred by the coiner. Perhaps the best way to illustrate the interrelation between word formation and word interpretation is to show the role of Onomasiological Types in the meaning-prediction process.

14.3.3 Onomasiological Types

One of the central assumptions of the model outlined is that the predictability of novel, context-free coinages is strongly influenced by the Onomasiological Type to which the interpreted word belongs. Onomasiological Types are conceptually based pendants of the traditional, formally grounded word-formation processes like compounding, prefixation, suffixation, etc. In Štekauer's onomasiological theory they result from a cognitive analysis of the 'motivating' objects. In particular, the selected features of the motivating objects constitute an *onomasiological structure* as a linearly ordered relation between semantic categories, such as Agent, Object, Instrument, Action, Location, Time, Manner, etc. The individual semantic

categories of the onomasiological structure are assigned morphematic representations, retrieved from the lexicon, by means of the MSAP. The principle is illustrated
in (1) in relation to giving a name to 'a device designed to feed (machines with
components)':

(1) a. Action   –   Instrument
         feed   *-er*

     b. Action   –   Instrument
         feed   *machine*

Example (1) illustrates that one and the same onomasiological structure may
underlie different traditional word-formation processes – suffixation and compounding in our example.

The onomasiological structure is not binary in its nature – it recognizes three
basic constituents:

(2) Determining   –   Determined   –   Onomasiological
     constituent   constituent   base
     of the mark   of the mark

The determining and the determined constituents of the mark correspond to
Marchand's unstructured determinant, the base corresponds to his determinatum.
From the interpretation point of view, the central position is assumed by the
determined constituent of the mark, standing for ACTION (which can be ACTION
PROPER, PROCESS, or STATE), because it expresses the relation between the base and
the determining constituent of the mark.

The onomasiological type is then determined by the interrelation between the
onomasiological structure and the morphematic (onomatological) structure. For
the purpose of the analysis of 'compounds' four out of five Onomasiological Types
are relevant.[9] In Onomasiological Type 1 each of the three constituents is morphematically expressed, as illustrated in (3):

(3) Object   –   Action   –   Instrument
     car   *feed*   *robot*

In Onomasiological Type 2 the determining constituent of the mark is not
morphematically expressed, as in (4):

(4) Object   –   Action   –   Instrument
                     feed   *robot*

The resulting unit is necessarily much more general, a hyperonym of the
compound in (3).

---

[9] Onomasiological Type 5 stands for 'Onomasiological Recategorization', traditionally called conversion or zero-derivation.

In Onomasiological Type 3 the determined (Actional) constituent of the mark is left unexpressed:

(5) Object   –   Action   –   Instrument
      car   robot

Apparently, this type, covering what has been traditionally called primary compounds, is the most demanding in terms of meaning predictability because of the absence of the most important, Actional, constituent in the morphematic structure.

Onomasiological Type 4 does not distinguish between the two mark constituents; rather it takes them as a single whole. It is this type that encompasses noun incorporation.[10] Thus, the verbal head functions as an onomasiological base and the incorporated noun as its mark, as in the following potential compound:

(6) Object   –   Action
      car   feed

Examples (3)–(6) show that one and the same onomasiological structure or similar structures may lead to different naming units, compounds in our cases.[11] The selection of any of these variants depends on a coiner's linguistic and extra-linguistic knowledge and experiences, preferences, fashionable trends, his professional expertise, education, age, etc. Obviously, this complicated situation at the level of word formation has its impact on the level of meaning predictability as already indicated in the previous brief comments. In the following subsections, the influence of the individual Onomasiological Types on meaning predictability is discussed in greater detail.

14.3.3.1 Onomasiological Type 1

OT1 mostly produces synthetic compounds, verbal compounds, or verbal-nexus compounds, such as *novel-writer, truck-driver, factory-automation, baby-sitting*, etc. OT1 establishes good preconditions for meaning predictability, because each of the constituents at the onomasiological level has its corresponding morpheme at the onomatological level, including the Actional constituent which is the key to understanding the semantic relation between the outer members of the onoma-

---

[10] While the majority of linguists would not agree with the assumption that in English there is a productive process of noun incorporation, we believe that the existence of, originally, back-formed words like *to vacuum clean, to babysit, to wiretap, to wirepull, to air-condition, to spotweld, to chainsmoke*, etc. gave rise to analogical formations not relying on 'longer' counterparts any more; the growing number of such formations may have triggered a synchronically productive process of noun incorporation. Such an account is also proposed by Kiparsky (1982) who explains the generation of these and other similar expressions as compounding, based on the rule $[Y\ Z]_X$, with X being V.

[11] Other options, including suffixation and conversion, are also available.

siological structure. Therefore, it might be assumed that predictability of the majority of OT1 compounds is very high.

For example, *piano-player* cannot but approach the maximum Predictability Rate (see section 14.3.6 below) because the Actional seme, onomatologically represented by the morpheme *play*, unambiguously relates the Instrument of Action (*piano*) and the Agent (*-er*). One of the central semantic components of *play* is [Human] because playing a piano requires conscious and purposeful training. Therefore, it may be predicted that the intended meaning of *piano-player* is 'a person who (professionally) plays a piano'. Certainly, the situation-conditioned interpretations are available, too ('a person just now playing a piano', 'an animal trained for playing a piano'); however, their Predictability Rate may be supposed to be low.

A lower Predictability Rate may be attached to words like *apple-eater* for the simple reason that this naming unit admits two competing readings as a result of the ambiguous nature of the base (Agent) and its morphematic representation (*-er*): they are 'a person eating an apple' and 'an animal eating an apple', because both readings are acceptable in terms of the relation between [Eating] and Agent. The next reading appears to be a figurative reading with a strong negative connotation (which is encoded neither in the onomasiological structure nor the onomatological structure), and therefore can only be inferred by having recourse to our extralinguistic knowledge and experience: 'a kind of mould or a pest playing havoc with one's crop of apples'.

Another model case of reduced predictability is due to the competition between two productive affixes, or better, WF rules, such as a large number of verbal compounds based on the rule Object–Verb Agent/Instrument. Compounds like *dishwasher, program generator, input extender, gap filler*, etc. can denote both a person and an Instrument, a fact which reduces their meaning predictability.

14.3.3.2 *Onomasiological Type 2*

In OT2 the determined constituent of the mark is expressed while the determining constituent is not (*lock pin, feed unit, plaything*). From this it follows that the Actional constituent of the semantic structure is present and used for the specification of the base in terms of what the object represented by the base does or what happens with it. The presence of this Actional constituent at the onomatological level facilitates the prediction process, and therefore the Predictability Rate of compounds belonging to OT2 is expected to be fairly high: we are pretty sure that *plaything* is 'a thing [Instrument] for playing [Action]', and that *feed machine* is 'a device [Instrument] used to feed [Action] (some Object) '.

Not all cases of this OT are that unequivocal. While we might predict that *lock pin* is 'a pin used for locking some other (unspecified) components or objects', it could just as well be 'a pin in a lock'. The obstacle to a high Predictability Rate in this case is the ambiguous status of the onomasiological mark – it may refer both to

ACTION and SUBSTANCE, which actually is ambiguity at the level of onomasiological types – the latter option shifts the compound under OT3.

14.3.3.3 *Onomasiological Type 4*

Before taking up OT3, let us note that OT4 is, from the meaning-predictability point of view, very advantageous because there is a direct semantic connection between the head which stands for Action and the unstructured mark which stands for Object, or some other semantic category. Therefore, a language user usually needn't select from many options, in contrast to OT3 described below. And so *to stage-manage, to baby-sit, to chain-smoke,* and *to air-condition* do not seem to be ambiguous. If we take examples of noun incorporation from other languages, their meaning predictability seems to be good, too. For example, Upper Necaxa Totonac *lakalása* 'slap someone in the face' (lit. 'face-slap-IMPF');[12] Lakota *phá kaksÁ* 'to behead' (lit. 'head INST-cut');[13] or Ket *iŋ-dɔn* 'to skin/to bark' (lit. 'skin$_N$/bark$_N$-remove'),[14] pose no substantial problems for interpretation. This is not to say that there are no ambiguous cases of noun incorporation. For illustration, it may be supposed that the predictability of Pipil *tan-kwa* 'to bite' (lit. 'tooth-eat')[15] or Mandarin Chinese *guaɪfenɪ* 'divide up (as though cutting up a melon)' (lit. 'melon-divide')[16] is lower.

14.3.3.4 *Onomasiological Type 3*

In the case of compounds without the determined constituent of the mark (traditionally called primary or root compounds), the situation is more complicated because the interpreter cannot unambiguously identify the logical-semantic relation between the two polar members of the onomasiological structure. The (theoretical) multiplicity of compatible semantic relations between the polar members is usually very high. This is the point where *extralinguistic factors* come to play a central role in the meaning-prediction process – obviously, in close cooperation with an interpreter's linguistic competence and intuition.

For example, when faced with a (possible) compound *baby book* an interpreter is able to identify the morphemes attached to the onomasiological structure. (S)he also knows the meaning(s) and therefore the semantic structure(s) of the determining constituent of the mark (*baby*) as well as the meaning(s) and the semantic structure(s) of the base (*book*).

It is postulated that this knowledge enables the interpreter to trigger the *matching process* which starts at the level of prototypical semes. To put it another way,

---

[12] Example by David Beck (personal communication).
[13] Example from de Reuse (1994: 209).
[14] Example from Werner (1998: 99).
[15] Example from Campbell (1985: 96).
[16] Example by Steffen Chung (personal communication).

what are matched first are the *prototypical features* of the motivating objects. This view corresponds with Miller and Johnson-Laird (1976: 291), who maintain that perceptual identification procedures are related to the perceptually salient features of the core of a concept, defined as 'an organized representation of general knowledge and beliefs about whatever objects or events the words denote – about what they are and do, what can be done with them, how they are related, what they relate to', as well as with that presented by Meyer (1993: 5), who assumes that 'interpreting novel compounds is based mainly on prototypical features of objects and of certain domains'.

In our example, a prototypical feature of the onomasiological base *book*, let us say, [For Reading], may be supposed to be taken as a reference point in scanning the hierarchical semantic structure of the onomasiological mark *baby*; the result of the scanning operation is the identification of [−Reading Capacity] as a relevant semantic component for the matching operation. In this way, the Agentive interpretation is automatically eliminated.

Since this matching operation failed, the matching process continues; now, the subsequent search appears to branch because there seem to be two matching operations as the next best candidates for evaluation. The interpreter may resume matching from the same semantic component of the Onomasiological Base, i.e. [For Reading], and search for a semantic component in *baby* that is compatible with it, thus identifying, for example, [+Perceptual Capacity]. In the relation of these two semantic components the latter assumes the logical-semantic function of Target of the overtly unexpressed Action:

(7) Target   ←   (Action)   –   Theme
     baby [Perception by listening]   [Reading] [For reading] *book*

Another possible combination is (8):

(8) Topic   –   (State)   –   Patient
     baby [Class of babies]   [Containing information   *book*
                                on taking care of babies]

and its individualized variant (9):

(9) Topic   –   (State)   –   Patient
     baby   [Single baby]   [Containing records   *book*
                             of one's baby]

The other line of the matching process takes another central, prototypical feature of *book* as a reference point, that is to say, [+Contains Drawings/Pictures], which yields reading (10):

(10) Agent   –   (Action)   →   Theme
     baby [Perception by   [Viewing]   *book*
             viewing]

Another matching operation combines [+Dimension] as a fairly general seman-tic component of *book* and one of the central and most specific semantic compon-ents of *baby* [+Small Size], this giving reading (11):

(11)   Quality   –   (State)   –   Patient
      baby [Small size]   *book* [Substance]

After completing the matching process (which may be conceived of as a trial-and-error process, which therefore also covers a number of other possible com-binations) the interpreter faces one or more readings complying with the semantic compatibility principle. However, it should be pointed out, the notion of semantic compatibility cannot be mixed with the notion of predictability. The former is much wider and also encompasses those combinations which are not easily pre-dictable. At this point it is the extralinguistic knowledge and experiences that are involved in the decision-making process aimed at the identification of the most predictable reading(s).

Exocentric compounds are also very interesting in terms of meaning predictabil-ity. Štekauer (2001) proposes to explain their formation by a two-step process in which only the first has word-formation relevance. So for example, on the basis of a conceptual analysis of *redskin*

(12)   The object to be denominated is HUMAN
      The HUMAN is characterized by the red colour of his/her skin

the onomasiological structure will be as follows:

(13)   Stative   –   State   –   Patient
      By applying the MSAP, we obtain:

(14)   Stative   –   State   –   Patient
      redskin   *person*

The auxiliary naming unit obtained is an endocentric compound. The second step consists in elliptical shortening, which is represented by bracketing the base member of the structure. The lexical and grammatical features of the complete naming unit passed over to its clipped version. This is indicated by an arrow:

(15)   redskin person →   redskin   [person]

The peculiarity of this type of compound bears upon the fact that as units of word formation they belong to a different onomasiological type (OT 3) than as units of the meaning-prediction act.

Similarly, *sabretooth* can be represented as follows:

(16)   Stative   –   State   –   Patient
      sabretooth   *tiger*

Due to the fact that this structure is reduced by elliptical shortening, what is encountered by the interpreter is the mere determining constituent of the onomasiological mark, this being clearly insufficient in terms of meaning predictability as there is no safe ground for an interpreter to determine the onomasiological structure of such a naming unit.

Exocentric compounds like *pick-pocket, kill-joy, wagtail, turnstone, catchfly* may be supposed to have a more favourable predictability. In word formation, they belong to OT1. The expression of the Actional constituent of the onomasiological structure (*pick, kill, wag, turn, catch*) makes it possible to relate the determining constituent of the mark (*pocket, joy, tail, stone, fly*) with the morphologically absent, but intuitively (in many cases) predictable base ('person' for the first two compounds and 'animal' for the next two compounds). The existence of OT-internal differences in predictability can also be identified in this group of compounds. A case in point is the last example, *catchfly*, where the Actional constituent represented by the morpheme *catch* indicates the Human or the Animal seme rather than Plant, thus significantly reducing the meaning predictability of *catchfly*.

This brief account suggests that a coiner's selection of an OT within the act of word formation greatly affects the meaning predictability of a novel compound. The OT of a particular naming unit establishes the basic (favourable or unfavourable) circumstances for the meaning-prediction act. There are, however, a number of other factors which co-determine the resulting predictability. The most important are discussed in the following sections.

14.3.4 Onomasiological Structure Rules

Onomasiological Structure Rules (OSR) provide another example of close inter-relation between meaning predictability and word formation. OSRs specify admissible arrangements of semantic categories at the onomasiological level. The meaning-prediction capacity of a language user is conditioned by his knowledge of OSRs that function as constraints on the interpretation of naming units. While one might surmise that this knowledge is an inherent part of a native speaker's competence this is, surprisingly, not quite so. Thus, Gleitman and Gleitman (1970) report that some of their informants were not able to interpret properly compounds like *house-bird glass*. They related their observation to the educational level of language users. Unlike graduate students and PhD's, secretaries with high-school degrees proposed various 'unacceptable' readings which corresponded rather to the compounds *glass house-bird, glass bird-house,* or a paraphrase like *a house-bird made of glass*. Gleitman and Gleitman conclude that there were 'very large and consistent differences among these subjects of differing educational background' (1970: 117) and that '[t]he less educated groups make more errors, and to a significant extent make different errors than the most-educated group' (ibid: 128).

Table 14.1 Violations of Onomasiological Structure Rules

Naming unit	Proposed reading	Appropriate naming unit
flower hat	'a flower in the shape of a hat'	*hat flower*
hill star	'a hill in the shape of a star'	*star hill*
	'a very high hill that "touches" the sky'	*star hill*
	'many stars at one place'	*star hill*
garden whisky	'vegetable meal with a little whisky'	*whisky garden*
	'very good fruit for somebody who likes this fruit as much as whisky'	*whisky garden*
age bag	'a period when bags were/are popular'	*bag age*
dog spade	'a dog for watching spades'	*spade dog*
	'the shape of a dog in the ground which is made with a spade'	*spade dog*
shape cloth	'a figurine for cloth makers'[a]	*cloth shape*
blondesjoker	'a blonde-haired woman who is good for a laugh'	*joke-blonde*
feather-dialer	'a person who decorates dials with feathers'	*dial-featherer*
anthraxist	'a person who fell ill due to anthrax'	*anthraxee*

[a] The inadmissibility of this reading is conditioned by the interpretation of this compound as an endocentric compound. As aptly noted by Rochelle Lieber, it wouldn't be anomalous if it's understood as an exocentric compound along the lines of *pickpocket*.

Similar cases are reported by Ryder (1994). For example, one of her native informants interpreted *quilt-horse* as 'a quilt made of horse-hair'.

My experiments (reported on in Štekauer 2005a) provide ample examples of inadmissible interpretation of possible context-free compounds due to the violation of OSRs. Examples are given in Table 14.1.

The inadequacy of the readings proposed can be judged from the Onomasiological Structure Rules imposing constraints on the arrangement of semantic categories at the onomasiological level. Examples of these rules are given in (17):

(17) a. The onomasiological base is on the right in English compounds.
  b. The Pattern seme is left of the State seme.
  c. The Quality seme is always left of the Patient seme.
  d. The Source feature is left of the Action seme.
  e. The Purpose seme is left-oriented.
  f. If the structure contains the Agent seme the Object seme is left of the Action seme. (Or, Action directed at Object is left-oriented in a structure with the Agent seme.)
  g. If the structure contains the Agent seme the Instrument seme is left of Action.

h. If the structure contains the Instrument seme and the Result seme, then the Result seme is the right-hand neighbour to the Action seme, and the Instrument seme is the left-hand neighbour to the Action seme.
i. If the structure contains both the Material seme and the Object seme, the material seme is a right-hand neighbour of Object.

A set of such rules makes it possible to decide whether a particular interpretation is admissible. For example, rule (17b) prohibits the reading 'a flower (Patient) in the shape of a hat (Pattern)' for *flower hat*. The naming unit corresponding to the proposed reading is *hat flower* because it has the required onomasiological structure (18):

(18)   [Pattern – (State) – Patient]

Rule (17f.) predicts that, in English, the Object of Action is, by default, a left-hand neighbour of the Actional constituent. Therefore, while

(19)   [Object ← Action – Agent]

is admissible for the reading 'a person (Agent) who tells/makes (Action) blonde (Object) jokes', the reading 'a blonde-haired woman who is good for a laugh' is controlled by the onomasiological structure given in (20):

(20)   [Quality – Patient]

and, for this reason, the corresponding naming unit must be *joker-blonde*.

14.3.5 Predictability and Productivity

At first sight it might seem that the predictability of novel, context-free naming units is in direct proportion to the productivity of WF rules. The reality is different. There are at least two crucial reasons preventing productivity from becoming a central predictability-influencing factor.

The first reason concerns the 'creativity within the productivity constraints' principle. This principle suggests that a coiner need not make use of the most productive WF rule if other options are available. Furthermore, while the coiner forms a new naming unit with a *single general* meaning, the number of possible compatibility-based combinations available to the interpreter usually abounds.

The second reason concerns the crucial difference that any treatment of the predictability–productivity relation must take into account. While predictability concerns the *meanings* of naming units, productivity usually pertains to *WF rules*, on the basis of which new naming units are generated. By implication, while productivity is about the *general*, predictability is about the *individual*.

Let us illustrate the point with one of my sample compounds. In the case of *baby book*, the predictable readings 'a book about babies and how to take care of them' and 'a book with photos of one's baby(ies)/album with records of baby's development (first steps, first word, . . .)' fall within one and the same conceptual category of Patients, here represented by the semantic structure of [Stative (= Theme) – (State) – Patient]. The latter, necessarily being a generalization, cannot discern the subtle, but vital, difference between these two distinct readings proposed for *baby book* by my informants.

Similarly, the predictable readings for *flower hat*, 'a hat with flowers on it' and 'a hat made of flowers', belong to a productive WF rule represented by the semantic structure [Stative (= Material) – (State) – Patient]. The predictable readings of *game wheel*, 'a wheel for playing roulette and casino games; a wheel in Wheel of Fortune-type games' and 'a wheel which is a part of a game equipment, a wheel with which a game is played', belong to a productive WF rule represented by the semantic structure of 'Process – Instrument'.

In any case, the role of the relation between productivity and predictability in the meaning-prediction process cannot be excluded. The process of predicting the meaning(s) starts at the phonological level and proceeds upwards through the onomatological level to the onomasiological level, with the 'interventions' of the interpreter's extralinguistic knowledge and experience. The identification of a specific morphological structure at the onomatological level is a precondition for the identification of a possible onomasiological structure, with the latter subsequently showing a language user the path to more specific readings. It may be assumed that an interpreter identifies the possible onomasiological structures on the basis of his/her knowledge of the productive rules of WF. It is here where the connection between WF productivity, on the one hand, and novel-coinage-meaning predictability, on the other, may be sought.

This connection does not mean that more productive WF Types/Morphological Types are automatically more predictable. As illustrated in 14.3.3.1, the existence of more than one productive WF rule increases the competition between the readings and reduces their meaning predictability.

14.3.6 Predictability Rate

Like WF productivity, meaning predictability is not an all-or-nothing notion. Instead it is assumed that it can be quantified, computed, and mutually compared. The calculation of the *Predictability Rate* (PR) is based on the following postulates:

1. The predictability of meanings of naming units correlates with the acceptability of these meanings to interpreters. It may be proposed that *acceptability* is a system-level analogue to Labov's speech-level term 'consistency' 'with which a given sample of speakers does in fact apply the term' (Labov 1973: 353).

2. Since there is no clear-cut boundary between acceptable and unacceptable meanings the predictability of the meanings of naming units is a *cline.*

Then, the Predictability Rate of a particular reading of a novel, context-free naming unit can be calculated as its frequency of occurrence weighted for the scores assigned:

(21) $PR = \frac{r}{R_{max}} \times \frac{p}{P_{max}}$

where r = the number of informants identifying a particular meaning as acceptable

R_{max} = the total number of informants

p = the sum total of the points assigned to a given meaning by all informants (on a scale from 1 to 10, where 10 stands for the highest acceptability of the meaning)

P_{max} = the maximum possible number of points assignable by all informants

For example, in my (2005a) experiments, the reading 'a book for babies (fairy tales, rhymes, pictures; drawings)' of the naming unit *baby book* was proposed by 38 out of 40 informants, i.e. the frequency of occurrence of this reading is 38/40 = 0.95. The scores assigned to this reading are 306 points of the total of 400 assignable points, which is 0.765. The resulting PR of this particular reading is therefore 0.95 × 0.765 = 0.727. It is much higher than the PR of, for example, 'a naive, babyish book', also proposed for this sample naming unit, because it was only proposed by 16 out of 40 informants (16/40 = 0.40), and its P_{max} quotient was merely 0.213, which gives the PR of 0.085.

By implication, this method of calculation of PR makes it possible to evaluate the strength of various readings proposed for a novel, context-free word, and thus determine the degree of their predictability.

14.3.7 Objectified Predictability Rate

While the PR value is sufficient to compare the meaning predictability of readings within one and the same naming unit it does not allow for comparing the predictability of readings of various naming units. The PR considers the predictability of a particular reading of a naming unit in isolation, regardless of the meaning predictability of the other possible readings of the same naming unit. It is assumed that the strength of the individual readings (i.e. their Predictability Rates) affect each other, which is reflected in their respective positions on the meaning-predictability scale. By implication, the individual readings *compete* with one another.

The concept of *Objectified Predictability Rate* (OPR) builds upon the notion of Predictability Rate, which is taken as a point of departure for subsequent calculations reflecting the differences in PRs of a certain number of the most predictable readings of a naming unit. It follows from the *Competition Principle* that OPR is directly proportional to the *Predictability Rate Gap* (PRG) between the most predictable reading and the next lower PRs of the same naming unit (and, by implication, to the Reading 1/Reading 2 and Reading 1/Reading 3 ratios), and indirectly proportional to the number of relatively strong non-top readings – the higher the number of such readings the lower the OPR. Let us illustrate these principles by an example:

Let us suppose that there are two naming units X and Y. Their three most predictable readings are X_1, X_2, and X_3, and Y_1, Y_2, and Y_3, respectively. Let us further suppose that X_1 and Y_1 are the top PR readings of their respective naming units and happen to have identical PRs of, let's say, 0.486. Furthermore, let us suppose that the PR of X_2 is 0.194 and that the PR of Y_2 is 0.362. Finally, let us assume that the third-rank readings' PRs are identical, for example, $X_3 = 0.088$, and also $Y_3 = 0.088$. This situation is given in (22):

(22)   Naming unit X   Naming unit Y

	PR		PR
X_1	0.486	Y_1	0.486
X_2	0.194	Y_2	0.362
X_3	0.088	$Y3$	0.088

Since the competition among predictable readings in the case of the naming unit Y is much tougher than in the case of X, intuitively, the actual (objectified) predictability of X_1 is higher than that of Y_1. This fact is captured by the proposed notion of OPR.

This type of relationship may be advantageously calculated using Luce's (1959) choice rule which makes it possible to weigh (in my case) the strength (PR) of the most predictable reading against the strength of any number of other competing readings (PRs). This rule was also applied by Gagné and Shoben (1997) for the calculation of the strength of the thematic relation which is the best candidate for the interpretation of a particular complex word.

The formula,[17] adapted for the calculation of the OPR, is as follows:

$$(23) \quad OPR = \frac{PR^{top}}{PR^{top} + PR^{top-1} + PR^{top-1}}$$

If formula (23) is now applied to (22), we get $OPR_X = 0.633$ and $OPR_Y = 0.519$. By implication, with other values identical it is the higher $PRG_{X_1-X_2}$ value compared to the $PRG_{Y_1-Y_2}$ value which is responsible for the higher OPR of X1. This result confirms our intuition according to which reading Y_1 faces much 'tougher

---

[17] In this formula, I relate the most predictable reading to rank-2 and rank-3 readings, as my experiments have shown that the PR of rank 4 is in the vast majority of cases insignificant.

competition' on the part of reading Y_2 than X_1 on the part of X_2. Consequently, the predictability of X_1 is much better than that of Y_1 in spite of these two having identical PR values.

From this it follows that a high absolute PR does not guarantee a high OPR: a naming-unit reading of lower PR may be comparably more predictable than a reading of another naming unit of a higher PR, if the former can take advantage of a considerable PRG. This postulate has been confirmed in my research on a number of occasions. For illustration, the top PR reading 'a hat with flowers on it' of a possible compound *flower hat* has the fourth highest PR (0.427) among the sample compounds, but ranked last in terms of its OPR due to tough competition on the part of the other two readings, 'a hat made of flowers' and 'a hat with flower design/pattern/ornaments'.

On the other hand, poor compatibility of the semes of the motivating units need not entail a poor OPR owing to the absence of any competition. For illustration, the top reading of one of my sample compounds *age bag* 'an old bag; a bag that looks old' has a very low PR (0.203), but due to the absence of competing readings (PR of Rank 2 = 0.017, PR of Rank 3 = 0.014), it has the highest OPR in the sample (0.744).

14.3.8 Prototypical features

There is an obvious tendency for the most predictable readings of compounds to be motivated by the combination of *prototypical features* of the motivating objects. *Figurativeness*, i.e. *semantic shift* (metaphor and metonymy), appears to be a serious obstacle to good meaning predictability.[18] This assumption only applies to cases in which one or both of the motivating constituents acquire figurativeness, as it were, within the process of conceptual combination. My (2005a) data provide numerous examples, including 'a book with a cover of a baby skin color', 'a book that smells like a baby', and 'one's favorite book' for *baby book*; 'a clumsy person with poor dancing skills' and 'an aggressive person' for *ball hammer*; 'a star that sleeps on a hill', 'Noah', and 'a famous actor who lives in Beverly Hills' for *hill star*; 'one's life' for *game wheel*; 'somebody very eccentric in dressing' and 'somebody who tries to be perfect in dressing' for *shape-cloth*; 'a group of people of the same age' for *age bag*; 'a spade by which a dog was/is killed' for *dog spade*; 'someone who talks softly on the phone' for *feather-dialer*, etc.

All these and other similar metaphorical interpretations remained isolated proposals restricted to a single informant. By implication, their PR is very low.

---

[18] For the same view see also Renouf and Bauer (2000: 254–5) who mention both metaphor and polysemy as major factors impeding a context-free interpretation of novel complex words.

The meaning predictability of new compounds based on a figurative meaning is a part of a broader problem bearing on polysemantic and homonymous lexemes that become constituents of new naming units because the one-to-many relation between form and meanings hampers the meaning-prediction process. Any necessity to select from optional meanings can be considered as a predictability-reducing factor as it potentially leads to a higher number of interpretations. However, its strength and effects are not directly proportional to the number of potential interpretations. They are influenced by the degree of institutionalization of the individual meanings, their respective relation to the other motivating constituent(s) of a coinage, and the effects of the other predictability-boosting and -reducing factors.

On the other hand, a well-established, i.e. *institutionalized figurative meaning* of a motivating constituent does not have a negative impact on meaning predictability. A case in point is the figurative, personified meaning of *star* in *hill star*. The most predictable reading in my experiment is one with the figurative meaning of the base: 'a person who is brilliant at hill climbing/running/cycling'.

Like figurative meanings, too general or too specific and idiosyncratic features tend to be a serious obstacle to meaning predictability. The research provided a number of readings of this kind, which, for this reason, were restricted to a single or two occurrences: 'a spade by which a dog was killed' for *dog spade* (any [Solid] SUBSTANCE can be used for this purpose); 'a hammer used for doing something to balls' for *ball hammer*; 'a person who constantly cracks stupid jokes' for *blondesjoker* (this can be any 'joker'); 'a book in the shape of a baby' for *baby book*; 'a hammer whose one part is spherical' for *ball hammer*; 'a hat with the odor of flowers' for *flower hat*; 'a special seat filled up with apple-juice' for *apple-juice seat*.

It may be concluded therefore that a conceptual combination based on prototypical features is a predictability-boosting factor but as with any other predictability-affecting factor, it is not a sufficient precondition for a high meaning predictability of novel, context-free compounds.

14.3.9 Extralinguistic knowledge and experiences

My research has confirmed the view that lexical meaning itself is not sufficient for interpreting/predicting the meaning(s) of novel compounds.[19] There is abundant evidence that mere meaning-identification, i.e. the comprehension of objects representing the individual compound constituents, is insufficient for the identification of acceptable/predictable readings. Thus, for example, the semantic structures of *baby* and *book* may indicate possible combinabilities: for instance, the semes

---

[19] Cf. e.g. van Lint (1982), Levi (1983), Cohen and Murphy (1984), Hampton (1987, 1988), Murphy (1988, 1990), and Wisniewski (1996).

[+Listening Capacity] [+Perception by Watching] of *baby* can be activated in combination with any of the semes [For Reading/Listening/ Perception by Watching], [Having Some Content], and/or [±With Photos/ Pictures] of *book*, but this combinability cannot identify the subtle semantic distinctions as represented by the three most predictable readings for this compound, 'a book about babies – how to take care of them', 'a book for babies', and 'a book with records of one's baby'. These readings, resulting from a conceptual analysis and evaluation of the possible relations between the objects conceptually processed and related within the new compound, reflect a language user's knowledge of the class of 'babies' and the class of 'books' and, crucially, also their experiences. Perfect knowledge of the prototypical features of 'book' and 'baby' can hardly be sufficient for proposing a reading referring, for instance, to records about one's baby. What is also needed is the knowledge of/experience with keeping records of baby development.

Similarly, the reading 'a spade used for scooping-up a dog's excrement' for *dog spade* cannot be inferred from the lexical meanings themselves. One must have the knowledge of/experience with spades from which one can infer that spades – apart from their basic function – can be and actually are sometimes used instead of shovels. In addition, this reading also requires the knowledge/experience concerning the habit (conditioned by relevant cultural habits/by-laws) of removing a dog's excrement.

The meaning subtleties of the individual predictable readings of *flower hat*, notably, 'a hat with flowers on it', 'a hat made from flowers', and 'a hat with flower patterns' also require a considerable amount of knowledge/experience. One should know that there are some traditions of decorating hats with flowers, and that rustic children have long enjoyed weaving flowers into a decorative cover of the head which, by being worn on the head, might be labelled as a 'hat'.

The reading of *apple-juice seat* as a place in a restaurant, bar, or café reserved for drinking apple-juice needs a huge amount of additional information: knowledge of the function and equipment of restaurants and similar establishments, knowledge of the existence of temperance bars for young people, and possibly experience with bars, a part of which is reserved for smokers and the other part for non-smokers, which may suggest that certain seats in bars may also be reserved for '(apple)-juice drinkers'.

Each of these and all the other predictable readings in my research illustrate *the significance of a language user's extralinguistic knowledge and experiences* for the meaning-prediction process.

In fact, every predictable meaning gives support to the assumption that for a language user to be able to predict the meaning of a naming unit he or she must:

(a) know the lexical meanings of the motivating constituents;
(b) be able to conceptually analyse the objects of extralinguistic reality which are covered by these lexical meanings; and
(c) identify their possible relations based on his/her knowledge and/or experiences.

14.3.10 Structural transparency

Another important condition of good predictability is structural transparency. An ambiguous morphological structure which admits more than one parsing makes the prediction process more demanding. Let us illustrate this case with *clamprod*, an example given by Libben, Derwing, and Almeida (1999: 385). This compound can be parsed into either *clamp+rod* or *clam+prod*, and even if the parsing process, which is vital to the subsequent interpretation, is 'highly correlated with semantic plausibility' (ibid.), the Predictability Rate may be expected to be reduced.

14.3.11 Single (rarely two) dominant reading(s)

My (2005a) experiments bear out the dominant position of a single (rarely two) strong reading(s) for almost all novel context-free compounds.[20] While rank-3 readings are in general of little significance in terms of meaning predictability, rank-4 readings are totally insignificant (the average PR value of my sample compounds falling within OT 3 was as low as 0.031). This brings us to one of the central conclusions of the presented meaning-predictability theory:

While there are many potential readings of novel, context-free naming units, it is usually only one or two that are significant in terms of meaning predictability.

This casts doubt on the widely encountered sceptical picture of the meaning interpretation of N+N compounds. The picture emerging from my research is much more optimistic.

14.4 PREDICTABILITY-BOOSTING FACTORS

Instead of conclusions, the following list identifies the factors which contribute to the meaning predictability of novel context-free compounds. While they indicate that meaning predictability results from the interplay of a large number of variables whose impact factor differs from case to case, it is important to stress that none of them is sufficient individually; rather, a good meaning predictability results from their synergic effect.

(1) Onomasiological Type 1 or 2
(2) Unambiguous onomasiological base and onomasiological mark

---

[20] This observation is also true of conversion. Cf. Štekauer, Valera, and Diaz (2007).

(3) Productive WF Rule underlying the compound

(4) Semantically compatible motivating words

(5) Motivation by a combination of prototypical semes reflecting the proto-typical features of the motivating objects

(6) Objective justification of a novel naming unit, i.e. the existence in extra-linguistic reality of a corresponding 'object'

(7) Reference to permanent, stable, and constant relations

(8) Productive Morphological Type underlying the naming unit

(9) Unambiguous interpretation of the underlying onomasiological and ono-matological structures – the principle of structural transparency

(10) Absence of competition, i.e. absence of other strong 'readings', implying a single strong predictable reading, a high PR Gap, and a high R1/R2 (R1/R3) ratio

(11) The possibility of interpreting the naming unit through an analogy-based template

(12) Knowledge of the meaning(s) of the motivating word(s), knowledge of the WF Rules, knowledge of the Onomasiological Structure Rules, and any other pertinent linguistic competence

(13) Well-established morphemes and affixes

(14) Relevant world knowledge of/experience with the object represented by a naming unit in question

C H A P T E R   1 5

CHILDREN'S ACQUISITION OF COMPOUND CONSTRUCTIONS

RUTH BERMAN

CHILDREN's comprehension and production of (mainly noun + noun) compound constructions have been the subject of substantial research over the past twenty years or so.[1] Studies relate to varied issues, including: pluralization in compounding as evidence for or against level-ordering constraints (Gordon 1985; Lardiere 1995a, b; Clahsen et al. 1996; Nicoladis 2005); prosodic factors (Fikkert 2001; Vogel and Raimy 2002); the contrast between root and derived or synthetic compounds – with deverbal heads in English (Clark, Hecht, and Mulford 1986; Murphy and Nicoladis 2006) and with derived nominal heads in Hebrew (Ravid and Avidor 1998); innovative compounding as evidence for children's lexical creativity (Berman and Sagi 1981; Clark 1981; Clark 1988; Becker 1994; Mellenius 1997); compounds in L2 and bilingual acquisition (Bongartz 2002; Nicoladis 2002

I am grateful to Wolfgang Dressler, Dorit Ravid, and Batia Seroussi for helpful feedback on an earlier draft and to the editors of the Handbook for their perceptive and valuable comments. Inadequacies are mine alone.

[1] That the topic is of relatively recent interest in child language research is suggested by the comprehensive survey in Mellenius (1997: Chapter 3). The term 'compound(ing)' does not appear in the index to Slobin (1985) on acquisition of some dozen languages.

Agothopoulou 2003; Nicoladis and Yin 2002; Nicoladis 2003) and in impaired language development (Dalalakis and Gopnik 1995; Clahsen and Almazan 2001).

In the present context, compounds are analysed as multifunctional constructions that serve different purposes, including lexical labelling of previously unnamed entities and semantic expression of relations between two or more nouns such as possession, hyponymy, or class inclusion. Compound constructions are viewed here as lying on a continuum. At one end are 'established' terms – ranging from frozen, typically idiomatic, to semantically transparent multilexemic items that form part of the familiar word-stock of adult speakers of the target language.[2] These may be extended by compounding as a means of new-word formation, whether for eventually conventionalized coinages or for idiosyncratic or occasional 'contextuals' (Downing 1977; Clark and Clark 1979). At the other end of the scale lie structurally productive compounds that are termed here 'open-ended', since (1) they can be reworded periphrastically and so alternate with semantically corresponding phrasal expressions and (2) their modifying element can be extended by syntactic operations like conjoining with other nouns in a way disallowed in established compounds (Berman and Ravid 1986; Borer 1988).[3] Compare, for example, idiomatic *beeline*, familiar *beehive, beekeeper, bee sting* with novel expressions like *bee wings*, alternating with *wings of a bee*, and novel *bee garden* 'a garden for / full of bees'.

15.1 THE MULTI-FACETED TASK OF ACQUIRING COMPOUND CONSTRUCTIONS

While compounding is 'a common way of introducing new words into the lexicon' (Gagné and Spalding 2006a: 9), it can also be seen as 'the part of morphology which is closest to syntax' (Dressler 2005: 29). As a result, children need to integrate

[2] The term 'lexicalized' is avoided, since lexicalization is essentially a matter of degree, and speaker judgements differ in how they rank compound expressions for familiarity (Berman and Ravid 1986). Besides, children's lexicon of established compounds will differ considerably from that of adults.
[3] Unfortunately, use of the term 'open-ended' conflicts somewhat with the terms 'familiar open-compounds' and 'novel modifier-noun phrases' used by Gagné, Spalding, and Gorrie (2005). However, it is appropriate to the case of Hebrew, as shown by comparing the following (where a caret ^ indicates a bound Genitive relation):

(i) Frozen, idiomatic, almost monolexemic: *orex^din* 'arrange(r) + GEN law' = 'lawyer'
(ii) Familiar, semantically transparent, potentially open-ended: *orex^iton* ('arrange(r) + newspaper') 'newspaper editor'
(iii) Non-established, fully open-ended: *orex^mesibot* (arrange(r) + parties) 'party giver'

The second, modifying element in (ii) – and the modifier in (iii) even more so – can be freely extended syntactically, from singular to plural or vice versa, by coordination with another modifier, or

knowledge at different levels of linguistic structure in order to comprehend and construct compounds. Phonologically, in English, for example, they need to recognize the peculiar prosodic contour associated with compound constructions, with main stress typically assigned to the initial, modifying element, and weaker stress on the head element that follows it (Alegre and Gordon 1996; Vogel and Raimy 2002); in Dutch, children might be aided in recognizing compound constructions, since these take stress on the main stressed syllable of the first prosodic word (Fikkert 2001); in Swedish, children produce the compound-particular fall-and-rise intonation contour with a relatively high pitch from as early as 2 years of age (Mellenius 1997); while in Hebrew, prosody appears to play little if any role in compound acquisition.[4]

Morphologically, in Germanic languages, children may need to know which if any 'linking element' occurs between the constituents of noun + noun compounds, as in Dutch *boek-en-legger* 'bookmark' vs. *boekwinkel* 'book store', or a phonological alternation as in German *händ-e-druck* 'handshake' (Neijt, Krebbers, and Fikkert 2002; Krott et al. 2007), as well as so-called 'liaison' elements in Swedish (Mellenius 1997). By contrast, English-acquiring children must observe the constraint on pluralization of the initial modifier (Gordon 1985; Nicoladis 2005).[5] In a case-marked language like Greek, they must learn the particular form of the root noun that occurs in compounds (Dalalakis and Gopnik 1995; Agathopoulou 2003). Relatedly, in Hebrew, children need to master morphophonological alternations on the bound stem form of the initial head noun, including suffixation and stem-internal changes (Berman 1988; Ravid and Zilberbuch 2003a).[6] Compare, for example, *ken* ~ *kinim* 'nest' ~ 'nests', *kiney^dvorim* 'nests + GEN bees' 'bee-hives'.[7]

---

paraphrased with the genitive marker *šel* 'of', thus: *orex^itonim* 'editor + GEN (of) *orex^itonim ve yarxonim;* 'editor of newspapers and magazines'; *orex šel ha-iton* 'editor of the newspaper'. These operations are prohibited in the case of fully established idiomatic compounds.

[4] I know of no detailed studies of Hebrew compound prosody. Bat-El (1993: 207) notes that 'the main stress of the rightmost [modifier] element is the main stress of the compound and secondary stress falls on the main stress of the first [head] element'.

[5] This language-specific constraint on pluralization of the initial (in English, modifying) element may be violated in some established compounds and in compounds preceded by an adjective, so that children also need to learn in what instances the constraint fails to apply (Alegre and Gordon 1996). Hebrew manifests a converse constraint to English: both the initial head and the second, modifying noun are generally pluralizable, but (indefinite) singular count nouns cannot occur as compound modifiers. Compare the ill-formed compound with a singular modifier *malkódet^axbar* 'trap + GEN mouse' '(a) mouse-trap', with well-formed compounds with a plural or a non-count modifying noun: *malkódet* ~ *malkodot^axbarim* 'trap ~ traps mice' = 'mice trap(s)', *malkódet^mávet* 'trap + GEN death' = 'death-trap', *malkódet^mištara* 'trap + GEN police' = 'police trap' respectively. This helps avoid ambiguity of definiteness, since Hebrew has no indefinite article. Thus, singular count noun modifiers can occur if the compound is definite, cf. *malkodet^ha-axbar* 'trap + Gen the-mouse' = 'the trap of the mouse'.

[6] I use the term 'stem' in preference to 'root', given the special connotation of the term 'root' in a Semitic language like Hebrew (Shimron 2003).

[7] The following conventions are adopted for Hebrew: (1) a caret ^ separates the initial, bound head noun from the following modifier noun; (2) in glossing compounds, the head noun is indicated

Other structural knowledge that children need to master in language-particular ways includes: which lexical categories can enter into compound constructions, what the order of the elements is, and how definiteness is marked. In Germanic languages, compounds are normally right-headed, with the modifier preceding the head noun. This incurs changes in basic VO order in English deverbal compounds, for example, *a person who pulls wagons~ wagon-puller* (Clark et al. 1986; Nicoladis 2003). They thus differ from the left-headed compound order of French (or Hebrew) and from periphrastic genitives in English (cf. *table legs~ legs of (a) table*). In Germanic and Romance languages, determiners precede the modifier–head compound construction, as in noun phrases in general. In contrast, Hebrew compounds observe the canonic left-headed direction of all nominal constructions in the language, but differ from other such constructions in definiteness marking, since the definite article *ha-* 'the' is attached internally to the modifier noun in compounds (cf. *ragley^ha-šulxan* 'table + GEN the-legs' = 'the table legs' ~ *ha-raglayim šel (ha)-šulxan* 'the legs of (the) table'). Definiteness marking in compounds thus presents Hebrew-acquiring children with difficulties through to school age and even beyond (Berman 1985; Zur 2004).

Semantically, children need to understand the relation of modification as providing information about the head and the nature of compounding as a means of semantic subcategorization (e.g. *cheese cake, chocolate cake,* and doubly compounded *birthday cake, ice-cream cake*). And lexically, they need to learn which combinations are conventionally established, frozen, or idiomatic compounds and what they mean in their language. For example, the same referent is labelled in English by the lexicalized compound *ashtray* but in Hebrew by a single, morphologically derived noun *ma'afera* (from *éfer* 'ash'); conversely, the object labelled by the monolexemic noun 'slippers' in English is referred to in Hebrew by the (well-established) compound noun construction *na'aley^báyit* 'shoes + GEN house'. As a third example of such arbitrary lexicalization processes, both languages refer to shoes with high heels by compound constructions, but English 'high-heeled shoes' involves a complex derived adjective as against the Hebrew bound noun + noun compound *na'aley^akev* 'shoes + GEN heel'.[8]

---

as + GEN, for 'genitive (case)'; and (3) Hebrew words with non-final stress are marked by an acute accent on the penultimate or antepenultimate syllable.

[8] Complex interweaving of different facets of linguistic knowledge is illustrated by children's coinages in Hebrew:
(1) Merav, aged 5;8, combines the idiomatic compound *kóva^yam* 'hat^sea' = 'bathing cap' with a contrasting novel compound, when she says *lo kóva^yam aval kóva^yabaša* 'not hat + GEN sea but hat + GEN dry-land', to mean she doesn't want to wear a bathing cap but a regular (sun) hat.
(2) Sivan, aged 7;3, says: *baláta šaked^marak* 'you + MASC-swallowed almond + GEN soup [=a soup almond]' (an innovative back-formation from conventional *škedey^marak* 'almonds + GEN soup' i.e. croutons – see note 5), to which her brother Assaf, aged 6;1, responds: *lo, ze haya bóten^marak, halevay še -yamtsíu marmeládat^marak* 'No, it was (a) peanut + GEN soup, I wish they'd invent marmalade + GEN soup'.

Detailed information on the occurrence of compounds in first-language acquisition is available mainly for English and Hebrew, two languages which differ markedly in how compounds are constructed, and where compounding is a structurally productive option, although more so in English.[9] This chapter focuses on noun + noun compounds, irrespective of whether so-called 'root' or 'synthetic' compounds. As noted, unlike English or Swedish, only noun + noun compounds are productive constructions in Hebrew (Clark and Clark 1979; Berman 1993a; Mellenius, 1997). Besides, Hebrew makes no structural distinction between so-called root and synthetic compounds, since the same word order and the same morphological alternations apply to compounds whether the head is a 'basic' or non-derived noun or a morphologically derived noun (e.g. *simla* 'dress' ~ *simlat^kala* 'dress + GEN bride' = 'bride's / bridal dress'; *simxa* 'happiness' ~ *simxat^kala* 'happiness + GEN (a) bride' = '(a) bride's happiness, happiness of a bride'; while clausal *ha-kala lovéšet simla* 'the-bride wears (a) dress' yields the derived action + noun compound *levišat^simla* 'wearing + GEN dress' = 'the wearing of a dress' – Ravid and Avidor 1998).

Against this background, the chapter presents cross-linguistic findings from experimental studies of how children construe compound constructions and from surveys of established and innovative compounds in children's naturalistic speech output (section 15.2). The developmental patterns that emerge from these varied sources are then traced from early preschool age to middle childhood and beyond (section 15.3). In conclusion, cross-linguistic differences in acquisition of compounding are attributed to the interplay of target-language typology and usage-based factors of frequency and register variation, with suggestions for further research in this domain (section 15.4).

15.2 CROSS-LINGUISTIC COMPARISONS: CHILDREN'S USE OF INNOVATIVE AND ESTABLISHED COMPOUNDS

In a series of structured elicitations, children aged three years to school-age were asked to derive new means for labelling agents and instruments that have no

---

[9] Hebrew compounding is mainly binominal. Compound verbs like English *whitewash, brainstorm* are structurally prohibited (Berman 2003), and it lacks particles to allow compound expressions like English *runaway, teach-in*. Adjective + noun compounds like *arukat^tvax* 'long + GEN.FEM range', *xamumey^móax* 'heated + GEN.PL brain' = 'hot-headed' are lexically restricted and typically high-register in usage, so largely irrelevant to child language input and output.

established lexical entry (English – Clark and Hecht 1982; Clark et al. 1986; Hebrew–Clark and Berman 1984; Icelandic – Mulford 1983). For example, to elicit an agent noun, the experimenter might say something like 'I have a picture here of a boy who likes to pull wagons. What would you call a boy who pulls wagons all the time, or someone whose job is to pull wagons?', and to elicit an instrument noun, children might be asked to give a name for a machine that is used 'to throw buttons', or a tool that we use in order 'to throw buttons'. In both English and Hebrew, less so in Icelandic, children sometimes selected compound forms to construct novel labels, and these became increasingly more complex and better formed with age. For example, English-speaking 3 year olds might say 'wagon-boy' or 'pull-wagon', 'puller-wagon', whereas 5 year olds would construct a more acceptable complex form like 'wagon-puller'. Hebrew-speaking children would initially use only the unmarked present-tense (also participial) form of the verb as a head noun, for example, for an instrument that is used *limšox agalot* 'to-pull wagons', 5 year olds might say *mošex^agalot* 'pull(s) ~ puller + Gen wagons', whereas older children would coin a derived noun head, for example, *mašxan^agalot* 'puller + GEN wagons' or simply *aglan* 'wagoner' (see, further, section 15.3 below).

Children acquiring English and Hebrew differed markedly in the extent to which they relied on compounding for coining labels for people and objects that habitually perform activities (Verb) on entities (Direct Object). Even the youngest English-speaking children used simple compound forms quite widely, and these continued to be a favoured option for the older children and the adults. In Hebrew, by contrast, children started to use compounds only around age 5, with a slight peak at age 7, while children and adults alike preferred monolexemic affixation over compounding for coining new terms – a finding indicative of more general typological preferences for new-word formation in the two languages. Moreover, compounding was more prevalent in Hebrew for instruments, and in English for agents – reflecting differences in the established lexicon, since Hebrew is largely lacking in terms like *policeman*, *fireman*, *doorman* (cf. forms produced by English-speaking 2- and 3-year-olds like 'wagon girl', 'wash man'), but has numerous established compounds for instruments like *mxonat^ktiva* 'writing machine' = 'typewriter', *tanur^bišul* 'cooking oven' (Ravid and Avidor 1998; Seroussi 2004). In Icelandic, also a Germanic language, Mulford's (1983) study revealed little reliance on compound constructions in coining novel terms for agents and instruments, with children preferring the suffix *-ari* increasingly from age 3 on, especially for agents. Moreover, as can be expected on typological grounds for a language of Romance origin, an unpublished study of agent and instrument nouns constructed by French-speaking children revealed that 5 and 6 year olds produced compound forms in these domains as little as around 5 per cent of the time (cited by Clark 1988).

Rather different issues motivate experimental studies in different Germanic languages that investigate children's observation of constraints on pluralization in English (Gordon 1985; Alegre and Gordon 1996) and of various linking elements on the initial, modifying element of compounds in Dutch (Neijt et al. 2002) and Swedish (Mellenius 1997). Gordon had children aged 3 to 5 years respond to a question like 'What do you call someone who eats _____?', with the missing modifier noun alternating between singular and plural items. He found that the overwhelming majority of children correctly avoided forms like *rats-eater, although once they knew the appropriate plural form of irregular nouns, they might use it in the same context, to produce, for example *mice-eater rather than grammatical mouse-eater. In an extension of this study, Alegre and Gordon (1996) tested children's ability to distinguish between phrasal and non-phrasal compounds. They found that children used their knowledge of the constraint on plural modifiers in compounds to impose a phrasal interpretation on the string red rats eater when it referred to an eater of red rats, as against a compound interpretation on the superficially similar string when it referred to a red eater of rats, that is, a rat eater that is red.

Swedish is another Germanic language for which detailed information is available on acquisition of compounding (Mellenius 1997). In one experiment, ten children aged 3;5 to 6;8 were asked to describe picture cards depicting two halves from a memory game 'patched together in two-by-two random combinations' (1997: 82).[10] In keeping with findings for English (Clark, Gelman, and Lane 1985), most of the children provided more compound constructions than other types of labels, and overall more than two-thirds of their responses took the form of compounds.[11] In production of linking elements, children were able to handle 'liaison forms' requiring deletion of -a – the most common final vowel in Swedish nouns, typically though not always deleted when the noun functions as a modifier – earlier than addition of -s (e.g. nöjes + resa 'pleasure trip' versus nöje 'pleasure'). Thus, in different Germanic languages, acquisition of noun plural inflections interacts with language-specific lexical knowledge of the particular 'linking' forms required or prohibited in constructing the initial modifying element of compound constructions.

Data from children's use of compound constructions in interactive conversations and monologic narratives make it possible to track occurrence of both established compounds – as evidence for compounding as a means for expressing relations between nouns – and innovative coinages, as evidence of productive knowledge of compounding. The relative productivity of compounding in child language is considered here by these two complementary criteria: how widely

[10] The term 'memory game' refers here to a game where participants have to find and match two halves of the same picture so that the combination yields a complete picture, say the top and bottom half of a doll, or the back and front of a boat. In the present case, the experimenter deliberately combined non-matching pairs, such as part doll and part boat, to elicit novel compounds.

[11] The authors note that this might be due to the elicitation materials no less than to a general preference for compounds over what they term 'descriptive phrases' in Swedish.

children use established compounds in their speech output, and how far they rely on compounding versus affixation for new-word formation.

With respect to 'established' or conventional noun compounds, Clark (1993: 151–9) concludes from her summary of databases in several languages that children acquiring Germanic languages 'make use of compounding very early in combining nouns' and that they rely extensively on compounding for coining novel nouns, more markedly in Dutch and German than in Icelandic or Swedish. Clark's findings are supported by Fikkert's (2001) study of twelve Dutch-acquiring children, nearly all of whom used several different established compound nouns as young as age 2 years or less, and by Mellenius's (1997) findings for Swedish-speaking children from around 3 years.

A very different picture emerges for Hebrew, which shows little reliance on established compounds in early child speech. In cross-sectional samples of adult–child conversations, Hebrew-speaking children aged 2 years or less produce almost no compounds; from age 3 they use on average fewer than five compounds (tokens) per 100 noun terms; and while compound occurrences rise somewhat among the 4- to 6-year-olds, they are used only sparsely by their adult interlocutors as well (Berman 1987). Longitudinal samples of four children aged 1;6 to 3 years in interaction with an adult caretaker (from the Berman corpus of CHILDES) show a similar pattern: Noun compounds accounted for around only 0.2 per cent of all the words used by the children (217 out of 103,226 tokens) and an almost equally negligible proportion of the word stock in the adult input (412 out of 245,384 tokens = 0.39%).[12]

The paucity of compound constructions in conversational Hebrew compared with English child language is supported by figures for conventionally established compounds in children's 'frog story' picture-book narratives (Berman and Slobin 1994).[13] For example, nine of the twelve English-speaking 4-year-olds used compounds at least once, often two or three different terms, e.g. *beehive, mud hole, baby frog, night-time, danger sign.* In contrast, only two Hebrew-speaking children of the twelve in this age-group used such constructions (e.g. *mišpáxat^cfarde'im* 'family + GEN frogs' = 'a family of frogs'), although they often use noun + noun phrases with the genitive particle *šel* 'of', in expressions like *ken šel dvorim* '(a) nest of bees', *ha-cincénet šel ha-cfardéa* 'the jar of the frog', *ha-géza šel ha-ec* 'the trunk of the tree'. Schoolchildren and adults made rather wider use of bound, so-called 'construct-case' compounds (Gesenius 1910; Borer 1988) in their narrations – e.g. *nexil^dvorim* 'swarm + GEN bees', *géza^ha-ec* 'trunk + GEN the tree', *karney^ha-áyil* 'horns + GEN the-deer' – also quite commonly in alternation with periphrastic

---

[12] I am indebted to Bracha Nir-Sagiv for calculating occurrences across the Hebrew databases of naturalistic speech samples and monologic texts.

[13] Children aged 3 to 9 years old, native speakers of five different languages, were asked to tell a story based on a picture-book without words that depicts the adventures of a little boy and his dog in search of a pet frog that had escaped from the jar where he was kept.

phrases with *šel* 'of '. These cross-linguistic contrasts are underlined by data from French-speaking children's narratives based on the same pictured storybook (Kern, 1996). Noun + noun compounds were almost never used by even the oldest French-speaking children (10- to 11-year-olds), with the marginal exception of (possibly appositive) terms such as *la famille grenouille, mama et papa grenouille*. This can be explained by the general preference in Romance for phrasal, prepositionally marked noun + noun constructions (e.g. *un nid d'abeilles*).[14]

Consider, next, cross-linguistic differences in use of compounding as a means for new-word formation. For English, Clark's extensive diary data revealed that her son Damon 'favoured compounding [over affixation, RAB] in innovative nominals. Before age 2;0, compounding accounted for all of his innovative nouns, and from 2;0 to 4;11, it accounted for over 70% of them' (1993: 146). J. Becker's (1994) case study of the conversational interactions of an English-speaking boy aged 2;4 to 5;0 years also shows compounding to be a favoured means of lexical innovation. Data from spontaneous innovations of a large number (n=274) of other English-speaking children 'showed almost identical patterns...the younger ones – under age four – relied on compounds 80 percent of the time, on zero-derived forms 7 percent of the time, and on suffixes just 13 percent of the time. Older children relied on compounds somewhat less often (63%) and on suffixes rather more (26%) than younger children' (Clark 1993: 148).

Swedish is like English in allowing a range of compound constructions, 'from N-N compounds as most productive, to V-V and Num-V as least productive' (Mellenius 1997: 25). Mellenius concludes from observation of two of her children that compounding is a favoured means of new-word formation in Swedish and that, in fact, children around age 3 to 6 years 'combine words into compounds in an unrestricted manner' (ibid.: 76), particularly when there is substantial contextual support for this process (see, further, section 15.3.2 below).[15]

In line with their infrequent use of established compounds, Hebrew-acquiring children rely relatively little on noun⌢noun compounding for new-word formation, even though the process is structurally quite unconstrained in Hebrew. Compound nouns accounted for less than 5 per cent of nearly one thousand innovative and unconventional lexical usages recorded in the naturalistic speech output of several dozen Hebrew-speaking children aged 2 to 8 years (Berman 2000). In an almost mirror image of the Germanic data, the vast bulk of children's lexical innovations are through affixation – primarily by means of set morphological patterns assigned

---

[14] These findings for noun + noun combining in children acquiring different languages are supported by data on bilingual and second-language acquisition that show the effect of frequency in learners' use of such constructions, for example, Nicoladis and Yin's (2002) study of four Mandarin Chinese–English bilingual children and Bongartz's (2002) comparison of Czech- compared with Chinese-speaking adult learners of English.

[15] Instances of compounding were clearly identifiable since they early on adhere to the peculiar stress pattern of Swedish compounds.

to a consonantal root but also linearly, by means of external suffixes – rather than by combining nouns to form novel lexical items (Ravid 1990; Berman 2000; Ravid 2006).

Clark et al. (1986) explain English-speaking children's preference for compounding over affixation as deriving from more general developmental principles, articulated in detail in Clark (1993). These include: (1) formal simplicity, such that children prefer to string words together rather than incorporate parts of words by affixation; (2) semantic transparency, revealing a one-to-one match between form and meaning, such that each word in a compound stands for a specific element; and (3) usage productivity (in the sense of how favoured a given device is in the ambient language, rather than in terms of structural constraints), such that the devices preferred by adult speakers for new-word formation in a given language will be those favoured by children as well. To this I would add the role of typological factors as interacting with frequency in the ambient language to account for these preferences – factors that, with age, come to outweigh the principles of structural simplicity and transparency (see section 15.4).

15.3 DEVELOPMENTAL PATTERNS IN COMPOUND ACQUISITION

This section reviews age-related developmental patterns that have been observed for different facets of compounding acquisition: comprehension (section 15.3.1), semantics (15.3.2), and morphosyntactic structure (15.3.3), supplemented by analysis of changes across time in the nature and function of compound constructions in Hebrew (15.3.4). It turns out that, while compound forms typically emerge as early as age 2 years or even before, the path to mastery may continue into and even beyond middle childhood (Berman 1987; Vogel and Rainy 2002; Ravid and Zilberbuch 2003a). Moreover, progress in command of the formal features of compounding is accompanied by age-related expansion and change in the function of such constructions in different target languages.

15.3.1 Comprehension

Children appear to understand compound constructions early on in different languages, typically before they are able to produce well-formed compounds. Clark and Barron's (1988) study of English-speaking children's judgements compared with their corrections of ungrammatical compounds is attributed to the fact that, in general, 'children understand linguistic forms before they can produce them correctly themselves', and that comprehension provides children with representations against which to judge the forms they hear. In a Hebrew-based study, children were tested for both comprehension and production of matching sets of novel compounds, including initial head nouns with the same form as the free noun in isolation and morphologically bound head nouns (Bilev 1985; Clark and Berman 1987). Three-year-olds identified the head noun appropriately in half the cases where the head noun was the same as its free form or had a feminine -*t* suffix (e.g. *karit* 'pillow' ~ *karit^tsémer* 'pillow + GEN wool' = 'wool pillow'; *buba* 'doll' ~ *bubat^tsémer* 'doll + GEN wool'). In contrast, the number of novel compound responses that the same children *produced* overall reached around 50 per cent only later, at age 4 to 5 years, taking until school-age to reach ceiling (Berman 1987).

Similar designs in English (Clark et al. 1985), Hebrew (Berman and Clark 1989), and Swedish (Mellenius 1997: Chapter 6) tested children aged 2 to 6 years for comprehension of the modifier–head relationship in novel 'root compounds' (e.g. *apple knife, boat ladder, mouse hat*), where both the head and modifier noun take the base form of the free noun. In both English and Swedish, children succeeded on this task around half the time by age 2;4, and reached nearly ceiling (over 80 per cent) by age 3;4. These parallel findings suggest that it takes children until around 3 years of age to identify the head as compared with the modifier, in two languages where the modifier precedes the head and is identifiable by a unique stress pattern, but without any surface morphological cue to specify which noun is head and which modifier. In contrast, in the parallel Hebrew study, even 2 year olds identified the head–modifier relation correctly nearly 80 per cent of the time. This precocious success on the task could be attributed to surface order and the idea that 'first is most important', since the head noun came before the modifying noun in the forms they heard. Besides, compounds are like *all* nominal constructions in Hebrew, with an initial head noun preceding its modifying elements (another noun in compounds, an adjective or adjective phrase, a prepositional phrase, or relative clause). That is, Hebrew-acquiring children are early on cued to the canonic right-branching nature of nominal constructions in their language, where the first element represents the entity being referred to and the elements that follow provide more information about that entity.

Children's construal of compound nouns might also be affected by the lexically determined factor of 'family size', defined by Krott and Nicoladis as 'the number of compounds sharing the modifier with the target compound' (2005: 140). This was suggested by the lexical-decision study of de Jong et al. (2002), cited as showing that participants recognized English compounds written as two words faster depending on the family size of the modifying noun. Krott and Nicoladis (2005) had children aged 3;7 to 5;9 explain 'why we say…' with the blanks filled in by established noun compounds in English, differing in the family size of either head or modifier or both. They found children more likely to mention modifiers of compounds with large rather than small family sizes, but this effect was less clear in the case of head nouns. Their conclusion that family size does not play a significant role in how preschoolers construe compounds in English is supported by the finding of Bilev's (1985) study on Hebrew, which controlled for family size of head nouns in established compounds likely to be familiar to children. For example, the nouns *kise* 'chair', *kóva* 'hat' – that have the same surface form when morphologically free or bound – and also *ugat*^ 'cake + GEN', *na'aley* 'shoes + GEN' – serve as heads of numerous established compounds, in contrast to other stimulus nouns in the study like *ganénet* 'nurseryschool teacher', *karit* 'cushion', *gamadey*^ 'dwarfs/elves + GEN', which rarely if ever occur as heads of established compounds. The Hebrew study, too, failed to elicit more or better compound responses in relation to family size of the head nouns, and this factor had no significant effect on either children's comprehension or production of compounds.

15.3.2 Lexico-semantic factors

In addition to a general understanding of the head–modifier relation, children need to assign an appropriate interpretation to this relation as expressing different types of subcategorization. Clark et al.(1985) propose that, initially, children interpret this relation not in the form of hyponymy from a generic to a superordinate entity ('a dog is a kind of animal $\sim$ pet', 'a cake is a kind of food $\sim$ dessert'), but in terms of class-inclusion ('a house-dog is a kind of dog', 'a chocolate cake is a kind of cake'). This finding is supported by children's spontaneous innovations of compounds – like the two Hebrew examples in note 8, where a 'land-cap' is coined in contrast to a 'sea-cap' (established term for 'bathing cap') or a 'soup marmalade' is coined to contrast with a 'soup-nut' (established term for a crouton). And it is consistent with research on children's acquisition of generic nouns in advance of superordinate terms. In fact, compounding may help children acquire the notion of subordinate members of a class, as in, say, *cheese cake, birthday cake, chocolate cake, wedding cake,* or Hebrew *na'aley*^*báyit* 'shoes + GEN house' = 'slippers', *na'aley*^*sport* 'shoes + GEN sport' = 'sneakers'.

The relation between the two nouns is another facet of compounding semantics that was examined, following Bilev (1985), by Clark and Berman (1987). Their test of children's comprehension and production of novel Hebrew compounds considered five different semantic relations between the head and modifier noun: Possession ('a blanket that a doll has, the blanket of a doll' > *a doll blanket*); Purpose ('a chair that a baby uses, a chair for a baby' > *a baby chair*); Container ('a box that holds buttons, a box that has buttons in it' > *a button box*); Material ('a cake that is made of sand, a cake from sand' > *a sand cake*); Location ('trees that grow in the mountains, trees in the mountains' > *mountain trees*). Counter to prediction, these different relations had no effect on either the number of compounds produced by the children or the ease with which they provided paraphrases identifying the different possibilities – even though some of the five relations seemed inherently more abstract and hence more difficult to process. For example, we assumed that temporal location (as in 'a night that exists in winter' > *a winter night*) would be more difficult than concrete relations like material (e.g. 'a pillow made out of silk' > *a silk pillow*), but this did not seem to affect either children's comprehension or production of the target constructions. Nor was the basic genitive relation of possession favoured over others – even though, as noted below, it appears to be the earliest noun + noun relation expressed by children.[16] Instead, morphological form rather than semantic content seems to be a determining factor in Hebrew-speaking children's processing of compound constructions (see section 15.3.4).

Mellenius (1997) designed an elaborate set of criteria for testing Swedish-speaking children's grasp of compounding semantics, testing the same children once a year over a period of four years, from age 7 to 10. She presented children with novel compounds constituted of two nouns in different semantic categories: for example, pairs where one noun denotes an animal and the other a kind of vegetation, or one an animal and the other something that grows on animals, or a man-made object plus a material, etc. The children's paraphrases to her question 'try to tell me what you think these (funny) words mean' yielded a role inventory of eleven categories: *location*, genitive, similarity, preference, *material*, *purpose*, obligation, *possession*, co-occurrence, source, and taste (the four italicized categories were also targeted in the Hebrew study described earlier). The two commonest interpretations were of Location (overwhelming preferred, for example, for both *fågelträd* 'bird tree' and *trädfågel* 'tree bird'), followed by Material (e.g. 95 per cent of the responses for *lädersko* 'leather shoe', as against the purpose interpretation preferred for *skoläder* 'shoe leather'). The paraphrases given by the children show that by age 7 years, children are in all cases able to identify the modifier–head relationship as such. Beyond that, Mellenius concludes that the semantic connection children attribute to the two nouns of a compound depends very largely 'on the semantics of the component nouns'. This is clearly the case where children are given novel terms in isolation, with no pragmatic or linguistic context to aid in their interpretation. Possibly for this reason, the developmental picture yielded by this facet of Mellenius's research is not too clear. Some nouns appeared to retain a stable interpretation across the four years of the study (e.g. *plåtbil* 'metal car' is given the sense of Material out of which the head is made), while others fluctuate (e.g. *bilplåt* 'car metal' is interpreted as expressing a relation of Location by half the 6-year-olds but of Purpose by half the older children).

---

[16] This finding is also interesting on language-specific grounds. In marked contrast to classical Hebrew, where bound compound (so-called 'construct state') constructions served the core genitive relation of possession (Gesenius 1910), in current Hebrew, possession is typically expressed periphrastically with the genitive particle *šel* (Berman 1988; Ravid and Shlesinger 1995).

The issue for child language here – as considered for English by Clark et al. (1985) and Windsor (1993) and for Swedish by Mellenius (1997) – is whether compound innovation serves mainly to express an inherent, permanent or a more incidental or transient relation between head and modifier. Taken together, findings from the very different English, Hebrew, and Swedish studies suggest that, in line with the pragmatically motivated idea of 'contextuals' (Clark and Downing 1977; Clark 1979), how children construe compound relations depends on the semantic function they meet in a particular communicative context. In other words, in the case of children's innovative constructions, compounds are highly 'context-dependent' and hence more likely to express temporary rather than intrinsic relations.

15.3.3 Acquisition of compound form and structure

In order to comprehend and produce compounds, children need, as noted, to attend to the peculiar phonological features of such constructions, including compound-specific prosodic contours, linking elements, and consonant clusters disallowed in single words. Relatively little research is available on acquisition of compound stress patterns, apart from suggestions to the effect that it is acquired as young as by age 2 in Dutch (Fikkert 2001), English (Clark et al. 1985) and Swedish (Mellenius 1997). As against this, in their comparison of compound versus phrasal stress in American English, Vogel and Raimy (2000) cite studies documenting the relatively late development of different prosodic structures in Dutch and British English. They presented children aged 5 to 12 years and a group of adults with N+N and N+A minimal pairs with contrasting stress pattern, for example, the compound *hot dog* as a type of food versus phrasal *hot dog* as a hot canine. Although they had not predicted this, they found a marked difference in response to known versus novel noun+noun combinations. Across age-groups, subjects gave an overwhelmingly phrasal interpretation to novel items (for example, they interpreted the string *rédcup* as a cup that is red – that is, as an adjective-plus-noun phrase, rather than as a novel compound naming a kind of flower). The authors explain this as owing to the fact that a novel compound like *rédcup* lacks an established lexical entry that it can be matched with. In contrast, the known items showed a clear age-related change, with an increasing preference for a compound interpretation, regardless of stress, among 11-year-olds and especially adults. The authors conclude that 'the knowledge required to distinguish between compound and phrasal stress is quite distinct from, and more abstract than, the ability exhibited by young children when they produce novel compounds with the correct stress pattern'. They suggest that command of compound versus phrasal stress in a language like English requires knowledge of higher-level prosodic constituents and the rules that govern them, and that only much later in development 'is the stress pattern separated from the morphological operation that combines individual lexical items into larger lexical items (i.e. compound words)'. Their study highlights the impact of familiarity with compounds on how they are interpreted across development. A rather different explanation for the late development of prosodic structures in English is suggested by Štekauer, Zimmerman, and Gregová (2007) in terms of the quite general oscillation of stress in compounds: their experimental study revealed significant individual differences in people's pronunciation of N+N compounds.

Similar studies might usefully be conducted in languages like Dutch or Swedish, not only for N+N versus A+N combinations, but for a range of compound constructions with prosodic contours that contrast with phrasal stress. As noted, Hebrew N+N compounds are not distinct from phrasal noun+noun combinations in prosody, but differ from them markedly in morphology and syntax. In periphrastic genitives with the particle *šel* both head and modifier noun are morphologically free (e.g. *rega'im šel emet* 'moments of truth' = 'reality') as against the morphologically bound head noun in compounds (cf. *rig'ey^émet* 'minute-s+GEN truth' = 'moments of truth, of true reckoning'). In contrast, in N+A phrases, the modifying (denominal) adjective agrees in number and gender with the (morphologically free) head noun (cf. *rga'-im amitiyim* 'moment-s true+PL' = 'true, authentic, real moments') (Ravid and Shlesinger 1987). As detailed further below, it takes Hebrew-speaking children until adolescence or beyond to command and alternate these two constructions appropriately (Ravid 1997; Ravid and Zilberbuch 2003b).

Acquisition of linking elements and plural marking on the modifying noun in Germanic compounds was earlier noted as arguing for or against level-ordering structural analyses. Another facet of acquisition of compound structure that has been studied quite widely for English is the impact of word-order changes and derivational morphology in Object Verb-*er* deverbal compounds (cf. established *truck driver*, innovative *wagon puller*). English-speaking children go through a stage where they produce ungrammatical compounds like *drive truck* or *pull wagon* for such constructions (Clark and Barron 1988). Relying on both spontaneous data and experimental elicitations, Clark et al. (1986) note that children 'typically acquire affixes like -*er* before they master the appropriate noun-verb word order, and they nearly always place -*er* on the appropriate base, the verb'. They identified three developmental phases in children's acquisition of O+V-*er* compounds: Given a cue such as being asked to label a boy who pulls wagons, they may start by giving the lone noun *puller*, or by merely juxtaposing V+N (e.g. *pull man, pull wagon*), followed by a derived compound without the required order inversion, V-*er*+O (e.g. *puller wagon*), and only subsequently the correct *wagon puller*. Murphy and Nicoladis (2006) tested the hypothesis that the frequency of different complex forms in the input language affects their acquisition of compound constructions by comparing deverbal compound production of British versus Canadian children. They had groups of 4- and 5-year-olds coin compounds by a task similar to that used by Clark and her associates, for example: 'Here is a machine that is watering a hat, brushing cows. What could we call that?' The Canadian children produced more O+V-*er* forms – e.g. *cow-brusher, hat-waterer* – and fewer (ungrammatical) V+O compounds (e.g. *brush-cow*) than their British English peers. The authors explain this by the fact that British English allows more V+O compound constructions (like *answer-phone*) – and possibly also more V+N compounds – than North American dialects of English. They interpret these findings as support for the role of frequency in the ambient dialect on the type of compound constructions coined by children, and also as putting into question the account proposed by Clark and her associates to the effect that children rely on phrasal ordering in producing OV-*er* type compounds.

These issues in children's acquisition of the ordering of elements in synthetic compounds deriving from Verb+Object combinations contrast with findings for Hebrew as typologically differing from both dialects of English as well as from French. First, in structured elicitations, Hebrew speakers across the board preferred to use monolexemic derived forms of the Object Noun rather than of the Verb; for example, *aglan* 'wagoner' from *agala* 'wagon' was commoner as a label for someone who pulls a wagon than *mašxan* 'puller' from the verb *li-mšox* 'to-pull'. Second, surface VO forms like *mošex agalot* 'pulls/puller/pulling wagons' – given mainly by the youngest children in the Clark and Berman (1984) study – constitute a well-formed compound N^N construction, since the head *mošex*, in the intermediate *benoni* form of the verb *li-mšox* 'to-pull', can be interpreted as either a participial or present tense verb and/or as an agent or instrument noun derived from the verb by syntactic conversion (cf. established *šomer^šabat* 'observe(r)+GEN Sabbath' = 'Sabbath observer', *holex^régel* 'walk(er)+GEN foot' = 'pedestrian'). Third, word-order errors in such constructions are not an issue, since the order of elements in the compound construction remains the same as clausal VO – for example, *li-mšox agalot* 'to-pull wagons' yields *mašxan agalot*. And this is true of other derived nouns – both heads and modifiers – that preserve the order of simple clause constituents, e.g. *šmirat^šabat* 'guarding+GEN Sabbath' = 'Sabbath observance' (cf. *anašim šomrim šabat* 'people observe Sabbath') or *kalbey^šmira* 'dogs+GEN guarding' = 'guard-dogs' (cf. *klavim(še)-šomrim* 'dogs (that-) guard+PL'). Rather, a major structural task for Hebrew-acquiring children is learning the appropriate morphological alternations required by the bound stem form of the initial head noun, as detailed below.

15.3.4 A long developmental route: The case of Hebrew

Compounding was characterized at the outset of this chapter as representing a possibly unique intersection of morphophonology, syntax, and lexicon in both structure and function, and hence, too, in acquisition. In tracing the developmental route of Hebrew-speaking children in acquiring compound constructions, this section aims at providing an integrative overall view of the domain. The path that emerges can be summed up as follows: (1) initial very early *lexicalized compounds* – at the stage of single words and early word-combinations; (2) subsequent *syntactic combination* of two associated nouns with juxtaposition the only formal operation – around age 2 to 3 years; (3) acquisition of relevant *lexico-syntactic knowledge* reflected in morphosyntactic processes of *new-word formation* including suffixation and stem change – age 3 to 5 years; (4) command of a full range of required *morphosyntactic changes* – beyond middle childhood to late grade-school age; and (5) finally, *syntactic productivity*, where different types of noun + noun constructions provide high-register, more formal means of expression– from high-school age into adulthood.

Below, these developmental phases are outlined and illustrated by data from naturalistic speech samples combined with experimental and semi-structured elicitations from older speaker-writers.

(1) UNANALYSED LEXICAL ITEMS (Single-word phase, age 1 to 2): To start, Hebrew-speaking children use well-established compound nouns as unanalysed amalgams, like other monolexemic nouns in their repertoire. This is evidenced by morphophonological blending – e.g. *yom^hulédet* 'day + GEN birth' = 'birthday' is pronounced as *yomulédet* and typically pluralized as *yomuladetim* ~ *yomuladetot* (cf. normative *yemey^hulédet*), *bet^šimuš* 'house + GEN use' = 'lavatory' also pluralized as *betšimúšim* (cf. normative *batey^šimuš*).

(2) N N JUXTAPOSITION (Early word-combinations, age 2 to 3 years): At this stage, children may combine two nouns in a structurally unmarked string, analogously to English-speaking 2 year olds – e.g. *fire-dog* for a dog found near a fire or *lion-box* for a box with a lion's head on the cover (Clark et al. 1985) – or 3 year olds' *pull man, pull wagon* (Clark et al. 1986). In Hebrew, these may yield well-formed combinations like *bakbuk tinok* 'bottle baby' = 'baby bottle ~ baby's bottle', or an ungrammatical string like *báyit a-kéle* 'house the-dog' = 'the dog's home, kennel' (cf. well-formed *bet^ha-kélev* or periphrastic *ha-báyit šel ha-kélev*). Semantically, early noun + noun combinations express mainly possessive relations between an inanimate head and an animate possessor as modifier. These are soon replaced by periphrastic genitives with the genitive particle *šel*, e.g. *ima šel Tali* '(the) Mommy of Tali', *ha-mita šel ima* 'the-bed of Mommy' = 'Mommy's bed', around age 2 to 3 years.

(3) INITIAL, PARTIALLY MARKED N^N COMBINATIONS (Basic morphosyntax, derivational morphology, age 3 to 5 years): Next, children will mark a range of nominal relations between two nouns by combining two nouns with, in some but not all cases, appropriate morphological adjustments on the head noun where required. That is, they may produce – from the head noun *uga* 'cake' – correct forms of both established *ugat^šókolad* 'cake + GEN chocolate' and innovative

ugat^šabat 'Sabbath cake'; at this stage, children may fail to produce other changes where required – e.g. **madafim sfarim* 'shelves books' in place of required *mada-fey^sfarim* 'shelves + GEN books' = 'bookshelves'; or they may use a bound genitive form of a noun in a phrasal context – e.g. **tmunat šel parpar* 'picture + GEN of (a) butterfly' vs. required *tmuna šel parpar* or compound *tmunat parpar*. (Berman 1987; Clark and Berman 1987).

In general, however, as noted earlier, when asked to coin names for agents and instruments, Hebrew-speaking children prefer affixation to compounding for new-word formation. Moreover, in two separate studies with different designs and populations, when children were provided with paraphrases requiring attention to two related nouns, they produced noun + noun combinations between only two-thirds and three-quarters of the time by age 5, and only 7-year-old schoolchildren responded at an adult-like level (Berman and Clark 1989; Clark and Berman 1987). These findings from structured elicitations are supported by naturalistic data revealing a general preference of Hebrew-speaking children for affixation rather than compounding as a device for new-word formation (Berman 2000).

(4) MORPHOSYNTAX OF COMPOUND CONSTRUCTIONS (Grade-school age, 7 to 12 years): Command of the formal structure of noun^noun compounds as a bound-head + free-modifier construction consolidates only around age 9, with stem-internal changes taking even longer. In a structured elicitation of novel compounds (Bilev 1985), 4 to 5 year olds were able to add final *-t* to the free feminine ending stressed *-a* (e.g. *uga* ∼ *ugat^šabat* 'cake ∼ cake-GEN Sabbath'); by age 5 to 6 years they changed the free masculine plural ending *-im* to *-ey* (e.g. given *tsiporim še-xayot ba-aá'ar* 'birds that-live in-the-forest', they produced the well-formed compound *tsiporey^yá'ar* 'forest birds'); but even 9 year olds made appropriate stem-internal changes only around three-quarters of the time (e.g. given *láyla šel xóref* 'night of winter' or *láyla še-yeshno ba-xóref* '(a) night that-is in-winter', they might produce incorrect *layl xóref* rather than required *leyl^xóref* 'winter night'; or given *praxim šel xag* 'flowers of holiday' = 'festival' or *praxim še-notnim be-xag* 'flowers (people) given on (a) holiday', they might say **praxey^xag* instead of required *pirxey^xag* 'flowers + GEN holiday' = 'holiday flowers'. Interestingly, a few such errors continue into adolescence and even adulthood (e.g. people use the free form of the noun *šemot* 'names' to form the established compound *šemot^mišpaxa* 'names-GEN family' = 'surnames' without the required vowel reduction, cf. normative *šmot^mišpaxa*). Definiteness marking in compounds, where the definite marker is affixed to the second, modifying noun rather than to the initial head, is a particularly late acquisition in Hebrew (Zur 1983, 2004). This is shown by errors in the few compound constructions that occurred in the oral 'frog-story' narratives of Hebrew-speaking 9 year olds (e.g. *ha-nexil^dvorim* 'the-swarm + GEN bees' in place of well-formed *nexil^ha-dvorim*). Analysis of noun + noun constructions in stories and essays written at school age reveals that 'by the end of grade school, complex

nominals still constitute a challenge to Hebrew writers' (Ravid and Zilberbuch 2003a).

(5a) PRODUCTIVE COMPOUNDING (Mastery of expressive options, from adolescence): By high school, Hebrew speaker-writers use compounding as a *structural device* for combining nouns in high-register style, typically in expository, scientific, and literary prose. That is, in more formal contexts, bound compounds – the 'construct state' constructions of traditional grammar – are selected in preference to periphrastic alternatives with the genitive particle *šel* or prepositional phrases and/or in alternation with N + A phrases with denominal adjectives. This is shown by analysis of biographical, expository, and encyclopedic Hebrew texts written by students and established authors (Ravid and Zilberbuch 2003a, b). A similar trend for greater, age-related use of bound N^N compounds in more formal written usage is shown by comparison of oral narratives and expository essays elicited from 9-year-old fourth-graders and 17-year-old eleventh-graders (Berman and Nir-Sagiv 2004). The younger children used very few, only lexicalized compounds in their oral narratives (e.g. *bet^sefer* 'house + GEN book' = 'school', *yom^sport* 'sports-day', *xadar^morim* 'room + GEN teachers' = 'staffroom'), and just about none in their compositions (two out of a total of 750 items). The older students likewise used few such constructions in their oral narratives (only five in all, also familiar or established expressions like *misxakey^yeladim* 'children's games', *malkat^ha-kita* 'queen + GEN the-class'), but they used far more – both tokens and types – in their essays (accounting for almost 10 per cent of the total number of words; and these included both familiar although high-register terms like *aruc^ha-yeladim* 'the children's channel', *misrad^ha-xinux* 'the Ministry of Education' and also innovative, syntactically productive strings like *memadey^ha-tofa'a* '(the) dimensions (of) the phenomenon', *ófi^ha-ben^adam* '(a) person's character').

These figures contrast markedly with the distribution of compound nouns in a comparable set of English-language texts, elicited by closely parallel procedures (Berman and Nir-Sagiv 2007): The English-speaking high-schoolers used compound nouns as freely in their oral narratives as in their more formal-style written essays (accounting for about 4 per cent of the total words in both text types), even though the latter typically manifested more formal, high-register language in English as in Hebrew (Bar-Ilan and Berman 2007; Ravid and Berman, in press). Taken together, these findings demonstrate that syntactic compounding by bound 'construct state' constructions of the type labelled here as N^N is a very late acquisition, and a hallmark of more formally monitored Hebrew prose style.

(5b) SYNTACTIC COMPOUNDING: 'DOUBLE COMPOUNDS': Hebrew has another, highly complex type of N^N compound construction, the so-called 'double compound': the head noun is suffixed by a bound pronominal form of the modifying noun to which it is linked by the genitive particle *šel* (e.g. *sipur-av šel Agnon* 'stories-his of Agnon' = 'Agnon's stories', *xaver-a šel Rina* 'boyfriend-her of Rina' = 'Rina's boyfriend'). Syntactically, these constructions require backwards pronominalization agreeing with the modifying noun in number, gender, and person; they are semantically far more restricted than N^N compounds or N *šel* N phrases; and they are confined to high-register, formal Hebrew (Ravid and Shlesinger 1995; Shlesinger and Ravid 1998). Structural complexity thus interacts with semantic productivity and low usage frequency to explain our finding that children never and educated adults only rarely use this construction.

In sum, the developmental patterns traced in this section indicate that initially, children acquiring two very different languages like English and Hebrew start out by treating compounds in much the same way, as unanalysed monolexemic labels, then as a means of juxtaposing two nouns with some unspecified semantic relation between them. Across age-groups, and most markedly in the preschool years, compound constructions serve as a means of new-word formation for labelling nominal referents from as young as age 2 in English, but only much later, and far less than affixation in Hebrew. Moreover, from around age 3, compound constructions reflect the impact of target-language structure and function. For example, English-acquiring children need to learn to manipulate deverbal compound formation, in the move from, say, *wagon-boy* to *push wagon* to *pusher wagon* to *wagon pusher*, while Hebrew-acquiring children take a long time to master the full range of morphological alternations required by noun compounds. And only once literacy is well established will they make use of compounding as a syntactic option for elevating the stylistic level of linguistic register in more formal, typically written contexts of use.

15.4 Discussion

Analysis of a range of other constructions has led me to argue that language acquisition depends on multiple factors and that the interplay between them changes over time (Berman 2004). In line with this non-monolithic view of the acquisition process and children's developmental path in moving 'from emergence to mastery', the following factors are considered below as impinging on compound acquisition in different languages: structural complexity (15.4.1), functional load (15.4.2), and the impact of target-language typology on form–function relations (15.4.3).

15.4.1 Formal factors of structural complexity

Among the principles she has formulated to explain children's lexical acquisition in different languages, Clark (1993) points to the principle of 'formal simplicity' as explaining, for example, the difficulty English-speaking children encounter in producing OV-*er* compounds in English or in alternating the morphological form of head nouns in Hebrew, or in assigning appropriate linking elements in Dutch or Swedish compounding (Mellenius 1997), while the structural complexity of 'double compound' constructions can account for their late acquisition in Hebrew. However, while structural difficulties clearly affect the *accuracy* of children's initial production of compound constructions, they do not seem to be crucial to the *extent* to which children in fact make use of such constructions in their own language production, nor do they appear to affect children's generally early comprehension of modifier–noun or noun–modifier relations. While formal simplicity together with the principle of 'semantic transparency' – the one-to-one mapping of form and meaning – may be important for children to initially break into the system, these alone cannot account for children's preference for compounding versus affixation as a means of new-word formation. Rather, increasingly with age and the development of a larger lexicon, features of target-language typology and frequency of usage in the ambient language outweigh structural difficulties that young children may initially encounter in constructing well-formed compounds.

15.4.2 Functional load: Linguistic and discourse functions

Another factor in compound acquisition concerns the linguistic function served by these constructions. In research on English and the other languages surveyed here, compound acquisition has been dealt with primarily as a means for new-word formation.[17] This might well be the major role of compounding among young English-speaking children, when the bulk of their vocabulary is still from the basic Germanic word-stock of their language (Anglin 1993; Carlisle 2000; Bar-Ilan and Berman 2007). On the other hand, where developmental data are available beyond early school age, a rather different picture emerges. As noted above, in Hebrew, compound constructions constitute a critical facet of acquisition of morphosyntax in what has been termed 'later language development' and access to a formal, more literate style of expression (Ravid and Zilberbuch 2003a; Berman 2004) so that, from around adolescence, speaker-writers use N^N construct-state compounds as structural alternatives to periphrastic prepositional phrases, increasingly alternated with high-register N + Denominal-A constructions.

Use of alternative means to meet the function of expressing relations between two nominals thus emerges as a facet of the 'rhetorical options' selected or preferred by speaker-writers for meeting different discourse functions out of the

---

[17] This also seems to be true of psycholinguistic research on compound processing (e.g. De Jong et al. 2002; Gagné and Spalding 2006b; Gagné et al. 2005).

range of available constructions in their language (Slobin 2004). This has been demonstrated for later language development in use of passives in different languages (Jisa et al. 2002), devices for agent downgrading in Spanish (Tolchinsky and Rosado 2005), and types of text-based clause linkage in English, Hebrew, and Spanish (Berman and Nir-Sagiv in press). These observations are supported by findings for acquisition of compounds in Hebrew, where compound constructions typically change not only in amount and form, but also in the linguistic and discourse functions that they serve across later, school-age language development.

15.4.3 Target language typology in form/function interrelations

English and Hebrew manifest clear typological differences in compounding, including (1) a distinctive stress pattern versus morphological change, (2) left versus right head-branching order, and (3) a large range of non-N+N compound types in English, where Hebrew has no equivalents to, say, A+N (*high school, sidewalk*), V+N (*playpen, push button*), Particle+N (*downstairs, backpack*), and no compound verbs (*whitewash, piggyback*), even though denominal verb-formation is morphologically productive (Berman 2003). Lexical innovations in both structured elicitations and naturalistic usage showed English-acquiring children to favour juxtaposing of two words for new-word formation whereas their Hebrew-acquiring peers prefer to coin new words by affixation. I suggest that this is due to the traditional typological distinction between English as more analytic and Hebrew as more synthetic, so that children acquiring these two languages will attend more to relations *between* words in English, and *inside* words in Hebrew. Thus, Hebrew-speaking children may rely less on compounding for coining new terms because they have numerous word-internal alternatives that are readily accessible from an early age for this purpose.

   The fact that preschoolers are from early on sensitive to the 'typological imperatives' imposed by their language (Berman 1986, 1993b) is attested by cross-linguistic research in different domains (e.g. Slobin 1996; Bowerman and Choi 2001). In the case in point, word-internal morphological processes – both linear to the ends of words and interdigited with consonantal roots – are typologically highly accessible and mastered early by children acquiring a Semitic language like Hebrew (Berman 1985; Shimron 2003). In contrast, more sophisticated derivational affixation is a late acquisition in English when applying to more advanced, high-register, Latinate elements of the lexicon (Nagy & Herman 1987; Carlisle, 2000).

   Frequency of occurrence in the ambient language interacts with structurally motivated typological factors. In line with usage-based theories of grammaticization (e.g. Bybee 2006), current psycholinguistic research demonstrates the acquisitional impact of frequency of distribution of particular constructions in naturalistic speech use. Such approaches view input as central to acquisition, in the sense that, based on frequency of occurrence (both types and tokens), certain concrete structures of the target language are stored and processed until they eventually become reformulated into more abstract linguistic representations (e.g. Cameron-Faulkner, Lieven, and Tomasello 2003; Tomasello 2003). In other words, the type of 'positive evidence' to which children are exposed plays a major role in acquisition (MacWhinney 2004). In the present context, children acquiring Germanic languages like English, Dutch, or Swedish are exposed early on to numerous exemplars of compound constructions. In contrast, the bulk of the content vocabulary that Hebrew-acquiring children hear around them is made up of morphologically complex items constructed out of consonantal roots plus affixal patterns, while the bulk of the noun + noun combinations that they hear and produce are in a phrasal form with the genitive particle *shel*.

Interestingly, these preferences reflect quite different historical developments. N + N compounding is a favoured device for the basic Germanic stock of everyday English – as in examples cited earlier from children's narratives – in contrast to higher-register, later-developing A + N phrases with Latinate denominal adjectives like *world order* ~ *universal arrangement, water bug* ~ *aquatic insect* (Levi 1976). In marked contrast, classical Hebrew N^N compounding has been largely replaced in everyday usage, hence in the input to young children, by periphrastic options (mainly with the post-Biblical genitive particle *šel*), while classical Semitic devices of affixation remain favoured for new-word formation – along with newer, more linear morphological devices (Ravid 2006). This line of reasoning explains why, although N^N compounding (as against compounding in general in languages like English or Swedish) is *structurally* highly productive in Hebrew, it is relatively marginal in actual occurrence in the language heard and hence used by young children.

These typological and usage-based factors intersect with level of usage and *linguistic register* to explain developments in acquisition of compound constructions. Recall that, in closely parallel sets of Hebrew texts, compounds were infrequent in the oral narratives of children and adults alike, occurring more in written essays only from high school up. In English, by contrast, compounds (mainly Germanic N + N forms) were quite common in English oral narratives from preschool on. This is understandable, since young English-acquiring preschoolers hear and use such constructions, together with a small group of native derivational suffixes like agentive *-er* or action nominal *-ing* (Clark 1993). At school age, as part of acquiring a 'literate lexicon', English speakers are exposed to more formal types of constructions, including Latinate denominal adjectives, on the one hand, and presumably (although to the best of my knowledge, this topic has not been investigated in English) a broader range of compound constructions, including denominal compound verbs and participial adjectives (*fine-tuned, clear-thinking*, etc.). In contrast, in order to acquire a formal written style of expression, Hebrew-speaking students need to master several high-register binominal constructions (N'N compounds, N+Denominal-A, and N-Pro šel N double compounds, which they master in that order). The fact that it takes so long for these constructions to consolidate derives from usage variables of low frequency in everyday register and conversational style, interacting with typologically motivated factors of formal complexity and the ready accessibility of structural alternatives.

15.4.4 Further directions

Usage-based explanations point to the need for detailed studies of the *relation between input and output* in compound acquisition – not in the behaviouristic sense of imitation or a one-to-one mapping of in-at-one-end, out-at-the-other, but by adopting a systematically tested, corpus-based account of the notion of 'frequency' in the ambient language. Current studies on a range of grammatical constructions demonstrate that caretaker input to young children in the critical period of early language acquisition is constrained in a non-obvious fashion. Compound acquisition in different languages affords a suggestive site for similar inquiries, beyond early acquisition and across school age.

A second possible line of investigation would be to compare acquisition and use of different types of *binominal constructions* – not only minimal pairs of N+N / A+N constructions (as in Vogel and Raimy's study) but, say, for English N+N compounds, Denominal-A+N phrases, possessives with *'s*, and phrases with genitive *of* (compare, say, *flower dress, flowery dress, flowered dress, floral dress*); and the full range of constructions noted earlier for Hebrew. Infelicitous strings of nominals or overuse of genitive phrases is common in the usage of even advanced learners of English as a second language from different language backgrounds. This, too, cannot be evaluated without a careful, usage-based analysis of these alternating, apparently 'synonymous' expressive options for combining two nouns in different languages.

Along the same lines, as initiated by the experimental studies of Eve Clark and her associates on coining labels for agent and instrument nouns, cross-linguistic research could be designed to compare the *alternative devices* favoured by children acquiring different types of languages for coining lexical items in a range of domains. Carefully controlled research of this kind could provide important further evidence for the role of target-language typology, usage frequency, and linguistic register in children's acquisition of compounds and related constructions.

Finally, given the rather ambiguous results of earlier, experimentally structured studies in different languages (as reviewed in section 15.3.2 above), further research is needed to ascertain which, if any, *semantic relation* is most favoured in compounding and which, if any, such relation is more basic or earlier acquired in different languages. Currently, the basic genitive category of possession appears to be the earliest-acquired noun + noun relation in both English and Hebrew – not through compound constructions but by inflection in English (*Mummy's bed*) and phrasally in Hebrew (*ha-mita šel ima* 'the-bed of Mummy').[18] This points to a more general methodological implication of the foregoing review of children's acquisition of compound constructions: the need to combine results of structured experimental elicitations with data from varied samples of naturalistic language use in different communicative contexts.

[18] The language-particular arbitrariness of the form–meaning relations of noun-noun constructions is demonstrated by another English/Hebrew contrast. The often highly lexicalized partitive relation is expressed periphrastically in English (e.g. *a cup of tea, box of matches*) in contrast to the container relation (*teacup, matchbox*). In Hebrew, both are typically compounded (*kos^te, kufsat^gafrurim*) – first showing up in children's usage in established expressions like *bakbuk^xalav* 'bottle (of) milk ~ milk bottle' (cf. possessive *bakbuk šel tinok* 'baby's bottle').

C H A P T E R   1 6

DIACHRONIC PERSPECTIVES

DIETER KASTOVSKY

16.1 TERMINOLOGY

This contribution will discuss aspects of the genesis and subsequent development of compounding in IE with a focus on the Germanic language family.[1] First, however, a clarification of the terminology employed here is indicated, since this is by no means uniform (cf. Aronoff 1994: 5 ff.), and notions such as 'root', 'stem', 'word' as defined below are used in rather different ways in the literature. Thus Bauer (1983: 20–1; 1988: 252–3) distinguishes between roots as forms which are not further analysable and which remain when all derivational and inflectional elements have been removed on the one hand, and stems, which remain when only the inflectional morphemes have been removed, on the other. Both roots and stems can be bound or free, i.e. can occur as 'words'. Thus, in *un-touch-able-s, touch* is a root, and *untouchable* a stem, but both are also words. Aronoff (1994: 32), on the other hand, distinguishes between words as syntactically free, (morphologically) simple or complex realizations of lexemes, stems as bound representations of lexemes 'that remain[s] when an affix is removed' (Aronoff 1994: 31), and roots as morphologically unanalysable entities, i.e. 'what is left when all morphological structure has been wrung out of the form' (Aronoff 1994: 40). In such a framework

I gratefully acknowledge Theresa Illés's help with the bibliography.
[1] For other IE languages, cf. the contributions in *Transactions of the Philological Society* 100:2, 3 (2002).

the term 'word formation' itself is problematic, since in highly inflectional languages the input to derivational processes would actually be stems, and these processes would again produce stems to which inflectional endings have to be added in order for these stems to become 'words', i.e. units to be used in syntactic constructions. It is for reasons such as these that I will adopt the term 'lexeme' instead of 'word' as central for the domain in question, which should therefore be called 'lexeme formation' rather than 'word formation' (cf. also Aronoff 1994: 13), since these processes deal with the formation of new lexemes, whose representations may or may not be words (free forms).

The lexeme can thus be defined as a simple or complex dictionary entry, that is, an abstract entity as part of the lexicon of a language, e.g. En. *do, doer, undo* or OE *drinc-(an)* 'to drink', *drinc-er-(e)* 'drinker', *win-drinc-er-(e)* 'wine-drinker', etc. Such lexemes are, at a more concrete level, represented by word-forms, which can be defined as the inflectional forms of a lexeme. Word-forms in turn appear as words in concrete linguistic utterances, that is, they are independent syntactic elements, which may be simple or complex, e.g. En. *man, mad, madman, madly, write, writers, or, the,* etc.; OE *lufian, lufode, lufu, luflice; drincan, druncon, windrinceras,* etc.

Word-forms as well as complex lexemes are derived from a basic lexical representation (base form) of the respective lexical item by adding the appropriate inflectional and/or derivational endings. The base form thus is that lexeme representation which acts as the input to morphological processes, whether inflectional or derivational. Depending on its morphological status, three types of morphological systems can be distinguished, which in turn provide the basis for a general morphological typology.[2]

(1) If the base form is an entity that can function as a word in an utterance without the addition of any additional morphological material, we speak of word-based morphology, e.g. En. *cat-s, cheat-ed, beat-ing, sleep-er.*

(2) The base form does not occur as an independent word, but requires additional morphological (inflectional and/or derivational) material in order to function as a word. It thus is a bound form, i.e. a stem, which can be defined as a word-class-specific lexeme representation stripped of any inflectional endings, which has to combine with additional derivational and/or inflectional morphemes in order to function as a word, cf. G. *bind-(-en, -e, -est, -er,* etc.); OE *luf-(-ian, -ie, -ast, -od-e,* etc.) = PG **luf-ōj-(-an)* 'love' vb., *luf-estr-(-e)* 'female lover'; PG **dag-a-(-z)* 'day', nom. sg., *a*-stem; PG **gast-i-(-z)* 'guest', nom. sg., *i*-stem; En. *scient-(-ist)* vs. *science, dramat-(-ic)* vs. *drama, astr-o-naut, tele-pathy;* Lat. *am-ā-(-re), hab-ē-(-re),* where *bind-, luf-, luf-estr-, *luf-ōj-, *dag-a-, *gast-i-, dramat-, astr-, -naut, tele-, -pathy, am-ā-, hab-ē-* are stems. In this case we speak of stem-based morphology (cf. also Beard 1981: 18, 123).

---

[2] For a more detailed discussion see Kastovsky (1992a: 397f.; 1992b: 415 ff.; 2006a: 58 ff.).

(3) The input to the morphological rule system can be even more abstract and may require additional morphological material just to become a stem. Such an abstract element will be called a root, which may be defined as the element that is left over when all derivational, stem-forming, and inflectional elements are stripped away. Such roots can either be affiliated to a particular word-class, or they can be word-class-neutral. In this case the word-class affiliation is added by a word-formative process, cf. IE roots like *wVr- 'bend, turn' (cf. L uer-t-ere 'turn', OE weor-þ-an 'become', wyr-m 'worm', etc.), with V standing for the ablaut vowel (cf. e.g. Kuryłowicz 1968: 200 ff.), or Semitic k.t.b. 'write'. In this case we speak of root-based morphology.

Since morphological systems undergo typological changes in this respect (cf. Kastovsky 1992b, 1996a), they are usually not completely homogeneous, but one or the other type may dominate. Thus, if all bases are necessarily words, and there is no affixation, we usually speak of an isolating language, e.g. Chinese; but this language seems to be on the verge of developing some kind of affixation, which would also make it a mixed type. Classical reconstructed IE was probably predominantly root-based and needed extensive stem-formative and inflectional processes, which interacted with each other and were not yet neatly separated as is the case in the IE daughter languages (cf. Kastovsky 1996a: 109 ff.). We thus had a mixture of root- and stem-based morphology at this stage, but cf. section 16.3.1 below for the potentially different status of earlier PIE. OE was predominantly stem-based, but partly already also word-based, whereas Modern English is basically word-based, and stem-based only in non-native lexeme formation. As we will see below, this is also relevant for the historical development of compounding.

16.2 THE DELIMITATION OF COMPOUNDING

16.2.1 The criterion of constituent wordhood

Compounds are usually defined as words which consist of two or more words: 'a syntactic word complex fused into one lexical unit is called a compound' (Brugmann 1889: 3);[3] similarly Carr (1939: xxii), Krahe and Meid (1967: 16). More recent definitions are also usually word-based, cf. 'when two or more words are combined into a morphological unit . . . we speak of a compound' (Marchand 1969: 11); 'compounding, or composition, is, roughly speaking, the process of putting

---

[3] 'Verschmilzt ein syntaktischer Wortkomplex zu einer Worteinheit, so nennt man diese ein Compositum'

two words together to form a third' (Bauer 1983: 11).[4] Such word-based definitions of compounding create some problems both synchronically and diachronically, if they are applied literally.

Marchand (1969: 1) defines words as 'the smallest, indivisible, and meaningful unit[s] of speech, susceptible of transposition in sentences'. This implies that words must occur as independent units in utterances, which would rule out compounds whose constituents do not occur outside the compound in question.

On the basis of this definition, formations like *Anglo-Norman*, *Balto-Slavic*, *concavo-convex*, *astro-physics*, etc., whose constituents *Anglo-*, *Balto-*, *concavo-*, *astro-* do not occur outside the respective compounds, would not count as compounds. But they are exactly parallel to the type *icy-cold*, *deaf-mute*, which is why Marchand (1969: 89–90) treats them as compounds despite the problematic status of their first constituents.

With *astro-naut*, *tele-gram*, etc., i.e. so-called neoclassical compounds (cf. Bauer 1983: 39, 213 ff.; Spencer 1998: 128), both constituents only occur in compounds, but clearly have lexical status, and the patterns are productive and match those of normal compounds (cf. *astro-naut* = *star-farer*, G. *Tele-phon* = *Fern-sprecher*). Such constituents have sometimes been referred to as 'combining forms', cf. the *OED* and Kastovsky (2000: 122). Marchand excluded such formations from his survey (Marchand 1969: 132, 218), because their constituents are not words and because they are coined on the basis of (neo-)Latin patterns. This is of course true, since the constituents had been stems as defined above in the source languages Latin and Greek, and not words. But their exclusion is nevertheless unsatisfactory, since this type is on the increase in all European languages, especially in technical jargon, and in view of the semantic parallels with native compound patterns. If we replace the word-based definition of compounding by a lexeme-based one, such inconsistencies can be avoided, because lexemes can be realized as words or stems and formations such as *Balto-Slavic*, *astro-naut* can be treated as stem compounds.

Another problem is posed by so-called synthetic compounds (Marchand 1969: 15 ff.), also called 'Zusammenbildungen' or 'verbal compounds' (cf. Roeper and Siegel 1978; Lieber 1983; Fabb 1998: 681 f.), whose second part is a deverbal noun or adjective. Formations such as En. *star-traveller*, *bread-cutter*, *oven-baked*, *soul-pinching*, G. *Autofahrer* 'car driver', *Weintrinker* 'wine drinker' would count as regular compounds, because *traveller*, *cutter*, *baked*, *pinching*, *Fahrer*, *Trinker* exist outside these compounds as well. But formations such as En. *star-farer*, *church-goer*; G. *Liebhaber* 'lover', *Landstreicher* 'tramp' are problematic, since *farer*, *goer*, *Haber*, *Streicher* (in the sense 'someone who loafs around') do not seem to exist as independent words: they only occur in these compounds. This type of formation is very old and goes back to IE, where the second members also often did not have independent status (see section 16.3.2). In view of the formal and semantic parallels between the first and the second

---

[4] For a more detailed discussion, see Chapter 1.

group, a homogeneous treatment is of course called for, no matter whether the second part exists as an independent derivative or not, as long as it represents a potential formation, a possible lexeme; cf. also Uhlich (2002: 406f.).

16.2.2 Compounding vs. affixation

A different problem is posed by the delimitation of compounding and affixation. It is of course well known that affixes frequently, though by no means always, go back to first or second members of compounds by progressive bleaching of their lexical content, cf. the suffixes En. *-hood*<OE *had* 'status, position', *-dom*<OE *dom* 'judgement, status, condition', adjectival and adverbial *-ly*<*lic* 'body'; similarly G. *-heit, -tum*; Fr. adverbial *-ment*<L *mente*<*mens*, etc. The same is true of many prefixes, which go back to prepositions or adverbs, e.g. En. *for-, be-, co-, en-, mid-*, etc. This was already realized by Brugmann (1889: 5), who pointed out that there is no hard and fast boundary between composition and simple lexical items because of such diachronic shifts. But when does such an element stop being a lexeme and turn into an affix?[5] This is both a synchronic and a diachronic problem, because the existence of a diachronic shift results in a synchronic cline, and it has two aspects, a theoretical-formal and a practical one.

From a formal point of view, it is the theoretical status of affixes which is at issue here: should these be treated as lexical entries on a par with regular lexemes or not? – a question that has been answered differently in different theories (cf. Beard 1998: 46 ff. with references), and which for reasons of space cannot be discussed here.

As to the practical demarcation, we have to reckon with a cline because of the diachronic shift. Sometimes, an intermediate category of 'semi-affix' has been introduced – see e.g. Marchand (1969: 356), who posits semi-suffixes such as *-like* (*manlike*), *-worthy* (*praiseworthy*), *-monger* (*whoremonger*), *-way(s)* (*sideways*), *-wise* (*clockwise*). But this is not really a solution, since it simply replaces a two-way by a three-way distinction, adding an additional stepping-stone on something which for diachronic reasons must be viewed as a cline, without providing criteria for the delimitation.

Sometimes semantics is invoked, but it is not really helpful. Thus it is argued that affixes are semantically less specific than full-fledged lexemes, but this is not borne out by the facts: affixes vary between having a very general, grammatical meaning, e.g. *-er* (*employer*) 'agent', *-ee* (*employee*) 'patient', etc., and a very specific lexical meaning, e.g. *mono-* (*monochromatic*) 'one', *bi-* (*bisexual*) 'two', *-teria* (*caketeria*) 'shop', *-gate* (*zippergate*) 'political scandal', *-age* (*anchorage*) 'fee', etc. As far as I can see, there is so far no semantic theory that allows us to clearly draw the line between

---

[5] Cf. the extensive discussion in Carr (1939: 344–75) and, for an attempt in connection with the description of Old English, Kastovsky (1992a: 363–4).

compounding and affixation on semantic grounds. We thus have to accept this indeterminacy, which reflects the diachronic development from lexeme to affix. Incidentally, this direction can also be reversed, that is, an affix can become an independent word, consider the history of *burger* (Marchand 1969: 213). This originated as a suffix from clipped *hamburger*, i.e. *cheese (ham)burger > cheeseburger, beefburger*, etc., but, as the name *Burger King* indicates, it has become an independent lexeme. Today, *burger*-formations will probably be interpreted by many speakers as compounds rather than as suffixal derivatives (cf. Beard 1998: 57).

16.3 THE GENESIS OF COMPOUNDING

16.3.1 Compounding as a result of univerbation in Indo-European

The genesis of compounding takes us back to the earliest stages of Indo-European, since compounds already existed in what Jacobi called the 'Indogermanische Ursprache', a stage preceding the 'Indogermanische Grundsprache' (Jacobi 1897: 1; Meier-Brügger 2002: 295).[6] These terms can probably be equated with what are now called Proto-Indo-European (PIE) and Indo-European, respectively, the latter representing the stage shortly before the split into the various IE daughter language families.[7] The basic assumption, already formulated by the Neo-Grammarians, is that compounds ultimately originated in syntactic constructions through some univerbation process:

If a syntactic word combination fuses into a single word unit, we call it a **compound**, e.g. Διόσκουροι 'Zeus's sons' from Διὸς κοῦροι, ModG *hungersnot* 'famine' from MHG *hungers nōt* 'hunger's need'

(Brugmann 1889: 3)[8].

Jacobi (1897:1) speaks of 'Zusammenrückung zweier Wörter' ('juxtaposition of two words'), and more recent treatments of the subject (e.g. Kuryłowicz 1964: 56, Krahe and Meid 1967: 17, Schindler 1997, Clackson 2002, Meier-Brügger 2002: 295, to mention only a few) endorse this syntactic origin of compounding, although they differ as to the details of this transformation from syntactic to morphological

---

[6] Pohl (1977: 65) opts for a later date, namely the end of the IE period.

[7] PIE can be dated to the fifth to fourth millennia BC, and the end of the Indo-European period to the later fourth millennium BC (Gamkrelidze and Ivanov 1995: 761 ff.).

[8] 'Verschmilzt ein syntaktischer Wortcomplex zu einer Worteinheit, so nennt man dies ein **Compositum** [emphasis by Brugmann], z. B. gr. Διόσκουροι 'des Zeus Söhne' aus Διὸς κοῦροι, nhd. *hungersnot* aus mhd. *hungers nōt*'.

structure. Syntactic origin does not mean, however, that all recorded compounds in the IE languages had been formed in this way, only that the category 'compound' as a prototype, distinct from syntactic constructions, came into existence in this manner, cf. Schindler (1997: 539): 'the prototypes of the IE compounds, which necessarily go back to a univerbation process'[9]). These prototypes could then act as the basis for analogical formations which did not necessarily have any direct syntactic source. In this way, the lexicon began to develop its own lexeme-based formation patterns independent of syntactic constructions, but incorporating syntactic properties, which had been inherited in the univerbation process. Since the possibility of univerbation always existed, new compound patterns could be added at any time, and these, at the morphological level, would reflect changes that had in the meantime taken place in syntax: 'the internal syntax of compounds can sometimes reveal much about the syntactic patterns of a language' (Clackson 2002: 163).

This reasoning also underlies the traditional explanation of the two compound layers found in IE, one called 'echte Komposita' ('primary compounds'), and a second one, called 'unechte Komposita', 'secondary compounds' (cf. Carr 1939: 309 ff.), or 'Juxtaposita' (Brugmann 1889: 23). In the first group, the first constituent is a pure root or a root followed by a stem-formative, cf. *rā̀ja-putra-* 'having a royal son', *rāja-putrá-* 'royal son', ἀκρό-πολις 'high city', *gud-hus* 'God-house' (cf. Jacobi 1897: 1). In the second group, the first constituent contains an inflectional ending, usually the genitive, but other cases also occur, e.g. IE *dems-potis- 'house-master' = 'master of the house', Skr. *divō-jā-s* 'heaven's child', L *aquaeductus* 'aqueduct' = 'conduit of water', OHG *donares-tag* 'Thursday' = 'day of Thor', OE *Tiwes-dæg* 'Tuesday' = 'day of Tiu' (cf. Carr 1939: 309 ff.). It is this latter type which most clearly documents the syntactic origin of compounding because of the presence of the nominal case/number inflection in the first constituent.

The difference between these two compound types is usually explained by assuming that the primary compounds go back to a period before the development of nominal inflection, or at least before inflectional endings for the nominative, accusative, and genitive became mandatory in syntactic constructions (cf. Brugmann 1889: 21, 23 ff.; Jacobi 1897: 1).[10] The syntactic function of the nouns was expressed by their position. Similarly, person/number inflection of the verb is regarded as a later development, that is, the verb could occur as a root followed by a stem-formative, which seems to have had derivative function just as the nominal stem-formatives did. Moreover, it is sometimes suggested that these roots were not really word-class-specific but received their word-class affiliation from stem-formatives and/or the inflectional endings (cf. Bader 1962: 127–30; Kastovsky 1996a: 110). If it is true that IE was preceded by such a stage where

---

[9] '…die Prototypen der idg. Komp., die ja auf Univerbierung beruhen müssen'
[10] For further references to this hypothesis, cf. Dunkel (1999: 50f.).

roots could occur without inflection in syntactic constructions, this PIE stage would have been characterized by a mixture of root- and word-based morphology, since at least some roots (e.g. root nouns like the antecedents of L *pes, pedis*, OE *fot* 'foot', and root verbs like the antecedents of Skr. *ás-mi* 'be', IE *$d^h\bar{e}$-* 'do') could occur as words without stem-formatives and inflectional endings. The majority of the roots, however, would at least have required stem-formatives to function as words, which at this stage apparently had primarily derivative function, adding word-class and probably also semantic information to an ambivalent root (cf. Jacobi 1897: 112; Pimenova 2004). But these stems would also occur as words without additional inflectional endings.[11] This would only change with the generalization of inflection, which would make stem-based morphology the dominant type and would marginalize word-based morphology until the modern period.

This analysis is, however, not generally accepted. Thus Dunkel (1999) rejects it altogether and argues that IE never went through a stage without inflection (Dunkel 1999: 51). Instead he assumes that these primary compounds arose through univerbation, with first constituents 'which were not really "endless" but only seemed to be so because they belonged to a category where a zero-ending was morphosyntactically regular' (Dunkel 1999: 56). But since the bare stem and a stem+zero are formally identical, and there does not seem to exist a functional opposition between them, the presence of a zero morpheme is rather difficult to prove, unless it could be shown that zero replaces some overt counterpart (cf. Kastovsky 1980: 230; 1996a: 105 ff.), which does not seem to be the case.

Pohl (1977: 65), on the other hand, generally assumes a more recent origin of compounds, shortly before the split of IE into the various daughter languages, by concurrent univerbation of stems and inflected forms, but does not rule out an inflectionless early phase. Others allow for an inflectionless phase, but argue that this is not really relevant for IE as such, since both types coexisted before the split, cf. Meissner and Tribulato (2002: 295). And Schindler simply states:

IE compounds are stem-compounds. The nominal categories (case, number), which are characterized by stress/ablaut and special endings, are neutralized in the first constituent of a compound . . . , with adjectives also gender distinctions.

(Schindler 1997: 537)[12]

Whether these two types of compounding thus really reflect two diachronic layers, one without inflection and one with inflection, must therefore be left undecided.

---

[11] Jacobi (1897: 111) argues 'dass in je höheres Alter wir zurückgreifen, um so mehr sein [i.e. IE] Charakter sich der Agglutination nähert' ('the further we go back, the more its [i.e. IE] character approaches agglutination'). Jacobi's classification as 'agglutinative' is not really adequate, however: the dominance of word-based morphology (or rather the absence of any inflectional morphology) would characterize this Proto-Indo-European stage as isolating.

[12] 'Idg. Komposition ist Stammkomposition. Die nominalen Kategorien (Kasus, Numerus), die durch Akzent/Ablaut und eigene Endungen charakterisiert sind, werden im Kompositionsanfangs-glied (KA) neutralisiert . . . , beim Adjektiv auch das Genus.'

But these two patterns certainly occurred side by side and both led to analogical new formations in classical IE.

Another important aspect concerns the subsequent status of the original stem-formatives and inflectional endings in the resulting compounds. In the long run both lost their original morphological function and developed into purely formal compound markers or linking elements ('Kompositionsvokal', 'Fugenelement'):

> Since morphologically unmarked compounds are stem-compounds, there is a *general tendency* to reinterpret inflectional material as belonging to the stem and to use these pseudo-stems multi-functionally, with the former endings merely functioning as composition morphemes.
>
> (Schindler 1997: 538)[13]

This is proved by modern examples where this morpheme could not have been the appropriate inflectional ending, e.g. G. *Liebesdienst* 'favour' (lit. 'service out of love'), *Universitätsbibliothek* 'university library': *Liebes, Universitäts* are not genitives of fem. *Liebe, Universität*, which are inflectionally unmarked. An interesting case are the German compounds *Gottesmutter* 'god's mother', parallel to the above with -*es*- as a linking element, and *Muttergottes* 'mother of God', the latter clearly the result of a recent univerbation process with *Gottes* a genuine genitive, cf. *das Haus Peters* 'the house of Peter'.

16.3.2 Indo-European compound types

Since Sanskrit is the IE language with the greatest variety of compounds and the Old Indian grammarians had developed an elaborate classification system, IE compounds are often classified on the basis of their Sanskrit counterparts (though this system is not used uniformly, cf. e.g. Brugmann 1889: 21–3, 82–9; Hirt 1932: 117 ff.; Carr 1939: xxvff.; Meier-Brügger 2002: 295 ff.). The following categories are found in the literature:

(1) *Tatpuruša* (also called 'verbale Rektionskomposita', 'verbal rectional compounds', or 'synthetic compounds'), e.g. En. *church-goer, chimney-sweep*;[14]

---

[13] 'Da bildungsmäßig unmarkierte Komp. Stammkomp. sind, besteht eine *generelle Tendenz* [emphasis by Schindler], flexivisches Material als zum Stamm gehörig umzuinterpretieren und diese Pseudostämme in beliebiger Funktion zu verwenden bzw. die einstigen Endungen als reine Kompositionsmorpheme zu gebrauchen.' Cf. already Brugmann (1889: 27) or Carr (1939: 268 ff., 309 ff.).

[14] Meier-Brügger (2002: 296–7) treats compounds with a verbal first constituent of the type Gk. *Mene-laos* '(someone) leading the people', Gk. *phere-oiko-s* '(something) carrying a house' = 'snail', En. *pickpocket* as 'inverted' verbal rectional compounds, i.e. also as members of this category, whereas Hirt (1932: 121) and others treat these as a separate type, sometimes also called 'imperative compounds', because the first constituent is interpreted as an imperative; but cf. Schindler (1997: 539), who rejects such an analysis.

(2) *Karmadhāraya* (also called determinative compounds), e.g. En. *blackbird, girlfriend, house-door*;[15]

(3) *Dvandva* (also called copulative[16] or coordinative compounds), e.g. Ved. *pánca-daśa* = Lat. *quīndecim* = G. *fünfzehn* = En. *fifteen*; Ved. *pitā-putráu* 'father and son', OE *aþum-swerian* 'son-in-law and father-in-law', *suhtorfœ-dran* 'nephew and uncle', En. *bitter-sweet*, G. *taubstumm* 'deaf and dumb', G. *Baden-Württemberg*, En. *Eurasia*;

(4) *Bahuvrīhi* (possessive or exocentric compounds), e.g. Gk. *rhodo-dakty lo-s* '(having) rose-fingers', G. *barfuβ*, En. *barefoot, paleface*;

(5) Prepositional rectional compounds, e.g. Gk. *en-deos* '(having) a God in oneself', *ein-al-ios* '(living) in the sea';

(6) Imperative compounds, e.g. *Mene-laos* '(someone) leading the people', En. *pickpocket* (cf. fn. 14);

(7) *Dvigu*, e.g. G. *Dreieck* 'three corner', En. *one-step* (with a numeral as first constituent);

(8) Verbal and nominal compounds with adverbial first constituent, e.g. Lat. *ad-ire* 'go to' = Got. *at-gaggan*, *at-gagg* 'access', OS *up-himil* 'the heaven above', Gk. *peri-idein* 'look around' = Got. *fair-weitjan*; and

(9) Iterative compounds, e.g. Ved. *dyávi-dyavi* 'day by day', En. *goody-goody, black-black* 'very black'.

Obviously, these classes are based on heterogeneous criteria such as word-class membership of the constituents, internal structure, and headedness. On the basis of the latter, we can distinguish two categories, endocentric and exocentric compounds. With the former, the head is contained in the compound itself, and the compound as a whole refers to a referent specified by the head, as in the classes (1), (2), (8), that is, a *church-goer* is basically a *goer*, a *blackbird* is basically a *bird*, etc. With the latter, the compound implies some referent which is not directly referred to by one of the constituents, for example a *paleface* is not a *face*, but 'a person having a pale face', and *Eurasia* is neither a part of Europe nor of Asia, but an entity consisting of both Europe and Asia; this category includes the classes (3)–(7), and possibly (9). Such exocentric compounds are sometimes also treated as zero derivatives (e.g. Marchand 1969: 380–9; Kastovsky 1992a: 394f.; 2002; 2006b: 242).

---

[15] *Karmadhārayas* are sometimes treated as a separate category from the synthetic *tatpuruša*-compounds, and sometimes as a subcategory of *tatpuruša*, when this is used as a cover term for both synthetic compounds with a deverbal second member and simple N/A+N compounds, since both can be interpreted as determinative compounds (cf. Carr 1939: xxvff., Clackson 2002: 164f.).

[16] The term 'copulative' is misleading, since genuine *dvandvas* are additive and denote a combination of two entities where none is dominant, e.g. OE *aþum-swerian* 'son-in-law and father-in-law', which might be regarded as exocentric rather than endocentric (cf. Kastovsky 2006b: 229). The copulative type *girlfriend, oaktree*, on the other hand, sometimes wrongly subsumed under the *dvandva* class, is determinative, i.e. endocentric, and therefore belongs to the *karmadhāraya* type.

Let me now turn to the actual genesis of the various IE compound types, namely the shift from a syntactic to a morphological-lexical construction. The hypothesis that compounding is ultimately due to a univerbation process dates back to the early days of IE studies; the first to investigate this univerbation process in detail was Jacobi (1897), and his analysis is still valid in principle, despite some modifications as to the details.

Jacobi investigated the following compound types: simple and synthetic compounds (i.e. *karmadhārayas* and *tatpuruśas*), imperative compounds, and *bahuvrīhi*-compounds. He assumed that the ultimate source of these compound types (with the exception of the type *tabletop, blackbird*) were so-called proto-relative clauses in attributive function. These were syntactic structures resembling present-day relative clauses but lacking some of their essential features, such as relative pronouns, verbs inflected for person and number, and full-fledged nominal inflection, or at least nominative, accusative, and (optionally) genitive markers.

These embryonic relative clauses[17] occurred as adjectival pre- or post-posed appositions to the nominal head, and from this appositional function it was only a small step towards fusion into a compound. It is therefore not surprising that the early 'transformational' word-formation theories, which integrated word formation into syntax, tried to capture this relationship by invoking transformations which explicitly converted relative clauses into compounds. See Lees (1960), Marchand (1965a, b; 1969: 31–59), and for a more general theoretical discussion, Brekle and Kastovsky (1977), Kastovsky (1996b); incidentally, the more recent alternative Lexicalist approach invokes syntactic analogues as well (cf. Chomsky 1970; Lieber 1983; Roeper and Siegel 1978; Selkirk 1982).

For the *karmadhāraya* compounds (A+N and simple N+N), Jacobi assumed as starting point a simple attributive relation between the constituents, which was inflectionally unmarked. The underlying semantico-syntactic relation was expressed by position, that is, by the structure modifier+head. This may have been similar to the situation in Modern English, where ' *Black* ' *Sea*, ' *black* ' *market* are regarded as syntactic groups, and ' *black₁ bird*, ' *Englishman* as compounds because of the stress difference (see e.g. Marchand 1969: 22f.).[18] This also corresponds to the assumption that the semantic relation between the constituents of N+N

[17] More recently, these structures have been regarded as a kind of parenthetical clause (cf. Olsen 2002: 247, 249), but this is in fact not much different from Jacobi's embryonic relatives, which are also parenthetical.

[18] Whether there was a formal phonological difference accompanying the shift from a syntactic phrase to a compound, or whether it was just 'semantic isolation', postulated as the most important feature distinguishing compounds from syntactic groups by, e.g., Paul (1920: 328 ff.) or Carr (1939: xxiii), is not discussed by Jacobi, but cf. Meier-Brügger (2002: 295): 'Das neue Nomen erhält einen eigenen Akzent und eine neue Bedeutung' ('the new noun receives its own stress pattern and a new meaning'). The stress difference (left-hand stress for compounds vs. level or right-hand stress for syntactic groups) is not unproblematic, however: cf. Bauer (1983: 105), Giegerich (2004) and chapter 1 above.

compounds is a very general one, which cannot be identified with a specific syntactic relationship (e.g. place, origin, etc.); thus *Papierkorb* is to be interpreted as 'basket – prepositional function – paper', i.e. as 'basket which has something to do with paper', cf. Coseriu (1977: 50f.) and already Brugmann (1889: 83 ff.)

In a recent paper presented at the 40th SLE meeting this September, Brigitte Bauer (2007) investigated nominal apposition in Indo-European, and it would seem that this structure is the origin of the IE copulative compound subtype represented by E *oaktree, girlfriend*, for which Jacobi did not discuss a syntactic source. The structures involved include forms like *Zeus patēr* 'Zeus father' = 'father Zeus', Skr. *ágne bhrātah* 'Agni brother' = 'brother Agni', where the second part is an apposition that acts as a kind of epithet or explanation of the preceding noun, usually being more general than the first constituent, especially in those instances where the preceding noun is a name. These structures might be traced back to a proto-relative of the type 'x (who is) y', which is very much in line with Jacobi's theory. The fact that such formations are relatively rare in the older IE languages may have pragmatic reasons: such appositions were not really necessary and mainly served stylistic purposes.

These N+N compounds have become a salient feature of Sanskrit and Germanic word formation, whereas in other IE language families such as Latin and the Romance languages, Celtic or Slavic, they are marginal and are replaced by syntactic phrases, very often of N+P+N (*maison de campagne* vs. *country-house, Sommerhaus*) or Denominal-A+N (*lumière solaire* vs. *sunlight, Sonnenlicht*, but also *solar flare*) structures.

While the derivation of these compounds from a simple N/A+N construction would seem to be unproblematic since both constituents occur as independent lexemes represented by words (but cf. below for a different interpretation), the genesis of the synthetic compounds (the *tatpuruṣas* or 'verbale Rektionskomposita'), whose second constituent is deverbal and often does not occur outside the compound in question (cf. Uhlich 2002: 405–7), as in Lat. *arti-fex* 'craftsman', *armi-fer* 'weapon-carrier', Got. *arbi-numja* 'heir', En. *chimney-sweep, church-goer*, etc. is less straightforward. The modern examples are predominantly nouns, but according to Jacobi (1897: 13, 16), adjectival synthetic compounds were much more frequent in the earlier stages of IE than nouns, and he suggested that the nouns should be regarded as substantivized adjectives.[19] The function of these formations was to convert a verbal expression (verb+dependent nominal / adverbial complement) into a nominal, i.e. a process of syntactic recategorization (cf. Kastovsky 1982: 182 ff.). In the absence of genuine relative clauses, Jacobi suggested as source a participial construction functioning as attribute to a nominal head. This had a special type of participle, a 'relative participle', as the second part of the emerging

---

[19] Cf. also Olsen (2002: 248 ff.), Uhlich (2002: 405) and the genesis of the *bahuvrīhis* below, which is similar.

compound type, 'because the compounds containing them from a semantic point of view correspond to relative clauses, more specifically relative clauses which attribute an apparently important property to the person or object to which they relate, or they designate, in substantivized form, the person or object which is implied in the nominative relative pronoun of the corresponding explicit paraphrase' (Jacobi 1897: 21).[20] While genuine agent or action nouns can occur independently, such relative participles only occurred in compounds. They resembled present participles, and were indeed replaced by them in individual daughter languages, cf. Lat. *bene-volus*>*bene-volens*, G. *wohl-wollend* 'benevolent', OE *sweord-bora* 'sword bearer' vs. *reord-berend(-e)* 'speech bearer' = 'human being' = 'speech-bearing (PTPL)'. Thus the OE formations in *-end(-e)* often occur both as nominal (synthetic) agent nouns and as participles, e.g. *sæ-liðend(-e)* 'sea-farer' and 'sea-faring' (cf. Kärre 1915 and Carr 1939: 211–15).

Jacobi (1897: 23) assumed that the relative participle did not imply any temporal specification but was generic, as befits compounds, whereas the present participle was temporally related to the tense of the main verb, as befits syntactic constructions. In this generic function, the noun + relative participle construction, though basically a syntactic recategorization, could also be used for naming, i.e. for creating epithets, the main function of lexical items, which explains the shift from a purely syntactic to a lexical unit and its nominalization as an agent or action noun. Both were thus substitutes for relative clauses, which according to Jacobi only emerged when the language developed a relative pronoun.[21]

The earliest structures seem to contain root-based deverbal derivatives (agent and action nouns) of the type Lat. *iu-dex* 'judge'<*iu-dik-s* 'who speaks the law', Gk. *boo-kleps* 'cattle-thief'<*klep-* 'stealing', Ved. *havir-ád-* 'eating the oblation', Skr. *veda-vid-* 'veda-knower, veda-knowing', etc. Olsen (2002: 249) traces these nominal forms back to adjectival (possessive) structures like 'vedic (is his) knowledge' = '(having) veda-knowledge', which are parallel to the structures underlying the *bahuvrīhis*, cf. below. In the Germanic languages, these compounds were usually characterized by the stem-formatives *-an-* and *-jan-*, cf. OE *sæ-lid-a* 'sea-farer', *yrfe-num-a* 'heir-taker, heir', *beag-gif-a* 'ring-giver'; Got. *arbi-num-ja* 'heir-taker, heir', OE *wæl-cyrge* 'who chooses the dead, valkyrie'. From there, the extension to suffixal derivatives in *-er(-)* for agent nouns, and *-ung/-ing* and other

---

[20] 'weil die mit ihnen gebildeten Composita inhaltlich Relativsätzen entsprechen und zwar solchen, die eine irgendwie wichtige Eigenschaft derjenigen Person oder Sache beilegen, auf welche sie sich beziehen, oder auch substantiviert diese Person oder Sache bezeichnen, welche immer in dem auflösenden Relativsatz durch das Pron. rel. im Nom. angedeutet wird'

[21] The fact that IE daughter languages can be subdivided on the basis of a relative pronoun isogloss *$k^{ho}is$/*$k^{ho}it^h$ vs. *yos/*yot^h (Gamkrelidze and Ivanov 1995: 339) indicates that indeed the development of relative pronouns took place during or after the first split of IE into daughter languages, i.e. after the development of these synthetic compounds, which are older than this split.

action-denoting suffixal derivatives was not difficult. And today such synthetic formations are extremely productive in all Germanic languages.

Another structure, discussed fairly controversially in the literature, is the exocentric compound type V+N, as in En. *pickpocket*, Gk. *Mene-laos* '(someone) leading the people', *phere-oikos* '(something) carrying a house along = snail', etc. (cf. Petersen 1914/15; Marchand 1969: 380 ff.), sometimes treated as inverted *tatpuruṣas* or imperative compounds (cf. note 14). With these, the first constituent seems to be verbal, but according to Osthoff (1878), who rejects the possibility of a verbal stem occurring as a determinant in a nominal compound in general, it had originally been a verbal noun, which only subsequently was reinterpreted as a verb. This had indeed been the case with the more recent Germanic type En. *whetstone*, G. *Schreibtisch* 'desk' – lit. 'write-table' which, however, has to be kept apart from this older type and belongs to the determinative type (cf. Carr 1939: 175 ff.).[22] Jacobi (1897: 52 ff.; cf. also Schindler 1997: 539), however, convincingly argues for the interpretation of the first part as an uninflected verbal stem. He assumes that such constructions go back to a stage when the verb was not yet obligatorily inflected for person and number in the third person but could occur as a bare stem, i.e. as a word. Moreover, while the synthetic compounds are traced back to attributively used preposed relative clauses (or parenthetical sentences), the *pickpocket* type evolved from a postposed appositive proto-relative clause, linked to the preceding noun by an *apo koinou* construction, i.e. one without a relative pronoun, where the subject of the proto-relative was coreferential with the nominal antecedent (Jacobi 1897: 55). This assumption is supported by the widespread existence of such constructions in the Germanic languages (cf. ModE *There's a man wants to see you*). An alternative interpretation as 'imperative compounds' (Darmesteter 1894: 168–234) is problematic in view of the late development of verbal inflection and is therefore rejected by Schindler (1997: 539; cf. also already Jacobi 1897: 73). This does not mean that a later reinterpretation along these lines might not have taken place, and modern formations such as *forget-me-not*, G. *Rühr-mich-nicht-an* 'don't touch me' seem indeed to be more readily interpreted as imperative constructions. The type itself is not too frequent in the early IE daughter languages, but is found more frequently in the later stages. The reason seems to be its colloquial status (cf. already Jacobi 1897: 73), e.g. in the function of nick-naming, which would not have made it into written records. Formations become very frequent in the emerging Romance languages and it is therefore sometimes assumed that the English type *pickpocket*, which begins to show up in early Middle English (there are no Old English examples), was influenced by French (cf. Fr. *coupe-gorge* = En. *cut-throat*, Fr. *coupe-bourse* = En. *cut-purse* from

---

[22] Note that in English this type is now rivalled by the type *writing table*, *swimming pool*, which resulted from the replacement of the participial *-ende* by *-ing*, leading to a formal merger of OE *-ung* / *-ing* action nouns and the participle, with a concomitant reinterpretation of the *-ing* forms as being equivalent to bare verbs, i.e. a functional equivalence of the types *whetstone* and *writing table*.

the twelfth and thirteenth centuries). But in view of German names such as *Fürchtegott* 'fear God', *Habedank* 'have thanks' going back to Middle High German where French influence was negligible (cf. also Carr 1939: 170–4), this does not seem likely. Rather, as Jacobi had suggested, the type had been part of spoken language and only surfaced in written language when spoken features entered written texts, probably in connection with name-giving.

The fourth group of IE compounds discussed by Jacobi are the *bahuvrīhi* compounds (*bahuvrīhi* 'having much rice'), which he also traced back to relative clause structures. More recent studies on IE word-formation, especially compounding, have suggested that this was perhaps the most important type for the genesis of compounds in Indo-European. IE *bahuvrīhis* occur both as adjectives and nouns. According to Brugmann (1889: 87), the type originated as regular A+N or N+N compounds (i.e. as *karmadhārayas*), which then 'mutated' into possessive adjectives with the meaning 'being / having x', and possessive nouns meaning 'someone who is / has x', by metonymic extension. This implies that *bahuvrīhis* would be younger than the 'unmutated' A/N+N compounds. Jacobi (1897: 84f.) argued, however, that the *bahuvrīhis* were as old as the other compounds or even older, and therefore rejected the mutation hypothesis. Instead, he again posited derivation from an *apo koinou* restrictive proto-relative structure, i.e. one without a relative pronoun, where the implied verbs *be* or *have* were missing (Jacobi 1897: 87 ff.). This lack of a verbal predicate facilitated the univerbation process.[23] Thus the adjective function would have been basic and the nominal function originated from the nominalization of the adjective. In view of the preponderance of adjectival *bahuvrīhis* in the older IE languages, this hypothesis is today generally accepted. See for example Schindler (1997: 537), who even suggests that the *tatpuruṣas*, too, go back to such possessive compounds, where the second constituent is a verbal noun stem, e.g. Gk. *taxy-bamōn* 'having fast strides' > 'striding fast'; cf. also Bader (1962: 127–30) and Uhlich (2002: 406) and the history of the *pickpocket*-type above.

Historically, the development thus was adjectival > substantival *bahuvrīhi*, but it is interesting to note that in the Germanic languages the relationship came to be reversed (cf. e.g. Kastovsky 2002). Thus, adjectival *bahuvrīhis* have basically died out except for a few relics like En. *barefoot*, G. *barfuß*, whereas the nominal *bahuvrīhis* of the *paleface* type have become very productive, especially as epithets. The adjectival *bahuvrīhis* have been superseded by the 'extended' *bahuvrīhis*, which are characterized by adjectival suffixes such as -*ed*, e.g. *hunchbacked*<*hunchback*, or -*ig*, e.g. G. *dickköpfig* 'pig-headed'<*Dickkopf*, overtly marking the word-class membership as adjectival, a process which had already started in OE and OHG.

---

[23] Cf. also Olsen (2002: 247) on the origin of *rhodo-daktylo-s*: 'This state of affairs is traditionally explained by means of a sort of sentence parentheses or relative clause of the type "a rose is the finger" or, in Schindler's interpretation "with finger a rose"'.

In this connection, another IE compound type should be mentioned which fits into this pattern, namely the prepositional rectional compounds, e.g. Gk. *en-deos* '(having) a God in oneself'. These are similar to the *bahuvrīhis* in that they represent a phrase which describes a characteristic feature of the head outside the phrase, except that in this case the phrase denotes a locative relation represented by a preposition and a noun, and not a property represented by an A/N+N structure. But as with the regular *bahuvrīhis*, the morphologically unmarked (or morphological zero) structure eventually came to be marked overtly by the addition of an adjectival suffix (cf. Lat. *sub-urb-an-us, cis-alp-in-us*, etc.) which has – as a loan pattern – become very productive in the modern language, cf. *trans-atlantic, pro-communist, anti-smoking campaign*, etc.

So far I have looked at nominal and adjectival compounds. There were of course also verbal compounds, but these were basically restricted to combinations of verbal roots with particles (adverbs, prepositions), parallel to nominal compounds occurring with adverbial/prepositional first members. Nominal stems as modifiers of verbal stems apparently did not occur in early IE, and only rarely in the daughter languages (cf. forms such as Lat. *patefacere* 'to open', lit. 'open-make', *anim-advertere* 'notice'<'turn the mind to', *vendere*<*venum dare* 'to sell'<'to give to sale'; OE *geþanc-metian* 'deliberate' = 'measure one's thought', *morgen-wacian* 'wake early'; G. *rad-fahren* 'to bike' = 'bike-drive', which represent univerbations). But recently, this type has become rather popular in Modern English as a result of the reinterpretation of denominal back-formations such as *stage-manage* 'act as stage-manager'<*stage-manager, proofread* 'do proof-reading'<*proof-reading* (Marchand 1969: 104–5), which formed the basis for analogical formations such as *machine-translate, thought-read, carpet-bomb, hull walk* (< *walk the hull), flash-freeze, quick-march, quick-frost*, etc. This pattern thus seems to be a typological innovation in that it verges on incorporation, that is, a syntactic complement of the verb is morphologically incorporated into a verbal compound. Another recent innovation are V+V compounds of the type *think-hiss, glide-walk, kick-start, strip-search*.

Compounds consisting of an adverb/preposition and a verb or noun probably also originated from a univerbation process in IE, and the cohesion between the particle and the verb was – at least in the beginning – rather loose, which is still reflected by the distinction between so-called 'separable' and 'inseparable' verbs in the Germanic languages, cf. OE, *under'standan* 'understand' and *'under, standan* 'stand under', or ModG *'über, setzen* 'to cross a river' (*Er setzte 'über*) vs., *über'setzen* 'to translate' (*Er' über'setzte*). Some of these preverbs eventually developed into prefixes, e.g. *be-* (*befall, benumb*), *ver-* (*verspielen* 'gamble away', *vertrinken* 'squander on drink'), but in English many of these ended up as parts of phrasal verbs such as *go out, eat out, eat up, use up, look up*, etc. Formations such as En. *outdo, outbid, overlook, overbid, underestimate* are intermediate between compounds and prefixations. Marchand (1969: 96 ff.) treats them as compound verbs, but in view of the

semantic behaviour of the preverbs, which have basically lost their locative meaning, an analysis as prefixal verbs might be more appropriate.

There is one interesting phonological problem with preparticle verbs (verbs
combined with an adverb or preposition as first constituent) and the corresponding nouns. In the Germanic languages, there is a general tendency for the nouns to
have the main stress on the particle (e.g. G. 'Ur₁ laub 'leave of absence', OE 'bi₁ gang
'worship$_N$') and the verbs to have the main stress on the verbal base, the prepar-
ticle/prefix being unstressed (e.g. G er'lauben 'to allow', OE beˈgangan 'to worship').
This has usually been explained by assuming that the verbal formations are
younger than the nominal ones and had only come into being in the Germanic
languages after the general fixing of stress on the first (= root) syllable, whereas the
nominal formations were already Indo-European and therefore underwent the
stress placement on the first syllables. But in view of the fact that combinations
with adverbs/prepositions and verbs also occur in other IE languages, this hypothesis is somewhat problematic. In a paper presented at the 5th SHEL Conference in
Athens, Georgia (October 2007), Donka Minkova proposed an alternative, very
plausible explanation, which assumes that both nominal and verbal formations
existed already in Indo-European, and that the stress difference was related to
syntactic stress. Since both verbal and nominal combinations originated in univerbation and for a long time must have been rather free collocations, it was their
syntactic function that determined stress, and not the general fixing of lexical stress
on the first syllable. The origin of the Germanic verb/noun stress opposition thus
was independent of the general stress development and reflected Germanic syntactic stress patterns, where nouns and verbs in combination with preposed
adverbs behaved differently.

16.4 CONCLUSION

As this survey has shown, compounding in IE had a syntactic origin: it goes back to
the progressive univerbation and concomitant lexicalization of syntactic phrases,
which were used attributively. The most important role seems to have been played
by the adjectival *bahuvrīhis* which apparently represented the oldest layer of
compounds; the *karmadhārayas*, *tatpuruṣas*, and the nominal *bahuvrīhis* as well
as the nominal *pickpocket*-type are younger and also ultimately have an adjectival
origin with subsequent nominalization. This hypothesis is neatly summarized by
Olsen:

it would be possible to envisage the compositional type as being derived from two basic
patterns: on one hand the synchronically transparent juxtapositions or 'co-compounds' like

the dvandvas and the case compounds, basically with two accents, on the other sentence parentheses consisting of an accented predicate and unaccented headword, leading to possessives and verbal governing compounds, whether ending in a simple zero grade root noun, one extended by *-t- (the type of Skt. -jit, -stut, -kr̥t etc.) as would seem to be regular after vocalic sonants and perhaps laryngeals, or a verbal noun of the *bʰoró's-type

(Olsen 2002: 249)

PART II

CHAPTER 17

....

TYPOLOGY OF COMPOUNDS

....

LAURIE BAUER

17.1 SOME PRELIMINARIES

....

In this chapter, I will first review some of the parameters along which compounds may vary and then consider the extent to which observing such variation brings us closer to a typology of compounds.

17.1.1 The universality of compounding

Compounding is usually defined, perhaps rather loosely, as the creation of words made up of two independent words (see e.g. Katamba 1994: 264; Plag 2003: 5). We have to understand 'word' in any such definition as meaning 'lexeme' (i.e. 'word' in the sense that *come, comes, coming, came* are all forms of the same 'word'), and also understand that the definition does not necessarily imply the presence of the citation form of the constituent lexemes in the compound. For example, the Latin compound *tridens* 'trident' has as its elements *tres* 'three' and *dens* 'tooth', yet the full form of only one of these appears in the citation form of the compound. However, on the basis of such a definition we would probably agree that the English

I should like to thank the editors and Salvador Valera for their helpful comments on earlier drafts of this chapter.

words *blackboard, ballpoint,* and *to freeze-dry* are compounds, and that is sufficient to allow a discussion to begin.

Compounding is sometimes (e.g. Fromkin et al. 1996: 54–5; Libben 2006: 2) suggested as a language universal. It certainly seems to be easy to learn for children acquiring languages which contain compounds (Clark 1993, but see also Berman, this volume) and also to be a phenomenon which is widespread in pidgins (Plag 2006a). Both of these seem compatible with a claim of universality. At the same time, grammars of individual languages not uncommonly claim that compounding is rare or unknown in that language (Nedjalkov 1997: 308 on Evenki; Fortescue 2004: 1394 on West Greenlandic; Zamponi, this volume). While the rarity of a phenomenon in any given language might not contradict a claim to universality, the lack of it certainly seems to. Even harder to deal with, perhaps, are descriptions of language from which it is not clear whether or not the language in question contains compounds. Consider a specific example.

Refsing's (1986) description of Ainu (a language isolate from Japan) does not talk of compounds at all. Neither does Shibatani's (1990) description. There are, however, a number of constructions which seem to have a similar function, some of which could no doubt have been called compounds. For instance, Ainu allows nominal attributives as in (1):

(1) *atuy asam*   bottom sea   'sea bottom'
     mosem apa   pole entrance   'entrance pole'
     kamuy napuri   mountain god   'holy mountain'
     supuya kur   trace smoke   'traces of smoke'

                                        (Refsing 1986: 160)

There are also various items termed 'postpositions' that are used to mark nouns as being attributive, as in the examples in (2):

(2) *rep un kurutar* open.sea's people 'foreigners'
     okkay ne po   man be child   'boy'
     cise kor nispa house have man   'head of the household'

                                        (Refsing 1986: 160–2)

Ainu also has incorporation, often included as a type of compounding, though the distinct semantic patterns shown by incorporation and determinative compounds usually lead to the two being treated differently in languages which have both. According to Shibatani (1990: 61–2), Ainu has direct-object incorporation, subject incorporation (where the subject is not an agent), and (Shibatani 1990: 72) adverb incorporation, as in (3):

(3) *cise-kar-as*   house-make-1PL.EX   'we made a home'
     sir-pirka   weather-good   'it is fine'
     a-tokyo-kikkik   1SG-thoroughly-beat   'I beat him up thoroughly'

So does Ainu have compounds or not? The answer is partly a matter of definition, partly a matter of analysis. But it is clear that straightforward claims for the
universality of compounding need to be taken with at least a grain of salt.

17.1.2 Compounds as words

Lieber and Štekauer (this volume) also point out that the definition of word is
fraught with problems. Since part of the definition of compounds is frequently that
they are single words, this adds to the problems of defining compounds. There may
be orthographic, phonological, morphological, syntactic, or semantic ways of
defining what a word is, and some of these will be reinterpreted in later discussion
here as ways of being sure that we are dealing with compounds. Again, this
indicates some of the problems in providing a good typology of compounding.

17.2 FORMAL MARKING OF COMPOUNDS

17.2.1 Phonological marking

Compounds are often differentiated from phrases by having the phonological
structure of single words. In a language like English, the stress pattern in compounds is often seen as indicating compound status (though see Bauer 1998b for a
dissenting view); in a language like Chukchi, vowel harmony may indicate that the
compound behaves phonologically as a single word (though there are many
languages with vowel harmony where compounds behave as two words in this
respect: Finnish and Turkish are examples).

In other instances, there may be phonological marking of compounds which is
rather more specific. In Bambara (a Mande language of West Africa), compounds
are treated just like derivatives in terms of their tonal patterns, showing only two
patterns: either all syllables have a high tone or, if the first syllable has a low tone, all
subsequent tones become high (Creissels 2004: 30–1). This is independent of the
lexical tone associated with later syllables. Thus *sàga sògo* 'sheep meat' means 'the
meat of the sheep', and is a syntactic construction, while *sàgasogo* (with high tones
on the last three syllables) is a compound, and means 'sheep-meat, mutton'. In
Fongbe (Lefebvre and Brousseau 2002: 224) there are also tonal sandhi phenomena
which are restricted to compounds.

The Japanese morphophonemic process called *rendaku* specifically marks compounds. In native Japanese compounds which are not coordinative (see 17.6.2) the
initial voiceless obstruent in the second element of a compound becomes voiced

(subject to certain other conditions, see Rosen 2003). So a sequence of *kuti* 'mouth' and *kuse* 'habit' gives *kutiguse* 'way of speaking', and *ike* 'arrange' and *hana* 'flower' together give *ikebana* 'flower arranging'.

17.2.2 Linking elements

Many languages have some kind of linking element between the two parts of a compound. Typically, whatever its etymological source, this element is semantically empty. A nice example is provided by a German word *Liebe·s·lied* 'love·LE·song'. While the linking elements in Germanic compounds in general derive from genitive and plural markers, and the suffix *-s* can be found in German with either of those meanings (genitive in *Das Auto mein·es Bruder·s* 'the car my·GEN brother·GEN', and plural in *die Auto·s* 'the(PL) car·PL'). However, neither of these morphs could occur following *Liebe*, since it is the wrong gender to allow an *s*-genitive and the wrong declension to allow an *s*-plural. The link in *Liebeslied* is thus simply that, and cannot be related to any other inflectional form. Greek, Khmer, Kuku Yalanji (North Queensland), Russian, Slave, and possibly Maori and Telugu are other languages with linking elements, or interfixes.

17.2.3 Internal inflection

The prototypical compound is simply the collocation of two unmarked lexemes, and, of course, in many languages in which there is no inflection, this is all that is possible. Even in inflecting languages, however, this seems to be an expected pattern. In Russian, for example, words patterned like *sport·klub* 'sports club' form an increasing number of compounds (Ward 1965: 144), and in Estonian we find words like *õlg-katus* 'straw roof' = 'thatched roof'.

However, in languages with inflection, there is always the possibility that one or more of the elements of a compound will contain its own inflection, independent of the inflection which is added to the compound as a whole to indicate its function in its matrix sentence. The most usual case here is that the modifying element carries some compound-internal inflection, while the head carries the inflection for the compound as a unit. What is crucial here is that the internal inflection does not vary as a function of the compound's role in its matrix sentence.

Various types of internal inflection are attested, depending on the word-class of the modifying element in the compound. Where the modifier is a noun, for example, it is common to find some case and/or number inflection on it. So Estonian, which we have seen has uninflected modifiers, also has instances like *riisi-puder* 'rice(GEN)-porridge', and Yimas marks the modifying element with an oblique case marker, as in *turuk·n namarawt* 'magic·OBL person'='magician'

(Foley 1991: 280). Some languages have more complex compounds with modifiers inflected for locative cases. Sanskrit allows these, as does Finnish, an example being *hattituksessa·olo·aika* 'government-in·existence·time'='period in government' (Karlsson 1999: 242). Under conditions which are difficult to specify, English appears to allow some plurals in modifying position (e.g. *suggestions box*), although it disallows plural modifiers elsewhere (e.g. *trouser-press*, not **trousers-press*, even though *trouser* is rarely attested outside the special register of tailoring). Examples such as *school concert* versus *schools concert* seem to imply that this is determined by the singularity/plurality of the entity denoted by the modifier, but such a conclusion is not necessarily supported by examples such as *sportsman* and *car-ferry*.

In some cases the inflection may take the form of a separate particle, as in Tamashek *tefæltelt ən bətˤron* 'lamp POSS gasoline'='gas-lamp' (Heath 2005: 263). Such cases look like the French *pomme de terre* 'apple of earth'='potato', which some scholars would treat as lexicalized syntactic phrases rather than as instances of word formation (Bauer 2001b).

Where verbs are concerned, these may appear in the stem-form (as in German *Trink·wasser* 'drink·water'='drinking water'; the infinitive of the verb is *trinken*), in the infinitive (as in the Danish equivalent *drikke·vand*), in a participial form (perhaps as in English, e.g. *drinking water*; several Dravidian languages have a class of verbal compounds with a past participle in the first element, like Tamil *kaṇṭu·piṭi* 'seen·grasp'='find'), or in some other form. For instance, there is much discussion in the literature as to what the form of the verb in French compounds like *porte-manteau* 'carry-coat'='coat hanger' really is, with many concluding that it is an imperative form. Only rarely are finite forms of verbs found inside compounds, though Hebrew has compounds like *gored shexakim* ('scrapes heights'='sky scraper') where the verbal element is ambiguous between a finite verb and a participle. In Kashmiri co-synonymic coordinative compounds, both elements seem to take tense inflection (*she:ra:npə:ra:n* 'decorate(PRST) decorate (PRST)'='is decorating') (Wali and Koul 1997).

Of these various patterns, only the instance where two unmarked words occur side-by-side is prototypically seen as being a compound; the other cases are usually classified as compounds because they otherwise behave like stem+stem compounds, or because, for other reasons, they appear to act as words.

Although inflection on the non-head element in a compound is usually constant in all forms of the compound's paradigm, there are instances where the non-head agrees with the head, as in Italian *mezza·luna* ('half·moon') plural *mezze·lune*, or *cassa·forte* ('box·strong'='safe'), plural *casse·forti* (Maiden and Robustelli 2000: 31; note the variable order of head and modifier in these examples). There is variation between *capo·cuochi*, with invariable first element, and *capi·cuochi*, with plural first element, as the plural of *capo·cuocho* ('head·chef') (Maiden and Robustelli 2000: 32).

17.3 HEADEDNESS

If we consider a simple compound consisting of just two elements like *flagpole*, we can say that the element *pole* is the more important of the two elements in a number of ways:

- A flagpole is a type of pole, not a type of flag; thus *flagpole* is a hyponym of *pole*, and *pole* is a superordinate term (or hypernym) for *flagpole*.
- It follows from this that in any situation in which we can use *flagpole*, we could use *pole*, but we could not use *flag* without changing the meaning. In other words, *pole* is obligatory in the construction *flagpole*.

This more important element in the construction is called the head of the construction, and if we look at a wider range of examples, we will find that there are other factors which help determine headedness or which tend to correlate with headedness.

Consider, for example, the word *grass-green*. *Green* is the head, because *grass-green* is a hyponym of *green* and because *green* is the obligatory element in the compound. But this is also related to the fact that *green* is an adjective, while *grass* is a noun. Although it will not always be the case, it tends to be true that compound adjectives have adjectival heads, and that compound nouns have nominal heads, and so on. That is, because of the hyponymy in compounds, the compound as an entity tends to belong to the same word-class as its head.

Next, consider the German compound *Hand·schuh* ('hand·shoe'='glove'). *Hand* is a feminine noun in German, and *Schuh* is a masculine noun. The gender of the compound *Handschuh* derives from the gender of the head of the compound, so that *Handschuh* is masculine. Masculine nouns in German can make their plurals according to a number of different patterns:

(4) *Dorn*   *Dornen*   'thorn'
     Stuhl   *Stühle*   'chair'
     Punkt   *Punkte*   'point'
     Wald   *Wälder*   'forest'

Because the plural of *Schuh* is *Schuhe*, the plural of *Handschuh* is *Handschuhe*. That is, the inflectional class of the compound as an entity follows from the inflectional class of its head. This may seem obvious, but there are exceptions such as English *to grandstand* having the past tense *grandstanded* and not *grandstood – and while this counterexample is usually said to exist because it is derived from the noun *grandstand* rather than direct from *grand* and *stand*, it makes the point that we cannot make assumptions about what is possible.

Note also that if we put the lexeme HANDSCHUH into a sentence such as 'the moths were in the gloves' *Die Motten waren in den Handschuhen*, the inflection for the dative case goes on the end of the head element, not on the modifying element.

There are compounds which may not have an obvious head. The English form *singer-songwriter*, for instance, does not have a head whose identity can be discovered by hyponymy: only the position of the external inflection may give us a clue as to which element is treated as the head in English. The French noun *porte-feuille* ('carry-leaf'='wallet') is masculine, even though the only noun element in the construction, *feuille*, is feminine. Words like this French example are sometimes said not to be headed, or to be exocentric, that is, to have their head or centre outside the construction itself.

17.4 THE ORDER OF ELEMENTS IN COMPOUNDS

We might expect headed compounds to show a regular order of head element and modifying element in any given language, that is to be either head-initial or head-final. Dutch is often cited as an example of a language which is regularly head-final. Maori is a language which appears to have head-initial compounds in productive formations. However, Bauer (2001b: 697) reports that in a sample of thirty-six languages, almost half had variable head–modifier order (more, if compound adjectives and compound verbs were considered as well as compound nouns). Furthermore, there seems to be an overall preference for right-headedness, even when the order of attributive adjective and noun is left-headed (Bauer 2001b). This could be related to the fact that left-headed compounds with inflection marked on their heads will have internal inflection; Maori is a language with virtually no inflection, and so the question seldom arises there. In Kisi (Atlantic) in some compounds the suffix of the first (head) noun is placed after the second (modifying) noun so that the compound as a whole appears to carry the external inflection:

(5) bɔlɔ·ó +   màlù·'ŋ   ⇒   bɔlɔ̀ŋ·màlù·ó
     bag·SUFF   rice·SUFF   bag PRON·rice·SUFF='rice bag'

(Childs 1995: 210)

(The suffixes are often homophonous with or related to pronouns and reflect noun classes.)

Some of the languages that display both orders of modifier and head have conflicting traditions passed down from different etymological sources. This is true of Vietnamese, for example, which has a native left-headed tradition and a Chinese right-headed tradition. A similar effect is found in Javanese, with a native Javanese pattern of modifier following the head, and a borrowed Sanskrit pattern of the modifier preceding the head (Ogloblin 2005). It is not clear how often such factors play an important role in the order of elements.

17.5 RECURSION IN COMPOUNDS

In the Germanic languages, compound structures are recursive: that is, a compound can be an element in another compound. For example, we can have a compound *notice board*, and another *Architecture School*. We can complicate the second to give *Auckland [Architecture School]*, and then complicate it again to give *[[[Auckland] [Architecture School]] [Library]]*, and then we can put all this together to give the attested form *Auckland Architecture School library notice board*. It is typical of such cases that they can be analysed as a series of binary structures, that is, every step along the way makes a division between two elements, although some of those elements contain several smaller elements. Although such constructions seem to be potentially unlimited, in practice any string of more than about five elements is very unusual in German (Fleischer 1975: 82) or English.

It has been suggested that recursion is one of the defining elements of compounds, but there appear to be languages which do not permit recursion, including Slovak (Štekauer and Valera 2007), and others such as Fongbe (Lefebvre and Brousseau 2002: 227) and Ngiti (Sudanic) (Lojenga 1994: 162–3) where recursion is extremely limited. We do not have sufficient information to see whether recursion or lack of recursion in compounds is the default, or whether either of these correlates with any other feature of compounding, though it would be something worth checking.

17.6 THE SEMANTICS OF COMPOUNDS

17.6.1 Endocentric versus exocentric

We have already seen section 17.3 that there may be grammatical reasons for distinguishing between endocentric compounds (compounds whose head or centre is one of the elements in the compound) and exocentric compounds (which are not hyponyms of either element of the compound). But while this distinction may have grammatical implications, it is, as expressed here at any rate, fundamentally a semantic distinction. There seem to be languages which allow only endocentric (e.g. Bahasa Indonesia: Štekauer and Valera 2007)[1] or only exocentric (e.g. Turkana: Dimmendaal 1983: 292) compounds.

The distinction between endocentric and exocentric is frequently drawn, and sometimes the term 'exocentric' is used as being equivalent to the Sanskrit term *bahuvrīhi*, while on other occasions *bahuvrīhi* compounds are seen as a subset of exocentrics. *Bahuvrīhi* literally means 'having much rice' and hence 'one who has much rice' and is an example of the type of compound it names; such compounds are sometimes called 'possessive compounds'. But a compound like *pickpocket* is an exocentric compound without being a possessive compound. It is suggested in Bauer (2008a) that possessive compounds are not really exocentric at all: rather they are synecdochic uses of headed compounds. In an example like English *greenshank* (type of sandpiper), it is quite clear that *green* modifies *shank*, since the bird denoted is one with green legs, and thus we seem to have a standard modifier–head construction. But the word as a whole is the name of one part of the bird used to refer to the whole, just as the *crown* can be used to refer to the monarchy. This is simply a figurative reading of the expression *greenshank*. It has nothing to do with there being a special kind of compound. Indeed, were it not for the stress, we might even query whether *greenshank* is a compound.

As is pointed out by Bisetto and Scalise (2005, this volume), the endocentric/exocentric distinction cross-cuts other distinctions drawn here.

17.6.2 Coordinative compounds

Coordinative compounds are those whose elements can be interpreted as being joined by 'and'. Some of these, but not all, fall under the heading of *dvandva* compounds. Two recent classifications of these compounds exist, with a large degree of overlap: those given by Wälchli (2005) and Bauer (2008b). A classification based on those two sources is presented in Table 17.1, with examples from a number of languages.

None of the types in Table 17.1 seems to be freely distributed through the languages of the world, even if we consider that almost any of the types illustrated can be found as nouns, adjectives, or verbs and sometimes adverbs. Coordinative compounds (sometimes under different labels, such as co-compounds, aggregative compounds, coordinate compounds, or copulative compounds) seem to be common in Eastern Asia and Southern Asia, becoming less common as we move westward across the Eurasian landmass, but rare in Africa, in the Americas, or in Australia. However, it is not sufficient simply to class these all together as a single

---

[1] I should like to thank Pavol Štekauer for making available to me his data file on compounding in a number of languages.

Table 17.1 Types of coordinative compound

Type	Subtype	Sub-subtype	Language	Example	Translation
Translative			French	[vol] Paris–Rome 'P–R [flight]'	'Paris–Rome flight'
Co-participant			German	russisch-türkischer [Krieg] 'Russian-Turkish [war]'	'Russo-Turkish'
Appositional			Dutch	eigenaar-directeur 'owner-director'	
Compromise			English	blue-green	
Generalizing			Mordvin	t'ese-toso 'here there'	'everywhere'
Dvandva					
	Additive				
		Family ties	Mlabri	mɤʔmɤm 'mother father'	'parents'
		Proper names	Hungarian	Budapest	
		Others	Sanskrit	ajāváyaḥ 'sheep goats'	'sheep and goats'
	Co-hyponymic		Vietnamese	ăn-uống 'eat drink'	'get nourishment'
	Co-synonymic		Mandarin	měi-li 'beautiful beautiful'	'beautiful'
	Approximate		Hmong	ob peb 'two three'	'some, a few'
	Exocentric		Khmer	khɔh trɤw 'wrong right'	'morality'

group, since the 'mother + father=parents' group seems no longer to be found as far west as that would imply, and the exocentric 'wrong + right=morality' seems to be even more restricted. On the other hand, the compromise type seems not to be found in South-East Asia (perhaps because of the potential ambiguity of forms as being exocentric or compromise compounds). Wälchli (2005) illustrates the higher use of coordinative compounds in general in the east than in the west of the Eurasian landmass, and much of the difference seems to lie in the greater use of co-synonymic compounds in languages like Vietnamese than in languages from further west. However, this does not correlate with any degree of analycity in languages like Vietnamese, because Polynesian and other isolating languages do not show the same use of co-synonymic compounds.

17.6.3 'Variable R' and endocentric compounds

Allen (1978) talks about the variable relationship between the two elements of an endocentric compound in English, and coins the term 'Variable R' for this well-known phenomenon. For instance, a sun cream blocks the sun('s rays), a face cream is applied to the face, a hormone cream contains hormones, and a rash cream is to cure the rash. This is often taken to imply that a compound represents the neutralization of several semantic relationships. How many relationships are involved is an open question. Granville Hatcher (1960) suggests four, Levi (1978) suggests about a dozen, Brekle (1970) suggests over one hundred, at the finest level of analysis. These particular suggestions are all based on the analysis of English, though similar suggestions have been made for other Germanic languages, at least. It is not clear whether such semantic variability is universally a feature of endocentric compounds, or whether Germanic languages provide some kind of extreme in this regard. It seems, for example, that while Classical Nahuatl illustrates a variable relationship between the elements of the compound, it does not permit such a wide range of meanings as English or Thai (Launey 2004; Fasold 1969). We do not have enough information to be able to tell whether there is any implicational relationship holding between such meanings such that the existence of an agentive reading will presuppose the existence of a locative reading, for example. However, locative readings do seem to be widespread in Germanic (Bauer 1978) and frequent in other languages that have compounds.

17.6.4 'Synthetic' compounds

Although many endocentric compounds show the kind of semantic ambiguity that is implicit in any analysis which sees the relationship between the elements as being underspecified, there is one type that is much more tightly constrained semantically. These are variously termed 'synthetic compounds' or 'verbal-nexus compounds'. In these compounds, the base in the head element is a verb, and the modifying element in the compound is interpreted as an argument of that verb. English examples are *bus-driver, mountain-climbing*, and *home-made*. There is a great deal of variation in the literature as to precisely what is classified as a synthetic compound. For some authorities, only the three affixes/processes illustrated can form synthetic compounds, so that while *home-maintaining* is a synthetic compound, *home-maintenance* is not.

There is also disagreement about precisely what arguments of the verb are permitted in the different kinds of synthetic compound. In the *bus-driver* type, where the subject role of the verb is filled by the -*er* suffix, the default pattern is for the modifying element to denote the direct object of the verb (so that *bus-driver* correlates with *someone drives the bus*). Forms like *cliffhanger, faith-healer,* and *town-crier* are thus either unusual types or not synthetic compounds at all, but primary compounds (sometimes unhelpfully termed 'root' compounds) just like *sheep-skin*. It is occasionally possible to find a compound which may have two possible readings along these lines, though actual misunderstanding is rare.

The *mountain-climbing* type is just like the *bus-driver* type in having a default reading in which the modifier is the direct object of the verb. In *mountain-climbing*, however, the subject-role is left unexpressed, and the focus is on the action. This again leaves unclear the status of examples like *consumer spending*, in which the modifier denotes the subject of the verb, or *sun-bathing*, where the modifier denotes the location of the action.

The *home-made* type is semantically more complex. This allows readings with subjects in the modifier (*man-made*) and with locations in the modifier (*home-made*), but only rarely with direct objects in the modifier (*heart-broken* – even that example is not clear since *heart* could be the subject as well as the object of *break*).

The major question here is whether synthetic compounds provide a definable separate set of compounds, or whether they are best treated just like primary compounds, or even (although this is denied by Baker 1988: 78–9) whether it is a limited kind of incorporation.

Many languages have constructions which clearly function like words like *bus-driver* in English. It is not always clear that these are compounds or, if they are, that they are a specific subset of compounds.

17.7 DOES THIS LEAD TO A TYPOLOGY?

Languages exploit the possibilities of compounding in a number of different ways. The main compound type in Hunzib is coordinative (van den Berg 2004), while in Chichewa (Bantu) (Mchombo 1998) and Kayardild (Evans 1995: 197) the main compounding process appears to be exocentric, and in English the main compounding processes are endocentric. In Warlpiri the most productive compound pattern is apparently synthetic (Nash 1986: 37; but see also Simpson, this volume). Wari' appears to have compound verbs to the exclusion of compound nouns, although it is perhaps arguable that we are dealing with serial verbs rather than compounding in this language (see Everett 1998). Tigre and Tigrinya (Semitic), to the extent that they have compounds at all, also appear to have verb compounds exclusively (Hetzron 1997). In contrast, English is sometimes said to have no compound verbs (Marchand 1969, but see Bauer and Renouf 2001). Fongbe is said only to have compound nouns (Lefebvre and Brousseau 2002, but see below 17.8) while Udihe appears not to have compound nouns, though it does have compound verbs and adjectives (Nikolaeva and Tolskaya 2001).

We have languages like the Germanic languages in which compounding is a major means of vocabulary expansion, and other languages, such as Turkana, where compounds are used only in the formation of names (Dimmendaal and Noske 2004).

Unfortunately we are not able to show that such variation is anything but random. We do not have evidence that any such facts correlate with anything else in the language structure. In many cases this is simply because we do not have good enough descriptions of word formation (and, specifically, compounding) in relevant languages, and in some cases this is due to problems of definition, mentioned at the outset. Most discussions of N+N compounding, for instance, will provide some examples of the construction, but few will give an exhaustive analysis of the types of semantic relationship that may hold between the two nouns. Thus we simply cannot determine whether there is an implicational scale of semantic relationships in such constructions. But since there is so much disagreement about how to specify the semantic relationships in those languages which are well-described (like English and German), it is not clear how helpful any such descriptions could be.

Given that English and Mandarin are fairly analytic languages and are described as having compounds, and that West Greenlandic is polysynthetic and described as not having compounds, we might expect compounding to be a feature of isolating languages, being replaced by incorporation in more complex languages. But Maori is largely isolating and has incorporation and Chukchi is polysynthetic and has compounds. In any case, Evenki and Turkana, said to have very few compounds, are not polysynthetic, but agglutinating languages. There may be some kind of statistical correlation here, but we do not have sufficient data to be able to see precisely how it might work: there is clearly no direct causal relationship.

There are clear areal preferences for particular compound structures: compound verbs in South America (possibly better thought of as serial verb constructions), coordinative compounds in South-East Asia, and so on. But again, it is not clear that this correlates with anything linguistic in the appropriate languages.

17.8 CONCLUSION

It has already been shown (Lieber and Štekauer, this volume) that there are many problems in defining a compound. In every case, a problem in definition leads to a problem in typology. If we include incorporation as compounding, there are more languages with compounds than if we omit it (for example, Kwakwala is said to have incorporation but not compounding: Štekauer and Valera 2007), there are more potential sets of implications, there are more compound-types which may be areally restricted, and so on. Fongbe is said (Lefebvre and Brousseau 2002: 221) to have only noun compounds, but it also has serial verbs and something that looks as though it may be a form of incorporation. Again definitions could change one's typological conclusions. It is not clear that there is any optimal point for the drawing of conclusions about 'compounding' which might help short-circuit the issue. Accordingly, many of the conclusions that can be drawn about universals of compounding or their typology are as provisional as the definitions.

Dressler (2006) suggests that we are in a position to provide a set of preferences for compounding. For instance, compound nouns will be more frequent than compound verbs, endocentric compounds more frequent than exocentric ones, and so on. I suspect that this is right if taken as a general view across languages, but wrong if it is taken to apply to individual languages. A serious consideration of this approach might lead to a different focus for questions, however. Instead of asking what structural factors are likely to presuppose the existence of, say, appositional compounding in a given language, we might start to ask what reasons there might be for languages to show patterns which run counter to general patterns of preference of the type Dressler (2006) discusses.

CHAPTER 18

....

IE, GERMANIC: ENGLISH

....

ROCHELLE LIEBER

It seems safe to say that compounding in English is one of the most extensively covered topics in the literature on word formation. Jespersen (1942) devotes two chapters of his *Modern English Grammar* to the subject, Marchand (1969) an entire section of his massive *The Categories and Types of Present-Day English Word Formation*. Within the generative tradition, the list of analyses is lengthy, including Lees (1960), Levi (1978), Bauer (1978, 1998a,b, 2001b), Allen (1978), Roeper and Siegel (1978), Selkirk (1982), Lieber (1983, 1992a,b, 2004, 2005), Botha (1984), Sproat (1985), Roeper (1988), Grimshaw (1990), Olsen (2000b), Štekauer (2005a), Plag (2006b), and of course a number of the chapters of this volume (DiSciullo, ten Hacken, Harley, Jackendoff, Lieber). I will not review this literature here, or revisit the many theoretical debates that the subject of compounding in English has engendered. My intent in this short chapter is to give a thorough description of the facts of compounding in English, looking not only at those areas of full productivity that have been extensively studied, but also at some compound types that are less productive and less well covered in the literature, and extending the discussion to several types of compounding that might be deemed at the limits of the process in English. In other words, this chapter will aim at broad empirical coverage in as theory-neutral a way as possible.

Of course, no description is completely theory-neutral. Any sort of organizing principle has some basis in theory, and our data must be organized somehow. I have therefore chosen to organize English compounding data roughly according to the classification of Bisetto and Scalise (2005, this volume), as this seems to be the best thought-out and most cross-linguistically applicable classification available. Most important is that the classification is cross-linguistically based: as discussions of compounding in English have tended in the past to confine themselves to root (primary) compounds and synthetic (deverbal, verbal nexus) compounds, the data section is intended to broaden our conception of compound types in English and allow English to be better seen in light of the facts of compounding in other languages.

In section 18.1 I give an overview of the data, considering coordinate, subordinate, and attributive types, as well as marginal types such as phrasal compounds, identical constituent (reduplicative) compounds, dummy compounds, neoclassical compounds, and items whose analysis arguably involves conversion or prefixation rather than compounding. Each main subsection will begin with a Table giving a working taxonomy of the compounds to be discussed. Section 18.2 will be devoted to issues concerning compounding in English such as headedness, the internal structure of compounds, the locus of inflection, and the presence or absence of linking elements.

We have already discussed the difficulty in identifying unequivocal criteria for compoundhood in the Introduction to this volume, so I will not revisit this topic here. However, where I touch on forms that fail some of the criteria for compoundhood or that have been analysed as the results of processes of word formation other than compounding (e.g. conversion, back formation, prefixation), I will point to possible alternative analyses.

18.1 DATA

As mentioned above, discussions of English compounding have frequently concentrated on two productive types, root compounds and synthetic compounds. The Bisetto–Scalise classification allows us to see that this division is rather limiting, and indeed inhibits cross-linguistic comparisons. I will start, however, with a brief discussion of the traditional classification of English compounds, and show how these types fit into the Bisetto–Scalise classification.

Synthetic compounds in English have traditionally been defined as compounds in which the second constituent is a deverbal element – either an -er nominal (*truck driver*), an -ing noun or adjective (*truck driving, hard-working*), or a passive participle (*hand-made, home-made*). Some theorists allow a broader range of deverbal nominalizations as the second constituents of synthetic compounds, including nominalizations in -al, -ance, -ment, and -ion (e.g. *trash removal, home maintenance, home improvement, car registration*). Root compounds are defined by default: they are not synthetic compounds. Indeed, root compounds need not consist of roots, if what we mean by roots in English is underived items: *maintenance schedule* or *driving school* would be classed as root compounds, even if their first constituents are derived, and indeed deverbal.

The Bisetto–Scalise (henceforth BS) classification divides the pie up somewhat differently. Synthetic compounds fall squarely into what BS call 'subordinate' compounds, that is, those compounds that express some sort of argumental relation between their constituents.[1] Many of the so-called root or primary compounds are subsumed under the attributive class in the BS classification. But some English compounds that would traditionally have been considered root or primary compounds fall into the subordinate class as well. The division is made not on the basis of the categorial composition of the compound, but on the basis of the grammatical/semantic relation between the constituents. In other words, non-synthetic N+N compounds can be classed as subordinate if they display an argumental (or quasi-argumental) relationship (e.g. *cookbook author*). Only where a clear argumental relationship between the compound constituents is lacking will compounds be classed as attributive.

The data I discuss below come from a number of sources – published works on compounding, the MORBO corpus, and my own relatively casual scrutiny of the *New York Times*.

18.1.1 Coordinate compounds

English is perhaps richer in coordinate compounds than might first be thought. Table 18.1 summarizes the main types.

Certainly endocentric N+N coordinates are not uncommon in English. Examples turned up in the New York Times include *publishing-magnate owner* (meaning 'owner and publishing-magnate') and perhaps *spiderman*. MORBO contains *comedy-drama*, *king-emperor*, and *secretary-treasurer*. A+A coordinates are also possible, although perhaps not common, and may have either a mixture reading (something which is *blue-green* is a colour between blue and green) or a simultaneous interpretation (for example, *deaf-mute*). V+V endocentric compounds can be found, but the type is unproductive: MORBO contains *trickle-irrigate*, and a few others come to mind (*slam-dunk*, *blow-dry*), but these are not freely formed.

---

[1] Bisetto and Scalise (2005) actually confine the class of subordinate compounds to those in which there is a relation of complementation between the two constituents, and in their contribution to this volume add the adjunct relation. This, however, would still require treating compounds with subject-oriented interpretations (e.g. *city employee*) as belonging to a macroclass different from those with object-oriented interpretations (e.g. *truck driver*), which seems counterintuitive. I have therefore broadened their definition of the subordinate class here.

Table 18.1 Coordinate Compounds

Endocentric		Exocentric		
simultaneous	mixture	relationship	collective	disjunctive
N+N producer-director	A+A blue-green	N+N parent-child (relationship)	N+N father-daughter (dance)	V+V pass-fail
V+V stir-fry		A+A English-French (negotiations)		
A+A deaf-mute				

Exocentrics seem quite productive, however, and can have a number of different interpretations. Generally, an exocentric N+N or A+A coordinate is possible when the two nouns or adjectives in question are semantically similar in some way (for example, both nouns denoting types of humans, countries, or even grammatical terms), and can either be given what I call a 'relationship' or 'between' interpretation, for example *doctor-patient (discussion)* or *subject-verb (agreement)* from the MORBO corpus, or a collective interpretation, as in *father-daughter (dance)*. Which interpretation the compound is given depends not so much on the compounded constituents themselves as on the noun they are predicated of. So, for example, *father-daughter* has the 'between' interpretation in *a father-daughter argument*, but the collective reading in *a father-daughter dance*. I have found only one exocentric coordinate compound in English that receives a disjunctive interpretation: *pass-fail (examination)*.

18.1.2 Subordinate compounds

English is rich in subordinate compounds. Table 18.2 summarizes the types to be found.[2]

Among the endocentric subordinate compounds, the most productive in English are of course the synthetic compounds. Note that while it is most typical for English synthetic compounds to exhibit what I call an 'object-oriented' interpretation (so a *truck driver* is someone who *drives trucks*), it is not impossible to find synthetics with 'subject-oriented' interpretations, specifically when the deverbal second constituent contains the patient suffix *-ee*, as in *city employee* (see Chapter 5, section 5.4.2). Adjunct interpretations are also possible, especially when the second

---

[2] Note that when I classify a compound as having one or another of these interpretations, I do not mean to assert that this is the only interpretation that the compound can have; I merely mean to suggest that it can have that interpretation (although sometimes other interpretations are available).

Table 18.2 Subordinate Compounds

		Endocentric				Exocentric
		verb-containing			verbless	
	synthetic	[V]N+N	[N+V]$_V$	N+[V]$_N$	table leg	pickpocket
object	truck driver	kick-ball	head-hunt	chimney sweep	cookbook author	cutpurse
subject	city employee	attack dog	machine-wash	sunrise		spoilsport
adjunct	home-made	skate park	spoon-feed	boat ride		

constituent is a passive participle. MORBO gives examples like *fresh baked* and *well preserved*. Compounds in which the second constituent is an *-able* adjective can also express an adjunct interpretation, for example, *machine-washable*.

Of course not all subordinate compounds in English are synthetics. Indeed, there are a number of types of greater or lesser productivity that display object-, subject-, or adjunct-oriented argumental relations. Generally these contain a constituent that either is a verb or arguably has undergone conversion from verb to noun. As Table 18.2 illustrates, one sort of compound that can be found in English contains as a first constituent a noun derived from a verb by conversion and as a second constituent a noun; the second constituent can bear any of the three relations to the first: object (*kick-ball, call girl*), subject (*attack dog, jump jet, call bird*), or adjunct (*skate park*). It is unclear to me whether the first constituent in such a compound must be a verb that has undergone conversion to noun, or whether it may also be an underived verb: consider, for example, compounds like *scrub woman* or *tow truck* (both subject-oriented), where a verb-to-noun conversion analysis for the first constituent seems less plausible.

Another sort that falls under the category of subordinate is the marginal class of compound verbs in English that is generally argued to be the result of back-formation, including *head-hunt, machine-wash, air-condition, spoon-feed,* and *babysit*. The MORBO corpus turns up only two of these (*color-code, blockbust*). It seems safe to conclude that back-formation does occur, and shows at least a small amount of productivity in English. Of course Ackema and Neeleman (2004) rightly point out that although the source of such compound verbs is likely to have been back-formation, from the point of view of the average native speaker, they are just compound verbs: native speakers need not have any sense of the historical origins of such forms.

We may also count among the subordinate compounds those compounds in English whose first constituent is a noun and whose second constituent is a noun formed by conversion from a verb. These include object-oriented examples (*chimney sweep, Mars probe, ball return, arachnid shower, baby care, blood test*), subject-oriented examples (*sunrise, sunshine, terrorist attack*), and adjunct-oriented examples (*boat ride, day care, telephone call, footwork*). The fact that a number of compounds of this type turn up both in the MORBO corpus and my examples from the *New York Times* suggests that this type displays at least some productivity.

It is important to note, of course, that it is not necessary for one of the constituents of a compound to be verbal or deverbal for the compound to be classed as subordinate. Indeed, simplex nouns that have relational or processual interpretations often permit complementation (e.g. *author of a book, leg of a table*), and therefore N+N compounds with such relational or processual nouns as their second constituents clearly fall among the subordinates in the BS classification: *cookbook author, table leg, gas price, justice role, team symbol* seem likely candidates. This group of compounds inevitably shades off into attributives, however, and it seems unlikely that we will be able to draw a clear line between N+N subordinates and certain kinds of N+N attributives.

Exocentric subordinates are not well-represented in English. Indeed, there are only a few examples with verbs as first constituent and nouns as second: *pickpocket, cutpurse, spoilsport, killjoy,* and perhaps a few others. Unlike the Romance languages, where this sort of compound is productive, it seems that English contains just a few survivals of a brief flowering of this pattern under the influence of French; Marchand (1969: 381) dates the appearance of the majority of this type to around the time of heaviest French influence on English, around AD 1300, and it is likely that this type has never been naturalized such that it displays any degree of productivity.

18.1.3 Attributive compounds

Perhaps the most productive type of compound to be found in English is the attributive compound (Table 18.3). As we saw above, not every N+N compound is attributive, but it seems safe to say that a great many N+N compounds are. N+N attributives appearing in the MORBO corpus and in my own survey of the *New York Times* include *high school, biofuels industry, immigration candidate, sister node, key word,* and *satellite nation.* It almost goes without saying that N+N compounds are coined with complete productivity in English. Attributives containing one or more adjectives also enjoy some degree of productivity, although they are certainly not as pervasive as N+N compounds. From MORBO and the *New York Times* we find A+N *bareback, barefoot, heavyweight, long-term, half-time;* N+A *dog-tired, jet-black, life-long, skin-tight, industry-wide;* and A+A *funny-peculiar.* It should be noted that some of the A+N compounds are purely exocentric (*bareback, barefoot*).

Booij (1992) argues that the sort of exocentricity displayed by compounds like *birdbrain, egghead,* and *redhead* should be attributed to a general process of

Table 18.3 Attributive Compounds

	Endocentric		Exocentric
N+N	dog bed, file cabinet	N+N	birdbrain, egghead
A+N	hard hat, blackboard	A+N	redhead, hardass
N+A	lemon yellow, ice cold		
A+A	red hot, wide awake		

metonymy at work in languages. That is, we assume that whatever process is at work when we use a simplex word like *the suits* to refer to the employees who wear suits is at work as well when we use a compound like *birdbrain* to refer to a foolish person. Indeed, there are compounds in English that can at the same time have endocentric and exocentric meanings, for example when we use the word *hard hat* to refer both to the helmet worn by construction workers and to the construction workers themselves.

One final type of attributive compound that I should discuss here is the type represented by forms like *long-legged* and *blue-eyed*. Marchand (1969: 265) treats these as exocentric, with an affix -*ed* attaching to a noun-phrase-like constituent: [[long leg] ed]. The motivation for this analysis is that items like *legged* or *eyed* are not freely occurring items. Still, it is not out of the question that these might be analysed as endocentric A+A compounds, in which the second constituent is an adjective derived from a noun: [long][[leg]ed]. Hudson (1975) and Ljung (1976), for example, point out that bare forms like *legged* and *eyed* are not impossible, just uninformative. We assume that certain sorts of entities have legs and eyes, and therefore bare adjectives like *legged* or *eyed* seem odd by themselves. But where an attribute (such as having a beard) is not taken for granted, both the bare adjective (*bearded*) and the compound (*grey-bearded*) are possible. Given this, it seems best to treat these as endocentrics.

18.1.4 Marginal types

18.1.4.1 *Phrasal compounds*

Phrasal compounds are items like *floor-of-a-birdcage taste, God-is-dead theology, over-the-fence gossip*, in which the first element is a phrase or even a sentence, and the second a noun. The phenomenon of so-called phrasal compounds was noted as early as the 1930s in the work of Mathesius and Vachek, who refer to them as 'quotational compounds'.[3] More recently they have been discussed by Botha (1980),

---

[3] Mathesius's ideas were first published in a posthumous volume edited by Vachek in 1961 (Vachek 1975, English translation).

Savini (1983), Toman (1983), Hoeksema (1985, 1988), Lieber (1988, 1992a), Bresnan and Mchombo (1995), and Lieber and Scalise (2006). Classing such items as compounds has been controversial. Lieber (1992a) argues that they are compounds on the grounds that, like canonical compounds, the first (phrasal) constituent cannot be separated from the second constituent (*a floor-of-a-birdcage salty taste). Bresnan and Mchombo (1995), on the other hand, dismiss this type of compound on the grounds that the first (phrasal) constituent is either lexicalized or 'quotative', by which they mean having the out-of-context nature of a quote. That neither of these is true is suggested by the phrasal compound I coined in the previous sentence: in the compound *out-of-context nature* we have no reason to believe that the phrasal constituent is either lexicalized (why would it be, as it's perfectly literal?) or quotative. Other examples from the MORBO corpus suggest the same: *one-hat-per-student stipulation, punch-in-the-stomach effect.*

In terms of the BS classification, it appears that phrasal compounds are generally endocentric attributive (*God-is-dead theology, floor-of-a-birdcage taste*), but they can be subordinate as well (*over-the-fence gossip, in-your-own-home care*[4]).

18.1.4.2 *Neoclassical compounds*

By neoclassical compounds I mean compounds formed on Greek and Latin bound roots, for example *psychopath* or *pathology*. Neoclassical compounds of course continue to be coined in English, especially in technical and medical fields – witness twentieth-century words for devices like the *telephone* or *phonograph*, or medical terms such as *angioplasty* or *arthroscopic*. Bauer (1998a) points out two issues that arise in the analysis of neoclassical compounds. First is the difficulty in differentiating neoclassical compounds as a distinct type, since it is sometimes impossible to distinguish such compounding from prefixation (*geo-morphology*) on the one hand, and blending and/or clipping (*Eurocrat, gastrodrama*) on the other. Indeed, neoclassical roots sometimes combine with non-neoclassical stems in English (e.g. *garbagology*). The second issue that Bauer raises concerns productivity: if a word-formation process can only be deemed productive if the coining of new forms is done unconsciously by the native speaker, we might hesitate to call neoclassical compounds productive. Nevertheless, new neoclassical compounds can be formed in English.

18.1.4.3 *Identical-constituent compounds*

Identical-constituent or reduplicative compounding is a phenomenon of collo-quial, mostly spoken English, including items like FRIEND *friend* or NERVOUS *nervous* which show stress on the left-hand constituent and typically pick out a prototypical or intensified exemplar of what is denoted by the second constituent. So a speaker of English might say FRIEND *friend* to distinguish an ordinary friend

---

[4] Compound found on the web 22 June 2007.

from a romantic interest, for example, or *NERVOUS nervous* to mean 'really nervous'. These have been discussed by Hohenhaus (1998, 2004) and Ghomeshi et al. (2004). Hohenhaus classes them as compounds, and although Ghomeshi et al. do not treat these items explicitly as compounds (indeed, they label the phenomenon 'contrastive reduplication'), they do analyse the reduplicated constituent as a 'free reduplicative morpheme' (2004: 342), which is consistent with a compounding analysis. They point out several characteristics of the phenomenon that suggest that compounding is the right analysis: (1) it is restricted to words (*FRIEND friend*)[5] or idiomatic or lexicalized phrases (*LIVING TOGETHER living together*); (2) it affects only lexical categories and not functional categories; (3) irregular inflection always copies (*GEESE geese*), but regular inflection can occur either on both constituents or on the compound as a whole (*GLOVE gloves* or *GLOVES gloves*). A key characteristic of reduplicative compounds is that they are unlexicalized, and indeed, according to Hohenhaus (1998) unlexicalizable.

18.1.4.4 *Dummy compounds*

Also unlexicalizable are the sort of compounds Hohenhaus has dubbed 'dummy compounds'. Hohenhaus (1998: 250) defines 'dummy compounds' as 'involving a semantically empty dummy-constituent (usually *thing* or *business*) in head position, whilst the first constituent is the "free" position (formally unspecified by the pattern), which is usually filled by some element from the context the compound as a whole deictically refers to'. For example, it is possible in colloquial English to refer to the trials involving accounting fraud in the Enron Corporation as 'that *Enron thing*', assuming in context that both speaker and hearers are aware of the situation referred to.

Dummy compounds are not in fact a distinct type of compound, but rather are probably the logical limit of attributive compounding, a limit we reach when the second constituent is sufficiently bleached of meaning that the speaker's intention can only be recovered from context.

18.1.4.5 *Compound or prefixation/conversion?*

Questions arise about whether to count complex words with preposition-like constituents as compounds. Here, there are two types to discuss.

The first consists of items like *overcoat, overfly, overabundant*, in which the prepositional constituent can arguably be analysed as a prefix rather than an independent stem. Although Marchand includes his discussion of complex words with *over-, out-,* and *under-* in his section on compounding, he is careful to point out (1969: 100) that, 'while verbs formed with preparticles are compounds insofar as they consist of two independent words, formally speaking, we note that the

---

[5] Included here are simplex, derived, and compounded words, as well as verbs with encliticized object pronouns (*LIKE'EM like'em*).

particles do not behave like substantives, adjectives, and verbs as first elements of compounds. Full words ordinarily do not change semantically when they become constituents of compounds.' In other words, as I argued in Lieber (2004), constituents like *over-* and *out-* differ from their prepositional counterparts in their semantics (often adding a meaning of 'excess' that is lacking in independent prepositions), and sometimes effect changes on the argument structure of the heads to which they attach.

The second type consists of complex nouns like *rip-off*, *cop-out*, and *put-down*. Although these items consist of two independent stems that are (in the nominal forms) inseparable, and although they show the characteristic left-hand stress pattern of English compounds, they are clearly not right-headed (see section 18.2.1 below). Further, they always correspond to verb-plus-particle combinations. They are therefore probably better analysed as the result of verb-to-noun conversion. Indeed they show the characteristic semantic profile of verb-to-noun conversion in English, where the resulting nouns typically are interpreted as 'an instance of V-ing'; in other words, just as *a throw* is interpreted as 'an instance of throwing', *a cop-out* is interpreted as 'an instance of copping out'.

18.2 General issues

General issues concerning the analysis of compounds in English have been well covered in the literature. I will merely reiterate main points here, adding reference to recent research where possible, concentrating on the linguistic as opposed to psycholinguistic literature. For a review of the latter, the reader is referred to the articles in Libben and Jarema (2006), as well as to Chapter 13 in this volume.

18.2.1 Headedness

It is uncontroversial that endocentric subordinate and attributive compounds in English are right-headed both in terms of syntax and semantics. Compounds take their category from the right-hand constituent; semantically they are hyponyms of that constituent, an observation that was encoded in Allen's (1978) IS A Principle. Right-headedness is, of course, the general case in Germanic compounds. As for the endocentric coordinate compounds (*producer-director*, *blue-green*, *stir-fry*), it is certainly possible to argue that they are double-headed, or that they have no head. There is little empirical basis in English for distinguishing the proposals. For example, as English nouns do not display grammatical gender, no argument from the gender of the compound as a whole is possible, and as for inflection, it is possible to argue that plural or possessive marking goes on the compound as a whole ([[*producer director*]s]), as opposed to the right-hand constituent. Exocentric coordinates, on the other hand, arguably have no head.

18.2.2 Internal structure

The internal structure of primary (root) compounds is relatively uncontroversial. Given the pervasive right-headedness of English compounds, structures like those in (1) would be typical:

(1)

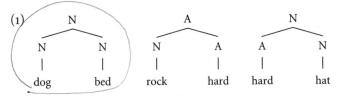

Over the years, however, there has been substantial debate over the internal structure of the synthetic compounds, with most theorists opting for the structure in (2), and a minority for (3).

(2)

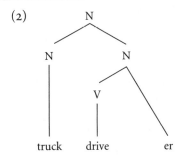

(3)

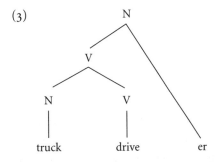

The debate hinges on whether one wants to postulate a type of compound (N+V) which is not productive in English as the base for the affixation of -*er*, -*ing*, and other nominalizing affixes, resulting in a type which is prodigiously productive.

A number of theorists including Lieber (1983), Fabb (1984), Sproat (1985), Ackema and Neeleman (2004), and Booij (this volume) have opted for this move, but others have eschewed it, among them Selkirk (1982), Booij (1988), and Lieber (1992a, 2004). Only rarely has ternary branching structure been advocated for such compounds (Štekauer 1998).

As I have observed elsewhere (Lieber 2005), analyses of compound structure (both root and synthetic) have often piggy-backed on developments in generative syntax, starting with the early days of transformational grammar in which Lees (1960) used a large variety of transformations in an attempt to capture the semantic relationships between the first and second constituents of compounds. More constrained versions of the Leesian transformational analysis were proposed by Levi (1978) and Bauer (1978), at the same time that Roeper and Siegel (1978) were arguing for what they called a 'lexical transformation', a rule which operated over subcategorization frames in the lexicon. During the heyday of Government-Binding theory, Roeper (1988) and Lieber (1992a) proposed syntactic analyses of synthetic compounds involving Head Movement. Most recently, Minimalist analyses have begun to appear, for example that of Roeper, Snyder, and Hiramatsu (2002), who use the operation of 'set merger' to derive root compounds.

The success and lasting value of such theories ultimately depend on empirical predictions, rather than theoretical fashion. The earliest of these theories (Lees 1960, Brekle 1970, Bauer 1978, Levi 1978), although ultimately unsuccessful, served to clarify that the semantic relationships between the first and second constituents of compounds in English are too open to be constrained by transformational rules. The second wave (Roeper and Siegel 1978, Lieber 1992a) highlighted some potential compounds that indeed seemed impossible in English, for example, synthetic compounds based on obligatorily ditransitive verbs (*shelf book putter, *shelf putter (of books), *book putter (on shelves)) or phrasal synthetic compounds (*apple on a stick taster). And most recently, Roeper et al.'s (2002) analysis has led us to explore whether there is a cross-linguistic correlation between productive N+N root compounding and complex predicate constructions. Ultimately, each of these theoretical forays serves to extend our understanding of the scope and limits of the phenomenon of compounding in English.

18.2.3 Interpretation

A number of generalizations about the interpretations of English compounds are well known: that the semantic relationship between the first and second constituents of root compounds is quite free (although as Štekauer [2005, this volume] points out, some interpretations are likelier than others for novel compounds); that the first constituent in compounds is non-referential (in other words, in a compound like *dog food* the first constituent cannot refer to any particular dog);

that the first constituent in synthetic compounds often (but not always) receives an 'object' interpretation.

One of the major goals of most analyses of English compounding over the last fifty years has been to account theoretically for such facts about compound interpretation. Indeed, examples of several current approaches are available in the first part of this volume (contributions by Jackendoff, Lieber, Booij, DiSciullo, Harley, Grzega, and Heyvaert). At least two major strands of analysis can be distinguished: those that attempt to attribute the interpretation of compounds purely to syntactic or morphological structure, and those that propose interpretive principles that are not directly tied to syntactic properties. Into the former camp fall Lees (1960), Bauer (1978), Levi (1978), Roeper (1988), Lieber (1992a), and Roeper et al. (2002). Among the latter are Allen (1978), Roeper and Siegel (1978), Selkirk (1982), Lieber (1983), Ryder (1990), Lieber (2004, this volume), and Jackendoff, this volume.

18.2.4 Locus of inflection and linking elements

English is, of course, a language that is poor in inflection. Generally speaking, where inflection does occur, it appears only on the second constituent of a compound: *dog beds*, but **dogs bed* (even if the item in question is a single large bed for multiple dogs!). There are, however, cases where it can be argued that the first constituent does bear a plural, or even a possessive inflection, for example, in *parks department* or *children's hour*, although Marchand (1969: 27) prefers to call the *-s/-'s* Linking Elements, on a par with those found in German and Dutch. The linking-element analysis receives some plausibility in light of examples like *oarsman* or *frontiersman*, where in the first case the denotee need not wield any more than one oar, and in the second neither a plural nor a possessive interpretation makes sense. It seems safe to say, however, that neither internal inflection nor the use of linking elements plays any strong role in English compounding.

CHAPTER 19

IE, GERMANIC: DUTCH

JAN DON

DUTCH is famous for its productive compound formation. Dutch native speakers easily make new compounds on the spot, and they also easily embed compounds in compounds leading to sometimes rather complex structures such as (1).

(1)   *weersvoorspellingsdeskundigencongres*
      weer[s].voorspelling[s].deskundige[n].congres
      weather.forecast.experts.conference

A look at a random front page of a Dutch nation wide newspaper (*NRC-Handels-blad*, 17 February 2007) yielded seven new compounds, 'new' in the sense that they could not be found in the most common Dutch dictionary (Van Dale Groot Woordenboek der Nederlandse Taal). Compound formation is without doubt the most productive morphological process in the language.

19.1 GENERAL CHARACTERISTICS

By considering the example in (1), we can point out several general characteristics of Dutch compounds.

   First, note that the compound is built from nouns. Nominal compounds are by far the most productive type, although other types (adjectival and verbal) exist and can also be formed productively. Even prepositional compounds exist, such as *voorover* (lit. 'for-over') 'headfirst', *achterin* (lit. 'back-in') 'in the rear', and *binnenin* (lit. 'inside-in') 'on the inside', but these seem not to be very productive and we will not discuss them here any further.

Second, (nominal) compounding is recursive. In our example, w*eersvoorspelling* is a compound, and *weersvoorspellingsdeskundige* again is a compound, and so is the word in (1) as a whole. Therefore, our example is a compound built from a compound, again built from a compound. The structure might be represented with the labelled bracketing in (2):

(2) $[[[[weer(s)]_N [voorspelling(s)]_N]_N [deskundigen]_N]_N [congres]_N]_N$

Native speakers of Dutch do not have any trouble further combining this word into a yet larger compound. It is not so clear what determines the upper limit, if there is one. To be sure, in practice compounds will not get much larger than the example in (1), but there does not seem to be any principled upper bound.

Third, derivational affixes freely occur inside the compounding structure: *-ing* as in *voorspelling* 'forecast' is a productive nominal derivational suffix. Other derivational affixes also freely occur inside compounds.

Fourth, compounds in Dutch are right-headed (Trommelen and Zonneveld 1986). This can be easily seen from at least three properties of compounds that are determined by their most right-hand member: category, gender, and meaning. So, the compound in (1) is a noun since the word *congres* 'conference' is a noun; furthermore, it is a neuter noun (rather than a common noun) since *congres* has neuter gender. The right-hand member of the compound also determines its meaning: it refers to a type of conference. Moreover, although plural formation in Dutch is predictable to a certain extent, the choice of allomorph is not fully predictable on purely phonological and/or morphological grounds. The right-hand member of a compound determines the choice of allomorph: there are no cases in which the compound gets a different plural allomorph than the plural of the right-hand member (i.e. the head).[1] Again, we will see that also in this respect other types of compounds exist, although right-headedness is the rule.

Fifth, compounds are built from stems. That is, although derivational affixes may freely occur within compounds, we hardly find any inflectional affixes within compounds. However, there are at least two potential counterexamples that the

---

[1] Another possible explanation for this observation is that plural formation involves a so-called 'head operation' (Hoeksema 1984). Head operations can be formally expressed as follows (cf. Hoeksema 1984: 50):

(i) F is a head operation iff F (Y) = Z and W = XY (where Y is the head of W) together imply that
   F (W) = X+F(Y) = X+Z

So, in a form (xy) in which y is the head, the head operation is the result of applying the operation to the head and then restoring the original relation between x and y. If 'head operations' exist and plural

reader should be aware of. In some cases, plural affixes seem to occur inside a compound. Consider the example in (3):

(3)   *deskundige-n-congres*
      'experts conference'

The plural of the noun *deskundige* is *deskundige-n*. Since a plural interpretation of the left-hand member of the compound is also applicable semantically, there seems little reason to doubt that the affix *-n* inside the compound is an inflectional affix. However, on closer inspection, we may be led to a different conclusion; we will come back to this issue below (section 19.3.2).

As a second potential source of inflectional affixes inside compounds we may think of examples that are built from full phrases including the inflectional material present in those phrases. Consider for example the constructions in (4):

(4)   *oude   muntenverzameling*
      'old   coins   collection'

The final schwa (spelled *e*) in *oude* 'old' is an inflectional affix, which is normally not present in compounding. This seems to indicate that in this case a whole phrase is part of a compound. Such examples have caught the attention of many authors (e.g. Botha 1981, Hoeksema 1985, Lieber 1992a) and the theoretical issue that these data pose is to what extent the morphology can be considered a separate domain of word formation, and if it can, how the relation with respect to the syntax should be defined. We will not discuss these examples here for reasons of space but leave it with the observation that embedding of phrases seems possible in compounds in Dutch.

The sixth general characteristic to be observed is that in between the nouns that constitute the compound we may find so-called 'linking morphemes' that do not seem to contribute anything to the semantics (or the syntax) of the compound. In the example in (1), we have put the linking morphemes (*-s*, *-n*) in brackets. Despite their semantic emptiness, native speakers share intuitions about where and which of these linking morphemes have to be inserted in a compound. In the literature some authors have argued that this is the result of analogy (Krott 2001) whereas others have argued that other determining factors are also at play (e.g. Neijt, Krebbers, and Fikkert 2002).

---

formation in Dutch is such an operation, then the fact that all plurals of compounds equal the plural forms of the heads of those compounds immediately follows. In (ii) we list several irregular morphological forms that do show up in case only the right-hand member of a compound requires them:

(ii)   kleinkind   kleinkinderen   'grandchild'
       bergvolk   bergvolkeren   'mountain people'
       vioolsolo   vioolsoli   'violin solo'

Seventh, in the compound in (5):

(5)   [[*weer(s)*]ₙ [*voorspelling*]ₙ]ₙ
        weather   forecast

we see that the noun *weer* stands in the same argument-relation to the deverbal noun *voorspelling*, as it would stand in a more or less parallel syntactic construction, like the one in (6):

(6)   [[*het   weer*]ₙₚ   *voorspellen*]ᵥₚ
        the   weather   forecast
       'to forecast the weather'

So, we may ask ourselves, as has been done in the literature (Roeper and Siegel 1978, Selkirk 1982, Lieber 1983, Grimshaw 1990, among others), whether this verb–argument relation is somehow at the base of this type of compound and the structure of the first half of the compound in (1) should be represented as in (7):

(7)   [[*weer-s voorspel*] *ing*]

Each of these seven general characteristics will be discussed in more detail in the following sections.

The organization of the rest of this chapter is as follows. In section 19.2 we will investigate different types of compounding in Dutch. Section 19.3 goes into some of the phonological properties of Dutch compounds; here we will also deal with the problem of the so-called 'linking' morphemes. In section 19.4 we will look into the structure of verbal compounds; here we will also look at some other compounds, which have been claimed to have a similar structure.

19.2 DIFFERENT TYPES OF COMPOUNDS

19.2.1 Nominal compounds

Let us first consider some examples of the most frequent type of compounds in Dutch, so-called N+N compounds:

(8)   N   N   COMPOUND   GLOSS
        vlees   *soep*   *vleessoep*   'meat soup'
        water   *fiets*   *waterfiets*   'water bike'
        computer   *spel*   *computerspel* 'computer game'

As we said above, any speaker of Dutch can add to this list an infinite number of examples: this type of compounding is fully productive. Also, these compounds make full use of recursivity, that is, we can easily embed compounds within compounds, within compounds, etc.:

(9) N (compound)   N   COMPOUND   GLOSS
     vleessoep   *bereider*   *vleessoepbereider*   'meat soup maker'
     waterfiets   *verhuur*   *waterfietsverhuur*   'water bike rent'
     computerspel   *winkel*   *computerspel winkel* 'computer game shop'

If we change the left-hand member of the compound into a verb(-stem), we still find full productivity:

(10) V   N   COMPOUND   GLOSS
     schuif   *deur*   *schuifdeur*   'slide door'
     speel   *veld*   *speelveld*   'play field'
     leer   *boek*   *leerboek*   'learn book'

Also, the verb stem may itself be derived or compounded:

(11) V   N   COMPOUND   GLOSS
     ver-koop   *techniek*   *verkooptechniek*   'sales-technique'
     af-haal   *chinees*   *afhaalchinees*   'take-away Chinese'
     zweef-vlieg   *toestel*   *zweefvliegtoestel* 'float-fly machine' (=glider)

However, examples of the type A+N seem to be much scarcer:

(12) A   N   COMPOUND   GLOSS
     hard   *board*   *hardboard*   'hard board'
     snel   *trein*   *sneltrein*   'express train'
     fris   *drank*   *frisdrank*   'fresh drink'

De Haas and Trommelen (1993: 390) note that 'almost exclusively Germanic adjectives (=monosyllabic, or bisyllabic with schwa in the second syllable) can be embedded in A+N compounds'.[2] So, apart from these Germanic adjectives (such as *hoog* 'high'; *laag* 'low'; *breed* 'broad'; *smal* 'narrow'; *klein* 'small'; *groot* 'big'; *dun* 'thin'; *dik* 'fat', etc.) Dutch hosts a large number of adjectives of Romance origin such as *flexibel* 'flexible', *corrupt* 'corrupt', *banaal* 'banal', which cannot be part of nominal compounds.

The semantics of the forms in (12) is not the same as the semantics of the nominal phrases that we can construct from the same stems. So, the phrase *snelle trein* 'fast train' does not refer to the same object as the compound *sneltrein* 'express train'.

Next to the examples in (12) in which the adjective is always a stem, we also find A+N compounds in which a schwa is added to the stem of the adjective:

---

[2] My translation (JD).

(13)

A (stem)	N	COMPOUND	GLOSS
wit	brood	wittebrood	'white bread'
wild	man	wildeman	'wild man'

Such forms are not easy to find, but there are far more examples of these A + schwa as left-hand member cases, if we also take into account examples with stress on the right-hand member:

(14)

A (stem)	N	COMPOUND	GLOSS
hoog	school	hogeschóól	'high school'
rood	kool	rodekóól	'red cabbage'
vast	land	vastelánd	'main land'

In all the examples discussed previously, main stress is on the left-hand member of the compound. In this respect, compounds can be easily distinguished from phrases since phrases have stress on their (mostly right-hand) head. The examples in (14) have precisely the same phonology as phrases: stress is on the noun (rather than on the adjectival part as in the examples in (12) and (13)), and the schwa is also present as an inflectional morpheme in the parallel phrases:

(15)   een hoge school   'a high school'
        een rode kool   'a red cabbage'

The difference between the phrases in (15) and the compounds in (14) is that the latter have a non-compositional semantics: *hogeschool* is an educational institution where a particular type (i.e. 'high') of education is given. The parallel phrase refers to simply any high school, like for example a school located in a high building. Such a school could never be referred to with the compound. So, we may want to analyse the compounds in (14) on the basis of their phonological resemblance to phrases as a kind of 'lexicalized phrase', whereas the examples in (13) are truly compounds. Note that the examples in (14) also contain an inflectional affix (-*e*), which adds to their original phrasal status.

In general nominal compounds are the most productive type in Dutch.

19.2.2 Adjectival compounds

Adjectival compounds (with an adjective as their right-hand member) are far less productive than the nominal compounds. Also, they can hardly be used recursively. So, we cannot embed an adjectival compound in an adjectival compound. Here are some examples of N+A compounds:

(16)

N	A	COMPOUND	GLOSS
steen	rood	steenrood	'stone red'
vrouw	vriendelijk	vrouwvriendelijk	'woman friendly'
doel	bewust	doelbewust	'target aware'

Note that the semantic relationships between the adjective and the left-hand noun can be rather diverse. So, in *steenrood*, *steen* modifies the meaning of *rood*: it is a particular kind of red. In *vrouwvriendelijk*, however, the noun refers to the object of *vriendelijk*: it means 'friendly towards women'. Also, in *doelbewust*, *doel* is the object of *bewust*: it means 'aware of his/her target'. Stress in the above cases lies on the right-hand member.

(17)

V	A	COMPOUND	GLOSS
fluister	*zacht*	*fluisterzacht*	'whisper soft'
drijf	*nat*	*drijfnat*	'soaking wet'
koop	*ziek*	*koopziek*	'buy ill' (i.e. 'buy compulsively')
leer	*gierig*	*leergierig*	'learn eager' (i.e. 'eager to learn')

Also in case the left-hand member is a verbal stem, we find that the verb can semantically be a modifier as for example in *fluisterzacht*, which means something like (only of noise) 'as soft as if one is whispering'. There is a small group of adjectives such as *ziek* 'ill', and *gierig* 'stingy' that allow for a kind of complement reading of the verbal stem. So, *leergierig* can be paraphrased as 'eager to learn'; *leer* 'learn' here is a kind of complement of *gierig*.

A+A compounds are a quite productive type. Mostly, the left-hand adjective modifies the right-hand adjective. This is the case in the following examples:

(18)

A	A	COMPOUND	GLOSS
donker	*blond*	*donkerblond*	'dark blond'
licht	*groen*	*lichtgroen*	'light green'
dicht	*bevolkt*	*dichtbevolkt*	'densely populated'

Note that Dutch adjectives can easily function as adverbs in syntax. For example the adjective *dicht* 'dense / close' is used as an adverb in the following sentence:

(19)   *De mensen staan dicht op elkaar*
       'The people stand close to each other'

So, one might argue that in the examples in (18) it is the adverb that is the left-hand member of the compound rather than the – phonologically identical – adjective. This would imply that (almost) all adjectives have a lexically stored adverbial counterpart, which would seem a rather unattractive solution. Another way to look at this issue is to claim that there is a kind of rule or principle that tells us that all adjectives in Dutch can act as adverbs, and that consequently, if these lexical items act as left-hand members of compounds, the adverbial reading is always possible, given an appropriate context.

There is also a small group of adjectives (such as *diep* 'deep' and *stom* 'stupid') that, if used in adjectival compounds, lose their original lexical meaning and only function as intensifiers:

(20)	A	A	GLOSS	COMPOUND	GLOSS
	stom	*dronken*	'drunk'	*stomdrunken*	'very drunk'
	stom	*verbaasd*	'surprised'	*stomverbaasd*	'very surprised'
	diep	*ongelukkig*	'unhappy'	*diepongelukkig*	'very unhappy'
	diep	*droef*	'sad'	*diepdroef*	'very sad'

19.2.3 Verbal compounds

Compounds with a verbal head come in two types: inseparable compounds and separable compounds. The latter are characterized by the fact that syntactic processes such as Verb Second (see e.g. Weerman 1989) and Verb Raising (see e.g. Evers 1975) only affect the stem of the verb and not the verb as a whole. As a consequence, the two parts of the word can be separated in a syntactic context. Consider the following sentences with the verb *opbellen*, which consists of a stem *bellen* 'ring' and a particle *op* 'on'.

(21) a. SUBORDINATE CLAUSE (no separation)

       dat   *ik*   *Iris*   *op-bel*

       that   I   Iris   PRT-ring

       'that I phone Iris'

  b. MAIN CLAUSE (separation under 'verb second')

       ik   *bel*   *Iris*   *op*

       I   ring   Iris   PRT

       'I phone Iris'

  c. 'verb raising'

       dat   *ik*   *Iris*   *op*   *probeer* *te*   *bellen*

       that   I   Iris   PRT   try   to   call

       'that I try to phone Iris'

Separable compounds often have idiosyncratic semantics: we cannot derive the meaning of the whole from the constituting parts. Furthermore, they can be morphologically derived and further compounded as shown by the following examples:

(22) *opbel*   'to phone'   *opbel-spel*   'phone-game'

      oplos   'to solve'   *oplos-baar* 'solvable'

      inkopen 'to buy'   *inkop-er*   '(professional) buyer'

In the literature there is much discussion about the question whether the separable compounds are indeed compounds (i.e. words) or whether they should be considered phrases. An analysis that considers separable compounds as words may account for their derivational and semantic properties, but the fact that they can be separated is not easily explained under such a view, since words are generally not separable. For those that argue in favour of a phrasal solution, the fact that idiosyncrasies in meaning may occur and that they can be easily derived are problematic. It would extend the limits of this contribution to discuss this issue in any detail. We refer the reader to (among others) Booij (1990), Neeleman (1994), Den Dikken (1995), Lüdeling (2001), Ackema and Neeleman (2004), Blom (2005), and references therein.

As said, these separable verbs stand in contrast to the inseparable ones. For example, the verb *rangschikken*, consisting of a noun *rang* 'rank' and the verbal stem *schikken* 'to arrange' is inseparable and thus the whole compound moves under V2 and VR:

(23)   a. *dat   Annelot   de   blokken   rangschikt*
           that   Annelot   the   blocks   arranges
           'that Annelot arranges the blocks'

       b. *Annelot rangschikt de blokken*

       c. *Annelot probeert de blokken te rangschikken*

The inseparability of these compounds goes hand-in-hand with another distinguishing property: in the inseparable compounds the prefix *ge-* shows up outside the compound as a whole, whereas in the separable cases, the prefix *ge-* separates the stem from the left-hand part. The examples in (24) illustrate this property:

(24)   a. *Jan   heeft   Iris   op-ge-bel-d*
           Jan   has   Iris   phoned
           'Jan has phoned Iris'

       b. *Annelot   heeft   de   blokken   ge-rangschikt.*
           Annelot   has   the   blocks   arranged
           'Annelot has arranged the blocks'

The formation of inseparable compounds is unproductive: speakers do not make this type of compound on the spot. New separable compounds are more easily made, especially with preposition-like elements as their left-hand member.

19.2.4 Exocentric compounds

Dutch also has a small, and nearly closed, group of exocentric compounds. They often refer to persons, and they typically are of the 'pars pro toto'-type. Here are some examples:

(25)   *rood-huid*   'red-skin'   American Indian
        snot-neus   'snot-nose'   arrogant youngster
        rood-borst   'red-breast'   robin

It can be easily seen that, semantically, the right-hand member of these compounds is not the head. Also, the gender of the right-hand member does not determine the gender of the whole:

(26)   *het hemd*   'shirt'   *de zwart-hemd*   'black-shirt'   fascist
       het bloed   'blood'   *de half-bloed*   'half-blood'   half-breed

This type of compounding is almost completely unproductive.

19.2.5 Left-headed compounds

One final type of compounds forms a small closed class. No new compounds can be formed in the same way. These compounds are characterized by the fact that they are left-headed. The left-hand member of the compound is a verbal stem and the compound as a whole is a verb. The right-hand member is a noun referring to a body part:

(27)   V   N   COMPOUND   GLOSS
       schud   *buik*   *schuddebuik*   'shake-belly'   shake with laughter
       reik   *hals*   *reikhals*   'reach-neck'   reach anxiously
       stamp   *voet*   *stampvoet*   'stamp-feet'   stamp with rage

19.3 THE PHONOLOGY OF COMPOUNDING

19.3.1 Stress

Most generally, we can say that the phonological form of a Dutch compound is the concatenation of the phonological forms of the compounding words (modulo linking morphemes, see section 19.3.2). The only structural additional property is that in general the left-hand member of the compound gets the main stress of the compound, whereas a secondary stress falls on the right-hand member (see Langeweg 1988, Visch 1989, Booij 1995: 115). The examples below illustrate this general stress pattern in different types of compounds:

(28)   a.   *brood + mes*   *bróódmes*   'bread-knife'
            slaap + kamer   *sláápkamer*   'sleep-room'
       b.   *donker + rood*   *dónkerrood*   'dark-red'
            diep + ongelukkig   *díepongelukkig*   'deeply-unhappy'
       c.   *rang + schikken*   *rángschikken*   'arrange'
            op + bellen   *ópbellen*   'phone'

Some compounds have different stress-patterns, though. Here are some examples:

(29)	*stad + huis*	*stadhúis*	'city hall'
	boer(en) + zoon	*boerenzóón*	'farmers' son'
	wereld + natuur + fonds	*wereldnatúúrfonds*	'WWF'

There are some lexemes that, if they occur as left-hand members of compounds, do not get the main stress. These lexemes include *stad* 'city', *staat* 'state', and *rijk* 'national'. But other exceptions exist and no clear pattern seems to be present. In the words of De Haas and Trommelen (1993: 389): 'As far as we can ascertain, there are no systematic reasons present that could explain these deviant stress-patterns in bipartite compounds.'[3]

Not specific for compounding but following from more general phonological rules in Dutch, we may observe final devoicing, stem-assimilation (progressive and regressive), nasal-assimilation, degemination and t-deletion. We will not go into these processes here, but refer to Booij (1995) for an overview of Dutch phonology.

19.3.2 Linking morphemes

A remarkable property of Dutch compounds is that the compound as a whole is often a little more than the sum, or more precisely the concatenation, of two stems. In many cases a so-called linking element is introduced between the two members of a compound. Here are some examples:

(30)	*weer-s-voorspelling*	'weather forecast'
	stad-s-vernieuwing	'city renewal'
	hond-e-hok	'dog-shed'
	huiz-en-rij	'house-row'

The linking element has either the form *-s*, schwa, or in a few cases *-er*. The schwa is spelled as *e* or *en*. Historically, in some compounds these linking morphemes are derived from case endings. In other cases they are derived from words that originally ended in schwa but that have lost this final schwa. After the loss of case endings as part of a more general process of deflection (see also Booij 2002a), these elements seem to have spread by analogy to different types of compounds, even to those of which the left-hand member is a verbal stem.

In the literature a much-debated issue is whether synchronically at least some of these linking elements are in fact plural morphemes. Booij and Van Santen (1998: 156–60) argue that in some cases a plural interpretation of the left-hand member is rather obvious:

---

[3] My translation (JD).

(31) *bedrijv-en-terrein* 'enterprise area'
       sted-en-raad   'cities council' (=council of more than one city)
       huiz-en-rij   'house row'

However, in other cases, the plural interpretation is absent:

(32) *bon-e-schil*   'bean peel'
       vrouwe-hand   'woman's hand'

And, in yet other cases, the contrast in presence or absence of the linking morpheme does not correlate with singular/plural interpretation:

(33) *boek-handel*   'bookshop'
       boek-en-kast 'bookcase'

Therefore, Booij and Van Santen also conclude that linking morphemes are distinct from plural markers.

It is clear from many studies into this phenomenon (Mattens 1970, 1984, 1987; Van den Toorn 1981, 1982) that the linking morphemes depend on the left-adjacent element. More specifically, we can state the following generalizations with respect to the linking elements (cf. Mattens 1970: 189, De Haas and Trommelen 1993: 379):

(34) a. If a word occurs with -*e(n)* as the left-hand member of a compound, its plural will also be marked with -*en*.

      b. If a word occurs with -*er* as the left-hand member of a compound, its plural will be marked with -*eren*.

So, the problem posed by linking morphemes is that they are not plural markers, and yet there is a clear connection between the form of the plural marker and the potentially occurring linking morpheme. Hoekstra (1996) connects the two in his analysis of linking morphemes in the following way. He assumes that many Dutch nouns have two stems: one with the linking morpheme, and one 'bare' stem without the linking morpheme. So, to give a few typical examples, the stems of the lexemes HUIS 'house', BOEK 'book', and KIND 'child' would be as in (35):

(35)   STEM I   STEM II
       HUIS   *huiz*   *huize*
       BOEK   *boek*   *boeke*
       KIND   *kind*   *kinder*

Following Hoekstra (1996), the stem *huize* is used when this lexeme occurs as the left-hand member of a compound. This same stem is used in the plural, thus explaining the correspondence in (34a). Along the same lines, the stem *kinder* is used as the left-hand member of a compound and also forms the basis for plural formation, in accordance with (34b).

19.4 SYNTHETIC COMPOUNDS

Synthetic compounds have raised a long debate about the question whether compounds are constructed in the lexicon, or result from syntax. Some researchers claim that compounds are the result of incorporation (Lieber 1992a, Ackema 1995, Kuiper 1999), while others (DiSciullo and Williams 1987, Booij 1988, Grimshaw 1990) claim that they are formed in the lexicon. Roeper (1988), following Roeper and Siegel (1978), argues that at least in English we should make a distinction between 'root compounds' (built in the lexicon) and 'synthetic compounds' (built in syntax). The latter type of compounds display several characteristics, which betray (in the view of Roeper) their syntactic origin. We will briefly discuss some Dutch data that pertain to this issue below.

One of those characteristics is the argument interpretation of the left-hand element in a compound of which the right-hand member is a deverbal noun as in (7) (here repeated for convenience) (see also Lieber 1983):

(36)   *weer(s) - voorspell-ing*
        weather - forecast

Another characteristic of such compounds is the possibility of control, as can be seen in the English example in (37) (from Roeper 1988: 189):

(37)   John enjoys rock-throwing for hours

Example (37) has an interpretation in which *John* is the subject of the throwing. According to Roeper this interpretation has a syntactic origin in which an IP with a PRO-subject underlies the compound. A third characteristic of synthetic compounds concerns their aspectual properties. Consider the example in (38) (from Roeper 1988: 187):

(38)   John enjoyed clam-baking for hours.

As Roeper points out the PP *for hours* modifies the verb *bake*. He assumes that progressive aspect presupposes an IP underlying the compound in (38), and hence a syntactic origin of these compounds.

Parallel Dutch constructions to the English examples in (37) and (38) are the ones in (39):

(39)   a. *Jan   houdt   van   urenlang   stenen   gooien*
           Jan   likes   of   hourslong   rocks   throw-INF
           'Jan likes rock-throwing for hours'

        b. *Jan   houdt   van   urenlang   oesters   bakken.*
           Jan   likes   of   hourslong   clam   bake-INF
           'Jan likes clam-baking for hours'

Like the English examples, these constructions may also involve control: there is an interpretation in which *Jan* is necessarily the subject of *stenen gooien / oesters bakken*, but also the non-control reading is possible (as in (37)).

However, it is not a priori clear whether such constructions in Dutch are truly compounds. One could also defend the position that these constructions involve nominalizations of (verbal) phrases. Ackema (1995) provides two tests to determine whether we are dealing with compounds or with phrases. Verb Raising provides an appropriate test, given the fact that true compounds always *can* raise as a whole (40a), although they may be separated as well (40b):

(40) a. *dat   Jan   het   probleem [t]   wil   oplossen*
         that   Jan   the   problem   wants   on-solve-INF
         'that John wants to solve the problem'

      b. *dat   Jan   het   probleem   op [t]   wil   lossen*
         that   Jan   the   problem   on   wants   solve-INF
         'that Jan wants to solve the problem'

Applying this test to the examples in (39a) shows that we may interpret these constructions as true compounds:

(41) a. *dat   Jan [t]   wil   stenen   gooien*
         that   Jan   wants   rocks   throw-INF
         'that Jan wants to throw rocks'

      b. *dat   Jan   stenen [t]   wil   gooien*
         that   Jan   rocks   want   throw-INF
         'that Jan wants to throw rocks'

A second test that Ackema (1995) uses to identify true compounds is the *aan het* construction. V′ as a complement to this construction is impossible:

(42) **Jan   is   aan   het   een   boterham   eten*
       Jan   is   on   the   a   sandwich   eat-INF
       'Jan is eating a sandwich'

However, the N+V combinations under scrutiny can function as complements of *aan het*:

(43) a. *Jan   is   aan   het   spelen*
         Jan   is   on   the   play-INF
         'Jan is playing'

      b. *Jan   is   aan   het   piano   spelen*
         Jan   is   on   the   piano   play-INF
         'Jan is playing the piano'

   c. *Jan is   aan het stenen   gooien*
      Jan is   on   the rocks   throw-INF
      'Jan is throwing rocks'

Nevertheless, Ackema (1995: 108) concludes: 'N-V compounding may be productive in Dutch, but it is hard to establish this with certainty. Due to the separability of most verbal compounds in Dutch they are hard to distinguish from syntactic phrases.'

Booij and Van Santen (1998: 165) provide yet another test for compoundhood of N+V combinations. The determiner element *geen* is used in order to negate NPs, where *niet* is used to negate verbal projections. (44) gives some relevant examples:

(44) a. *ik   kan   geen   huis   kopen*
       I   can   none   house   buy
       'I cannot buy a house'

    b. **ik   kan   niet   huis   kopen*
       I   can   not   house   buy

    c. **?ik kan   geen   adem   halen*
       I   can   none   breath take

    d. *ik   kan   niet   adem   halen*
       I   can   not   breath take
       'I cannot breathe'

So, *huis kopen* in (44a) is a VP in which the object is negated, whereas *adem* in (44c) is not an object NP but is 'incorporated' in the verb. Many examples allow for both possibilities; however, if we turn back to the examples in (39), we can see that both *stenen gooien* and *oesters bakken* are not compounds according to this test:

(45) a. *ik   kan   geen   stenen   gooien*
       I   can   none   rocks   throw
       'I cannot throw rocks'

    b. **?ik kan   niet   stenen   gooien*
       I   can   not   stones   throw

(46) a. *ik   kan   geen   oesters bakken*
       I   can   none   clams   bake
       'I cannot bake clams'

    b. **?ik kan   niet   oesters bakken*
       I   can   not   clams   bake

We should add here that the intuitions with respect to the examples in (45b) and (46b) are rather subtle and seem to depend on the extent to which a particular activity can be considered a conventionalized activity always involving the same rules or a particular technique. So, once we tell native speakers before judging these sentences that in order to bake oysters you need a particular technique, or a procedure involving a particular instrument, they are more easily inclined to accept (46b). The upshot seems to be that a compound reading is possible only once a more or less idiosyncratic reading becomes available.

An interesting generalization is drawn by Ackema and Neeleman (2004), who claim that V-headed compounds are only possible if they are embedded. Consider the data in (47):

(47)   a.   *stenen-gooi-er*
             'rock-thrower'
       a'. **Jan stenengooit naar auto's*
             'John rockthrows at cars'

       b.   *appel-pluk-machine*
             'apple-picking-machine'
       b'. **Jan appelplukt in Frankrijk*
             'John apple-picks in France'

       c.   *lang-haar-ig*
             'long-hair-y'
       c'. **Jan heeft langhaar*
             'John has longhair'

The compounds in the examples a', b', and c' are all ill-formed. Conversely, as soon as these compounds are embedded, as the other examples show, the structures become fine. Ackema and Neeleman argue that syntactic structures, if they are possible, block morphological structures (*pace* Elsewhere Condition-related blocking). The well-formed examples in (47) have no competing syntactic structure, whereas there is a regular syntactic structure available as an alternative for the other constructions. Applying this reasoning to the examples in (45) and (46), we may say that if the suffix *-en* is a nominalizing affix, the embedded compound structures should be fine as compounds. If, however, the *-en* suffix is a verbal affix, the structures should only be well-formed as regular VPs.

CHAPTER 20

IE, GERMANIC: GERMAN

MARTIN NEEF

20.1 INTRODUCTION

German is notorious for its ability to form 'awful' long compounds. Sometimes, compounds fill a whole line in written text. They immediately catch the reader's eye because they are usually written without blanks or hyphens in between. There is no maximum upper limit for the length of a German compound. One of the most famous examples is *Donaudampfschifffahrtsgesellschaftskapitänsmütze*. This word is known by almost every German child, and it is the basis for internet surveys looking for the longest word in German. A structural analysis of this word is the following (with LE denoting 'linking element'):

(1) *Donau dampf schiff fahrt   s   gesell   schaft s kapitän s mütze*
    Danube steam ship journey LE journeyman SUFFIX LE captain LE cap
    'Cap of the captain of the Danube steam ship company'

It is easy to make this word even longer. To talk about the hook to locate this entity on, the word *Haken* 'hook' may simply be added to the right, yielding *Donaudampfschifffahrtsgesellschaftskapitänsmützenhaken*.

Compounding is a highly productive means of lexeme formation in German. Many compounds are ad-hoc formations that never enter dictionaries. Therefore, it is hard to assess the share of compounds in the German vocabulary. German contains compounds with different structures. Moreover, there are some marginal types that may or may not be classed as compounds. This structural diversity will be discussed in this chapter, giving details of structural types and an overview of the main focus of contemporary theoretical discussions concerning compounding in German. A short overview of the rich history of the linguistic treatment of compounding in German is given in Olsen (2000a: 898). Detailed databases are presented in Ortner and Müller-Bollhagen (1991) and Pümpel-Mader et al. (1992). The German term for compounding is either *Komposition* lit. 'composition' or *Zusammensetzung* lit. 'putting together'. The latter term is the same for the process and the result while the former allows a distinction between these two notions as in English, with *Kompositum* denoting the result, the compound.

Compounding is a type of lexeme formation. The following presentation of linguistic properties of compounds will therefore be organized along the following generally assumed structure of lexemes (in a slightly different order), concentrating on such properties of compounds that go beyond the properties of their constituents.

(2)   Phonological form
      Grammatical features
      Argument structure
      Semantic form

20.2 GRAMMATICAL FEATURES: HEADEDNESS

Compounds by definition consist of at least two morphological elements. Typically, these elements are lexemes in their own right. The grammatical features of the compound are the same as those of its right-hand constituent. Virtually no exceptions to the right-headedness of German compounds are reported. The head in German determines several different grammatical features, most importantly word-class. German has three open word-classes – noun, adjective, and verb – that allow the formation of new compounds. New nominal and adjectival compounds are quite frequent, while the productivity of verbal compounds is restricted. The following lists (cf. Fleischer and Barz 1992, Meibauer 2001) give a survey of structural types of compounds consisting of stems of differing word-class, beginning with nominal compounds.[1]

---

[1] The dot in the compound denotes the beginning of the second constituent.

(3) N → N+N   *Holz·haus* 'wooden house'   *Freiheits·kampf* 'fight for freedom'
                Merkel·rede 'Merkel-speech'   *Helfers·helfer* 'accomplice'
     N → A+N   *Groß·segel* 'mainsail'   *Dunkel·kammer* 'dark-room'
     N → V+N   *Web·fehler* 'weaving flaw'   *Radier·gummi* 'rubber'
     N → P+N   *Neben·frau* 'concubine'

Among the nominal compounds, the type N+N is the most productive one. First constituents can be simple or complex generic nouns or proper names. Even self-compounding occasionally occurs (cf. Günther 1981) as in the lexicalized noun *Helfers·helfer* or in the recent formation *Film·film* (special category of movies by commercial television company Sat.1).[2] Some types of adjectives are not allowed in A+N compounds, as can be seen in the ungrammatical forms *Farbig·graphik* 'colour print' and *Rosa·wein* 'rosé wine'. Wiese (1996b: 103–5) assumes that this restriction is prosodically conditioned in that adjectives ending in an unstressed full syllable (or in Wiese's terms: in a bisyllabic foot) are ruled out as first elements of nominal (as well as of adjectival) compounds. On the other hand, Eisenberg (1998: 218–19) claims that the restriction mentioned is morphologically conditioned, with suffixed adjectives being ruled out as first members in nominal compounds. Both explanations have a number of counter-examples.

The next group are adjectival compounds:

(4) A → N+A   *fleisch·farben* 'flesh-coloured'   *herz·zerreißend* 'heartbreaking'
     A → A+A   *alt·klug* 'precocious'   *alt·eingeführt* 'introduced long ago'
     A → V+A   *treff·sicher* 'accurate'   *fahr·tüchtig* 'able to drive'

Adjectival compounds can be composed with basic adjectives as well as with both present participles and past participles as second members (*herzzerreißend, alteingeführt*). On a certain abstract level, participles are inflectional forms of verbs, and so should be considered as verbs. To maintain the idea of headedness, a different level has to be relevant for the determination of word-class in compounds (or word-class-changing inflection has to be taken into account). With respect to words like *fahrtüchtig*, their status as compounds is disputed. This is because the meaning of the free element *tüchtig* 'efficient' is not preserved in the complex word. Therefore, some linguists distinguish a productive semi-suffix *-tüchtig* from the free stem *tüchtig*, interpreting *fahrtüchtig* as belonging to a different category than compound (cf. Barz 2005: 757f).

Finally, verbal compounds have to be examined:

---

[2] Donalies (2004) regards self-compounding as an instance of reduplication, but usually reduplication is defined as a kind of derivation. Most linguists assume that reduplication does not exist as a productive process of lexeme formation in German.

(5) V → N+V   *rad·fahren* 'to cycle'   *lob·preisen* 'to praise'
     V → A+V   *trocken·legen* 'to drain'   *froh·locken* 'to rejoice'
     V → V+V   *kennen·lernen* 'to get to know' *schwing·schleifen* 'to grind
                                                  by swinging'

     V → P+V   *an·rufen* 'to call'   *unter·lassen* 'to refrain from'
               'durch·schneiden 'to cut through' *durch·'schneiden* 'to intersect'

The examples in the rightmost row are inseparable verbs; the other examples
are separable ones. The last line shows a minimal pair differentiated by stress
pattern only. P+V compounds are often classified as particle compounds.
Whether verbal compounds are compounds in a strict sense or something else
(sometimes called 'pseudo-compounds') is generally disputed (e.g. Eisenberg
1998: 225–7).

   Other grammatical features are also determined by the right-hand element. This
is especially evident for nouns. The following list shows that both inherent and
external features of compounds are supplied by the head of the structure (linking
elements in part obscure these regularities; cf. section 20.3.1):

(6) a. GENDER
         ($Dampf_{MASC}$·$schiff_{NEUT}$)$_{NEUT}$ 'steamship'   ($Schiff_{NEUT}$·$fahrt_{FEM}$)$_{FEM}$ 'shipping'

     b. PLURAL
         $Dampf_{SG}$ – $Dämpfe_{PL}$ 'steam' $Schiff_{SG}$ – $Schiffe_{PL}$ 'ship'
         $Dampf·schiff_{SG}$ – $Dampf·schiffe_{PL}$ $*Dämpfe·schiff_{PL}$

     c. GENITIVE
         $Haus_{NOM}$ – $Hauses_{GEN}$ 'house' $Herr_{NOM}$ – $Herren_{GEN}$ 'master'
         $Haus·herr_{NOM}$ – $Haus·herren_{GEN}$ 'host' $*Hauses·herr_{GEN}$

In a sense, the head also determines that the whole construction is a compound. If
the right-hand element of a word is a stem (i.e. the formal side of a lexeme) and the
left-hand element as a whole is something other than an affix, then the whole
construction is called a compound in German. The left-hand member allows for
quite diverse structures:

(7) a. *der Aber-da-hört-sich-doch-gleich-alles-auf-Blick*
                               'the this-puts-a-stop-to-everything look'
     b. *die Just-in-time-Garantie*   'the just-in-time guarantee'
     c. *der US-Präsident*   'the president of the USA'
     d. *O-Beine*   'bendy legs'

Examples (7a) and (7b) are phrasal compounds, a type that has received much
discussion in German linguistics (e.g. Leser 1990, Wiese 1996a, Meibauer 2003). The
left-hand member in (7a) is a full sentence; many other types of phrases are
reported in this structural position as well. The left-hand element in (7b) is an
English phrase, yielding a German compound. Other types of left-hand elements

are abbreviations and single letters. In summary, it seems that the structure of left-hand members of nominal compounds is unconstrained in German. This poses theoretical problems especially for derivational approaches to morphology, in particular for theoretical positions subscribing to the Lexical Integrity Hypothesis (defined in a way that word formation is ordered prior to syntax; cf. Borer 1998: 152–3).

20.3 PHONOLOGICAL FORM

20.3.1 Linking elements as stem allomorphy

Many compounds in German do contain extra segments that are missing in its constituents when they appear as free forms. The compound based on the words *Kapitän* and *Mütze* is *Kapitänsmütze* instead of *Kapitänmütze. These segments (marked by bold) are called linking elements (German *Fugen*). According to Barz (2005: 722) about 30 per cent of all compounds contain a linking element. The central questions concerning this subject from a linguist's perspective are: What is the distribution of linking elements? What is their function? Some analyses treat linking elements as discrete constituents, yielding ternary structures. Coordination reduction, however, shows that it is the first constituent the linking element belongs to (Fuhrhop 1998: 187):

(8)   *Kapitänsmützen und Admiralsmützen*   'caps of captains and admirals'
      Kapitäns- und Admirals+ mützen
      **Kapitän- und Admiral+ smützen*

This analysis is further corroborated by the fact that only compounds with nouns or verbs as first constituents may have linking elements, irrespective of the word-class of the second element. Historically, linking elements stem from genitive and plural morphemes. Consequently, linking elements are regarded as morphemes in many studies, even in synchronic ones (Augst 1975, Gallmann 1999). The term morpheme, however, suggests that linking elements have meaning or grammatical function, a view that has been questioned in recent times (e.g. Becker 1992, Ramers 1997, Fuhrhop 1998). The following data illustrate the issue:

(9)   a. *Boots·bau*   *Jahres·beginn*
          boat·building   year·beginning
          'building of boats'   'beginning of a year'

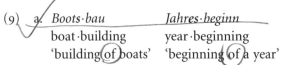

b. *Eier·likör*   *Hunde·rennen*
   egg·liqueur   dog·racing
   'advocaat'   'dog racing'

c. *Wochen·ende*   *Professoren·gattin*
   week·end   professor·wife
   'weekend'   'wife of a professor'

d. *Auto·sammlung*   *Nagel·fabrik*
   car·collection   nail·factory
   'car collection'   'nail factory'

e. *Liebes·brief*   *Arbeits·amt*   Geburtstag.
   love·letter   work·office
   'love letter'   'employment office'

The left-hand members of the compounds in (9a) are formally similar to the genitive singular of the basic lexemes; those in (9b–c) correspond to the nominative plural and those in (9d) to the nominative singular. In (9a–b), the meanings of the compounds are consistent with the respective inflectional categories as can be seen both in a paraphrase and in the translation. In the data in (9c–d), form and meaning are incompatible. The linking elements in (9c) suggest a plural reading although the semantic interpretation forces a singular interpretation of the first constituent. The first constituents in (9d) have the form of the singular, but a plural interpretation is called for. The data in (9e) shows linking elements that do not correspond to any inflectional marker of the respective lexeme. These linking elements are called 'unparadigmatic', as opposed to the 'paradigmatic' ones in (9a–c). In general, thus, it is reasonable to regard linking elements as functionally different from inflection markers.

Another putative function of linking elements discussed in the literature is a euphonic one: they are said to improve the compounds' pronunciation (e.g. Donalies 2005: 45). The fact, however, that a compound that usually contains a linking element sounds strange when pronounced without it, only shows that the unconventional word goes against the habits of language users. In order to prove the pronunciation hypothesis it would be necessary to show that a specific phonological context strictly demands some kind of linking element. No such proof has been given so far. Quite the reverse, the following data show that linking elements are not phonologically conditioned:

(10) a. *Mund + Pflege → Mund·pflege*   *Hund + Pflege→Hunde·pflege*
        mouth + care 'oral hygiene'   dog + care 'care of dogs'

     b. *Wind + Park → Wind·park*   *Kind + Park → Kinder·park*
        wind + park 'park of wind turbines'   child + park 'park for children'

   c. *Bank+Raub → Bank·raub* and *Bänke·raub*
       bank/bench+robbery 'bank robbery' and 'robbing of benches'

   d. *Kiefer+Bruch → Kiefer·bruch* and *Kiefern·bruch*
       jaw/pine +break 'fractured jaw' and 'breaking of pines'

The first constituents of the compounds in (10a) and in (10b) perfectly rhyme as free forms but behave differently with respect to linking elements when combined with the same second constituent. The compounds in (10c) and in (10d) consist of homophonous lexemes as first constituents that show a different linking behaviour. Obviously, linking elements do not have a general phonological function.

   As a conclusion, a number of linguists assume that linking elements have no function at all in compounds (e.g. Barz 2005: 720, but cf. e.g. Wegener 2003). Nevertheless, there are certain regularities in the distribution of linking elements. In order to understand these regularities, it is necessary to somewhat broaden the notion of linking element. In the following list, which draws upon a presentation in Becker (1992: 11), all the different segments that may appear between two parts of a compound are listed and other sound modifications are included too. Among them is pure umlaut or umlaut in combination with added segments as well as the subtraction of segments. The examples are restricted to N+N compounds. The same diversity can be found in N+A compounds while V+X compounds only have zero or schwa as linking elements.

(11) a. *e*   Tag+Buch   *Tagebuch*   'diary'
     b. *er*   Kind+Garten   *Kindergarten*   'kindergarten'
     c. *s*   Wirt+Haus   *Wirtshaus*   'tavern'
     d. *es*   Jahr+Zeit   *Jahreszeit*   'season'
     e. *n*   Affe+Haus   *Affenhaus*   'ape house'
     f. *en*   Präsident+Wahl   *Präsidentenwahl* 'presidential
                                                                election'
     g. *ns*   Name+Tag   *Namenstag*   'name day'
     h. *ens*   Herz+Wunsch   *Herzenswunsch*   'dearest wish'
     i. umlaut   Mutter+Heim   *Mütterheim*   'mother house'
     j. umlaut+*e*   Gans+Braten   *Gänsebraten*   'roast goose'
     k. umlaut+*er*   Buch+Regal   *Bücherregal*   'bookshelf'
     l. subtraction of *e* Sprache+Insel   *Sprachinsel*   'linguistic
                                                                enclave'
     m. replacement of *e* by *s* Geschichte+Buch *Geschichtsbuch* 'history book'
     n. ø   Büro+Tür   *Bürotür*   'office door'

Despite this general diversity of linking elements in German, most lexemes have only one form as first parts of compounds. According to August (1975: 134), only ten percent of nominal lexemes have more than one linking form. In these latter cases, there is typically one productive form while the others appear in lexicalized compounds only. An example for this is the lexeme MANN 'man'. In the actual vocabulary of German at least four different linking types can be observed (12a). Newly coined compounds, however, always take one and the same linking element as in the nonce-words in (12b):

(12)   a. *Männer·freund* 'man's man', *Manns·bild* 'fellow', *Mannes·alter* 'manhood', *Mann·decker* 'centre-half'

      b. *Männer·album, Männer·erbe, Männer·frost, Männer·philosophie, Männer·bearbeitung*
        man + album/ inheritance/ frost/ philosophy/ treating

This can be modelled using the concept of stem-form paradigms (Fuhrhop 1998). Lexemes in German have at least one general stem-form, a default. Some have a larger stem-form paradigm comprising deviating forms for specific structural positions as well as the default for all other contexts. A specific structural position for nouns is the left-hand membership in compounds. Thus, linking elements are an instance of stem-allomorphy (cf. also Becker 1992, Booij 2005a: 88). From this perspective, several minor regularities for specific stem forms can be detected, but many lexemes have idiosyncratic properties.

20.3.2 Stress and structural ambiguities

Each word in German has one (primary) stressed syllable. A compound consists of two elements that in isolation are stressed on one syllable each. Since a single compound can only have one stressed syllable, the question is which of the constituents will contain this stressed syllable. A straightforward hypothesis would be that it is the head that is stressed. This, however, is not the case in German. At least all nominal compounds in (3) are stressed on the first constituent. Therefore, Donalies (2005: 56) proposes initial stress to be the regular pattern for German compounds, but in passing she mentions difficulties with more complex compounds. Taking also complex compounds into account, a more promising rule is the following one which can be found in different formulations in several textbooks (e.g. Wiese 1996b: 298):

(13)   In a compound, the second constituent is stressed if it is a compound by itself; otherwise, the first constituent is stressed.

Consequently, in complex compounds stress may be a decisive factor to distinguish meaning. The following example is a compound with two readings, correlating with two different stress patterns (similar examples are discussed in Wiese 1996b: 298 and Meibauer 2001: 35):

(14)

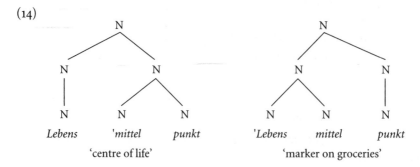

If rule (13) is the general compound stress rule in German, then a number of compounds have irregular stress (cf. Wiese 1996b: 300–2). In some cases, the data can be explained as showing conventional contrastive stress:

(15)   a. *Hundert.'eins*   'one hundred and one'
         b. *'Nord{bahn·hof}*   'North station'

The first example is a compound with two stems only; thus stress should be on the first constituent but is on the second. The second example has a compound as its second constituent which should carry main stress according to the rule, but stress is on the first constituent. In both cases it can be argued, however, that the stress pattern has a contrastive function. Both words belong to lexical fields whose members are distinguished by the elements focused on by stress only. In this way, *Nordbahnhof* contrasts e.g. with *Westbahnhof* 'West station'. Contrastive stress of this type is conventional and, thus, lexicalized.

20.4 SEMANTIC FORM: THE INTERPRETATION OF COMPOUNDS

The semantic aspect of compounds is sometimes taken to be the dominant one. Donalies (2005), for example, distinguishes two major classes of compounds based on their different semantic interpretation, with other distinguishing features being subordinate to this first level. In the presentation chosen here, semantics is just one level of analysis besides three others (cf. also Štekauer, this volume, on the interpretation of novel compounds).

The basis of semantic analysis is the principle of compositionality. According to this principle, a complex linguistic expression is compositional if its meaning is determined by both the meanings of its parts and the way it is structured.

The relevant structural property of compounds is headedness. A majority of compounds is interpreted in such a way that grammatical and semantic head coincide. According to such a determinative reading, the meaning of a compound with the constituents AB is 'B that has something to do with A'. In principle, every compound with a binary structure can be interpreted in a determinative way, for example all the compounds in (9). The best studied type of this class is N+N compounding. For example, a *Fisch·frau*, lit. 'fish·woman' is a woman that has something to do with fish. Heringer (1984) gives possible specifications for the relation between the two components, with more interpretations being possible:

(16)   a. woman who sells fish
     b. woman who has brought fish
     c. woman standing close to fish
     d. woman eating fish
     e. woman looking like a fish
     f. spouse of a fish
     g. woman and fish at the same time (i.e. mermaid)
     h. woman having Pisces as zodiac sign (German *Fisch*)
     i. woman as cold as a fish

In cases like these, the context is responsible for the exact interpretation, and a speaker cannot always be sure that the hearer is able to understand the compound in the intended way. Following Fanselow (1981), many attempts have been made to identify preferred interpretation strategies. In effect, however, any interpretation that is pragmatically sensible is a possible one (cf. Haspelmath 2002: 87). In this sense, the meaning structure of determinative compounds is underspecified.

In the actual vocabulary, however, a familiar compound typically has a usual interpretation drawn from the open set of possible interpretations. *Fischfrau* is an atypical example of an established compound in that there is no usual reading available. The compound *Haustür*, in contrast, usually refers to a door leading into a house. In order to evoke a different interpretation of this compound, the linguistic or non-linguistic context has to supply strong enough clues to make such an understanding possible. For example, when walking through a corridor inside a building and seeing several doors with pictures on them, one of them depicting a house, it may be quite clear that one should open this door when asked to enter the *Haustür* (and not, e.g. the *Fischtür* 'fish-door').

Another subgroup of determinative readings is based on analogy. Given that there exists a compound with a usual reading, another compound may be formed in relation to this model. An example is the compound *Haus·mann* that in principle denotes a man who is in some relation to a house. The specific reading 'househusband', however, takes the usual compound *Hausfrau* 'housewife' as its model.

There are also types of semantic interpretation where the grammatical head is not the semantic one, namely in copulative compounds (which are still right-headed grammatically). The meaning of a compound AB in a copulative reading is 'A and B', showing a coordinative structure. As is typical for coordination, the coordinated elements must be of the same type, both formally and semantically. Two classes of words are discussed as copulative compounds:

(17) a. *rot-grün*   'red and green'
          schwarz-rot-gold   'black and red and golden'
          Dichter-Maler-Komponist   'poet and painter and composer'
      b. *Hosen·rock*   'pant·skirt'
          Kinder·pilot   'child pilot'
          Kino·café   'cinema and café'
          nass·kalt   'chilly and damp' (lit. 'wet·cold')

The data in (17a) are copulative compounds in a narrow sense (cf. Becker 1992: 27–9). They have formal properties different from determinative compounds in that they allow more than two immediate constituents, they have stress always on the last constituent, irrespective of its internal structure, and they lack linking elements. In spelling, they are typically written with hyphens. The data in (17b) may be interpreted in a coordinate way but in a determinative way as well without yielding a real difference (cf. Breindl and Thurmair 1992). Formally, these words resemble determinative compounds with respect to binarity, stress, linking elements, and spelling. Therefore, it is more convincing not to treat them as copulative compounds (Becker 1992, contrary to e.g. Wegener 2006: 427).

Furthermore, there are some exocentric compounds in German (Donalies 2005: 58–60). Examples are *Rot·haut* 'redskin' and *Blond·schopf* 'blond person' (lit. 'blond·hair'), both denoting persons that have the features expressed in the compound. Exocentric compounds have a grammatical head but lack a semantic one. Formally, they resemble determinative compounds. This type of lexeme formation is unproductive in German.

Finally, many words that look structurally like compounds have a non-compositional interpretation, due to the process of lexicalization. For example, *Eselsbrücke* is composed of the nouns *Esel* 'donkey' and *Brücke* 'bridge', but the meaning is 'mnemonic trick'. A determinative interpretation of this compound is, of course, also viable. Examples for different types of non-compositional compounds are given in (18):

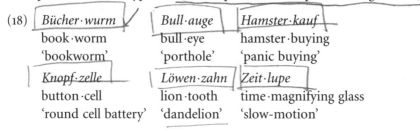

(18) | *Bücher·wurm* | *Bull·auge* | *Hamster·kauf* |
     | book·worm | bull·eye | hamster·buying |
     | 'bookworm' | 'porthole' | 'panic buying' |
     | *Knopf·zelle* | *Löwen·zahn* | *Zeit·lupe* |
     | button·cell | lion·tooth | time·magnifying glass |
     | 'round cell battery' | 'dandelion' | 'slow-motion' |

20.5 ARGUMENT STRUCTURE: INHERITANCE AND SATISFACTION

The final level of lexemes to be discussed is the level of argument structure. Compounding in German does not lead to the introduction of new arguments but the argument structure of embedded elements may become effective. Typically, the embedded element is a verb and the resulting compound contains a deverbal noun as its head. Such compounds are called 'synthetic compounds' (German *Rektionskomposita*). Clear examples are the following:

(19)   a.   *Appetit·hemm.er*   b.   *Farb·geb.ung*
           appetite·suppress.SUFF   colour·give.SUFF
           'appetite suppressant'   'coloration'

The second constituents of these words are not free words in the way that a noun like *woman* is free. In this feature, the data resembles other compounds like *blau-äugig* 'blue-eyed' although the second element is denominal here instead of deverbal. A number of linguists take this feature to be decisive and combine both types of words under the term 'Zusammenbildungen'. Many analyses take phrases to be the bases of this type of words. The properties of these compounds, however, clearly differ from those of phrases (cf. Leser 1990).

Moreover, the noun *Hemmer* is in the same way free or not free as its basic verb *hemmen* is. This latter word is a transitive verb demanding a subject and an accusative object in its grammatical domain in order to be well-formed. The same holds for the noun *Hemmer*, which has inherited the object argument from the base in its derivation while the subject argument has been suppressed. The derived noun, too, needs the realization of its arguments in some grammatical domain. There are two types of domains available: the first is the position of the first element of a compound, yielding the compound *Appetithemmer* with an argument structure that is fully satisfied, and the other one is the syntactic position of complement, yielding the synonymous phrase *Hemmer des Appetits*. Semantically, synthetic compounds are determinative compounds. The semantic relation between the first and the second constituent, however, is not constrained by general conceptual categories but by grammar proper. The only way to interpret the noun *Appetithemmer* is to give *Appetit* the role of the internal argument of the embedded verb. Synthetic compounds have been a main focus of study in word-syntactic approaches (cf. Olsen 1986, Rivet 1999).

In a comparable fashion, there are governed readings with compounds having a truly free right-hand member:

(20)   a. *Jazz·fan* 'jazz-fan', *Britney-Spears-Schwester* 'sister of Britney Spears'
       (but: *Kranken·schwester* 'nurse')
       b. *Brief·schreiber* 'letter-writer', *Helfers·helfer* 'accomplice'
       c. *Fahrer* 'driver', *Auto·fahrer* 'driver of a car', *Unfall·fahrer* 'driver at fault in
       an accident', *Geister·fahrer* 'ghost-driver/ person driving in the wrong
       direction'

The heads in (20a) are relational nouns. These nouns are free words that may
appear in sentences without the related entity being expressed explicitly. If they are
the head of a compound, however, the non-head must be interpreted as this related
entity. The second example in (20a) is different because *Schwester* is both a
relational noun ('sister') and a sortal noun ('nurse'). Therefore, both a relational
and a free interpretation are available. The deverbal heads in (20b) differ from the
examples in (18) in that they are free nouns, due to lexicalization. In these cases, a
governed reading is available when the semantics suggest it (e.g. *Briefschreiber*) but
other readings are possible as well. Since dative arguments are never inherited by
-*er*-suffixation, first elements in compounds with a head noun based on a dative
verb cannot be interpreted in a governed way. For example, a *Helfershelfer* (based
on the verb *helfen* 'to help' with a dative argument) is not a person to help someone
who helps others but an accomplice. Thus, the semantics of the compound is non-
transparent. The examples in (20c) show the diversity of interpretation strategies:
the nominalization *Fahrer* lost its internal argument by lexicalization. Since a car
may be an internal argument of a driving-action, the interpretation of *Autofahrer*
depends on the argument structure of the embedded verb. An accident, on the
other hand, does not fit this semantic criterion; therefore *Unfallfahrer* needs some
other kind of interpretation, in this case a lexicalized one. A ghost may also be an
internal argument of a driving-action, but in the case of *Geisterfahrer* there is also a
lexicalized reading available independent of the argument structure. Lexicalized
readings are customary and therefore preferred context-free.

20.6 BORDERLINE CASES OF COMPOUNDS

In the pertinent literature, more kinds of German words are discussed as subtypes
of compounds. A first type is blends (German *Kontaminationen* or *Kofferwörter*):

(21)   a. Kur+Urlaub   *Kurlaub*   'cure+holiday'
       b. Winter+Intermezzo   *Wintermezzo*   'winter+intermezzo'
       c. ja+nein   *jein*   'yes+no'
       d. Tomate+Kartoffel   *Tomoffel*   'tomato+potato'

Blends consist of two lexical stems but in the process of compounding some segments are left out. This is most likely if the ending of the first stem and the beginning of the second one sound the same or are written the same. Then this reoccurring sequence is realized only once (21a, b). Blends also occur if this feature is not contained in the basic material (21c, d). It is yet to be specified whether there are strict regularities as to what segments have to be left out in blends as well as which stem appears first and which one second. This is due to the fact that blends typically have a copulative reading. Therefore, the elements of a blend have to have the same word-class and they have to fall into the same semantic field. In this sense, blending is an iconic way to form copulative compounds. Naturally, blends lack linking elements. The stress pattern of a blend typically equals the pattern of one of the two basic stems. A weak tendency in blends is having the same number of syllables as the longer one of the two basic stems. Blending is a type of language pun. It appears most frequently in literature and in advertising. Only a few blends are part of the general vocabulary (*jein* as well as the English borrowings *smog* and *brunch*).

Another minor type of compounding is *Zusammenrückungen* (cf. Fleischer 2000).

(22) *Hand·voll*   hand·full   'handful'
      dort·hin   there·to   'there'
      Tu·nicht·gut   do·not·good   'good-for-nothing'
      Drei·käse·hoch   three·cheese·high 'tiny tot'
      Vater·unser   father·our   'Our Father'

These lexemes result from the fusion of words that frequently appear adjacent to each other in sentences. The resulting words quite often are not right-headed and they lack linking elements altogether. They may be regarded as conversions of phrases rather than true compounds. This process is not productive in German.

Finally, words like the following are also discussed as compounds (e.g. Donalies 2005):

(23) *Thermo-stat* 'thermostat', *Phono-logie* 'phonology'

These neoclassical compounds (German *Konfixkomposita*) differ from typical compounds in that at least one of the basic elements is a bound form. These bound forms, however, differ from affixes in certain respects like appearing in both first and second position of a word or in combining with each other to form a whole word (cf. Elsen 2005, Schu 2005). Linguists are not unanimous as to whether this type of productive lexeme formation belongs to either compounding or derivation or forms a main type of its own.

CHAPTER 21

IE, GERMANIC: DANISH

LAURIE BAUER

21.1 INTRODUCTION TO DANISH

Danish is a North Germanic language spoken by approximately five million people in Denmark, northern Germany, the Faroe Islands, and Greenland. It is closely related to Swedish, and has historically borrowed a great deal of vocabulary from varieties of German and, in recent years, from English.

Danish is a verb-second language in main clauses (see (1)), and main clauses are distinguished from subordinate clauses by the relative position of verbs and adverbials (see (2)). Adjectives precede their heads when they are used attributively, and agree for gender and number in indefinite NPs (see (3)) and are inflected for definiteness in definite NPs (see (4)). They are also inflected for degree. Nouns carry inherent gender, either common gender (marked on singular articles with forms ending in *-n*) or neuter gender (marked on singular articles with forms ending in *-t*), and inflect for number and definiteness when the noun is not premodified (see (5)).

(1) *Folk   elsker deres   born   som   regel*
     People love   their   children   as   rule
     'As a rule people love their children'
     Som regel elsker folk deres børn
     Deres børn elsker folk som regel
     *Som regel folk elsker deres børn

I should like to thank Hans Basbøll, Alex Klinge and Salvador Valera for their helpful comments on earlier drafts.

(2) a. *Han   er   ikke   kommet*
      He   is   not   come
      'He hasn't come'

    b. *Jeg   ved   at   han   ikke   er   kommet*
      I   know   that   he   not   is   come
      'I know he hasn't come'

(3) a. *Et   stort   hus*
      a   big (NEUT)   house (NEUT)
      'a big house'

    b. *En   stor   bil*
      a   big (COM)   car (COM)
      'a big car'

    c. *store   huse*
      big (PL)   houses
      'big houses'

    d. *store   biler*
      big (PL)   cars
      'big cars'

(4) a. *Det   store   hus*
      the   big   house (NEUT)
      'the big house'

    b. *den   store   bil*
      the   big   car (COM)
      'the big car'

    c. *de   store   huse*
      the   big   houses
      'the big houses'

    d. *de   store   biler*
      the   big   cars
      'the big cars'

(5) a. *Huset   er   stort*
      House(DEF)   is   big (NEUT)
      'the house is big'

    b. *bilen   er   stor*
      car(DEF)   is   big (COM)
      'the car is big'

    c. *husene   er   store*
      houses(DEF)   are   big (PL)
      'the houses are big'

d. *bilerne*   *er*   *store*
   cars(DEF)   are   big (PL)
   'the cars are big'

Note that adjectival inflection is ambiguous between definite and plural, so that it is not necessarily clear what the final -*e* (pronounced /ə/) represents in *de store huse*. Adverbial marking is homophonous with the neuter inflection for adjectives, so that *stort* can mean 'greatly' as well as 'big (NEUT)' (whether this is homonymy or polysemy is a matter which need not be debated here). Adverbial -*t* (often not pronounced) is frequently omitted from adjectives ending in -*ig*. The precise use of the final orthographic <t> here has recently been the subject of prescriptive interference from the Danish Language Council, Dansk Sprognævn.

Verbs do not agree for person or number, but are inflected for tense (either past or non-past), for participial forms, and for the infinitive. Verbs also inflect for a synthetic passive (historically a middle voice). The forms for a regular verb such as *arbejde* 'to work' are thus *arbejde* (infinitive), *arbejder* (present tense), *arbejdede* (past tense), *arbejdende* (present participle), *arbejdet* (past participle), *arbejd* (imperative) and passive/middle versions of the present and past tenses with a final -*s*.

Danish is a stress-timed language, with stress falling on the initial syllable of the root of the word. A millennium of consonant lenition (sometimes followed by consonant reinstatements) has left the Danish spelling system a rather indirect guide to the pronunciation of Danish words, with many diphthongs represented as sequences of vowel and consonant letters. Standard Danish (*Rigsmål*), based on the pronunciation of Copenhagen, also has an important contrastive prosodic phenomenon called the *stød* or 'glottal catch'. The *stød* corresponds to the tones of Norwegian and Swedish, and occurs on syllables which have a sufficiently sonorous moraic structure to allow it. In such syllables it is contrastive, so that /man/ means 'one (impersonal pronoun)' (cf. German *man*) while /man'/ means 'man' (cf. German *Mann*). Phonetically, the *stød* is realized by laryngealization of the relevant sonorant (whether it is a vowel or a consonant). Local dialects exhibit differences in their use of *stød*, and in southern parts of Denmark there is no *stød* or *stød* occurs irregularly.

On the basis of this thumbnail sketch of Danish, we are in a position to start considering the compounds of the language.

21.2 INTRODUCTION TO COMPOUNDING

Where compounding is concerned, Danish is a fairly typical Germanic language. Because premodifiers have to be marked for definiteness (see (4) above), only adjectives are permitted as premodifiers. Verbs, adverbs, sentences, and nouns are morphologically unsuited to appear in this position (Klinge 2005). English, which no longer has this structural restriction on premodifiers, seems able to use other word-classes in this function relatively freely, as in (6). If Danish wants to do this, it has to create an adjective or a compound in which the premodifying element is included in the same word as its head (cf. (7)).

(6)   ADVERBS, PARTICLES: *the then king; the in thing*
       VERBS: *a can-do attitude*
       SENTENCES: *give-me-the-money-or-I'll-blow-your-brains-out scenarios*
       NOUNS: *an iron bar; his student experiences*

(7)   *den daværende konge* 'the then-being king'
       drikkevand 'drink(INF)-water'
       hvorfor-skal-man-op-om-morgenen-stemme   'why-must-we-(get)-up-in-the-morning voice'
       en jernstang 'an iron-bar'; *hans studenteroplevelser* 'his student-LE-experiences'

    This does not, however, explain the occurrence of adjective + noun compounds in Danish, although they seem to have existed since the period of Early Middle Danish (Skautrup 1944, I: 294). There is a consistent semantic difference between an adjective + noun compound and an adjective + noun phrase. The adjective in adjective + noun compounds is always a classifying adjective. Consider the example of *den hvide vin* 'the white wine'. In this example, *hvid* 'white' is gradable and sub-modifiable, so that we can say *den ikke særlig hvide vin* 'the not particularly white wine', *den gul-hvide vin* 'the yellowish-white wine', and so on. On the other hand, the compound *hvidvin* simply contrasts with red wine and with rosé, independent of its actual colour. Consequently, the adjectival part of *hvidvin* cannot be independently modified, and *den gule hvidvin* 'the yellow white-wine' is not a contradiction in terms. Likewise there is a difference between *en lille finger* 'a little finger', which is simply a matter of the finger's size, and *en lillefinger* which is the fifth finger of the hand. Examples like *centralvarme* 'central heating', *national-følelsen* (EB 2)[1] 'national pride', *passiv-rygning* (BT 26) 'passive smoking', whose adjectives might be expected to be classifying under their normal readings, confirm the general trend but stress the nameability of the concept labelled. Keller (1978: 577) says of comparable constructions in German that they indicate that Latinate

---

[1] Examples which can be found in dictionaries are not given a source, while examples which are not completely lexicalized but which are attested are provided with a source. The sources used here are BT (*BT* newspaper, 28 June 2006), EB (*Ekstra Bladet* 28 June 2006), FS (Peter Høeg, *Frøken Smillas fornemmelse for sne* [Miss Smilla's feeling for snow], Copenhagen: Rosinate, 1992), and PL (Astrid Lindgren, *Pippi Langstrømpe* [Pippi Longstocking], translated into Danish by Anine Rud, Copenhagen: Gyldendal, 1945).

suffixes are not recognized as derivational endings in adjectives, implying that Germanic suffixes are never found in adjectives in this position (see also Fleischer 1975: 84) – something which appears to be largely true in Danish as well.

There are both phonological and morphological grounds for saying that these compounds are single words. Phonologically, the vast majority of them take stress on the initial element, and carry a single main stress for the compound, just as a non-compound lexeme would carry a single main stress. Basbøll (2005: 496–500) points out that although loss of *stød* in the first element of compounds has been stated to be the norm, this is true only of lexicalized compounds, and that the relationship between the presence or absence of *stød* and compound morphology is far more complex. Morphologically, at least where nouns are concerned, we have evidence for single-word status from definiteness inflection. While a single noun can take a postposed definite article, as in *hus·et*, a premodified noun must take a preposed definite article, as in *det store hus* (see (4) and (5) above). Thus, when we discover that the definite form of *hvidvin* is *hvidvin·en* and not **den hvidvin*, we have evidence that *hvidvin* is a single word and not a noun with an independent premodifier.

21.3 Compound nouns

21.3.1 Endocentric

The most common pattern for compound nouns in Danish is for endocentric noun + noun formations, with variable semantic relations holding between the elements, as is illustrated in Table 21.1.

There are many ways of analysing the wide range of semantic relationships which hold between the elements of these compounds, and the analyses which have been proposed for other Germanic languages (e.g. by Granville Hatcher 1960, Lees 1960, Žepić 1970, Brekle 1970, Levi 1978), are equally valid for Danish. However, what these analyses show is that there is no agreement about the level of abstraction at which the semantic analysis should be carried out, with the number of semantic categories being proposed varying from one to over a hundred. Examples such as *mælketand* 'milk tooth' (with a corresponding figure also in Dutch, English, French, German, Italian, and Spanish) *bjørn·e·tjeneste* 'bear·LINK·service' = 'ill turn', *brand·mos* 'fire·moss' = 'water moss' suggest that it is not likely to be easy to find an exhaustive list of semantic relationships between the elements of a compound if those relationships are too specific. On the other hand, Søgaard (2005) argues that theories that do not give precise meanings for the links between

Table 21.1 Noun + noun compounds

Compound	Gloss	Translation	Semantic relation
barn·e·dåb	child·LE·baptism	'christening'	process in which someone baptises a child
barn·e·barn	child·LE·child	'grandchild'	the child *of* one's child
død·s·straf	death·LE·penalty	'death penalty'	the penalty *is* death
drab·s·sag	murder·LE·case	'murder case'	case *involving* murder
fod·bold	foot·ball	'football'	the ball is controlled *by the use of* the feet
læge·sprog (BT 4)	doctor·language	'doctor talk'	language *produced by* doctors
lag·kage	layer·cake	'layer cake'	the cake is *made up of* layers
lunge·betændelse	lung·inflammation	'pneumonia'	inflammation *in* the lungs
lyn·kursus (BT 16)	lightning·course	'short course'	course *resembling* lightning (in its speed)
mælk·e·produkt (BT 4)	milk·LE·product	'milk product'	product *derived from* milk
miljø·ministerium	environment·ministry	'ministry of the environment'	the ministry *deals with* the environment
morgen·mad	morning·food	'breakfast'	the food is eaten *in* the morning
myg(g)·e·stik	mosquito·LE·sting	'mosquito bite'	the mosquito *creates* the bite
reklame·pause (BT 15)	advertisement·pause	'commercial break'	break *for* advertisements
sol·crème	sun·cream	'sun-tan lotion'	the lotion *protects against the effects of* the sun

compounds miss ambiguous readings of compounds. The case will not be argued further here, but is of general importance in developing a theoretical description of compounds in Germanic.

Much of the Danish literature on compounding focuses on the linking elements which are found between the elements of nominal compounds (Spore 1965: 215–16;

Table 21.2 Linking elements

Link	Examples
no link	*dag·penge* (day·money = 'per diem') *dyr·læge* (animal-·doctor = 'vet') *land·mand* (land·man = 'farmer') *landvej* (land·way: *ad* ~ = 'overland') *ord·bog* (word·book = 'dictionary') *øje·klap* (eye·patch)
s-link	*amt·s·læge* (county-LE·doctor) *dag·s·orden* (dag-LE·order = 'agenda') *land·s·mand* (land-LE·man = 'fellow countryman') *universitet·s·forlag* (university-LE·press)
e-link	*dyr·e·handler* (animal-LE·trader = 'pet shop owner'), *hest·e·vogn* (horse-LE·cart = 'horse and cart') *jul·e·dag* (christmas-LE·day) *land·e·vej* (land-LE·way = 'main road')
er-link	*blomst·er·bed* (flower-LE·bed) *student·er·liv* (student-LE·life)
(e)n-link	*rose·n·gård* (rose-LE·yard = 'rose-garden'), *øje·n·læge* (eye-LE·doctor = 'ophthalmologist')

Hansen 1967, II: 296–301; Diderichsen 1972: 63–4; Allan, Holmes, and Lundskær-Nielsen 1995: 543–6). The various possibilities are illustrated in Table 21.2.

These linking elements are generally historically derived from genitive forms or plural forms (though the *e*-link is sometimes derived from the word *og* 'and' as in *hestevogn*). Although there are many instances where readings based on the genitive or the plural would not make sense, naïve speakers often feel that the *s*-link gives a genitive feel to the compound and that the *e*-link and *er*-link give, where appropriate, a plural feel. The *e*-link no longer conveys any genitive impression to naïve speakers.

The examples in Table 21.2 are deliberately chosen to indicate that no absolute generalizations about the form of the link (if any) exist as long as we seek generalizations over the established lexicon. This is consistent with the case in the other Germanic languages (see Botha 1968 for Afrikaans, Krott, Baayen, and Schreuder 2001 for Dutch, Dressler et al. 2001 for German). There are, however, many generalizations to be made, based both on form and on meaning. In general we can say that a particular left-hand element in a compound selects a particular linking element, particularly in productive use, and that instances such as *land*- versus *lands*-, illustrated in Table 21.2, where the two modes of linking lead to different semantic interpretations, are rare. In accordance with this generalization, many suffixes call forth a particular linking element: for example nouns ending in -*tet* always have an *s*-link, as do nouns ending in -*dom*, -*ion*, -*ning*, -*skab*, etc. (Allan et al. 1995: 544–5). Note that these suffixes include both native and borrowed affixes.

There are also instances where there is variation. Allan et al. (1995: 545) give *tid(s)·nød* 'shortage of time' and *kartotek(s)kort* 'filing card' as examples. A quick Google search suggests that this is correct, although the forms with -*s*- are clearly preferred.

More interesting is the claim (e.g. Allan et al. 1995: 545) that three-element compounds bracketed as [[AB][C]] are likely to get an *s*-link at the end of the B-element, which will distinguish them from compounds bracketed as [[A][BC]]. Minimal pairs between these two bracketings are vanishingly rare, but there are a number of compounds of the appropriate form which do show the *s*-link: *rød·vin·s·glas* 'red·wine·LE·glass', contrast *vin·glas* 'wine glass'. Similar claims are made for other Nordic languages (e.g. Thráinsson et al. 2004: 207 for Faroese; Mellenius 2003: 77 for Swedish). A count of clear three-term compounds from a single source (EB) was made to check this. Of eighty three-term compounds,[2] fifty-five were bracketed as [[AB][C]] and twenty-five as [[A][BC]]. Of the former, thirty had an *s*-link at the major break. It is clear that this use of an *s*-link can be no more than a tendency. Among the twenty-five words with the reverse bracketing, only three had an *s*-link between elements two and three. Of the fifty-five, only four had an *s*-link between elements one and two, while six of the twenty-five had an *s*-link in this position.

It is hard to say whether these link-forms should be treated as inflectional forms of the lexeme or not. The fact that they are not predictable would count against such an analysis, while their frequency might count in favour of it. However, independent of the analysis that these linking elements are given, we can say that the general rule for Danish compounds is that the first element does not change its inflectional form when the compound as a whole takes a different inflection. Thus the plural of *mand·drab* (man·killing = 'homicide') is *manddrab*, not **mænd·drab* (men·killing), even though several men would have to be killed for a plural to be meaningful. There are marginal exceptions. The plural of *barn·e·barn* (child·LE·child = 'grandchild') is *børn·e·børn* (children·LE·children), even when the grandchildren all belong to the same parents. The plural *bønder·gård·e* (farmers·yard·PL = 'farms') is now yielding to *bonde·gård·e* 'farmer·yard·PL', in line with the singular *bondegård*. Such inflected first elements appear to be dying out in the Nordic languages, being more common in conservative Icelandic than in innovative Danish, and less common in modern Danish than previously (see Hansen 1967, II: 107).

There are a few instances like *bom·uld* (?·wool = 'cotton'), *brom·bær* (?·berry = 'blackberry'), *jom·fru* (?·woman = 'virgin') where the construction looks like

[2] No compound type was counted more than once; compounds including initialisms were ignored; loan compounds were ignored; compounds which showed subsequent affixation before being included in the three-term compound were not included. The results might by chance under-represent the number of *s*-links in such words, since the newspaper considered was published during the soccer world cup, and *fodbold* 'football', which does not take an *s*-link, was a common first element in the observed compounds, occurring six times.

a compound but one element (in these instances, the first) has no independent existence. Such forms seem to arise through a loan process, *bom·uld* being cognate with German *Baum·wolle* (tree·wool), *brom* being cognate with English *bramble*, and *jom·fru* being cognate with German *Jung·frau* (young·woman = 'virgin').

Although it is unusual, the first element in a compound of this type can be separately modified. The norm is illustrated by *de små side·veje* (the small side·streets) (FS 208) where the adjective modifies the compound as a whole. Even examples like *ægte pels·frakker*[3] (genuine fur·coats) show agreement between the adjective and the head of the compound, rather than with the modifier to which they belong semantically (Klinge 2005). Despite widely cited apparent counterexamples like *kold smørrebrød·s·jomfru* (cold open-sandwich·LE·shop-assistant) or the attested *det tysk-østrigske grænse·område* (the German-Austrian border·area) (BT 3) it seems that such examples as *mærkelige snegle·huse* (strange snail·houses = 'strange snail shells') (PL 20) are not ambiguous in Danish as they might in principle be in English.

Adjective + noun compounds generally have a stem-form adjective which is unavailable for sub-modification in the initial position. Thus, given *stor·køb* (big·purchase = 'wholesale'), which is a neuter noun, we do not find **stor·t·køb* (big·NEUTER·purchase) or **meget stor·køb* (very big·purchase) or **størst·køb* (biggest·purchase). There are a number of exceptions to this general rule. Words like *ny·t·år* (new·NEUTER·year = 'new year') might not be compounds but lexicalized syntactic expressions. The same cannot be true for *små·kage* (small(PL)·cake = 'cookie') which has a suppletive plural form in the first element. The origin of the <e> in *stor·e·tå* (big·LE·toe) (more common than the alternative *stortå*) is unclear. In such words, however, the form of the adjective is fixed for all inflectional forms of the compound as a whole: *storetå, storetæer, storetåen*, etc.

Some examples of adjective + noun compounds are given in (8). Unlike what happens in most other compounds, the semantic relation between the head and its modifier seems to be consistent in these cases. Although adjective + noun compounds seem to be productive in principle, very few new such forms are found.

(8)	*høj·sæson*	high·season	'high season'
	let·sind	light·mind	'rashness'
	lige·mand	equal·man	'equal'
	lige·vægt	equal·weight	'balance'
	lille·bil	little(SG)·car	'taxi'
	polar·eskimo	polar·eskimo	'polar Eskimo'
	(FS 214)		
	rød·kål	red·cabbage	'red cabbage'
	små·kage	small(PL)·cake	'biscuit'

---

[3] www.mingler.dk/user/skovfinken/perma/2007/08/02/s_tl_dog_til_10 accessed 9 August 2007.

Rare lexicalized examples such as *barn·lille* (child·little = 'little one'), where the adjective follows the noun, are used as pet names, and *fader·vor* (father·our = 'Lord's prayer') is a similarly old-fashioned construction (Hansen 1967, II: 312). Similar modifier-final constructions are found in some place names.

In verb + noun compounds, the verb is, in productive use, in the infinitive form, unless the verb infinitive ends in -*ere*, when the final -*e* may be dropped: *punkter·kunst* (puncture-art = 'stippling'). Hansen (1967, II: 315) lists a number of lexicalized examples where the stem-form appears to have been used instead, or where some other form is used. Some regular examples are given in (9).

(9)
bære·pose	carry·bag	'carrier bag'
drikke·vand	drink·water	'drinking water'
folde·pung (FS 217)	fold·purse	'coin purse'
fortælle·kunst	tell·art	'narrative art'
koge·punkt	boil·point	'boiling point'
leje·tyv (EB 14)	hire·thief	'thief who is a hired hand'
leve·tid	live·time	'lifetime'
lokke·mad	tempt·food	'bait'
løbe·bane	run·track	'running track'
løbe·tid	run·time	'currency'
måle·fejl	measure·error	'error in measurement'
rulle·stol	roll·chair	'wheelchair'

It can be seen from the examples in (9) that the semantic relationship between the modifying verb and the head noun is variable. The noun may indicate the actor in the action of the verb, the object of the action of the verb, the location of the action of the verb, the instrument with which the action of the verb is carried out, or the thing which is made up by the action of the verb. While these semantic relations seem to cover most verbs of this type, the list is not exhaustive.

Compound nouns with other word-classes in the modifying position are illustrated in (10). It is not clear whether these types are still productive in Modern Danish. Hansen (1967, II: 314) cites a single recent (at that time) nonce-formation.

(10)
da·tid	then·time	'past'
efter·år	after·year	'autumn'
om·vej	about·way	'detour'
over·tøj	over·clothes	'top clothes'
på·skud	on·shot	'excuse'
sammen·komst	together·coming	'get-together'
selv·had	self·hatred	'self-hatred'
til·tro	to·belief	'faith'
udenom·s·snak	round_about·LE·talk	'prevarication'
under·titel	under·title	'subtitle'

Clearly, there are different degrees of lexicalization illustrated here, with the motivation for *påskud* being completely lost. *Sammenkomst* (and there are many words similar in structure) is probably to be understood as a nominalization from the verb *komme sammen* (come together). Note that deictics which appear in modifying position do not refer, so that *datid* does not refer to a particular 'then', and the same is true of *jeg·følelse* (I·feeling = 'self-consciousness'), *her·komst* (here·coming = 'extraction, lineage'), etc.

Finally, there are a number of coordinative compound nouns in Danish (see Bauer 2008b for general discussion). Some examples are given in (11). Despite the clear grammaticality of this type, such compounds are not particularly widely used. There do not appear to be exocentric subtypes of coordinative compound in Danish.

(11) *hest·e·vogn*   horse·LE·cart   'horse and cart'
      Jesusbarnet   Jesus·child(DEF)   'baby Jesus'
      Lolland-Falster   (two adjacent islands) the two islands seen as a
                                                    geographical unit
      øl(l)·e·brød   beer·LE·bread   dish made of beer and
                                                    rye-bread
      prins·gemal (EB 15)   prince·consort
      saft·e·vand   juice·LE·water   'diluted cordial'
      Slesvig-Holsten   Schleswig-Holstein
      smør(r)·e·brød   butter·LE·bread   'open sandwich'
      vidunder·barn (BT X 2) miracle·child

To illustrate the productivity of compound nouns in Danish, 100 different examples were taken from one of my sources (BT). Of these, just fifty were listed in Vinterberg and Bodelsen (1966). While there are problems with using a translating dictionary for such an exercise, and an old one at that, we can counterbalance this by saying that a further eleven of the compounds would be item-familiar to modern Danish speakers. This still leaves a very large percentage of nonce-formations.

21.3.2 Exocentric

Danish also has exocentric compound nouns. These are much rarer than their corresponding forms in English (see, though, Bauer 2008a), and it is not clear that they are productive in all the uses in which they can be found. They are usually made up of an adjective + noun, though there are occasional noun + noun forms, and they are used largely to name plants and animals, though nicknames for people may also be created in this way. Some examples are presented in (12).

(12)   *grå·skæg*   grey·beard
       gul·bug   yellow·belly   'warbler'
       kort·læbe   short·lip   'wood sage'
       lækker·mund   delicious·mouth   'gourmet'
       være en   'have a sweet tooth'
       lang·øre   long·ear   'long-eared bat'
       Lang·strømpe (PL)   long·stocking
       Rød·hætte   red·hood   'Little Red Riding Hood'
       storke·næb   stork·beak   'crane's bill geranium; pantograph'
       tusind·ben   thousand·leg   'millipede'

21.4 Compound adjectives

A selection of compound adjectives is presented in Table 21.3. The first elements in such compounds can be a number, a particle, an adjective (often with adverbial force), a noun, or a verb. The adjective itself can be a simple or derived adjective, or can be a participle. In some cases it may not be clear what word-class the first element belongs to. There is a link element following a noun which would take a link in a noun + noun compound. There are also problems with bracketing in some cases, as illustrated in Table 21.3. *Overnaturlig* must be bracketed as [over] [natur·lig], since there is no independent *overnatur*, but *overvægtig* is probably [over·vægt][ig].

The semantics of these compounds is slightly obscure. Those which are made up of noun + adjective can usually be interpreted as 'adjective Preposition noun' (with the preposition being variable), but in some cases such a gloss seems insufficient. There are also coordinative adjectival compounds, illustrated in (13), where a different set of meanings is required.

(13)   *bitter-sød*   'bitter-sweet'
       dialogisk-lyrisk   'dialogical-lyrical'
       døv·stum   deaf·dumb
       filosofisk-historisk 'philosophical-historical'
       grå-blå   'grey-blue'
       hvid·rød   'white-red' (e.g. of the Danish flag)
       tysk-østrigsk (BT 3) 'German-Austrian'

Table 21.3 Compound adjectives

Adjective	Gloss	Translation	Structure
18-årig	18-yearly	'18-year-old'	[AN]ig
død·træt	death-tired	'exhausted'	NA
elle·vild (EB 4)	elf·wild	'wildly enthusiastic'	NA
flaske·grøn	bottle·green	'bottle green'	NA
før·sproglig	before·linguistic	'pre-lingual'	PA
høj·lys	high·light	'broad' (of daylight)	AA
jern·hård	iron·hard	'hard as iron'	NA
kaffe·gul (EB 17)	coffee·yellow	'stained yellow by coffee'	NA
køre·teknisk (EB 3)	drive·technical	'(course) in driving technique'	VA
lyse·rød	shine·red	'pink' (light red)	VA
mad·glad	food·happy	'fond of good food'	NA
morgen·frisk	morning·fresh	'refreshed after a good night's sleep'	NA
natur·tro (EB 21)	nature·true	'true to life'	NA
ny·født	new·born	'new-born'	AA
over·natur·lig	over·nature·al	'supernatural'	P[N-lig]
over·vægt·ig	over·weight·y	'over-weight'	[PN]ig
rekord·høj (BT 36)	record·high	'at a record high'	NA
ret·tro·ende	right·believe·ing	'orthodox'	N/AParticiple
snot·dum	snot·stupid	'extremely stupid'	NA
splint·er·ny	splinter·LE·new	'brand new'	NA
stryge·fri	iron·free	'non-iron'	VA
tro·fast	believe/f·firm	'faithful'	N/VA
verden·s·kendt	world·LE·known	'known throughout the world'	NParticiple

21.5 COMPOUND VERBS

Compound verbs in Danish fall into two main classes. The first and numerically more important of these is verbs with a particle in the first element. The second has a noun, adjective, or verb (usually a noun) in the first element. Orthogonal to this distinction is one between separable and inseparable verbs. Although this distinction has been widely studied in Dutch and German (Lüdeling 2001, Kemenade and Los 2003), I am unaware of any comprehensive study of the Danish phenomenon. In most cases, where there is a difference in meaning between separable and inseparable verbs, the separable one is more literal than or more old-fashioned

(14) a. *Pia **fast·gjorde** mig hurtigt til seng·en*

      Pia firm·made me quickly to bed·the

      'Pia quickly tied me to the bed'

      *han **gjorde** mig **fast***

      he made me firm

      'he tied me up'

b. *[vi] har ret til at . . . **i·land·sætte** passagerer under rejse·n*

      [we] have right to to in·land·set passengers during voyage·the

      'we have the right to send passengers ashore during the voyage'

      *Der var kommet flere skibe til by·en for at **sætte** mennesker **i land**.*

      there were come more ship(s) to town·the for to set people in land

      'Several ships had come to the town to set passengers off'

c. *Er det lovligt at **ud·sende** regninger på den måde?*

      is it legal to out·send bills on that way

      'Is it legal to send out bills in that way?'

      *de vil undlade at **sende** regninger **ud** til forbrugere*

      they will omit to send bills out to consumers

d. *Australiens opposition·s·parti opfordrer landets premier·minister til at **under·skrive** Kyoto·aftalen*

      Australia's opposition·LE·party exhorts the_country's premier·minister to to under·write Kyoto·agreement(DEF)

      'Australia's opposition party is demanding that the country's prime minister should sign the Kyoto agreement'

      *nogle skoler vil føle det som en stor lettelse bare at kunne **skrive** aftale·n **under***

      some schools will feel it as a big relief just to can write agreement·the under

      'Some schools will find it a great relief just to be able to sign the agreement'

e. *jeg måtte lige **rådspørge** mig med fru Wiki om det*

      I must(PST) just counsel·ask me with Mrs Wiki about that

      'I just had to seek advice from Mrs Wiki[pedia] on that subject'

      *i er velkommen til at **spørge** mig **til råds***

      you(PL) are welcome to to ask me to counsel

      'You are welcome to ask me for advice'

f. *Når du **op·tager** noget via DR 1 f. eks*

      When you(SG) up·take something via Denmark's Radio 1 for example

      'When you record something from DR1, for example'

      *Han finder sig en plads, og **tager** noget **op** af sin taske*

      he finds himself a place and takes something up from his bag

      'He finds a seat and takes something out of his bag'

*Jeg synes jeg netop **tager** noget **op** til debat*

I think I precisely take something up to debate

'I thought I'd just start a debate about something'

g. *Under Bedømmelse **ud·går** obligatorisk seminar i kultur·modul*

under judgement out·goes obligatory seminar in culture·module

'According to the judgement the obligatory seminar in the cultural module is dropped'

*jeg tager et bad og **går ud** i by·en*

I take a bath and go out in town··the

'I'll take a bath and go to town'

h. *FOA lader bod **til·falde** medlemmer·ne*

FOA lets fine to·fall members·the

'FOA will let its members pick up fines'

*Det er svært at **falde til** i et nyt område*

it is hard to fall to in a new area

'It is hard to settle in a new area'

i. *Vi arbejder istedet for at **små·snakke** om liggyldigheder*

we work instead for to small(PL)·talk about trivialities

'We work instead of chatting about trivialities'

*snakke små(t)

j. **opskrige*

*hun er meget hurtig til bare at **skrige op** så snart noget ikke passer hende*

she is very quick to just to shout up so soon something not suits her

'She is very quick to complain if something doesn't suit her'

k. **færdigtale*

*Må jeg ha' lov til at **tale færdig**!*

may I have law to to speak finished

'May I finish, please?'

l. *Jeg **underviser** i engelsk og dansk*

I teach in English and Danish

'I teach English and Danish'

*vise under

than or more formal than the inseparable equivalent. Some examples are given in (14), taken from the Internet.

In general, noun + verb compounds tend to be inseparable and particle + verb verbs tend to be separable, but as can be seen from the examples in (14), there is a great deal of variation.

21.6 COMPOUNDS IN OTHER WORD-CLASSES

There are prepositions, adverbs, and conjunctions which contain two lexemic stems, although it may not always be clear whether they are best seen as compounds or as lexicalizations of syntactic structures. Some examples are given in (15).

(15)
bag·efter	back·after	'afterwards'
der·med	there·with	'thereby'
efter·som	after·as	'whereas'
for·fra	before·from	'from the beginning'
hjemme·fra	home·from	'from home'
høj·lydt	high·loudly	'loudly'
i·gennem[4]	in·through	'through'
i·morgen	in·morning	'tomorrow'
langt·fra	long(ADV)·from	'far from'
ned·ad	down·to	'downwards'
og·så	and·so	'also'

21.7 NON-COMPOUNDS

There are some constructions which might look like compounds, which it is probably helpful to distinguish from compounds. Some examples are given in (16), along with a reason as to why these might be treated as something other than a compound.

---

[4] The *i* in such words is usually omitted under composition: *gennem·brud* 'break through'.

(16)   *hulter til bulter*   ? to ?   'all over the place'   the construction
                                                                  is basically
                                                                  syntactic, though
                                                                  including unique
                                                                  morphs
       må·ske   may·happen   'perhaps'   probably a piece
                                                                  of lexicalized
                                                                  syntax
       forglem-mig-ej   forget-me-not   lexicalized syntax

21.8 CONCLUSION

The above is a very brief overview of compounding in Danish. The tyranny of word limits means that there are many marginal examples which have not been discussed, but the broad outline of the way in which compounds work in Danish should be clear. Compounding in Danish is an extremely productive means of word formation, both in terms of providing a large number of established forms and in terms of being used to create nonce-formations. There are some interesting differences between what happens in Danish and what happens in West Germanic, though such differences are never central.

CHAPTER 22

IE, ROMANCE: FRENCH

BERNARD FRADIN

22.1 INTRODUCTION

This chapter aims first to give an overview of native compounding in French (section 22.2). Its second goal is to sketch a description of the two most widespread and productive types among these compounds, V+N (22.3) and N+N (22.4), with a discussion of previous analyses.

22.2 AN INVENTORY OF FRENCH COMPOUNDS

22.2.1 Principle A

Principle A is a restatement of a proposal made by Corbin, which says that lexical units that can be straightforwardly generated by other components of grammar are not the concern of compounding (Corbin 1992: 50).

(1)   Principle A: Compounds may not be built by syntax (they are morphological constructs).

This criterion helps us to delineate what the respective properties of syntax and morphology are. Assuming that compounds are singular word-forms in syntax, Principle A forces us to determine whether clauses (2a) and (2b) are conjunctively satisfied:

(2)   a. The sequence of elements could have been generated by syntax.
      b. The phonology of the sequence of elements is that of a syntactic unit.

If they are, it means that the expression in question is not the concern of morphology. If they are not, it normally means that the expression pertains to morphology. In French, only (2a) is in force, while in English both clauses are (see however Bauer, 1983: 104–9). According to (2a), expressions in (3) are not compounds insofar as they correspond to phrases generated by syntax that can freely occur in texts, as shown in (4).

(3)   a. *sans papier*   'person without (identity) papers' lit. 'paperless'
         hors-la-loi   'outlaw' lit. 'out the law'

      b. *pied-à-terre*   'pied-à-terre' lit. 'foot on ground'

      c. *va et vient*   'comings and goings'; 'two-way wiring'
         boit-sans-soif 'drunkard' lit. 'drink without thirst'
         guérit-tout   'cure-all' lit. 'cure everything'

(4)   a. *Il s'est retrouvé **sans papiers**.*
         'He found himself without (identification) papers.'
         *Quand Condorcet fut mis **hors la loi**…*
         'When Condorcet was outlawed'

      b. *Le cavalier mit **pied à terre**.*
         'The horseman dismounted.' (lit. 'put his foot on ground')

      c. *Jean **boit sans soif** ni envie, simplement par habitude.*
         'John drinks without being thirsty and without desire, only as a habit'

Whereas all expressions in (3) are Ns (and X°), they correspond respectively to a PP in (4a), a nominal locution in (4b), and a VP in (4c). This change is an instance of lexicalization, and in the present case of univerbation (Schwarze 2007), which takes place when the property described by the expression in question is considered such a characteristic feature of some entity in a context, that the expression is used as the denomination of this entity (Bauer 1983: Chapter 3).

Principle A also allows us to dismiss examples (5) as compounds, since these expressions are sentences, as indicated by the inflectional marks they contain that become lexicalized through a mechanism known as 'delocutive derivation'.[1]

---

[1] This term aims at capturing the idea that the original meaning of the expression crucially refers to the utterance of the expression, for example, *sauve-qui-peut* describes a situation in which people shout 'sauve qui peut'.

(5) *décrochez-moi ça*   'cheap second-hand clothes' shop' lit. 'reach me down'
     rendez-vous   'appointment, date' lit. 'go to (somewhere)'
     sauve-qui-peut   'run for your life' lit. 'save who can'

By the same token, the nouns in (6a) must not be considered as compounds insofar as 'they are instantiation of the syntactic structure [N PP]$_{NP}$, a noun phrase consisting of a head followed by a PP complement', as Booij rightly put it (2005a: 83).[2]

(6) a. *avion à réaction*   'jet plane'
         serpent à sonnettes   'rattlesnake'
         chambre d'hôtes   'guest room'

     b. *poêle à frire*   'frying pan'
         fer à souder   'soldering iron'

The same reasoning leads us to conclude that the nominal expressions in (7) are not compounds either, since they instantiate two possible NP syntactic substructures in French, namely N + A (7a) and A + N (7b). The expressions in question can generally occur in sentences where they are plain NPs and have no idiomatic meaning, as shown in (8).[3]

(7) a. *nature morte*   'still life' lit. 'nature dead'
         guerre froide   'cold war' lit. 'war cold'

     b. *beaux-arts*   'fine arts' lit. 'beautiful arts'
         premier ministre 'prime minister'

(8) *De sorte que ce triste local et cette **nature morte** inspirent… plus de mélancholie que de curiosité.* DUSAULX, 1788 (in Frantext)
     'So that this mournful place and this dead nature inspire more melancholy than curiosity.'
     *Le **premier ministre** qui est entré portait un chapeau.*
     'The first minister who went in was wearing a hat.'

This conclusion has far-reaching consequences insofar as many linguists assume that (3) and (6)–(7) are genuine compounds (Darmesteter 1894, Bally 1950, Riegel, Pellat, and Rioul 1994; Gross 1996, Mathieu-Colas 1996), without any sound

---

[2] The same reasoning extends to (6b). Actually, expressions (6) are not NPs but Ns, since they can co-occur with a DET and an A: *Un gros avion à réaction* 'a big jet plane'. Nevertheless, Booij's comment is not invalidated, since he intended to say that these expressions are generated with an NP structure. The fact that the NP category becomes an N category is a direct effect of lexicalization.

[3] This point remains to be settled more firmly. In a few cases the actual sequence A + N or N + A does not seem to have existed before the appearance of the frozen phrase in question. For instance, there is no occurrence of *guerre froide* between 1700 and 1950 in the Frantex corpus, while there are 161 of such occurrences from 1950 up to 2000. Moreover, many complex nouns such as (7) originated in older stages of French, when the grammar of the internal NP was slightly different from what it is now. Combinations that were still possible a few centuries ago may not be allowable nowadays.

Table 22.1 Lexical categories in French compounds

	N	A	V	ADV
N	**N** prêtre-ouvrier (cf. Table 22. 2) poisson-chat jupe-culotte	**N** coffre-fort guerre-froide N < PSTPT chassé-croisé roulé-boulé	**V** maintenir saupoudrer	*
A	**N** basse-cour beaux-arts N < Vinf franc-parler faux marcher	**A** aigre-doux (cf. Table 22.2) A < PTCP nouveau né faux fuyant	*	*
V	**N** brise-glace tire-bouchon	**N** gagne-petit pète-sec	**V** saisir-arrêter (cf. Table 22.2)	**N** couche-tard passe-partout
ADV	**N** malchance malheur	**A** malpropre bienheureux A < PRSTPT moins disant malvoyant	**V** maltraiter bienvenir	—

argument and simply because they have never addressed the issue raised by Principle A. They confuse compounding with idiomaticity.

Normally, whenever an expression cannot be generated by syntax, Principle A tells us that the expression in question is the concern of morphology (cf. 22.3.1).[4] The polylexemic units examplified in (3) and (5)–(7) are nominal locutions whose abstract versions are phrasemes (Mel'čuk 1993: 56). Phrasemes, on a par with lexemes, ought to be listed in the lexicon since they have an idiosyncratic meaning (they are listemes in Di Sciullo and Williams's (1987) terms).

22.2.2 Overview

In French, the compounds and their constituents exhibit the combination of lexical categories given in the unshaded cells of Tables 22.1 and 22.2. For clarity, coordinate

---

[4] The possibility that an expression pertains neither to syntax nor to prototypical morphology is left open.

compounds have been mentioned but will be discussed below. Letters in bold indicate the category of the entire compound.

Table 22.1 reads as follows:

- *poisson-chat* 'cat-fish' is an **N** formed from two Ns, *poisson* 'fish' and *chat* 'cat'
- Dotted lines have been added when one constituent at least is generated with a category that differs from the actual one e.g. *roulé-boulé* 'roll' is an **N** formed from two Ns, *roulé* and *boulé* (both 'roll'), which come from past participles
- Double-lined cells indicate the productive patterns; their discussion is postponed until sections 22.3 and 22.4
- The shaded cells contain expressions that are not compounds according to Principle A
- Starred cells indicate that the sequences do not exist as constituents either in syntax, or in morphology
- The dash notes a gap: all instances of pattern **ADV ADV** belong to syntax and are related to the expression of degree e.g. *assez vite* 'fast enough', or high degree when the adverb is repeated e.g. *Elle est descendu, vite vite à la cuisine* (GIONO, in Frantext) 'She went down, very quickly to the kitchen'.

The N+A and A+N cases have already been illustrated in (7). For the sake of completeness, I have added examples (9a) and (9b), where the N originates in past participle and infinitive respectively.

(9)   a. *chassé-croisé*   'chassé-croisé' (dancing); 'to-ing and fro-ing'
      jeté-battu   'grand jeté' (dancing)
   b. *franc-parler*   'outspokenness'

As for the remaining cases, two points have to be kept in mind. First, they appear here as the result of the systematic category scanning imposed by the table. It is far from certain, however, that they must be considered as true instances of compounding. Second, they represent a very small number of lexemes (around one hundred all together), some of them vestigial and most of them exhibiting idiosyncratic properties in consequence of their intricate history.

If we lay out the compounds exhibiting an X+X pattern in Table 22.1, we obtain Table 22.2. It must be said straightaway that the V+V pattern is non-existent, insofar as only four examples are attested, all pertaining to the language of the law.

As for A+A compounds, only those with an allomorphic first element (*sino-*) or a linking element (*balladur-o-* < *Balladur*, former French prime minister) are truly productive. The others seem restricted to domains linked with perception (colour, taste), which limits their expansion.

In conclusion, we are left with four productive patterns: N+N coordinate (*auteur-compositeur*) and subordinate (*poisson-chat*), V+N (*brise-glace*), and A+A (*sino-coréen*). In what follows, I will focus on the first three, which raise more challenging issues for morphology than the last one.

Table 22.2 Lexical categories in co-ordinated compounds

N+N	A+A	V+V
Plain N	Plain A	Infinitive V
prêtre-ouvrier 'worker priest' *auteur-compositeur* 'author-composer'	*aigre-doux* 'sour-sweet' *sourd-muet* 'deaf-mute' *vert-bleu* 'green-blue'	*saisir-arrêter, saisir-brandonner* 'to distrain upon'
	Allomorphic A *sino-coréen* 'Sino-Korean' *balladuro-giscardien*	–

22.3 FRENCH V+N COMPOUNDS

The issues that have been repeatedly discussed regarding V+N compounding in French concern its nature (syntactic vs. morphological, 22.3.1) and the status of the verb (tensed vs. other, 22.3.2). I also discuss the semantic relationship between the constituents (22.3.3) and the phonological constraints (22.3.4).

22.3.1 Syntax or morphology

The view according to which V+N compounds are constructed by syntax has been defended in several influential accounts. The first one is Darmesteter's, who argues that the entire compound originates in an imperative sentence. His analysis will be discussed in 22.3.2.

The crucial point is to establish whether expressions like (10) can be generated by syntax or not. If they cannot, then Principle A allows us to conclude that they are constructed by morphology.

(10)	*essuie-mains*	'hand towel'	lit. 'wipe hands'
	porte-drapeau	'standard bearer'	lit. 'bear standard'
	tire-bouchon	'corkscrew'	lit. 'pull cork'
	abat-jour	'lampshade'	lit. 'weaken light'

This has already been conclusively demonstrated by Corbin (1992: 48–9): these expressions cannot occur in sentences, as the examples in (11) show. We can only have (12), but in this case what follows the verb is a full-fledged NP:

(11)   *Ce tissu essuie mains.   lit. 'This cloth wipes hands'
        *Pierre porte drapeau.   lit. 'Peter bears standard'

(12)   Ce tissu essuie les mains.   'This cloth wipes the hands'
        Pierre porte un drapeau.   'Peter bears a standard'

The distribution of V+N compounds contrasts sharply with that of frozen NPs in (3), where the expressions in question do appear in sentences since they are phrases, cf. (4c). Another distributional difference lies in the fact that while V+N compounds are commonly used to express the institutionalized function a human being performs in a society (e.g. *servir de NP* 'serve as NP') or, simply, an activity which allows us to socially identify the compound's referent, such a use is definitely impossible for complex nouns derived from frozen NPs (cf. (13), (14)). On the other hand, the latter are frequently used as nicknames, as *fend-le-vent* 'one who shows off', *boit-sans-soif* (cf. (15)).

(13)   Pierre était porte-drapeau en chef.
        'Peter was chief standard bearer.'

(14)   *Pierre était fend-le-vent en chef à Trois-Rivières
        'Peter was the chief of those who showed off at Three-Rivers'

(15)   On l'avait surnommé (fend-le-vent / boit-sans-soif / *porte-drapeau).
        'He has been nicknamed (lunge-toward-the-wind / drink-without-thirst / standard-bearer)'

This runs afoul of the analysis of Di Sciullo and Williams (1987), which makes no distinction between these two types of complex lexical units. On the contrary, I claim that Ns such as *boit-sans-soif*, *fend-le-vent*, and other frozen NPs are stored in the lexicon (in accordance with Di Sciullo and Williams's proposal), while V+N compounds are constructed by morphology.

22.3.2 The nature of the first constituent

Theoretical discussion has focused on the first element of the compound, the only one which is really problematical. A neutral formulation of the question is given in (16) and the answers that have been proposed are listed in (17):

(16)   In compounds $[X N2]_N$, what is the nature of X?

(17)   a. X is a deverbal N, derived from a V through a zero-morpheme suffixation
           (Scalise, Bisetto, and Guevara 2005: 140) $(= [[V+\emptyset]_{N_1} N2]_N)$.
        b. X is a V in the imperative 2SG (Darmesteter 1894).
        c. X is a V in the indicative 3SG (nineteenth-century grammars).

    d. X is a V, head of a VP which includes the N and is immediately
       dominated by an N (Di Sciullo and Williams 1987) (= [[X N2]$_{\text{VP}}$]$_{\text{N}}$).
    e. X is a verbal stem (*thème verbal*) of the V (Bauer 1980).

Analysis (17a) is adopted in several works by Bisetto and Scalise, where they
contend that V+N compounds in Romance are endocentric and are a mirror
image of Germanic secondary compounds of the type [N1 [V-er]$_{\text{N2}}$]$_{\text{N}}$ e.g. *taxi-
driver*. This account predicts that the first element could normally occur as a
converted V in the language, in a way similar to what we observe for most
Germanic *V-er* nouns like *driver*. This prediction is not borne out, however. Either
the nouns do not exist at all as example (b) of Table 22.3 shows; or, when they exist,
it is difficult to see how they semantically combine with N2 to yield the meaning of
the compound. For instance, if the converted V *coupe* has the same meaning as in
(la) coupe du bois 'cutting down trees', it remains to explain why *coupe-légume*
denotes an object and not an event.

    This analysis also predicts that the gender of the compound should be the same
as the gender of the converted first element. But this prediction is disconfirmed,
since V+N compounds are always masculine while the account in question
predicts they will be feminine.

    Darmesteter postulates basic structures (18) for *porte-drapeau* 'standard bearer'
and *serre-tête* 'headband' (Darmesteter 1894: 183). Subsequent formal changes
transform the sentence into a nominal compound.

(18)   '*toi, porte*:IMP *(le) drapeau!*'   'You, bear (the) standard'
       '*toi, serre*:IMP *(ma) tête!*'   'You, tighten (my) head'

He several times alludes to expressions with an overt imperative marking, like
rendez-vous in (5), as arguments supporting his view. However, such lexemes are
always derived through delocutive derivation and the very fact that a trace of the
imperative is still visible enforces this analysis. This contradicts analysis (17b).
Another problem is that the latter has to stipulate a fixed feature value for the
imperative (viz. 2SG), while complex NPs as in (5) allow all range of values for the
imperative (Bauer 1980). An additional problem arises whenever the compound's
denotatum is not an agent but a place as in *passe-plat* 'serving hatch' lit. 'hand
meals', which denotes a hole in a wall which the meals are handed through. The

Table 22.3 Compounds and converted first element

VN	Gloss	Converted N: FEM	Gloss
(a) *coupe-légumes*	'vegetable cutter'	*coupe*	'cutting (down)'
(b) *brûle-parfum*	'perfume burner'	**brûle*	—

Table 22.4 Phonological stems of verbs PORTER, TORDRE, **and** SOUTENIR

Lexeme	Stem 1 PRST.SG	Stem 2 PRST.3PL	Stem 3 PRST.1/2PL; IMPF
PORTER	/pɔʁt/	/pɔʁt/	/pɔʁt/
TORDRE	/tɔʁ/	/tɔʁd/	/tɔʁd/
SOUTENIR	/sutjẽ/	/sutjɛn/	/sutən/

present assessment forces us to conclude that Darmesteter's account is a failure. Most arguments against (17b) carry over to (17c).

Di Sciullo and Williams postulate a VP node in order to capture the fact that N2 is interpreted as the direct argument of the transitive verb occurring as the compound's first constituent (cf. (19)).[5]

(19)   [$_N$ [$_{VP}$ [$_V$ porte][$_N$ drapeau]]]

For the sake of discussion, suppose that we adopt (19). This analysis has to explain why a V may occur without any morphosyntactic marking although it heads a syntactic VP. This problem is the mirror-image of Darmesteter's. If no marking is assumed, a theory of ellipsis is required, which should make explicit in what situation the deletion of obligatory inflectional marks is licensed. A more serious problem arises with compounds the N of which has to be interpreted as the subject of the V and not as its direct object, for example *appuie-tête* 'head-rest', where the head rests on the compound's denotatum. Such compounds clearly cannot be accounted for by Di Sciullo and Williams's theory.

If we assume that compounding involves two lexemes, analysis (17e) follows quite naturally. It can be given a precise form if we take advantage of recent accounts of verbal inflection in French (Bonami and Boyé 2003, 2006). A French verb is associated with one or several phonological stems in the lexicon. Each stem is indexed to a subpart of the verbal paradigm. Each of these subparts corresponds to (groups of) cells in the paradigm where suppletion may happen for one verb of the language at least. The set of all stems of a verb constitutes its 'stem space'. Table 22.4 shows three of these stems for the verbs PORTER 'bear', TORDRE 'twist', and SOUTENIR 'support'.

The default stem for derivational rules is stem 3, e.g. *souten-ance* 'defence'< SOUTENIR, *tord-able* 'twistable' < TORDRE. As for compounding, the phonological default stem is stem 1 as shown in Table 22.4 (Bonami, Boyé, and Kerleroux 2008). Graphemically, the situation is more complicated for historical reasons. Generally,

---

[5] The following variant of this analysis is proposed by Lieber (1992a): [$_N$ [$_{VP}$ [$_V$ brise] [$_N$ glace]] Ø]. This analysis falls under the various criticisms levelled against other accounts or a combination thereof.

the stem corresponds to the actual graphemic stem of the present third-person singular, e.g. *porte-drapeau, tord-boyau* 'rot-gut (whiskey)', but not always, e.g. *soutien-gorge* lit. 'support-breast' = 'bra' (Villoing 2008).

22.3.3 The semantic relationship between constituents

22.3.3.1 *The V*

In the overwhelming majority of V + N compounds, the V is an action verb and the compound denotes either an agent (e.g. *porte-drapeau*) or an instrument (e.g. *ouvre-boîte* 'can-opener'). However, a wider range of denotata can be observed, as attested in Table 22.5, where Agent and Patient are defined according to the criteria given by Dowty (1991) and Davis and Koenig (2000), Causative corresponds to a cause that has no control over what is caused, and Locative denotes the place where the event the verb denotes occurs (in Fr. *lieu scénique*).

As expected, the Patient type remains very uncommon inasmuch as it constitutes the mirror-image of the Agent type: what the V + N denotes is what is affected by the process described by the verb (more examples in Fradin 2005). The locative type is widely illustrated by place names (e.g. *Jappeloup* 'place where wolf yelps' lit. 'yelp wolf'), and also by functional objects whose functionality crucially involves location, e.g. *passe-plat* or the above-mentioned *appuie-tête*. One can come across new Event and Causative types in corpora or on the Web, e.g. *pousse-plante* 'lighting fixture that makes plants grow', which indicates that these types are

Table 22.5 The compound's denotata in V + N compounds

Denotatum	Example	Glosses
Agent	*porte-drapeau*	'standard bearer' lit. 'bear standard'
	perce-oreille	'earwig' (insect) lit. 'drill ear'
Instrument	*tournevis*	'screwdriver' lit. 'turn screw'
	réveille-matin	'alarm clock' lit. 'wake up morning'
Event	*remue-ménage*	'hurly-burly' lit. 'move/shift housekeeping'
	baise-main	'kissing a woman's hand' lit. 'kiss hand'
Causative	*pisse-chien*	'plant which makes dogs pee' lit. 'pee dog'
	pense-bête	'aide-mémoire' lit. 'think beast (= people)'
Locative	*coupe-gorge*	'dangerous back alley' lit. 'cut throat'
	passe-plat	'serving hatch' lit. 'pass meal'
Patient	*broute-biquette*	'honeysuckle' = 'plant that goats graze' lit. 'graze goat: DIM'
	gobe-mouton	'thing that sheep swallow' lit. 'swallow sheep'

Table 22.6 The semantic role of N2's denotatum

Denotatum	V	Example	Glosses
Agent	T	*broute-biquette*	'plant that goats graze' lit. 'graze goat:DIM'
		croque-monsieur	'toasted cheese sandwich with ham' = 'X that a sir crunches' lit. 'crunch sir'
	I	*trotte-bébé*	'child walker'
Means	T	*cuit-vapeur*	'steam cooker' lit. 'cook steam'
Locative	I	*traîne-buisson*	'bird who shuffles along under shrubs' lit. 'shuffle shrub'
Temporal	T	*réveille-matin*	'alarm clock' = 'clock that awakens people in the morning' lit. 'awaken morning'
Patient	T	*ouvre-boîte*	'can opener' lit. 'open can'
		trompe-valet	'kind of pear' lit. 'deceive manservant' (because it seems not to be ripe when it is)
	I	*saute-bouchon*	'champagne' lit. 'pop cork' (because it makes the cork pop)

slightly productive. If we compare the range of denotata given in Table 22.5 with that allowed by other word-building processes, we see that the situation is more or less the same: derivational processes involving a V yield a type of derived lexeme for most kinds of semantic argument the verb can take. This fact has been acknowledged in French for *-IER*, *-ABLE*, and *-ET* suffixations (Fradin 2003a: Chapter 9; Hathout, Plénat, and Tanguy 2003).

22.3.3.2 *The N*

In a parallel way, the semantic role played by the N2's denotatum is not uniform, as shown in Table 22.6 (T, I = transitive, intransitive verb). In fact, types with N2 denoting a temporal interval[6] or a means are limited to the ones given here and those denoting locative are very rare and have an archaic flavour.

If we compare the first and last rows, we see that the N2s swap their semantic role and also that the compound's denotata swap correlatively (cf. first and last row of Table 22.5).

The data mentioned in Table 22.6 raise problems for the classical analyses examined so far. For the VP analysis, V+Ns in the first series are problematic because the semantic role of N2 and that of the compound's denotatum are the inverse of what it predicts; V+N compounds whose V is intransitive are out of reach of this analysis, since it postulates that N2 has to be the 'external argument' of

---

[6] *Lève-tôt* 'early riser', *couche-tard* 'late-bedder' can be analysed as frozen (incomplete) NPs, cf. *Jean se couche tard* 'John goes to bed late'.

Table 22.7 Phonological structure of V in French VN compounds

Type	Structure	Number	Example
1	σ	126	*porte-drapeau, trotte-bébé, ouvre-boîte, tourne-vis*
2a	σσ	4	*démonte-pneu* 'tyre lever'
2b	V.σ	17	*abat-jour, emporte-pièce* 'punch', *essuie-main*
2c	ʁV.σ	6	*repose-tête, remonte-pente* 'skilift', *réveille-matin*

the V; finally, V + Ns where N2 is temporal or locative are problematic because N2 is not, strictly speaking, an argument in a VP insofar as it denotes a place or an interval within which what the V describes takes place. An analysis of data mentioned in Table 22.6 is sketched in Fradin (2005).

22.3.4 Phonological constraints

The optimal word in French is dissyllabic (cf. Kilani-Schoch and Dressler 1992; Plénat 1998, 2008) and this ideal seems to have a direct bearing on the phonology of compounding. If we rely on data provided by Villoing (2002), we see that most Vs in V + N compounds are monosyllabic (126 of a total 153 verbs used in more than 2,000 different V + Ns) as shown in Table 22.7 (Villoing 2008). True dissyllabic V are very few (2.61 per cent), if we agree with Plénat (1999) that initial onsetless syllables are extrametrical in French and consequently should not be counted in the prosodic calculus (cf. Type 2b). This amounts to saying that the verb is monosyllabic in this case.

Moreover, it is well-known that all consonants are not equally suitable to constitute an onset and that /ʁ/, and liquids in general, are among the less suitable for this purpose. To that extent, the verbs of Type 2c could be considered as monosyllabic insofar as their first syllable is defective, since it begins with /ʁ/. Correlatively, the just-mentioned constraints could explain why there is no verb from the second conjugational group, the first stem of which is always dissyllabic (e.g. /fini/ 'finish' and no verbs suffixed in -*ifier* or -*iser* (-*ify* or -*ize*) in V + N compounding.

22.4 DESCRIPTION OF NN COMPOUNDS

In French, as in Romance in general (Rainer and Varela, 1992), it is much more difficult to state what counts as a compound for N + N than for V + N constructions. The reason for this stems from the fact there are many different N+N constructions and while some of them are clear instances of NPs, the syntactic status of many others remains to be settled (cf. 22.4.3). Hence, Principle A is more difficult to apply. Therefore, the scope of this section will limit itself to surveying the main types of N+N constructions and establishing which ones can safely be considered to be morphological compounds.

22.4.1 Coordinate compounds

The first type consists of coordinate N+Ns (20). When the Ns denote an individual, each N has a distinct referent and the compound's denotatum is said to be the sum of these referents.

(20) a. *Piémont-Sardaigne* 'Piedmont-Sardinia', *Bosnie-Hercégovine* 'Bosnia-Herzegovina'

b. *physique-chimie* 'physics-chemistry' (as a teaching discipline)

Noailly (1990: 70, 78) argues that whenever these N+Ns are arguments of some predicate in a sentence, the sentence's meaning implies the coordination of the predicate applied to each N. In other words, entailment (21) should hold, as (22) is supposed to show:

(21) X N1N2 Y ⇒ X N1 Y & X N2 Y

(22) a. *La physique-chimie manque d'étudiants.*
    'Physics-chemistry lacks students'

b. *La physique manque d'étudiants et la chimie manque d'étudiants.*
    'Physics lacks students and chemistry lacks students'

However, the validity of (22) is disputable because the very fact that the compound's denotatum corresponds to the cumulation of the denotatum of each N is questionable. Actually these N+Ns are denominations of something that is a unit from a juridical point of view only (the law (20a), teaching (20b)), on the model of what we have for pen names, e.g. *Boileau-Narcejac* (two people but one crime story author). If true, this means that genuine *dvandva* compounds are rare, if they exist at all.

Test (21) allows us nevertheless to contrast coordinate compounds (20) with (23), which denote a unique referent combining properties of both N1 and N2. N+N compounds (23) do not pass test (21), as (24) shows. On the other hand, they can be paraphrased according to schema (25a), which has a generic reading, a possibility excluded for compounds (20), as shown in (25c).

(23) *chanteur-compositeur*   'singer-composer'
    hôtel-restaurant   'hotel-restaurant'

(24) a. *Pierre a rencontré le chanteur-compositeur.*
          'Peter met the singer-composer.'

      b. #*Pierre a rencontré le chanteur et Pierre a rencontré le compositeur.*
          'Peter met the singer and Peter met the composer.'

(25) a. N1N2 is an N1 that is also an N2 and vice versa

      b. *Le chanteur-compositeur est un chanteur qui est aussi un compositeur et un compositeur qui est aussi un chanteur.*
          'The singer-composer is a singer who is also a composer and a composer who is also a singer.'

      c. **La physique-chimie est une physique qui est aussi une chimie et une chimie qui est aussi une physique.*

          *'Physics-chemistry is physics which is also chemistry and chemistry which is also physics.'

Constructions like (23) were considered typical N+N compounds by Corbin (1992). They are numerous and relatively productive in the domains given in (26) (cf. Noailly, 1990: 80):

(26) Crafts *boulanger-pâtissier* 'baker-confectioner', *plombier-zingueur* 'plumber-zinc worker', *enseignant-chercheur* 'teacher-researcher'
      Machines *moissonneuse-batteuse* 'combine harvester', *machine-outil* 'machine-tool', *étau-limeur* 'shaper'
      Functional object or place *canne-épée* 'swordstick', *bar-tabac* 'bar-tobacconist', *salon-salle à manger* 'living-dining room'
      Hybrid entities *chien-loup* 'wolfhound', *attentat-suicide* 'suicide attack'

The respective order of the Ns can be reversed in most N1N2 compounds of type (23) without changing the denotatum (e.g. *pâtissier-boulanger*). They have a received order, however, which seems mainly dictated by prosodic or pragmatic constraints (cf. remarks about the latter in Olsen 2001).

22.4.2 Subordinate N+N compounds

While the compounds in (23) entail both clauses instantiated in (27), as schema (25a) states, the N1N2 expressions in (28) only entail (27a) as (29) shows.

(27) a. 'an N1N2 is an N1'
      b. 'an N1N2 is an N2'

(28) a. *requin-marteau* 'hammerhead' lit. 'hammer shark', *tétras-lyre* 'black grouse' lit. 'lyre grouse', *homme-grenouille* 'frogman', *camion-toupie* 'ready-mix truck' lit. 'concrete-mixer truck' *guerre-éclair* 'blitzkrieg'

    b. *camion-citerne* 'tanker truck', *voiture-balai* 'broom wagon' (bicycle racing competitions), *livre-phare* 'leading book' lit. 'lighthouse book'

(29) a. *Un requin-marteau est un requin.*   'a hammerhead is a shark'
      b. **Un requin-marteau est un marteau.* 'a hammerhead is a hammer'

Although only inference (30a) holds for these expressions (cf. *Marie a vu un requin-marteau* 'Marie saw a hammerhead shark' ⇒ *Marie a vu un requin* 'Marie saw a shark'), it can be argued that (29b) is entailed in a figurative way, provided that we can specify the particular property Q of the compound's referent according to which the predication in question is true (cf. (31)).

(30) a. X N1N2 Y ⇒ X N1 Y
      b. X N1N2 Y ⇒ X N2 Y

(31) *Un requin-marteau est un marteau du point de vue de la forme.*
      'A hammerhead is a hammer from the point of view of its shape'

The property in question may concern a physical dimension (shape, length, weight), an intrinsic capacity (slowness: e.g. *justice escargot* 'slow justice'; quickness: e.g. *guerre-éclair*; strength: e.g. *attaquant-bulldozer* 'bulldozer-attacker'; duration: e.g. *discours fleuve* 'lengthy discourse' lit. 'discourse river') or a function (cf. (28b)). In most cases, Q corresponds to a salient property of the compound's referent. It is quite clear that the meaning of N+Ns of this type is metaphor-based, if we agree that a metaphor is the understanding of one concept in terms of another (Benczes 2006).

    Although many of them have long been considered subordinate compounds, their status as a lexeme or as a syntactic unit is difficult to establish for others. The fact that their semantics requires interpretive patterns of the kind we need to account for some types of derived lexemes (Fradin 2003b) could be taken as an argument for considering them morphological units. The fact that many of them are coined on the fly, as in (32), and never become lexicalized cannot be put forth as an argument against their compound status, since in languages where compounding is a very productive process (German), not all such compounds are lexicalized. If the same can be true in French, then all expressions discussed in this section could perfectly well be regarded as compounds.

(32) *Des malfaiteurs ont défoncé lundi au **camion-bélier** la devanture d'un distributeur de billets à Villiers-sur-Marne. (20 minutes, 11 September 2007)*
      'Gangsters smashed down the front of a cash dispenser with a ram-lorry at Villiers-sur-Marne on Monday.'

22.4.3 Two-slot nominal constructs

N + N sequences exemplified in (33) do not pass test (21), as expected (cf. (34d)), but do pass test (30a) insofar as they conform to (27a)(cf. (34c)).

(33) a. *impression laser*   'laser printing'
          roman photos   'photo novel'
          espace fumeurs   'smoking area'

      b. *alliage haute température*   'high temperature alloy'

      c. *responsable surgelés*   'manager in charge of deep-freeze products'
          langage auteur   'author language' (in computer science)
          impôt sécheresse   'tax for dryness'
          randonnée pêche   'hike for angling'
          accès pompiers   'entrance for firemen'

(34) a. *Une randonnée pêche est une randonnée.*
          'A hike for angling is a hike'

      b. *Jean organise des randonnées pêche.*

      c. ⇒ *Jean organise des randonnées.*

      d. ⇒ *Jean organise des randonnées et Jean organise une pêche.*

However, these constructs completely differ from the subordinate compounds discussed in 22.4.2. First, in no way does N2 express a property that could be ascribed to N1's referent on a metaphoric (or whatever) ground, in a parallel way to what we have in (31). This is so because no dimension of comparison whatsoever is conceivable as (35) attests.

(35) **Un responsable surgelés est des surgelés du point de vue de?*?*
       'A manager in charge of deep-freeze products is a deep-freeze product from the point of view of??'

Second, while the relationship between the Ns in subordinate compounds N1N2 is internal, in the sense that it is based on a salient property of the compound's denotatum (cf. *requin-marteau*), I would claim that it is external in constructs (33), for two reasons. On the one hand, you generally cannot deduce from the mere inspection of the construct's denotatum that the latter possesses an intrinsic property which sets it apart from objects commonly denoted by N1. For instance, no special property distinguishes an *accès pompiers* 'entrance for firemen' from an ordinary entrance, except the fact that somewhere there is a sign posted saying 'accès pompiers'.[7] Notice also that N2 never introduces a semantic predicate that N1 would be an argument of (in contrast to (28b)). On the other hand, these

---

[7] This feature does not hold true when one of the Ns denotes a material object e.g. *roman-photos* 'photo-novel'.

constructs usually denote entities that belong to a conceptual or technological classificatory system and N2 provides a clue about the place the construct's referent occupies within the classification in question. For instance, *responsable surgelés* denotes a type of manager among many others (~*jouets, charcuterie* '~toys, delicatessen') in the domain of food retailing (Fradin 2003a: 204).

Third, all the expressions in (33) also exist with a preposition heading a PP including either an N that can be bare (cf. (36a)) or an (incomplete) NP (cf. (36b)).

(36)   a. *impression* [$_{pp}$ *par laser*]
        roman [$_{pp}$ *avec (des) photos*]
        espace [$_{pp}$ *pour (les) fumeurs*]

        b. *responsable* [$_{pp}$ *pour* [$_{np}$ *les surgelés*]]
        alliage [$_{pp}$ *à* [$_{np}$ *haute température*]]
        langage [$_{pp}$ *de l'auteur*]

This property clearly distinguishes these expressions from all compounds that have been discussed so far and suggests that they have a syntactic origin. It also explains (i) why the value of the number feature can be distinct for the two Ns e.g. *roman*: sG*photos*:PL, and (ii) why the second member of these expressions can be an NP, as in (33b). Many such expressions generally have both structures, the one with the preposition being the oldest one (e.g. *stylo à bille* / *stylo-bille* 'ballpoint-pen').

22.4.4 Identificational N + Ns

I borrow from Noailly (1990) the term *identificational* to name the last N+N expressions we have to examine. These are exemplified in (37).

(37)   *l'institution Opéra*   'institution of Opera'
        la catégorie adjectif   'adjective category'
        le facteur coût   'cost factor'
        la filière bois   'wood industrial sector'
        la fée électricité   'electricity fairy' (electricity is a fairy   presumably because it makes wonders)

In contradistinction to those discussed in the preceding sections, these expressions satisfy (30b) although they also conform to (27a), as (38) shows:

(38)   a. *Jean étudie la catégorie adjectif* ⇒ *Jean étudie l'adjectif.*
        'Jean studies the adjective category' 'Jean studies the adjective'
        la filière bois se développe ⇒ ?*le bois se développe.*
        'The wood industrial sector developes.' '?Wood develops.'

        b. *la catégorie adjectif est une catégorie.*
        'The adjective category is a category.'
        la filière bois est une filière.
        'The wood industrial sector is a sector.'

Actually, these expressions even entail (39a), as (39b) attests:

(39) a. 'DET$_{DEF}$ N2 is an N1'

b. *L'Opéra est une institution.*   'Opera is an institution.'
  L'adjectif est une catégorie.   'Adjective is a category.'

From this point of view, these expressions behave exactly like sequences (40), where N2 is a proper name and N1 expresses a socially recognized category:

(40) a. *le président Mandela*   'president Mandela'
   b. *la région Bourgogne*   'Burgundy region'

(41) a. *le président Mandela est un président.*
   b. *Elle a traversé la région Bourgogne* ⇒ *Elle a traversé la Bourgogne.*
    'She travelled across Burgundy region' 'She travelled across Burgundy.'

(42) *Mandela est un président.*   'Mandela is a president.'
   La Bourgogne est une région.   'Burgundy is a region.'

Similarly, in (37) N1 gives us the type according to which N2's denotatum can be classified and referred to in a certain domain of knowledge or action. If we agree that expressions (40) are in the realm of syntax and therefore need not be accounted for by morphology, we must conclude that the same holds for (37) as well, which is felicitous, since they are quite unlike prototypical compounds.

22.5 CONCLUSION

This chapter provides a survey of expressions that can potentially be considered as instances of native compounding in French. Eventually, only three of these belong to compounding and prove productive: V+N compounds, coordinate and subordinate N+N compounds.

The discussion of V+N compounds shows that they cannot be conceived of as VP constructs and that V corresponds to the verb's phonological third stem. Moreover, the variety of semantic roles the N can exhibit in V+N is equivalent to the variety we find in sentences, a fact incompatible with their being considered as VPs. This fact means that we have to give up the idea according to which compounding is 'syntax in morphology' (Anderson 1992: 293).

While V+N constructions are very specific and exclusively dedicated to compounding, the situation is the reverse with N+N constructions: the form is unspecific and the range of interpretations is very large, hence the difficulty in picking out the ones which are a matter of compounding. For those which are compounds (i.e. coordinate and subordinate N + N compounds), they only allow one type of strictly formatted semantic relationship. Then, while the interpretation of V + N tends to exhaust the semantic possibilities permitted by the relationship existing between V and N, in N + N compounds the nature of the relationship follows a constrained pattern.

CHAPTER 23

IE, ROMANCE: SPANISH

LAURA MALENA KORNFELD

23.1 INTRODUCTION

The present chapter offers a short review of the characteristics of compounding in Spanish, presenting not only the main patterns of compounds but also the empirical and theoretical problems they pose for the literature on Spanish morphology.

The main types of Spanish compounds are presented here with observations on their internal structure and analysis of the formal relations between their constituents. I intend to lay out the problems that compounds would cause to a strict Lexicalist view of grammar (such as DiSciullo and Williams 1987), which has prevailed in the description of Spanish morphology. In my view, the problems in the analysis of many properties of compounds have their origin in the attempt to keep some premises of the Lexicalist approach 'untouched'. I claim that these premises, being false, condition a wrong analysis of the phenomena they are meant to describe. The present chapter intends to change this tendency by proposing a new direction to re-examine the data from a critical point of view.

23.2 TYPES OF SPANISH COMPOUNDS

There are some topics concerning the description of compounding that can be repeatedly found in the generative literature on Spanish morphology. One of these is the traditional distinction between 'proper' and 'improper' compounds or, in other words, between lexical compounds (that result from a 'process of compounding that operates on words') and syntactic compounds (that imply a 'process of reinterpretation that operates on syntactic constructions'), following Val Alvaro (1999: 4760). Val Alvaro assumes that prototypical lexical compounds have phonological amalgamation of their constituents and morphological unity. The first characteristic implies one main stress and morphological juncture, by means of elision of phonological material or insertion of linking elements and phonological endings; thus, *telaraña* 'net-spider' ('cobweb') has phonological amalgamation (by means of elision of phonological material), while *tela de araña* 'net of spider', with the same meaning, does not. On the other hand, morphological unity implies marginal and unique inflection in the second constituent: compare the plural *telarañas* 'net-spider(PL)' with *telas de araña* 'net(PL) of spider', which does not have marginal inflection. However, a quick review of the different types of compounds makes it possible to corroborate that the behaviour of compounds with the same pattern or internal structure is not uniform. Thus, almost all the patterns of compounding present some variation in the formal properties of compounds. Morphophonological (and consequently orthographical) variations can be found even in the same word, as in the oscillation between the forms with and without phonological amalgamation and morphological unity *medialunas* 'half(SG)-moons' / *medias lunas* 'half(PL) moons' ('croissants'), or *casaquintas* 'house(SG)-villas'/ *casas quintas* 'houses(PL) villas' ('country houses'). For this reason, the majority of compounding patterns in Spanish have been considered by some authors as improper or syntactic compounds and by other authors as prototypical or lexical compounds (see, for instance, Varela 1990 vs. Rainer and Varela 1992 on P+N compounds; Rainer and Varela 1992 vs. DiSciullo and Williams 1987 on N+N and N+*de*+N compounds), perhaps with the sole exception of V+N compounds, uniformly defined as lexical in the literature.

Another repeated topic in the literature is the distinction between endocentric and exocentric compounds, which refers to the possibility of recognizing one constituent as the head of the unit.[1] Basically, some compounds permit us to identify a head constituent, while others do not. Since phrases are, in principle, always endocentric, exocentricity is considered as a proof of the non-syntactic

---

[1] The notion of *head* employed here is the usual one in the literature on morphology, according to which the head of a morphologically complex word would be a constituent with the same category as the whole, and, on a semantic level, a kind of hypernym of the complex.

(i.e. lexical/morphological) nature of the compound. This distinction has also given rise to some puzzles, to which we will come back in the third section of the chapter.

I will now review briefly the main types of Spanish compounds. The presentation is organized observing the internal structure of the compounds, and not their output lexical category (since – as we will see – the same compound can function alternatively as an adjective or as a noun). I will only mention the productive patterns, which can be used in order to create new words, putting aside all obsolete types (as in *sopicaldo* 'soup-*i*-stock' = 'poor quality soup' or *altiplanicie* 'high-*i*-plain' = 'high plain') or the patterns that create a very reduced set of words (for instance, the pattern Adv + V in *malvender* 'badly-sell' 'sell off cheap' or *malgastar* 'badly-spend' = 'waste'), as well as compounds formed with Greek or Latin stems, which present other peculiarities and pose other theoretical problems. This review is restricted, then, to the patterns that permit a productive creation of new compounds constituted by Spanish free morphemes.[2]

23.2.1 V + N

V + N is a compounding pattern common to several Romance languages, although relatively rare in the rest of the Indo-European languages. The pattern implies the relation between a transitive verb and a noun that, in syntax, would be a direct object complement:[3] in this way, in *espantapájaros* 'scares-birds' [scarecrow], *pájaros* 'birds' is a plausible direct object for the verb *espantar* 'to scare'. The same could be said about *abrelatas* 'opens-cans' ('can opener'), *abrepuertas* 'opens-doors' ('door opener'), *ayudamemoria* 'helps-memory' ('memory aid'), *chupamedias* 'sucks-stockings' ('boot-licker'), *comeniños* 'eats-children' ('child eater'), *cortacésped* 'cuts-lawn' ('lawnmower'), *cubrecama* 'covers-bed' ('bedspread'), *cuentakilómetros* 'counts-kilometres' ('mileometer'), *rompecabezas* 'breaks-heads' ('puzzle').[4]

The examples in (1) illustrate the parallelism between the internal structure of a compound V + N and the one in an analogous VP:

---

[2] The examples presented correspond to different Spanish varieties, particularly Argentine Spanish.
[3] We can find very few exceptions to this generalization, as the cases of *girasol*, 'turns-sun' ('sunflower') (verb + complement of a PP) or *pagadios*, 'pays-God' (verb + subject). Related cases are the coordinated verbs in *correveidile*, 'run-go-*i*-tell-him/her' ('gossip') or *subibaja* 'goes-up-*i*-goes-down' ('seesaw'), that Rainer and Varela (1992: 127) consider to be a different pattern.
[4] There is a debate in the traditional and generative literature about the nature of the verbal constituent in V + N compounds. Some authors assume that the V is a stem (root + thematic vowel), while others claim it is the third person singular of the present tense (i.e. the Spanish non-marked verbal form). As seen in the glosses, we adopt the second view.

(1)   a. *En   el   campo   hay   un* [$_{X^0}$ *espantapájaros*].
           in   the   field   there-is   a   scares-birds
           'There is a scarecrow in the field.'

      b. *Ese   muñeco* [$_{SV}$ *espanta* [*pájaros*]].
           this   puppet   scares   birds.

In general, the V + N pattern is very productive in the creation of instrumental nouns: *abrelatas* 'opens-cans' ('can opener'), *lavaplatos* 'washes-dishes' ('dish-washer'); and agentive nouns: *matasanos*, 'kills-healthy (people)' ('physician'), *cuidacoches* 'cares-cars' ('car watcher'). It has rightly been noted that, although they often function as nouns, they can also be adjectives (cf. Rainer and Varela 1992: 129; Val Alvaro 1999: 4793), as in *una tarjeta abrepuertas* 'a card opens-doors' ('a key-card') or *un alumno chupamedias* 'a student sucks-stockings' ('a student who is a boot-licker').

A problem concerning the analysis of V + N compounds is their exocentricity, that is, the fact that none of the constituents may apparently function as the head (see note 1). It seems evident that the head of *espantapájaros* is neither the verb *espanta* (since it does not have the category of the whole) nor the noun *pájaros* (which has the 'right' category, but lacks all semantic relation with the meaning of the compound). In any case, there exist several 'endocentric' analyses of V + N compounds, that propose, for instance, the reanalysis of the (originally inflectional) final *-a/-e* of the first constituent as a derivational suffix (cf. Varela 1990) or the existence of a derivational zero-affix that subcategorizes a VP and determines the nominal category of the compound (cf. Lieber 1992a for French V + N compounds).

23.2.2   P + N

The nature of the P + N pattern has been intensely discussed in literature on Spanish grammar, where we can find very different analyses. In traditional grammars, P + N compounds such as *sinvergüenza* 'without-shame' ('shameless') or *contraluz* 'against-light' ('back light') are considered lexical or proper because of their frequent phonological amalgamation (e.g. RAE 1931), but some morphologists put them among syntactic compounds given their similarity with PPs (e.g. Rainer and Varela 1992). There are also analyses suggesting that a process of prefixation is involved, in which case these forms would be derived words and not compounds (e.g. Varela 1990 or Varela and García 1999). By including them in the present chapter, we reject the latter approach, since the elements appearing in the first position (*sin* 'without', *contra* 'against', *entre* 'between', *sobre* 'over') are Spanish prepositions that have the same meaning in compounds as they usually have in syntax. Therefore, the P + N pattern can be simply described as the combination of free morphemes.

P + N compounds are never formed with the so-called 'light' prepositions (mainly *de* 'of', *en* 'in', and *a* 'to'), which produce, instead, idioms that can be eventually lexicalized later on (such as *enseguida* 'in-consecutive' = 'immediately' or *acerca* 'to-near' = 'about', cf. Masullo 1996).[5] The first constituents are, then, 'full' prepositions from a semantic point of view, such as *contra* (e.g. *contraargumento* 'against-argument' = 'counterargument', *contraluz* 'against-light' = 'back light', *contraindicación* 'against-indication' = 'contraindication', *contracultura* 'against-culture' = 'counter-culture'), *entre* (e.g. *entretiempo* 'between-time' = 'break', *entrepierna* 'between-leg' = 'crotch', *entretelones* 'between-curtains' = 'behind-the-scenes'), *sin* (e.g. *sin techo* 'without-roof' = 'homeless', *sin papeles* 'without-documents' = 'undocumented', *sinvergüenza* 'without-shame' = 'shameless', *sinrazón* 'without-reason' = 'mistake', *sinsentido* 'without-sense' = 'nonsense'), or *sobre* (e.g. *sobrepeso* 'overweight', *sobreprecio* 'over price' = 'surcharge', *sobretecho* 'over roof' = 'outer tent'). However, notice that other 'full' prepositions, such as *con* 'with', *desde* 'from', and *hacia* 'towards', cannot appear in this kind of compound.

Like V + N compounds, P + N compounds have a predictable syntactic form and are perfectly parallel to PPs, as (2) shows:

(2)   a. *Carlos   es   un* [$_{X^0}$ *sinvergüenza*].
         Carlos   is   a   without-shame
         'Carlos is a shameless (man)'

      b. *Carlos   es   un   político* [$_{PP}$ *sin*   [*vergüenza*]]
         Carlos   is   a   politician   without   shame

P + N compounds have also been considered exocentric units, like the V + N ones, since they are often used as nouns (a fact that 'prefixal' analyses claim as a proof of their derivational nature). It is possible to try a slightly different analysis: the combination of a preposition with its nominal complement may function in syntax as a PP (i.e. with an adjectival distribution) and in fact P + N compounds have this function in sequences such as *carrera contrarreloj* 'race against-clock' ('timed race') or even *político sin vergüenza/ sinvergüenza* 'politician without shame/ shameless', which actually may be alternatively understood as a PP, as suggested in (2b), or as a compound. PPs and adjectives are liable to be recategorized as nouns, as Rainer and Varela (1992: 121) have remarked, and, when seen in this way, the nominal category of P + N compounds is fully predictable.

23.2.3   N + N

N + N compounds are not so common or productive in Romance as they are in Germanic languages, but all the same there are a number of neological forms,

---

[5] We are not considering here the forms created from Greek or Latin prepositions such as *anti, pro, pre, post*, which are very productive in word formation, since these forms cannot be free morphemes in Spanish syntax (but see note 13).

which is a sign of their relative productivity. Some N+N compounds exhibit phonological amalgamation and marginal inflection, as *aguanieve* 'water-snow' ('sleet'), *casaquinta* 'house-villa' ('country house') or *bocacalle* 'mouth-street' ('street intersection'), sometimes with a shortening of the first element, as *cantautor* 'sing-author' ('singer-songwriter'). In the majority of N+N compounds, however, the nominal constituents are morphophonologically independent: *arco iris* 'bow iris' 'rainbow', *bar restaurante* 'bar restaurant', *barco tanque* 'ship tank', *buque escuela* 'ship school' (='training ship'), *carta bomba* 'letter bomb', *casa cuartel* 'house barrack', *célula madre* 'cell mother' ('stem cell'), *ciudad dormitorio* 'town dormitory' ('bedroom-community'), *centro-izquierda* 'centre-left' (political party). They are all classified as endocentric compounds, in which the first noun is the head of the compound, although two subtypes are usually distinguished (cf. Rainer and Varela 1992: 125–6). In the so-called 'coordinative' N+N compounds, both nouns seem to have the same hierarchy from a semantic point of view, which could be paraphrased by 'an object that is both N_1 and N_2' (for instance, *casaquinta* 'house-villa'='country house', *pollera pantalón* 'skirt trousers'='trouser-skirt'). On the other hand, in 'subordinative' N+N compounds, the second noun indicates a property of the class referred to by the first noun, which could be paraphrased by 'an N_1 that is like a N_2', as in *célula madre* 'cell mother' ('stem cell') or *perro policía* 'dog police' ('German shepherd dog').[6]

With respect to the characterization as proper or improper, in Spanish grammars N+N compounds are usually considered not as 'syntactic' as the N+*de*+N or N+A ones. Rainer and Varela (1992) and Val Alvaro (1999), who assume the traditional characterization, recognize, however, that there is a 'fuzzy border' between N+N compounds and appositions. Indeed, there exists a significant parallelism between N+N compounds and the so-called restrictive apposition, as illustrated in (3) (and in fact DiSciullo and Williams 1987: 81–2 consider the French equivalent to N+N compounds as lexicalized phrases that keep their phrasal nature):

(3) a. *cantante   autor*
        singer   author
        'singer-songwriter'

    b. *un   clérigo poeta   autor   de   miles   de   versos*
       a   priest   poet   author   of   thousands   of   verses
       deleznables
       futile (from Rainer & Varela 1992: 119)

---

[6] In our view, some cases presented in the literature as examples of N+N compounds, such as *viaje relámpago* 'trip lightning' ('flying trip') or *periodista estrella* 'journalist star' ('star journalist'), correspond actually to the resemantization of the second noun; because of that, it would be more appropriate to define these nouns as 'new adjectives' that produce systematic and transparent paradigms (e.g. *visita/ vuelo/ guerra/ ataque relámpago* 'lightning visit/ flight/ war/ attack', *redactor/ futbolista/ empleado/ alumno/ profesor estrella* 'star writer/ soccer-player/ employee/ student/ professor'), as Val Alvaro (1999: 4785) suggests.

23.2.4 A+A

A+A compounds are very similar to N+N compounds, since in both cases the compounds show a relation of coordination/juxtaposition between elements of the same category. A+A compounds present different levels of formal 'cohesion' with respect to the processes of phonological amalgamation and marginal inflection indicated by Val Alvaro (1999). Thus, there are some compounds with an interfixal *i* (such as *agridulce* 'sour-*i*-sweet' = 'sweet and sour', *blanquiceleste* 'white-*i*-sky-blue') or shortening of the first element (e.g. *semio-lingüístico* 'semiolinguistic', *socioeconómico* 'socioeconomic') – in both cases with obligatory marginal inflection – as well as compounds with less or null phonological amalgamation and with or without marginal inflection: *árabe-israelí* 'Arab-Israeli', *sordomudo* 'deaf-mute', *(clase) media alta* '(class) middle-high' ('upper middle (class)'). Morphophonological variations can be found even in the same word: *semánticos-pragmáticos* 'semantic(PL)-pragmatic(PL)' / *semántico-pragmáticos* 'semantic(SG)-pragmatic (PL)' or *verdes-azules* 'green(PL)-blue(PL)' / *verde-azules* 'green(SG)-blue(PL)'.

23.2.5 N+*de*+N

N+*de*+N compounds are constituted by two nouns related by the Spanish 'default' preposition in the nominal domain, *de*,[7] as in *agente de seguridad* 'agent of security' ('security officer'), *barco de vapor* 'ship of steam' ('steamboat'), *bautismo de fuego* 'baptism of fire', *bicicleta de montaña* 'bike of mountain' ('mountain bike'), *bodas de plata* 'wedding of silver' ('silver wedding'), *botas de lluvia* 'boots of rain' ('rubber boots'), *caja de música* 'box of music' ('music box'), *calidad de vida* 'quality of life', *canción de cuna* 'song of cot' ('lullaby'), *cara de bebé* 'face of baby' ('baby face'), *casa de campo* 'house of country' ('country house'), *cerebro de mosquito* 'brain of mosquito' ('pea brain'), *diente de leche* 'tooth of milk' ('milk-tooth'), *ojo de buey* 'eye of bull' ('porthole'), *patas de rana* 'legs of frog' ('fins'), *torre de marfil,* 'tower of ivory' ('ivory tower').

The formal parallelism between N+*de*+N compounds and phrases is evident and, in fact, these compounds can never produce morphophonological words (i.e. with phonological amalgamation and morphological unity). For these reasons, N+*de*+N compounds are placed within the set of syntactic or improper

---

[7] The default nature of *de* is supported by the multiplicity of the semantic relations between the two nouns that this preposition can express ('possession', 'substance', 'part–whole', 'origin', 'function', 'domain', etc.), by its functioning as a mere grammatical marking in the relation between deverbal nouns and their arguments (e.g. *la contaminación del agua* 'the pollution of the water', *la pesca de ballenas* 'the fishing of whales', *la decisión del presidente* 'the decision of the president'), and by the fact that it is the sole Spanish preposition that can appear as a sentinel in nominal ellipsis and other anaphoric phenomena (e.g. *el hijo de Juan y el e de Pedro,* 'the son of Juan and the *e* of Pedro', cf. examples (12) and Brucart 1987).

compounds in the literature on Spanish morphology (cf., for instance, Rainer and Varela 1992, Val Alvaro 1999). However, some morphologists have suggested that N + *de* + N compounds should be considered as 'real' compounds – with the same status as V + N compounds, for instance – given that they imply a conceptual unit and that it is impossible to make syntactic operations within the unit (cf. DiSciullo and Williams 1987), as shown in examples (6)–(7) below. On the other hand, from the point of view of acquisition, N + *de* + N compounds have been compared with English N + N compounds because of their great productivity in Romance languages (Snyder and Chen 1997).

23.2.6 N+A / A+N

These compounds are usually grouped under the label of improper compounds, because of the obvious syntactic nature of the relation between nouns and adjectives (cf. Rainer and Varela 1992, Val Alvaro 1999). However, there is a restricted subset of forms with phonological amalgamation and marginal inflection, including forms with the linking vowel *i* (e.g. *pelirrojo* 'hair-*i*-red' = 'red-haired', *manicorto* 'hand-*i*-short' = 'stingy') and other words whose formal unity seems to be the result of accidental phonological or metrical factors: thus, two-syllables words are 'better candidates' than longer words for phonological amalgamation and marginal inflection (e.g. *aguafuerte* 'water strong' = 'etching' vs. *agua mineral* 'water mineral' = 'mineral water'), but other differences seem to be attributable to purely 'euphonic' effects (e.g. *malapata* 'bad-leg' = 'hard luck' vs. *mala suerte* 'bad luck'). Compounds of the type of *pelirrojo* or *manicorto* are considered adjectives, although they may often function as nouns (see Val Alvaro 1999).

Among the adjectives that constitute these compounds, there are qualifying adjectives in prenominal position (e.g. *malapata* 'bad-leg' = 'hard luck', *altavoz* 'high-voice' = 'loudspeaker', *malasangre* 'badblood' = 'heartache', *librepensador* 'freethinker') or postnominal position (*marea roja* 'tide red' = 'red tide', *fiebre amarilla* 'fever yellow' = 'yellow fever', *caja negra* 'box black' = 'black box', *aguardiente* 'water-burning' = 'liquor', *aguafuerte* 'water strong' = 'etching', *bicho raro* 'bug strange' = 'weirdo'), as well as relational adjectives (*pastor alemán* 'shepherd German' = 'German shepherd dog', *escalera mecánica* 'ladder mechanic' = 'escalator', *portero eléctrico* 'porter electric' = 'door intercom'). Because of the usual classification in Spanish traditional grammar of quantifiers as prenominal adjectives, cases such as *medianoche* 'middle night' ('midnight'), *medialuna* 'half moon' ('croissant'), *ciempiés* 'one hundred feet' ('centipede'), *milhojas* 'one thousand leaves' ('puff pastry'), in which the first element is a quantifier, are generally included in the set of A + N compounds.

With respect to the determination of the head, some N + A compounds are considered exocentric, since the noun cannot be a semantic hypernym of the whole, e.g. *piel roja* 'skin red' ('redskin'), *carapintada* 'face-painted' ('special forces soldier'), *caradura* 'face-hard' ('cheeky devil'). Nonetheless, most N+A compounds are endocentric: thus, *fiebre amarilla* 'fever yellow' 'yellow fever' is a kind of fever, *escalera mecánica* 'ladder mechanic' ('escalator') a kind of ladder, etc., although the meaning of the compound is often metaphoric, as in *malapata* 'bad-leg' ('hard luck') or *aguardiente* 'water-burning' ('liquor').

Briefly, following the mainstream literature on morphology, Spanish compounds are mostly nominal, although A+A compounds (such as *agridulce* 'sweet and sour') are always adjectives and some N+A, V+N, and P+N compounds can also function as adjectives (e.g. *muchacho pelirrojo*, 'boy hair-i-red' = 'red-haired boy', *tarjeta abrepuertas* 'card opens-doors' = 'key-card', *carrera contrarreloj* 'race against-clock' = 'timed race', respectively). The relations established between the constituents of the compound are invariably syntactic and can be reduced to two cases: either it is the relation expected between a head and its complement (as in P+N, A+N, N+N, N+*de*+N compounds) or a relation of coordination/ juxtaposition (as in A+A and most N+N compounds).

23.3 DISCUSSION

In the previous section, I have presented the different types of Spanish compounds in the way they have usually been described in the relevant literature. In the present section I will explain some aspects that might challenge the division of labour among the different grammatical components if a strict separation of morphology and syntax (i.e. a real Lexicalist view of grammar) is assumed, as occurs, in fact, in the most part of the descriptive literature of Spanish (see Varela 1990, Rainer and Varela 1992, Varela and García 1999, Val Alvaro 1999, Varela 2005, among others).

The first aspect has to do with the fact that the relation between the constituents of compounds can always be explained by syntactic properties of Spanish. That is to say, the combination is always predictable from a syntactico-semantic point of view. Thus, as has already been remarked, V+N compounds consist of a transitive verb and a noun that might be its direct object in syntax; neither intransitive verbs nor nouns that could not constitute a plausible direct object from a semantic point of view can be found as part of these forms. As (4) shows, a compound combining a verb with a non-plausible direct object is equally odd in the equivalent sentence:

(4)   a. *Ese   es   un   ??espantamesas.*
       this is   a   ??scares-tables

    b. *Ese   es   un   muñeco   que   espanta   ??mesas.*
       this is   a   puppet   that scares   ??tables

Moreover, the more subtle formal properties of compounds are a direct reflex of sentential syntax: thus, the noun is usually plural if it is countable (cf. (5a)) and singular if it is uncountable (cf. (5b)), just as we would expect within a VP:[8]

(5) a. *espantapájaros* / *cuentakilómetros* / *cascanueces*   / *abrepuertas*
         scares-birds   / counts-kilometres / cracks-nuts   / opens-doors
         'scarecrow   / mileometer   / nutcracker   / door-opener
         / *levantavidrios*
         / raises-glasses
         / glass-raiser'

     b. *guardapolvo*   / *tragaluz*   / *quitaesmalte*   / *ayudamemoria*
        shelters-dust   / swallows-light   / removes-polish / helps-memory
        'overalls   / skylight   / polish remover / memory aid'

Something similar can be said about the rest of Spanish compounds, which also have predictable properties from the syntactico-semantic point of view, as has already been remarked.

The perfect parallelism between the properties of compounds and phrases in Romance languages has led scholars to question whether it makes any sense to duplicate the rules of syntax in morphology, since what determines the relation between *espanta* and *pájaros* in *espantapájaros* is, in short, the syntactic component (DiSciullo and Williams 1987: 79–83). For these authors, assuming that morphology contains rules related to the combination of a transitive verb with a direct object would result in a general lack of economy for grammar. But then, if compounds result from the simple combination of words following syntactic rules, what is 'special' about compounds with respect to phrases? Or, in other words: why are they regarded as the product of morphology and not of syntax?

The justification for regarding compounds as words (and not phrases) is based on evidence showing that they are syntactic atoms in the sense of DiSciullo and Williams (1987), which additionally implies that they exhibit a number of formal properties. Thus, their constituents cannot be separated by determiners or quantifiers (6) nor be modified in an independent way (7):

(6) a. *Encontró   en   la   orilla   una   estrella   de (*l)*
        found   in   the   shore   a   star   of (*the)
        mar
        sea
        'She found a starfish on the shore.'

---

[8] In fact, the presence of inflectional marks in countable nouns is one of the most solid proofs that constituents of compounds should be regarded as words rather than stems (despite the ambiguity in the case of the verbal constituent).

b. *Es   un   abre*   (**muchas*)   *latas.*
  is   a   opens   (*many)   cans
  'It is a can-opener.'

(7)   a. *Es   un   abre*   [*latas*   (**grandes*)].
    is   a   opens   cans   (*big)
    'It is a can-opener.'

    b. *La   habitación   tiene   un   ojo*   (**grande*)   *de   buey.*
      the   room   has   a   eye   (*big)   of   bull
      'The room has a porthole.'

    c. *una   mujer*   (??*excelente*)   *policía*
      a   woman   (??excellent)   police
      'a police woman'

    d. *Tiene   un   perro   policía$_i$*   (*, *que   pro$_i$ es   una   profesión   terrible*).
      has   a   dog   police$_i$ (*, that   pro$_i$ is   a   profession   terrible)
      'He has a policedog.'

As an additional proof of the syntactic opacity of compounds, notice that, if some kind of lexical substitution is made, the referential value of the compound is lost (cf. *chupamedias* 'sucks-stockings' / ??*chupazoquetes* 'sucks-socks', *espantapájaros* 'scares-birds' / ??*espantaves* 'scares-flying animals').

From data similar to (6)–(7), DiSciullo and Williams (1987) propose the notion of *syntactic word*: some compounds in Romance languages must be produced by the rules of syntax and then relabelled as words by means of a peripheral morphological rule which enables them to occupy a head position ($X°$). In other words, syntactic words are created by means of a (morphological) reanalysis rule applied to phrases ($XP \rightarrow X°$). In this sense, Romance compounds should be distinguished from English compounds, which, following DiSciullo and Williams, are produced by specific morphological rules of stem combination. DiSciullo and Williams assume, then, that Romance languages lack morphological compounding and have only lexicalized phrases (i.e. syntactic objects listed in the lexicon) and syntactic words, created by the $XP \rightarrow X°$ rule.

Setting aside the theoretical problems that this view poses for a Lexicalist framework, I can provide empirical arguments that indicate that the notion of syntactic word is, at least, debatable. The first empirical argument is that compounds can contain phrases (in a way similar to English, Dutch, and Afrikaans compounds, as described by Lieber 1992a). This possibility makes it unlikely that they could really occupy an $X°$ position, which is a fundamental characteristic of syntactic words. For instance, V + N compounds – i.e. the prototypical proper compounds in Spanish (and whose status as compounds has never been challenged in the literature) – can be formed by two coordinated verbs (see examples in (8a)) or by a verb and a direct object expanded by means of coordination (8b) or of a nominal complement (8c):

(8) a. *un* [[*lava   y   limpia*] *faros*]   / [[*lava   y   seca*] *ropas*]
        a   washes and cleans headlights /   washes and dries   clothes
        'an [artefact that] washes and cleans headlights / washes and dries clothes'

    b. *un* [*cubre* [*piletas   y   carpas*]] / [*cubre*
        a   covers swimming-pools and tents   /   covers
        [*piletas   y   carritos*]]
        swimming-pools and   trolleys
        'a [fabric that] covers swimming-pools and tents / swimming-pools and trolleys'

    c. *proyectiles de tipo* ['*perfora   [chalecos' antibalas*]]
        projectiles of kind   perforates- vest   anti-bullets
        'projectiles that perforate bullet-proof vest'[9]

These data may be contrasted with the examples usually discussed in the literature insisting on the opacity of compounds (see examples in (6)–(7) and also Varela 2005: 75, who presents data incompatible with (8a/b)). And, crucially, there is no coherent way to account for data such as (8) from a Lexicalist perspective. Any possible explanation in terms of either coordination, ellipsis (cf. Varela 2005: 63–4), or complementation would mean that syntactic operations can apply within syntactic atoms, in direct contradiction of the strict Lexicalist principles assuming the total opacity of these units. Parallel data to (8) exist for P+N and N+*de*+N compounds:

(9) a. *un   sin   techo ni   hogar /   un   sin-techo*
       a   without roof nor   home /   a   without-roof
       (*ni   paredes, ni   ventanas ni   puertas*)
       (nor   walls   nor   windows nor   doors)
       'a homeless homeless' / 'a homeless wall-less, window-less, door-less'

    b. *dientes permanentes y   de   leche*[10]
       teeth   permanent   and of   milk
       'permanent and milk teeth'

Interestingly, the cases in (8) and (9) are much more complex from a theoretical point of view than the examples analysed by DiSciullo and Williams (1987), which only show the existence of syntactic relations between heads and complements

---

[9] All the controversial data in this chapter (cf. specially examples in (8) and (9)) may be checked in Google.
[10] Obviously, coordination is impossible in the case of metaphorical units, such as *ojo de buey* 'eye of bull' ('porthole') or *luna de miel* 'moon of honey' ('honeymoon').

within compounds (see (6)–(7)). Moreover, examples in (8) and (9) are in radical contrast with the syntactic opacity that is characteristic of all inflectional and derivative Spanish suffixes (with the exception of -*mente*) and a substantial part of Spanish prefixes:

(10)   a. *[*am*   y   *odi*]ó,   *[*nominaliza*   y   *verbaliza*]*ción*
            *[lov   and   hat]ed,   *[nominaliz   and   verbaliz]ation

        b. *in* [*útil*   y   *capaz*],   *re [*hacer*   y   *escribir*]
            *un [useful   and   capable],   *re [make   and   write]

It is obvious that the probability of phrases appearing within a compound as in examples (8)–(9) is very low, but, evidently, it is above zero. Therefore, these data allow us to question the assumption of an essential distinction between words and phrases (or, in other words, that there exists a clear-cut separation between morphology and syntax). Nonetheless, the prohibition on functional elements such as determiners or quantifiers appearing within compounds, illustrated in (6), is strictly respected (in other words, determiners and quantifiers do seem to be limited to sentential syntax).

On the other side, we have already remarked that a property that the literature on Spanish compounds usually takes as a sign of the lexical or morphological nature of certain compounds is exocentricity (i.e. apparent absence of a head), while syntactic constructions are always endocentric. This is the case with V + N or P + N compounds, in which – as has been observed – it is not easy to identify a constituent that functions as the 'head' of the construction (see footnote 1).

However, the existence of exocentric compounds in Spanish seems to be dependent on a much more general property: as Kornfeld and Saab (2003, 2005) have noted, apparent 'exocentricity' can be found also in 'normal' syntactic constructions with nominal anaphora,[11] which do not involve word formation at all:

(11)   a. *Había*   *dos*   *vestidos:*   *el*   *e*   *más*   *elegante*   *era*
            there-were   two   dresses: the   *e*   most   elegant   was
            azul (*e*='vestido')
            blue (*e*='dress')
            'There were two dresses: the most elegant one was blue.'

        b. *¿Te*   *gusta*   *el*   *e*   *más*   *elegante*   *o*   *el*   *e*   *más*
            you   like   the   *e*   most   elegant   or   the   *e*   most
            raro? (*e*='humano')
            odd (*e*='human')
            'Do you like the most elegant one or the oddest one?'

---

[11]   *Anaphora* is here used in the traditional sense of Hankamer and Sag (1976), involving merely an empty (or pronominal) category that is syntactically or pragmatically controlled.

(12) a. *Hay   dos   vestidos: el   e   de   arriba   me   gusta*
      there-are two   dresses: the   e   of   above   me   like
      más (e= 'vestido')
      most (e= 'dress')
      'There are two dresses: I like the one above better.'

    b. *El   e   de   arriba   me   tiene   bronca (e=* 'humano')
      the   e   of   upstairs   me   has   hate (e= 'human')
      'My upstairs neighbour hates me.'

(13) a. *Había   dos   vestidos: compré   el   e   que   te*
      there-were two   dresses: bought-I   the   e   that   you
      gustó (e= 'vestido')
      liked (e= 'dress')
      'There were two dresses: I bought the one you liked.'

    b. *Saludé   al   e   que   te   gusta (e=* 'humano')
      said-hello-I the   e   that you   like (e= 'human')
      'I said hello to the one you like.'

The nature of this kind of construction has been extensively discussed in the literature. Kornfeld and Saab (2005) observe that in examples such as (11)–(13) there are actually two different phenomena. In one case there is nominal ellipsis, in which the semantic interpretation of the omitted noun is identical to an antecedent (*vestido*, in the (a) examples); in the other case, the empty noun is interpreted, by default, as 'human' (see the (b) examples).[12] The relevant literature has often emphasized one or the other case in order to propose unitary explanations for the examples (cf. for instance Brucart 1987 or Bosque 1990), although neither of the phenomena can be clearly explained in terms of the other.

It sounds reasonable to believe that the existence of anaphoric phenomena such as these also influences different processes of word formation, for instance conversion from A to N, as in *el tonto* 'the fool [one]' or *el impermeable* 'the waterproof' [raincoat], a process that is much more frequent in Spanish than in languages that lack nominal ellipsis, as English. In the specific case of compounds, anaphoras are involved in the apparent 'exocentricity' of different patterns. Thus, the 'normal' category for a P+N compound is the one corresponding to a PP (with an equivalent distribution to an adjective in the nominal domain). Its use in contexts of omission of the noun as in (14) is what leads to its 'recategorization':[13]

---

[12] There is as well a third possibility: the factive interpretation, as in *El que hayas venido me conmovió* 'The [fact] that you have come moved me'.

[13] This analysis can also be applied to the cases of word formation involving Greek/ Latin 'prepositions', such as *anti* in *antimisil* 'against missile' ('antimissile') or *inter* in *interclubes* 'among clubs' ('interclub'). The established literature assumes that *anti* or *inter* should be prefixes and involve derivational processes, since they cannot function as free morphemes in Spanish syntax (see, for instance, Varela and García 1999 and Varela 2005). The problem with this idea is that the resulting

(14) a. *un* *político*   *sin*   *vergüenza* → *un* e *sinvergüenza*
         a   politician without   shame   → a   e   without shame
         → *un* *sinvergüenza*
         → a   shameless [person]

    b. *un* *juicio*   *sin*   *sentido* → *un* e *sinsentido*
         a   statement without sense   → a   e without sense
         → *un* *sinsentido*
         → a   nonsense

A similar explanation can be proposed for the so called 'exocentric' N+A compounds, such as *piel roja* 'skin red' ('redskin') or *carapintada* 'face-painted' ('soldier'): they are originally adjectives, their exocentricity being the superficial
consequence of the presence of a nominal anaphora with the interpretation
'human', as can be observed in the paraphrases in (15):

(15) a. *un* *hombre* *piel* *roja* → *un* e *piel* *roja* → *un* *piel* *roja*
         a   man   skin   red   → a   e skin   red   → a   red   skin

    b. *un* *militar* *cara* *pintada* → *un* e *carapintada* → *un*
         a   soldier face   painted   → a   e face-painted   → a
      carapintada
      face-painted [soldier]

The case of V+N compounds seems less obvious; nonetheless, in these compounds also, a predicative construction is often reanalysed as a noun by virtue of
the anaphoric processes already described. If anaphoras are involved in the category of V+N compounds, it is easy to explain why V+N compounds can be
alternatively nouns or adjectives, as examples in (16) show, and also why the gender
of V+N compounds sometimes depends on an elided noun (16a):[14]

(16) a. *una* *máquina* *tragamonedas* ('*una* *máquina* *que* *traga*
         a   machine   swallows-coins   ('a   machine   that   swallows

words do not seem to have the expected category for the combination of a prefix with a noun: they
often function as As (as in *escudo antimisil* 'shield antimissile' or *crema antiarrugas*, 'cream anti-
wrinkle') and not as Ns. In order to solve this problem, it is usually assumed that *antimisil* or
antiarrugas are actually nouns in apposition. However, it seems much more plausible to assume
that the complex functions in a similar way to *sinvergüenza* 'without-shame' ('shameless') (that is, as
PP/adjective), given that the normal syntactic function for *antiarrugas* 'anti-wrinkle' is modifying a
noun. Therefore, the prepositional character of *anti, inter, pro*, etc. is kept and they are more like
compounds than derivational words.

[14] For a complete analysis, see Kornfeld (2005), where V+N compounds are considered as
complex heads created in syntax that can include some phrasal projections, as the ones illustrated
in (8), but, crucially, never involve certain functional categories such as I or D. In this analysis, V+N
compounds function originally as adjectives, but can be recategorized as nouns by the anaphoric
processes already mentioned. It is worth noticing that analyses of V+N compounds that include null
categories have been previously proposed in generative literature, for instance in Contreras (1985) and
DiSciullo (1992b) for Italian V+N compounds.

| monedas') | → | una | tragamonedas |
| coins') | → | a(FEM) | slot machine |

b. un/a   chico/a   cuidacoches   ('un/a   chico/a   que   cuida
   a   boy/girl   cares-cars   ('a   boy/girl   that   cares
   coches') →   un/a   cuidacoches
   cars') →   a(MASC/FEM)   car-watcher

To sum up, it can be remarked that, on the one hand, the case of compounds with an expanded or coordinated constituent shows that establishing a clear-cut boundary between compounds and phrases is almost impossible. This explains why intermediate categories such as *syntactic words, syntactic compounds, lexicalized phrases*, etc. are so common in the literature, as well as the debates and controversies about the lexical/ morphological or syntactic nature of particular patterns of compounds.

On the other hand, the parallelism between the exocentricity of certain compounds and the phenomena of nominal ellipsis and other anaphoric elements suggest that the study of the general syntactic properties of Spanish should say more about compounds than the proposal of specific ad hoc properties. And, additionally, this would make it possible to explain several properties of Spanish (nominal ellipsis, categorial conversion, 'exocentric' compounds, Greek/ Latin compounding, etc.) with only a few rules, which is an epistemological desideratum.

23.4 CONCLUSIONS

The brief review in this chapter suggests that in the case of Spanish compounds it is not possible to separate morphology from syntax.

From an empirical point of view, one of the most important conclusions is that it is difficult to obtain interesting generalizations by focusing on the patterns of internal structure of Spanish compounds, since compounds with the same internal structure behave in syntax in radically different ways. On the other hand, although morphophonology supplies more transparent and less debatable criteria, it leads also to a great degree of arbitrariness, since the same pattern alternatively can or cannot produce unitary words, depending on random or non-grammatical factors such as the number of syllables or metrical reasons.

Another relevant result is that compounds present more syntactic transparency than would be expected. On the one hand, their constituents may be phrases, as we have seen with the case of V + N compounds, the most prototypical examples of Spanish compounds. This implies that the constituents of compounds (and not compounds themselves) are syntactic atoms (i.e. minimal elements manipulated by syntax). On the other hand, a property considered as typical of certain compounds (exocentricity, as opposed to the obligatory endocentricity of phrases) has proved to be a consequence of a normal syntactic phenomenon in Spanish (nominal anaphoras). Both empirical arguments explain why there is so much controversy in the literature about the syntactic or the lexical nature of this or that compound, and also call into question the importance of these debates.

From the theoretical point of view, the data strongly indicate that the simplistic Lexicalist view that morphology produces words and syntax produces phrases (predominant in Spanish literature) cannot be maintained. In spite of their greater adequacy to the data, reanalysis rules of the kind proposed by DiSciullo and Williams (1987) should also be abandoned, at least if these rules are assumed to apply before syntax (see Lieber 1992a for a similar criticism of the strict Lexicalist views based on data from different languages). Additionally, this permits us to question wordhood as a prime or real principle of grammar, something that the theoretical frameworks proposing a complete 'deconstruction' of grammar (such as Distributed Morphology, cf. Halle and Marantz 1993) have repeatedly suggested. Therefore, given that compounds can include certain syntactic structures, it seems more plausible to conceive of them as the product of a 'reduced syntax' (or microsyntax, in Benveniste's 1966 proposal), in which certain properties of 'real' syntax are available while other properties are not.

CHAPTER 24

IE, HELLENIC: MODERN GREEK

ANGELA RALLI

24.1 DEFINITION – BASIC CHARACTERISTICS

Compounding is a widespread process in Modern Greek (hereafter Greek), which creates morphologically complex words from the combination of two stems, most of which are linked together by the vowel /o/. Greek compounds belong to the three major grammatical categories, i.e. nouns, adjectives, and verbs:

(1) a. *domat-o-salata*[1]   < *domat-*[2] *salata*
        tomato salad   tomato salad

     b. *mavr-o-aspros*   < *mavr-*   *aspros*
        black (and) white   black   white

     c. *pijen-o-erxome*   < *pijen-*   *erxome*[3]
        come (and) go   go   come

---

[1] Greek examples are given a broad phonological transcription. Stress is not marked in the examples, unless it is necessary for the purposes of argumentation.

[2] Stems end in a hyphen in order to show that the inflectional ending is missing.

[3] There is no overt infinitival form in Greek. Conventionally, verbal compounds are given in the first person singular of the present tense.

There are also adverbial compounds (2), which are not primary formations, in that they are built on the basis of adjectival compounds with the addition of the adverbial ending -*a*:

(2)   a. *kakotixa* < *kakotix-*   -*a*
          unluckily   unlucky   -ly

      b. *kakotixos* < *kak-* *tix-*   -*os*
          unlucky   bad   luck   INFL

Crucially, compounds are inflected at the right-hand edge, and are phonological words, that is they contain one stress, which falls on one of the last three syllables. Very often, their stress and inflectional ending may be different from those of the second constituent part, when it is used as an autonomous word (see section 24.3 for an explanation):

(3)   Compound-inflectional ending < stem1-inflectional ending
      likóskil-o[4]   < *lík-os*
      wolf-dog   wolf
      stem2-inflectional ending
      skíl-os
      dog

24.2 COMPOUND MARKER

As already mentioned, the internal constituents of Greek compounds are linked together by the vowel /o/. Items such as this -*o*- are traditionally called 'linking elements' (Scalise 1992), 'interfixes' (Dressler 1984), or 'confixes' (Mel'čuk 1982). As shown by Ralli (2007, 2008a), -*o*- is a semantically empty element, which originates from an ancient thematic vowel, and synchronically does not belong to any of the compound members. As an illustration, consider the example *psarovarka* 'fish boat' (< *psar-* 'fish' + *varka* 'boat'), where the inflected form of the first constituent is *psari* 'fish' and not **psaro*. Following Booij (2005a), we could assume that *psaro-* is an allomorphic variation of the stem *psar-*, which is used in word formation. However, this is not an economical solution, since the form *psaro-* is restricted to compounding (see *psarovarka*), while in derivation only *psar-* is used (see *psar-as*

---

[4]   -*o* is the inflectional ending of the fifth class of neuter nouns (e.g. *likoskilo*), carrying the features of nominative/accusative/vocative singular. -*os* characterizes the first class of masculine nouns (e.g. *likos, skilos*). It carries the features of nominative singular. See Ralli (2000, 2005) for the inventory of nominal inflection classes in Greek.

'fisherman'). Moreover, it is worth stressing that -*o*- cannot be an inflectional ending, in spite of the fact that in certain cases (see the nominative singular of neuter nouns in -*o*, e.g. *vun-o* 'mountain-NOM.SG'), its form coincides with the inflection of the first constituent part when taken as an autonomous word. For instance, in the neuter form of an adjectival coordinative compound like *asprokokino* 'white and red' (< *aspr-* 'white' + *kokino* 'red'), the form *aspro* could have been considered as the inflected type of the nominative singular of 'white'. However, when the compound is used in the plural, *aspro* remains unchanged, and only the second member *kokino* 'red' acquires the appropriate plural form *kokina* 'red.PL'. Compare *asprokokina* 'white (and) red.PL' vs. **asprakokina* 'white.PL (and) red.PL'. The impossibility of changing form depending on the morphosyntactic context proves that *aspro* is not a fully inflected word, but must be analysed as a combination of the stem *aspr-* with a fixed element -*o*-.

In Ralli (2007, 2008a) I argue that items such as this -*o*- constitute markers, the primary function of which is to indicate the process of compound formation.[5] As already known, both inflection and derivation involve their own functional elements (i.e. affixes), which differentiate them from other linguistic processes. In this spirit, I have proposed that compounding, being a word-formation process, also needs its own functional element that renders it distinct from the other two processes. Seen as a simple marker, and being semantically empty, this element has no affixal status, and does not need to be assigned any derivational (or even inflectional/morphosyntactic) properties. It is just a morphological element, deprived of any meaning, whose function is to indicate the word-formation process of compounding.

Furthermore, in Ralli (2007, 2008a) I have suggested that the occurrence of a compound marker, as well as its systematic or non-systematic form, depends on a number of parameters, which refer to the typology of the particular language we deal with. For instance, I have argued that in an inflectionally rich language like Greek, the existence of -*o*- is related to the paradigmatic character of inflection, and its systematic use and form are due to the fact that morphologically complex Greek words are stem-based. These two parameters explain the absence of markers in languages the inflection of which has no particular paradigmatic character (e.g. English), and also account for the rather unsystematic behaviour of compound markers in languages with word-based morphology (e.g. German).

Generally, -*o*- does not surface when the second constituent begins with a vowel, as in the example *aɣrianθropos* 'wild man' (< *aɣri-* 'wild' + *anθropos* 'man'). However, there are also examples where -*o*- appears even in front of a vowel (see *vorioanatolikos* 'north-east' < *vori-* 'north' + *anatolikos* 'east'). Crucially, the existence of these examples reinforces the hypothesis of -*o*- having the function of a compound marker,

---

[5] A more or less similar idea is found in Mel'čuk (1982), where the so-called 'confix' is assumed to indicate the combination of two roots to form a compound.

since in coordinative compounds, like *vorioanatolikos,* whose members are in a rather loose structural relation, the presence of a compound marker ensures a high degree of cohesion between the constituent parts.

24.3 STRUCTURE

As already pointed out in the previous sections, the stem plays an important role in the formation of Greek compounds. In fact, compound structures, in their vast majority, have a stem as their first constituent.[6] As far as the second constituent is concerned, compounds are distinguished into those whose second member is a stem and those whose second member is a word (see Drachman and Malikouti-Drachman 1994, Nespor and Ralli 1996, Malikouti-Drachman 1997). According to Ralli (2007), compound structures are generally determined on the basis of two criteria: the position of stress, and the form of the inflectional ending. Formations which diverge as far as the position of stress is concerned, and inflect differently from the second constituent when used as an autonomous word, are considered to display a stem as their right-hand member.[7] On the contrary, formations whose second part is a word preserve both its stress and inflection. Following these criteria, [stem stem] and [stem word] are the two possible structures of most Greek compounds.[8] This point can be illustrated by the following examples (inflectional endings and other irrelevant parts, which appear when stems are used as autonomous words, are given in parentheses):[9]

---

[6] There are only a few compounds whose first constituent is a word, namely those with certain adverbs (e.g. *eksoji* lit. 'out-earth', 'out-place' < *ekso* 'out' + *ji* 'earth'), and numerals (e.g. *peninda-δraxmo* 'fifty drachmas (bill)' < *peninda* 'fifty' + *δraxm(i)* 'drachma' [Greek currency before Euro]).

[7] Note that there is no inflection class specific to compounds. Compounds whose second member is a stem may inflect differently from their second constituent when taken in isolation, but their particular inflection class belongs to the set of the eight inflection classes of Greek nouns and adjectives.

[8] Two more structures, [word stem] (ia) and [word word] (ib) can also be detected in the language, but only a handful of examples belong to them. In both cases, and as already mentioned in footnote 6, the first constituent is an uninflected adverb or numeral, i.e. a word without any inflectional part, since inflection is not generally allowed within Greek compounds.

(i) a. word stem: *eksóporta*   < *ékso*   *pórta*
            outdoor   out   door
    b. word word: *ksanaγráfo* < *ksaná*   *γráfo*
            write again   again   write

[9] *-i* of *rízi* and *-a* of *γál(a)* are parts of the stem, while *-o* and *-os* of *péfko* and *δásos* respectively are the inflectional endings. *-os* is not put in parenthesis because it is the inflectional ending of the compound as well.

(4)   a. [stem stem]:   *rizóγalo*   <   *ríz(i)*   *γál(a)*
                            rice pudding   rice   milk
      b. [stem word]:   *pefkoδásos*[10] <   *péfk(o)*   *δásos*
                            pine forest   pine   forest

We observe that *rizóγalo* (4a) is stressed on the antepenultimate syllable, and inflects differently from its second member, *γál(a)*, which bears a ø inflectional ending. On the contrary, with respect to stress and inflection, *pefkoδásos* (4b) does not diverge from its second inflected constituent *δásos*. Note that the different behaviour of the two examples is not due to headedness, since, as argued in section 24.5, both examples are endocentric and right-headed. It can be explained though if we appeal to the different structures which are responsible for their formation, along the lines of Nespor and Ralli (1996). In (4b), the second constituent is a fully inflected word. As such, it keeps its stress and inflectional properties when it undergoes compounding.[11] As opposed to it, the second constituent of formations like the one in (4a) is a stem, in other words a morphological category which is neither a phonological word nor a fully inflected item. Thus, when it is combined with another stem it is submitted to laws and properties which are specific to compounding: a compound-specific stress rule places stress on the antepenultimate syllable of the formation (e.g. *rizóγalo*) when an *-o* inflectional ending is added to it.

Furthermore, on the basis of these considerations, it follows that compounds exhibit a binary structure. As with other grammatical structures, it can be recursive, in the sense that more constituents can be added to the left of the structure, according to the patterns described above. The compound *meγalokapnemboros* 'big tobacco merchant', for instance, is analysed as [[*meγal*]-[*kapn-emboros*]] (< *meγal-* 'big' + [*kapn-* 'tobacco' + *emboros* 'merchant']).

It is also important to add that, beside inflection, which does not appear within compounds – although with some exceptions[12]– derivation is also excluded. As argued by Ralli and Karasimos (2007), the particular absence of compound-internal inflection is due to a constraint, the so-called *Bare Stem Constraint*, according to which in languages with stem-based morphology, like Greek, the bond between the two constituents of a compound word is better guaranteed if the first stem is as bare as possible, that is a stem without any suffixes.

---

[10] As explained in section 24.2, *-o-* in *pefkoδásos* is a compound marker, and not an inflectional ending.

[11] Nespor and Ralli (1996) have proposed that the preservation of its properties is due to the *Structure Preservation Principle*, as has been formulated by Emonds (1985).

[12] See Ralli (2007) for certain fossilized cases of compound-internal inflection originating from Ancient Greek.

24.4 COMPOUND-INTERNAL RELATIONS

With respect to the functional relation between the two compounding parts, Greek compounds can be divided into two basic categories: those which display a dependency relation (5a) and those whose parts are coordinated (5b):

(5) a. *aɣrioɣata*   < *aɣri- ɣata*
        wild cat   wild cat

     b. *laðoksiðo*   < *lað- ksið(i)*
        oil (and) vinegar   oil   vinegar

The first category corresponds to what Bloomfield (1933) calls *determinative compounds*, but also appears under the Sanskrit term *tatpurusha*. It includes subordinative and attributive compounds.[13]

(6) a. Subordinative compounds: *nixtopuli*   < *nixt- puli*
                                  night bird   night bird

     b. Attributive compounds: *xazokoritso* < *xaz- korits(i)*
                                  silly girl   silly girl

Coordinative compounds have their members in an additive relation, and are also given the Sanskrit name *dvandva* compounds.[14] It is worth noting that coordinative compounds became productive in Greek after the Hellenistic period (3rd c. BC – 3rd c. AD) (Browning 1969), and belong to all three major grammatical categories:

(7) a. Verbs: *aniɣoklino*   < *aniɣ- klino*
                     open (and) close   open close

     b. Nouns: *alatopipero*   < *alat- piper(i)*
                     salt (and) pepper   salt   pepper

     c. Adjectives: *ɣlikopikros*   < *ɣlik- pikros*
                     sweet (and) bitter   sweet bitter

Note that in coordinative compounds, constituents of the same category are juxtaposed, and express a parallel or an opposite meaning. For instance, *alat-* 'salt' has a parallel meaning to *piperi* 'pepper' and *aniɣ-* 'open' has an opposite meaning to *klino* 'close'. Moreover, in verbal compounds, constituents display a parallel argument structure, as coordinative constituents do not generally differ in transitivity.

---

[13] See also Bisetto and Scalise (2005, and this volume) for a cross-linguistic classification of compounds.

[14] I choose not to include appositive compounds (e.g. *iθopios-traɣuðistis* 'actor-singer') in this category. Following Ralli (2007), these are not typical Greek compounds but belong to a special category of multi-word units.

The kinds of functional relations between the first and the second compounding parts do not seem to differ from the functional relations found in corresponding phrases when the same constituents participate in such constructions as independent words. However, compounds seem to be different from phrases when it comes to form, meaning, and structure in general. Structurally, the first constituent is always a stem, quite often the second one is a stem too (section 24.1), and there is a compound marker between the two members (section 24.2). Phonologically, compounds undergo certain rules of lexical phonology, a compound-specific stress rule (section 24.3), and semantically, they often develop a semi- or non-compositional meaning (e.g. *psixokori* 'adopted daughter' < *psix-* 'soul' + *kori* 'daughter').

24.5 HEADEDNESS

The majority of Greek compounds are endocentric and right-headed. The head is responsible for transmitting to the compound its morphosyntactic features, but not the form of the inflectional ending (*contra* Zwicky 1985), since, as already mentioned, there are headed [stem stem] compounds which display a different ending from the one of the head (second constituent) when taken in isolation. Endocentric compounds may belong to all three major categories and their constituents are in a subordinative or in an attributive relation.

Headedness should not normally apply to coordinative compounds, which have their items juxtaposed one after the other. This absence of head makes certain compounds consisting of two items of the same category display an unfixed order between their constituent parts. For instance, A + A compounds like *pikroɣlikos* 'bitter-sweet' (< *pikr-* 'bitter' + *ɣlikos* 'sweet') and *kitrinoprasinos* 'yellow (and) green' (< *kitrin-* 'yellow' + *prasinos* 'green') may appear as *ɣlikopikros* 'sweet-bitter' and *prasinokitrinos* 'green (and) yellow' as well. However, not all coordinative compounds show this free constituent order. Most N + N and V + V formations have a rather fixed order, which, as I argued in Ralli (2007), is mostly for pragmatic reasons. For instance, compounds like *alatopipero* 'salt (and) pepper' (< *alat-* 'salt' + *piper(i)* 'pepper') and *troɣopino* 'eat (and) drink' (< *troɣ-* 'eat' + *pino* 'drink') do not appear as **piperoalato* 'pepper (and) salt' and **pinotroɣo* 'drink (and) eat' respectively, because 'salt' and 'eating' are probably considered to have priority over 'pepper' and 'drinking'.

It is worth noting that in Greek, a considerable number of compounds constitute exocentric formations, i.e. constructions without a head, such as the following examples:

(8)   a. *anixtoxeris*   < *anixt-*   *xer-*
          open-handed   open   hand

      b. *kokinomalis*   < *kokin-*   *mal-*
          red-headed   red   hair

Exocentric compounds were abundant in Ancient Greek (see Tserepis 1902), and are still very productive today, especially in Modern Greek dialects. Ralli (2007) has proposed that while these constructions contain no head within the confines of the two stems, a suffix, which is added to the compound structure as a whole, assumes the role of the head, that is, the role of the element which gives the construction its basic morphosyntactic features. In the examples above, this suffix has the form of *-i-* (*-s* is the inflectional ending). It should be specified that this suffix has derivational properties: it bears a lexical meaning ('the one who has the property of...') and the feature of gender (gender in Greek is a property of stems and derivational affixes, see Ralli 2002). Moreover, it displays an allomorphic variation (*-iδ-*) in the paradigm of the plural number, which is not typical of the inflectional endings:

(9)   [Stem-derivational suffix-inflectional ending]
      a. Singular: [*kokinomal-i-s*]   [*anixtoxer-i-s*]
      b. Plural: [*kokinomal-iδ-es*]   [*anixtoxer-iδ-es*]

24.6 SYNTHETIC COMPOUNDS

Synthetic compounds are particularly developed in Greek. They consist of a verbal (10a) or a deverbal head (10b), and a noun at the non-head position:

(10) a. *xartopezo*   < *xart-*   *pezo*
          play cards   card   play

      b. *eleokalierjia* < *ele-*   *kalierjia*
          olive cultivation   olive   cultivation

A typical property of synthetic compounds is the internal theta-role saturation. For instance, in the examples above, the stems *xart-* and *ele-* satisfy the Theme role of the verb *pezo* 'play' and the underlying verb *kaliergo* 'cultivate', respectively. Crucially, not only a Theme, but a wide range of theta-roles seem to be saturated inside Greek synthetic compounds:

(11) a. Agent: *θalasoδarmenos*   < *θalas-*   *δarmenos*
                    sea beaten   sea   beaten

b. Instrument: *kondaroxtipima*   < *kondar-* *xtipima*
                 pole stroke, joust   pole   stroke

c. Location: *nerovrastos*   < *ner-*   *vrastos*
                 boiled in water   water   boiled

d. Goal: *aɣrotoδanioδotisi*   < *aɣrot-* *δani-*   *δotisi*
                 farmer-loan-giving   farmer   loan   giving

e. Material   *petroxtistos*   < *petr-*   *xtistos*
                 stone-built   stone   built

As shown by Ralli (1992) and Di Sciullo and Ralli (1999), compound-internal theta-role saturation is often facilitated by the rich suffixation which characterizes the Greek language. For instance, the agent role could not be saturated if the head constituent were not a derived item. This is illustrated by the ungrammaticality of a compound such as **θalasoδerni* 'sea beats', where the stem *θalas-* 'sea' functions as the subject (external argument) of the verbal head *δerni* 'beats'.[15] Nevertheless, the presence of a suffix such as *-men(os)* on the deverbal head *δarmenos*[16] 'beaten' transforms this function into one of a *by*-phrase, renders the structure a possible site for theta-role saturation, hence, making grammatical a compound like the one in (11a).

It should be noted though that, with the exception of the agent role, theta-role saturation is common within compounds with a verbal head. The theme role appears more frequently (e.g. *afisokolo* 'stick posters' < *afis-* 'poster' + *kolo* 'stick'), but also other roles, such as the instrument (e.g. *kondaroxtipo* 'hit with a pole' < *kondar-* 'pole' + *xtipo* 'hit'), the location (e.g. *ematokilo* 'steep in blood' < *emat-* 'blood' + *kilo* 'roll'), and the material (e.g. *plakostrono* 'pave (a surface) with tiles/slates' < *plak-* 'tile, slate' + *strono* 'spread/cover).

24.7 BORDERLINE CASES

In Greek, as in other languages, there is no clear borderline between derivation and compounding. Suffice it to mention the property of categorial neutrality that is shared by prefixes and the left-hand constituents of compounds. In fact, a considerable number of prefixed structures have usually been confused with compounds, and vice versa. For example, there is a long tradition in Greek grammars of treating verbs preceded by preverbs as compounds (cf. Triantaphyllidis 1941), and not as

---

[15] In the literature, the impossibility of the subject appearing within compounds is assumed to be due to the *First-sister Principle*, as proposed by Roeper and Siegel (1978).

[16] *δern-* and *δar-* are allomorphs of the verb 'to beat'.

462   IE, HELLENIC: MODERN GREEK

derived words, in spite of the fact that several preverbs are not separable items, and
have no prepositional or adverbial use, at least on synchronic grounds[17] (e.g.
anaɣrafo 'write on' < *ana-* + *ɣrafo* 'write', *kataɣrafo* 'write down/register' < *kata-*
+ *ɣrafo* 'write', *epiɣrafo* 'inscribe' < *epi-* + *ɣrafo* 'write', etc.). It is only recently that
Greek preverbs have been analysed as instances of prefixes (see Holton, Mackridge,
and Philippaki-Warburton 1997; Ralli 2002, 2004), on the basis of several criteria
of structural (combinability properties) and semantic (unclear lexical meaning)
nature, which distinguish prefixes from adverbs and prepositions.

Another typical borderline case is a set of formations consisting of one stem and
one bound deverbal element, that is, an element which cannot appear as an
autonomous word with the appropriate inflectional ending (similar constructions
exist in the vocabulary of other languages, under the heading of neoclassical
formations):

(12) a. *ktinotrofos*   < *ktin-*   *-trof-* (< verb *trefo*)
          cattle-breeder   animal/beast   to raise

      b. *anθropofaɣos*   < *anθrop-*   *-faɣ-* (< verb *troo*)[18]
          cannibal   man   to eat

      c. *kinonioloɣos*   < *kinoni-*   *-loɣ-* (< verb *leɣo*)
          sociologist   society   to talk

In Ralli (1992, 2008b), I argue that these formations constitute a specific type
of compounds, very productive in Greek, which share properties with derivational
structures (e.g. boundness, closed-class right-hand heads). However, they are
governed by the basic structural principles of compounds and there is substantial
evidence for their [stem stem] structure, compound-internal theta-role saturation,
and compound marking. In addition, in Ralli (2008b) I demonstrate that their
second bound constituent is a deverbal noun which cannot be treated as an affix,
since it bears a lexical meaning, inherits the argument structure of its root verb
(e.g. *angeliofor(os)* 'lit. who brings messages, messenger' < *angeli-* 'message/
announcement' + *-for-* (< *fero* 'bring/carry'), and may combine with a prefix
(e.g. *afor(os)* 'lit. who has not been put on, infertile, barren' < *a-* + *-for-* (< *fero*
'bring/carry')).

Crucially, the adoption of a specific category of bound stems, beside that of
regular ones (i.e. those that can become words with the addition of an appropriate
inflectional ending), raises an issue as to whether there are distinct boundaries
between the various morphological categories, that is affixes, stems, and words. As I
argue in Ralli (2005), these categories are placed in a morphological continuum,[19]

---

[17] One of the main reasons for such a position is the fact that most of these preverbs are formally
identical to ancient adverbs or prepositions, and diachronically derive from them.

[18] There are two basic allomorphic variations of the verb stem with the meaning of 'eat': *tro-* (the
present stem) and *faɣ-* (the aorist stem).

[19] See Bybee (1985) for the general notion of the continuum in linguistic theory.

which is determined on the basis of properties such as structural boundness and lexical meaning. Affixes and words occupy the two poles. Stems and bound stems are situated in the middle, with bound stems occupying a position between stems and affixes. This approach accounts for the similarities that may be shared by different categories, such as, for example, the boundness property displayed by both affixes and bound stems.

CHAPTER 25

....

IE, SLAVONIC: POLISH

....

BOGDAN SZYMANEK

25.1 INTRODUCTION

....

The Polish word *wideofilm* means 'video film', as might be expected. But, perhaps surprisingly, Polish *film wideo* means the same, i.e. again 'video film'. The thing is that the two expressions differ in structure and grammatical status. The former item is a compound, ultimately a borrowing from English, while the latter is a somewhat irregular syntactic phrase of the noun + relational-adjective type. However, since a derived denominal adjective from the indeclinable noun *wideo* does not seem to exist in Polish,[1] *wideo* is used attributively here, as a substitute for a full-fledged adjective, with its head noun on the left. By contrast, the head (*film*) appears on the right in the compound. The majority of Polish compounds are right-headed.

Compounding accounts for a relatively small section of the Polish lexicon of morphologically complex words, compared to a language like English. However, the process is fairly productive in Modern Polish. Moreover, there are specific types

---

[1] The neologistic adjective ?*wideowy* is not attested in dictionaries but it may be spotted in Henryk Grynberg's prose (Grynberg 2000: 5): 'Adam Bromberg...nagrał na taśmach dźwiękowych i *wide-owych* wiele gawęd o doświadczeniach swojego burzliwego życia.' ('Adam Bromberg...recorded, on audio and *video* tapes, many tales recounting the experiences of his stormy life' – emphasis added, translation mine). Incidentally, the basic form *wideo* gets about 6,180,000 hits on Google while ?*wideowy* gets only four (8 July 2007).

of compounds and areas of the vocabulary which, in recent years, have shown a remarkable spread or revitalization of this morphological process. The main focus of this survey will be on the structural diversity and certain formal properties of Polish compounding which set it apart from compounding systems in many other languages. It needs to be stressed, though, that the situation one finds in Polish is, by and large, representative of the whole group of Slavonic languages. Polish compounds, as well as compounds in many other languages, also pose notorious problems of a semantic nature, like their classification and interpretation. Due to space limitations, this complex subject-matter will just be outlined in what follows. For a more detailed account, see e.g. Kurzowa (1976) and Grzegorczykowa and Puzynina (1999), probably the most authoritative and comprehensive sources on Polish compounds available to date.

The bulk of the relevant data consists of compound nouns, i.e. output forms whose category is N, while the input constituents may have a variety of syntactic labels. Characteristically, though, the rightmost input element is either N or V (see below). Output forms which belong to the class of compound adjectives are also varied, in terms of their internal structure, and fairly common in Polish. Hence, focusing on the output category, I divide the following discussion into two main parts: compound nouns and compound adjectives, interpreted as output categories (sections 25.2 and 25.3, respectively). For the sake of completeness, one should note that formation of compound verbs is unproductive in contemporary Polish, although a few older (often obsolete and lexicalized) coinages of this type do exist; e.g. *lekceważyć* 'snub, disregard' < *lekce* 'lightly, little (obs.)' + *ważyć* 'weigh'; *zmartwychwstać* 'rise from the dead' < *z* 'from' + *martwych* 'dead GEN. PL' + *wstać* 'rise'. Also, as far as function words are concerned, traditional grammar books identify the class of compound prepositions, i.e. combinations of two prepositions, like *z* 'from' + *nad* 'over, above' > *znad* 'from above'; *po* 'on/along' + *przez* 'through' > *poprzez* 'through(out)'. However, by definition, this set is extremely limited and so negligible in the context of this survey.

25.2 COMPOUND NOUNS

Where English frequently has an N+N compound, Polish may have (i) a noun phrase with an inflected noun modifier (usually in the genitive), (ii) a noun phrase incorporating a prepositional phrase modifier, or (iii) a noun phrase involving a denominal (relational) adjective as a modifier, as is illustrated below:

(1)   a. *telephone number*
          i. *numer telefon-u*
          ii. **numer do telefon-u*
          iii. **numer telefon-icz-n-y*

       b. *computer paper*
          i. **papier komputer-a*
          ii. *papier do komputer-a*
          iii. *papier komputer-ow-y*

       c. *toothpaste*
          i. **past-a zęb-ów*
          ii. *past-a do zęb-ów*
          iii. **past-a zęb-ow-a*

Evidently, alternative structures are often available, cf. *papier do komputera* vs. *papier komputerowy* 'computer paper'. The kind of construction may depend on a variety of factors which need not concern us here. What is important is the fact that the Polish expressions just cited are syntactic objects, and that they may involve both inflection and derivation, but not compounding.[2] That is to say, there are no compounds like **komputeropapier* or **telefononumer*, to parallel the English counterparts. This may partly explain why the number of nominal compounds is not so spectacular in Polish. Quite simply, certain functions that are served by compounding in other languages tend to be realized by syntactic, inflectional and/or derivational means in Polish. However, there is a wealth of evidence to demonstrate that nominal compounding is, relatively speaking, a live process in Polish, too.

Typically, a compound noun (or adjective) in Polish must involve a so-called linking vowel (interfix, intermorph, connective) which links, or separates, the two constituent stems. As a rule, the vowel in question is *-o-*, but there are other possibilities as well which surface in compound nouns incorporating some verbs or numerals in the first position. In the latter case, the intermorph is *-i-/-y-* or *-u-*, respectively (see Grzegorczykowa and Puzynina 1999: 458). Consider the following straightforward examples where the linking element appears in bold type, hyphenated for ease of exposition:[3]

(2)   STEM 1   STEM 2   COMPOUND N
       gwiazd-a 'star' + *zbiór* 'collection' > *gwiazd-**o**-zbiór* 'constellation'

---

[2] According to some Polish authors (see e.g. Jadacka 2006: 120), fixed nominal phrases like *pasta do zębów* 'toothpaste', *drukarka laserowa* 'laser printer', etc. ought to be viewed as a special type of a generally conceived category of compounding: the so-called 'juxtapositions' (Pol. *zestawienia*).

[3] Occasionally I will use hyphens to separate the elements of a compound, but it must be borne in mind that, according to the spelling convention, the majority of Polish compounds are written as one word, with no hyphen. Exceptions involve some coordinate structures like *Bośnia-Hercegowina* 'Bosnia-Herzegovina' or *czarno-biały* 'black and white'.

siark-a 'sulphur'	+ *wodór* 'hydrogen'	> *siark-o-wodór* 'hydrogen sulphide'
star-y 'old'	+ *druk* 'print, n.'	> *star-o-druk* 'antique book'
żyw-y 'live'	+ *płot* 'fence'	> *żyw-o-płot* 'hedge'
łam-a-ć 'break'	+ *strajk* 'strike'	> *łam-i-strajk* 'strike-breaker'
mocz-y-ć 'soak, v.'	+ *mord-a* 'mug, kisser'	> *mocz-y-morda* 'heavy drinker'
dw-a 'two'	+ *głos* 'voice'	> *dw-u-głos* 'dialogue'[4]
dw-a 'two'	+ *tygodnik* 'weekly'	> *dw-u-tygodnik* 'biweekly'

Prosodically, the compounds are distinguished from phrases by the fact that they receive a single stress on the penultimate syllable (in accordance with the regular pattern of word stress in Polish). Thus, for instance, STA·RY·DRUK 'old print' (phrase) vs. sta·RO·druk 'antique book' (compound).

Morphologically, the typical presence of the interfix (usually -*o*-) does not exhaust the range of formal complications. In fact, there may be no interfix at all, in certain types of compounds. In some cases, the lack of an interfix seems to be lexically determined. For instance, most combinations involving the noun *mistrz* 'master' as their head have no linking vowel (e.g. *balet-mistrz* 'ballet master', *kapel-mistrz* 'bandmaster', *zegar-mistrz* 'clockmaker'; but *tor-o-mistrz* 'railway specialist', *organ-o-mistrz* / *organ-mistrz* 'organ specialist'). In other cases, the omission of the intermorph seems to be due to the phonological characteristics of the input forms: if the final segment of the first constituent and/or the initial segment of the second constituent is a sonorant, the combination is likely to be realized without any intervening connective (e.g. *pół-noc* 'midnight', *trój-kąt* 'triangle', *ćwierć-nuta* 'quarter note, crotchet', *noc-leg* 'lodging, accommodation', *hulaj-noga* 'scooter' (see Kurzowa 1976: 68). The intermorph is not isolable, either, in some compounds involving so-called initial combining forms, particularly when they end with the vowel -*o*, identical with the default connective; cf. *eurowaluta* 'Eurocurrency' (other examples of the same type: *eko-*, *narko-*, *porno-*, *neo-*, *auto-*, *foto-*, *krypto-*, *makro-*,

---

[4] The intermorph -*u*-, which appears in some compound nouns and adjectives when it follows a numeral is, in fact, heavily restricted in its distribution: it mainly appears after the numerals *dwa* 'two' (*dwudźwięk* 'double note', *dwutorowy* 'double-track') and in combinations thereof (e.g. *dwanaście* 'twelve' > *dwunastolatek* 'twelve-year-old, *dwadzieścia* 'twenty' > *dwudziestozłotówka* 'twenty zloty note', *dwieście* 'two hundred' > *dwustustronicowy* 'two-hundred-page') as well as *sto* 'one hundred' (*stulecie* 'century'; exception: *stonoga* 'centipede') plus the following combinations of *sto*: *dwieście* 'two hundred' (*dwustu-*), *trzysta* 'three hundred' (*trzystu-*), *czterysta* 'four hundred' (*czterystu-*, e.g. *czterystumetrowiec* '400-metre runner'). With most of the remaining numerals, the principal intermorph -*o*- is used (cf. *Pięcioksiąg* 'Pentateuch', *osiemnastolatek* 'eighteen-year-old', *osiemdziesięciopięciostronicowy* 'eighty-five-page'); after *pięćset* 'five hundred' and higher round hundreds no intermorph is used (e.g. *pięćsetlecie* 'five-hundredth anniversary'). Cf. also the irregular allomorphy *trzy-*/*trój-* 'three'; the latter variant, with no intermorph, is used in a few lexicalized combinations (e.g. *trójskok* 'triple jump', *trójwymiarowy* 'three-dimensional' vs. *trzyczęściowy* 'three-part', *trzydrzwiowy* 'three-door').

mikro-, *pseudo-*, etc.). Finally, there is no intermorph in many recent neologisms or loan adaptations evidently modelled on the English pattern; cf. *seksskandal* or *seksafera* 'sex scandal'.

Another feature that blurs the picture is the frequent occurrence of co-formatives, that is, morphological elements which, side by side with the interfix itself, contribute to the structure of a given compound. Thus, for instance, fairly common are compound nouns of the following structure: STEM1+interfix+STEM2+suffix, that is, there is both an interfix and a suffix which jointly function as exponents of the category (hence the Polish traditional term: *formacje interfiksalno-sufiksalne*). Consequently, *nos-o-roż-ec* 'rhinoceros' incorporates the input forms *nos* 'nose' and *róg* 'horn' (with stem-final palatalization), followed by the obligatory noun-forming suffix *-ec* (cf. **nos-o-róg*). The compound is then structurally analogous to its counterparts in Czech and Slovak (*nosorožec*), while in Russian the equivalent is simply *nosorog*, with no suffix. Consider a few more Polish examples:

(3) STEM 1   STEM 2   COMPOUND N
     dług-i 'long'   *dystans* 'distance' *dług-o-dystans-owiec* 'long-distance runner'
     obc-y 'foreign'   *kraj* 'country'   *obc-o-kraj-owiec* 'foreigner'
     drug-a 'second'   *klas-a* 'form'   *drug-o-klas-ist(a)* 'second-form pupil'
     prac-a 'job'   *daw-a-ć* 'give'   *prac-o-daw-c(a)* 'employer'[5]
     gryź-ć 'bite'   *piór-o* 'pen'   *gryz-i-piór-ek* 'pen-pusher'

It may be seen that each of the compounds on the list ends in a suffix. The suffixes *-ec*, *-owiec*, *-ist(a)*, *-c(a)*, and *-ek* are quite common in this function, so that they may be said to do some of the formative work, as far as compounding is concerned, together with the linking vowel.

Various other Polish compounds end in a suffix, too, which has a fundamentally different status though, since it is inflectional. However, as we shall see, it may also have an important role to play, from the point of view of word formation. Incidentally, it will be noticed that the examples of compounds given so far are all masculine nouns, which typically have no overt inflectional ending in the nominative singular (e.g. *gwiazdozbiór-ø*, *nosorożec-ø*). Here the gender of the whole combination is inherited from gender specification on the head (in case it is nominal). Thus *gwiazdozbiór* is masculine because *zbiór* is masculine, etc. Yet, in quite a few compounds there is a gender-class shift, for instance from feminine to neuter or masculine, as in the following examples:

---

[5] When looked at from another angle, *pracodawca* 'employer', literally 'job giver', is clearly reminiscent of the type of synthetic compounds like *jobseeker*, *truck driver* in English. Other Polish examples of the same class: *kredytodawca* 'lender' (lit. 'credit giver'), *kredytobiorca* 'borrower' (lit. 'credit taker'), *cudotwórca* 'miracle-worker', etc. Consider also the analogy between Pol. *praw-o-daw-ca* 'legislator' (< *prawo* 'law' + *dawca* 'giver'), Slovak *zákon-o-dar-ca* and Czech *zákon-o-dár-ce*.

(4) STEM 1   STEM 2   COMPOUND N
     wod-a 'water'   *głow-a* 'head'   *wod-o-głowi-e* 'hydrocephalus'
                       [+feminine]   [+neuter]
     płask-a 'flat' *stop-a* 'foot'   *płask-o-stopi-e* 'flat foot'
                       [+feminine]   [+neuter]
     czarn-a 'black' *ziemi-a* 'earth' *czarn-o-ziem-ø* 'black earth'
                       [+feminine]   [+masculine]

Thus, the compound status of *wodogłowie* (rather than **wodogłowa*) is signalled by two things: first, the presence of the usual connective *-o-* and, second, the gender-class modification, which results in a distinct paradigm of declension (cf. a few forms in the singular: *głow-a* NOM, *głow-y* GEN, *głowi-e* DAT vs. *wodogłowi-e* NOM, *wodogłowi-a* GEN, *wodogłowi-u* DAT, etc.). Thirdly, in fact, one could mention the characteristic palatalization of the stem-final consonant in the [+neuter] compounds above (throughout the paradigm). Due to this effect, the paradigmatic shift may be looked upon as a significant co-formative which, together with the intermorph *-o-*, defines the structure of the compound in question (hence the Polish term: *formacje interfiksalno-paradygmatyczne*). In fact, the shift of paradigm need not result in gender modification; for instance, the Slovak noun *slov-o* 'word' and the compound *tvar-o-slov-ie* 'morphology' are of the same gender (neuter) but their respective declensional paradigms are distinct. The same property is illustrated by the Polish compound *pust-o-słow-ie* 'verbosity' [+neuter] < *pust-y* 'empty' + *słow-o* 'word' [+neuter].

On some accounts, this formal type is also extended to cover masculine compounds which have a verbal root as their second element, with a zero marker of the NOM SG. For example: Polish *ręk-o-pis-ø* 'manuscript' < *ręk-a* 'hand' + *pis-(ać)* 'write'; likewise Russian *rukopis'*, Slovak and Czech *rukopis*. Further Polish examples are given below:

(5) STEM 1   STEM 2   COMPOUND N
     korek 'cork'   *ciąg(nąć)* 'pull'   *kork-o-ciąg-ø* 'cork-screw'
     śrub(a) 'screw, n.' *kręc(ić)* 'twist' *śrub-o-kręt-ø* 'screwdriver'
     paliw(o) 'fuel' *mierz(yć)* 'measure' *paliw-o-mierz-ø* 'fuel indicator'
     piorun 'lightning' *chron(ić)* 'protect' *piorun-o-chron-ø* 'lightning conductor'
     drog(a) 'road' *wskaz(ać)* 'indicate' *drog-o-wskaz-ø* 'signpost'
     długo 'long, adv.' *pis(ać)* 'write'   *długo-pis-ø* 'ballpoint pen'[6]

---

[6] Since adverbs do not inflect, the *-o* vowel in *długo-pis*, etc. may be interpreted not as an intermorph but rather as an integral element of the input form, at least in those cases where an adverb in *-o* exists.

Paradigmatic conversion (from V to N) of verbal roots of the kind listed in (5) is corroborated by the fact that some such elements may appear as independent nominals – products of paradigmatic derivation; for instance, *ciąg-nąć* 'to pull, drag' > *ciąg* 'pull, draught, bender'. However, **kręt, *mierz, *chron*, etc. are never used as independent nouns.

Taking into account the syntactic category of the input forms which participate in the coining of compound nouns in Polish, one needs to point out that, evidently, not all theoretically possible combinations are actually attested. To generalize, one can say for instance that only noun and verb stems may appear as second-position (final) constituents (see below). Alternatively, the verbal stems in question may be interpreted as (potential) nouns, too – products of verb-to-noun conversion. Incidentally, it is enough to distinguish between the first and second constituent, since nominal compounds in Polish hardly ever contain more than two elements (in obvious contradistinction to, say, English compounds). In particular, recursion, which is perhaps evidenced by certain types of compound adjectives in Polish (see next section), is not really corroborated by the facts of N+N combination. To sum up, I list below the major syntactic types of compound nouns, with examples involving an intermorph only:

(6)   STEM 1   STEM 2   EXAMPLE
    N   N   *ocz-o-dół* 'eye socket'
                     (< *oko* 'eye' + *dół* 'pit')
    V   N   *łam-i-strajk* 'strike breaker'
                     (< *łamać* 'break' + *strajk* 'strike')
    A   N   *ostr-o-słup* 'pyramid'
                     (< *ostry* 'sharp' + *słup* 'pillar')
    Num   N   *dw-u-głos* 'dialogue'
                     (< *dwa* 'two' + *głos* 'voice')
    N   V   *wod-o-ciąg* 'waterworks'
                     (< *woda* 'water' + *ciagnąć* 'pull, draw')
    Adv   V   *szybk-o-war* 'pressure cooker'
                     (< *szybko* 'fast' + *warzyć* 'cook')
    Pron   V   *sam-o-lub* 'egoist'
                     (< *sam* 'oneself' + *lubić* 'to like')
    Num   V   *pierw-o-kup* 'pre-emption'
                     (< *pierwszy* 'first' + *kupić* 'buy')

However, as has been pointed out, the intermorph (interfix) need not be the only exponent of the compounding operation. It may co-occur with a derivational suffix, as a co-formative. Hence we get the following distributional pattern, illustrated below with compounds involving a noun in the head position ('plus' means presence and 'minus' means absence of an affix):

(7) INTERFIX SUFFIX EXAMPLE
     +   +   *nos-o-roż-ec* 'rhinoceros'
                      (< *nos* 'nose' + *róg* 'horn')
     +   −   *krwi-o-mocz* 'haematuria'
                      (< *krew* 'blood' + *mocz* 'urine')
     −   +   *pół-głów-ek* 'halfwit'
                      (< *pół* 'half' + *głowa* 'head')
     −   −   *balet-mistrz* 'ballet master'
                      (< *balet* 'ballet' + *mistrz* 'master')

As may be seen, the full range of theoretically available options is actually attested (although with different degrees of productivity). A complete formal classification would have to superimpose yet another feature, namely the presence or absence of the paradigmatic marker, often appearing in place of an overt suffix. Thus, for instance, *nos-o-roż-ec* contains the suffix *-ec* while, say, *głow-o-nóg* 'cephalopod' has none; in the latter, the compounding operation is manifested by a paradigmatic (gender) shift: from [+feminine] (*noga* 'leg') to [+masculine].

According to traditional accounts, Polish nominal compounds of the kind illustrated so far (or: compounds in the strict sense of the term) need to be distinguished from a specific structural variety of so-called solid compounds (*zrosty*; see e.g. Nagórko 1998: 195). The differentiating feature is the degree of formal coalescence of the two constituents which participate in a compound word. Thus, while compounds proper normally reveal the presence of the intermorph, which is not structurally subordinated to either the first or the second constituent, the solid compounds are originally based on fixed syntactic phrases, and hence incorporate the first lexeme, syntactically dependent on the following item, complete with one of its inflectional endings (usually a single vowel). That is to say, the lexeme in question appears under the guise of its particular word-form which is petrified in the compound (the lexeme does not inflect). For instance, consider the phrase *oka mgnienie* 'a blink of an eye' and the corresponding solid compound noun *okamgnienie* 'blink, flash' (cf. German *Augenblick*). The two expressions differ orthographically but, more importantly, the former is a syntactic object (phrase) while the latter is a single lexical item. In both cases, the ending *-a* in *oka* is simply an inflectional desinence (selected by the rules of government) as it marks the genitive singular of the noun *ok(o)* 'eye'. Yet, the order of the constituents may be reversed only in the case of the syntactic phrase: cf. *mgnienie oka* vs. **mgnienieoka*. As is evidenced by other comparable pairs, solid compounds may also differ from their phrasal counterparts in terms of stress placement: just like compounds at large (or most other words) they receive a single stress on the penultimate syllable; cf. *dobranoc* 'good night' (do·BRA·noc) < *dobra noc* 'a good night' (DO·bra·NOC). The pattern under discussion is completely unproductive but worth illustrating with two more examples: *psubrat* (obsolete) 'rogue' < *psu* 'dog. DAT.SG' + *brat* 'brother. NOM.SG', *wniebowzięcie* 'Assumption' < *w* 'in' + *niebo* 'heaven. ACC.SG' + *wzięcie* 'taking. NOM.SG'. According to traditional norms of usage, a few solid compounds may have their first constituent inflected (optionally), which leads to the following free variants: *Wielkanoc* 'Easter' (< *Wielka Noc* 'great night'), genitive singular *Wielkanocy* or *Wielkiejnocy*; *rzeczpospolita* 'republic (of Poland)', genitive singular *rzeczpospolitej* or *rzeczypospolitej*, etc.[7]

A pattern of compounding which is certainly more significant in Modern Polish, due to its increasing productivity, is the use of so-called combining forms, that is, elements which typically occur in neoclassical compounds like *morfologia* 'morphology' but may also be found in hybrid combinations (see below). Common initial combining forms are, for instance, *auto-* (*autocenzura* 'self-censorship'), *foto-* (*fotografia* 'photograph(y)'), *krypto-* (*kryptokomunista* 'crypto-communist'), *makro-* (*makroekonomia* 'macroeconomics'), *mikro-* (*mikrochirurgia* 'microsurgery'), *multi-* (*multikino* 'multi-screen'), *neo-* (*neofita* 'neophyte'), *poli-* (*poligamia* 'polygamy'), *pseudo-* (*pseudoeksperyment* 'pseudo-experiment'). The list of popular final combining forms includes the following items: *-fobia* (*ksenofobia* 'xenophobia'), *-fonia* (*radiofonia* 'radio broadcasting'), *-grafia* (*bibliografia* 'bibliography'), *-logia* (*neurologia* 'neurology'), *-metria* (*geometria* 'geometry'), *-metr* (*amperometr / amperomierz* 'ammeter'), *-nomia* (*autonomia* 'autonomy'), *-skopia* (*bakterioskopia* 'microscopic study of bacteria'), etc. These and other combining forms are often found in combination with native Polish stems, thus producing instances of hybrid formations; for instance: *eksżołnierz* 'ex-soldier', *fotokomórka* 'photocell', *kryptopodatek* 'crypto-tax', *makrowspólnota* 'macro-community', *pseudokibic* 'pseudo-fan', *hełmofon* 'headset', *światłoterapia* 'phototherapy'. There are also cases where both Greco-Latinate constituents (initial and final) have been replaced to produce a uniformly native combination; cf. *światłowstręt* 'photophobia').[8]

---

[7] In a handful of solid compounds, usually place names (toponyms), the first (and the second) constituent must be inflected; for instance, the A+N combination *Białystok* 'place name' (lit. 'white slope') – gen. sg. *Białegostoku*, loc. sg. *Białymstoku*, etc. This fact contradicts Dressler's (2006: 27) remark about such nouns, namely that they may have 'single or double inflection' – the genitive singular form **Białystoku* is unacceptable. Consider also *Krasnystaw* 'place name' – gen. sg. *Krasnegostawu*, dat. sg. *Krasnemustawowi*. The lexical status of such combinations is enhanced by the regular stress placement on the penultimate syllable, throughout the paradigm. Due to that, stress may actually fall on the internal inflection *-y* in the nominative forms. Notice, additionally, that in derivatives from such names the internal inflection is replaced with the linking vowel *-o-*, typical of ordinary compounds: *białostocki*, *krasnostawski* (adjectives), *białostocczanin*, *krasnostawianin* (inhabitant). On the other hand, a number of Slavic Christian names are, etymologically, solid compounds, too, whose first element is uninflected, as a rule; cf. the following male first names involving the root *Bóg* 'God' as their first element: *Bogusław*, *Bogusława* (GEN), *Bogusławowi* (DAT); *Bogumił*, *Bogumiła* (GEN), *Bogumiłowi* (DAT); *Bożydar*, *Bożydara* (GEN), *Bożydarowi* (DAT). In another name, *Bogdan* (etymology: (*przez*) *Boga dany* '(by) God given'), the inflectional ending of the first constituent has been lost, throughout the paradigm: *Bogdana* (GEN), *Bogdanowi* (DAT).

[8] For more examples and a general discussion on the status of hybrid formations in contemporary Polish morphology, see Waszakowa (2004, 2005). Jadacka (2001: 98) gives numerous examples of recent neologisms which belong to the type under discussion.

When analysed from the functional perspective, the Polish noun compounds present themselves as a highly diversified class. First, there are a number of examples of coordinate structures like: *klubokawiarnia* 'a café that hosts cultural events' (<*klub* 'club'+*kawiarnia* 'café'), *kursokonferencja* 'training conference' (<*kurs* 'course, training'+*konferencja* 'conference'), *marszobieg* 'run/walk' (<*marsz* 'walk'+bieg 'run'), *chłoporobotnik* 'a peasant farmer who works in a factory' (<*chłop* 'peasant'+*robotnik* 'manual worker'), etc. It may be argued that a combination of the type in question is semantically headed by both constituents and hence their order is potentially reversible (cf. ?*kawiarnioklub*, ?*biegomarsz*; see Kurzowa 1976: 59). A formal variant within this class are juxtapositions like *klub-kawiarnia* 'a café that hosts cultural events' (cf. *klubokawiarnia* above) or *trawler-przetwórnia* 'factory trawler'. As may be seen, there is no intermorph here. Instead, both constituent nouns are hyphenated and they inflect. The type is then formally similar to so-called copulative (*dvandva*) juxtapositions, evidenced by proper names like *Bośnia-Hercegowina* 'Bosnia-Herzegovina' or *Alzacja-Lotaryngia* 'Alsace-Lorraine'. Here, again, both constituents may inflect (cf. *Bośni-Hercegowiny* GEN, *Bośnią-Hercegowiną* INSTR, etc.). Yet, in terms of headedness, the situation seems to be different here: neither constituent functions as the head.

However, the majority of Polish N+N or A+N compounds are hierarchically structured and subordinate, with the right-hand constituent functioning as the head. For example: *światłowstręt* 'photophobia', *gwiazdozbiór* 'constellation', *czarnoziem* 'black earth', *drobnoustrój* 'micro-organism'. All the examples on this list are endocentric, in other words the compound may be interpreted as a hyponym of its head (thus, for instance, *światłowstręt* 'photophobia' means 'kind of phobia', etc.).[9] Exocentric combinations are also fairly common regardless of whether or not the compound incorporates an overt suffix. For instance, *nosorożec* 'rhinoceros' and *stawonóg* 'arthropod' denote 'kinds of animals' although their second constituents make reference to horns or legs, respectively (*róg* 'horn', *nog-a* 'leg'). Other examples of the exocentric type: *trójkąt* 'triangle' < *trój-* 'three'+*kąt* 'angle'; *równoległobok* 'rhomboid' <*równoległy* 'parallel'+*bok* 'side'; *obcokrajowiec* 'foreigner' <*obcy* 'foreign'+*kraj* 'country'. Here the head of the compound is either unexpressed, as in *trój-kąt* '(a flat figure with) three angles' or is vaguely symbolized by the final suffix, as in *obc-o-kraj-owiec* 'a person from a foreign country, foreigner'. According to an alternative interpretation, the latter example might be viewed as endocentric rather than exocentric, assuming that the meaning of 'person' is directly encoded by the suffix *-owiec*. Structures of the kind just illustrated are also right-headed, in themselves, since the first two constituents function as a complex, right-headed, modifier with respect to the implied head of the compound.

---

[9] Left-headed N+N compounds are truly exceptional (Grzegorczykowa and Puzynina 1999: 461); cf., however, *nartorolki* 'grass skis' when paraphrased as 'skis with (small) rollers/wheels'. In order to be consistent with the right-headed endocentric pattern, the form should rather be: (*)*rolkonarty*.

However, in exocentric compounds with a verbal element, this element mirrors the head of the corresponding verb phrase, regardless of whether it appears in the first or second position in the compound. This is illustrated with the following examples where the verb stem appears in bold face:

(8)   V+N   N+V
   łam-i-strajk 'strike breaker'   *list-o-nosz* 'postman'
      lit. 'sb. who breaks a strike'   lit. 'sb. who carries letters'
   baw-i-dam-ek 'ladies' man'   *lin-o-skocz-ek* 'tightrope walker'
      lit. 'sb. who amuses/entertains ladies'   lit. 'sb. who jumps (on) a tightrope'

The examples presented so far give the correct impression that the semantic structure of Polish nominal compounds is quite diversified and, at times, fairly complex and/or ambiguous. However, due to space limitations, it is hardly possible to give a full-fledged semantic classification of the data under discussion (for details, see Kurzowa 1976 or Grzegorczykowa and Puzynina 1999). Suffice it to say that, by and large, the semantic categories that are discernible are reminiscent of those normally established in the context of ordinary (e.g. affixal) derivation of Polish nouns. Thus, one can identify, for instance, formations that are agentive (*listonosz* 'postman', *dobroczyńca* 'benefactor'), instrumental (*gazomierz* 'gas meter'), locative (*jadłodajnia* 'eating place'), resultative (*brudnopis* 'rough draft'), attributive (*lekkoduch* 'good-for-nothing'), that denote activities (*grzybobranie* 'mushroom picking'), states/conditions (*płaskostopie* 'flat foot'), or inhabitants (*Nowozelandczyk* 'New Zealander'), etc. For a detailed interpretation of the semantics of Polish nominal compounds in terms of thematic relations, see Sambor (1976).

25.3 COMPOUND ADJECTIVES

Just like compound nouns, compound adjectives show a variety of structural patterns. Again we see the characteristic appearance of interfixes, in the form of linking vowels (-*o*- and -*u*-), which bind together the constituent stems. For instance, *dług-o-ziarn-ist(y)* (*ryż*) 'long-grain (rice)', *ciemn-o-brąz-ow(y)* (*stół*) 'dark-brown (table)'; or *dw-u-maszt-ow(y)* (*statek*) 'two-masted (ship)', *st-u-piętr-ow(y)* (*budynek*) 'hundred-storey (building)'.[10]

---

[10] Because the Polish adjective must agree in gender (also number and case) with its head noun, examples of adjectives are cited here in their form of nom. sg. masc. when they are given in isolation or in the proper gender form (MASC / FEM / NEUT) of nom. sg. when a particular adjective appears in context. Hence the inflections may vary; e.g. *ciemnobrązow-y* (MASC) / *ciemnobrązow-a* (FEM) / *ciemnobrązow-e* (NEUT.) for 'dark-brown'.

The interfixes co-occur with a range of adjective-forming suffixes (co-forma-tives). The suffixes are familiar from plain adjectival derivation and so, for instance, when the second constituent is a noun, the suffix may be any of the following: *-ow-* (*dwumaszt-ow-y* 'two-masted'), *-n-* (*wielobarw-n-y* 'multicoloured'), *-an-* (*elanobawełni-an-y* 'polycotton'), *-sk-* (*wysokogór-sk-i* '(high) mountain, alpine'), *-ist-/-yst-* (*grubokośc-ist-y* 'big-boned'), *-ast-* (*ostrokanci-ast-y* 'sharp-edged'). In case of verb-stems used as final elements, one may identify the following suffixes: *-n-* (*szybkostrzel-n-y* 'quick-firing'), *-czy-* (*dźwiękonaśladow-cz-y* 'sound-imita-tive'), *-ł-* (*długotrwa-ł-y* 'long-lasting'). Additionally, since numerous compounds with a verbal head actually incorporate a participle form (regular or lexicalized), one may come across the participial endings such as *-ąc-* (*słodkobrzmi-ąc-y* 'sweet-sounding') and *-an-* (*wysokozaawansow-an-y* 'highly advanced').

For noun- and verb-final compounds, the choice of the suffix is dictated by a simple rule (Kallas 1999: 519): the compound adjective takes the suffix that is also used to form a corresponding derived (denominal or deverbal) adjective. This principle is illustrated below:

(9)

SUFF	N / V	DERIVED A	COMPOUND A (X+N / V)
-ow-	*maszt* 'mast'	*maszt-ow-y*	*dwumaszt-ow-y* 'two-masted'
-n-	*barw-a* 'colour'	*barw-n-y*	*wielobarw-n-y* 'multicoloured'
-an-	*bawełn-a* 'cotton'	*bawełni-an-y*	*elanobawełni-an-y* 'polycotton'
-sk-	*gór-a* 'mountain'	*gór-sk-i*	*wysokogór-sk-i* 'alpine'
-ist-	*kość* 'bone'	*kośc-ist-y*	*grubokośc-ist-y* 'big-boned'
-ast-	*kant* 'edge'	*kanci-ast-y*	*ostrokanci-ast-y* 'sharp-edged'
-cz-	*tworz-y-ć* 'create'	*twór-cz-y*	*rakotwór-cz-y* 'carcinogenic'
-ł-	*trw-a-ć* 'last$_V$'	*trwa-ł-y*	*długotrwa-ł-y* 'long-lasting'

The afore-mentioned rule has certain exceptions, though. First of all, no usual denomi-nal suffix is used in case of adjectival compounds (or premodified possessional adjec-tives) with a final noun which refers to an inalienably possessed, salient body-part of a human or animal. Instead of an overt suffix, one uses here the method of paradigmatic (inflectional) derivation, which produces the following formal contrasts:[11]

(10)

N	DERIVED A	COMPOUND A (A+N)
głow-a 'head'	*głow-ow-y*	*twardogłowy* 'hard-headed'
nos 'nose'	*nos-ow-y*	*długonosy* 'long-nosed'
ok-o 'eye'	*ocz-n-y*	*niebieskooki* 'blue-eyed'
ręk-a 'arm, hand'	*ręcz-n-y*	*jednoręki* 'one-handed'
skór-a 'skin'	*skór-n-y*	*czerwonoskóry* 'red-skinned'
uch-o 'ear'	*usz-n-y*	*długouchy* 'long-eared'
włos-y 'hair'	*włos-ow-y*	*jasnowłosy* 'fair-haired'
dziób 'beak'	*dziob-ow-y*	*ostrodzioby* 'sharp-beaked'

[11] See Szymanek (1996: 261) for more data; consider also similar contrasts in Slovak: *ok-o* 'eye' > *oč-n-ý* (adj.) / *modr-o-ok-ý* 'blue-eyed', *ruk-a* 'arm, hand' > *ruč-n-ý* (adj.) / *dlh-o-ruk-ý* 'long-armed', etc.

| *łusk-a* 'scale' | *łusk-ow-y* | *srebrnołuski* 'silver-scaled' |
| *płetw-a* 'fin' | *płetw-ow-y* | *długopłetwy* 'long-finned' |

As may be seen, this remarkable pattern is fairly regular and relatively productive, given the low number of inalienably possessed, salient body-parts. It is functionally analogous to the English type of compound adjectives in -*ed* like *blue-eyed*. It ought to be stressed that the adjectival forms in -*i/-y* like -*głowy* above may only appear in compounds (with premodification) but not on their own. This fact can be explained along the lines suggested in Booij (2005a: 218) for the corresponding English combinations like *red-faced* vs. ?*faced* (see also Lieber, Chapter 18, for more discussion and references). The shorter forms, arguably well-formed, are said to violate a general pragmatic restriction called Non-Redundancy Constraint: 'It is expected that human beings have a face, and hence it does not seem to make much sense from a pragmatic point of view to say *My husband has a face*. Hence the use of such adjectives is infelicitous ... unless they are embedded in a compound' (Booij 2005a: 218–19). By analogy, assuming that the paradigmatic formative is a distinctive marker of possession in the Polish adjectives, formations like *głowy*, *oki*, etc. (cf. above) are all ruled out, in contradistinction to their generally relational, suffixal counterparts (*głowowy*, *oczny*, etc.).

Apart from the systematic sub-regularity just discussed, the principle according to which the suffix in the compound is copied from a simpler adjective is rarely violated, though. Nevertheless, one may find a few offending counterexamples: *język* 'tongue' > *dwujęzycz-n-y* 'bilingual' but *język-ow-y* (adj.); *czas* 'time' > *równoczes-n-y* 'simultaneous' but *czas-ow-y* (adj.), *linia* 'line' > *prostolinij-n-y* 'straightforward, guileless' but *lini-ow-y* (adj.) (Kurzowa 1976: 96).

Another look at instances of compound adjectives which incorporate a verbal head as the final constituent reveals that the verb stem is usually preceded by a noun or an adverb, as illustrated in (11) and (12) below:

(11)	NOUN	VERB	COMPOUND ADJECTIVE
	dźwięk 'sound'	*naśladować* 'imitate'	*dźwiękonaśladowczy* 'onomatopoeic'
	dźwięk 'sound'	*chłonąć* 'absorb'	*dźwiękochłonny* 'sound-absorbent'
	owad 'insect'	*(za)bijać* 'kill'	*owadobójczy* 'insecticide'
	rak 'cancer'	*tworzyć* 'create'	*rakotwórczy* 'carcinogenic'
	rop-a 'oil'	*nosić* 'bear$_V$'	*roponośny* 'oil-bearing'
	kwas 'acid'	*odpierać* 'resist'	*kwasoodporny* 'acid-resistant'
	ciepł-o 'warmth'	*lubić* 'like$_V$'	*ciepłolubny* 'stenothermic'
	bramk-a 'goal'	*strzelać* 'score'	*bramkostrzelny* 'scoring (many) goals'

(12)	ADVERB	VERB	COMPOUND ADJECTIVE
	lekko 'lightly'	*strawić* 'digest'	*lekkostrawny* 'light, easily digestible'
	szybko 'quick(ly)'	*strzelać* 'fire'	*szybkostrzelny* 'quick-firing'
	blisko 'close'	*znaczyć* 'mean$_V$'	*bliskoznaczny* '(nearly) synonymous'

| *długo* 'long' | *trwać* 'last$_V$' | *długotrwały* 'long-lasting' |
| *wszystko* 'all' | *wiedzieć* 'know' | *wszystkowiedzący* 'omniscient' |

It ought to be added that neither of the types exemplified above are very productive in contemporary Polish. In fact, the majority of existing formations contain a handful of recurring verb-based terminations like *-bójczy*, *-chłonny*, *-twórczy*, *-nośny*, *-odporny* (see above). Combinations of compound-final verbs with preceding numerals or adjectives are extremely rare (however, cf. respectively *dwuznaczny* 'ambiguous' and *żyworodny* 'viviparous').

Now we need to take a look at the range of possible structures which involve an adjective in the final position. Predictably, the most common type are combinations A+A. It ought to be stressed that, within this type, one can identify two structural subclasses (see Kallas 1999: 514): coordinate combinations like (*sklep*) *owocowo-warzywny* 'fruit and vegetable (shop); greengrocer's', (*dział*) *ekonomiczno-finansowy* 'economy and finance (department)', (*sieć*) *wodno-kanalizacyjna* 'water and sewage (system)' and modifier-plus-head combinations (with subordination) like *teoretycznonaukowy* 'scientific, with emphasis on theory', *historycznoliteracki* 'concerning historical aspects of literature'.[12] Compounds of the former class (i.e. coordinated ones) are normally hyphenated. Another remarkable feature of structurally coordinated compounds is that they show recursion, that is, more than two adjectives may be used within one compound word; cf. (*stosunki*) *polsko-rosyjsko-ukraińskie* 'Polish-Russian-Ukrainian (relations)'. This seems to be the only area of Polish compounding where recursion is not ruled out.

The domain of colour terms suggests another, strictly morphological division. Apart from combinations of denominal adjectives there are numerous instances of compounds involving two qualitative, simplex adjectives. Thus, for instance, forms like *biało-czerwony* 'white and red' are to be classified as coordinations of two qualitative (simplex) adjectives while examples like *ciemnoczerwony* 'dark red', *jasnożółty* 'light yellow', *jaskrawozielony* 'bright/vivid green' show subordination of the first (modifier) element. Of course, there are also 'mixed' cases, where a qualitative adjective is followed by a derived (relational) one, or vice versa.

Adjectives premodified by nouns, adverbs, and numerals are much less common and quite often the combination is lexicalized. The type N+A may be illustrated with the following examples: *wodoszczelny* 'waterproof', *wiarygodny* 'credible', *prawdopodobny* 'probable'.

Summing up this section, let us stress that a precise semantic interpretation of a compound adjective would have to pay heed to its immediate context, that is (typically) the head noun it modifies. This has hardly been attempted here. Other analytic hurdles include the notorious problems of paraphrase, double motivation, and lexicalization.

---

[12] Alternatively, certain combinations of this formal type may be interpreted as being motivated by corresponding noun phrases: e.g. *teoria literatury* 'theory of literature' > *teoretycznoliteracki*.

CHAPTER 26

SINO-TIBETAN: MANDARIN CHINESE

ANTONELLA CECCAGNO AND BIANCA BASCIANO

26.1 INTRODUCTION

While in some languages compounding can be considered peripheral, in Chinese compounding is the most productive means of word formation. It has been shown that approximately 80 per cent of Chinese words are compound words (Xing 2006: 117). In the corpus of neologisms proposed in *The Contemporary Chinese Dictionary* (2002) more than 90 per cent of all new words are compounds.[1] Therefore analysing Chinese compounds means analysing the most significant morphological phenomenon of that language.

Over time different theoretical approaches have been adopted in the analysis of Chinese compounds. In this article, starting from the classification of compounds

The general outline of the work was discussed jointly by the authors, however Antonella Ceccagno is responsible for sections 26.1, 2, 3.1 and Bianca Basciano for sections 26.3.2-4. This research has been also made possible with the help of PRIN 2005 funds.

[1] For an analysis of the data of the corpus, see Ceccagno and Basciano (2007). The examples presented in this article mainly come from this corpus. Glosses are those given by the dictionary.

argued for by Bisetto and Scalise (2005), we will put forth a redefinition of their macro-types in order to be able to undertake an in-depth analysis of Chinese compounding.

One widely discussed theoretical issue in the literature is the morphological position of the head in the languages of the world. This article discusses headedness in Chinese compounds and proposes a new Head Position Principle, which challenges some widespread assumptions and could well be of interest for the analysis of headedness in other languages.

In our analysis of Chinese compounds we have identified a phenomenon never analysed before, namely the formation of new compounds from underlying compounds, which we name 'metacompounding'. These compounds have implications for headedness.

26.2 CLASSIFICATION OF CHINESE COMPOUNDS

Over time different approaches have been adopted for Chinese compounds (Chao 1948; Lu 1964; Chao 1968; Tang 1989; Packard 2000). These approaches generally focus only on one aspect: the relationship between the constituents (Xia 1946, cited in Pan, Ye, and Han 2004), semantics (Li and Thompson 1981), syntactic description (Chao 1948; Lu 1964; Chao 1968; Tang 1989), form class description (Packard 2000).[2]

In analysing Chinese compounds we follow the works of Ceccagno and Scalise (2006, 2007), who propose a comprehensive analysis able to take into account the whole set of category, functional, and semantic levels: the lexical category of the constituents, their grammatical relationship, the semantics of the constituents, the semantics of the compound, and the position of the head (if any). Following their approach, we posit that in the absence of one of these components the analysis is incomplete if not misleading.

For Chinese compounds we adopt the classification argued for by Bisetto and Scalise (2005), who single out three macro-types in compounding (subordinate, attributive, and coordinate). Each type may be endocentric (with a lexical head) or exocentric (without a lexical head).

However, in our view, the proposed distinction between subordinate and attributive compounds seems not to be able to account for all the varieties existing in natural languages. In particular, following this classification scheme, a number of Chinese compounds do not easily fit in one or the other macro-type. Therefore we propose a modification of the scheme put forth by Bisetto and Scalise, through a

---

[2] The lack of space prevents us from commenting directly on these approaches in this article.

redefinition of the macro-types. In the following section we shall illustrate our definition and description of the three macro-types.

26.2.1 Subordinate compounds

We define subordinate compounds (SUB) as those in which constituents have an argument–head (or head–argument) relation. A first type shows either a verbal or deverbal head which projects an argument satisfied by the non-head constituent. Among subordinate compounds there are also those with a verbal head which takes another verbal constituent as its complement. Examples are presented below:

(1) 毒犯 *dúfàn* [N+N]$_N$ 'drug+vendor' = 'drug trafficker'

(2) 通关 *tōngguān* [V+N]$_V$ 'clear out+customs' = 'clear the customs'

(3) a. 走高 *zǒugāo* [V+A]$_V$ 'climb+high' = 'climb up; rise'
     b. 入住 *rùzhù* [V+V]$_V$ 'come into/enter+live/stop' = 'move into'

(4) 竞买 *jìngmǎi* [V+V]$_V$ 'compete+buy' = 'compete to buy'

毒犯 *dúfàn* (1) is a compound with a deverbal head, where the noun constituent acts as its argument.

通关 *tōngguān* (2) is a verbal compound of the verb+object type, where the leftmost constituent is the head of the compound. What characterizes this type of compound is that the noun is apparently subcategorized for by the verb. In fact, the noun constituent acts as the internal argument of the verb. However, it should be noted that the noun does not saturate an argument position, as demonstrated by the possibility of taking an additional object, which is the real argument: 投资五千欧元。 *tóuzī wǔqiān ōuyuán* 'put money 5,000 euro' = 'invest 5,000 euros'.[3]

走高 *zǒugāo* and 入住 *rùzhù* (3) are verbal compounds of the resultative type, also called verb-complement constructions (cf. Zhu 1982; Huang 2006), in which the verb (or adjective)[4] on the right expresses the result of the activity conveyed by the first element.[5]

---

[3] Verb+object compounds represent a widely discussed issue since they may fall in between morphology and syntax. In lexicalist approaches many criteria have been proposed in the attempt to solve this problem. Chao (1968), Li and Thompson (1981), Huang (1984), Chi (1985), Dai (1992), and Packard (2000) propose different criteria to distinguish verb+object compounds from phrases: lexicality or specialization of meaning; inability of the verb and object to be moved or separated; one of the constituents being a bound root, i.e. being unable to occupy a syntactic slot; exocentricity of the construction; the construction allowing an additional object. However, even the most convincing criteria sometimes seem not to work.

[4] Notice that in Chinese adjectives are often treated as verbs (cf. Li and Thompson 1981, among others); one of the strongest pieces of evidence in favour of this analysis is that adjectives in this language can function as the predicate of a sentence without needing any copula (cf. Li 1990).

[5] Different approaches to the formation of resultative verb constructions have been proposed: lexical (Li 1990, 2005); syntactic (Huang 1992); both lexical and syntactic (Cheng 1997); constructional (Huang 2006).

竞买 *jìngmǎi* (4) is a compound of the serial-verb type, in which the event expressed by the verb on the right depends on the one expressed by the verb on the left. As far as we know, this kind of compound has never been discussed in the literature, which has focused instead on resultative compounds (often referred to as resultative serial-verb constructions). What we call serial-verb compounds show the same relation between the constituents as that shown by syntactic serial-verb purpose-clause and complement-clause constructions (Li and Thompson 1981).[6]

A second type of subordinate compound shows a relational noun as head, where the non-head acts as a semantic argument saturating the noun head, as in:

(5)   警嫂 *jǐngsǎo* [N+N]$_N$ 'police+sister' = respectful term for a policeman's wife

(6)   价差 *jiàchā* [N+N]$_N$ 'price+difference' = 'price difference'

26.2.2 Attributive compounds

Attributive compounds (ATT) are those in which the constituents have a modifier–head relation. These can be compounds where:

(a) the non-head is an adjective or a noun which expresses a property of the head, as in 主页 *zhǔyè* [A+N]$_N$ 'main+page' = 'homepage' or 地价 dìjià [N+N]$_N$ 'earth+price' = 'bottom price';

(b) the non-head constituent acts as an adjunct modifying the head, as in 口算 *kǒusuàn* [N+V]$_V$ 'mouth+(to) do a sum' = '(to) do a sum orally'; or as in 跃增 *yuèzēng* [V+V]$_V$ 'leap+increase' = 'grow by leaps';

(c) a verbal non-head acts as a modifier of the head, as in 卖点 *màidiǎn* [V+N]$_N$ 'sell+point' = 'selling point'.

26.2.3 Coordinate compounds

Coordinate compounds (CRD) are those that show a logical coordination between the constituents ('and'), as in 蔬果 *shūguǒ* [N+N]$_N$ 'vegetables+fruit' = 'vegetables and fruit', or a semantic relation of synonymy, as in 靓丽 *liànglì* [A+A]$_A$ 'pretty+beautiful' = 'pretty/beautiful'; antonymy, as in 呼吸 *hūxī* [V+V]$_V$ 'exhale+inhale' = 'breathe' or 大小 *dàxiǎo* [A+A]$_N$ 'big+small' = 'measure';

---

[6] In Chinese, serial-verb constructions do not indicate a single construction with its own properties but a number of different constructions with different properties. The only common feature is that they are a sequence of two verbs without any overt coordinating or subordinating markers between them. Serial-verb purpose-clause constructions are those constructions where the first event is done for the purpose of achieving the second. In a complement-clause construction the second verb is subcategorized for by the first verb.

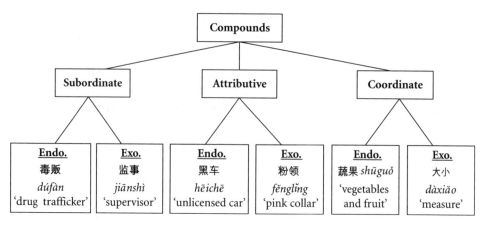

Figure 26.1 Classification of Chinese Compounds

redundancy, as in 松树 *sōngshù* [N + N]$_N$ 'pine + tree' = 'pine tree'; or reduplication, as in 大大 *dàdà* [A + A]$_{Adv}$ 'big + big' = 'enormously'.

Figure 26.1 shows the classification scheme whereby compounds are classified according to the new definitions of macro-types, illustrated with Chinese examples.

26.3 HEADEDNESS IN CHINESE COMPOUNDS

26.3.1 Different theoretical approaches

The issue of identification of the head in compounding is of particular interest. From the 1980s there has been a steady development in the theory with Williams (1981), Selkirk (1982), Trommelen and Zonneveld (1986), and Di Sciullo and Williams (1987) assuming that the position of the head is invariably on the right and Scalise (1984), Corbin (1987), and Varela (1990) claiming that in compounding Romance languages heads are consistently on the left.[7]

The different positions of morphological heads in the different languages studied induced Bisetto and Scalise (2002) to conclude that the position of the head in all of the languages of the world is a parameter that needs to be set.

As far as Chinese compounding is concerned, back in 1968, Chao (1968: 372) distinguished between coordinate and subordinate compounds in Chinese, saying that in coordinate compounds 'each constituent is a centre while in a subordinate compound only the second constituent is the centre' (we assume 'centre' to be the

---

[7] For a discussion of the development of the theory of headedness in compounding see Scalise, Bisetto, and Guevara (2005).

equivalent of head). Therefore, according to Chao Chinese has both right-headed and left-headed compounds.

Huang (1998) instead reached the conclusion that: 'Chinese is a headless language in its morphology since neither the rightmost nor the leftmost member of a compound uniquely determines the category type of a compound' (for a critical analysis of Huang's positions, see Ceccagno and Scalise 2007). Huang reached this conclusion after observing that compounds with the same structures can have different output categories. For example, [V + N] compounds can be nouns as well as verbs, and sometimes adjectives. What Huang failed to consider is the relation between the constituents. In fact, the position of the head also depends on the relation holding between the two constituents. For example, in a compound such as 卖场 *màichǎng* 'to sell + place' = 'big marketplace for selling commodities', with a $[V+N]_N$ structure, the head is the noun constituent and the verb acts as a modifier, i.e. 'the place in which one sells'. On the other hand, in a $[V+N]_V$ compound, such as 投资 *tóuzī* 'to put + money' = 'to invest', the head is the left constituent, the verb, while the noun acts as its internal argument. Finally, a $[V+N]_N$ compound such as 监事 *jiānshì* 'supervise + matter/responsibility' = 'supervisor' has the same structure and the same output category as the compound in the first example, but the relation between the constituents is completely different: it is an exocentric compound where the constituents have a verb–argument relation. The examples highlight not only how input and output categories are important, but also that the relation between the constituents of a compound contributes to determining the position of the head.

Starosta et al. (1998) claimed that Chinese compounds are right-headed and 'it may be that many of the words which are not right-headed are also not compound words'.

Packard (2000) proposed the generalization (Headedness Principle) according to which 'All verbs have a verb on the left; and all nouns have a noun on the right'. However, this generalization only applies to subordinate compounds, and it does not take into account the fact that verbs can be right-headed in attributive compounds. Further, Packard fails to acknowledge the existence of coordinate two-headed compounds and exocentric compounds, which are quite widespread in Chinese compounding.

These limitations in Packard's generalization have been highlighted by Ceccagno and Scalise (2006), who were also the first to delve into the issue of headedness and exocentricity in Chinese. Their data showed the prevalence of right-headed compounds. Left-headed compounds did exist in their corpus (of the verb + object and resultative types); however the fact that these left-headed compounds fall in between morphology and syntax – in that it is not always clear whether they are compounds or phrases – led them to assume that 'the canonical position of the head in Chinese compounds is on the right and that the so-called verb-object compounds and resultative compounds are an exception to this principle'.

On the basis of Ceccagno and Basciano's (2007) analysis of a corpus of disyllabic neologisms we will discuss headedness patterns in the different macro-types and illustrate a new Headedness Principle.

26.3.2 Headedness among macro-types

Among endocentric subordinate compounds, those with noun output are right-headed. Examples of nominal right-headed compounds are presented in Table 26.1.[8]

Subordinate verbal compounds are of the verb+object type, resultative type, and serial-verb type. We consider resultative verbs as left-headed. In the literature resultative compounds are generally considered left-headed: Lin (1990), Li (1990, 2005), Cheng and Huang (1994), Cheng (1997), Packard (2000), and Sun (2006) all assume that these constructions exhibit a verb–complement relation, where the resultative verb (on the right) acts as a complement of the verb on the left.[9]

Besides, on the basis of the corresponding syntactic structures, we assume that serial-verb compounds too are left-headed.

Therefore, all subordinate verbal compounds are left-headed. Table 26.2 shows an example for each type. The behaviour of Chinese subordinate compounds appears to be in line with the generalization in Packard (2000). This generalization however does not apply to attributive and coordinate compounds (or to exocentric compounds).

Endocentric attributive compounds, as already observed by Ceccagno and Scalise (2007), behave in a straightforward manner: they are always right-headed. The output can be either a noun, a verb, or an adjective. Table 26.3 shows examples of attributive compounds.

Finally, coordinate compounds are two-headed. As stated by Sun (2006), the constituents of coordinate compounds are coordinate in nature or are parallel with each other within a semantic domain. According to Chao (1968), in Chinese

---

[8] In the tables in this Chapter, *Pinyin* represents the official romanization method for Chinese; *Cat* (Category) can be: A(djective), V(erb), N(oun), or Adv(erb); and *Head* (position) can be: r (right), l (left), b (both), or n (none = exocentric compounds).

[9] Starosta et al. (1998) put forth an analysis of Chinese resultative compounds which considers resultative verbs as derived words headed by the resultative suffix on the right. For some Chinese resultative compounds, such as 攀高 *pāngāo* 'climb + high' = 'climb up/rise' it would seem possible to propose an analysis similar to that proposed for resultative compounds in English or for prefixed verbs in Russian (see, for instance, Spencer and Zaretskaya 1998), where the element corresponding to 高 *gāo* in these constructions, although syntactically a secondary predicator, expresses the core semantic predicator, so that semantically the verb stem is subordinated. Cheng and Huang (1994) argue against this analysis based on semantic criteria, claiming that only syntactically relevant considerations can reveal the head constituent of a resultative compound. They assume left-headedness, claiming that headedness in resultative compounds derives from the event structure. Li (1990) assumes left-headedness on the basis of the argument structure.

Table 26.1 Subordinate right-headed compounds

Compound	Pinyin	Class	Struct	Cat	Head	Gloss
网民	wǎngmín	SUB	[N+N]	N	r	net + people = 'netizen'
毒犯	dúfàn	SUB	[N+N]	N	r	drug + criminal = 'drug criminal'

Table 26.2 Subordinate left-headed compounds

Compound	Pinyin	Class	Struct	Cat	Head	Gloss
禁毒	jìndú	SUB	[V+N]	V	l	prohibit + poison = 'ban the sale and abuse of drugs'
告破	gàopò	SUB	[V+V]	V	l	inform + crack into pieces/expose the truth = 'make known that a mystery has been cracked'
入住	rùzhù	SUB	[V+V]	V	l	enter + live/stop = 'move into'
攀高	pāngāo	SUB	[V+A]	V	l	climb + high = 'climb up; rise'

Table 26.3 Attributive compounds (right-headed)

Compound	Pinyin	Class	Struct	Cat	Head	Gloss
主页	zhǔyè	ATT	[A+N]	N	r	main + page = 'homepage'
猫步	māobù	ATT	[N+N]	N	r	cat + walk = 'cat's walk'
完胜	wánshèng	ATT	[A+V]	V	r	whole + win victory = 'win a complete victory'
突审	tūshěn	ATT	[Adv+V]	V	r	unexpectedly + interrogate = 'interrogate sb. by surprise'
函售	hánshòu	ATT	[N+V]	V	r	letter + sell = 'order by mail'

coordinate compounding each constituent is a 'centre'. Anderson (1985) argues that neither constituent can exclusively be considered as the 'centre'. According to Packard (2000), in these compounds neither constituent has a modifying or subordinate relation to the other: these compounds have a juxtapositional, flat form, in which the two morphemes are structurally parallel.

Different criteria contribute to show that Chinese coordinate compounds are two-headed. First, from the semantic point of view, in coordinate compounds both constituents equally contribute to the interpretation of the whole compound. Second, criteria such as inflection of the head constituent, gender, etc. – which in other languages help to establish which constituent formally acts as the head[10] – do not

---

[10] According to different criteria, coordinate compounds in Germanic languages are considered right-headed, taking on the morphosyntactic properties of the rightmost constituent. For a discussion of copulative compounds in German and English, see Olsen (2001).

Table 26.4 Coordinate compounds (two-headed)

Compound	Pinyin	Class	Struct	Cat	Head	Gloss
餐饮	cānyǐn	CRD	[N+N]	N	b	food + drinks = 'food and drink'
峰位	fēngwèi	CRD	[N+N]	N	b	peak + place = 'peak'[a]
打压	dǎyā	CRD	[V+V]	V	b	hit + suppress = 'combat and suppress'
亮丽	liànglì	CRD	[A+A]	A	b	bright + beautiful = 'brilliant/bright and beautiful'

[a] This kind of compound, redundant compounds, only on the basis of semantic criteria, can possibly be considered right-headed, since the left-constituent is a subgroup of the rightmost constituent. These compounds behave like similar compounds in other languages, for example the English *palm-tree*.

exist in Chinese. Therefore, it cannot be established which constituent provides the morphosyntactic properties to the whole compound. Third, the fact that Chinese compounds – as we will see below – seem not to have a canonical position for the head, in that Chinese productively forms both right-headed and left-headed compounds, also strengthens the conclusion that coordinate endocentric compounds are two-headed. Table 26.4 shows examples of two-headed coordinate compounds.

Finally, in Chinese exocentric compounds do exist and can be found in all macro-types. Table 26.5 shows an example of each of the many exocentric structures available.

26.3.3 Headedness in metacompounding

Some compounds at first appear to be exocentric, but in fact are not so. They represent a particular phenomenon that we call 'metacompounding' or compounds formed from compounded constituents (for further reading, see Ceccagno and Basciano, forthcoming). This is a mode of compound formation in which at least one of the constituents refers to an underlying compound that does not appear on the surface. The constituent on the surface is therefore a truncated form of the underlying compound. In order to clarify the semantics, the lexical category, or the head of the compound, an analysis of the underlying compounds is required, too.

In a compound like 义拍 *yìpāi* the analysis of the surface compound would be as in (7):

(7)   义拍 *yìpāi* ATT [A+V]$_N$ 'righteous + pat/take' = 'charitable auction'

At first the compound seems to be exocentric. Moreover, from both the structural and semantic point of view, the analysis of the compound appears to be problematic. This would not be the case if we were to analyse the second constituent of the compound, 拍 *pāi*, as a truncated form of the underlying compound, 拍卖 *pāimài* ('auction'). The analysis of the compound will thus be as follows (8):

Table 26.5 Exocentric compounds

Compound	Pinyin	Class	Struct	Cat	Head	Gloss
楼花	lóuhuā	SUB	[N+V]	N	n	floor+spend/use='building that is put up for sale before it is completed'
网虫	wǎngchóng	SUB	[N+N]	N	n	net+insect='internet buff; web enthusiast'
胆小	dǎnxiǎo	SUB	[N+A]	A	n	guts/ courage+small='coward'
地震	dìzhèn	SUB	[N+V]	N	n	earth+shake='earthquake'
文胸	wénxiōng	SUB	[V+N]	N	n	conceal+breast='bra'
割肉	gēròu	SUB	[V+N]	V	n	cut with a knife+meat='sell sth. at a price lower than its original price'
失范	shīfàn	SUB	[V+N]	A	n	lose/deviate from the norm+model = 'irregular'
黄毒	huángdú	ATT	[A+N]	N	n	pornographic+poison='pornographic books'
色狼	sèláng	ATT	[N+N]	N	n	lust+wolf='sex maniac'
蹦床	bèngchuáng	ATT	[V+N]	N	n	bouncing+bed='trampoline'
婚介	hūnjiè	ATT	[N+V]	N	n	wedding+introduce='matchmaking'
速递	sùdì	ATT	[A+V]	N	n	fast+hand over/pass='express delivery'
互动	hùdòng	ATT	[Adv+V]	N	n	mutually+move='interaction'
航拍	hángpāi	ATT	[V+V]	N	n	navigate (by water or air)+take a photograph = 'aerial photograph'
高发	gāofā	ATT	[A+V]	A	n	high/above the average+deliver='frequent'
花心	huāxīn	ATT	[A+N]	A	n	attractive but unreal or insincere+heart='unfaithful'
频密	pínmì	ATT	[Adv+A]	A	n	frequently+close/dense='frequent'
梯次	tīcì	ATT	[N+N]	Adv	n	steps+order='by echelon or by group/ in order of age, size, etc.'
东西	dōngxī	CRD	[N+N]	N	n	east+west='thing'
天天	tiāntiān	CRD	[N+N]	Adv	n	day+day='everyday'
联动	liándòng	CRD	[V+V]	N	n	unite+move='chain effect/reaction'
高矮	gāoǎi	CRD	[A+A]	N	n	high+low='height'
大大	dàdà	CRD	[A+A]	Adv	n	big+big='enormously'

(8)

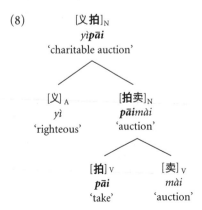

Thus, in itself the compound 义拍 *yìpāi* presents both semantic and categorial opacity, and it is not possible to identify the head. However if we consider the underlying compound, the structure of the surface compound and its meaning become clear and the head can be identified.

The compound in (9) refers to two underlying compounds:

(9)

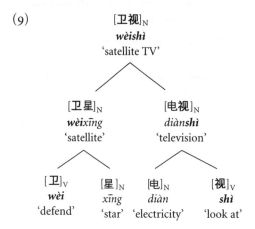

What could appear as a $[V+V]_N$ coordinate compound would be unfathomable from the semantic point of view if we did not refer to the underlying compounds 卫星 *wèixīng* and 电视 *diànshì* 'satellite + TV' = 'satellite TV'. Further, if we consider the two underlying compounds, the input lexical categories are not $[V+V]$, but rather $[N+N]$, and the compound is not exocentric but rather endocentric with head on the right; lastly, it is no longer a coordinate but rather an attributive compound. Therefore the whole structure of the compound changes when we refer to the underlying compounds.

Summing up, we define as metacompounds those compounds that require reference to their underlying compounds in order to ascertain semantics, lexical category, or head of the compound. A metacompound could be depicted as an iceberg, only the tip of which can be seen, but whose morphology can only be explained by reference to the submerged part.[11]

In conclusion, with the caveat of checking the underlying compounds, as far as headedness is concerned, metacompounds behave in the same manner as regular compounds.

---

[11] Metacompounds are in a way similar to so-called blends (*motel* from 'motor hotel') and truncated compounds in Russian (Molinsky 1973; Billings 1998), as in *partorg* from 'partтījnyj + organizаtor' ('(political) party organizer'). The main difference lies in the nature of the truncated constituents, which in metacompounds are compound words. The phenomenon of metacompounding can be somehow related to Chinese phenomena such as abbreviations (cf. Ling 2000), or 'stump compounds' (cf. Li and Thompson 1978). Tibetan exhibits a phenomenon that is similar to metacompounding, called 'clipping' (Wälchli 2005). Further cross-linguistic investigations could show whether similar phenomena exist in other languages of the Sino-Tibetan family.

26.3.4 A new Head Position Principle

As a result of our analysis of the corpus of disyllabic neologisms, we are able to state that right-headed, left-headed, and two-headed compounds, alongside exocentric compounds, do exist in Chinese (Ceccagno and Basciano, 2007).

Left-headed compounds cannot be considered a peripheral phenomenon – as would be the case with right-headed compounds in Romance languages – but are rather a central feature of Chinese compounding. Furthermore, a distinctive element of Chinese is the productivity[12] of two-headed endocentric coordinate compounds.

This prompts us to propose a Head Position Principle for Chinese compounding. Unlike other languages for which the position of the morphological head has been studied and where the compound's canonical head has been identified to be either on the right (Germanic languages) or on the left (Romance languages), Chinese does not have a canonical position for the head. In Chinese, endocentric compounds exhibit head on the right, head on the left, and both constituents as heads.

Interestingly enough, if we were to exclude coordinate two-headed compounds, among endocentric compounds a pattern could be singled out. Nominal compounds are straightforwardly right-headed, while verbal compounds can be both right-headed (attributive) and left-headed (subordinate).

This feature of compounds in Chinese can have an impact on the theory of the head(s) in compounding in general. First, the hypothesis according to which the location of the head in compounds is a binary parameter is clearly challenged by Chinese (for further reading on parametric linguistics cf. Kayne 2000; Longobardi 2003; Gianollo, Guardiano, and Longobardi 2008). Second, our generalization on Chinese compounding – that in compounding multiple locations of heads do exist – could also apply to other languages.

26.4 CONCLUSION

In the analysis of Chinese compounds we have adopted a comprehensive approach which takes into account the semantics, the lexical categories, and the relationship between the constituents of compounds (Ceccagno and Scalise 2006). In order to analyse Chinese compounds, we have modified the classification scheme put forth by Bisetto and Scalise (2005) by redefining the three macro-types they suggest.

---

[12] We do not intend productivity as a value determined by means of statistical measurements, but rather in the sense of wider or lesser presence in our corpus.

This article has also addressed the question of headedness in Chinese. Packard (2000) and Huang (1998) are the pioneers who undertook to adopt new theories in the analysis of Chinese compounds. Their conclusions on the position of the head in Chinese compounding, however, are either groundless (Huang) or only pertinent to subordinate compounds (Packard). We have reached different conclusions and have shown that Chinese compounding consistently produces right-headed compounds (nouns, verbs, and adjectives), left-headed compounds (verbs), two-headed compounds (nouns, verbs, and adjectives), and exocentric compounds, too.

We have thus been able to put forth a new generalization on headedness in Chinese compounding. Like a Cerberus, Chinese compounds exhibit three head positions, none of which can be considered peripheral. By showing that at least in one language the morphological head cannot be identified on the basis of a single position (on the right *or* on the left), our results challenge the overall theory on headedness in compounding.

....

CHAPTER 27

AFRO-ASIATIC, SEMITIC: HEBREW

....

HAGIT BORER

27.1 INTRODUCTION

....

That Hebrew does have compounds is very clear, given the possible concatenation of two nouns, as in (1a–c), with a meaning that is neither compositional nor predictable from the individual N components:

(1) a. *orex*   (*ha-*)*din*
      editor   (the-)law
      '(the) lawyer'

    b. *melaxex*   (*ha-*)*pinka*
       chewer   (the)-bowl
       '(the) sycophant'

    c. *beyt*   (*ha-*)*sefer*
       house   (the-)book
       '(the) school'

What is trickier, however, is setting a precise boundary between the clear compounds in (1), and noun concatenations such as those in (2), which are syntactically productive and which have a meaning entirely predictable from their parts:

(2) a. *orex*   (*ha-*)*ma'amar*
      editor   (the-)article
      '(the) editor of (the) article'

b. *melaxex*   (*ha-*)'*esev*
   chewer   (the-)grass
   '(the) (one who) chews grass'

c. *beyt*   (*ha-*)*sar*
   house   (the-)minister
   '(the) house of (the) minister'

The structures in (2) (construct nominals) have been discussed extensively in the generative literature in the past decades, and there is a consensus that regardless of their specific analysis, they are clearly creatures of the syntax. In turn, the nominals in (1) and in (2) share some major structural properties, making it implausible that their respective derivations follow entirely distinct routes. Distinctions between the two groups exist, however, suggesting that their paths do diverge, at some point. At the end of the day, then, any investigation of the shared and disjoint properties of compounds (as we shall refer to the combinations in (1)) and constructs (the combinations in (2)) perforce bears on how word formation operations should be modelled, relative to, or within, the syntax.

Section 27.2 of this chapter is devoted to reviewing, largely following Borer (1988), the grounds for assuming that the paradigm in (1) – but not in (2) – is associated with compounding. In section 27.3 I show that there are at least two distinct types of N + N constructs; one, labelled here an *R*-construct, whose non-head is referential, and another, an *M*-construct, whose non-head is a modifier. I will further show that *M*-constructs, but not *R*-constructs, share important properties with compounds. Finally, section 27.4 is a sketchy outline of an analysis of constructs and compounds in Hebrew.

27.2 CONSTRUCTS AND COMPOUNDS

27.2.1 Similarities

27.2.1.1 *Phonological*

Phonologically, N + N combinations, both constructs and compounds, are prosodic words. Combinations such as those in (1)–(2) have only one primary stress falling on the non-head. A variety of phonological operations sensitive to stress placement take place in both constructs and compounds in an identical fashion: for example, non-final (short) vowels of the head are subject to deletion on a par with such pre-penultimate vowel deletion in stress-suffixed forms (e.g. pluralization) (cf. (3)). Further, feminine singular forms ending in *-á* when free, and masculine plural forms ending in -*ím*, when free, exhibit a distinct bound form for the head both in compounds and in constructs (compounds in bold) (cf. (4)):

(3) a. *báyit*   *ha-báyit*
        'house.SG'   'the-house'

     b. **beyt**   **midráš**   *beyt*   *morá*
        house   sermon   house   teacher
        'religious school'   'house of a teacher'

(4) a. *šmira*   *batím*
        guarding.FEM   houses

     b. **šmirat sáf**   *šmirat*   *yeladím*
        guarding threshold   guarding children
        'gate keeping'   'guarding children'

     c. **batey**   **midráš**   *batey*   *morót*
        houses   sermon   houses   teachers
        'religious schools'   'teachers houses'

27.2.1.2 *Syntactic*

The head of the construct cannot be directly modified. While in free nominals a modifying adjective occurs between the head and any additional non-head constituent, in the construct, the modifying adjective must follow the non-head; indeed, it must follow all construct non-heads, if there is more than one. An identical restriction holds for compounds:

(5) *ha-bayit*   *ha-xadaš*   (free nominal)
     the-house   the-new
     'the new house'

(6) a. *beyt*   *mora*   *xadaš*   (construct)
        house   teacher   new
        'a new teacher's house'

     b. **beyt*   *xadaš*   *mora*
        house   new   teacher

(7) a. **beyt**   **xolim**   *xadaš*   (compound)
        house   patients   new
        'a new hospital'

     b. **beyt*   *xadaš*   *xolim*
        house   new   patients

The definite article, *ha-*, cannot be realized on the head of either constructs or compounds. In turn, when it is realized on the (last) non-head, the entire expression, with the bare leftmost N as its head, is interpreted as definite, triggering, subsequently, definite agreement on a modifying adjective (compare (8) with (9) for constructs and (10) for compounds; definite agreement involves the reiteration of the definite article *ha-* on the adjective):[1]

(8) *ha-bayit*   *ha-xadaš*   (free nominal)
     the-house.MASC   the-new.MASC

(9) a. **ha-beyt*   *(ha-)mora*   *(ha-xadaš)*   (construct)
        the-house.MASC   (the-)teacher.FEM   (the-new.MASC)

     b. *beyt*   *ha-mora*   *ha-xadaš*
        house.MASC   the-teacher.FEM   the-new.MASC
        'the new teacher's house'

(10) a. **ha-beyt*   *(ha-)xolim*   *(ha-xadaš)*
        the-house.SG   (the-)patients.PL   (the-new.SG)

     b. *beyt*   **ha-xolim**   *ha-xadaš*
        house.SG   the-patients.PL   the-new.SG
        'the new hospital'

We return below to some additional syntactic similarities between compounds and *some* constructs, but not others.

27.2.2 Differences

27.2.2.1 *Constituent structure*

While constructs allow the modification of the non-head, such modification is impossible for compounds without the loss of the non-compositional reading:

(11) a. *beyt*   *ha-talmidim*   *ha-xadašim*
        house.SG   the-students.PL   the-new.PL

     b. **beyt**   **ha-xolim**   *ha-xadašim*
        house.SG   the-patients.PL   the-new.PL
        'the new patients' house; *the new hospital; the hospital for the new patients'

While the non-head in constructs may be coordinated (cf. (12)), such a coordination is excluded with a non-compositional (compound) reading (cf. (13)):

(12) a. *beyt*   *talmidim*   *ve-talmidot*
        house   students.MASC.PL   and-students.FEM.PL

     b. *gan*   *perot*   *ve-yerakot*
        garden   fruits   and-vegetables
        'a garden of fruit and vegetables'

(13) a. **beyt*   *xolim*   *ve-xolot*
        house   patients.MASC.PL   and-patient.FEM.PL

[1] For some potentially complicating factors, see Engelhardt (2000) as well as Danon (2001, 2008b).

b. *gan   yeladim   ve-xayot*
   garden   children   and-animals
   '*a kindergarten and a zoo'; 'a kindergarten and animals'; 'a garden for children and animals'

   cf: *gan   yeladim   gan   xayot*
       garden   children   garden   animals
       'kindergarten'   'zoo'

While a pronoun may refer to the head of a construct (excluding the non-head), (cf. (14a–b)), such reference is impossible with a non-compositional (compound) reading (cf. (15)):

(14) a. *hu   bana   li   šney   batey   'ec   ve-exad   mi-plastik*
         he   built me   two   houses   wood   and-one   of-plastic
         'he built for me two wooden houses and one of plastic'

      b. *'amdu   šam   šney   batey   morot   mi-xul*
         stood   there   two   houses   teachers   from-abroad

         ve-'exad šel mora   mi-be'er   ševa
         and one   of teacher from Be'er   Sheba
         'there were two houses there of teachers from abroad, and one of a teacher from Be'er Sheba'

(15) **hu   bana   lanu   shney   **batey xolim**   ve-exad   le-yetomim*
      he   built us   two   houses-patients   and-one   for-orphans
      'he built for us two hospitals and orphanage'

      cf. ***beyt   xolim   beyt   yetomim***
          house   sick   house   orphans
          'hospital'   'orphanage'

Finally, while at least prescriptively the head of the construct may not be coordinated directly, the entire construct may be coordinated with the identical non-head realized as a pronoun on the second conjunct, as illustrated in (16):

(16) a. *beyt   ha-mora$_i$ ve-xacer-a$_i$*
         house   the-teacher$_i$ and-yard-her$_i$
         'the teacher's house and her yard'

      b. *beyt   mora$_i$ ve-xacer-a$_i$*
         house   teacher$_i$ and-yard-her$_i$
         'a teacher's house and her yard'

Such coordination is not possible for compounds, nor is any pronominal reference to the non-head allowed without a loss of non-compositional meaning:

(17) a. *mitat   (ha-)xolim$_i$ ve-beyt-am$_i$*
         bed   (the-)patients$_i$ and house-theirs$_i$
         '*(the) patients' bed and their hospital'

b. **beyt**   (**ha-**)**xolim**ᵢ   **ve-mitat-am**ᵢ
house (the-)patientsᵢ and bed-theirsᵢ
'(the) patients'ᵢ home and theirᵢ bed'; 'the/a hospital and their bed' (with
reference of 'their' vague)
cf. **beyt**   (**ha-**)**xolim**
house   (the-)patients
'(the) hospital'

(18) **'iš**   (**ha-**)**sefer**ᵢ   **ve-beyt-o**ᵢ
man   bookᵢ   and-house-hisᵢ
*'the/a scholar and the school'; 'the/a scholar and his house'
cf. **iš**   (**ha-**)**sefer**   **beyt**   (**ha-**)**sefer**
man   (the-)book   house   (the-)book
'(the) scholar'   '(the) school'

27.2.2.2 Definiteness spreading

While the definite determiner in both constructs and compounds may only be
realized on the last non-head member, in the construct, the definiteness marked on
that non-head is associated not only with the entire expression, as already noted,
but also with the non-head itself. If the construct has more than two members,
such definiteness comes to be associated with every single noun in it, as can be
illustrated through the obligatoriness of agreement on adjectives modifying such
non-heads:[2]

(19) a. *delet*   *beyt*   *ha-mora*   *ha-vatiqa*   *ha-xadaš*
door.FEM house.MASC the-teacher.FEM the-senior.FEM the-new.MASC
'the door of the new house of the senior teacher'

b. *delet*   *beyt*   *ha-mora*   *ha-vatiqa*   *ha-xadaša*
door.FEM house.MASC the-teacher.FEM the-senior.FEM the-new.FEM
'the new door of the house of the senior teacher'

c. *delet*   *beyt*   *ha-mora*   *ha-xadaš*   *ha-levana*
door.FEM house.MASC the-teacher.FEM the-new.MASC the-white.FEM
'the white door of the new house of the teacher'

Not so in compounds, where the non-head, although directly marked by a definite
article, is not even referential. The 'orphans' under discussion in (20a) not only
need not be specific, they need not exist altogether, nor does the 'king' (20b) need
to be a specific one or to exist. The expression is best translated as 'prince', rather
than 'a king's son':

----

[2] The order of adjectives in constructs mirrors that of the nouns. As such cases of centre embedding
tend to deteriorate rather rapidly, all exemplifications in (19) involve only two-adjective combinations.
As we shall see shortly, definiteness spreading is relevant to R-constructs, but not to M-constructs.

(20) a. *beyt   ha-yetomim*
         house the-orphans
         'orphanage'

      b. *ben   ha-melex*
         son   the-king
         'prince'

27.2.2.3 *Semantic headedness*

Adapting somewhat the 'IS A' condition of Allen (1978), we note that a construct
IS A modified version of its head. Not so compounds, where such semantic
connection does not typically obtain:

(21) a. *beyt   mora*   IS A *bayit*
         house teacher   IS A house

      b. *šomer   mexoniyot* IS A *šomer*
         guard   cars   IS A guard

(22) a. *beyt   sefer* IS NOT (necessarily) A *bayit*   cf. *beyt   sefer*
         house book   IS NOT (necessarily) A house   house book
                                                                 'school'

      b. *yošev roš*   IS NOT A *yošev*   cf. *yošev roš*
         sitter head   IS NOT A sitter   sitter head
                                                                 'chairman'

Summarizing thus far, we note that the lack of compositional reading for some
N+N combinations correlates directly with syntactic opacity. In turn, cases of
compositional readings correlate with syntactic transparency. The label 'compounds' thus appears well deserved for the former.

This said, a closer scrutiny reveals that at least some compositional N+N
combinations are not as syntactically distinct from compounds as may be pre-
sumed on the basis of the comparison just outlined. We now turn to the discussion
of these combinations.

27.3 MODIFICATION CONSTRUCTS

27.3.1 *M-constructs vs. R-constructs – the syntax*

Construct formation is an extremely heterogeneous phenomenon which is
not restricted to N+N combinations. In turn, even within the class of N+N

combinations (by far the largest construct group) we find diverse properties associated with distinct subtypes. A full review of all construct types is outside the scope of this chapter, but with the properties of compounds in mind, I will focus here on the properties of modificational constructs (henceforth *M*-constructs; broadly speaking, a type of Modificational Genitive as discussed in Munn 1995 and others), and whose syntactic properties are closer to those of compounds. *M*-constructs are illustrated in (23), to be contrasted with the constructs in (24):

(23) *beyt*   (ha-)'ec;   *kos*   (ha-)mic;   *signon*   (ha-)ktiva;
     house   (the-)wood;   glass (the-)juice; style   (the-)writing;
     '(the)wooden house';   '(the) juice glass'; '(the) writing style';
     magevet (ha-)mitbax
     towel   (the-)kitchen
     '(the) kitchen towel'

(24) *beyt*   (ha-)mora;   *gag* (ha-)bayit; *na'aley* (ha-)yalda;
     house   (the-)teacher; roof (the-)house; shoes   (the-)girl;
     mexonit (ha-)nasi
     car   (the-)president

The intuitive meaning difference between the two groups of constructs is clear, but considerably more crucial is the fact that they are syntactically distinct. Most saliently, the non-head of *M*-constructs is not referential and is interpreted as a modifying property, while the non-head of the constructs in (24) (henceforth *R*-constructs) must be referential.[3] In (25), we list syntactic differences, in turn illustrated by the contrasts between (26a–f) and (27a–f):[4]

(25) The non-head in *M*-constructs –
      a. cannot be modified by a definite adjective ((26a) vs. (27a));
      b. when indefinite, can only be modified by a property modifier ((26b) vs. (27b));
      c. cannot be pluralized, unless the plural itself is interpreted as a property ((26c) vs. (27c));
      d. cannot be quantified ((26d) vs. (27d));

---

[3] The term *R*-construct is used here for all constructs with a referential non-head (broadly, the Individual Genitives of Munn 1995 and subsequent literature). Constructs in Event Derived Nominals are formed of the head N and one of the arguments. Since arguments are perforce referential, all such constructs are *R*-constructs. For some previous discussion of this distinction within Hebrew constructs see Hazout (1991); Dobrovie-Sorin (2003).

[4] Dobrovie-Sorin (2003) likewise draws a syntactic distinction between (our) *R*-constructs and *M*-constructs, and suggests that compounds are related to the latter. Dobrovie-Sorin's (2003) syntactic analysis of these structures, however, cannot be adopted. See Borer (2008) for a fuller review.

e. does not allow pronominal reference ((26e) vs. (27e));

f. does not allow determiners or adjectives that entail reference ((26) vs. (27f)).

(26)   a. *beyt*   *ha-mora*   *ha-vatiqa*
    house   the-teacher   the-senior
    'the house of the senior teacher'

   b. *beyt*   *mora*   *vatiqa*
    house   teacher   senior
    'a house of a senior teacher'

   c. *beyt*   *(ha-)morot*
    house   (the-)teachers
    '(the) teachers' house'

   d. *beyt*   *šaloš/harbe*   *morot*   /   *beyt*   *kol*   *mora*
    house   three/many   teachers   house   every   teacher
    'a house of three/many teachers'   'every teacher's house'

   e. *beyt*   *(ha-)mora*ᵢ   *ve-rahite-ha*ᵢ
    house   (the) teacherᵢ   and furniture-herᵢ
    'the/a teacher's house and her furniture'

   f. *beyt*   {*'eyze*}   *mora*   {*kolšehi/mesuyemet*}
    house   {some}   teacher   {some/specific}
    'a house of some/a specific teacher'

(27)   a. *beyt*   *ha-zxuxit*   {**ha-xadaša;*   *??ha-venezianit*}
    house   the-glass   {*the-new;   ??the-Venetian}
    'the [{*new; ??Venetian} glass] house'

   b. *beyt*   *zxuxit*   {**xadaša;*   *venezianit*}
    house   glass   {*new;   Venetian}
    *'a [new glass] house'; 'a [Venetian glass] house'

   c. **beyt*   *(ha-)zxuxiot*   *kir*   *(ha-)levenim mic*   *(ha-)tapuzim*
    house   (the-)glasses   wall   (the-)bricks juice   (the-)oranges
    *'(the-) (multiple) glasses' house'   '(the) brick wall'   '(the) orange juice'

   d. **kir*   *me'a/harbe*   *levenim*   **beyt*   *kol*   *'ec*
    wall   hundred/many   bricks   house   every   wood
    *'a wall of hundred/many bricks'   *'a house from every (type of) wood'

   e. **xalon*   *(ha-)zxuxit*ᵢ   *ve-dalt-a*ᵢ
    window   (the-)glassᵢ   and-door-herᵢ
    *'the/a glass window and its door'

   f. **xalon*   {*'eyze*}   *zxuxit*   {*kolšehi/msuyemet*}
    window   {some}   glass   {some/specific}
    *'a window of some/specific glass'

27.3.2 *M*-constructs, compounds, and pre-N+N Determiners

As the reader has no doubt noted already, the behaviour of *M*-constructs is suspiciously similar to that of compounds. The similarity is further supported by a development in spoken Modern Hebrew which affects *M*-constructs and compounds, but not *R*-constructs. Specifically, the placement of the definite article in constructs is shifting in spoken Modern Hebrew from a realization on the non-head to a realization on the head itself. In such cases, the entire construct is definite. The non-head, however, cannot be independently marked with a definite article (cf. (30)), and is not interpreted as definite, as illustrated by (28)–(29):[5]

(28) COMPOUNDS
    a. *ha-yom   huledet   šeli*
       the-day birth   mine
       'my birthday'

    b. *ha-beyt   sefer   ha-ze*
       the-house book the-this
       'this school'

    c. *ha-beyt   xolim   ha-'ironi*
       the-house patients the-municipal
       'the municipal hospital'

    d. *ha-'orex   din ha-ca'ir*
       the editor law the-young
       'the young lawyer'

(29) M-CONSTRUCTS
    a. *ha-kos   mic   ha-zot*
       the-glass juice the-this
       'this glass of juice'

    b. *ha-magevet   mitbax   ha-meluxlexet   ha-zot*
       the-towel   kitchen the-dirty   the-this
       'this dirty kitchen towel'

    c. *ha-mic   tapuzim   šeli*
       the-juice oranges mine
       'my orange juice'

    d. *ha-signon   dibur   šelo*
       the-style talking his
       'his talking style'

[5] The reanalysed definite marker appears to require some anchoring in the form of an additional demonstrative, adjective, or PP.

(30)   a. *ha-yom   ha-huledet;   *ha-beyt   ha-sefer;   *ha-orex   ha-din
          the-day   the-birth   the-house   the-book   the-editor the-law
          (the birthday)   (the school)   (the lawyer)

       b. *ha-kos   ha-mic;   *ha-magevet ha-mitbax;   *ha-signon ha-dibur
          the-glass the-juice the-towel   the-kitchen the-style   the-talking

When applied to constructs with a (contextually plausible) referential non-head, such placement of the definite article has the effect of converting them, however implausibly, to *M*-constructs (cf. (31)): the non-head acquires a property interpretation, disallowing definite and non-property modification of the non-head; it cannot be pluralized or quantified, and pronominal reference to it becomes impossible (cf. (32)):

(31)   a. ha-tmunot   muzeon   ha-ele
          the-pictures museum   the-these
          *'these pictures of the museum'
          (ok: 'these museum-type pictures')

       b. ha-beyt   mora   ha-xadaš
          the-house   teacher   the-new
          (*'the new house of the teacher')
          (ok: 'the new teacher-type house')

       c. ha-na'aley   yalda   ha-xumot
          the-shoes   girl   the-brown.PL
          (*'the brown shoes of the girl')
          (ok: 'the brown girl-type shoes')

(32)   a. *ha-simlat   rof'a   (ha-)vatiqa
          the-dress   physician   (the-)senior
          'the dress of the/a senior physician'

       b. *ha-simlat   rof'ot
          the-dress   physicians
          'the physicians' dress'

       c. *ha-simlat   kol   rof'a
          the-dress   every   physician
          'the dress of every physician'

       d. *ha-simlat   rof'a$_i$ ve-rahite-ha$_i$
          the-dress   physician$_i$ and-furniture-her$_i$
          'the physician's dress and her furniture'

       e. *ha-simlat   {'eyze}   rof'a   {kolšehi/mesuyemet}
          the-dress   {some}   physician   {some/specific}
          'the dress of some/a specific physician'

Siloni (2001) notes that when semantically definite determiners such as *oto* 'the same' and the (post-nominal) demonstrative *ze* are used with N + N compounds, the entire expression is definite, but not so the non-head. This, Siloni reasons, suggests that while definiteness does spread from the non-head to the head, indefiniteness does not, and is rather associated independently with each N member of the construct. However, the properties of *oto* and *ze*, as it turns out, are exactly identical to those just outlined for the reanalysed definite article *ha-* when it occurs on the head – they are only compatible with *M*-constructs and are strictly barred in the context of referential non-heads:

(33) a. *'oto*   *'orex*   *din ca'ir* / *'orex*   *din ca'ir* *ze*
     same.MASC editor.MASC law young   editor.MASC law young this.MASC
     'the same young lawyer'   'this young lawyer'

   b. *ota*   *kos*   *mic* / *kos*   *mic* *zot*
      same.FEM glass.FEM juice   glass.FEM juice this.FEM
      'the same glass of juice'   'this glass of juice'

(34) a. *oto*   *beyt*   *mora*   (*vatiqa*)
         same.MASC   house.MASC   teacher   (*senior)
         'the same [(*senior) teacher's house]'
         / *beyt*   *mora*   (*vatiqa*)   *ze*
            house.MASC   teacher   (*senior)   this.MASC
            'this [(*senior) teacher's house]'

     b. **ota*   *simlat*   *rof'ot*
        same.FEM   dress.FEM   physicians
        'the same [dress of physicians]'
        / **simlat*   *rof'ot*   *zot*
           dress.FEM   physicians   this.FEM
           'this [dress of physicians]

     c. **ota*   *simlat*   *kol*   *rof'a*
        same.FEM   dress.FEM   every   physician
        'the same [dress of every physician]'
        / **simlat*   *kol*   *rof'a*   *zot*
           dress.FEM   every   physician   this.FEM
           'this [dress of every physician]'

     d. **ota*   *simlat*   *rof'a*ᵢ   *ve-rahite-ha*ᵢ
        same.FEM   dress.FEM   physicianᵢ   and-furniture-herᵢ
        'the same [dress of a physician] and her furniture'
        / *simlat*   *rof'a*ᵢ   *zot*   *ve-rahite-ha*ᵢ
           dress.FEM   physicianᵢ   this.FEM   and-furniture-herᵢ
           'this [dress of a physician] and her furniture'

e. *ota   simlat   {'ezye}   rof'a   {kolšehi/mesuyemet}
   same.FEM   dress.FEM   {some}   physician {some/certain}
   'the same [some/specific] physician's dress'
       / simlat   {'eyze}   rof'a   {kolšehi/mesuyemet}   zot
          dress.FEM   {some}   physician {some/specific}   this.FEM
          'this (some/specific) physician's dress'

The absence of indefiniteness spreading exactly in these contexts follows now directly from the very same factor which excludes definite modification for such a non-head – as the non-head is not referential in *M*-constructs and compounds, it is neither sensibly definite nor sensibly indefinite. Not so the non-head in *R*-constructs, which is referential, and where both definite and indefinite spreading hold as traditionally described.[6]

27.3.3 *M*-constructs vs. compounds

Are *M*-constructs compounds, then? Even more significantly, are all Det+N+N combinations, including those in (31) and (33b) compounds? In terms of their interpretation, they most certainly come closest to the properties of typical English primary N+N compounds nevertheless. The answer to this must be 'no'. Some crucial distinctions do remain between *M*-constructs and compounds, both with and without a preceding determiner, mandating a separate treatment. Specifically, although the modification of the non-head in *M*-constructs is limited, as compared with *R*-constructs, it is possible: not only by adjectives (providing they refer to properties) but also by a PP and through the non-head itself heading a construct. Such modification is never possible in compounds without the loss of non-compositional meaning (cf. (35)–(36)). It further remains possible to coordinate the non-head in *M*-constructs (with and without a preceding Det), whereas such coordination remains incompatible with non-compositional reading (cf. (37)–(38)), and finally, reference to the head of *M*-constructs with a pronoun, never possible in compounds, is possible in *M*-constructs (cf. (39)–(40)):[7]

(35) a. *mitkan 'energiya tiv'it*   / *ha-mitkan 'energiya tiv'it   ha-ze*
        facility energy   the-natural / the-facility energy   natural the-this
        'a/this natural energy facility'

---

[6] For a fuller analysis of the exclusion of referential DP non-heads in the context of pre-N+N determiners, see Borer (2008).

[7] [N + [N+N]] compounds (non-compositional) do occur, just in case the embedded [N+N] itself is a compound:

i. *oxel   lexem xesed*
    eater bread compassion
    eater ['charity']
    'charity receiver' (derogatory, implies laziness)

b. *na'aley yaldat   rexov   / ha-na'aley yaldat   rexov   ha-'ele*
   shoes   girl   street   / the-shoes   girl   street   the-these
   '(these) street girl shoes'

c. *mic* [*tapuzim mi   sfarad*] / ha-*mic* [*tapuzim mi-sfarad*]   ha-ze
   juice [oranges from spain] / the-juice [oranges from-spain] the-this
   '(this) juice from Spanish oranges'

(36) a. **beyt xolim   xroniyim   /*ha-beyt*
   house-patients chronic.PL /the-house
   xolim   xroniyim   ha-ze
   patients   chronic.PL the-this
   'a/this hospital for chronic patients'

b. **beyt   xoley   Alzheimer /*ha-beyt*
   house   patients   Alzheimer /*the-house
   xoley   Alzheimer ha-ze
   patients Alzheimer the-this
   'the/this hospital for Alzheimer patients'

c. **beyt   xolim   me-'ayarot   pituax   /*ha-beyt*
   house   patients   from towns   development / the-house
   xolim   me-'ayarot pituax   ha-ze
   patient from towns development the-this
   'a/this hospital for patients from under-developed towns'

(37) a. *beyt   'ec   ve-levenim / ha-beyt   'ec   ve-levenim ha-ze*
   house   wood   and-bricks / the-house   wood   and-bricks the-this
   'this/a house of wood and bricks'

b. *'aron   magavot ve-sdinim   / ha-'aron   magavot ve-sdinim   ha-xadaš*
   cabinet towels   and-sheets / the-cabinet towels   and-sheets the-new
   'the/a (new) cabinet for towels and sheets'

(38) a. **beyt   xolim   ve-yetomim   / *ha-beyt   xolim   ve-yetomim   ha-ze*
   house   patients and-orphans / the house   patients   and-orphans the-this
   'a/this hospital and orphanage'

b. **gan   yeladim ve-xayot   / *ha-gan   yeladim ve-xayot   ha-ze*
   garden children and-animals / the-garden children and-animals the-this
   'a/this kindergarden and zoo'

(39) a. *hu bana lanu   šney batey   'ec   ve-'exad mi-levenim*
   he built for. us two   houses wood and-one from-bricks

b. *ha-magavot   mitbax   šekanita   yoter šimušiyot*
   the-towels   kitchen   that-you-bought more useful
   me-ha-'ele   le-ambatia
   than-the-those for-bathroom

Table 27.1 Compounds, R-constructs, and M-constructs

	Compounds	M-constructs	R-constructs
a. Semantic compositionality	No	Yes	Yes
b. Coordination	No	Yes	Yes
c. Pronominal reference to the head	No	Yes	Yes
d. [N+N]+N structures	Yes	No	No
e. Non-head modification	No	Property modification only	Yes
f. Free pluralization of non-head	No	Property reading only	Yes
g. Pronominal reference to the non-head	No	No	Yes
h. Cardinals or quantifiers w/the non-head	No	No	Yes
i. (In)definiteness spreading	No	No	Yes
j. Reanalysed DEF placement	Yes	Yes	No
k. Determiners and reference denoting adjectives w/non-head	No	No	Yes

(40) a. *hu   bana   lanu   šney   batey   xolim   ve-'exad   le-yetomim
       he   built   for. us two   houses patients and-one   for orphans
       *'he built for us two hospitals and one orphanage'

   b. *ha-batey   xolim   yoter   muclacim   me-ha-ele   le-yetomim
      the-houses   sick   more   successful   than-the-those   for orphans
      *'the hospitals are better than the orphanages'

Finally, we observed that the non-head in *R*-constructs and in *M*-constructs may itself be a construct, but not so for compounds. Significantly, however, the compound *as a whole* can, at least at times, function as a head of a construct, never a possibility for either *M*-constructs or *R*-constructs:

(41) [beyt   sefer]   sade;   [beyt   xolim]   sade;   [begged   yam]   meši;
      house   book   field   house   patients field   suit   sea   silk
      'field school'   'field hospital'   'silk bathing suit'

      ['orex   din]   xuc;
      editor   law   out
      'external lawyer'

      [yošev   roš]   mo'aca;   [beyt   mišpat]   'al
      sitter   head   council   house   court   up
      'council chairman'   'higher court'

Table 27.1 summarizes the diagnostics of compounds, *R*-constructs, and *M*-constructs, before we turn to some speculations on the theoretical ramifications of this three-way distinction in section 27.4.

27.4 STRUCTURAL CONSIDERATIONS

27.4.1 *R-constructs and M-constructs*

Effectively, Table 27.1 suggests that there are three types of nominal constructs in Hebrew. Only one of them allows for a referential non-head (*R*-constructs), and only one of them can be semantically and syntactically opaque. Considerations of scope exclude a detailed analysis of these distinct types. A sketchy outline of such an analysis, however, is attempted in the next few paragraphs (and see Borer 2008, for a fuller treatment).

Seeking to account for the referentiality, or lack thereof, of the non-head, suppose we assume (following Munn 1995) that the non-head in *R*-constructs (Individual Genitives) is a full DP, while the non-head in *M*-constructs (Modificational Genitives) and compounds is not a full DP.[8] In fact, even the projection of a #P (Quantity Phrase) non-head in *M*-construct and compounds appears unwarranted given (h) in Table 27.1. Rather, the non-head appears to be either a ClP (Classifier Phrase) or an NP, a predicate.[9] Assume now that non-heads in N+N constructs always merge in the specifier of some nominal functional projection associated with the head N. If the non-head is a full DP, it will be interpreted referentially, as a possessor, as an argument, or as bearing a part–whole relation with the head. If, on the other hand the non-head is a predicate, it will be interpreted as a modifier.[10] Finally, regardless of the merger site of the non-head, the order *Head–Non-head* is generated, I assume, through the movement of N to a functional head above the relevant specifier, in line with Ritter's original (1988) analysis and much subsequent work. Schematic structures for *R*-constructs and *M*-constructs are given in (42)–(43):

(42) R-CONSTRUCT

$[_{FP}$ N $[\ldots [_{specifier} [_{DP}Non\text{-}Head]$ N$\ldots [_{NP}$ N$]]]]$

(43) M-CONSTRUCT

$[_{FP}$ N $[\ldots [_{specifier} [_{ClP/NP}Non\text{-}Head]$ N$\ldots [_{NP}$ N$]]]]$

In Borer (1996, 1999) I propose that the phonological word properties of constructs are derived through the syntactic incorporation of the non-head into the head (see also Shlonsky 1990). As Siloni (1997) points out, however, such an

---

[8] For a similar claim for some construct nominals see Danon (2008b). See Dobrovie-Sorin (2003) for the claim that these non-heads must be bare Ns, a claim which, I believe, cannot be sustained.

[9] As is argued extensively in Borer (2005a), 'plural' marking is a Classifier, not a Number (#) specification.

[10] A maximal #P will presumably be interpreted as a measure phrase. We set this case aside. That modifiers, including adjectives and PPs, may merge as specifiers is explicitly suggested in Cinque (2000) and pursued for Hebrew by Shlonsky (2000) and by Sichel (2000). I depart from the Cinque model in assuming that modifiers can be licensed by *any* functional specifier.

incorporation account must allow for violations of the Coordinate Structure Constraint (e.g. in (12), (37)) (and see also Benmamoun 2000 for Arabic). Rather crucially, the coordination of non-heads *is* possible for *M*-constructs, making it untenable that the *M*-construct, but not the *R*-construct, is derived through incorporation.

In Borer (2005a, b, forthcoming), I argue that morphophonological merger rules affecting constituent structure do not exist. Constituent-structure-forming operations as well as recursion are, rather, within the province of the syntax alone. Word formation, in turn, consists of two components – one, morpheme-based, is syntactic and recursive (see section 27.4.2 below). The other, a-morphemic, involves the phonological spell-out of non-hierarchical formal syntactic features on L-heads (e.g. *dance*.PST. $\Rightarrow$ /dænst/; *sing*.PST $\Rightarrow$ /sang/) very much in line with the approach to (much of) inflectional morphology put forth by the Word and Paradigm approach (see in particular Beard 1995, Anderson 1992). It therefore follows that if the construct is not formed by syntactic incorporation, it fails to involve an incorporation altogether. We must therefore conclude that the word properties of constructs derive from liaison, the assignment of pure prosodic structure to syntactic constituents, often resulting in the emergence of bound forms conditioned exclusively by phonological string adjacency (with clitics being the prime comparison class).[11]

If on the right track, we do not expect constructs to be syntactically uniform, a conclusion that is independently extremely plausible. The essence of the construct diagnostics, it would appear, involves a bare head form of *any* category, an obligatorily *nominal* non-head, and the prosodic-word properties of the output. Beyond that, we do not expect, nor do we find, syntactic similarities between constructs formed from N + N combinations, A + N combinations, Participle + N combinations, Cardinal + N combinations, Q + N combinations, and P + N combinations, exemplified by (44a–f):[12]

(44) a. *yefe*   *(ha-)ʿeynayim*   A + N
         beautiful   (the-)eyes
         'beautiful of eyes'

      b. *kotev*   *(ha-)maʾamar*   PTPL + N
         writer   (the-)article
         'the writer of the article'

---

[11] I thus reject explicitly the phonological merger approach put forth by Benmamoun (2000) and adopted in Siloni (2001).

[12] The existence of P + N constructs is an inevitable conclusion from the properties of prepositions which are attested as a bound plural form in conjunction with pronominal complementation (cf. (44f)). See also the archaic form in (i):

i.   *al-ey*   *kinor*
     on-[PL.MASC.BOUND FORM]   violin
     'on violin' (e.g. in the context of playing 'on' it)

c. *šlošet   ha-dubim*   Cardinal + N
   three   the-bears
   'the three bears'

d. *rav   nocot;   mrube   yeladim;*
   multiple   features;   multiple   children;
   'of many features';   '(one with) many children';
   mu'at   emca'im   Qu + N
   few   means
   '(one of) few means'

e. *rov   ha-no'ar;   kol   ha-kita;*   Qu + N
   most   the-youth;   all   the-class
   'most of the youth';   'all the class'

f. *al   ha-šulxanot;   aleyhem*   P + N
   on   the-tables;   ON-PL-PRON
   'on the tables';   'on them'

27.4.2 Deriving compounds

I concluded in section 27.4.1 that the prosodic-word properties of both
M-constructs and *R*-constructs do not involve any change in constituent structure,
and are rather a phonological liaison. Given this conclusion, one plausible assumption concerning Hebrew compounds would be that they are not a morphological
formation altogether, but rather a species of idioms with a syntax and morphology
identical to that of constructs. This conclusion, however, is unsatisfactory. First,
unlike idioms, and with the exception of plural inflection, compounds never
involve any functional material otherwise attested in constructs – no (non-
affixal) articles, no adjectives, no pronouns, etc., all potentially possible in idiomatic expressions. Second, languages do not typically exhibit an 'idiom strategy',
with idioms systematically formed from one syntactic structure, and yet constructs
are, by far, the language's predictable source for compound formation. Finally, that
compounds, but not any other constructs, can themselves head a construct argues
in favour of them having a distinct structure.

Note now that intriguingly, no syntactic problem faces an incorporation account
for compounds. The Coordinate Structure Constraint (CSC) invoked to exclude
incorporation in at least some cases of *M*-constructs and *R*-constructs is tangential,
for the simple reason that non-head coordination never occurs with compounding.
Suppose, then, that syntactic incorporation may take place where licit (i.e. when the
CSC is not violated), and that compounds are formed through such an incorporation.

What are the unique properties of compounds such that they can be attributed
to incorporation? By assumption, these could not be the phonological word-like

properties of compounds, as these are shared with constructs, which do not involve incorporation.

Suppose we assume that incorporation is an operation which merges predicates (<et>), and that both N and N+CL are of type <et>, but # and D are of type <e>. Suppose we assume further that incorporation may not proceed past functional heads (*contra* Baker 1988). It now follows that if #P or DP project, incorporation cannot take place, thereby excluding incorporation in (non-coordinated) *R*-constructs, and excluding the formation of compounds with referential non-heads. We now also derive the obligatoriness of non-referential non-heads in compounds, accounting for their affinity with *M*-constructs.

Why, the reader may now wonder, is incorporation necessary for the formation of compounds? Such a question, however, appears to be ill-phrased. Incorporation is not necessary for compounds. Rather, compounds, by definition, are constructs that have undergone incorporation. Elaborating, suppose we re-examine the entire logic of the distinction between compounds and constructs. Assuming no pre-theoretical category of 'compounds', what we have done, in actuality, is diagnose three types of nominal constructs, distinguished from each other along syntactic and semantic lines. Having called one of these groups 'compounds' already implies some conclusions on our part concerning the properties of that group. Those conclusions are not based on the phonological properties of that group, as these are identical to those of other construct types. They are not based on the syntactic properties of that group either, as those syntactic properties in and of themselves do not classify that group as what is traditionally referred to as 'compounds'. Fundamentally, then, we labelled that group 'compounds' because of its semantic non-compositionality, a key factor in the diagnostic of compounds, proceeding then to ask whether non-compositional constructs have syntactic properties which distinguish them from those of compositional constructs. Having answered this question in the affirmative, we then proceeded to propose that they involve a unique syntactic derivation – incorporation – which is impossible for *R*-constructs and at the very least unnecessary for *M*-constructs, thereby attempting to relate the possibility of incorporation with the emergence of a non-compositional meaning.[13]

Reformulating the original question, then – what is it about incorporation which allows a non-compositional meaning?

By way of offering an answer, suppose we define (morpheme-based) morphology as the syntactic merger of L-head predicates in general, either with each other (i.e. *incorporation*, giving rise to e.g. English compounding) or with functional morphemes, including L-affixes, where by L-affixes we refer to affixes that are themselves categorically marked (e.g. [N *-ation*], [A *-al*]). According to this view morphology is not a separate component, but a generalization over a class of particular syntactic operations and their outputs.

---

[13] Incorporation in non-coordinated *M*-constructs (with compositional meaning) may arguably be ruled out by considerations of economy.

We may now define the constituents of the morphological stratum (but not those of higher phrasal strata) as the input to encyclopedic searches. In other words, encyclopedic interpretation, as linked to phonological spell-out, confines its searches to L domains (with the intended meaning), with interpretation for bigger syntactic domains requiring compositionality.[14] The boxed combinations in (45a', b') are now possible targets for an encyclopedic search. Their pre-incorporation components, as in (45a, b) can only be searched separately, and put together compositionally. It thus follows that 'compounds' must undergo incorporation, insofar as by definition, their 'holistic' meaning can only be assigned on the basis of the post-merger structure.

(45)   a. $[_{FNP1} \boxed{N_1}$ $[[_{CLP} \boxed{N_2 + CL}$ $[_{NP2} \cancel{N_2}] \ldots$

     a'. $[_{FNP1} \boxed{N_1 + [N_2 + CL]}$ $[[_{CLP} [\cancel{N_2} + \cancel{CL}]$ $[_{NP2} \cancel{N_2}] \ldots$

     b. $[_{FNP1} \boxed{N_1}$ $[$ $[_{NP2} \boxed{N_2}] \ldots$

     b'. $[_{FNP1} \boxed{N_1 + N_2}$ $[$ $[_{NP2} \cancel{N_2}] \ldots$

(FNP= some functional projection in the N extended projection)

We can now explain in full the distinctions between compounds and M-constructs in Table 27.1. The impossibility of coordinated non-heads in compounds follows from the fact that compounds are formed by syntactic incorporation. The impossibility of pronominal reference to the head follows from the fact that the compound is assigned an encyclopedic interpretation as a whole. As the head is not assigned any reference or meaning independently of the compound, pronominal reference to it in exclusion of the non-head is impossible. The exclusion of modification for the non-head is likewise excluded, as the non-head does not effectively exist as an independent meaning to be modified.

And finally, that compounds, but not M-constructs, can themselves head a construct follows from the existence of an N constituent $[_N N+N]$ formed by the incorporation. No such constituent exists in either M-constructs or R-constructs.

We have now derived in full the properties of compounds without recourse to non-syntactic operations, or to syntactic structures that are not otherwise available.[15]

---

[14] For the relations between PF and encyclopedic searches, see Marantz (1996). This description, we note, covers not only the output of word formation (internal merger), but external merger as well, to wit, 'lexical insertion', insofar as it concerns the properties of any merged L-heads.

A few comments are warranted (and see Borer 2008 for a fuller execution). First, note that phrasal idioms are now excluded, as whole units, from the domain of encyclopedic searches. Rather, we must assume that an encyclopedic entry such as *kick* makes reference to the relevant reading of *kick* in the context of *bucket* (and, presumably, the entry for *bucket* references *kick* in a similar fashion.) See Harley and Noyer (1999) for an explicit suggestion along these lines. Second, the system explicitly allows for separate searches for the L subparts of mergers within the morphological stratum. Thus N+N may remain compositional, as may the L in any L+Affix combination, thereby allowing compositional morphological operations.

Finally, this execution entails that copies are not assigned meaning by the encyclopedia, a direct result of the fact that the encyclopedia operates on (syntactically annotated) PF representations.

[15] For completeness's sake, we note that synthetic compounds, just like other compounds, have non-referential non-heads, and altogether share the properties of compounds discussed thus far. It

27.5 CONCLUSION

Beyond establishing the existence of compounds in Hebrew, I investigated the systematic relations which hold between their properties and those of construct nominals. The typology that emerges is given in (46):

(46)

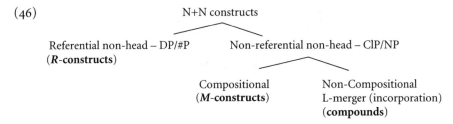

Crucially, while the properties of compounds are syntactically entirely regular, their formation through the merger of two L-stems results in allowing the encyclopedia to search for their PF representation, thus potentially associating them with non-compositional meanings. At least for Hebrew compounds, then, there is no need for any recourse to a non-syntactic component of word formation or an independent grammatical lexicon, nor is it necessary to define a specialized syntactic component dedicated to the formation of 'words'. What is needed is a clearer delineation of the domain which falls under the jurisdiction of encyclopedic searches, independently needed within any model involving late insertion.

follows that synthetic compounds cannot be derived from Complex Event Nominals, in the sense of Grimshaw (1990). This is further supported by the fact that Event Nominals (in their construct form) allow for event modification (ia), strictly barred in synthetic compounds (ib), as illustrated in (ic). Therefore at least Hebrew synthetic compounds do not differ from 'primary' compounds, and their non-head is a modifier and not an argument. The appearance of complementation relation between the head and the non-head thus must be otherwise accounted for. See Borer (forthcoming) for some relevant discussion.

i. a. *šmirat   ran   'et   ha-bayit   be-mešex   30   ša'ot/   be-hac'laxa*
       guarding Ran   DOM* the-house for   30   hours/ successfully
       'Ran's guarding of the house for 30 hours/successfully'

   b. *šmirat   saf   šomer   saf*
       guarding threshold   guard   threshold
       'gate keeping'   'gate keeper'

   c. **šmirat   ha-saf   be-haclaxa/   be-mešex   šanim   rabot*
       guarding the-threshold   successfully/ in-duration   years   many
       (literal (absurd) reading only)

* DOM = Direct Object Marker.

CHAPTER 28

ISOLATE: JAPANESE

TARO KAGEYAMA

A prominent feature of Japanese morphology is the pervasiveness of compounds in both lexical and syntactic domains, as opposed to the rather modest affixes and inflections. Concerning English compounds, Lieber (1992b: 80) observes that the least productive are those containing verbs. In Japanese, on the contrary, the most productive and most widespread are compounds involving verbs and other predicates. This chapter provides an overview of the richness and intricacy of Japanese compounds and illuminates their intriguing properties, not found in well-studied European languages. Section 28.1 is addressed to lexical compounds, and Section 28.2 to syntax-related compounds. Section 28.3 pinpoints their theoretical implications.

28.1 REPRESENTATIVE TYPES OF LEXICAL COMPOUNDS

In general, compounds are diagnosed by the absence of case markers, inflections, and other functional categories from the non-head position. Thus in Japanese, *huru-hon* 'old-book' = 'used book' is a compound while *huru-i hon* 'old-INFL book' is an NP; *hon-yomi* 'book reading' is a compound while *hon-o yomi(-nagara)* 'book-ACC read(-ing)' is a VP.

Japanese compounds embrace morphological objects of various sizes – bound morphemes, words, and larger morphological units (Word-Plus or W$^+$: section 28.2.1) – and items of all vocabulary strata: the native Japanese stratum, the Sino-Japanese (S-J) stratum comprising Chinese elements, and the foreign stratum including loans from languages other than Chinese. Of these, morpheme-level compounding is limited to S-J bound morphemes, whereas compound formations at word- and W$^+$-levels apply regardless of the vocabulary strata. This section presents the repertoire of Japanese lexical compounds, using the following lexical categories: N, V, A, VN (verbal noun: noun-like verbs that need a light verb *suru* 'do' to carry tense), and AN (adjectival noun: noun-like adjectives that take the -*na* inflection instead of the adjectival inflection -*i* in prenominal position).

28.1.1 Head structures in compounds

In terms of headedness, Japanese compounds are predominantly right-headed but display left-headed, double-headed, and headless (exocentric) structures as well.

28.1.1.1 *Right-headed compounds*

The right-hand head structure, by far the most productive pattern, is exemplified in (1).

(1) a. Compound nouns: N+N *ha-burasi* 'tooth-brush', A+N *maru-gao* 'round-face', V+N *yude-tamago* lit. 'boil-egg' = 'boiled egg', N+[$_N$ V] *hon-yomi* 'book-reading', AN+N *yuuryoo-kabu* lit. 'excellent-stock' = 'blue-chip stock'

   b. Compound verbs: N+V *ti-basiru* lit. 'blood-run' = 'get bloodshot', V+V *hasiri-deru* lit. 'run-go.out' = 'run out', A+V *tika-yoru* lit. 'near-approach' = 'go near', AN+V *kooka-sugiru* lit. 'expensive-exceed' = 'be too expensive'

   c. Compound adjectives: N+A *kuti-gitanai* lit. 'mouth-dirty' = 'foul-mouthed', A+A *hoso-nagai* lit. 'thin-long' = 'long and narrow', V+A *musi-atui* lit. 'steam-hot' = 'sultry'

   d. Compound VNs: N+VN *isi-kettei* lit. 'mind-decide' = 'decision making', VN+VN *zyutyuu-seisan* lit. 'receive.order-produce' = 'production-to-order', AN+VN *huhoo-tooki* lit. 'illegal-throw.away' = 'unlawful dumping'

   e. Compound ANs: N+AN *isi-hakuzyaku* lit. 'will-weak' = 'weak-willed', VN+AN *kokyuu-konnan* lit. 'breathe.difficult' = 'have difficulty breathing'

A more and more complex compound can be built by recursively adding a new head to the right. In special cases the left-hand member may be expanded to phrases to make so-called 'phrasal compounds', but the head on the right has no capacity for phrasal expansion (Namiki 2001).

28.1.1.2 *Left-headed compounds*

The left-headed structure, a reflection of Chinese syntax, is strictly confined to morpheme-level S-J compounds with a verbal element (VN) on the left and an internal argument on the right.

(2) a. Transitive VN + Object N: *soo-kin* lit. 'send-money' = 'remit', *sen-gan* lit. 'wash-face' = 'wash one's face'

   b. Intransitive VN + Locative Complement N: *ki-koku* lit. 'return-country' = 'return to one's country', *tai-sya* lit. 'leave-office' = 'leave the office (for the day)'

   c. Unaccusative VN of appearance + Subject N: *syuk-ka* lit. 'go.out-fire' = 'for a fire to break out', *raku-rai* lit. 'fall-lightning' = 'for lightning to strike (something)'

Three points deserve special mention. First, these are truly left-headed because the VN determines the transitivity of a whole compound. In (2a), *soo-kin* 'send money' is transitive because *soo-* 'send' is transitive and in (2b), *ki-koku* 'return to one's country' is intransitive because *ki-* 'return' is intransitive. Second, not all S-J compounds of the morpheme level are left-headed. Following Chinese word order, combinations of an adjunct and a VN like *doku-satu* lit. 'poison-kill' = 'to kill with poison', as well as compound nouns like A + N *ryoku-tya* 'green-tea' and N + N *syo-mei* 'book-name', are right-headed. Third, the standard right-headed structure obtains if a left-headed S-J compound is embedded in a larger compound of any vocabulary stratum, as in [*soo-kin* (send-money)] + [*hoohoo* (method)] 'the method of remittance'.

28.1.1.3 *Double-headed or coordinate compounds*

Coordinate or *dvandva* compounds, composed of two (or more) members functioning as heads on an equal footing, are spread across all lexical categories: N + N *niti-bei* 'Japan-USA', [$_N$ V] + [$_N$ V] *kasi-kari* 'lending-borrowing', V + V *imi-kirau* 'detest-hate', A + A *hoso-nagai* lit. 'thin-long' = 'long and narrow', AN + AN *zyuu-koo-tyoodai* lit. 'heavy.thick-long.big' = 'big and heavy'. Semantically, these compounds are divided into three groups: (i) a holistic type, where the coordinated elements together refer to one conceptual unit, as in *oo-bei* lit. 'Europe-America' denoting 'the West'; (ii) a relational type, where the compound represents the notion of 'between X and Y', as in [*niti-bei*]-*kankei* '[Japan-USA] relationship'; and (iii) a separate-reference type, where each of the coordinated elements has a syntactically visible reference. (Curiously, 'copulative compounds' like *singer-songwriter* seem to be systematically missing in Japanese, where the conjunctive morpheme *-ken-* '-cum-' is used instead.) Of these, only type (iii) can be identified with

what Wälchli (2005) calls 'co-compounds'. Co-compounds of this type are characterized phonologically by a high pitch on the initial mora followed by a sharp drop
of pitch, and syntactically by the visibility of each member to sentential anaphora,
as in *Huu-hu-wa* ([husband-wife]-TOP) *tagai-o* (each.other-ACC) *hagemasita*
(cheered) 'The husband and wife cheered each other up'. These idiosyncrasies are
suggestive of their status as W^+ (section 28.2.1).

28.1.1.4 *Headless or exocentric compounds*

Exocentric compounds in Japanese present more fascinating problems than headed
compounds. The basic mechanism of creating exocentric compounds is metonymy, which in Japanese is manifested in several types: (i) entity-to-entity mapping
(e.g. *aka-boo* 'redcap', which refers to a person who typically wears it), (ii) event/
state-to-entity mapping, and (iii) entity-to-event/state mapping. Of these, the
latter two types are intriguing because they involve category change. Type (ii) is
exemplified by the formula 'N + nominalized V', which, compared with the unproductive *pickpocket* type in English, is frequently exploited in Japanese to name
agents, instruments, products, and other concrete entities that figure prominently
in the events or states described by the compounds (Sugioka 2005).

(3)   EVENT/STATE-TO-ENTITY METONYMIC MAPPING
   a. person: *e-kaki* lit. 'picture-drawing' = 'painter', *kane-moti* lit. 'money-
      having' = 'moneyed person'
   b. instrument: *tume-kiri* lit. 'nail-cutting' = 'nail clipper', *neko-irazu* lit. 'cat-
      being.unnecessary' = 'rat poison'
   c. product: *tamago-yaki* lit. 'egg-frying' = 'fried eggs, omelette'
   d. resultant state: *hada-are* lit. 'skin-getting.rough' = 'state of one's skin being
      rough'
   e. place: *mono-oki* lit. 'thing-keeping' = 'storeroom'
   f. time: *yo-ake* lit. 'night-being.over' = 'daybreak'

For example, the nominalized verb *kaki* 'drawing, writing' acquires a specific
meaning of agent when compounded with a concrete noun on the left, as in
e-kaki 'picture-drawing' (Kageyama 2001b). It is not feasible to derive such
exocentric compounds directly from VP structures, because their corresponding
tensed compound verbs like **e-kaku* lit. 'to picture-draw' are non-existent.

   Type (iii) is embodied by compound ANs of the form A + N, as in (4).

(4)   ENTITY-TO-STATE METONYMIC MAPPING
      hutop-para lit. 'fat-belly' = 'big-hearted, generous', *tuyo-ki* lit. 'strong-mind'
      = 'aggressively confident', (S-J) *syoo-sin* lit. 'small mind' = 'timid'

Here the entity nouns on the right are augmented with adjectives on the left and
shift to a new category of AN (adjectival noun), signalled by the *-na* inflection in

prenominal position as in *hutop-para-na hito* 'a big-hearted person'. Unlike the English *-ed* in *big-hearted*, this *-na* ending itself has no ability to change categories. Another manifestation of type (iii) metonymy is shown in (5), where the original entity meaning changes to an activity meaning.

(5)   ENTITY-TO-EVENT/ACTIVITY METONYMIC MAPPING
    huka-zake lit. 'deep-liquor' = 'drink too much', *ami-mono* lit. 'knit-thing' = 'do knitting', *hari-gami* lit. 'post-paper' = 'post up a bill', *oki-tegami* lit. 'leave-letter' = 'leave a note'

The activity meaning of these compounds is demonstrated by their occurrence as objects of *suru* 'do', as in *huka-zake-o suru* lit. 'do heavy drinking'.

The nature of the exocentric compounds of types (ii) and (iii) could be linked to the general tendency in Japanese for the left-hand element in a complex word to exert a strong influence on the whole word in such a way as to change its meaning and even the category. For example, the concrete noun *te* 'hand' takes on an activity meaning 'to shake hands' (said of dogs) when combined with the honorific prefix *o-*, as in *o-te* 'handshake'. Presumably, the same mechanism will account for a special group of AN-creating prefixes that express the presence or absence of a certain property, such as *mu-* 'absent, non-existent', used as in *mu-sekinin* lit. 'no-responsibility' = 'irresponsible', and *yuu-* 'existent', used as in *yuu-gai* lit. 'existent-harm' = 'harmful' (cf. Kageyama 1982).

This subsection has outlined four kinds of head structure in Japanese lexical compounds. If we take recursivity as an indicator of productivity, only the right-headed and double-headed structures are identified as truly productive. Although left-headed S-J compounds are semantically transparent thanks to the ideographic nature of Chinese characters representing each morpheme, they are never recursive. Exocentric compounds are not recursive, either, and their formation should be ascribed to what Lyons (1977: 549) called 'creativity' (the language-user's ability to extend the system by means of motivated, but unpredictable, principles of abstraction and comparison) rather than 'productivity' (built-in rule). However, the wealth of exocentric compounds illustrated in (3), (4), and (5), which are created frequently and rather systematically, should not be underestimated. Creation of such exocentric compounds is a prerogative of morphology not found in syntactic structure.

28.1.2 Argument relations in verbal compounds

Abundance of compounds containing verbs is a major trait of Japanese. The possible ranges of argument relations available inside verbal compounds are summarized in Table 28.1.

The principal targets of verbal compounding are internal arguments, i.e. transitive objects, intransitive locative complements, and, contrary to Selkirk's (1982)

Table 28.1 Functions of compounded nouns

	Transitive object	Unaccusative subject	Intransitive locative complement	Adjunct
S-J compounds	*aku-syu* 'shake hands'	*tei-den* 'for power to fail'	*tyaku-sui* 'land on water'	*yuu-soo* 'send by mail'
	shake-hand	stop-electricity	land-water	mail-send
native verbal compounds	*ko-sodate* 'child rearing'	*zi-suberi* 'land-slide'	*sato-gaeri* 'homecoming'	*mizu-arai* 'washing in water'
	child-raise	land-slide	home-return	water-wash
native N+V verbs	*tema-doru* 'take time'	*nami-datu* 'for wave to rise'	*su-datu* 'fly from the nest'	*te-watasu* 'hand over'
	time-take	wave-rise	nest-fly	hand-give

'no subject condition', unaccusative subjects. Even compounding of indirect objects, allegedly non-existent according to Fabb (1998), is marginally available, as in S-J *ta-gon* 'say to others' and native *oya-makase* 'leave to one's parents'. Besides, adjuncts freely participate in lexical compounds.

The widely-accepted generalization that agents or external arguments are excluded from compounds is confronted with (apparent) counterexamples in Japanese. First, compounds involving unergative subjects occur in two patterns: (i) what looks like an unergative subject is actually an adjunct representing a metaphorical manner of action, as in *kaeru-oyogi* lit. 'frog-swim' meaning 'swim like a frog'; (ii) the whole word constitutes an exocentric compound naming a concrete entity, as in *inu-basiri* lit. 'dog-run' denoting a narrow concrete path surrounding a building. These two patterns are idiosyncratic naming and have no productivity.

Combinations of agents and transitive VNs, however, present a fairly productive pattern (Kageyama 2007).

(6) a. [*Spielberg* | *seisaku*]-*no*   *eiga* (' | ' stands for a short pause characteristic of W⁺)
     [Spielberg | produce]-GEN   movie
     'a movie produced by Spielberg'

   b. *Kono   eiga-wa   [Spielberg | seisaku]   desu.*
     this   movie-TOP   [Spielberg | produce]   is
     'This movie is a Spielberg production.'

The compound in (6) consists of the agent 'Spielberg' and the transitive predicate 'produce'. A hallmark of such compounds is that they do not express the agent's action per se (eventive predication) but provide a characterization of a distinct property which their modified noun has acquired through the agent's particular action (property predication). Because of this, they must be used adjectivally. In Japanese, this is the only productive pattern of agent compounding, and hence the standard 'internal argument constraint' is still valid for compounds of eventive predication.

To recapitulate, the argument relations available in Japanese verbal compounds are generally limited to internal arguments and adjuncts, as predicted by the standard theory of argument linking (Lieber 1983). However, agent-incorporating compounds of property predication are a new discovery that calls for theoretical inspection.

28.2 REPRESENTATIVE TYPES
OF SYNTAX-RELATED COMPOUNDS

This section introduces several types of compound that pertain to the morphology–syntax interface, focusing on two theoretical issues: (i) the category problem, namely how or to what extent morphological objects differ from syntactic phrases (section 28.2.1); and (ii) the component problem, namely where in the grammar compounding takes place (section 28.2.2).

28.2.1 The category problem: Phrase-like compounds

Japanese has three distinct classes of compounds that ostensibly involve phrases.

(7) a. PHRASAL COMPOUNDS
     [$_{NP}$kirei-na mati]-zukuri lit. '[clean-INFL town]-making' = 'construction of a clean town', [$_{NP}$karaoke to geemu]-taikai lit. '[karaoke and game]-tournament'

     b. POSSESSIVE COMPOUNDS
     hi-no-de lit. 'sun-GEN-rise' = 'sunrise', ama-no-zyaku 'devil's advocate'

     c. W$^+$-LEVEL COMPOUNDS (Kageyama 2001a)
     booeki-gaisya | syatyoo   (' | ' stands for a short pause.)
     trading-company | president
     'president of a trading company'

First, phrasal compounds have their non-heads stretched to phrasal categories. The stretched non-heads must always be on the left-hand side and are categorially limited to NPs with adjectival or other modifiers as in the first example in (7a), or

Table 28.2 Morphosyntactic properties of word–level and W⁺–level compounds

	A. Intrusion of phrasal and functional categories	B. Syntactic deformation	C. Syntactic analysability
word–level	No, except for phrasal and possessive compounds	No	No
W⁺–level	No	No	Yes; internal structure is visible to syntax

coordinated NPs as in the second example; inflected VPs, TPs, or CPs as in the English *an [ate too much] headache* (Lieber 1992a) are impossible. Second, possessive compounds, like *girls' school* and *spider's web* in English (Taylor 1996), are lexicalizations of NPs with the genitive particle *-no* inside. Despite their syntactic flavour, those two types of phrase-like compounds exhibit all the traits of lexical words in terms of compound accent, limited productivity, and lexical conditioning.

From this vantage point, W⁺-level compounds in (7c) look like genuine phrases at first blush, because they lack all the characteristics of lexical compounds: they are pronounced like two independent words, are completely productive, and are immune from lexical conditioning.

28.2.1.1 *Word Plus*

Whereas morpheme- and word-level compounds are fully integrated into a phonological unit, W⁺ compounds retain the accent of each member with a slight pause in between. Despite the phrase-like pronunciation, W⁺ compounds qualify as full-fledged words because of the exclusion of a functional category (8a) and the impossibility of partial deletion (8b).

(8)   a.   [*siritu-*(*no)   *daigaku*] | [*kyoozyu*]
        private-(*GEN)   university | professor
        'professor at a private university'

      b.   *A-wa   [*siritu-daigaku* | ~~*kyoozyu*]~~ *de*,   *B-wa*
        A-TOP   [private-university | ~~professor]~~ and   B-TOP
        [*kokuritu-daigaku* | *kyoozyu*]   *desu.*
        [state-university | professor]   is.
        'A is a professor at a private university, and B a professor at a state university.'

Table 28.2 summarizes the morphosyntactic characteristics of W⁺ compounds as compared with those of lexical word-level compounds.

Like word-level compounds, W⁺ compounds resist intrusion of phrasal and functional categories, and their internal structure cannot be syntactically deformed by deleting or replacing part of them. While these two results are well expected, Column C indicates an outstanding property of W^+ compounds, namely that their internal structure is visible to syntax. Specifically, part of W^+ compounds can be coreferential with a syntactic phrase, in blatant violation of Postal's (1969) anaphoric island constraint. There is even a determiner-like prefix, *doo* 'the same', which is dedicated to making its base noun anaphoric (Kageyama 2001a). (9) shows how this anaphoric prefix refers to its antecedent.

(9) *Daitooryoo-wa asu   yuukoo-zyooyaku$_i$ -ni tyoo'in-suru yotei-da.*
      president-TOP   tomorrow amity-treaty-DAT   sign   schedule-is
      $[_{W+}$ *Doo zyooyaku$_i$* | *saisyuu-an*]   *niyoruto*...
      $[_{W+}$ same   treaty | final-version] according.to
      'The President is going to sign the amity treaty. According to the final version of that treaty, ...'

In previous research, the three properties listed in Table 28.2 are all subsumed under the rubric of 'lexical integrity' or 'syntactic atomicity' (Di Sciullo and Williams 1987). The behaviour of W^+ compounds reveals that this notion needs to be disintegrated into two components: one related to the properties of Columns A and B, and the other related to the property of Column C.

Intrusion of phrasal and functional categories (Column A) and syntactic deformation of word-internal structure (Column B) have to do with the morphological coherence of compounds. The well-formedness of word structure is determined by morphological conditions which are at work in the morphological plane, whereas phrases and sentences are built up in the syntactic plane (cf. Di Sciullo 2005a). Given this architecture of grammar, exclusion of functional categories and prohibition of syntactic deformation fall out naturally. In short, syntax has no say about the internal composition of words. Let us call this 'syntactic indeformability'. The fact that W^+ compounds are endowed with syntactic indeformability is sufficient evidence to establish their word status.

Now, violation of the anaphoric island constraint (Column C) has a different nature from syntactic indeformability. Participation in anaphoric relations does not impair the morphological integrity of W^+ compounds but only makes reference to information contained in them. This property, call it 'syntactic analysability', will also account for why W^+ compounds are pronounced like phrases.

28.2.1.2 *Argument inheritance from non-heads*

Another phenomenon at the morphology–syntax interface is argument inheritance from the non-head position. In $V_1 + V_2$ compound verbs, the argument structure of a whole compound is normally determined by V_2. However, the compound verbs which express an activity (V_1) concomitant with motion (V_2) permit projection of arguments from V_1 as well as from V_2. (10) illustrates how the arguments of *sagasi-mawaru* 'walk about looking for someone/something' are realized.

(10) *Keisatu-wa yama-kara umi-made hannin-o* $[_V[_V sagasi]$- $[_V mawat]]$-ta.
      police-TOP [hill-from beach-to] [criminal-ACC] [look.for]- [go.round]-PST

'The police searched various places from the hills to the beach for the suspect.'

N + V compounds also allow inheritance from the non-head. In (11), the external modifier ('of my father, who died last year') realizes the inalienable possessor argument of the relational noun 'grave'.

(11) *kyonen   nakunat-ta   titi-no   [haka-mairi]*
      last.year die-PST   father-GEN   [grave-visit]
      lit. 'a grave-visit of my father, who died last year' = 'a visit to the grave of my father, who died last year'

   Examples like (10) and (11) demonstrate that Di Sciullo and Williams's (1987) claim that argument inheritance takes place only from the head is too strong. In Japanese, the non-head is permitted to discharge its argument in syntactic structure on condition that the inherited argument does not conflict with the arguments discharged by the head.
   The two phenomena introduced in this subsection, Word Plus and inheritance from non-heads, suggest that although morphology and syntax are organized in independent components, words and phrases as linguistic objects form a continuum.

28.2.2 The component problem: Compound formation in syntax

What I call the 'component problem' concerns the locus of compound formation in the system of grammar. In the literature, there have been two opposing views on this problem, strong lexicalism and strong syntacticism. Recently, however, what once appeared to be a paragon of syntactic compound formation, namely Baker's (1988) incorporation in polysynthetic languages, has been subjected to lexical treatments (Rosen 1989; Spencer 1995), and it now appears that only a highly limited set of data provides truly effective motivation for syntactic incorporation (Baker, Aranovich, and Golluscio 2005). Viewed in this light, the demonstration of the existence of syntactic compounding in Japanese will be profoundly significant.

28.2.2.1 *Verb incorporation*

Japanese has two types of V + V compound verb, lexical and syntactic, whose similarities and differences are summarized in Table 28.3 (Kageyama 1989).
   Columns A and C together show that both types of compound verb make up a word unit. The differences reside in Columns B and D.

Table 28.3 Lexical vs. syntactic V+V compounds

	A. Compound accent	B. Semantic relations	C. Syntactic indeformability	D. Syntactic analysability
Lexical	Yes	Varied as in (10)	Yes	No
Syntactic	Yes	Complementation	Yes	Yes

In lexical compound verbs, the two members hold a variety of semantic relations as in (12) (Kageyama 1993, Matsumoto 1996, Fukushima 2005, Yumoto 2005).

(12) a. means: *osi-akeru* lit. 'push-open(tr.)' = 'to open by pushing'
   b. manner: *korogari-otiru* lit. 'roll-fall' = 'to fall rolling; roll down'
   c. cause and result: *aruki-tukareru* lit. 'walk-get.tired' = 'to get tired from walking'
   d. coordination: *naki-sakebu* lit. 'cry-shout' = 'to cry aloud while weeping'
   e. complementation: *mi-nogasu* lit. 'see-fail' = 'to miss'

Lexical compound verbs, though numerous, lack full productivity. Also, although there appears to be a systematic combinatory restriction to the effect that a transitive verb can go with another transitive verb or an unergative verb but not with an unaccusative verb (Kageyama's (1999) Transitivity Harmony Principle), the systematicity is sometimes blurred by apparent counterexamples emerging from back-formation or analogical creation.

By contrast, syntactic compound verbs are produced freely and unconsciously insofar as the head verb is chosen from a set of approximately thirty designated verbs including those in (13) (Kageyama 1989).

(13)   V-*hazimeru* 'begin to V', V-*oeru* 'finish V-ing', V-*tuzukeru* 'continue V-ing', V-*kakeru* 'be about to V', V-*sokoneru* 'fail to V', V-*kaneru* 'cannot afford to V', V-*wasureru* 'forget to V', V-*naosu* 'V again', V-*okureru* 'be late in V-ing', V-*sugiru* 'V excessively'

Since the non-head V is always in a complementation relation with the head V, the meanings of syntactic compound verbs are determined purely compositionally.

The crucial difference now boils down to syntactic analysability (Column D of Table 28.3). Unlike lexical compound verbs, syntactic compound verbs permit their non-heads to be analysed syntactically in such a way that set expressions like *soo suru* 'do so' and honorific verbal complex *o-V-ni naru* 'HONORIFIC-V-DAT become' are split up as in (14).

(14)   a. [$_{VP}$...   *soo*...t$_i$]   [$_V$ *si$_i$-hazimeru*]
                    so   [do-begin]
       'begin to do so'

       b. [$_{VP}$... *o-kaki-ni*...t$_i$]   [$_V$ *nari$_i$-hazimeru*]
          HONORIFIC-write-DAT   [become-begin]
          'begin to write'

Such disrupted constituent structures can be derived only by assuming that the complement verbs *si* 'do' and *nari* 'become' are incorporated with the head verb 'begin', leaving the remnants behind in the complement clauses.

28.2.2.2 *VN incorporation*

In the light verb construction, the main verb *suru* 'do' takes a complement clause headed by a VN, from which the VN is optionally incorporated with the verb to make up a compound *VN-suru* (Kageyama 1982).

(15) *London-ni* [$_{VN}$ *syuttyoo*]-*o* [$_V$ *suru*] → *London-ni* [$_V$ [$_{VN}$ *syuttyoo*]-*suru*]
     London-LOC   business.trip-ACC do   London-LOC [$_V$ business.trip-do]
     'to make a business trip to London'

Matsumoto (1996) provides the example in (16), arguing that the VN *rakka* 'fall' and the verb *suru* 'do' do not form a word because only the VN is deleted in B's utterance.

(16)   A: *Sore-wa*   *rakka*   *si-masi-ta*   *ka*?
          it-TOP   fall   do-POLITE-PST   Q   'Did it fall?'

       B: *Hai, Ø*   *si-masi-ta.*
          yes,   do-POLITE-PST   'Yes, it did.'

This argument, however, looks at only one side of the coin – the syntactic analysability of *VN-suru* – and misses the other side, namely its syntactic inde-formability shown in (17):

(17)   a. * [*totuzen-no*   *rakka*]-*suru*
            [sudden-GEN   fall]-do
            'to have a sudden fall'

       b. * *Akai*   *huusen-wa*   [*rakka-si*],   *aoi*   *huusen-wa*
            red   balloon-TOP   [fall-d̶o̶]   blue   balloon-TOP
            [*zyoosyoo-si-ta*].
            [rise-do-PST]
            'The red balloon fell and the blue one went up.'

The seemingly contradictory observations in (16) and (17) indicate that a VN and *suru* are separate constituents at some stage of syntactic structure and are later merged into a compound.

28.2.2.3 Post-syntactic compounding

What Shibatani and Kageyama (1988) termed post-syntactic compounds provide even more compelling evidence for syntactic incorporation.

(18)   *kyoozyu-ga*   *London-o*   *hoomon*   *no*   *ori...*
       professor-NOM   London-ACC   visit   GEN   occasion
       'when the professor visited London'
       → *kyoozyu-ga*   [$_{VN}$ *London:*   *hoomon*]   *no*   *ori...*
          professor-NOM   [London: visit]   GEN   occasion

In (18), the object *London* is incorporated with the VN *hoomon* 'visit', with a short pause (:) inside. While this phonological break coincides with that of W$^+$ compounds, post-syntactic compounds cannot be identified with lexically derived W$^+$ compounds. A reliable diagnosis is the availability of the subject honorification prefix (*go-*) on the head VN.

(19)   *kyoozyu-ga*   [*Yooroppa:*   *go-taizai*]   *no*   *ori*
       professor-NOM   [Europe: HONORIFIC-stay]   GEN   occasion
       'when the professor stayed in Europe'

Lexical compounds are incapable of containing the subject honorific prefix, because this prefix is a marker of syntactic subject–verb agreement. Now the fact that the head of a post-syntactic compound can bear the honorific prefix as in (19) demonstrates that this compounding is really syntactic.

The syntactic nature of post-syntactic compounds is reinforced by contrasting them with lexical compounds. First, as shown in Table 28.1, lexical compounds can contain not only internal arguments but also adjuncts and indirect objects. Post-syntactic compounds, in contrast, reject adjuncts and indirect objects altogether.

Second, lexical compounding contributes to changing the grammatical functions of the NPs that are not compounded.

(20)   *tomodati-o/*ni*   [$_V$ *yuuki-zuke-ru*]
       friend-ACC/*DAT   courage-give-PRES
       'to give the friend courage'

In (20), the ditransitive verb *zuke-ru* (variant of the base form *tuke-ru* 'add, give'), which by itself takes an accusative Theme object and a dative Goal object, marks the Goal object in the accusative when it is compounded with a Theme argument. By contrast, post-syntactic compounding never alters the grammatical functions of unincorporated NPs, as shown by (21), where the unincorporated Goal object ('winner') retains its original dative case.

(21)   *Kaityoo-ga*   *yuusyoosya-ni/*o*   [*medaru: zootei*]   *no*   *sai*
       president-NOM   winner-DAT/*ACC   [medal: award]   GEN   occasion
       'when the president awarded the medal to the winner'

Third, consider duplication of supposedly incorporated nouns. Morpheme-level S-J compounds exhibit all of what Rosen (1989) termed 'compounding type', 'noun doubling type', and 'modifier stranding type' for Noun Incorporation languages.

(22) a. Compounding type
         (*syoosetu-o) doku-syo lit. 'to read-**book a novel**'
      b. Noun doubling type
         gakuhi-o soo-**kin** lit. 'to send-**money the tuition fee**' = 'to remit the tuition fee'
      c. Modifier stranding type
         hidari-asi-o kos-setu lit. 'to **bone**-break **the left leg**' = 'to break the bone of the left leg' (Note: the stranded modifier is marked in the accusative rather than the genitive.)

By contrast, post-syntactic compounds are strictly of the compounding type, rejecting noun doubling and modifier stranding.

While Baker's (1988) original scheme was to derive the grammatical function changing and modifier stranding in NI languages as byproducts of syntactic incorporation, Rosen (1989) and Spencer (1995) have shown that these phenomena are properly accounted for by lexical operations on argument structure or Lexical Conceptual Structure (LCS). The Japanese data in (20) and (22) buttresses such a lexical analysis because those compounds are unquestionably lexical. Particularly noteworthy is the fact that among the various types of lexical compounds, it is the S-J morpheme-level compounds that permit noun doubling and modifier strand-ing, as in (22). This can be correlated with the fact that the languages Baker (1988) treated are all polysynthetic, which means that incorporation in those languages applies to bound morphemes. If noun doubling and modifier stranding are reducible to the level of LCS (Sadler and Spencer 1998), both Baker's data and S-J compounds in Japanese will be unified as morpheme-level compounding that creates new LCS representations.

In sharp contrast to lexical compounds, post-syntactic compounds tolerate neither noun doubling nor modifier stranding. This suggests that incorporation in syntax is a simple movement that is irrelevant to noun doubling and grammatical function changing. There still remains the problem of modifier stranding, which, as Baker et al. (2005) argue, has much to do with number and gender agreement between modifiers and head nouns. Since Japanese lacks overt modifier–head agreement, prohibition of modifier stranding in post-syntactic compounds might plausibly be reduced to lack of such agreement features. Note finally that post-syntactic compounding is not a case of Pseudo Noun Incorporation (Massam 2001), i.e. a phrase structure in which an NP directly merges with a V, because the incorporated Ns in Japanese post-syntactic compounds are not NPs.

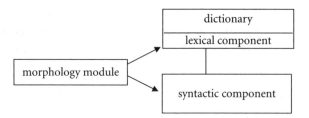

Figure 28.1 Modular morphology

28.3 CONCLUSION

In surveying the representative compound types in Japanese, this chapter has paid special attention to verb-based compounds, because their peculiarities have po-tential to contribute to theorizing the architecture of grammar. The Japanese data will be shaped into a model of grammar (Figure 28.1) in which an independent module of morphology globally constrains the well-formedness of compounds that are built up in the lexical and syntactic components.

This 'Modular Morphology' model (Shibatani and Kageyama 1988), which is consonant with Borer's (1998) Parallel Morphology or Ackema and Neeleman's (2004) Parallel Representation model but incompatible with Distributed Morph-ology, can resolve both the category problem and the component problem in an appealing way. As to the component problem, it allows compounding to take place in both the lexical and the syntactic component while at the same time prohibiting syntactic deformation of all kinds of morphological objects regardless of the locus of their creation. As regards the category problem, postulation of W^+ as a morphological category accounts for its syntactic analysability while maintaining its syntactic indeformability.

URALIC, FINNO-UGRIC: HUNGARIAN

FERENC KIEFER

29.1 INTRODUCTION

The purpose of this paper is to provide an overview of the data of compounding in Hungarian and to point out some controversial issues concerning both the empirical data and the analysis of some types of compounds. In establishing the types of compounds we are going to restrict ourselves to the discussion of productive root compounds. This survey will be followed by a discussion of deverbal compounds concentrating on features which are typical of Hungarian. A separate section will be devoted to the discussion of particle verbs, which have some features in common with compounds. The chapter concludes with a brief disussion of some residual problems such as inflection and compounding, derivation outside compounding, exocentric compounds, and coordinative compounds.

As in many other languages, in Hungarian compounding is one of the main ways by which new words are formed. Compounds appeared very early in the history of Hungarian but a large number of compounds in present-day Hungarian were artificially coined during the language reform movement in the second half of

The present paper is partly based on the author's earlier work on compounding in Hungarian, esp. Kiefer (1992a, b, 2000, 2001, 2002).

the eighteenth century and in the beginning of the nineteenth century. German influence is quite apparent as testified by the huge number of loan translations – *eső + kabát* 'raincoat', G. *Regenmantel; állás + pont* 'point of view', lit. 'standpoint', G. *Standpunkt; tükör-tojás* 'fried egg', lit. 'mirror egg', G. *Spiegelei* – which gives a Germanic touch to Hungarian compounding.

29.2 PRODUCTIVE PATTERNS OF ROOT COMPOUNDS

The productive patterns of compounding[1] in Hungarian are all endocentric and right-headed and are formed by mere concatenation. N + N compounds are particularly productive – practically any two nouns can be concatenated to form a new compound: *olaj + ezredes* (lit. 'oil officer') meaning 'an army officer involved in black oil business'; *ár + vadász* (lit. 'price hunter') 'person comparing prices in order to find the best price'; *atom + vonat* (lit. 'atom train') 'train transporting nuclear waste'. In addition, N + N compounds are recursive and have a binary structure (indicated by brackets): *vér + nyomás* 'blood-pressure', [*vér + nyomás*] + *mérő* 'blood-pressure measuring', [*vér + nyomás + mérő*] + *készülék* 'blood-pressure measuring apparatus', [*vér + nyomás + mérő + készülék*] + *gyártó* 'blood-pressure measuring apparatus producer', [*vér + nyomás + mérö + készülék + gyártó*] + *üzem* 'blood-pressure measuring apparatus producing factory', etc. The other existing patterns are less productive. In some cases the possible combinations are semantically restricted by the head. For example, in A + A compounds with a colour word as head, the non-head is normally *light* or *dark*. The productivity of compounding patterns is a matter of degree rather than absolute. It should also be made clear that productive compounding does not necessarily mean that the meaning of the compound is predictable on the basis of the meaning of its parts. In the case of N + N compounds, for example, normally the only semantic feature which can be predicted is that the thing denoted by the head has something to do with the thing denoted by the non-head. In this sense, too, compounding differs from derivation: in the case of productive derivation the meaning of the derived word can always be predicted from the meaning of its parts.

Example (1) shows the productive compounding patterns in Hungarian (in what follows word boundaries will be denoted by ' + ' and, whenever necessary, morpheme boundaries by '#').

---

[1] For the notion of productivity in compounding see Dressler and Ladányi (2000).

(1)   a. N + N *adó + kártya* 'tax card', *beton + elem* 'concrete slab', *bank + automata*
          'bank automaton, ATM'

      b. A + N *fehér + gazdaság* 'white/legal economy', *fekete + szoftver* 'black/illegal
          software', *kereső + gép* 'search engine'

      c. N + A *oszlop + magas* 'pillar high, high as a pillar', *euro + kompatibilis* 'euro-
          compatible', *szolárium + barna* 'solarium brown, tanned in a solarium'

      d. A + A *bal + liberális* 'left-liberal', *forró + nyomos* 'hot + trail$_{Adj}$' = 'having to
          do with a person following a hot trail'

      e. N + V *tény + feltár* 'fact + explore/disclose' = 'explore/disclose the facts',
          város + néz   'town + look' = 'do   sightseeing',   *ház + kutat*   'house +
          search' = 'search sb's premises'

Notice, however, that (1e) are backformations from the deverbal compounds
tény + feltárás 'revealing of the facts', *város + nézés* 'sightseeing', *ház + kutatás*
'house search, perquisition' rather than primary compounds, consequently they
can be dropped from list (1). In addition to (1a–d), we may encounter a number of
V + N compounds as well: *lát + lelet* 'medical report' from *lát* 'see' and *lelet* 'report',
lak + bér 'rent' from *lak* 'dwell' and *bér* 'rent', *véd + levél* 'letter of protection' from
véd 'protect' and *levél* 'letter'. However, most of the V + N compounds were
artificially coined in the nineteenth century during the language reform movement;
others were formed by analogy but the pattern has never become productive. We
may thus conclude that the productive compounding patterns are formed from the
categories N and A only.

29.3 DEVERBAL COMPOUNDS

29.3.1 Action nouns as heads

It has been pointed out by several authors (e.g. Di Sciullo and Williams 1987) that
in compounds the non-head may, but need not satisfy one of the arguments of the
head. It seems to be clear, however, that both 'satisfaction' and 'argument' must
mean something different from what they mean in syntax. In contrast to syntax the
alleged argument of a deverbal head (the non-head) cannot be modified, it cannot
take the plural, and it always has a generic meaning. A syntactic argument clearly
behaves differently from that. Moreover, if the head has two obligatory internal
arguments only the object argument can appear in non-head position, as in the
case of the verb *kölcsönöz vki vkinek* 'lend to somebody', the oblique argument
cannot even be spelled out syntactically. Consider

(2) a. *Péter   pénzt   kölcsönöz   Annának.*
      Peter   money-ACC   lend   Ann-DAT
      'Peter lends Ann money.'

     b. **Péter   pénzkölcsönzése   Annának*
      Peter   money-lending-POSS   Ann-DAT
      'Peter's money lending to Ann'

Consequently, it seems to be more adequate to say that the non-head may be interpreted as a semantic argument (corresponding to a thematic role of the verb) of the head in certain cases.

Similarly to many other languages, in the case of a deverbal head derived from a transitive verb the non-head may correspond to the Theme argument, but never to the Agent argument.

(3) *levél + írás* 'letter-writing', *újság + olvasás* 'newspaper-reading', *ebéd + főzés* 'dinner-cooking', *utca + söprés* 'street-sweeping', *zene + hallgatás* 'music-listening', *tévé + nézés* 'TV-watching'

The derivational morphology of action nouns is very regular in Hungarian. The only productive suffix is *-ás/-és*, which is attached to the verbal stem: *olvas#ás* 'reading', *főz#és* 'cooking', *hallgat#ás* 'listening', *csökken#és* 'decrease'.[2] The deverbal noun may have a complex event, a simple event, and/or a result reading; Hungarian does not differ from other languages in this respect. The same deverbal noun, for example, *aláír#ás* 'signing, signature', may exhibit all three readings, as illustrated in (4a–c).[3]

(4) a. *A szerződésnek az elnök által való aláírása ünnepélyes külsőségek között történt.* (complex event)
      'The signing of the contract by the president took place with all due solemnity.'

     b. *A szerződések aláírása sokáig tartott.* (simple event)
      'The signing of the contracts took a long time.'

     c. *Az elnök aláírása olvashatatlan ezen a szerződésen.* (result)
      'The president's signature is illegible on this contract.'

What makes Hungarian noteworthy is the regularity of its morphology. Compare H. *aláírás* En. *signing* and *signature*; H. *írás* En. *writing* and *document*; H. *igazolás* En. *certifying* and *certificate*. In Hungarian the result noun normally has the same form as the event noun.

The regularity of Hungarian morphology can also be observed in deverbal compounds. In (5) the head *vágás* 'cutting' is derived from the verb *vág* 'cut':

---

[2] The two forms of the suffix are due to vowel harmony. There are a few exceptions which can be explained by lexical blocking.

[3] Cf. Laczkó (2000: 304–18).

(5)   *fa + vágás* 'wood-cutting', *disznó + vágás* 'pig-killing', *haj + vágás* 'haircut'

The drawback of this regularity is, of course, multiple polysemy, which has to be resolved contextually.

Transitive verbs with an articleless singular object noun are considered to be complex verbs because they denote a generic activity: *levelet ír* 'letter write, to do letter writing' is not the same as *ír egy levelet* 'to write a letter'. The object NP with an indefinite article refers to a single entity; the articleless object noun, on the other hand, does not refer to any concrete letter – the verb phrase expresses the complex activity of letter writing. Complex verbs show a number of similarities with compounds: they bear compound stress (the first syllable of the articleless object noun is stressed, the verb remains unstressed), the articleless noun precedes the verb (it occupies the non-head position),[4] they cannot be modified or pluralized, and the non-head has a generic meaning.[5] Examples are given in (6).

(6)   *level#et ír* 'letter-ACC write', *újság#ot olvas* 'newspaper-ACC read', *ebéd#et főz* 'dinner-ACC cook', *utcá#t söpör* 'street-ACC sweep', *zené#t hallgat* 'music-ACC listen', *tévé#t néz* 'TV-ACC watch'

The similarity between (6) and the deverbal nouns in (3) is striking. In spite of this similarity, however, the deverbal nouns cannot be derived from the complex verbs in (6) for the following reason. The object noun in (6) is marked by the accusative suffix *-(V)t*, which does not appear in the corresponding deverbal noun and there is no way to explain why it should be deleted during derivation. The accusative case is assigned to the object noun by the verb in syntax and spelled out in phonology. Moreover, suffixed nouns can never appear as arguments of a deverbal noun:

(7)   **level#et írás* 'letter-writing', **újság#ot olvasás* 'newspaper-reading'

Consequently, we have to assume that deverbal nouns and complex verbs are formed independently of each other.

Let's turn now to the problem of the subject argument in compounds. In English subject arguments may never appear in non-head position. Compare now the English examples in (8a,b) with their Hungarian equivalents.

(8)   a. **Leaf-falling makes a big mess.*
          'A lombhullás nagy szeméttel jár.'

      b. **Glass-breaking can be caused by sound waves.*
          'Üvegtörés hanghullámokkal is létrehozható.'

---

[4] The word order is normally SVO.

[5] Complex verbs are similar to compounds in other ways, too: in order to be able to form such a verb the activity denoted by the verb must be institutionalized. That is, one can express the activity of reading a letter, an article, a book by a complex verb but not the activity of reading ads or slips of paper. Cf. Kiefer (1990).

The Hungarian equivalents of (8a,b) are fully grammatical: *lomb+hullás* 'leaf-falling' and *üveg+törés* 'glass-breaking' are both impeccable deverbal compounds, in which the non-head is interpreted as the Patient argument of the head.

In (9) more examples are given for compounds whose head is derived from an intransitive verb and whose non-head is interpretable as the subject argument of the verb.

(9) a. *liba+gágog#ás* 'gaggling of a goose/geese', *kutya+ugat#ás* 'barking of a dog/dogs', *macska+nyávog#ás* '(cat's) mewing', *légy+zümmög#és* 'buzzing of a fly/flies'

   b. *rózsa+nyíl#ás* 'opening of a rose/roses', *orgona+virágz#ás* 'blooming of a lilac/lilacs', *gyümölcs+ér#és* 'ripening of fruit'[6]

In (9a) the head is derived from a verb denoting sound emission of an animal, and in (9b) from verbs denoting phenomena of nature. The examples can easily be multiplied. The non-head in (9a) is certainly not a typical agent: a goose does not act intentionally. Moreover, nouns referring to a human being cannot usually occur in that position.[7] If we call the non-typical agent Actor, the following generalization holds: the non-head of a deverbal compound in which the head is derived from an intransitive verb of 'emission of sounds' may be interpreted as the Actor argument of the base. In the case of heads derived from verbs denoting phenomena of nature the entity denoted by the non-head undergoes a change of state; consequently, it may correspond to the Patient argument of the head.

In sum, then, we get the following picture.

(10) a. The non-head of a deverbal compound in which the head is derived from a transitive verb may satisfy the Theme argument of the base.

   b. The non-head of a deverbal compound in which the head is derived from an intransitive verb may satisfy either the Actor or the Patient argument of the base. The choice depends on the semantics of the base: verbs denoting phenomena of nature require a Patient argument, emission of sound verbs an Actor argument.[8]

---

[6] Note the regular morphology of the deverbal head in all these examples. Note furthermore that the examples in (9b) involve unaccusative verbs, which in English do not seem to allow synthetic compounds. Cf. Grimshaw (1990: 69).

[7] There are a few exceptions, though. Cf. *gyermek+sírás* 'child crying, crying of children'; *gyermek+nevetés* 'child laughing, laughing of children'.

[8] In some cases the non-head may also be interpreted as the Instrument argument of the deverbal head. For example, on one of its readings, the verb *fűt* 'heat' takes an Agent, a Theme, and an Instrument argument. Yet without strong contextual support there is no **ház+fűtés* 'house heating', **lakás+fűtés* 'apartment heating', **szoba+fűtés* 'room heating'. The verb seems to systematically select the Instrument argument: *szén+fűtés* 'coal-heating', *víz+fűtés* 'hot-water heating', *gőz+fűtés* 'steam-heating', *gáz+fűtés* 'heating by gas', etc.

The same non-head may be interpreted either as a Patient or as a Theme argument depending on whether the base is intransitive or transitive:

(11) a. *ár + csökkenés* 'decline in prices', *ár + drágulás* 'increase in prices', *ár + kiegyenlítődés* 'levelling of prices'

  b. *ár + csökkentés* 'reduction of prices', *ár + drágítás* 'running up of prices', *ár + kiegyenlítés* 'levelling off of prices'[9]

In other cases the deverbal noun must be interpreted as a result nominal, e.g. *bolha + csípés* 'flea-bite', *kutya + harapás* 'dog-bite', *disznó + túrás* 'rooting of pigs', *macska + karmolás* 'cat's scratch', *nyúl + rágás* 'damage done by rabbits'. These compounds are interpreted as the result of perfective events, that is, *bolhacsípés* 'flea bite' cannot be related to *egy bolha csíp* 'a flea bites' (which has also a generic reading) but only to *a bolha megcsip valakit* 'the flea bites somebody' (with the perfective/resultative verb *megcsíp*). Similarly, *kutyaharapás* 'dog-bite' is the result of the event *megharap valakit a kutya* 'the dog bites somebody' (with the perfective verb *megharap*), and *macskakarmolás* 'cat's scratch' the result of the event *megkarmol valakit a macska* 'the cat scratches somebody' (with the perfective verb *megkarmol*). The fact that we are concerned with a perfective-resultative event explains the result meaning.[10] The head has no event reading, hence the non-head cannot be interpreted as a semantic argument of the base. Nevertheless it does have a subject-like reading, which must be due to the related resultative structure: a flea bites somebody and the result is a flea-bite.

In a considerable number of deverbal compounds there is no systematic relation whatsoever between the head and the non-head. Some examples are given for transitive bases in (12a), for intransitive ones in (12b).

(12) a. *fej + számolás* (lit. 'head + counting') 'mental arithmetic', *részvét + látogatás* (lit. 'compassion + visit') 'visit of condolence', *császár + metszés* (lit. 'emperor + cut') 'Caesarean section', *világ + kiállítás* (lit. 'world + exhibition') 'world fair'

  b. *öröm + rivalgás* (lit. 'joy + shouts') 'shouts of joy', *magas + ugrás* (lit. 'high + jump') 'high-jump', *vak + repülés* 'blind flying', *szamár + köhögés* (lit. 'donkey + cough') 'whooping cough'

As expected, the meaning of such compounds is largely unpredictable. It does not even make much sense to speak of a result reading in such cases.

The event reading of deverbal compounds can be identified by means of aspectual verbs such as *kezd* 'begin', *befejez* 'finish', *abbahagy* 'stop', *tart* 'last',

---

[9] The last examples in (11a,b) contain the verbal particle *ki*, the causative suffix *–it*, and in the case of (11a) the decausativizing suffix *-őd(ik)*. The morphological structure of *kiegyenlítődés* is thus [[ki + [egyenl + ít] + őd] + és].

[10] Compare in this respect the deverbal compound *kutya + ugatás* 'barking of a dog', which comes from *a kutya ugat* 'a/the dog barks' with the generic meaning of the NP.

történik 'happen, occur'. It may also be useful to make use of the postposition *alatt/ közben* 'during'. Compare, once again, *kutya + ugatás* 'barking of a dog/dogs' and *kutya + harapás* 'dog-bite'. While *kutya + ugatás alatt* 'during the barking of a dog/ dogs' is fully grammatical, **kutya + harapás alatt* 'during dog-bite' is unacceptable. Once a deverbal compound has been formed no other argument of the base can occur in the VP, which means that deverbal compounds can never have a complex event reading.

The deverbal compounds in (13) have an event reading, as testified by the compatibility with aspectual verbs in (13a, b) and with the temporal adverb közben 'during' in (13c).

(13) a. *A   kutyaugatás   éjfélkor   kezdődött.*
         the   dog barking   midnight.at   started
         'The (dog's) barking started at midnight.'

      b. *Az   üvegtörés   ötkor   következett be.*
         the   glass-breaking   at.five   occurred
         'The glass broke at five o'clock.'

      c. *Újságolvasás   közben   ne   zavarj.*
         newspaper-reading   during   not   disturb
         'Don't disturb me when I am reading the newspaper.'

Let's conclude this section by looking at some differences between the nominalized forms of simple verbs and those of particle verbs. Most Hungarian verbs can be prefixed by a verbal particle, which typically turns the imperfective base verb into a perfective one, but it may also add some further semantic material to the base.[11] Their respective nominalized forms exhibit interesting differences.

(14) a. *vizsgáztatás*   'examination'   from the imperfective verb *vizsgáztat*
      b. *le + vizsgáztatás*   'examination'   from the perfective verb *levizsgáztat*

(15) a. *simogatás*   'stroking'   from the imperfective verb *simogat*
      b. *meg + simogatás*   'stroking'   from the perfective verb *megsimogat*

The imperfective form may have both a simple event and a complex event reading, the perfective form has a complex event reading only. In the latter case the object argument must accompany the deverbal noun.

(16) a. *A vizsgáztatás sok időt vett igénybe.*
         'The examination took a long time.'

      b. **A levizsgáztatás sok időt vett igénybe.*
         'The examination (PRF) took a long time.'

      c. *A diákok levizsgáztatása sokáig tartott.*
         'The examination (PRF) of the students took a long time.'

---

[11] Particle verbs, too, are considered to be complex verbs.

Compounds with heads derived from particle verbs are relatively rare, but there are some examples:[12]

(17) a. *ér+elmeszesedés* 'arteriosclerosis, hardening of the arteries' from the particle verb *el+meszesedik* 'harden'; *ár+kiegyenlítődés* 'levelling of prices' from the particle verb *ki+egyelítőd(ik)* 'be levelled'

b. *kormány+átalakítás* 'reconstruction of the government' from the particle verb *át+alakít*; *fa+kitermelés* 'wood-felling' from the particle verb *ki+termel* 'exploit'; *csont+átültetés* 'bone grafting' from the particle verb *át+ültet* 'transplant'

The interpretation of the compounds in (17a) is not different from the ones where the base is intransitive and particleless: the non-head is interpreted as the Patient argument of the base. Similarly, in the case of (17b) the non-head is interpreted as the Theme argument of the base. In general, however, compounds cannot be formed with heads derived from particle verbs. The following forms are not even possible as potential words:

(18) **újság+elovasás* 'reading of a newspaper' (the head contains the particle *el*); **kéz+megmosás* 'washing of hands' (the head contains the particle *meg*); **pénz+megtalálás* 'finding of the money' (the head contains the particle *meg*); **mese+elmondás* 'telling a tale' (the head contains the particle *el*)

The reason for the ungrammaticality of the forms in (18) is this: the head in (18) requires a definite or specific noun as a Theme argument, it does not tolerate nouns with a generic reading. Definiteness or specificity is expressed by the definite or indefinite article, which appears in possessive constructions: *az újság/egy újság elovasása* 'the reading of the/a newspaper'. Evidently, the non-head cannot take any article in compounds. The verbs from which the heads in (17) are derived behave differently: they are compatible with nouns with a generic reading. In other words, while *szervet ültet át* 'to transplant an organ', *fát termel ki* 'to fell trees' are possible constructions, **mesét mond el* 'to tell tales', **pénzt talál meg* 'to find money' are not. Recall that the articleless nouns normally have a generic reading. The different behaviour of the two types of deverbal nouns can be explained if we realize that there is an important difference between the verbs underlying the deverbal nouns in (17) and (18). In the case of (17) the particle has a word-formation function and brings about a completely new meaning: *termel* 'produce' – *ki+termel* 'exploit'; *ültet* 'plant (seeds, flowers)' – *átültet* (in (17)) 'transplant (an organ)'. In the case of (18), on the other hand, the particle has a perfectivizing/resultative function only: *olvas* 'read' – *elolvas* 'read through'; *mond* 'say' – *elmond* 'tell'. Note that it is a

---

[12] Some of these compounds may have been formed in one single step.

typical feature of perfective verbs that they require a definite or specific object. We have thus arrived at the following generalization:

(19)   In the case of particle verbs, deverbal compounds can only be formed if the particle has a word-formation function.

29.3.2 Agent nouns

Agent nouns are productively formed by the suffix -ó/-ő: ír 'write' – ír#ó 'writer', olvas 'read' – olvas#ó 'reader', gondolkod(ik) 'think' – gondolkod#ó 'thinker', szerel 'mount, install' – szerel#ő 'technician', fűt 'heat' – fűt#ő 'heater'. The same suffix is also used to form nouns denoting an instrument (vés + ő 'chisel' from vés 'chisel', ás + ó 'spade' from ás 'dig') and places (tárgyal#ó 'conference room' from tárgyal 'negotiate, discuss', internetez#ő 'public place where one has access to the internet'). In the latter two cases the derived noun loses the argument structure of the base completely; in the case of agent nouns, however, a Theme argument may appear in non-head position.

(20)   regény + író 'novel-writer', kazán + fűtő 'boiler-man', autó + szerelő 'car mechanic/fitter', levél + író 'letter-writer', újság + olvasó 'newspaper-reader'

It is equally possible to form compounds with heads derived from particle verbs:

(21)   csont + átültető 'transplanter of bones', népesség + összeíró 'census taker', fa + kitermelő 'tree feller'

And, once again, it is impossible to form compounds of type (22):

(22)   *újság + elolvasó 'newspaper reader' from the perfective verb el#olvas'; *gyűr-ű + megkereső 'ring seeker' from the perfective verb meg#keres 'seek, search'; *tévé + megnéző 'TV watcher' from the perfective meg#néz 'watch, look'

The reason for the ungrammaticality of (22) is the same as in the case of action nouns: in (21) the head is derived from particle verbs where the function of the particle is to derive a verb with non-compositional meaning, whereas in (22) the main function of the particle is to perfectivize.

There is yet another feature of agent nouns which deserves to be mentioned. The productive reading of agent nouns can be paraphrased as 'occasional performer of the activity denoted by the base verb'. This means that the primary meaning of író 'writer' is not the name of a profession, but a person who happens to be writing something. Similarly, the primary meaning of fűtő 'heater' is not the name of a profession either, but the incidental performer of heating. This distinction has important syntactic consequences. Consider:

(23) a. *Anna olvasó.
          'Ann is a reader.'

      b. Anna a könyv olvasója.
          'Ann is the reader of the book.'

(24) a. Anna író.
          'Ann is a writer.'

      b. Anna a levél írója.
          'Ann is the writer of the letter.'

Example (23a) is ungrammatical because olvasó 'reader' cannot mean 'someone whose profession is reading', in contrast to (24a), where író 'writer' has an institutionalized meaning. (23b) and (24b) show that both agent nouns may have an 'incidental performer of an activity' reading which takes an object argument on that reading. The possessive construction in (23b) and (24b) is the source of the compounds könyv+olvasó 'book reader' and levél+író 'letter writer'. Agent nouns with institutionalized meaning don't have any argument structure, hence the question of argument satisfaction does not arise.

   Agent nouns derived from perfective/resultative verbs which denote an incidental performer of the activity expressed by the verb always require an object argument:

(25) a. *a   felrobbantó
           the   blower-up
           'the person who blows up something'

      b. a   híd   felrobbantója
          the   bridge   blower-up
          'the person who has blown up the bridge'

This explains why such deverbal nouns never get institutionalized.

   All agent nouns derived by the suffix -ó/-ő inherit the object argument from the base verb (as in other languages, the subject argument is satisfied by the suffix), and this argument may appear as a Theme argument in compounds. Institutionalized deverbal nouns don't have any arguments, they function as 'root' nouns, and they form root compounds. Yet, the non-head in such compounds may be interpreted as a kind of object argument, e.g. regény+író 'novel writer', újság+olvasó 'newspaper-reader'. These compounds are interpreted on the basis of what constituted the input to institutionalization, similarly to the case of compounds which have a 'result nominal' meaning.[13]

---

[13] Cf. the examples in (11) and the discussion there.

29.4 SOME NOTES ON PARTICLE VERBS

In Hungarian, particles have been developed from adverbs or postpositions and some of them are still undistinguishable from adverbs. In spite of the fact that particle verbs are separable from the verbal base, they are, in many respects, very similar to compounds: they carry compound stress, they behave like compounds with respect to ellipsis and, when nominalized, they become inseparable.

(26)   a. *újjá+épít* 'rebuild' from *új* 'new', *já* translative case suffix, *épít* 'build'

   b. *újjá   hidat   építenek*
      particle   bridge-ACC   build
      'it is a bridge/bridges that they are going to rebuild'

(27)   a. *újjáépít#és* 'reconstruction, rebuilding'
   b. **újjá hidat épités,*újjá hídépités*

(28)   a. *újjá+épít#hető* 'reconstructable'
   b. *újjá is építhető* 'is reconstructable after all'

(29)   a. *újjáépíthető#ség* 'reconstructability'
   b. **újjá is építhetőség*

The particle and the verb can be interrupted by practically any constituent, and, under certain circumstances, the particle can also be moved into a postverbal position. The nominalized form does not allow any interruption, as shown in (27b). The participial adjectival form in (28a) is still interruptible but when a noun is formed from it by the suffix *-ság/-ség* nothing can be inserted between the particle and the rest of the word: (29b) is ungrammatical. Let us next have a look at elliptical constructions.

(30)   a. *fel+ír vagy le+ír* 'note or copy'
   b. *fel- vagy le+ír*

(31)   a. *fel+megy vagy fel+mászik* 'go or climb up'
   b. *fel+megy vagy -mászik*

Forward and backward ellipsis is a typical feature of compounds, but with derivational affixes ellipsis is only exceptionally possible.[14]

   In sum, then, particle verbs show compound-like behaviour and can be considered a special type of Adv+V compound, at least lexically. Syntax has, then, to take care of the syntactic behaviour of particle verbs. How to do this best remains a controversial issue, however.

---

[14] Cf. Kenesei (2000: 81–7) for a discussion of the problem of ellipsis in morphology.

29.5 INFLECTION AND COMPOUNDING

In Hungarian there are some morphologically marked compounds as well, in which the non-head is inflected, e.g. *bűn#be+esés* 'fall into sin' from *bűnbe esik* 'fall into sin', where the the noun is marked by the illative case suffix *-ba*; *fej#en+állás* 'head-stand' from *fejen áll* 'stand on one's head', where the noun is marked by the superessive case suffix *-n*; *nagy#ra+becsülés* 'high esteem' from *nagyra becsül* 'esteem highly', where the noun is marked by the sublative case suffix *-ra*. These compounds have all been formed directly from the corresponding verb phrases and they do not represent productive patterns. Less frequently, though, morphological marking may also appear on the head (*város+ház#a* 'city hall', where the head is marked by the possessive suffix *-a*, lit. 'house of the city') or on both the head and the non-head (*bolond#ok+ház#a* 'madhouse', where the non-head is marked by the plural suffix *-ok* and the head by the possessive suffix *-a*, lit. 'house of the mad'). The sources of these compounds are possessive constructions.

Inflection may never appear inside compounds in productively formed compounds. As expected, inflectional suffixes are attached to the head.

29.6 DERIVATION OUTSIDE COMPOUNDING

Compounds may undergo various derivational processes. Nouns, whether compound or simple, may be suffixed by the diminutive suffix *-ka/-ke* or *-(V)cska/-(V)cske*. Consider the diminutive forms of the N+N compounds in (1):

(32)   [*adó+kártyá*]#cska 'small tax card', [*beton+elem*]#ecske 'small concrete slab'

They may also be the input to the adjective forming rule in *-(V)s*:

(33)   [*adó+kártyá*]#s 'with a tax card', [*beton+elem*]#es 'with a concrete slab'

Similar things are true of the A+N compounds, as shown in (34):

(34)   [*kereső+gép*]#ecske 'small search engine', [*fekete+szoftver*]#es 'with black/ illegal software'

More interestingly, verbs, too, can be derived from compounds. Let us take the N+N compound *tök+mag* 'pumpkin seed'. In addition to the diminutive [*tök+mag*]#ocska 'little pumpkin seed' and the adjective [*tök+mag*]#os 'with pumpkin seed' we also have [*tök+mag*]#ozik 'eat pumpkin seed'. Since any verb can be nominalized by the suffix *-ás/-és*, we also get [[*tök+mag*]#oz]#ás 'eating pumpkin seed'. The verb can also take the diminutive suffix -gat, which yields [[tök + mag] #oz] #gat 'eat pumpkin seed now and then' and, once again, this form can be nominalized, etc. Note that the Theme argument is incorporated into the meaning of the verb, consequently no further semantic argument may accompany the nominalized form.

29.7 EXOCENTRIC COMPOUNDS

Bahuvrīhi compounds can be formed with some regularity to denote types of people just as in English and other Germanic languages: *kopasz + fej* 'bald-head', *nagy + orr* 'big-nose', *hosszú + láb* 'long-leg'. Their underlying structure is (35):

(35)   [Det [Adj N-Suffix] EMBER]$_{NP}$

where EMBER means 'man' and the suffix is -*ú*/-*ű*, which is an argument-taking suffix: **fej#ű* 'head-Suff', **orr#ú* 'nose-Suff' are ungrammatical.

29.8 COORDINATIVE COMPOUNDS

Coordinative compounds are two-headed; they occur with verbs only: *ad-vesz* 'give-take', *jön-megy* 'come-go', *üt-ver* 'hit-beat', *eszik-iszik* 'eat-drink'. Both verbs take inflectional suffixes: *ütött#te-ver#te* 'he/she hit and beat him/her', *ev#ett-iv#ott* 'he/she ate and drank'. One of the conditions to get such compounds is that the two verbs must have related meanings. Though this seems to be a necessary condition it is certainly not sufficient. The following forms are unacceptable in spite of the semantic relatedness of the two verbs: **sír-bőg* 'cry-howl', **rohan-szalad* 'run-rush', **szeret-imád* 'love-adore'. Coordinative compounds cannot be formed productively.

29.9 CONCLUSION

In this chapter we started out with an overview of the productive compounding patterns in Hungarian and showed that these patterns all involve the categories N and A. All productive compounds are formed by mere concatenation. What makes Hungarian special are the following features:

   (i) The nonhead of a deverbal compound may satisfy the subject (Actor or Patient) argument of the base.

  (ii) Deverbal nouns derived from particle verbs can only serve as heads in compounds if the particle has a word-formation function, i.e. the semantic contribution of the particle to the base is more than just perfectivization.

 (iii) Agent nouns with institutionalized meaning cannot be formed from perfective/resultative verbs.

It has also been shown that 'bare noun + verb' constructions and particle verbs have a number of features in common with compounds. Hungarian is an agglutinative language with a regular and rich morphology. Regularity is reflected, among others things, by the fact that the only suffix used to derive action nouns is -ás/-és, and the only suffix to derive agent nouns is -ó/-ő. In addition, there are various ways to derive new derivatives from compounds, which testifies to the richness of morphological means in Hungarian.

CHAPTER 30

....

ATHAPASKAN: SLAVE

....

KEREN RICE

COMPOUNDS in the Athapaskan language Slave ([slevi]), also called Dene ([dɛne], a language of northern Canada, have a set of properties that raise interesting analytic challenges. One is perhaps common to many languages, and concerns the definition of a compound, a problem that can be viewed in two ways. First, there are words which are called compounds in the Athapaskan literature based on morphophonological properties and, in some cases, diachronic knowledge, but in which one (or more) of the elements do not occur independently. Second, there are forms that are ambiguous between compounds and phrases. The existence of such words points to the slipperiness of the concept of compound: there are prototypical cases that all would agree are compounds, but there are also non-core cases, one of which might be argued to consist of morphologically simplex words from a lexical perspective and a second that might be treated as phrases rather than words. There is no a priori best way of categorizing such cases.

A second challenge to understanding Slave compounds relates to the phonological patterning of fricative-initial stems as a non-initial element of a compound. Stem-initial fricatives alternate between voiceless and voiced in Slave. The conditions that determine the distribution of voicing are interesting, and complex, and occupy much of this paper.

Many thanks to the editors and to Leslie Saxon for very helpful advice. This work is funded by the Canada Research Chair in Linguistics and Aboriginal Studies held by Keren Rice.

I begin with a discussion of the definition of compound in the Athapaskan literature (section 30.1), and then provide an overview of the lexical categories that enter into compounds in Slave (section 30.2). Following this I examine structural, semantic, and phonological properties of compounds, proposing a division of compounds into three major types that are distinguished in their structures, semantics, and phonologies (sections 30.3 through 30.6).

30.1 WHAT IS A COMPOUND?

How 'compound' is defined is much discussed in the morphology literature. Fabb (1998: 66), for instance, defines compound very generally: 'a word consisting of two or more words'; Crystal (2003: 92) characterizes a compound as 'a linguistic unit which is composed of elements that function independently in other circumstances'. As the term 'compound' is used in the Athapaskan literature, a compound may fail to meet these definitions in two separate ways. First are words that are considered to be compounds where one unit of the compound (or both) is not found as an independent word. In this case, the compound meets the definitions of compound in one way – it is an independent word – but fails to meet them in another way: the pieces need not be words on their own. Second are ambiguities in whether a sequence is best considered a single word – a compound – or a phrase. In this case, the compound meets the definitions in that the units that compose it are words, but challenges the definition in that it is not clear if the compound is a single word or a phrase. I address these issues in this section.

30.1.1 Non-free forms in compounds

In Slave there are words that are identified as compounds where the pieces of the compound are not independent words.

First are compounds where the form that a noun takes differs depending upon whether it is independent or the right-hand member of the compound, as opposed to the left-hand member of a compound. Thus a morpheme may have a special form that is found only as the first element of a compound, called a compound form of the noun in the Athapaskan literature. For instance, in many Slave dialects the word for 'eye', when independent, begins with [d], while as the first member of a compound, it begins with [n] or [r], depending on dialect.[1] Thus the stem of 'eye'

---

[1] I group together what are often called North Slavey and South Slavey as a single language, spelled Slave. I draw examples from different dialects (there are two dialects of North Slavey, Hare and Sahtú), as they are similar in how they pattern with respect to compound formation. Examples come from my

is *da*, the form that occurs when it is possessed or incorporated (body parts seldom occur truly independently), but the compound form is *na* or *ra*. (The underlying form is /na/; the initial /n/ hardens to [d] when the form is the stem; it remains [n] or becomes [r], depending on dialect, when it is in the compound form.) Example (1b), from the Hare dialect, shows the form of this morpheme when it is not in a compound, in this case in the possessive construction, with a possessive noun suffix. (1c) provides a compound with this morpheme as the second element. Finally the forms in (1d) illustrate the compound form of the morpheme, [ra].

(1)   a. lexical entry
        /na/   'eye'

      b. independent form²
        -*dá* 'eye, possessed form'
        da 'eye' +' PNS

      c. right-hand member of compound
        saşǫ́ da   'glasses'
        saşǫ́ 'metal' + *da* 'eye'

      d. left-hand member of compound
        ***ra** tú*   'tears'
        ra 'eye' + *tu* 'water' +' PNS
        ***ra** ta*   'forehead'
        ra 'eye' + *ta* 'above'

A similar phenomenon is found with this morpheme in other Athapaskan languages. For instance, in Witsuwit'en (Hargus 2007: 250), the morpheme for 'eye' is *neɣ*, while the compound form *ne* occurs in -*ne-duts* 'eyebrow' (*ne* 'eye, compound form' + *duts* 'curly').

In addition to compounds with nouns that have special shapes found only as the first element of a compound, Slave compounds can be unusual in a second way: there are nouns that do not occur independently, but are found only in compounds or as an incorporate in a verb. For instance, the compound form *tɛh*- 'water' is the

---

fieldwork (see Rice 1989), dictionaries (Monus and Isaiah, n.d.), and texts. I use standard orthography with two exceptions: where the orthography uses the symbol {e} for a vowel of the quality [ɛ] and the symbol {ə} for a vowel of the quality [e] or [ie], I use the phonetic symbols for these vowels; and I use a raised comma for a glottal stop – the standard orthography uses a glottal stop. Nasalization is indicated by a hook beneath a vowel, and high tone is marked by an acute accent. Note the following symbols: gh = voiced velar fricative; dh = voiced dental fricative; zh = voiced alveopalatal fricative; sh = voiceless alveopalatal fricative; ł = voiceless lateral fricative. Symbols such as d, dz, g represent voiceless unaspirated stops and affricates; t, ts, k, etc. are voiceless aspirated stops and affricates; t', ts', k', etc. are glottalized. Forms are labelled for dialect; dialects differ largely in phonological ways that are not relevant to this particular topic. I write compounds with a space between the elements of the compounds to aid in identification of the pieces. The abbreviation 'PNS' is used for 'possessive noun suffix.'

² Body parts are generally possessed, seldom occurring in a truly independent form. Possession is indicated in the Athapaskan literature by a hyphen preceding a stem.

first element of many compounds (2a, b, c) and an incorporate in a verb (2d), but does not occur independently – the independent form is *tu*.[3]

(2) a. *th zaá*   'polar bear' (all)
         th 'water' + *za* 'bear' + *é* PNS

     b. *th tl'o*   'water grass' (all)
         th 'water' + *tl'o* 'grass'

     c. *tɛh tl'uh* 'ice line' (all)
         tɛh 'water' + *tl'uh* 'rope'

     d. *tɛh-ɛtla* 's/he goes into water' (all)
         tɛh 'water' + *hɛ-tla* 'one goes'

While *tɛh* is not an independent word in Slave, it is in some Athapaskan languages, having the meaning 'under water' (e.g. Witsuwit'en *tɛχ* 'under water' – Hargus 2007: 245).

Another compound form of 'water' exists, *ta*. It is illustrated in subordinate compounds in (3) and in attributive compounds in (4); see section 30.2 for definitions of these terms. Basically, the first member of the compound characterizes the second in subordinate compounds, while the second describes the first in attributive compounds. This form is reconstructed as a prefix, **taʾ:-* 'into water' (Krauss and Leer 1981), yet in the words in (4), it is the semantic head.

(3) SUBORDINATE COMPOUNDS
     a. *ta ghú* 'white cap' (all)
         ta 'water' + *ghu* 'tooth' +' PNS

     b. *ta ché* 'mouth of river' (Sahtú, South Slavey)
         ta 'water' + *ché* 'tail'

(4) ATTRIBUTIVE COMPOUNDS
     a. *ta h ɬo*   'deep water' (all)
         ta 'water' + *h* compound formative + *ɬo* 'much'

     b. *ta dhɛɛ* 'open water' (South Slavey)
         ta 'water' + *dhɛɛ* 'warm, hot'

Words with components that are not found independently and are not identifiable in meaning synchronically are considered to be compounds in the Athapaskan literature as well. For instance, the Slave word *xahfí* 'stovepipe elbow' appears to be a compound composed of two morphemes, *xah* and *fí*. While the meaning of the second can be identified – 'head' – the meaning of the first is not known. Nevertheless, it is classified as a compound based on form: few morphemes in

[3] As discussed later in this chapter, fricatives participate in voicing alternations. I write the fricatives here in the form that they appear in on the surface in the compound in question. See section 30.3 for detailed discussion.

Slave consist of more than one syllable, and consonant clusters occur only at morpheme boundaries. Similarly, in Witswit'en Hargus (2007: 252) treats the word *c'ɛldzin* 'moon, moonlight' as a compound: the second piece, *dzin* 'day', is recognizable while the first, *c'ɛl*, cannot be assigned an independent meaning and does not occur on its own. Further examples are given in (5), some with one piece identifiable in meaning and some with neither piece clearly identifiable.

(5)   a. *tɛh waá*   'mink' (Hare, Sahtú)
         tɛh 'water' + *waá* '?'

      b. *bɛh k'ái*   'seagull' (Hare, Sahtú)
         bɛh '?' + *k'á* '?' + *i* nominalizer

      c. *xah tonɛ*   'stranger' (all)
         xah '?' + *tonɛ* '?'

      d. *dah ghoo* 'gooseberry' (all)
         dah 'above' + *ghoo* 'thorn?'

      e. *dah káa*   'strawberry' (all)
         dah 'above' + *káa* 'be flat?'

The examples discussed above are lexicalized units, similar to cranberry words in English. They are identified as compounds in the literature based on phonological and morphological criteria. In (5d, e) for instance, the first element is an uninflected postposition (see (15) below), and the second, while I cannot identify the meaning, is the head, identifying the compound as a noun. In examples like (5a), semantics suggests a compound: the first noun describes the second. These are not productively formed compounds, but nevertheless they appear to be compounds structurally.

   In the sense that compounds are defined as words that consist of two (or more) units, one or the other or both of which might not occur independently, the Athapaskan use of the term compound differs from that of the general literature. In these cases, it is by and large phonological and morphological criteria that suggest compound status as opposed to single morphemes or affixed forms.

30.1.2 Compounds or phrases?

The definition of compound is slippery in a second way, in that it is sometimes difficult to draw the boundary between a compound word and a phrase. In such cases, meaning is used as a criterion to suggest compound status: an apparently phrasal unit is considered a compound if the meaning is not directly ascertainable from the meaning of the individual elements of which it is composed. Consider, for instance, the form in (6).

(6)   ['ı̨hbé gǫ] ke   'running shoes, sneakers' (Hare, Sahtú)
       'ı̨hbé 'summer' + go pronoun + ghǫ 'for' + ke 'shoes'

The meaning suggests that this unit is lexically formed, since it is not clear that 'shoes for summer' are sneakers. Thus (6) is a compound consisting of a postpositional phrase followed by a noun. The same construction is also used productively, as in (7).

(7)   [déline gots'ɛ] dɛné   'Deline people' (all)
       déline 'Deline (place name)' + go pronoun + ts'ɛ 'from' + dɛnɛ 'person'

Possessive phrases present a similar issue. In many cases a noun followed by a possessed noun can be identified as a compound, lexically formed, based on meaning.

(8)   a.   dlǫ béré   'cheese' (Hare)
            dlǫ 'mouse' + bér 'food' + é PNS

       b.   tsá wé   'fur'
            tsá 'beaver' + wé 'fur'

In these examples, the meaning is not compositional.

However, it is not always clear whether a construction such as those in (8) is better treated as a compound or as generic possession, and phrasal in nature. The examples in (9) show generic possession, or at least are translated as generic possession.

(9)   a.   chı̨a kw'ɛné   'bird's legs' (Sahtú)
            chı̨a 'bird' + kw'ɛn 'bone' + é PNS

       b.   'ɛkwę́ dzáré   'caribou's leg' (Sahtú)
            'ɛkwę́ 'caribou' + dzár 'leg' + é PNS

       c.   'ı̨ts'é ghú   'moose tooth' (Hare, Sahtú)
            'ı̨ts'é 'moose' + ghu 'tooth' + ' PNS

The similarity between these possessed forms and compounds in (8) suggests that one path of development of subordinate compounds is through generic possession.

30.1.3 What is a compound? A summary

The very definition of compound in Slave is faced with challenges. Can a compound contain elements that do not occur independently? Can a word be defined as a compound if one or both of the pieces that make it up cannot be identified as meaningful? The term compound, as used in the Athapaskan literature, includes such forms, based largely on phonological properties. Is there a well-defined way of distinguishing whether an apparently phrasal structure is a phrase or a compound?

Some phrases are treated as compounds in the Athapaskan literature, based on meaning. The existence of forms such as those discussed in this section suggests that, not surprisingly, some compounds develop historically out of phrases, with drifts of meaning, loss of meaning, and reduction of form. The term compound is used more broadly in the Athapaskan literature than in Fabb's and Crystal's definitions, and these different perspectives raise the question of whether it is possible to draw a single line as to what constitutes a compound cross-linguistically, or whether there will inevitably be language-particular factors that enter in to defining this term.

30.2 THE CATEGORIES OF COMPOUNDS

Having clarified the use of the term 'compound' in the Athapaskan literature, I now outline the categories of compounds found in Slave.

Compounds in Slave involve items from several lexical categories, with the majority functioning as nouns. A few examples of Noun + Noun compounds are given in (10).

(10)   [N + N]$_N$ COMPOUNDS
    a. *dlǫ béré*   'cheese' (Hare)
        dlǫ 'mouse' + *bér* 'food' + *é* PNS
    b. *k'ále mįhé* 'spider's web' (South Slavey)
        k'ále 'spider' + *mính* 'net' + *é* PNS
    c. *yú kǫ́ę́*   'store' (all)
        yú 'clothing' + *kǫ́ę́* 'house'
    d. *jíyɛ tú*   'wine, juice' (all)
        jíyɛ 'berry' + *tu* 'water' +' PNS

Either member of a Noun + Noun compound can be desentential, as in (11) and (12); a nominalizer may or may not be present on the desentential element.

(11)   FIRST NOUN DESENTENTIAL
    a. *[mɛ-t'áh*   *ná'ets'ɛnɛlu]*   *tɛn-é*
        3-by means of   unspecified subject sew   container-PNS
        'sewing machine case' [lit. 'one-sews-with-it container'] (South Slavey)
    b. *[dɛshįté*   *bɛ-hé*   *'ɛk' ɛrá'ɛts' ɛrɛhsi]*   *dɛshin-é*
        wood.mat   3-with   unspecified subject wash   stick-PNS
        'mop handle' [lit. 'one-washes-the-floor-with-it stick'] (Hare)

(12) SECOND NOUN DESENTENTIAL
  a. ʾɛk'a [dɛ́k'on-i] 'candle' [lit. 'fat that burns'] (Hare)
     fat   3 burns-NOML

  b. ʾɛdįtl'éh [ɛjįh] 'gramophone' (South Slavey)
     paper   3 sings

The morphology of Noun + Noun compounds is discussed in section 30.3.

Noun compounds consisting of a Noun followed by a Postposition are also found.

(13) [N + Postposition]ₙ
  a. dɛshį ta   'bush' (Hare)
     dɛshį 'wood' + ta 'among'

  b. tu mbah   'shore' (South Slavey)[4]
     tu 'water' + mbah 'along'

  c. nɛ yíi   'mine' (Sahtú)
     nɛ 'ground' + yíi 'in'

  d. xéh ts'ę́   'evening' [note xéh not used independently] (all)
     xéh 'evening' + ts'ę́ 'to'

  e. xah wɛrɛ   'leader' (Hare, Sahtú)
     xah '?' + wɛrɛ 'before'

  f. tu gá   'white line on water' (Hare)
     tu 'water' + gá 'along'

  g. lu k' ę́   'spring' (Hare)
     lu 'ice' + k'é 'after'

  h. k'oh shį   'nape' (Hare)
     k'oh 'neck' + shį 'underneath, at bottom of'

  i. ghǫ́ yíi   'nostril' (all)
     ghǫ́ 'nose' + yíi 'in'

While the compounds in (10)–(12) are right-headed, those in (13) are left-headed; the same is true of the compounds in (14) below.

Noun compounds composed of a noun followed by an uninflected verb form exist. I call the second element of these compounds a verb stem, abbreviated as 'Stem'. They do not appear independently: in a verb, pre-stem inflectional material is required. Examples are given in (14); see section 30.4.

(14) [N + Stem]ₙ
  a. tɬ'o tsę   'onion' (Sahtú, South Slavey)
     tɬ'o 'grass' tsę 'smell'

---

[4] This example is perhaps a N + N compound, as the second component, mbah, can also be translated as 'edge'. Further work on the use of this morpheme is required to sort out whether it is a noun or a postposition.

b. *fí 'alɛ*   'pillow' (Hare)
  fí 'head' + *'al* 'handle 3 dimensional object' + *ɛ* suffix

c. *łɛ́h t'ɛ́h*   'bread' (Sahtú, South Slavey)
  łɛ́h 'flour' + *t'ɛ́h* 'cook, burnt'

d. *dlǫ da solɛ*   'shrew' (Hare)
  dlǫ 'mouse' + *da* 'chin' + *solɛ* 'be pointed'

Postposition + Noun compounds also occur, forming nouns. The most common are formed with the postposition *dah* 'above, upon'.

(15) [Postposition + N]$_N$
  a. *dah kǫ́ę́*   'attic' (all)
    dah 'above' + *kǫ́ę́* 'house'

  b. *dah nɛ́nɛ́* 'plateau' (all)
    dah 'above' + *nɛn* 'land' + *ɛ́* PNS

  c. *dah t'oo*   'stage, platform' (all)
    dah 'above' + *t'oo* 'nest'

  d. *dah yah*   'snow on trees' (all)
    dah 'above' + *yah* 'snow'

In the examples in (15), the postposition is uninflected. In other cases the postposition is inflected; the examples in (16) occur with the pronominal *go*, called an areal pronoun or a space-time prefix in the Athapaskan literature. This prefix indicates that the object in question occupies space or time.

(16) [Pronoun + Postposition + N]$_N$
  a. *[got'áh] yú* 'underwear' (all)
    go pronoun + *t'áh* 'inside of small area' + *yú* 'clothing'

  b. *[gok'ɛrí] 'e* 'jacket' (Hare)
    go pronoun + *k'ɛrí* 'inside of' + *'e* 'clothing'

  c. *[got'áh] ke* 'socks' (South Slavey)
    go pronoun + *t'áh* 'inside of small area' + *ke* 'shoe'

There are compounds with a postpositional phrase as first member.

(17) [[Postpositional Phrase] + N]$_N$
  a. *[tu gǫ] ke*   'waders' (Hare)
    tu 'water' + *go* pronoun + *ghǫ* 'for' + *ke* 'shoe'

  b. *[tu gǫ] tɛnɛ*   'water pail' (Hare)
    tu 'water' + *go* pronoun + *ghǫ* 'for' + *tɛnɛ* 'container'

  c. *[bɛshuts'įhtį gǫ] ts'ɛ́rɛ́* 'sleeping bag' (Hare)
    bɛshuts'įhtį 'one sleeps' + *go* pronoun + *ghǫ* 'for' + *ts'ɛ́rɛ́* 'blanket'

  d. *['įhbɛ́ gǫ] ke*   'running shoes, sneakers' (Hare)
    'įhbɛ́ 'summer' + *go* pronoun + *ghǫ* 'for' + *ke* 'shoe'

e. *[mɛhchį́ gha] tlɛh*   'gasoline' (South Slavey)
   mɛhchį́ 'sled' + *gha* 'for' + *tlɛh* 'oil'

While these are phrasal in the sense that they involve a postpositional phrase, their meaning suggests compound status, as discussed in section 30.1.2.

Compounds can enter into further compounds, as in (18).

(18) a. *[xa tɛnɛ] tl'ulɛ́*   'basket handle' (all)
         xa 'root' + *tɛnɛ* 'container' + *tl'ul* 'rope' + *ɛ́* PNS

      b. *[gah wɛ́h] [tl'á 'e]*   'rabbit skin pants' (Hare, Sahtú)
         gah 'rabbit' + *wɛ́h* 'skin' + *tl'á* 'bottom' + *'e* 'clothing'

      c. *[k'áy t'uɛ́] mį́*   'willow-bark net' (all)
         k'áy 'willow' + *t'uɛ́* 'bark' + *mį́* 'net'

The compounds discussed so far are nouns. There are also compound postpositions, although such compounding appears to be lexically frozen and meanings are not always transparent.

(19) [Postposition + Postposition]_P
      a. *ts'ɛ́ts'ɛ*   'against' (all) (Rice 1989: 310)
         ts'ɛ́ 'to' + *ts'ɛ* 'from'

      b. *ts'ɛ 'ónɛ́*   comparative (i.e. 'X-er than') (all) (Rice 1989: 310)
         ts'ɛ 'from' + *'ónɛ́* 'beyond'

To summarize, the following compound types occur in Slave:

(20) NOUN   POSTPOSITION
      N + N   P + P
      N + Stem
      N + Postposition
      Postposition(P) + N

While compounds are usually right-headed, N + Stem and N + Postposition compounds are left-headed.

In the remainder of the discussion, I focus on noun compounds, and Noun + Noun and Noun + Stem compounds particularly, examining the internal morphology, semantics, and phonology of such compounds. See Rice (1989) for details.

30.3 CLASSES OF NOUN + NOUN COMPOUNDS

Noun + Noun compounds in Slave divide into two major types, as discussed in Rice (1989). First are what I will call subordinate compounds; I call these type 1 compounds in Rice (1989). In these compounds the first member of the compound is, in some way, subordinate to the second: the first noun represents a characteristic of the second – the particular relation might be one of possession or ownership, of modification, of association with a particular property, or of use for. Second are what I will dub 'composed of' compounds, labelled type 2 compounds in Rice (1989). In these compounds, the second member is composed of the first member. A few examples of each type are given in (21).

(21)   a. SUBORDINATE
           da tlɛh   'soap' (face + lard)
           nę 'ɛdɛhtl'ɛ́hɛ́   'map' (land + paper + PNS)

       b. 'composed of'
           dɛchį łuh   'wooden spoon' (wood + spoon)
           satsǫ́ tɛnɛ   'tin can' (metal + container)

Subordinate and 'composed of' compounds differ in the semantic relationship between the pieces, and structural and phonological differences between the compound types are found. A third compound type, attributive compound, composed of a noun followed by a stem, is discussed in section 30.4.

I begin with a study of 'composed of' compounds.

30.3.1 'Composed of' compounds

'Composed of' compounds consist of two (or more) elements that enter into a particular semantic relationship with one another where the object in question has properties of both nouns: these compounds can be paraphrased as 'N2 made of N1.' A number of examples are given in (22).

(22)   a. *kwe gohkwį*   'stone axe' (Sahtú)
           kwe 'stone' + *gohkwį* 'axe'

       b. *naya ts'ah*   'toque' (Sahtú)
           naya 'wool' + *ts'ah* 'hat'

       c. *xa tɛnɛ*   'basket' (all)
           xa 'root' + *tɛnɛ* 'container'

       d. *tthe shíh*   'rock mountain' (South Slavey)
           tthe 'stone' + *shíh* 'mountain'

       e. *gohtl'ɛ́h ndu*   'mud bar' (South Slavey)
           gohtl'ɛ́h 'mud' + *ndu* 'island'

       f. *lálɛníh 'e*   'sweater' (Hare)
           lálɛní 'wool' + *h* + compound formative[5] + *'e* 'clothing, shirt'

[5] The use of the compound formative *h*, as in this example, is another interesting problem in Slave; I do not pursue this here. See Rice (1989) for further examples.

g. *'ɛdhɛ́h thɛ*   'hide belt' (South Slavey)
   'ɛ unspecified possessor + *dhɛ́h* 'hide' + *thɛ* 'belt'

h. *dɛghoni tl'á'e*   'caribou skin pants' (Hare)
   dɛghoni + 'caribou' + *tl'á* 'bottom' + *'e* 'clothing'

i. *satsǫ́ xoo*   'metal snare' (Sahtú, South Slavey)
   satsǫ́ 'metal' + *xoo* 'snare'

j. *dɛchįká 'ɛlá*   'scow' (all)
   dɛchį 'wood' + *ká* 'flat' + *'ɛlá* 'boat'

k. *golǫ dhɛ́h nimbáa*   'moosehide tent' (South Slavey)
   golǫ 'moose' + *dhɛ́h* 'skin' + *nimbáa* 'tent'

In (22k), *golǫ dhɛ́h* 'moosehide' is a subordinate compound; it forms a 'composed of' compound with *nimbáa* 'tent.'

I propose that nominal 'composed of' compounds have the structure in (23).

(23)   N
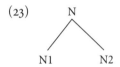
   N1   N2

The order of the nouns is fixed, with N1 describing what N2 is composed of.

The structure in (23) is based on morphological and phonological evidence. Morphologically each member of a 'composed of' compound can stand as a noun on its own, without additional morphological trappings. Phonologically these compounds are distinct from subordinate compounds, discussed below. I present the phonological evidence here, although its significance will become apparent only when subordinate compounds are considered.

In Slave, fricatives participate in voicing alternations. Simplifying, alternating fricatives are voiceless word-initially, and voiced when something precedes (I modify this statement later); there are also non-alternating voiced fricatives. In 'composed of' compounds, an initial fricative of N2 is voiceless, as (21b) and (22d, g, i) illustrate. The initial fricatives of these morphemes are subject to voicing: they voice when the morpheme occurs in the possessive construction, for instance, as in (24). Note that laterals are considered to be fricatives in the Athapaskan literature since they participate in voicing alternations.

(24) [ɬ]*uh*   'spoon'   -[l]*uhɛ́*   'spoon, possessed form' (South Slavey)
      [x]*óo*   'snare'   -[gh]*óó*   'snare, possessed form' (all)
      [sh]*íh* 'mountain'   -[y]*íhɛ́* 'mountain, possessed form' (South Slavey)
      [th]*ɛ*   'belt'   -[dh]*ɛɛ́* 'belt, possessed form' (South Slavey)

The failure of fricative voicing to affect the initial element of the second member of a 'composed of' compound is, I suggest, attributable to the structure of the

compound. While voicing of fricatives affects stem-initial consonants when the stem
is preceded by morphological material, conditions for voicing are more stringent:
the fricative voices only when the fricative-initial element and the preceding lexical
material stand in a non-symmetric relationship with one another, as discussed in
sections 30.4 and 30.5 below. The structure in (23) thus does not present the
appropriate environment for fricative voicing, as the relationship is symmetrical.

In phrasal structures involving two noun stems as well, if one noun directly
follows another, no voicing of an initial fricative of a non-initial noun is found, as
seen by the failure of the initial /s/ to voice in the word *sah* 'bear' in (25).

(25) *tsá*   *tɛhk'ái*   *sah/*zah*   *hɛ́*
      beaver   muskrat   bear   and
      'beaver and muskrat and bears' (Sahtú)

In the phrasal possessive construction, on the other hand, a stem-initial fricative of
the possessed noun is voiced, as in (26), where in (26a) the initial /tl/ is historically
*ɬ, and thus the voiced form in the possessive is not unexpected.

(26) a. *Charlie* *lįɛ́*   'Charlie's dogs' (all)
          tlį   'dog'
      b. *t'ɛrɛ*   *dhɛɛ́* 'the girl's belt' (South Slavey)
          thɛ   'belt'

Characteristics of 'composed of' noun compounds are summarized in (27).

(27) CHARACTERISTICS OF 'composed of' COMPOUNDS
     Structure: [[N1] [N2]] ₙ
     Semantics: N has properties of both N1 and N2; specifically, N2 made of N1
     Phonology: N1 and N2 pattern as independent words

30.3.2 Subordinate compounds

Subordinate compounds in Slave are more complex than 'composed of' compounds. As noted above, subordinate compounds evince a wider range of meanings than do 'composed of' compounds and differ in structural and phonological
terms as well. While I call all compounds discussed in this section subordinate
compounds, there are subclasses within this group.

I begin the presentation of subordinate compounds around meanings, following
Rice (1989), and then examine their structural and phonological aspects.

In subordinate compounds, the first noun in some way characterizes the second
noun. Subordinate compounds divide into two classes morphologically: those
with a suffix on the second noun, called the possessive noun suffix (PNS) in the
Athapaskan literature, and those without it. This suffix has two forms – one, -ɛ́, is
associated very generally with alienable possession and the other, high tone, with

inalienable possession. While these suffixes are often called possessive noun suffixes, this name provides only a very general guideline to their usage (see Rice 1989: 215, Wilhelm and Saxon 2007 for discussion). As discussed in Rice (1989), the suffix indicates a relationship between components that is broader than possession in its strictest sense. The possessive noun suffix demands that an argument in addition to the head be present, either lexically, as in a compound, or syntactically, as in the possessive and some other constructions.

In subordinate compounds the second noun may belong to, be used by, used for, associated with, or consist of the first noun. The various usages are elaborated below.

The examples in (28) illustrate the relationship that N2 belongs to or is associated with N1. The first noun can occur independently, and the second noun has the possessive noun suffix.

(28) 'belong to, associated with'
    a. *k'alɛ mįhé*   'spider's web' (South Slavey)
        k'alɛ 'spider' + *mính* 'net' + *-é* PNS

    b. *'idi kónɛ́*   'lightning' (Hare)
        'idi 'thunder' + *kón* 'fire' + *-é* PNS

    c. *ts'uh dzégé*   'spruce gum' (Hare)
        ts'uh 'spruce' + *dzég* 'gum' + *-é* PNS

    d. *tsá dhɛ́h*   'fur' (South Slavey)
        tsá 'beaver' + *thɛh* 'fur' +' PNS

    e. *ts'ét'uri fé*   'pipe' (Hare)
        ts'ét'uri 'tobacco' + *fe* 'stone' +' PNS

    f. *tsáwé dɛchiné* 'stretcher for furs' (Sahtú)
        tsáwé 'fur' + *dɛchin* 'stick' + *-é* PNS

    g. *'ɛhdzoi bɛ́ré*   'bait for trap' (Hare)
        'ɛhdzoi 'trap' + *bɛ́r* 'food' + *-é* PNS

    h. *nɛ 'ɛdɛhtl'éhé* 'map' (South Slavey)
        nɛ 'land' + *'ɛdɛhtl'éh* 'paper' + *-é* PNS

    i. *'ɛráke ké*   'mukluk' (Hare)
        'ɛráke 'Inuit' + *ke* 'shoe' +' PNS

    j. *'ɛnáke 'é*   'parka' (Sahtú, South Slavey)
        'ɛnáke 'Inuit' + *'e* 'clothing' +' PNS

    k. *ts'éku 'é*   'dress' (all)
        ts'éku 'woman' + *'e* 'clothing' +' PNS

    l. *tl'éhzɛ́lé*   'trigger' (all)
        tl'éh 'flint' + *sɛ́l* 'hook' + *-é* PNS

    m. *'ah chonɛ́*   'fog' (Sahtú, South Slavey)
        'ah 'fog' + *chon* 'rain' + *ɛ́* PNS

> n. *nahtɛnɛ kónɛ́* 'electricity' (South Slavey)
> *nahtɛnɛ* 'thunder' + *kón* 'fire' + *ɛ́* PNS

Subordinate compounds can have the meaning that the second noun is associated with the first, or has the property of the first. The examples in (29) involve second nouns with the possessive noun suffix.

(29) 'associated with, having the property of'

> a. *[ɬɛts'ɛgǫ] dɛnɛ́*   'soldier' (Sahtú)
>   *ɬɛts'ɛgǫ* 'war' (deverbal: literally 'one fights') + *dɛn* 'person' + *ɛ́* PNS

> b. *['ik'ǫ́] dɛnɛ́*   'medicine man, shaman' (all)
>   *'ik'ǫ́* 'medicine' + *dɛn* 'person' + *ɛ́* PNS

The subordinate compound construction is found with compounds with the meaning 'N2 used by or for N1', as in (30) and (31).

(30) 'used by or for'

> a. *'ah tl'ulɛ́*   'babiche' (all)
>   *'ah* 'snowshoe' + *tl'ul* 'string' + *ɛ́* PNS

> b. *kw'ih wɛ́*   'mosquito net' (Sahtú)
>   *kw'ih* 'mosquito' + *wɛ* 'skin' +' PNS

> c. *chǫ ts'árɛ́*   'rain hat' (South Slavey)
>   *chǫ* 'rain' + *ts'ár* 'hat' + *ɛ́* PNS

(31) a. *mí kwe*   'sinker for net' (Sahtú)
>   *mí* 'net' + *kwe* 'rock'

> b. *lidí tɛnɛ*   'pot for tea' (all)
>   *lidí* 'tea' + *tɛnɛ* 'container'

> c. *tl'o mbɛh*   'scythe' (South Slavey)
>   *tl'o* 'grass' + *mbɛh* 'knife'

The second noun may or may not appear in suffixed form: in (30) the suffix is present, while in (31) it is not. Rice (1989: 187–8) suggests that when the suffix occurs, the relationship between the nouns of the compound represents a type of inalienable possession, with N2 being an integral part of N1, while in the absence of the suffix, the relationship is alienable, with N2 used for but not an integral part of N1. Alternatively, the compounds might simply be lexically listed with or without a suffix, as suggested by Wilhelm and Saxon (2007).

The subordinate compound construction is also used with the meaning 'N2 consisting of or made with N1':

(32) a. *jíyɛ tú*   'wine, juice' (all)
>   *jíyɛ* 'berry' + *tu* 'water' +' PNS

b. *k'į tué*   'syrup' (all)
    k'į 'birch' + *tu* 'water' + *é* PNS

(33) *'εhts'oi ke* 'beaded slippers' (all)
    'εhts'oi 'bead' + *ke* 'shoe'

These differ from 'composed of' compounds: beaded slippers, for instance, are not shoes made of beads, but rather shoes decorated with beads; wine is not water made of berries, but rather liquid from berries, and so on. The examples in (32) have a suffixed N2, while those in (33) have an unsuffixed N2. Rice (1989: 188) points to a difference in alienability, with the second noun in a non-possessed form when the relationship is not integral.

Subordinate compounds thus encompass a range of meanings. The second member may be suffixed or not – with a suffix, there is generally an intimate relationship between the elements of the compound that is missing when there is not a suffix present.

In terms of phonology, subordinate compounds share properties with the possessive construction and postpositional phrases. In the possessive construction, a fricative-initial stem differs phonologically from the form in isolation: an initial fricative of the possessed item is voiced. This is illustrated in (26); additional examples are given in (34).

(34) a. *shį*   'song'
    gah yíné 'rabbit's song' (Sahtú, South Slavey)
    gah 'rabbit' + *yin* 'song, possessed form' + *-é* PNS

   b. *sa*   'month, sun'
    -zaá   'month, sun, possessed form' (all)
    za 'month, sun, possessed form' + *-é* PNS

   c. *łε*   'smoke'
    go-łεré 'its smoke' (e.g. from fire) (Sahtú)
    go 'areal' + *łεr* 'smoke, possessed form' + *-é* PNS

Several of the compounds in (28) through (33) have a fricative-initial stem as the second noun. Note that in these cases, the fricative is consistently voiced. Some examples are repeated in (35); the focus here is on the fricative and complete morphological breakdowns are not given.

(35) a. *tsá **dhéh***   'fur'
    tsá 'beaver' + *dhéh* 'fur, possessed form'

   b. *tl'εh zélé*   'trigger'
    tl'εh 'flint' *zél* 'hook, possessed form' + *-é* PNS

Similarly, in a postpositional construction, an initial fricative of the postposition is voiced.

(36)   -ghá   'for; near, nearby' (all)
       -dhene 'around' (South Slavey)
       -dhee   'ahead of, before' (South Slavey)

The phonology of subordinate compounds suggests a structural resemblance to possessive and postpositional constructions. The postpositional construction takes a postposition as its head: an initial fricative of the head undergoes voicing. The possessive construction has been treated in different ways in the Athapaskan literature. (Note that there are differences between alienable and inalienable possession that I abstract away from here; see Rice 2003 and Wilhelm and Saxon 2007 for discussion.) One possible structure is given in (37), from Wilhelm and Saxon (2007).

(37)

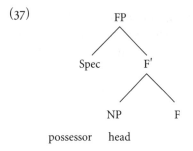

The possessor is a specifier, while the possessed noun is a head; 'F' represents a functional projection that is realized morphologically as the possessive noun suffix.

Important to this discussion is the relationship of the head noun to what precedes it. In the possessive construction, the head follows a non-head. In this configuration, a stem-initial fricative is voiced, unlike in the 'composed of' configuration. 'Composed of' and subordinate compounds differ in their morphological structures, and these structural differences are reflected in the phonology through voicing alternations.

Subordinate compounds bear a resemblance to the possessive construction and the postpositional construction in their phonology – all involve voicing of an initial fricative of the second noun. Subordinate compounds in which the relationship between the two nouns is one of inalienability or where one noun is an integral part of the whole are also similar to the possessive construction in their morphology – the compounds, like the construction, occur with the possessive noun suffix. Voicing affects a head, triggered by a non-head. Characteristics of subordinate compounds are summarized in (38).

(38)   CHARACTERISTICS OF SUBORDINATE COMPOUNDS
       Structure: [N1 [N2]] N
       Semantics: N1 characterizes N2 in some way
       Phonology: N2 patterns as a head and N1 as a dependent

30.4 ATTRIBUTIVE COMPOUNDS

A third class of noun compounds occurs in Slave: attributive compounds. These are composed of a noun followed by a stem, and, as discussed earlier, are left-headed, with the right-hand member characterizing the left-hand member. Examples are given in (39).

(39) a. *tl'o tsę*   'onion' (Sahtú, South Slavey)
         tl'o 'grass' + *tsę* 'smell'

   b. *łéh t'éh*   'bread' (Sahtú, South Slavey)
         łéh 'flour' + *t'éh* 'cooked'

   c. *'ɛk'a k'ǫ*   'candle' (South Slavey)
         'ɛk'a 'fat' + *k'ǫ* 'burn'

   d. *tu dhɛɛ*   'soup' (South Slavey)
         tu 'water' + *dhɛɛ* 'warm'

   e. *dlǫ da solɛ* 'shrew' (Hare)
         dlǫ 'mouse' + *da* 'face, chin' + *solɛ* 'pointed'

   f. *da t'éh*   'brant' (species of goose) (all)
         da 'beak' + *t'éh* 'burnt, cooked'

   g. *daɛtị lú*   'large round needle' (Hare)
         daɛtị 'needle' + *lú* 'round'

   h. *libó ghínɛ*   'bowl' (all)
         libó 'cup' + *ghínɛ* 'round'

   i. *ke ch'ịlɛ*   'high heel shoes' (all)
         ke 'shoe' + *ch'ịlɛ* 'pointed'

   j. *tl'uh gǫ*   'babiche' (all)
         tl'uh 'string' + *gǫ* 'dry'

   k. *'ɛtthę́ gǫ*   'dry meat' (South Slavey)
         'ɛtthę́ 'meat' + *gǫ* 'dry'

These compounds have a noun as their first element. The second element is called a qualifier in Rice (1989); in San Carlos Apache de Reuse (2006: 288–90) identifies cognate elements as 'Noun plus Adjectival Verb Stem' compounds, where the adjectival verb stem modifies the noun. In attributive compounds, the second element modifies the first. Attributive compounds are nouns, with the left-hand element functioning as the head. The second element, when inflected for aspect and person, is a verb stem, although it is uninflected in compounds.

In terms of phonology, the second member, when fricative-initial, begins with a voiced fricative. Based on the analysis of the environment for fricative voicing proposed so far, this might suggest that the second member is the head of the compound and the first member a non-head. If so, there is a mismatch between heads from the perspective of phonology (right-hand head) and heads from the perspective of meaning (left-hand head). Alternatively, the statement of the environment for voicing in section 30.3.1 might require revision: voicing affects the second member of the compound when the relationship between the units in the compound is not symmetrical, independent of the way the asymmetry goes. If these compounds have a structure along the lines of (40), where the second element modifies the first, then this reworking of the environment for fricative voicing is appropriate.

(40)   [[N] Stem]

The stem modifies the noun, parallel to the way one noun modifies another in subordinate compounds; the difference between the compound types concerns the position of the head.

Properties of attributive compounds are summarized in (41).

(41)   CHARACTERISTICS OF ATTRIBUTIVE COMPOUNDS
        Structure: [[N1] Stem] $_N$
        Semantics: Stem identifies an attribute of N1
        Phonology: Stem is affected by fricative voicing

30.5 MORE ON FRICATIVE VOICING

As we have seen, fricative voicing affects a stem-initial fricative in the second member of a compound when one characterizes or modifies the other and the meaning relationship is not 'composed of'. There is another condition on fricative voicing, one that can be observed when compounds are possessed.

Recall that in the possessive construction, an initial fricative of the possessed noun is voiced (26). When a fricative-initial compound is possessed, the fricative generally is voiceless, independent of compound type, as illustrated in (42a), (43a), (44a), while the noun on its own is affected by voicing when it is possessed, as shown in the (b) forms below.

(42) 'composed of' COMPOUND
    a. *xa tɛnɛ*   'basket'
       -xa tɛné 'basket, possessed form'
       xa 'root' + *tɛnɛ* 'container'
    b. *-ghá*   'root, possessed form'

(43) SUBORDINATE COMPOUND
    a. *sadzéé*   'watch, clock'
       -sadzéé 'watch, clock, possessed form'
       sa 'sun, month' + *dzé* 'heart' + *é* PNS
    b. *-zaá*   'sun, month, possessed form'

(44) ATTRIBUTIVE COMPOUND
    a. *ɬéhtʼéh*   'bread'
       -ɬéhtʼéhé 'bread, possessed form'
       ɬéh 'flour' + *tʼéh* 'cooked, burnt'
    b. *-lézé*   'flour, possessed form'

The failure of voicing in these forms suggests the need for an additional condition on fricative voicing. In order to determine this condition, further examples where fricatives fail to voice where voicing might be expected require consideration.

(45) a. [s]*úhga*   'sugar' (all)
       -[s]*úhgá*   'sugar, possessed form'
    b. [th]*átsʼɛhʼoni*   'chewing tobacco' (South Slavey)
       thá 'mouth' + *tsʼɛhʼon* 'one keeps default object' + *i* nominalizer
       -[th]*átsʼɛhʼoné*   'chewing tobacco, possessed form'
    c. [s]*ótsʼɛdéya*   'necklace' (all)
       só 'around' + *tsʼɛdéya* 'one places string-like object'
       -[s]*ótsʼɛdéyaé*   'necklace, possessed form'

In both long monomorphemic items (45a) and in polymorphemic deverbal nouns (45b, c), a voiceless fricative occurs in the possessed form. In Rice (1988) I propose a structural analysis for the failure of voicing in these forms, suggesting, essentially, that default values fill in cyclically. Two alternative hypotheses are available. First, there could be a prosodic condition on voicing, such that long words – basically, words of two or more syllables (not counting suffixes) – are not subject to voicing. Second, given that morphemes in general are monosyllabic in Slave, it is possible that a word such as *súhga* 'sugar' is treated as if it were morphologically complex, and voicing alternations are possible only with morphologically simplex forms. In both cases complexity is appealed to – prosodic in one case and morphological in the other; I do not have evidence that provides a way to decide between these alternatives.

30.6 ADDITIONAL CHALLENGES
FOR VOICING ALTERNATIONS

In this section I consider some exceptions to the generalizations about voicing alternations of fricatives. While generally the first member of a compound begins with a voiceless fricative when possessed, as discussed in section 30.5, sometimes an initial fricative of the first member is voiced. Examples are given in (46).

(46)   a. *-ghu kwę́*   'gums' (Sahtú)
          ghu 'tooth' + ' PNS + *kwę́* 'flesh'
          cf. *lɛ-xu-déhk'a*   's/he grinds teeth' (Hare)
          xu 'tooth (incorporated form)'

      b. *-ghǫ́ kw'ɛ́nɛ́*   'nose ridge' (Sahtú)
          ghǫ́ 'nose' + *kw'ɛ́n* 'bone' + *ɛ́* PNS

In Rice (1989) I suggest that these possessed compounds have a different structure from the subordinate compounds discussed earlier, namely [Possessor [Noun] [Noun]], while subordinate compounds have the structure [Possessor [Noun [Noun]]]. The proposed structure for nouns such as those in (46) is indicated both by the voicing and by the presence of the possessive noun suffix on the first noun, when the phonology and morphology of that noun is such that the presence of this suffix can be detected. The reasons why these compounds would differ in structure from the others are not clear.

While the examples in (46) involve body parts, there are other cases where a voiced fricative occurs, unexpectedly, where the noun is not a body part; I mention these for completeness. (47a) and (48a) give nouns and possessed forms; (47b) and (48b) are compounds with the nouns in (47a) and (48a) as first member, and (47c) and (48c) are possessed forms of the compounds. The first noun is affected by voicing in the compound.

(47)   a. *tlį*   'dog' (Sahtú, South Slavey)
          -lįé   'dog, possessed form'

      b. *tlį kǫ́ę́* 'dog house' (Sahtú, South Slavey)
          tlį 'dog' + *kǫ́ę́* 'house'

      c. *-lį kǫ́ę́* 'dog house, possessed form'

(48)   a. *łu*   'ice' (Sahtú)
          -luré   'ice, possessed form'

      b. *łu kǫ́ę́*   'ice house' (Sahtú)

      c. *-lu kǫ́ę́* 'ice house, possessed form' (Sahtú)

These compounds involve the noun 'house' as second element. An initial fricative of the first noun is voiced when the compound is possessed; these differ from the compounds in (46) in that the first noun does not have the possessive noun suffix, although this suffix occurs with the noun when it is possessed. These compounds suggest that the facts are more complex than presented so far, and additional work towards understanding of the full range of compound structures is required. They perhaps also suggest that a full understanding of compounds lies not only in synchrony, but also in diachrony. While compounding is productive and much is predictable, compounds also exhibit unpredictable properties in terms of phonology and semantics both, indicating that at least some lexical specification is required.

30.7 CONCLUSION

Three major types of nominal compounds exist in Slave – 'composed of' compounds, subordinate compounds, and attributive compounds – with semantic, structural, and phonological criteria that define and differentiate them. 'Composed of' compounds involve two elements both of which have properties of a head; these pattern as separate and distinct words phonologically. Subordinate compounds encompass a range of meanings in which the first noun in some way characterizes the second; the second noun is the head. Attributive compounds are composed of a noun followed by a stem; in these the second element presents an attribute of the first. If voiced fricatives are analysed as being found when the second element is a head and the first element is not, then attributive compounds present a mismatch between phonology and morphology in that the second noun appears to be a head from the perspective of the phonology, but a modifier from the perspective of the morphology; the first noun appears to be the head from the perspective of morphology but not from the perspective of phonology. Alternatively, the voiced fricative might begin the second element when one of the members of the compound is a head and the other a non-head, regardless of the ordering of these two elements. The environment of voicing alternations for fricatives thus presents a major issue in Slave.

CHAPTER 31

IROQUOIAN: MOHAWK

MARIANNE MITHUN

MOHAWK is a language of the Iroquoian family of northeastern North America, spoken in Quebec, Ontario, and New York State. Like other Iroquoian languages, it is polysynthetic: words, particularly verbs, can consist of many meaningful parts (morphemes). Often what is said in a single verb in Mohawk would be expressed in a multi-word sentence in other languages such as English. This fundamental difference in grammatical structure raises interesting questions about the boundaries between morphology and syntax. Perhaps the most intriguing involve a robust kind of noun + verb compounding called noun incorporation.

31.1 MOHAWK WORDS

Because Mohawk has such elaborate morphology, words are usually classified according to their internal morphological structure. Words fall into three clear morphological types: particles, nouns, and verbs.

31.1.1 Particles

By definition, particles have no internal structure, apart from some formed by compounding. Particles serve a wide variety of syntactic and discourse functions, among them various kinds of adverbials (*á:re* 'again', *átste* 'outside', *ó:nen* 'at this time'), pronominals (*ì:'i* 'I myself, me, we ourselves, us', *ónhka* 'someone, who'), qualifiers and quantifiers (*akwáh* 'quite, just, very', *é:so* 'much, many', *áhsen* 'three'), grammatical markers (*iáh* 'no, not', *kén* interrogative), conjunctions (*káton* 'or', *tánon* 'and', *tsi* 'as, how, while'), and other expressions (*hánio* 'Come on, let's', *ió:* 'you're welcome', *kóh* 'Here!' [offering something], *kwé:* 'hi'). Some words that are used as nominals syntactically are particles, that is, they have no internal morphological structure, such as *takò:s* 'cat' (from Dutch *de poes*), and *rasós* 'gravy' (from French *la sauce*).

Some particles can be seen to be shortened forms of verbs. The particle *wá:s* 'Go away!' is from an old verb *wá:se* (*wa-s-e* TLOC 'away'-2SG.IMP.AGT-go). In this form the original verb root -*e*- has completely disappeared.

A number of particles are actually compound forms. The tag *kwi'* is a shortened form of two particles, *ki'* 'just' and the tag *wáhi'* 'isn't it'. Both the full and contracted forms are in current use. The proximal demonstrative *kí:ken* 'this' was formed from the combination *ken* 'here' and the verb *í:ken* 'it is'. The long form is now heard only in one community. The shorter form is often further reduced phonologically to *kí:* and even *ki*. Its distal counterpart shows a parallel history: *tho í:ken* ('there it.is') > *thí:ken* > *thí:* > *thi*. The compound particles are not the result of the kind of word-formation process we usually classify as prototypical compounding. No speaker decided to create a new particle by combining two old particles. They are, rather, the descendants of frequent collocations, which have, over time, come to be thought of as single units.

31.1.2 Nouns

Basic Mohawk nouns have clear morphological structure. They consist of a gender prefix, a noun stem, and a noun suffix. The stem may be a simple monomorphemic root, like -*kar*- 'story' in (1), or derived from a verb, like -*wisto-hser*- 'butter' in (3).[1]

(1) BASIC NOUNS
    a. *oká:ra'*   b. *okónhsa'*
        o-kar-a'   o-konhs-a'
        NEUT-story-NSUFF   NEUT-face-NSUFF
        'story'   'face'

---

[1] Examples are given in the community orthography. It is essentially phonemic. Most of the symbols represent sounds close to their IPA values. In addition, the digraphs *en* and *on* represent nasalized vowels: a nasalized caret and nasalized high back vowel [ʌ] and [u] respectively. *i* represents a palatal glide before vowels, the apostrophe ' represents glottal stop, and the colon : represents vowel length. An acute accent over vowels (*á*) represents high or rising tone on a stressed syllable, and a grave accent (*à*) a tone that rises higher then descends steeply on a stressed syllable.

Possession can be indicated by a possessive prefix in place of the gender prefix.
Alienable and inalienable possession are distinguished by the prefix paradigms.

(2) POSSESSED NOUNS
     a. *akká:raʼ*   b. *kkonhsà:ke*
        ak-kar-aʼ   k-konhs-aʼ-ke
        1SG.AL-story-NSUFF   1SG.INAL-face-NSUFF-place
        'my story'   'my face'

An example of a complex noun stem is in (3). The stem for 'butter' was derived
from the verb root -*wisto*- 'be cold' plus the nominalizer -*hser*-.

(3) DERIVED NOUN STEM
     owistóhseraʼ
     o-wisto-hser-aʼ
     NEUT-be.cold-NOML-NSUFF
     'cold one' = 'butter'

    Morphological nouns serve as referring expressions and syntactic arguments. For
various reasons they are much less frequent in speech than nouns in many other
languages. One is that many lexical expressions for entities are actually morphological verbs. Another, as we shall see, is the existence of noun incorporation.
    There is essentially no noun + noun compounding at the root or stem level. One
and only one noun root or stem can serve as the base of a morphological noun.
There are, however, some word + word compounds. These are generally recent
creations, probably coined under the influence of English. The terms below are
from Kahnawà:ke, near modern Montreal.

(4) NOMINAL COMPOUNDS
     a. *kátsheʼ*   *káhi*
        jug   fruit
        'pear'
     b. *akohsá:tens* *ohsò:kwaʼ*
        horse   nut
        'horse chestnut'
     c. *arawé:n*   *othè:seraʼ*
        oat   flour
        'oatmeal'

The term *kátsheʼ* 'jug' originated in Mohawk, but it was apparently derived from a
verb. This verb root no longer occurs on its own, but it requires the nominalizer -*ʼt*-
when it is incorporated, as in *katsheʼtíz:io* (ka-tshe-ʼt-iio NEUT-ʔ-NOML-be.nice)
'nice jug'. The term *akohsá:tens* 'horse' is actually a morphological verb 'it carries
one on the back', but it has been lexicalized as a nominal. The term *arawé:n* 'oat'

was borrowed from French *avoine*. Each of the terms in (4) designates an introduced item.

31.1.3 Verbs

The most common words in speech and the largest portion of the lexicon are
morphological verbs. All verbs contain minimally a pronominal prefix referring to
the core arguments of the clause and a verb stem. Verbs other than commands also
contain an aspect suffix.

(5) BASIC VERB
    a. *Shehró:ri*   b. *Khehró:rihs*
       she-hrori   khe-hrori-hs
       2SG/FEM.SG-tell   1SG/FEM.SG-tell-HAB
       'Tell her!'   'I tell her.'

Morphological verbs can also be more complex.

(6) MORE COMPLEX VERB
    Aonsakonwaia'tisákha'.
    a-onsa-konwa-ia't-isak-ha-'
    OPT-REP-3PL/FEM.SG-body-seek-AND-PRF
    'They should go back to look for her.'

They may contain various pre-pronominal prefixes, like the optative 'should' and
the repetitive 'back' in (6), and various derivational suffixes, such as the andative
'go and' here. They may also contain a noun stem incorporated immediately before
the verb root, such as *-ia't-* 'body' in (6).

    Morphological verbs serve a wider variety of syntactic functions than nouns. As
in other languages, they can serve as predicates, accompanied by lexical nominals
and other elements. Since they contain pronominal reference to their core arguments, they can serve as complete grammatical sentences in themselves. They can
also serve as syntactic nominals and adverbials. In the example below, P identifies
morphological particles, and v verbs.

(7) MORPHOLOGICAL VERBS IN USE (Rita Konwatsi'tsaién:ni Phillips, speaker, p.c.)

P	V	P	V
Ísi'	*nónhskwati*	*she's*	*niió:re'*
isi'	na'-w-ahskw-ati	she's	ni-io-r-e'
yonder	PRTV-NEUT-bridge-be.beyond	formerly	PRTV-NEUT-extend-STA
yonder	so it is bridge beyond	formerly	so it is far

V
niekonnéhtha'
n-ie-konn-e-ht-ha'
PRTV-TLOC-ZO.PL.AGT-go-INST-HAB
over there they go with purpose

P	V
ne	*tionnhónhskwaron.*
ne	te-io-onnhonhskwar-ont-e'
the	DUP-NEUT.ZO.PAT-jowl-be.attached-STA
the	it is doubly jowl attached

'The cows used to pasture way over on the other side of the bridge.'[2]

There is essentially no verb + verb compounding in modern Mohawk at the root, stem, or word level. There is evidence that there may have been verb + verb compounding in the past. A very few modern verb roots show traces of two verbal elements. One is the root -*oha*- 'remove from water, fish out', which appears to be composed of the verb roots -*o*- 'be in water' and -*haw* 'take', both of which persist in modern Mohawk. Noun + verb compounding, like that seen in (6) *aonsakonwaia'-tisákha'* 'they should look for her' (-*ia't-isak*- 'body-seek'), *ísi' nónhskwati* 'it is on the other side of the bridge' (-*ahskw-ti* 'bridge-be.beyond'), and *tionnhónhskwaron* 'cow' (-*onnhonhskwar-ont* 'jowl-be.attached') is, by contrast, pervasive, productive, and powerful. It is this construction that will be our focus here.

31.2 NOUN INCORPORATION

Mohawk noun incorporation consists of the compounding of a noun stem with a verb stem to form a new verb stem. As was seen earlier, basic Mohawk nouns consist of a gender prefix, a noun stem, and a noun suffix. Only the noun stem is incorporated, not the whole noun word.

(8)   BASIC INCORPORATION

a. *oká:ra'*	b. *wákien'*	c. *wakká:raien'*
o-**kar**-a'	wak-ien-'	wak-**kar**-a-ien-'
NEUT-**story**-NSUFF	1SG.PAT-have-STA	1SG.PAT-**story**-JR-have-STA
'story'	'I have it'	'I have a story.'

[2] Genders are masculine, feminine/indefinite, neuter, and zoic. Feminine indefinite forms are used for indefinite persons ('one') and for certain female persons. Neuter forms are used for inanimate objects, and feminine zoic for larger animals and other female persons. For the most part, neuter and zoic pronominals have the same forms.

If an incorporated noun stem ends in a consonant, and the following verb stem begins in a consonant, a stem joiner vowel -*a*- is inserted between the two, as in -*kar-a-ien* 'story-JOINER-have' above.[3] (The verb root -*ien*- 'lie, have' begins with a palatal glide, represented by orthographic *i*. In penultimate position, the joiner vowel does not bear stress unless the preceding syllable is closed.) Only morphologically well-formed noun stems can be incorporated. Verbs that have become lexicalized as nominals must be overtly nominalized before they can be incorporated. The word *atekhwà:ra* 'table' originated as a morphological verb: 'one's meal is set on it' (*w-ate-khw-a-hra* NEUT-MID-meal-JR-set.on). It can be incorporated, but only with the overt nominalizer -'*tsher*-: *watekhwahrà tsherí:io* 'it is a nice table' (-*iio* 'be nice').

It was noted earlier that Mohawk verbs often correspond to full, multi-word sentences in other languages, such as *aonsakonwaia'tisákha* 'they should go back to look for her' and *wakká:raien* 'I have a story'. One might wonder whether these are in fact single words. Mohawk word boundaries are actually clear from a variety of criteria.

The first is the view of speakers. If speakers are asked to repeat a sentence word by word, they do it without hesitation and without variation from one time to the next or from one speaker to the next, whether or not they have ever read or written their language. The sole exceptions are some compound particles like those described in section 31.1.1. When speakers hesitate with those, they are accurately reflecting the transitional status of the forms.

There are also phonological clues to wordhood. Each word (except certain un-stressed particles) contains one and only one primary stress. Stress is basically penultimate, apart from epenthetic vowels. Words end after the syllable following the stress. Furthermore, phonological processes operate across morpheme boundaries in ways they do not operate across word boundaries. The word *iontenonhsatar-iha'táhkhwa* 'one heats one's house with it' > 'heater', for example, begins with the prefixes *iaw-ate*- (INDEF.AGT-MID-), but the combination is pronounced *ionte*-. Most pronominal prefixes containing a masculine participant begin with *r*- word-initially but *h*- word-internally: *rak-hró:rihs* 'he tells me', *wa-hak-hró:ri'* 'he told me'.

There are clear morphological cues to word boundaries. Both nouns and verbs have strong internal morphological structure. They are essentially templatic: morphemes are strictly ordered within the word. One cannot, for example, shift prefixes or suffixes around to alter scope relations, as in some languages. If one hears a negative, contrastive, coincident or partitive prefix, one knows this is the beginning of a verb. If one hears a post-aspectual suffix, it is the end.

Mohawk words are strong cognitive units. Speakers know the meanings of words of course, but they do not necessarily have a conscious knowledge of the identities of individual morphemes (unless they have become linguists). Speakers are often initially surprised to learn that *atekhwà:ra* 'table' contains the root -*khw*- 'food,

---

[3] The term 'stem joiner' is used in the Iroquoianist literature for linking elements similar to the vowels that join elements of compounds in languages like German and Greek.

meal', though after a moment's thought, they realize that it is true. Few would be able to identify the root -*khw*- however. Speakers never pause within words to choose a morpheme then continue, as one might pause between words in a sentence. If for any reason they are derailed mid-word (something that rarely happens), they simply begin the word again. They have a strong sense of words as units: they know which words exist in the language and which do not. The inventory of existing words varies from community to community and even from speaker to speaker, something speakers notice immediately and comment on. The morphology is highly productive, but speakers are generally aware of innovations.

All of these criteria converge to delineate words in the same way. The strength of the Mohawk verb as a phonological, morphological, and cognitive unit, alongside of its correspondence with multi-word sentences in many other languages, raises interesting issues about the boundaries between morphology and syntax. For this reason, the Mohawk incorporation construction has been the subject of an extensive literature, including but by no means limited to Mithun (1984, 1986a, b, 1996, 1999, 2001a, b, c), Baker (1988, 1996, 1999), and Rosen (1989).

31.3 DETERMINER PHRASES?

Cross-linguistically, markers of definiteness, gender, number, and case are not included when nouns are incorporated into verbs. Mohawk provides no exception. We do find Mohawk constructions like those in (9), (10), (11), and (12) where demonstratives, quantifiers, and other modifiers appear outside of verbs containing incorporated nouns.

(9)   DEMONSTRATIVE *kí:ken* 'this' (Awenhráthen Joe Deer, speaker)
        Ne: *ki:*   *wà:kehre*   *kí:ken*   *ki:*
        it is   this   I thought   this   **this**

        akenikaratónhahse'.
        a-keni-kar-aton-hahs-e'
        OPT-1/2.DU-story-say-BEN.APPL-PRF

        'I thought that I would tell you guys **this** story.'

(10)   QUANTIFIER *é:so'* 'much, many, a lot' (Watshenní:ne' Sawyer, speaker, p.c.)
        Thó   *né:*   *ki:*   *iah*   *é:so'*   *teionkwahwístaien'*
        tho   ne: ki: iah   eso'   te-ionkwa-hwist-a-ien-'
        there   it.is   this   not   much   NEG-1PL.PAT-money-JR-have-STA
        there   it is   this   not   much   did we money have
        'At that time we didn't have **much** money.'

(11) MODIFIER *ò:ia'* 'other' (Watshenní:ne' Sawyer, speaker, p.c.)

    Shé:kon   *ò:ia'*   *wakká:raien'.*
    shekon   o-hi-a'   wak-kar-a-ien-'
    still   NEUT-other-NSUFF   1SG.PAT-story-JR-have-STA
    still   other   I story have
    'I have still **another** story.'

(12) MODIFIER *iohsté:ris* 'it is funny' (Watshenní:ne' Sawyer, speaker, p.c.)

    Wakká:raien',
    wak-kar-a-ien-'
    1SG.PAT-story-JR-have-STA
    'I have a story,

    iohsté:ris   *wakká:raien'.*
    io-hsteris   wak-kar-a-ien-'
    NEUT.PAT-be.funny   1SG.PAT-story-JR-have-STATIVE
    a **funny** story.'

The existence of examples like (9)–(12) might suggest that noun incorporation constructions are built up from sentence structures much like those in English, in which the noun originates as a constituent of a determiner phrase ('this [story]', 'much [money]') and is then moved into the verb by syntactic rule, 'stranding' any demonstratives, quantifiers, or other modifiers. In fact these sentences do not in the end constitute evidence for such a process. Words like *kí:ken* 'this', *é:so* 'many, much', *ò:ia'* 'other', and *iohsté:ris* 'funny' all occur on their own in construction with verbs that contain no incorporated noun.

(13) *Kí:ken* 'this' ALONE (Rita Konkwatsi'tsaién:ni, speaker, p.c.)

    E'thó   *kì'*   **kí:ken**   *ronahstoróntie'.*
    e'tho   ki'   kí:ken   ron-ahstor-on-tie'
    there anyway this   MASC.PL.PAT-be.fast-STA-PROG
    '**These** (**boys**) were hurrying along.'

When there is an incorporated noun, the external elements are not necessarily coreferential with or even pertinent to it. In (14) 'many' has nothing to do with the incorporated 'mind'.

(14) *É:so'* 'many' ALONE (John Maracle, speaker)

    É:so   *ní:*   *sewake'nikónhrhen*
    eso'   ne i'i   se-wake-'nikonhr-hen
    many   the myself REP-1.SG.PAT-mind-fall.STA
    'I've forgotten **many** [tree names] myself.'

The word *ò:ia'* is a perfectly formed morphological noun meaning 'other one(s)'. It occurs on its own as a lexical argument.

(15)   *Ò:ia'* 'other' ALONE (Frank Natawe, speaker, p.c.)
      Ó:nen   *wahónttoke'*
      onen   wa-hon-at-tok-e'
      then   FAC-MASC.PL.AGT-MID-notice-PRF
      'Then they noticed

      ò:ia'   *ohnà:ken'*   *tahón:ne'.*
      o-hi-a'   ohna'ken'   ta-honn-e-'
      NEUT-other-NSUFF   behind   CIS-MASC.PL.AGT-go-STA
      other   behind   they are coming
      another (group) coming along behind them.'

Mohawk has no lexical adjective category. Concepts expressed by adjectives in other languages are typically expressed by stative verbs in Mohawk. The word *iohsté:ris* is a stative verb 'it is funny'. It can stand alone as a predicate or a clause and, like other verbs, it can serve as a referring expression with no further marking: 'funny one'.

(16)   *Iohsté:ris* 'it is funny' (Joe Awenhráthen Deer, speaker)
      Ah   *tsi*   *iohsté:ris*   *kì:.*
      ah   tsi   io-hsteris   kiken
      oh   how   NEUT.PAT-be.funny.STA   this
      'Oh how funny this is.'

Since all of these words can function as referring expressions on their own, there is no evidence that they represent the remnants of a larger determiner phrase that contained a noun at some earlier stage of derivation which was subsequently moved into the verb.

31.4 POSSESSION

As seen earlier, possession can be expressed on nouns by means of possessive prefixes.

(17)   POSSESSED NOUN (Charlotte Bush, speaker, p.c.)
      Tanon' *thó* *iehonátie's*   *kí:ken* *raonahthén:no.*
      tanon'   tho   ie-hon-atie'-s   kiken   raon-ahthenno
      and   there TLOC-MASC.PL.PAT-lose-HAB   this   MASC.PL.AL-ball
      'And they would throw **their** ball in there.'

Such constructions are much rarer than their English counterparts, however. Often verbal constructions are used instead.

(18) VERB (Charlotte Bush, speaker, p.c.)
      Né:'e   tehonta'enhrané:ken   *wáhe.*
      ne'   te-hon-at-a'enhr-a-nek-en   wahe'
      it.is   DUP-MASC.PL.AGT-MID-fence-JR-be.adjacent-STA   TAG
      '**Their** fences were next to each other, you know.'

(19) VERB (Ida Nicholas, speaker, p.c.)
      Khehsennahrónkhahkwe'   *se's.*
      khe-hsenn-ahronk-hahkwe'   se's
      1SG/3-name-hear-HAB.PST   formerly
      'I used to hear **her** name.'

It has sometimes been proposed that such constructions can be understood as the result of syntactic movement, of a 'possessor raising' process whereby possessed nouns in constructions like that in (17) are incorporated into the verb and the possessor moved into an argument position (Baker 1999). In fact these constructions do not actually express possession. A better translation of (18) is 'they were neighbours', and of (19) 'I used to hear about her'. The noun + verb compound stems are recognized lexical items with meanings 'be neighbours' and 'hear about'. The sentence in (18) is about neighbours, not their fences, and (19) about a woman under discussion, not her name. Possessors of entities evoked by incorporated nouns often do appear as core arguments of the clause, particularly where inalienable possession is concerned, such as body parts. This is not surprising. An event or state that affects a part of my body (having a headache, breaking my leg) significantly affects me. In Mohawk, the most significantly affected animate participant is typically cast as a core argument. As can be seen in the examples above, however, the incorporated noun need not be an inalienable possession. In fact, it need not be a possession at all. The structure itself does not specify or even imply a possessive relationship.

The pronominal prefixes in the three verbs in (20) are all the same: *-honwa-* 'they/him'. It could be argued that in the second verb *iahonwaia'ténhawe'* 'they took him' the masculine singular element refers to the possessor of the incorporated noun stem *-ia't-* body'. It is clear, however, that in the third verb *wahonwanhó:ton* 'they locked him up' the masculine pronominal 'him' does not refer to the possessor of the door. It refers to the one primarily affected by the jailing, the prisoner.

(20) VERB (Watshenní:ne Sawyer, speaker, p.c.)
      Wahonwaié:na'.
      wa-honwa-iena-'
      FAC-3PL/MASC.SG-grab-PRF
      '**They** arrested **him**.'

Iahonwaia'ténhawe'	*karihtòn:ke*
ia-honwa-ia't-enhaw-e'	ka-rihton-'ke
TLOC-3PL/MASC.SG-body-take-PRF	NEUT-police-place

'They took him to the police station . . .'

tanon'	*wahonwanhó:ton*
tanon'	wa-honwa-nh-oton-'
and	FAC-3PL/MASC.SG-door-close-PRF

'. . . and they locked him up.'

The incorporated noun -*ia't*- 'body' in the second verb *iahonwaia'ténhawe'* 'they took him away' actually reflects an interesting lexical pattern. A large number of compound verb stems have as their first member one of three noun roots: -*ia't*- 'body', -*'nikonhr*- 'mind', or -*rihw*- 'matter, affair, idea, word, news, reason, time, etc.'. We saw another verb with -*ia't*- 'body' in (6): *aonsakonwaia'tisákha'* 'they should go back and look for her'. The verb root -*isak* 'seek, look for' is used alone for looking for an inanimate object, but in combination with -*ia't*- 'body' when it means looking for a person or animal. This particular verb was used in (6) to describe two boys looking for their cow. There are thus two verb stems in the lexicon: -*isak* 'seek (an inanimate object)' and -*ia't-isak* 'seek (an animate being)'. We saw an example of the incorporated noun -*'nikonhr*- 'mind' in example (14): *É: o ní: sewake'nikónhrhen* 'I myself have forgotten a lot' ('I am mind-fallen again'). Forgetting is classified as a mental activity, but the mind is not a core argument of the clause. The speaker was talking about forgetting names of trees. An example of the third noun root, -*rihw*-, is in (21).

(21) INCORPORATED -*rihw*- 'matter, idea, etc.' (Tiorhakwén:te' Joe Dove, speaker)

Wahèn:ron	*iáh*	*teharihwanòn:we's*
wa-ha-ihron-'	iah	te-ha-rihw-a-nonhwe'-s
FAC-MASC.SG.AGT-say-PRF	not	NEG-MASC.SG.AGT-**matter**-JR-like-HAB

'He said he doesn't approve [of people speaking Mohawk in that place].'

31.5 THE NOUN–VERB RELATIONSHIP

If noun incorporation is to be described as a syntactic process, a precise specification of the syntactic role of the noun at each point is necessary. Syntactic accounts of noun incorporation have generally taken as their point of departure transitive clauses with lexical direct objects. The direct object is then moved to a position inside of the verb. Many Mohawk clauses with incorporated nouns are indeed

translated into English clauses with transitive verbs and direct objects, like that in
(22). A group of friends had been discussing the poor corn crop.

(22) INCORPORATED OBJECT? (Josephine Horne, speaker, p.c.)
      Tánon'   *karì:wes*   *tsi*   *niió:re'*
      tanon'   ka-rihw-es   tsi   ni-io-r-e'
      and   NEUT.AGT-time-be.long   as   PRTV-NEUT.PAT-reach-STA

      ientewanénhstake'
      i-en-tewa-nenhst-a-k-e'
      TLOC-FUT-1PL.EX.AGT-**corn**-JR-eat-PRF

      'And it will be a long time before we'll eat **corn**.'

Intransitive verb roots also occur with incorporated nouns:

(23) But INTRANSITIVE ROOT: (Tiorhakwén:te' Joe Dove, speaker)
      Konkwe'táksen   *kén?*
      k-onkwe't-aks-en   ken
      1SG.AGT-**person**-be.bad-STA   Q
      'Am I a bad person?'

It is difficult to argue that 'person' in (23) is structurally a direct object. An attempt
to identify the root 'be bad' as an 'unaccusative' verb runs up against the problem
that it occurs with pronominal agents rather than patients. There is actually no
consistent syntactic or even semantic relation between incorporated nouns and the
verb roots that incorporate them.
      The verb stem -*atkenni* 'compete' can be seen on its own in (24). The same stem
appears with the incorporated noun 'garden' in (25). The garden is not a syntactic
argument. It simply indicates a kind of competition, qualifying the competing.

(24) VERB 'compete' (Kaia'titáhkhe' Jacobs, speaker, p.c.)
      Tiótkon   *ok*   *nahò:ten'*   *tiorihón:ni.*
      tiotkon   ok   naho:ten'   t-io-rihw-onni
      always   some   thing   CIS-NEUT.PAT-matter-make

      tehonatkénnion.
      te-hon-at-kenni-on
      DUP-MASC.PL.PAT-MID-compete-STA

      'Always for some reason they were competing with each other.'

(25) VERB 'compete' WITH INCORPORATED NOUN (Tiorhakwén:te' Joe Dove, speaker)
      Sok   *né:*   *wa'thonthehtakén:ni*
      sok   ne: wa'-t-hon-at-heht-a-kenni-'
      so   it.is   FAC-DUP-MASC.PL.AGT-MID-**garden**-JR-compete-PRF
      'So then they competed with their gardens.'

The incorporated noun 'hand' in (26) is also not a direct object. The closest semantic characterization of its role might be as a source.

(26) SOURCE NOUN: (Watshenní:ne Sawyer, speaker, p.c.)
    Tóhsa   *kí:ken*   *tesatsha'nén:tonhk*
    tohsa'   kiken   te-s-at-hsi-a'nenton-hkw
    PROH   this   DUP-2SG.AGT-hand-fall-CAUS-INST.APPL
    ne   *ohwísta'*
    ne   o-hwist-a'
    the   NEUT-money-NOUN.SUFFIX
    'Don't let the money just slip out of your hand, slip through your fingers.'

The incorporated noun 'container' in (27) is also not a direct object or semantic patient. If anything, it indicates a location.

(27) LOCATION NOUN (Kaia'titáhkhe' Jacobs, speaker, p.c.)
    Wahohonwì:sere'
    wa-ho-honw-i'ser-e'
    FAC-MASC.SG.PAT-boat.shaped.container-drag-STA
    'He was container-dragged' = 'He rode off.'

The incorporated noun 'wind' in (28) represents a kind of instrument or means.

(28) INSTRUMENT NOUN (Rita Konwatsi'tsaién:ni Phillips, speaker, p.c.)
    Wahonatewerá:ienhte'.
    wa-hon-ate-wer-a-ien-ht-e'
    FAC-MASC.PL.PAT-MID-wind-JR-fall-CAUS-PRF
    'They were hit by a **wind**.'

One might argue that the problem is one of translation of the verb root. The same Mohawk verb root can, however, occur with incorporated nouns with quite different semantic roles. The verbs in both examples in (29) are based on the root -*itahkhe*-. The first incorporates the noun -*ia't*- 'body'; the second -*hah*- 'road'.

(29) VERB ROOT -*itahkhe*- 'be moving' (Charlotte Bush, Kaia'titáhkhe' Jacobs, speakers, p.c.)
    a. *Tóka'*   *ótia'ke*   *ákte'*   *nihatiia'titáhkhe'.*
       toka'   otia'ke   akte'   ni-hati-ia't-itahkhe-'
       maybe   other   nearby   PRTV-MASC.PL.AGT-**body**-be.in.moving-STA
       'Maybe some of them were riding in another car.'
    b. *Ó:nen*   *nì'*   *ken'*   *tahonathahitáhkhe'*
       onen   ohni'   ken'   ta-hon-at-hah-itahkhe-'
       now   also   here   CIS-MASC.PL.AGT-MID-**road**-be.in.moving-STA
       'And now here they come, walking down the road.'

The variety of relations that hold between the members of these noun + verb compounds is much like what we find with noun + noun compounds in English. There is no constant semantic relation. The first noun must simply be 'appropriately classificatory' in the sense of Zimmer (1972) and Downing (1977). It is no accident that so many incorporated nouns in Mohawk are translated as direct objects or intransitive subjects in English. These are the kinds of participants that tend to shape the nature of an action or state, such as eating meat but drinking water.

Incorporation also fails to show a consistent syntactic effect on the argument structure of the resulting complex verb stem. Both transitive and intransitive verb roots incorporate. When a transitive verb incorporates, the resulting stem can be intransitive, transitive, or both. When it is transitive, the incorporated noun may or may not have anything to do with any core arguments of the clause. In 'They should body-seek her', the body is that of the cow being sought. In 'The boys were wind-hit' the only argument is the boys. Such grammatical fluidity is typical of word formation: speakers extend existing patterns to create labels for the concepts they wish to name.

After a noun + verb stem has been formed, it can be extended to new contexts with different argument structure. The verb stem -nh-oton 'door-close' (actually 'opening-cover') is used as an intransitive verb meaning 'close the door', as might be expected. As we saw in (20), it is also now used as a transitive 'lock someone up'. The verb -renn-ot- 'song-stand' was originally used intransitively for singing. It can be seen in (30) as a transitive.

(30)   ARGUMENT STRUCTURE SHIFT (Tiorhakwén:te' Joe Dove, speaker)
    O'nó:wa'   *ne:'*   *thaterennótha'.*
    o-'now-a'   ne'   t-ha-ate-renn-ot-ha'
    NEUT-dome-NSUFF   that   DUP-MASC.SG.AGT-MID-song-stand-HAB
    'He plays the guitar.'

Speakers could create such a sentence only if the verb stem 'song-stand' was stored as a lexical whole to mean 'sing, play', not as a predicate with direct object.

31.6 SEMANTIC TRANSPARENCY
AND IDIOMATICITY

A feature sometimes cited as a difference between morphological and syntactic formations is semantic transparency. Noun incorporation structures show a cline of semantic transparency. Some noun + verb compounds have meanings that are exactly what would be predicted from the meanings of the parts, such as 'person-be.bad' = 'be a bad person' and 'corn-eat' = 'eat corn'. For perhaps the majority, the original semantic basis for the formation can be discerned after the fact, but the meaning could not be predicted precisely. An example is in (31).

(31) IDIOMATIC 'go to church' (Charlotte Bush, speaker, p.c.)
   Ri'kèn:'a   wahaterennaiénhna.
   ri-'ken = 'a   wa-ha-ate-renn-a-ien-hna-'
   1SG/MASC.SG-be.sibling.to = DIM   FAC-MASC.SG.AGT-MID-song-JR-lay-PURP-PRF
   I am older sibling to him   he went to lay down his songs/prayers
   'My younger brother went to church.'

The verb is understood as the label for the event as a whole. This speaker would have used the same construction even if her brother had simply sat in the back with no intention of praying. Another example is 'word-be.good' = 'be free'. The speaker was saying that livestock was not fenced in.

(32) IDIOMATIC 'be free' (Watshenní:ne Sawyer, speaker, p.c.)
   Akwé:kon   *katshé:nen*
   akwekon   ka-tshenen
   all   NEUT-domestic.animal
   'All the animals

   enhskontatewenní:iohne'.
   en-s-kont-atate-wenn-iio-hne-'
   FUT-REP-ZO.PL.AGT-REFL-word-be.good-PURP-PRF
   they were going to be word good
   were free.'

Noun incorporation constructions are generally formed for a purpose, so their meanings are not necessarily precisely equivalent to the meanings of their components even at the moment of their creation. Once they have become lexicalized, they are continually being extended to new contexts, and their meanings can shift accordingly, without regard to their original components. Such processes are typical of Mohawk incorporation. The verb *-hsw-a-neta'* 'back-layer' is used for putting another blanket on: *Takshwa'néta'* 'Put another blanket on me'. The same verb has been extended metaphorically to mean give someone moral support, covering their back. The verb *-'nikonhr-iio* 'mind-be.good' means 'be patient': *ro'nikonhrí:io* 'he is patient'. The same verb stem with incorporated noun 'mind' is used for geraniums: *ioti'nikonhrí:io* 'they are patient' because they are so hardy. The verb *tontahshako'nikonhrotakwenhátie'*, based on the stem *-'nikonhr-ot* 'mind-stand', was used to describe a man who was very controlling to his wife: 'he goes along un-standing her mind' = 'he rules her at every turn'.

The set of noun + verb compounds in the lexicon is a repository of idiomaticity, the ways ideas are conventionally expressed. The noun root -*nonhs*- 'house' appears in numerous noun + verb compounds. It actually rarely occurs in an independent noun. It is almost always incorporated into one verb or another, the default being the verb -*ot* 'stand': *kanónhsote'* 'standing house'. When one talks about burning a house, however, a different noun is incorporated: -*non'kw*-.

(33)   HOUSE BURNING (Tiorhakwén:te' Joe Dove, speaker)
        Né: ki'   thí:ken   né: rotenon'kwatékton
        ne: ki'   thiken   ne: ro-ate-non'kw-atek-t-on
        that   in.fact   that   it is MASC.SG.PAT-MID-house-burn-CAUS-STA
        'That's the guy that burned the house.'

The root -*non'kw*- does not seem to appear in any other constructions with this meaning. Its meaning here is only inferred from the meaning of the whole verb (33).

The same noun root is not necessarily incorporated into every verb pertaining to a particular referent. The verb stem usually used to talk about possession of livestock or pets is -*nahskw-a-ien*- 'domestic.animal-JR-have'. The kind of animal can be specified with a separate nominal: *akohsá:tens wakenáhskwaien'* 'I have a horse', *è:rhar wakenáhskwaien'* 'I have a dog'. Two men had been discussing how people used to help each other out. Those who had horses would take them around to help others plough their gardens. One of the men mentioned a particular individual he had known.

(34)   HORSES (Awenhráthen Joe Deer, speaker)
        Tiótkon's   *ne:'*   *ronáhskwaien'.*
        tiotkon = 's   ne:'   ro-nahskw-a-ien-'
        always = formerly   that.on   MASC.SG.PAT-domestic.animal-JR-have-STA
        'He always had animals (horses).

        A: sok   ki   ne:'
        ah   and.the   this.one   it is
        Oh yes, then this guy

        enhaia'taniión:ten'   *ne:'*
        en-ha-ia't-a-niionten-'   ne'
        FUT-MASC.SG.AGT-body-JR-suspend-PRF   that.one
        would hitch the horse(s) up [and then they'd plough].'

No separate lexical nouns were necessary, because horses were an ongoing topic of conversation. In the first sentence the incorporated noun is -*nahskw*- 'domestic animal', while in the second, it is -*ia't*- 'body'. The reason is simple: the verb stem for keeping livestock is -*nahskw-a-ien*-, while the verb stem for hitching up horses is -*ia't-a-niionten*-.

31.7 PRODUCTIVITY

Another difference sometimes cited between morphological and syntactic processes is their productivity. Word-formation processes show a wide range of productivity, from those barely or no longer productive (like English *-th* of *warmth*) to those used so pervasively in new formations that speakers barely notice the neologisms (like *-ness* of *political correctness*). Mohawk noun incorporation shows a similar range of productivity. The productivity of noun incorporation is not characteristic of the process as a whole, any more than the productivity of derivation is constant for all derivational affixes. Each noun stem and verb stem has its own degree of productivity with respect to incorporation. Some nouns occur only incorporated, such as *-nahskw-* 'domestic animal'. Some are usually incorporated, some occasionally, some rarely, and some never. A similar continuum can be seen with verbs. Some verbs always incorporate, some usually incorporate, some sometimes incorporate, and some never incorporate. The difference is not purely semantic: the root *-íio* 'be good' always incorporates, while the root *-ianer-* 'be good' never does.

If noun incorporation were fully productive in the way syntactic processes have been assumed to be, we would expect it to occur consistently in a given syntactic context. It does not. One speaker was describing the events in the Pear Film, created by Wallace Chafe and his collaborators with the goal of eliciting parallel narratives in different languages without translation. The film shows a sequence of events but contains no language. The Mohawk speaker's description opened with the sentences in (35). (The description was entirely in Mohawk.)

(35)   THE PEAR STORY (Kaia'titáhkhe' Jacobs, speaker)
['What I watched took place in the morning, I believe, because I heard a rooster crow.']

Kí:ken	*rón:kwe,*	*kwah*	*í:kehre'*
this	man	just	I believe

kátshe'	*káhi*	*rahiákwahs*
ka-tshe'	ka-ahi	ra-ahi-akwa-hs
NEUT-jug	NEUT-fruit	MASC.SG.AGT-fruit-pick-HAB

'This man was picking pears.'

['He was wearing something like a bag']

Tho	*kí'*	*iehréta's*	*kí:ken*	*kátshe'*	*káhi.*
tho	ki'	ie-hr-eta'-s	this	jug	fruit
there	in.fact	TLOC-MASC.SG.AGT-insert-HAB			

'And he was putting the pears in there.'

The lexical nominal *kátshe' káhi* 'pear' was used to direct special attention to this significant referent, around which the story revolves. The nominal appears early in the first clause, when it is first introducing the pears, but late in the second, when it is simply reiterating the reference.

Interestingly, the noun root -*ahi*- 'fruit' is incorporated into the first verb 'pick' but not the second verb 'insert'. The reason is simple. There exists a lexical item 'fruit-pick' but no lexical item 'fruit-insert'. Fruit-picking is a nameworthy activity, but fruit-inserting has apparently not achieved this status. The verb 'insert' does appear with other incorporated nouns, as in the stem for burying a person: -*ia't-a-ta*- 'body-JR-insert'. In this speaker's description of the film, the noun -*ahi* was also incorporated into other verbs. At a certain point, while the pear picker is up in the tree, a boy comes along on a bicycle, steals one basket of pears, and rides off.

(36) FURTHER INCORPORATED FRUIT (Kaia'titáhkhe' Jacobs, speaker, p.c.)
      rohianenhskwenhátie'
      ro-**ahi**-nenhskw-en-hatie'
      MASC.SG.PAT-**fruit**-steal-STA-PROG
      'he was going along having stolen the fruit.'

The boy hits a rock and falls, scattering the pears all over the ground. The noun 'fruit' is not incorporated because there is no stem 'fruit-scatter' in the lexicon. Reference to the fruit is reiterated after the verb with the more general independent noun 'fruit' sufficient in this context:

(37) INDEPENDENT 'FRUIT' (Kaia'titáhkhe' Jacobs, speaker, p.c.)
      Sok   wa'tewaré:ni'   *kí:ken   káhi.*
      sok   wa'-te-w-areni-'   kiken   ka-ahi
      and   FAC-DUP-NEUT.AGT-scatter-PRF   this   NEUT-fruit
      'And it scattered, this fruit.'

As the story progresses, the noun 'fruit' appears incorporated in various other verbs. Three boys come along and help the pear thief up from his fall. In gratitude, he gives each a pear. The scene then shifts as we watch the three trudge off.

(38) FURTHER INCORPORATED FRUIT (Kaia'titáhkhe' Jacobs, speaker, p.c.)
      Akwé:kon   *skatshon*   *ronahiaientátie'*
      akwekon   skat-shon   ron-**ahi**-a-ient-atie'
      all   one-each   MASC.PL.PAT-**fruit**-JR-have-PROG
      all   each   they were **fruit** having along

      ótsta'   *tsi*   *nihonahiá:kon*   *ki:*   *kátshe*   *káhi.*
      otsta'   tsi   ni-hon-**ahi**-ak-on   this   jug   fruit
      gee   how   PRTV-MASC.PL.PAT-**fruit**-eat-STA
      gee   how   so they were **fruit** eating
      'They were each going along with a fruit, really eating the fruit, the pears.'

Much later, after a series of events centring on the pears, we return to the pear picker, who climbs down out of the tree to find one of his baskets of pears missing. At this point the fruit is mentioned only with the incorporated root -*ahi*-, part of the lexicalized stem, -*ahi-nenhskw*- 'fruit-steal'. An external nominal was unnecessary because the pears were such a well-established part of the scene, but the presence of the incorporated root does help to keep reference alive.

(39)   No LEXICAL NOMINAL (Kaia'titáhkhe' Jacobs, speaker, p.c.)
['This man couldn't figure out what had happened,']
ónhka'   *wahonwahianénhsko'.*
onhka'   wa-honwa-ahi-nenhsko-'
who   FACTUAL-3.INDEF/MASC.SG-**fruit**-steal-PRF
'who had stolen the fruit'

Like other languages, Mohawk offers its speakers a variety of devices for invoking referents, among them full lexical nominals of varying degrees of specificity, demonstratives, and pronominals. Mohawk offers an additional device as well in noun incorporation. Though its occurrence is governed first by the combinations that happen to be established in the lexicon, it can help to keep reference alive over the course of speech.

31.8 REFERENCE

Incorporated nouns in Mohawk are not usually referential. They typically serve as qualifiers, narrowing the semantic scope of the verb: -*onkwe't-iio* 'be a good person', -*enhniser-iio* 'be a good day, be fine weather'. In some cases, however, incorporated nouns do introduce referents in Mohawk. Noun stems may be incorporated into 'light' verbs, verbs with minimal semantic content of their own. When the pear picker in the Pear Film has filled his apron, we see him climb down out of the tree. There on the ground are three baskets. The speaker introduced them as follows.

(40)   REFERENT INTRODUCTION (Kaia'titáhkhe' Jacobs, speaker, p.c.)
Áhsen ní:kon   *wa'thé:raien'*
ahsen ni-k-on   w-a'ther-a-ien-'
three   PRTV-NEUT.AGT-number.STA   NEUT.AGT-basket-JR-lie-STA
'There are three baskets lying

kahentà:ke   *tho.*
ka-hent-a'ke   tho
NEUT-ground-place   there
on the ground there.'

The incorporation allows the expression of a single idea, the presence of baskets, in a single word. The light verbs such as 'sit', 'stand', 'lie', 'have', etc. provide a vehicle for moving referents onto the scene. Such constructions are not uncommon.

31.9 CONCLUSION

The fact that Mohawk verbs with incorporated nouns are usually translated into multi-word sentences in English has understandably prompted some descriptions of them as syntactic formations. It is important, however, to distinguish the formation process from its effects. Replacing a simplex verb with a complex verb can indeed have syntactic consequences, shifting the argument structure of the clause. But replacing one lexical verb with another can have syntactic consequences in any language. In this sense, incorporation is not significantly different from word-formation processes like that linking *able* and *enable*.

The recognition that the products of Mohawk noun incorporation are not always perfectly regular semantically or syntactically has prompted some analysts to distinguish two types of incorporation, one syntactic and one morphological. The first is described in the same terms as sentence formation. The second consists of the irregular residue. But such a theoretical distinction is difficult to reconcile with the range of formations that actually occur. Mohawk verb stems formed by incorporation fall along a continuum of semantic transparency, much like those formed by other derivational processes. Even when they are fully transparent like 'domestic.animal-have', speakers recognize them as lexical items in their language. Substituting a synonym for the component noun or verb stem would not yield a usable lexical item. Similarly, it is difficult to specify the exact syntactic structures that serve as input to incorporation, or consistent, predictable syntactic structures that result. Both input and output possibilities are fluid, with no sharp distinction between 'regular' and 'irregular'.

Mohawk incorporation also shows a continuum of productivity. The productivity is tied to individual noun and verb stems rather than to the process as a whole, just as the productivity of derivational processes is tied to individual affixes or other word-formation processes.

It remains to be seen whether a sharp distinction can ultimately be maintained between processes of word and sentence formation. Nevertheless, Mohawk noun incorporation clearly shares the fundamental properties of other word-formation processes. It provides a tool for creating lexical items, verb stems that are learned and used as units. Many excellent speakers never create new stems on their own, but the lexical inventory is available to all.

CHAPTER 32

ARAWAKAN: MAIPURE-YAVITERO

RAOUL ZAMPONI

32.1 BACKGROUND

UNDER the (compound) name Maipure-Yavitero, three languages of northeastern Amazonia, constituting a subgroup of the northern division of the Arawakan (or Maipuran) family, are gathered together. The languages in question are Maipure, Yavitero (or Parene), and Baniva (or Baniva/Baniwa of Guainía).

Of the three members of the Maipure-Yavitero group, only Baniva has speakers today. The language is spoken in the villages of Maroa and La Comunidad and in the area of the Casiquiare river in the Venezuelan state of Amazonas, along the Caño Aki (a tributary of the Guainía) in Colombian territory, and along the Xie river (a tributary of the Rio Negro) in Brazilian territory (Warekena dialect), by about 1,200 people altogether. Yavitero, whose last speaker died in 1984, was spoken in the basin of the Atabapo river (Amazonas). Maipure, once spoken along the Ventuari, Sipapo, and Autana rivers (Amazonas) and, as a lingua franca, in the Upper Orinoco region, became extinct around the end of the eighteenth century.[1]

---

[1] A co-dialect of Maipure, or perhaps a closely related language, was spoken by the Avane (Awani) along the Autana and Sipapo rivers. Of this variety, only eighteen words survive (see Zamponi 2003: 9–10).

For all three Maipure-Yavitero languages, at least a grammatical outline and a word list is available. Zamponi (2003) is a grammatical sketch of Maipure, furnished with a classified word list, based on all its extant available eighteenth-century material (mainly from the Italian missionary Filippo Salvatore Gilij). For Yavitero, we are fortunate to have a 240-page 'salvage' grammar and vocabulary (Mosonyi 1987), a dissertation written at the Universidad Central de Caracas, on which an outline included in Mosonyi and Mosonyi (2000: 594–661) is based. The Warekena dialect of Baniva is analysed by Aikhenvald (1998), while the dialect of Maroa is described grammatically by Mosonyi and Camico (1996), republished in Mosonyi and Mosonyi (2000: 184–223), and lexically by González Ñáñez (1996), a basic vocabulary.

Drawn together on the basis, especially, of shared lexical innovations (see Zamponi 2003: 8), Baniva, Yavitero, and Maipure also have a significant common stock of grammatical morphemes that they share with other languages of the Arawakan family (or of its Northern division) or are exclusive to them (a personal prefix *ni-* '2PL/3PL', instead of reflexes of Proto-Arawakan *hi-* '2PL' and *na-* '3PL'; and a relativizing enclitic *-li*, multifunctional, that seems to originate from a nominalizing suffix; Zamponi 2005).

Further lexical innovations and phonetic developments which characterize Yavitero and Baniva, and which Maipure ignores (see Zamponi 2003: 9), suggest identification, in the context of Maipure-Yavitero, of a Baniva-Yavitero subunit and, therefore, articulation of the whole subgroup as it appears in Figure 32.1.

Like other Arawakan languages of the area, Maipure, Yavitero, and Baniva are agglutinating, suffixing with few prefixes, and strictly head-marking. They have open classes of nouns, verbs, adjectives, and adverbs, and closed classes of pronouns, demonstratives, quantifiers, numerals, adpositions, and particles. Shared nominal categories are (optional) number and possession (alienable vs. inalienable, as in other Arawakan languages). Verbal categories include person and number. A number of suffixes and enclitics are used for tense reference and various aspectual and modal meanings. Further modal and aspectual specifications are expressed by serial verb constructions.

Branches Languages († extinct)
1. Maipure†
    a. Maipure† (plus Avane†)
2. Baniva-Yavitero
    a. Baniva (including Warekena)
    b. Yavitero†

Figure 32.1 Internal classification of Maipure–Yavitero

32.2 LANGUAGES WITH FEW COMPOUND WORDS

Yet another common feature of Maipure, Yavitero, and Baniva is represented by the scarce weight that the technique of compounding assumes in coining new words. Compounds that have as their constituents two or more freestanding stems closely linked phonologically and operating syntactically as a single word are uncommon in the three languages. Out of about 450 attested lexical items of Maipure, only nine compound words were identified. The compound words discovered in Yavitero are even fewer. In his grammar of 1987, Mosonyi highlights only four of these forms, which, out of the total of about 1,500 (native) lexical items gathered together by him, represent a mere 0.27 percent.[2] Baniva would appear to make use of compound words to a greater extent than Yavitero, within the limits of a language where compounding is not particularly productive (Aikhenvald 1998: 321) or frequent (Mosonyi and Mosonyi 2000: 201), however. The compound words of Baniva quoted in the grammatical descriptions of Aikhenvald and Monsonyi and Camico are six in all and very few can be added to these by examining González Ñáñez's vocabulary, in spite of the rather ample lexical coverage provided by this work (about 1,100 items).

A more or less strong resistance to forming compounds was also observed in other Arawakan languages, in distinct contrast with the propensity for compounding of other Amazonian languages, as for example the isolate Yaruro (Mosonyi and Camico 1996: 29). In Maipure-Yavitero (and in other Arawakan languages), the preferred method of creating new words is affixation, which allows deriving, for example, 'ghost of one killed in war or in a private feud' from (that which Gilij 1782: 14 renders as) 'devil' (*wasúli*) in Maipure, 'advice' from 'see' in Yavitero, and 'drunk and useless' from 'die, faint' in Baniva.[3]

MAIPURE (Gilij 1782: 15)

(1) *Makapu-mi-né*   *wasule-ná-mi*
     name-NOM.PAST-NF   devil:POSS-HUMAN-REMAINS
     'the ghost of the late Makapu'

YAVITERO (Mosonyi 1987: 47)

(2) *níta-ta-hitsi*
     see-CAUS-NOM
     'advice'

---

[2] All identified compounds of Yavitero and Maipure are here given.
[3] The Maipure, Yavitero, and Baniva examples are presented in phonemic transcription, tentative in the case of the Maipure ones.

BANIVA (Warekena dialect) (Aikhenvald 1998: 321)

(3)   *wiyuá-yua-daɟu-mi*
       die/faint-RED-ADJ-PEJ
       'drunk and useless'

32.3 CHARACTERISTICS OF COMPOUND WORDS

The few word-level compounds recorded in Maipure-Yavitero languages are composed of no more than three stems. They are all nominal and at least one of their components is a noun (stem).

Compound words in Maipure-Yavitero are distinguished from phrases in various ways. First, in Maipure, Yavitero, and the Warekena dialect of Baniva, they manifest only a single primary stress.[4] Second, in Maipure and Baniva, they present the same morphophonological changes that occur on affix + root boundaries ($i + i > i$ in Maipure and $V + V > V$ in Baniva) (4, 6).

BANIVA (of Maroa) (Monsonyi and Camico 1996: 29)

(4)   *dékamêwa* 'government property'   *-déka*   'property'
                                            amêwa   'government'

At least in Maipure, compounds, like other words, can also have derivations by the morphological processes of affixation, as indicated by the following examples.

MAIPURE (Gilij 1782: 160, 380)

(5)   a. *ka-ani-kiwakane-kiní*   b. *ma-anitu-tení*
          ATTR-son-father-ATTR   PRIV-son + mother-PRIV
          'one who has a husband'   'one who has not a wife'

A further characteristic of compound words in Maipure-Yavitero is that their meaning is not readily predictable from the meanings of their component morphemes.

---

[4] Stress in other dialects of Baniva can occur on more than one syllable of a word, whether it be compound or not. In these varieties stress is of three types: it may be accompanied by high pitch both on the stressed syllable and the unstressed syllables that follow (*á*), by low pitch both on the stressed syllable and the unstressed syllables that follow (*à*) or by high pitch exclusively on the stressed syllable (*â*) (see Mosonyi 2002).

As far as can be observed, two types of compound word may be distinguished in Maipure-Yavitero: genitive (endocentric) and deverbal (exocentric).

Genitive compound words are structurally identical with genitive noun phrases consisting in a sequence possessor–possessed in Maipure and, unusually in the Arawakan context, possessed–possessor both in Yavitero and Baniva. The referent of the noun corresponding to the possessed items is always inalienably possessed in such compounds, ergo possession is marked by simple juxtaposition of terms. (Note that the inalienably possessed noun undergoes shortening in (8).)

MAIPURE (Gilij 1782: 380)

(6) *anítu* 'wife'   *-áni* 'son'
                       -ítu 'mother'

BANIVA (Warekena dialect) (Aikhenvald 1998: 320)

(7) *panátaḻi* 'kitchen'   *-pána* 'house (poss.)'
                             táḻi   'oven'

YAVITERO (Mosonyi 1987: 45)

(8) *ínesimasi* 'pustule, pimple'   *-ínesinaha* 'egg'
                                      símasi   'fish'

Interestingly, in three genitive compound nouns of Yavitero and in the Baniva equivalents of two of them composed by noun stems cognate to those that constitute the corresponding Yavitero forms, the sequence in which possessor and possessed follow each other is the mirror image of that in which they occur in syntactic noun phrases in the two languages, that is, the same one observed in Maipure genitive constructions.[5]

YAVITERO (Mosonyi 1987: 45)

(9) a. *máhatsia*   'wax'   *máha*   'bee'
                                      -tsiá   'excrement'

     b. *haníḻihuḻisi* 'door'   *haní-ḻi* 'house' (house-NPOSS)
                                      -húḻisi 'eye'

     c. *káḻihuḻisi*   'brand, torch' *káḻi*   'fire'
                                      -húḻisi 'eye'

BANIVA (of Maroa) (González Ñáñez 1996: 13, 28)

(10) a. *mápatsià*   'wax'   *máːpà*   'bee'
                              -tsià   'excrement'

---

[5] Other exceptions to the usual order possessor–possessed in the Warekena dialect of Baniva are reported by Aikhenvald (1998: 296).

b. *paniṣ́ipừli* 'door'   *panî-ṣ́i* 'house' (house-NPOSS)
                          -púḷì 'eye'

In all probability, such compounds bear a trace of a syntactic pattern that has disappeared in Yavitero and, by now, is completely marginal in Baniva, stably retained only by Maipure.

A genitive compound analogous to those denoting 'wax' in Yavitero and Baniva (9a, 10a) is attested for Maipure (11), but with the noun 'honey', rather than 'bee' (cognate, however, to the Yavitero and Baniva terms for 'bee'), as possessed item.

MAIPURE (Gilij 1782: 377)

(11)   *mapaiká* 'wax'   *mápa* 'honey'
                         -iká 'excrement'[6]

The Maipure equivalent of the compounds denoting 'door' in (9b) and (10b) is also a genitive compound, but semi-opaque. It includes two elements, which do not exist as independent stems, corresponding to the nouns 'mouth' and 'house' in other Arawakan languages. The first one of them is, in fact, synchronically connected also to the Maipure term for 'mouth', *-numakú*, appearing to lack the final syllable, corresponding to a fossilized noun classifier meaning 'container, cavity, hole' (Zamponi 2003: 26) of Proto-Arawakan ancestry (*-Vku* or *-VkHu* 'container, cavity, hole'; Payne 1991: 384).[7]

MAIPURE (Gilij 1782: 377)

(12)   *penúma* 'door'   *pe* < Proto-Arawakan *pe* 'house' (Payne 1991: 408)
                         núma < Proto-Arawakan *numa* 'mouth' (Payne 1991: 413)

Compounds of the deverbal type consist of a verb stem and a subject or object constituent preposed to it. They are attested for Maipure and Baniva, but not for Yavitero. In (13a) and (14a), the constituent in initial position is the subject of the verb member, while in (13b) and (14b) it is its object.

MAIPURE (Gilij 1782: 377, 380)

(13)   a. *weni-kania-nikú*   b. *eka-ti-kania-tá*
          water-be-inside   eat-NOML-be-CAUS
          'jug'   'dinner table' (*ekatí* 'food', *-kaniatá* 'make be')

---

[6] Maipure *-iká* is cognate with Yavitero *-tsiá* and Baniva *-tsià* (Proto-Maipure-Yavitero *tika*, Proto-Arawak *itik[a]/[i]*; Payne 1991: 401).

[7] In various Arawakan languages of the Rio Negro basin, including Baré, Piapoco, and Baniwa (of Içana-Kurripako), the term for 'door' is a (transparent) genitive compound which literally means 'mouth of the house'.

BANIVA (Warekena dialect) (Aikhenvald 1998: 322)

(14) a. *mawáli-ʃia*
      snake-live
      'São Gabriel da Cachoeira'

b. *pana-táma-li*
      house:POSS-dance-REL
      'house of dance, longhouse'

The deverbal compound in (13a) also contains an adverb after the verb stem, as we can note. Compounds with *-kanía* and *nikú*, like this, might have been freely constructed in Maipure, as suggested by the following entries from a word list in Gilij (1782: 375–84): *yema-kania-nikú* 'snuff box', *kuyaluta-kania-nikú* 'book case', *kantiriti-kania-nikú* 'candlestick'.

For the Warekena dialect of Baniva a certain variation is reported as to whether constructions such as (14b) are treated as compound or as two independent words (Aikhenvald 1998: 322). The pausal form of (14b), for example, can be either *pana-táma-li-hĩ* or, broken up by the pausal marker *-hṼ*, *pána-hã táma-li*. In the latter case, it cannot be treated as a compound.[8]

32.4 PHRASAL AND CLAUSAL COMPOUNDS

The compounds that have been examined up to this point contrast, in the three Maipure-Yavitero languages, with (less infrequent) clusters of words not linked phonologically, with each component retaining its own word stress(es), that have become stable lexicalized expressions with an idiosyncratic meaning. Such word clusters correspond to descriptive noun phrases of two types: possessive noun phrases – both inalienable, expressed without any marker of possession (15a), and alienable, expressed with a suffixed marker of possession (17b, 19b) on the possessed item or (in Maipure and Yavitero) a stem-final change to /e/ (see *aláta* 'banana' > *aláte* in Maipure) (15b) – and adjectival noun phrases (16a, 16b, 18a, 18b, 20a, 20b).

MAIPURE (Gilij 1780: xxxviii, 213; 1781: 27; 1782: 377)

(15) a. *urúpu   sakalé*
      star   spit
      'dew'

b. *kurúmu   aláte*
      black.vulture banana:POSS
      'cambur (banana plant)'

(16) a. *mápa   panakalé*
      honey   planted
      'sugar cane'

b. *wéni   malikiní*
      water white
      'Rio Branco'

---

[8] The pausal form is the form, typical of native languages of the Upper Rio Negro region, in which a word may appear in front of a pause.

YAVITERO (Mosonyi 1987: 45, 170)

(17) a. *síhu   síha*   b. *tsáhua-ne   haní-ḷi*
         head   stone   hat-POSS   house-NPOSS
         'stubborn person'[9]   'eaves'

(18) a. *kuáiḷi   ka-yánane-mi*   b. *iḷwaḷi-mi   káhahi*
         jaguar   ATTR-drawing-ADJ   be.big-ADJ   hand/finger
         'butterfly jaguar'   '(his) thumb'

BANIVA (of Maroa) (González Ñáñez 1996: 8, 40; Mosonyi and Camico 1996: 29)

(19) a. *pána   é:tenêḷu*   b. *mulú:pà-ḷe   wítsi*
         house   old.man   canoe-POSS   air
         'old person's home'   'airplane'

(20) a. *wâụṣ*ⁿⁱ   *têwa-ḷi*   b. *apìbu-ṣ*ⁿⁱ   *ṣ*ⁿ*útsi-ḷi*
         jaguar   be.yellow-ADJ   finger-NPOSS   be.big-ADJ
         'cougar'   '(his) thumb'

The Maipure numerals 'five', 'ten', 'twenty', 'forty', and 'sixty' (in all probability coined after the white invasion) are also (dual stress) lexical phrases.

MAIPURE (Gilij 1781: 334, Hervás y Panduro 1786: 104)

(21) *papéta-ri   kapi-tí*
      one + CL:HUMAN-EMPH   hand-NPOSS
      'five' (lit. 'only one single hand')

(22) *apanúme-ri   kapi-tí*
      two + CL:HUMAN-EMPH   hand-NPOSS
      'ten' (lit. 'just two hands')

(23) *papéta   kamoné:*
      one + CL:HUMAN   man
      'twenty'

(24) *awanúme   kamoné:*
      two + CL:HUMAN   man
      'forty'

(25) *apekiwá   kamoné:*
      three + CL:HUMAN   man
      'sixty'

While the numerals 'six' and 'eleven' are based on clauses.

---

[9] Literally, 'stone head'. As in Baniva (Aikhenvald 1998: 298), a genitive construction could be used to express the meaning 'made out of' in Yavitero.

MAIPURE (Gilij 1781:334)

(26) *papéta*   *yaná* *páuⱡia*   *kapi-tí*   *puⱡená*
      one + CL:HUMAN   ?   other   hand-NPOSS   relative
      'six' (Gilij: 'One takes one from the other hand')[10]

(27) *papéta*   *yaná* *ki-tí*   *puⱡená*
      one + CL:HUMAN   ?   foot/toe-NPOSS   relative
      'eleven' (Gilij: 'One takes one of the toes')

32.5 AN APPARENT CASE OF INCIPIENT COMPOUNDING

The nominalization, by means of the feminine suffix -*yawa* or its non-feminine counterpart -*ne*, of the clause 'his eye is sleepy' (i.e. 'he is tired') implies an unexpected stress shift in Yavitero: the stress of the second component (*húäisi*) is moved one syllable to the right.

YAVITERO (Mosonyi 1987: 46)

(28) *táhu-ne*   *huⱡísi*
      be.sleepy-NF   eye
      'sleepy-head'

According to Mosonyi, the displacement of stress that may be observed in this context would be indicative of a state of incipient fusion.

32.6 COMPOUND WORDS IN LANGUAGES WITH FEW COMPOUND WORDS

With apparently only few exceptions (e.g. the Wakashan languages Nootka and Makah – Davidson 2002: 92, and the extinct Andean isolate Mochica – Hovdhaugen 2004: 69), all natural languages that have been studied contain compound

---

[10] *yaná* is perhaps cognate with Tariana -*dyánata* 'follow'; cf. the numeral 'six' in Tariana (Aikhenvald 2003: 218), *peme-kapí pá:-na dyánata-na* (one + SIDE + INDEF-hand one-CL:VERTICAL follow-CL: VERTICAL), literally 'the side of one hand and one which follows'. The (inalienably possessed) noun -*puⱡená* also denotes a thing of the same kind as another.

Table 32.1 Incidence of compounding and derivation in selected languages

Compounding	Derivation	Examples
Absent or limited	Productive	Nootka, Makah, Evenki, Maipure-Yavitero languages
Productive	Absent or limited	Mandarin, Mulao (Tai – Kadai – Wang and Zheng 1993: 26), Moré (Chapakuran – Angenot-de Lima 2001: 267)
Productive	Productive	Tümpisa Shoshone (Uto-Aztecan – Dayley 1989: 233, 240); Vogul (Uralic – Riese 2001: 56); Ainu (isolate – Tamura 2000: 193)
Limited	Limited	Atjnjmathanha (Australian phylum – Schebeck 1974: 50), Tol (Mesoamerican isolate – Holt 1999: 38–9)

words in their lexicon. The formal shape and the productivity of compounding, as is known, however, differ from language to language. If, on the one hand, we find languages where compounding is an extremely productive word-formation process (e.g. Kayardild, Australian phylum – Evans 1995: 197; Classical Nahuatl, Uto-Aztecan – Sullivan 1998: 263; Mandarin and many other isolating languages), on the other we find languages where, as in Baniva and apparently Maipure, compound words are infrequent (e.g. Yurok, Algic – Robins 1958: 14; Thompson, Salishan – Thompson and Thompson 1992: 109; Turkana, Nilo-Saharan – Noske 2000: 783; Menya, Angan – Whitehead 2004: 42) or, as in Yavitero, particularly rare (e.g. Evenki, Altaic – Nedjalkov 1997: 308). Languages with few or very few compound words do not, however, seem to represent a particularly wide sample of natural languages. In the majority of cases, in languages where compounding is not productive, as in Maipure-Yavitero, or completely or almost totally inoperative, as in Nootka, Makah, and Evenki, the method for coining new words used (most frequently) is derivation. Compounding and derivation are not always, however, means of word formation which complement each other. Even though there are many languages in which compounding occupies a prominent place but derivation is limited or non-existent, there are also examples of languages in which both compounding and derivation are productive, and languages in which neither compounding nor derivation is well attested (see Table 32.1).

Languages with few compounds tend to have compounds among nouns (the word class where compounds often concentrate even in the languages which make extensive use of compounding) and not among verbs, as happens in Maipure, Baniva, and Yavitero (and also, for example, in Yessan-Mayo, Sepik-Ramu – Foreman 1974: 20 – and Lillooet, Salishan – van Eijk 1997: 54). Only a small number of languages with few compounds do not have compound nouns. One of these is the above-mentioned Evenki whose only compound words are a few verbs and one adverb (Nedjalkov 1997: 308).

CHAPTER 33

....

ARAUCANIAN: MAPUDUNGUN

....

MARK C. BAKER AND
CARLOS A. FASOLA

MAPUDUNGUN is the primary member of the small Araucanian family – its greater genetic affiliation is uncertain – and is spoken by some 300,000 Mapuche people in central Chile and adjoining areas of Argentina (Augusta 1903, Smeets 1989, Salas 1992, Loncon Antileo 2005). The most common word order is Subject–Verb–Object, but word order is fairly free: the subject often comes after the verb instead of before it, and the object sometimes comes before the verb rather than after it (Smeets 1989, Loncon Antileo 2005). Noun phrases are not marked for case, but agreement with both the subject and the object appears on the verb in a way that is sensitive to the person hierarchy. The language can be classified as polysynthetic in both the informal sense and in the more technical sense of Baker (1996) (M. Baker 2006).

Compounding is frequent and productive in Mapudungun, and constitutes an important part of the language's overall polysynthetic quality. Different types of compounds can be distinguished, with some cross-cutting similarities. Perhaps the most interesting theoretical issues that are raised by compounding in Mapudungun stem from the fact that different ordering principles apply to different kinds of compounds. These principles are at least partly independent of what categories are involved in compounding. We illustrate this by discussing in some detail the three most prominent kinds of compounding in Mapudungun: V+N compounding, N+N compounding, and V+V compounding. We then touch more briefly on other sorts of compounds in the language, including those that contain an adjectival root.

33.1 VERB+NOUN COMPOUNDING

The best-known and best-studied type of compounding in Mapudungun is the joining of a verb root and a noun root to form a larger verbal stem. Two full-sentence examples that contain this sort of compounding are:[1]

(1) a. *Ñi   chao   kintu-waka-le-y.*   (Sa:195)
         my   father   seek-cow-PROG-IND.3SG.SBJ
         'My father is looking for the cows.'
     b. *Ngilla-kofke-n.*   (EL)
         buy-bread-IND.1SG.SBJ
         I bought the bread.

Additional examples that illustrate the scope of the phenomenon are given in (2) (Smeets 1989: 421).

(2) a. *entu-poñu-n*   take.out-potato-INF   'to dig up potatoes'
     b. *kintu-mara-n*   look.for-hare-INF   'to hunt hares'
     c. *llüka-lka-che-n*   become.afraid-CAUS-person-INF   'to frighten people'
     d. *kücha-kuwü-n*   wash-hand-INF   'to wash one's hands'
     e. *nentu-antü-n*   take.out-day-INF   'to fix a date'
     f. *are-tu-ketran*   borrow-TR-wheat   'borrow wheat'
     g. *püto-ko-n*   drink-water-INF   'to drink water'

In these compounds, the noun root is interpreted as the theme/direct object argument of the verb root. Examples like (1a) are thus roughly equivalent to sentences like (3), in which there is no compounding, but the verb takes a direct object in the syntax.

(3) *Ñi   chao   kintu-le-y   ta chi   pu   waka.* (Sa:195)
     my   father   seek-PROG-IND.3SG.SBJ   the   COLL   cow
     'My father is looking for the cows.'

---

[1] The data that this article is based on comes from four main sources, which we abbreviate as follows: A = Augusta (1903); Sm = Smeets (1989); Sa = Salas (1992); EL = Elisa Loncon Antileo (2005) and/or personal communication. If no attribution is given for one member of a list of examples, then it is taken from the same source as the closest example above it that has an attribution.

The examples in (1) and (2) thus count as a kind of noun incorporation, of the sort studied for other languages in Mithun (1984), Baker (1988, 1996), Rosen (1989), and other works. The compound verbs in (1) and (2) are morphologically intransitive; for example, there is no marker of object agreement on the verb in (4) (*ngilla-waka-fi-n, buy-cow-3SG.OBJ-1SG.SBJ). The incorporated noun can be referred to by pronouns in discourse, as shown in (4), but it cannot be doubled or modified by material outside the verbal complex, as shown in (5).

(4) *Ngilla-waka-n.   Fei   langüm-fi-n.   (Baker et al. 2005)
     buy-cow-1SG.SBJ   then   kill-3OBJ-1SG.SBJ
     'I bought a cow. Then I killed it.'

(5) *Pedro   ngilla-waka-y   tüfa-chi   (waka).   (Baker et al. 2005)
     Pedro   buy-cow-IND.3SG.SBJ   this-ADJ   cow
     'Pedro bought this cow.'

Mapudungun V+N compounding thus counts as type III noun incorporation within the typology of Mithun (1984): incorporated nouns are active in the discourse, but cannot function as 'classifiers' that are doubled by more specific external noun phrases.

Since verb+noun compounding is a (superficially) detransitivizing process in this language, nouns cannot generally be compounded with intransitive verb roots. Such compounding is possible, however, if an NP interpreted as the possessor of the noun is present in the sentence to function as its grammatical subject, as shown in (6).

(6) a. *af-kofke-y.   (EL)
         end-bread-IND.3SG.SBJ
         'The bread ran out.'

     b. af-kofke-n
         end-bread-IND.1SG.SBJ
         'My bread ran out.'

Baker, Aranovich, and Golluscio (2005) argue that noun incorporation in Mapudungun is a syntactic process, the result of moving the head noun of the thematic object out of the noun phrase that it heads in the syntax and adjoining it to the head of the verb phrase. Their argument is based partly on the fact that the noun is active in the discourse in examples like (4), and partly on the fact that the incorporated noun root can be understood as standing in a possessee–possessor relationship with an NP (e.g. the null first person singular pronoun in (6b)) that appears outside the verbal complex, where it was 'stranded' by movement of the head noun. Unlike other well-studied languages with syntactic noun incorporation, however, the noun root comes immediately after the verb stem, not immediately before it, as observed by Golluscio (1997). Mapudungun thus falsifies an

absolute interpretation of Baker's (1996) observation that syntactically incorporated nouns always appear to the left of the incorporating verb (see also Kayne 1994
on heads generally adjoining to the left of other heads). That observation turns out
to be a statistical tendency, but not an inviolable universal.

The head–non-head order of V + N compounds in Mapudungun also stands out
in some language-internal comparisons. The language contains occasional examples of N + V compounds as well, although this order is much less common:

(7) a. *Ngillañ-yew-fu-yngün.*   (EL)
       brother.in.law-carry-IMPED-3DU.SBJ
       'The two of them were brothers-in-law.'

    b. *ad-tripa-n*   (A: 271)
       face/appearance-go.out-INF
       'to turn out like the original'

These examples are also different from the ones in (1)–(6) in that there is not a
clear-cut predicate–argument relationship between the verb root and the noun
root; if anything, the nouns seem to play a quasi-predicative role in (7). Since these
examples are less productive and less semantically transparent, it is plausible to
think that they are formed in the lexicon, rather than in the syntax via head
movement. If so, then the order of head and non-head differs in Mapudungun
depending on the component in which the compound is formed: syntactically
constructed combinations are head-initial, whereas morphological combinations
are head-final.

Morpheme order in compounds also contrasts with morpheme order in derivational morphology in Mapudungun. Verbalizing affixes are always suffixes in
Mapudungun. In other words, the verbal head follows its nominal argument if
the verbal head is an affix, whereas the opposite order is characteristic of productively formed compounds. Typical are the examples in (8), which involve the
common and productive verbalizing affix *-tu* (Smeets 1989: 161).

(8) a. *kofke-tu-n*   bread-VBLZ-INF   'to eat bread'
    b. *pulku-tu-n*   wine-VBLZ-INF   'to drink wine'
    c. *kitra-tu-n*   pipe-VBLZ-INF   'to smoke a pipe'
    d. *tralka-tu-n*   gun-VBLZ-INF   'to shoot a gun'
    e. *mamüll-tu-n*   wood-VBLZ-INF   'to fetch wood'

These examples are semantically comparable to the compounds in (1) and (2) in
that the noun seems to function as the internal argument of the verbal morpheme;
compare, for example, (2g) with (8b). Nevertheless, the order is markedly different:
the noun root comes before the verbal head in (8b), but after it in (2g). It is
apparently not the case, then, that the same morpheme-ordering principles apply
to compounds and affixed forms in Mapudungun (contrary to, for example, Di
Sciullo and Williams 1987 and Lieber 1992a). Rather, the stipulated attachment

properties of affixes can override the general ordering principles that are seen in compounds, where no lexically specific affixation features are involved.

33.2 NOUN + NOUN COMPOUNDING

Although they have received less attention, noun + noun compounds are also common and very productive in Mapudungun. (9) gives some examples.

(9) a. *mapu-che*   land-people   'the Mapuche people'   (EL)
    b. *mapu-dungun*   land-words   'the language of the Mapuche'
    c. *ilo-korü*   meat-soup   'soup containing meat'
    d. *mamüll-wanglu*   wood-chair   'wooden chair'
    e. *küna-ruka*   bird-house   'birdhouse'
    f. *wingka-kofke*   whiteman-bread   'European-style bread'
    g. *kutran-che*   sickness-person 'sick person'   (Sm: 148)
    h. *wariya-che*   town-people   'townspeople'
    i. *pulku-fotilla*   wine-bottle   'wine bottle' (a particular type
                                                              of bottle)

These are very similar to noun + noun compounds in English and other Germanic languages. As in English, the second noun is the head of the construction, and the first noun is interpreted as some kind of modifier of it. For example, the Mapuche are a kind of people who have a special relationship to the land, not a kind of land that relates somehow to people. Also as in English, the exact semantic relationship between the two parts of the compound is underspecified and can cover a broad range of meanings.

There is, however, a productive vein of noun + noun compounding that has the opposite morpheme order. The following compounds are left-headed, not right-headed:

(10) a. *nge-trewa*   eye-dog   'dog's eye, the eye of a dog'   (EL)
     b. *saku-kachilla*   sack-wheat   'a bag of wheat'
     c. *longko-waka*   head-cow   'cow's head'
     d. *lüpi-achawall*   wing-chicken   'chicken wing'
     e. *longko-kachilla* head-wheat   'a head of wheat'
     f. *namun-mesa*   leg-table   'table leg'
     g. *ilo-trewa*   meat-dog   'dog meat'
     h. *lichi-waka*   milk-cow   'cow's milk'
     i. *molifüñ-che*   blood-person   'human blood'
     j. *fotilla-pulku*   bottle-wine   'a bottle of wine'
                                           (one that actually contains wine)

What distinguishes these compounds from the ones in (9) is that the head noun in (10) is relational, and takes the second noun as its argument. Many of these examples involve body parts, or some other kind of part–whole relationship. Others involve a relationship between a container and a substance that it contains (10b, j), or a substance and the entity that it has been extracted from (10g–i). Indeed, sometimes the same two nouns can stand in either a modificational relationship or in an argumental relationship; this results in minimal pairs like (9i) and (10j), in which different semantic relationships between the nouns correspond to different orders of the roots (Smeets 1989: 173).

Evidence that the examples in (10) are N + N compounds, not syntactic combinations of noun and noun phrase complement (as Smeets 1989: 173–6 claims) comes from the fact that the second member of this construction cannot be a proper name or a full NP with an explicit determiner:[2]

(11)   a. *nge   tüfachi   trewa   (EL)
             eye   this   dog
             'an eye of this dog'

       b. *nge   Antonio
             eye   Antonio
             'Antonio's eye'

       c. *nge   ñi   chaw
             eye   my   father
             'my father's eye'

Also relevant is the fact that combinations like those in (10) can incorporate as a unit into a verb:

(12)   Antonio   ngilla-ilo-trewa-y.   (EL)
       Antonio   buy-meat-dog-IND.3SG.SBJ
       'Antonio bought some dog meat.'

Given that only the head noun of a noun phrase can incorporate into the verb, and other NP-internal material is stranded by noun incorporation (Baker 1988), (12) shows that *ilo-trewa* must count as a single N° in the syntax. Therefore, it is a compound.

What are the theoretical implications of this variation in the headedness of noun + noun compounds in Mapudungun? Notice that there is no similar variation in N + N compounds in English: *table-leg* and *dog-meat* are head-final, just as *townspeople* and *birdhouse* are. Nor is there any direct motivation for these orders in the phrasal syntax of Mapudungun: modifiers generally come before nouns in

---

[2] We credit Elisa Loncon with the view that the examples in (10) are compounds, and thank her for the supporting data in (11) and (12).

Mapudungun syntax, but so do possessors, even inalienable possessors (Smeets 1989: 170–1):

(13) *tüfa-chi   kawellu   ñi   pilum*   compare: *tüfa-chi   pilun-kawellu*
      this-ADJ   horse   POSS   ear   this-ADJ   ear-horse
      'the ear of this horse'   'this horse-ear'

One can, however, discern a similarity between order in V+N compounds and order in N+N compounds. In both domains, when the non-head is interpreted as an argument that bears a thematic relationship to the head, the non-head follows the head. In contrast, when the non-head is interpreted as a modifier, with an underspecified semantic relationship to the head, then the non-head precedes the head in both domains. There is a superficial difference in that most V+N compounds are head-initial, whereas the majority of N+N compounds are head-final, but this simply follows from the fact that most verbs are thematic-role assigners, whereas most nouns are not. Once this is factored out, the core ordering principle is seen to be the same in both domains.

This parallelism can perhaps be pushed one step further. Above we claimed (following Baker et al. 2005) that V+N=V combinations are formed by adjoining the noun to the verb in the syntax, as a result of movement, whereas N+V=V combinations are formed in the lexicon. Now the modificational N+N compounds in (9) are exactly the kind that Baker (2003: 271–5) argues must be formed in the lexicon, before referential indices are assigned to the noun roots in the syntax. By parity of reasoning, we tentatively conclude that the N+N compounds in (10) have the order that they do because they, like the V+N compounds in (1) and (2), are formed by noun incorporation in the syntax. If so, then the examples in (10) are the first known cases of noun incorporation into a noun – a sort of construction that is theoretically possible within the framework of Baker (1988), but which has never been documented.

The order of morphemes in N+N compounds can also be compared with the order of root and affix in noun-to-noun derivational morphology. Mapudungun has a productive noun forming suffix-*fe*, which attaches to nouns to form a new noun that means 'person who (habitually, professionally) makes X'.[3]

(14) a. *ilo-kulliñ-fe*   meat-cattle-er   'butcher; one who
                                           makes animal meat'(Sm:411)

      b. *kofke-fe*   bread-er   'baker'   (A: 247)

---

[3] There is an alternative analysis of these examples in which they are not immediately relevant to the point at hand. *Fe* also attaches productively to verb stems, to create agentive nominals (e.g. *küdau-fe* 'work-er'). Moreover, Mapudungun allows verbs to be zero-derived from nouns, with the verb meaning 'to make an X' (e.g. *ruka-n* house-INF 'to make a house'; see Smeets 1989: 154). Hence, it is possible that the proper analysis of (14c) is only [$_N$ [$_V$ ruka$_N$+Ø]-fe] and never [$_N$ [$_N$ ruka]-fe]. We leave this matter open.

    c. *ruka-fe*   house-er   'architect'
    d. *zapato-fe*   shoe-er   'shoemaker'

The grammatical head in these examples is the affix, and there is presumably a function–argument relationship between the two morphemes, not merely a relationship of modification. Nevertheless, the head is final, not initial as it is in compounds with a function–argument relationship. This replicates what we saw in (8): the morphological attachment properties of an affix (whether it is stipulated as being a prefix or a suffix in the lexicon) override the general principles of ordering that hold in compounds.

For completeness, we mention that we have seen no sign of *dvandva*-type compounds in Mapudungun, which have conjunctive meanings like those that are found in many South Asian languages. Thus, Mapudungun has no known compounds of the type 'father-mother', with the meaning 'parents'. The fact that a certain formal type of compounding is common and productive in a language (here N + N compounding) does not mean that it can do everything that can be done semantically by that type of compounding in other languages.

33.3 Verb + verb compounding

The third salient kind of compounding in Mapudungun is verb + verb compounding. This is the least studied type of compounding in Mapudungun, and is arguably the least well-understood type cross-linguistically. Many cases seem to be at least partially idiomatic, and it is not always clear which element of the compound is the head. We can, however, present some interesting examples, make some comparisons, and draw some tentative conclusions.

The following selection (15) contains examples which seem to be more or less compositional, with the normal lexical meanings of both verb roots discernible in the meaning of the compound.[4]

(15) a. *weyel-kon-n*   swim-go.in-INF   'to go in swimming' (A: 269)
      b. *anü-n-püra-m-n* sit-INF-go.up-CAUS-INF 'to make sit up'
      c. *rüngkü-kon-n*   jump-go.in-INF   'to go in jumping'

---

[4] We omit from our discussion aspectual combinations in which the second verb is semantically bleached; some or all of these may now be affixes that have developed historically from verbal roots. Examples include morphemes like *meke* 'spend time X-ing', *fem* 'do X immediately', *(kü)le* 'be X-ing', *ka* 'do X various times', *nie* 'have'. For some remarks on these, see Smeets 1989: 419–20. Other verbal compounds seem similar to light verb constructions in other languages; see (21) below for a brief discussion.

d.	*fuli-naq-n*	scatter-fall-INF	'to fall and scatter' (A: 270)
e.	*weyel-nopa-n*	swim-cross-INF	'to swim over to here' (A: 272)
f.	*fitra-lef-tripa*	get.up-run-leave	'get up and run out' (Sa: 189)
g.	*rapi-tripa-n*	vomit-go.out-INF	'to go out by vomiting' (A: 271)
h.	*wüño-kintu-n*	come.back-look-INF	'to look back' (A: 272)
i.	*kon-kintu-n*	go.in-look-INF	'to look into'
j.	*wüño-weu-tu-n*	come.back-win-TR-INF	'win back' (A: 276)
k.	*witra-nentu*	pull-take.out	'to pull out' (Sm: 416)
l.	*ultra-nentu*	push-take.out	'to push out, away'
m.	*meñku-ñ-püra-m*	carry.in.arms -INF-go.up-CAUS	'to carry up'
n.	*kücha-nentu-n*	wash-take.out-INF	'wash out' (A: 270)
o.	*trana-künu-n*	knock.down-leave-INF	'to leave something fallen' (A: 262)
p.	*anü-künu-n*	sit-leave-INF	'to leave something sitting'
q.	*sera-kunu*	close-leave	'to leave something closed' (Sa: 190)

For many of these, it is not clear what the relationship between the two verbs is. Many of them consist of a manner-of-motion verb followed by direction-of-motion verb (15a–f, k–n). Many also seem to have a conjunctive meaning, in which the associated NPs are interpreted as the subject and/or object of both verbs equally. Two examples in actual sentences are:

(16) a. *Witra-ñ-püra-m-fi-y-u*   *tüfa-chi*   *mesa.* (Sm: 417)
           pull-INF-go.up-CAUS-3SG.OBJ-IND-1DU.SBJ   this-ADJ   table
           'We lifted up this table.'

      b. *Rumé*   *ayü-w-üy-ngün*   *pülle-tu-pe-fi-lu*   *ti*   *füchá*   *üñüm* (Sm: 496)
          very   love-REFL-   near-TR-see-   the   big   bird
                   IND-3PL.SBJ   3OBJ-PTPL
          'They were enthusiastic when they came close to and saw the airplane.'

It is not clear which verb, if either, is the head. But Smeets (1989: 416) observes that, as a rule, when the argument structures of the two members of a compound differ, the compound derives its valence from the second member of the compound. That seems particularly clear for the compounds that end with *künun* 'leave' in (15o–q); these are compounds of an intransitive verb plus the transitive verb 'leave', resulting in a transitive verb. (15b) probably also fits this pattern, and (15h–j) might too. So for those verb + verb compounds in (15) that have a clear and unique head, the head is final.

There is another productive pattern, however. A modal, aspectual, or causative verb can compound with any other verb, and when it does, the modal/aspectual verb comes first:[5]

(17) a. *kim-rüngkü*   know-jump   'to know how to jump' (Sa: 192)
     b. *küpa-ülkatu*   want-sing   'to want to sing'
     c. *pepi-nengüm*   be.able-move   'to be able to move'
     d. *pepi-trepe-l*   be.able-wake-CAUS   'to be able to wake X up'
     e. *wüño-kutran-tu-n*   return-sick-VBLZ-INF   'to fall ill again' (A: 276)
     g. *af-nak-üm*   stop-go.down-CAUS   'to stop taking down' (Sm: 416)
     h. *ngilla-azoti*   make(lit. buy)-scourge 'to have X scourged' (A: 277)

The first verbs in these combinations are exactly the sorts of verbs that take VP complements in many other languages (Wurmbrand 2003a). In fact, all these verbs except perhaps *küpa* 'want' can be used as independent verbs that take fully clausal complements in Mapudungun. (18) and (19) give near-minimal pairs, one with V + V compounding, and one without.

(18) a. *Kim-tuku-fi-n.*   (Sm: 219)
       know-put.at-3OBJ-1SG.SBJ
       'I know how to put it.'

     b. *Iñche   kim-ün   fey   ñi   küpa-ya-l*   (Sm: 258)
       I   know-1SG.SBJ   he   POSS   come-FUT-NOML
       'I have learned (come to know) that he will come.'

(19) a. *Af-dungu-y-iñ.*   (Sm: 418)
       stop-speak-IND-1PL.SBJ
       'We stopped speaking.'

     b. *Af-a-y*   *kewa-n.*   (Sm: 243)
       stop-FUT-3SG.SBJ   fight-INF
       'The fighting will stop.' ('it/she/he will stop fighting')

A verb incorporation account is thus natural for the examples in (17), (18a), and (19a). These six verbs (among others) can select a propositional complement. This complement may be expressed either as a full clause, with tense and all the other usual functional categories, or it can be a bare verb phrase. If it is a full clause, the functional categories block incorporation of the verbal head of the complement

---

[5] Unlike Salas (1992), Augusta (1903), and Pascual Masullo (personal communication), Smeets (1989) treats these as auxiliary-plus-main-verb constructions, not as verb-verb compounds. It is unclear what her reason for doing this is. Taking the modal/aspectual verbs to be auxiliaries makes them exceptional in two respects. First, inflectional morphology goes on the main verb, not on the 'auxiliary' (see (18a) and (19a)), the opposite of what one sees in auxiliary constructions in Indo-European languages. Second, the 'auxiliary' is required to come immediately before the associated verb – a surprising requirement in a language that otherwise has rather free word order. Both these anomalies disappear if we take these to be verb + verb compounds, as other authors do.

into the higher verb, resulting in (18b) and (19b). But if the complement is a bare VP, incorporation is not blocked; the head verb of the complement can move to adjoin to the higher predicate. More precisely, the complement verb adjoins to the right of the selecting verb, just as an incorporated noun adjoins to the right of the verb that selects it in Mapudungun. We thus find argument-taker–argument order in these V+V compounds, just as we did in the V+N compounds in (1) and the N+N compounds in (10).

In contrast, it is far from clear what sort of syntactic structure the V+V compounds in (15) could be derived from; there is no obvious paraphrase for these examples in which the two verb roots are separate. Hence it is plausible that all or many of these examples are derived in the lexicon, with the first verb functioning as a modifier of the second verb, which determines the argument structure of the whole. If that is correct, then lexically formed V+V compounds have the order modifier–modified, parallel to what we found for modificational N+V and N+N compounds. It seems, then, that the same ordering principles apply to V+V compounds as apply to the other types – although the exact nature of many V+V compounds is not as clear as one would like.

Finally, we can compare compounding with derivational affixation once again. The causative morpheme *-l* is like the morphemes in (17) in that it is plausibly analysed as a verbal head that takes a VP as its argument, based on similar periphrastic constructions in other languages (e.g. English [$_{VP}$*make* [$_{VP}$*someone talk*]]). But *-l* is a bound affix, not a root. Furthermore, it follows the verb root that expresses its argument, in contrast to the order seen in (17):

(20) a. *dungu-l* talk-CAUS   'to make someone speak' (Sm: 396)
      b. *küpa-l*   come-CAUS   'to bring'
      c. *ürkü-l*   be.tired-CAUS   'to make tired'
      d. *putu-l*   drink-CAUS   'to make someone drink'

These examples can be compared especially with (17h), which is also a kind of causative construction. Again, the morpheme order in instances of derivational morphology is systematically different from the morpheme order in semantically comparable compounds, as a result of the particular attachment properties of the affixes.

It may be, however, that the attachment properties of affixes in Mapudungun are not ultimately all that idiosyncratic. The reader has probably noticed that all of the derivational affixes presented are, in fact, suffixes (see (8), (14), and (20)). Indeed, virtually all affixation in Mapudungun is suffixation. The examples with affixation are also somewhat different from comparable compounding examples in that the meanings of the affixes are vaguer and more general than those of any particular root. This is especially evident in (8), where the verbal suffix *-tu* can variously be translated as 'eat', 'drink', 'use', or 'get', depending on the meaning of the noun it combines with. It could be that this semantic fact about affixation determines the morpheme order, rather than any stipulated morphological properties of the affix. In other words, these examples might illustrate a third general principle of morpheme order in Mapudungun, that 'light verbs' follow the complement that provides the lexical meaning, where a 'light verb' is a verb that has a very general ('bleached') meaning, contributing aspectual information or argument structure properties to the construction it appears in, but little or no encyclopedic meaning. This generalization could perhaps also account for the morpheme order in verb + verb compounds like the following:

(21)   a. *rütre-n-tüku-n*   push-INF-put-INF   'to push' (A:267)
        b. *pütre-n-tüku-n*   burn-INF-put-INF   'to set on fire'
        c. *rütre-wül-n*   push-give-INF   'to give a push' (A:273)
        d. *kintu-wül-n*   look-give-INF   'to give a look' (A:272)

Pursuing this idea further would require being much more specific about what exactly a light verb is, and what the nature of its relationship to its complement is than we can be here. We simply mention it as an intriguing possibility for future work.

33.4 OTHER TYPES OF COMPOUNDING

N + N compounds, V + N = V compounds, and V + V compounds are salient parts of Mapudungun, and are explicitly discussed in Smeets (1989), Loncon (2005), and other descriptive works. But there are probably some other, less salient types as well, which we mention here.

Let us consider first what other kinds of compounds one might expect to find, given the informal theoretical observations that we have made so far. In particular, suppose that two roots of any category can be compounded together in Mapudungun, and that all combinations are subject to two general ordering principles: argument-takers come before their arguments, and modifiers come before their heads (perhaps because the former are derived in the syntax, and the latter are created in the lexicon). Given these simple and general principles, what other types of compounds should be found in Mapudungun?

One additional type that we should look for is verb-and-noun compounds in which the noun is the head – compounds comparable to *drawbridge* or *runway* in English. Given that nouns rarely or never take verbs/verb phrases as arguments, we would expect the verb to function as a modifier of the head noun in this sort of compound, not as its argument. Given the general ordering principles, the verb should come before the noun, not after it. We should not be surprised, then, to observe V+N=N compounds in Mapudungun, and (22) shows that we do observe them.

(22) a. *tripa-che*   go.out-person   'foreigner'   (Sa: 219)
      b. *trem-che*   grow-person   'a grown-up'   (Sm:149)
      c. *anü-ruka*   sit.down-house   'a house with a
                                               round roof' (Sm: 423)
      d. *chafo-kutran*   cough-illness   'a coughing disease'

In contrast, we do not expect N+V=N compounds, nor have we found any.

We mention in passing that there are also some exocentric V+N=N compounds in Mapudungun, comparable to *scarecrow* and *pickpocket* in English, although Smeets (1989: 423) says that this process is not productive. Two examples are *trari-kuwü* (bind-hand) 'bracelet' and *shiwill-ko* (stir-water) 'porridge'. These cases are like the V+N=V compounds discussed in section 33.1 in that the noun stem functions as the semantic (theme) argument of the verb. Hence, it is consistent with our generalization that the verb comes before the noun. The difference is that the verb is not the head of the compound in these cases, because they are nouns, not verbs: a bracelet is neither a type of hand, nor a type of binding, but rather something that one binds around one's hand.

Now we add adjectives into the mix. What kinds of compounds should they appear in? In principle, an adjective could combine with a root of any category, and it could function as either the head or the non-head of the compound. But adjectives generally do not enter into function–argument relationships as either the argument-taker or as the argument, for principled reasons (see Baker 2003: Chapter 4). Hence compounds that include an adjective will be modificational compounds, and should fall under the modifier–head rule. In fact, an adjectival root can come before a noun, adjective, or verb head in a modificational compound, as shown in (23).

(23) a. *pichi-che*   little-person   'child'   (A+N=N, EL)
         pichi-achawall   little-chicken   'chick'
         kochi-kofke   sweet-bread   'sweetbread, cake'
         awka-waka   wild-cow   'wild cow'
         fücha-chaw   old-father   'grandfather'   (Sm: 149)
      b. *lig-karü*   white-green   'light green'   (A+A=A, EL)
         kum-karü   deep-green   'dark green'
         kurü-kelü   black-red   'dark red'   (Sm: 149)
      c. *küme-künü-n*   good-leave-INF   'to leave
                                                     something good'   (A+V=V, EL)
         karü-la-n   green-die-INF   'to die by accident'
         ngellu-miawu-n   difficult-walk-INF   'to walk with
                                                     difficulty'

For A+N combinations with very compositional meanings, it is not immediately obvious whether they are compounds or phrases. However, some of them can be incorporated into the verb as units, proving that they count as a single N° in the syntax (compare (12) above):

(24) *Ngilla-küme-pulku-a-n.*   (EL)
      buy-good-wine-FUT-1SG.SBJ
      'I will buy good wine.'

It is also significant that we have not found any clear examples of compounds with the opposite headedness, compounds of the form N+A=N or V+A=V. Hence the expectation is confirmed that all compounds involving adjectives fall under the general modifier–modified rule for Mapudungun – perhaps the result of their being formed in the lexicon, not in the syntax by way of head movement. If these are less salient than some of the other types of compounding, that might simply be the result of there being fewer adjective roots to work with. But more systematic work on compounds that involve adjectives is called for before these conclusions can be considered firm.[6]

Finally, for the sake of completeness, we mention that there may also be compounds in Mapudungun that involve functional categories. For example, complex determiners can be built up out of simple determiners; hence Smeets (1989: 118–19) mentions 'compound' forms like *fey-ta* 'that-the', *fey-ti* 'that-the', *fey-ta-ti* 'that-the-the', *fey-tüfa* 'that-this' (p. 110), *ta-ti* 'the-the', *ta-ñi* 'the-my' (p. 120), *fey-(ta)-engu* 'that-the-they.DU' (pp. 120–1), and so on. Of course the system for doing this is limited, because the range of determiners is limited. These examples might be compared to the very limited range of compound prepositions allowed in English (*into* and *onto* but not *underto*, *onfrom*, etc.). Also worth noting is the common word *fey-pi* 'that-say', which seems to be a compound of a demonstrative and a verb:

(25) *Fey-engu*   *fey-pi-e-new:* . . .   (Sm: 478)
      that-they.DU   that-say-INV-1SG.SBJ.3OBJ
      'The two of them said this to me: . . .'

The head verb is the final member of the compound here. If the demonstrative is an expression of the direct object argument of the verb, then the order is argument–verb, in marked contrast to the verb–argument order that is found when a noun is incorporated. This could point to some principled difference in how compounding/incorporation applies to functional categories as opposed to lexical categories.

---

[6] In principle, our theoretical expectations would also permit N+A=A compounding and V+A=A compounding, but we have not found examples of these types. We do not know whether this is merely an accidental gap in our data, or whether these sorts of compounds are truly absent in the language. If they are absent, this could be a sign that the adjective category is a closed class in Mapudungun, so new members of the category cannot be freely coined or constructed.

Or it could be that the demonstrative is really interpreted as an adverbial, to be more accurately glossed as 'X said thusly'. If so, then (25) has the modifier–head order that is normal for Mapudungun. In general, the issue of compounds that involve functional categories as one or both members of the compound is one that merits further work.

33.5 CONCLUSIONS

In conclusion, we have seen that virtually all formal types of compounding are productive in Mapudungun – although not all types have all the meanings that one might imagine for them. In particular, Mapudungun is rich in compounds with a modificational interpretation and in compounds with a function–argument interpretation, but seems rather poor in compounds with a conjunctive interpretation.

The order of the two elements in a simple binary compound varies in an interesting way. The head of the compound is not in one consistent location within the compound, the way it is in English. Rather, there are two major ordering principles for compounds: an argument-taker comes before its argument, and a modifier comes before the term it modifies. These generalizations cut across the different formal types of compounds, explaining why some noun-and-verb compounds are right-headed and some are left-headed, and similarly for noun + noun compounds and verb + verb compounds. It is thus not the categories of the roots involved in the compound that are crucial for determining the structure of those compounds in Mapudungun, but rather the kind of semantic condition that holds between them. It may seem that compounding is predominantly head-final in this language, but that is probably an artefact of the fact that all categories can participate in modification, whereas only some categories (verbs and relational nouns) are argument-takers.

More speculatively, we have conjectured that the differences in order might ultimately be signs of differences in where and how the compounds are constructed. Modifier–head order could be the result of adjoining on the left in the lexicon, whereas head–argument order could be the result of adjoining on the right in the syntax. This is largely an extrapolation from Baker et al.'s (2005) view that V + N compounds result from syntactic incorporation in Mapudungun, and Baker's (2003) view that modificational N + N compounds must be built in the lexicon. If the extrapolation is correct, then the unusual property of Mapudungun – that the order of adjunction is different in the two generative components – provides an unusually clear window into the question of which types of word formation are syntactic and which are not.

CHAPTER 34

PAMA-NYUNGAN: WARLPIRI

JANE SIMPSON

34.1 INTRODUCTION

The structure of Warlpiri words is integrally bound with the word-classes of Warlpiri, the morphological fact that the language is generally suffixing, the morphosyntactic fact that the language is underlyingly right-headed (in that it has case-suffixes, and that objects precede verbs in non-finite clauses), and the semantic preference for entities to precede attributes, but not determiners, in noun phrases.

In Warlpiri there are two main open classes of words: nominals and preverbs. Verb roots are a closed class of less than 150, which may be monosyllabic (a list is given in Nash 1986: 242–6). Nominals include words that denote entities, words that denote properties, and words that may denote either. Free nominals must be two or more syllables long, and must end in a vowel. Thus, to historical monosyllables or consonant-final roots are added synchronically inseparable augments such as -pa or -ki or -ku. For example, proto-Pama-Nyungan *calañ; 'tongue' (Alpher 2004) is realized in Warlpiri as *jalanypa*. Preverbs (Nash 1982) are a class of words found in many Australian languages which combine with verbs to form verbal words that denote events and states. For example, *karri-mi* 'to stand' combines with the preverb *jaa-*, to form *jaa-karrimi* 'to be agape'. They may be monosyllabic, as *jaa-*, and may end in a consonant, as *rdilypirr-karrimi* 'to be perforated', but the consonant-final forms often have alternants with the same augments as nouns, *rdilypirrpa*, and then are freer in distribution and in terms of what can suffix to them. By far the most productive way of creating new words in Warlpiri is the joining of preverb and verb.

34.2 NOMINALS

Plenty of nominal + nominal compounds are attested in the *Warlpiri Dictionary* (Laughren in prep.). However, these do not seem to have the same productivity as nominal + nominal compounds in English.

In Warlpiri, attributes may be predicated of entities by juxtaposition, without the need for a copula. Often, but not always, the nominal denoting the entity precedes the nominal denoting the attribute, as in (1). In this example 'curved beak' is predicated of the subject of the sentence, via part–whole syntax (Hale 1981).

(1)   *Lapaji, lapaji = ji*   *ka*   **lirra**   **narntirnki!**   *nyina,*
      Port.Lincoln.Ringneck = EUPH   AUX   mouth   curved   sit.NONPST
      'The Port Lincoln Ringneck Parrot, the Port Lincoln Ringneck Parrot has a curved beak.'
      (Warlpiri Dictionary *lapaji*, HN: 598–9)[1]

Example (2) shows that the sequence can act as a single phrase.

(2) *Ngamirliri,*   **kakarda**   **kirrirdi** = *yijala* *kuja* = *ka*   *nyina,*
     Stone.curlew   nape   long = also   thus = AUX   sit. NONPST
     parrulka = piya,   **wurliya** = *ju* **wita** = *lku*   *ka*   *wapa -*
     bush.turkey = like   foot = EUPH   small = then   AUX   move.NONPST
     wuurnpa.
     narrow.
     'The Stone Curlew, which also has a long neck, like a bustard, has little feet. They are narrow.' (Warlpiri Dictionary *ngamirliri*, HN: 587–9)

Note that the two nominals precede the auxiliary. Since the auxiliary appears in second position, a group of words preceding it is arguably a single constituent (Hale 1973), regardless of whether the first element has a discourse marker attached, as the euphony marker = *ju* in *wurliya* = *ju*. Thus (2) shows that the sequence N N can occur as a single constituent, presumably NP, although it could also be interpreted as a compound. The main predicator here is a stance verb (*nyina*) or motion verb (*wapa*) used as a copula. Such phrases are quite common.

---

[1] Codes after an example sentence refer to its source.

Similar structures of entity–attribute are found in words for natural kinds (animals and plants), but are deemed frozen in Nash (1986: 39). Many consist of body parts with following modifiers of the body part (Warlpiri Lexicography Group 1986); the term gives a characteristic property of the animal's appearance. Semantically they are exocentric compounds, syntactically they have a head–modifier structure:

kuna-maju 'emu'	*kuna* 'anus, shit'	*maju* 'bad'
milpa-rtiri 'Spectacled Hare-wallaby'	*milpa* 'eye'	*tiri* 'red'
ngalya-turlkunku 'cat'	*ngalya* 'forehead'	*turlkunku* 'bulging'
jaka-larra 'small tree with double-pointed prickles'	*jaka* 'rear, backside'	*larra* 'split'

These terms may coexist with everyday terms, or they may come to be the everyday term for the entity. Some words appear to be old compounds, often with recognizable first members and reduplicated second members (Nash 1986:120), e.g. *ngapurlu-punngu-punngu* 'multi-barbed spear' (*ngapurlu* 'nipple').

The strategy of creating a name for some entity by creating a compound describing some distinctive property of it (such as 'red eye') resembles another strategy – using a noun with a derivational case-suffix[2] to express a distinctive property. Echidnas for example can be called *jiri-parnta* (spike-having), and scorpions are *kana-parnta* (digging stick-having).

Body-part attribute structures are also used to attribute properties. Many sequences of body-part–attribute, such as *milpa-liirlki* 'cross-eyed' (lit. 'eye-white'), are given as compounds in the *Warlpiri Dictionary*. The meaning of the whole is transparently derived from the meanings of the parts, and there are no clear phonological differences between the phrase and the compound. So the justification for calling them compounds is less clear, except perhaps when used as nicknames for people: *Jurru-yarlu* 'Baldy' ('head-bare'), *Lirra-wantiki* 'Loud-mouth' ('mouth-wide'), or when the meaning is not transparent, as in *jalanypa-mulyu-mulyu* ('tongue-nose-nose') 'rapid repeated movement of tongue in and out of mouth'.

Body parts are also used to denote the seats of emotions, and the same entity–attribute structure is used for properties of behaviour and attitude:

jurru-marntarla 'insensitive and stubborn person'	*jurru* 'head'	*marntarla* 'gidgee tree'
kuna-liirlpari 'brave, courageous'	*kuna* 'anus, shit'	*liirlpari* 'white'
lirra-wilji 'keep on insisting loudly'	*lirra* 'mouth'	*wilji* 'insistent'

---

[2] 'Derivational case suffix' is a label for suffixes with meanings such as 'having', 'lacking' which are derivational in that they are used to derive new words, but are like case-suffixes in that there may be agreement, e.g. *yiljirli-kirli panu-kurlu* (lit. 'claw-with lot-with') 'with lots of claws' or, as is common in Warlpiri noun phrases, just the last word is marked with case, *watiya panu-kurlu* (lit. 'tree lot-with') 'with many trees' (Nash 1986, Simpson 1991). They are discussed later in this chapter.

Other types of semantic relation are seen, but none are particularly productive.[3]

The difficulty of distinguishing between phrases and compounds is found in other Australian languages; Baker has suggested for Ngalakgan that apparent compounds are in fact phrases which are interpreted as predicates, rather than as nominals (Baker 2006).

One area in which endocentric compounds are noticeably absent concerns place-names. Many English place-names consist of a place-label and a descriptor: the River Murray, Murray Bridge, Mount Murray, Murray Island, and so on. Place-labels like 'mountain, hill, plain, island' are rarely found in indigenous Australian place-names (Hercus and Simpson 2002), and Warlpiri is no exception. Place-names often denote water sources, but the names don't consist of compounds of descriptors with words like 'water-hole', 'creek', 'rock-hole', or 'soakage'. Instead, they may be unanalysable, or may contain derivational case-suffixes, e.g. *Yankirri-kirlangu* 'emu-belonging', or may contain small clauses.

Endocentric compounds are rare; even the apparently left-headed *langa-parraja* ('ear-coolamon') 'bat-ears, ears which stick out' noted by Nash (1986: 39) can also be used metonymically as a descriptor of a class of animals, and this is how a Warlpiri lexicographer, the late Paddy Patrick Jangala, defined it.

(3)   ***Langa-parraja*** = *ji,*   *ngulaji*   *mujunyku,*   *tankiyi*   *manu*
       ear-coolamon = EUPH,   that   rabbit,   donkey   and
       walpajirri,   *yangka*   *pilirripilirri-kirli.*
       rabbit.eared.bandicoot   the   flat-with
       '*Langa-parraja* is like rabbits, donkeys and bandicoots with flat ears.' (PPJ 10/85)

---

[3] They include:

- compounding a larger body part with something that narrows the denotation:
  lirra-pinpinpa 'lip'   *lirra* 'mouth'   *pinpinpa* 'thin'
  milpa-ngipiri 'eyeball'   *milpa* 'eye'   *ngipiri* 'egg'
- compounding a body part with a property to describe a resulting state, not a 'kind-of':
  langa-larra   'ear-split'   'ear-mark'
  mulyu-larra   'nose-split'   'bloody nose, nose-bleed'
- forming compound expressions of time by compounding the words for 'sun' or 'shade' with the position of the sun: *yama-karlarra* 'shadow-west' 'sunrise'
- compounding two partial antonyms:
  jaka-ngalya 'some of this and some of that'   *jaka* 'rear, backside'   *ngalya* 'forehead'
  nyurnu-wankaru ' brothers, sisters, where at least   *nyurnu* 'dead'   *wankaru* 'alive'
  one is dead and at least one is alive'
  pirdangirli-kamparru 'one behind the other'   *pirdangirli* 'behind'   *kamparru* 'ahead'
  kankarlu-kanunju 'up and down, one on top of the other' *kankarlu* 'up'   *kanunju* 'down'

This last can be metaphorically extended to 'be in two minds':

(i)   *Nyina*   *ka-rna*   *kankarlu-kanunju.*
      sit.NONPST   PRES-1SBJ   up-down
      'I'm in two minds (about it).' (PPJ 24/10/86)

A curious group of seemingly right-headed endocentric compounds occurs with words associated with the *jukurrpa*, 'the Dreaming' (the creative and omnipresent ancestral time). A person's own ancestral entity (totem) is also called *jukurrpa*, and that person can be named for that dreaming, e.g. *Ngapa-jukurrpa* 'Water-dreaming' or *Wampana-jukurrpa* 'hare.wallaby-dreaming'. Dreamings in their manifestations as men can be named using *ngarrka* 'man' or *wati* 'man' instead of *jukurrpa*: *Ngatijirri-ngarrka* 'Ancestral Budgerigar men', *Yarla-ngarrka* 'Ancestral Yam man', *Karnanganja-wati* 'Ancestral Emu man'.

It is tempting to relate these apparently anomalous right-headed forms to some polysyllabic, productive derivational case suffixes with meanings such as 'associate of' (*-wardingki*), 'denizen of' (*-ngarna(rra)* and *-ngawurrpa*), which, semantically, seem to be creating meanings that resemble right-headed structures. These suffixes never occur as free words. They attach to terms for places or areas: *yawulyu-wardingki* 'person associated with women's ceremonies', *pirli-ngarnarra* 'rocky hill dweller', *wilpayi-ngawurrpa* 'creek dweller'. But they appear in places where they clearly act more like case inflections than the second elements of compounds. They can attach to phrases (4), or be spread over both parts of a phrase (5), like normal case-suffixes.

(4) *Manu   miyi   ngirriri-ngirriri   watiya   wita-wita-ngawurrpa   manu*
      and   fruit round   tree   small-small-denizen   and
      miyi   ngakurru-nyayirni   ngayaki=ji.
      fruit   sweet.and.juicy-very   bush.tomato = EUPH
      'And the fruit is round and grows on small bushes [=is a denizen of small bushes] and its fruit is very sweet and juicy, the bush tomato.' (Warlpiri dictionary, *ngayaki*, PPJ 9/86)

(5) *Ngulaju   lalkapurra   wita-nyayirni   watiya-ngawurrpa   wita-ngawurrpa.*
      that   grub.sp.   small-very   tree-denizen   small-denizen
      'It is a small *lalkapurra* grub which lives on a small bush.' (Warlpiri Dictionary, *jakarla-payipayi* Rosie Napurrurla)

There are also some productive suffixal formatives which have the same form as free nominals, and attach to nominals and nominalized verbs. The resulting structures fit the strict definition of compounds as involving two free words when the formative attaches to a nominal, but they do not fit the definition when the formative attaches to a nominalized verb, since the latter never appear on their own. They must be followed by a suffix or a bound verb. Hence these formatives have been treated as suffixes, rather than as compounding nouns (Nash 1986: 25), but they clearly derive from compounds. An example is *panu* 'many', which as a suffix *-panu* means 'doing, typically to excess, some action' and attaches to nominals denoting activities and to nominalized verbs. This suffix is very productive.

On nominal: *yinka-panu* 'a real laugher' *yinka* 'laughing'

On nominalized verb: *pinja-panu* 'a real fighter' *pi-nyi* 'to hit'

Similar forms include *palka* 'thing, presence, fruit, body', *-palka* 'one able to', and *wita-wangu* (lit. 'small-without') 'very big, really big', *-wita-wangu* 'excessively, very much'.

There are a number of other rarely attested polysyllabic formatives which do not appear as free words, and which Nash (1986: 26) suggests may historically be the final part of N + N compounds.[4]

As Nash (1986: 37) notes, a productive pattern consists of forming a nominal denoting an actor or instrument by joining a nominal with a following deverbal nominal with the Nomic or Agentive ending.

kuyu-pantu-rnu	meat-pierce-AGEN = meat-piercer	'eagle-hawk'
yapa-nga-rnu	person-eat-AGEN = people-eater	'cannibal'
ngardanykinyi-nga-rnu	mistletoe-eat-AGEN = mistletoe-eater	'Mistletoe-bird'

The most common usage may often be metaphorical:

mulyu-paka-rnu	nose-hit-AGEN = nose hitter	'dense underbrush'
purturlu-paju-rnu	back-cut-AGEN = back cutter	'joker'

Usually, the base verb is transitive, and the first nominal corresponds to the object of the verb. The order Object–Verb mirrors the syntactic order that is found in non-finite nominalized clauses, where the object (if expressed) or other complement normally directly precedes the verb, which has led to Warlpiri being described as syntactically right-headed. But the association between the noun and the verb is not strictly that of object and verb. For example *milpa-nya-ngu* 'eye-see-er' is not someone who looks at eyes, but rather someone who stares a lot, and by metaphoric transfer, someone who is covetous. Sometimes the connection is obscure: *Lama-pakarnu* and *yarnma-pakarnu* are both glossed as 'skinny', as are *yarnma* and *lama*, while *pakarnu* is 'hitter'. The same occasional lack of transparency is true of English right-headed synthetic compounds: the relationship between the meanings and functions of *back* and *bite* and the meaning of *back-biter* is not transparent.

Sometimes an overt case-marker signals that the nominal does not bear the semantic role of the Object in the corresponding main clause: e.g. examples discussed in Hale (1967) and Nash (1986): *ngulya-ngka nyina-ngu* (burrow-LOC sit-AGEN) 'hole-dwellers', *mina-ngka nyina-ngu* (nest-LOC sit-AGEN) 'nest-dwellers'.

---

[4] An example is the ending *-marramarra* which is attested on only a few forms: *ngalyarrpa-marra-marra, jilja-marra-marra, yilyampuru-marra-marra* 'multiple sand-hills, continuous sand-ridges' (*ngalyarrpa, jilja, yilyampuru* 'sand-hill'), *marliri-marramarra* 'string of claypans' (*marluri* 'claypan'). The fact that it attaches to the augmented form *ngalyarrpa* shows that it attaches to a free-standing nominal. This contrasts with some lexicalized noun-suffix forms in which the suffix attaches to the unaugmented form, e.g. *ngalyarr-ngarna* 'creeper-twine' ('sand.hill-denizen').

Two rare examples in which the nominal is the agent are: *ngaju-wiri-manu* (I-big-cause-AGEN) 'one grown up by me' (Laughren p.c. 1994), and the complex *jaka ngawarra-rlu-ka-ngu* (rear flood-ERG-carry-AGEN) 'eroded buttocks' (insult) (Jeanie Nungarrayi Herbert p.c. to D. Nash 1994). The verbs *wiri-ma-ni* and *ka-nyi* take Ergative subjects in main clauses. The absence of the Ergative case on *ngaju* may reflect the fact that Ergative case may be omitted on first and second person singular pronoun subjects of transitive verbs in certain positions.

It is unusual for a deverbal noun created with the Nomic or Agentive ending to appear without a preceding nominal (exceptions include *karla-ngu* 'digging stick' from *karla-mi* 'to dig', and *pangu-rnu* 'digging scoop' from *pangi-rni* 'to dig'). The question arises as to whether a compound like *yarla-karla-ngu* 'yam-digger' (used of a person) is right-headed, that is, *yarla-karla-ngu* is a kind of digger. However, on its own, *karlangu* is usually used not of a person but of a digging-stick. This makes it a little problematic to argue that semantically *yarla-karla-ngu* is right-headed. More generally, the fact that deverbal nouns with the Nomic or Agentive are mostly the right-hand element of compounds, and are very rare without preceding nouns, makes it somewhat harder to justify considering these compounds as having the deverbal noun as the semantic head.

In sum, nominal compounds in Warlpiri are overwhelmingly semantically exocentric, and syntactically, the structure of most mirrors the syntax of corresponding phrases.

34.2.1 Words for new things

If N + N compounding were productive, we might expect to find it used a lot in words for new concepts (for which Warlpiri speakers have needed to find many words). In fact this doesn't happen much, as, in modern written Warlpiri, the major strategy is borrowing from English, including compounds such as 'health worker' which act as single units. Only a few words for new things are derived through exocentric body-part–attribute compounds:

langa-kirrirdi 'donkey'	*langa* 'ear'	*kirrirdi* 'long'
jurru-pirrjirdi 'buffalo'	*jurru* 'head'	*pirrjirdi* 'strong'
ngalya-larra 'rolled oats'	*ngalya* 'forehead'	*larra* 'split'
ngalya piirn-pari 'white person, European'	*ngalya* 'forehead'	*piirn-pari* 'whiteish'

For some of these, there are more commonly used terms: *tangkiyi* 'donkey', *kardiya* 'white person'. The strategy is the same as with other words for animals – picking out a salient feature of the thing concerned and describing that feature. Similar to this is the strategy of forming words for new things through exocentric forms with derivational case-suffixes meaning 'having' or 'belonging':

pangki-kirli, pangki-parnta[5] ('skin-having') 'orange, citrus fruit'	*pangki* 'skin'
kalaja-kurlangu ('foot.area-belonging') 'toilet, lavatory'	*kalaja* 'foot end of sleeping area where people urinate'

This strategy is also used for names of institutions; for example *Kurdu-kurdu-kurlangu* 'children-belonging' is the name of the Yuendumu child care centre. Occasionally the two strategies are combined into endocentric compounds: *turaki jaka-kurlu* ('vehicle backside-with') 'pick-up truck, utility truck'.

One example of an agentive compound is *pirlirrpa-ma-nu* (spirit-catch-AGEN) 'camera', including video camera, but *pitiyawu* 'video' and *kamira* 'camera' are also used.

34.3 VERBS

Having productive ways of creating verbs is a necessity in Warlpiri, since the class of monomorphemic verbs in Warlpiri is small and closed (Nash 1982, 1986; Laughren 2007). Monomorphemic verbs range from those with general meanings which appear as part of many complex verbs, such as *nyinami* 'to sit', *yirrarni* 'to put', *pakarni* 'to strike', to those with much more specific meanings, which appear in fewer complex verbs, such as *kapatimi* 'be uneasy in a place or situation'. We have seen that it is hard to distinguish nouns created by compounding from noun phrases in Warlpiri. It is also difficult to characterize compound verbs, but for different reasons.

The structure of all complex verbs is X+finite verb, and there are four main ways of creating them. However, none of these falls clearly inside the strict definition of compounding as joining together two words which can appear independently. Two involve elements which are definitely not free words. The other two involve either the word class of preverb, whose position is determined by that of the verb, or words which can be construed as preverbs or nominals.

The first way, [V-inf]$_N$+V, consists of taking a nominalized verb (which cannot stand on its own as an independent word) and adding one of a small group of free verbs: *kiji-rninja-parnka-mi* 'go and throw' (*kiji-rni* 'to throw', *parnka-mi* 'to run'). The second verb is restricted – usually a verb of motion – and the meaning is not always the same as the free verb in isolation. If either verb is transitive, then the

---

[5] *-kirli* and *-kurlu* are used in the Yuendumu and Lajamanu dialects of Warlpiri, while *-parnta* is used in the Hanson River and Willowra dialects.

resulting complex verb is transitive, and has an Ergative subject. Thus in (6) the transitive verb *kiji-rni* would normally take an Ergative subject, but the intransitive verb *parnka-mi* takes an unmarked subject, while in (7) the nominalized verb *yukanja* is intransitive and the finite verb *yirrarni* is transitive. In both cases the subject has Ergative case (Simpson 2001).

(6) *Lulju*   *ka=lu*   *kiji-kiji-rninja-parnka*   *yurrampi-rli.*
     dirt.heaps   AUX=3PL.SBJ   throw-throw-INF-run-NONPST   honey.ant-ERG
     'The honey ants run back and forth dumping dirt.' (Warlpiri Dictionary *lulju*)

(7) *Pirlijimanu-rlu*   *wiyarrpa*   *yuka-nja-yirra-rnu.*
     policeman-ERG   poor.thing   enter-INF-put-PST
     'The policeman put the poor fellow in (jail).' (Warlpiri Dictionary *yirra-rni*)

So this strategy consists of joining a bound infinitive to a free verb. The resulting form has the tense/aspect markers atttached to the free verb, but the case-marking of the subject may be determined by that demanded by the bound infinitive.

   The second way, N + -V, consists of taking a nominal X and adding to it a bound verb *-jarri-mi* 'to become X', or adding a bound verb *-ma-ni* 'to cause to become X' or 'to act in relation to X' (both transitive) or 'to move somewhere in X manner' or 'make X noise' (both intransitive) among other meanings. The verbs created with *-jarri-mi* are intransitive and have subjects unmarked for case, as do the intransitive verbs created by *-ma-ni*. The transitive verbs created with *-ma-ni* have Ergative subjects. Thus, if we allow for at least two verbs *-ma-ni*, the case-frame of the whole complex verb is determined by the case-frame of the bound.

   The meaning of the nominal can be quite indeterminate, as can be seen by the fact that this structure is the standard way of borrowing new verbs from English or Kriol into Warlpiri, e.g. *riiti-ma-ni* 'to read', *jingkapat(i)-jarri-mi* 'to think about'. *Riiti* and *jingkapat* do not generally occur on their own. The nominal normally has the form of a free nominal (at least two syllables, vowel final), but Laughren (2007) notes that the nominal preceding *-ma-ni*, but not that preceding *-jarri-mi*, can be a consonant-final bare root: *karaly-ma-ni* or *karalypa-ma-ni* 'make something smooth', *karalypa-jarri-mi* 'become smooth'. A few examples of case-marked nominals have been found: *[langa-kurra]-jarri-mi* ear-ALL-become-NONPST ('to take in, understand'), *[langa-kurra]-ma-ni* ear-ALL-cause-NONPST 'to make someone understand' (Laughren 2007). The nominal may not be a nominalized verb, with the rare exception of case-marked nominalized verbs with *-ma-ni* as in *yula-nja-ku-ma-ni* (cry-INF-PURP-cause-NONPST) 'to make someone cry' (Nash 1986: 43).

   So this strategy consists of joining a free nominal to a bound verb. The resulting form has the tense/aspect markers attached to the bound verb, and the case-marking of the subject is determined by that demanded by the bound verb.

   The third way, N + V, consists of taking a nominal X and adding a free verb to it. Thus, *larra* 'split', which we have seen can be compounded with nouns in *mulyu-larra* 'nose-bleed', can be compounded with a verb to mean 'split by V-ing', e.g. *larra-kati-rni* 'tread on something and split it' (*kati-rni* 'to tread'), *larra-ya-ni* 'come to be split' (*ya-ni* 'to go'). The case-frame of the whole complex verb is determined by the case-frame of the final verb.

In such cases, it has usually been assumed that X is both a nominal and a preverb. If X is a nominal, then it must be at least two syllables long and vowel-final. If X is a preverb then it may appear as a consonant-final bare root (and some when acting as preverbs are only attested as bare roots): *jiirlpa* 'rising/setting of celestial body', *jiirl(pa)-wanti-mi* 'to set' (*wanti-mi* 'to fall'). The border between preverb and nominal is unclear. One test that Nash proposes is morphological: if the form can take a case ending in another context, then it can be a nominal; if it never appears in other contexts with case endings, then it must be a preverb.

The fourth way, PV + V, or V + PV, consists of taking a preverb and adding a verb to it: *jirrnganja-karri-mi* 'to stand accompanied by something' (*karri-mi* 'to stand'). Many preverbs have two forms, a bare root form which may be monosyl-labic and end in a consonant, and a form which conforms to the minimal word constraint of being at least two syllables long and ending in a vowel.

34.3.1 Preverbs

Preverbs themselves, while they can be reduplicated, are mostly monomorphemic, and show no evidence of internal structure resembling compounding. They may be productive creators of complex verbs, occurring in complex verbs with many monomorphemic verbs, or they may be unproductive, occurring with one or two verb roots. The verbs which they occur with may themselves be complex; thus in (8) a preverb which adds a Dative argument occurs as the initial element to a verb which consists of a Kriol loanword *warrki* followed by the bound verb *-jarri-mi* 'become'.

(8) *Manu* **ngirrilypa-warrki-jarri-mi**   *ka=rlipa=rla*   *pawuju-ku*
     and   close.by-work-become-NONPST   AUX=1PL.EX.SBJ=3DAT   boss-DAT
     warrki-ngka   *kutu=juku.*
     work-LOC   close=still
     'Or we work alongside the boss at work, really close by.' (Warlpiri Dictionary, *ngirrilypa*, jne)

Preverbs normally don't change the transitivity of a sentence (and thus the case of the subject), but some productive preverbs do add arguments with Dative case, which may act syntactically like Objects or Adjuncts depending on the preverb (Nash 1982; Simpson 1991; Legate 2002). (9) illustrates a preverb *jirrnganja* adding a Dative adjunct, *ngapa-ku palka-ku* 'water-DAT really.present-DAT' to a verb which would not normally take a Dative adjunct.

(9)   *Ngapa-ku   ka = rla   palka-ku   **jirrnganja-karri**   kartaku.*
      water-DAT   AUX = 3DAT   actual-DAT   accompanied-stand.NONPST   billycan
      'The can is standing with water (in it).' (Warlpiri Dictionary *jirrnganja-*)

Many preverbs can be reduplicated, and add quantifying or distributive meanings
to the resulting complex. Unlike nominals and verbs in Warlpiri, preverbs have
syntactic restrictions as to where they appear. They usually precede the verb, but
occasionally can directly follow it, as in (10) (note that in this case they must have
the form of a free word, i.e. at least two syllables and vowel-final, and so in the
example the consonant-final preverb *yaarl-* has the augment *-pa* added). Lexicalized
and unproductive preverbs cannot do this.

(10)   *ngula   yangka   kuja = ka = rla   jupujupu   kuyu   karli-mi*
       that   the   thus = AUX = 3DAT   soup   meat   flow-NONPST
       yaarl-yaarlpa,   rdiparl-pi-nja-warnu.
       on.top-on.top   knock-hit-INF-after
       'And the soup spills over her, having been knocked.' (Warlpiri Dictionary
       pupu-, PPJ)

When they precede the verb, they may have temporal clitics (11), directional
clitics (12), or second-position auxiliary clitics (11) attached. Again, if the preverb is
consonant-final, the form with the augment *-pa* must be used to provide a vowel
for consonant-initial clitics to attach to.

(11)   **Yaarlpa** = *lku = lpa = rla*   *parntarri-ja yangka yinya mingkirri-ki = ji.*
       on.top = then = AUX.past = 3DAT   crouch-PST the   yon   anthill-DAT = EUPH
       'He then collapsed over the top of that ant hill.' (Warlpiri Dictionary *yaarl-*,
       Winnie-W)

(12)   *Kalaka = ji   **walya   yaarlpa** = rni   wanti.*
       otherwise = 1OBJ   dirt   on.top = hither   fall.NONPST
       'Otherwise the dirt might fall down on me.' (Warlpiri Dictionary *yaarl-*,
       HN:1508)

So preverbs are not entirely free, but not entirely bound either. Note that in all
these examples the minimal word form of the preverb is used. A bare consonant-
final root is not possible in inverted structures or with clitics attached.

Nash (1982: 190) provides a table classifying these ways of forming new verbs
according to four properties: whether or not a directional clitic can attach to the
initial element, whether or not a second-position auxiliary can intervene between
the initial element and the finite verb, whether or not the order of the initial
element and the finite verb can be reversed, and whether or not the initial element
and the verb can occur separately. To these Laughren (2007) adds a further
property: whether or not the initial element can be consonant-final, i.e. a bare
root. She argues for a basic two-way split between tightly bound compound verbs

Table 34.1 Properties of initial elements in complex verbs

Possibility of...	Compound verb	⇒		⇐	Complex phrasal verb
	Conson-ant-final initial element	directional clitic on initial element	AUX clitic between V and initial element	reversal of initial element and V	both ini-tial element and V occurring independently
Type 1					
N-inf+V	n/a	yes	no	no	no
Type 2					
N+jarrimi	no	yes	rare	no	no
N+mani (tV)	yes	yes	rare	no	no
N+mani (iV)	yes	yes	rare	no	no
Type 3					
N/Pv V	yes	yes	yes	yes	yes (as N)
Type 4					
Frozen preverb	yes	no?	no	no	no
Other preverb	yes	depends on mean-ing	yes	yes	no
Dative adjunct preverb	no?	no	yes	yes	sometimes
Dative object preverb	yes	yes	yes	yes	sometimes (as post-position)

'consisting of a basic verb to which a modifying preverbal morpheme is directly attached', and more loosely bound phrasal verbs 'consisting of a basic verb to which a modifying preverbal morpheme which may be directly attached to the inflecting verb or which may host a number of enclitic morphemes including the deictic spatial morphemes, or the auxiliary element consisting of a tense/aspect marking base and pronominal enclitics'.

Table 34.1 summarizes Nash's and Laughren's properties of initial elements in complex verbs. The properties are arranged from left to right according to how tightly bound the resulting structure is if the property is positively attested. The most tightly bound are Laughren's compound verbs, which can include bare roots, the least tightly bound are Laughren's complex phrasal verbs.

In the course of a detailed discussion of the meanings of preverb+verb combinations, Nash (1982) observes that there is a cline from lexicalized combinations
of preverb and verb which cannot be split from the following verb, through semi-
productive combinations of preverb and verb which can be split, and where the
meaning of the whole is not always transparently derivable from the meaning of the
parts, through to highly productive preverbs, such as the preverbs which add
Dative arguments or adjuncts, which occur with lots of different verbs and create
combinations whose meanings are mostly compositional.

Some initial elements can form either compound verbs or complex phrasal
verbs: thus the productive Dative object preverb *yaarl(pa)* which occurs with
many verbs can be compounded as a bare root *yaarl-*, in which case it is tightly
bound and no directional clitic or auxiliary clitic can intervene between it and the
verb, or it can appear as a minimal word *yaarlpa*, in which case it is part of a
complex phrasal verb and for example directional clitics can attach to it (12).

Productive preverbs can be added to verbs which are themselves complex.
Productive preverbs occur commonly with lexical and semi-productive pre-
verb+verb combinations, as the outermost preverb. There are rare example of
three preverbs, e.g. (13):

(13) *Ngapa＝ju   milpirri   yirra-rninja-rla kankarlarra-ngurlu-kankarlarra-*
                                                      ngurlu
      water＝EUPH rain.cloud put-INF-after   above-from-above-from
      yaarl-   yurrurluku-   pirri-   -ma-nu.
      on.top- moving.down.and.away.from- landing- -cause-PST
      'After the rain clouds had all amassed from up above they then came down
      and settled over the top of it.' (Warlpiri dictionary *yurrurluku*, Dinny:
      Warntapi)

In this example, *yaarl-* is a productive preverb, *yurrurluku* is recorded with at
least seven other verbs. *Pirri* is recorded as a preverb with other verbs, but the
combination *pirri-ma-ni* 'to land on' appears to be idiosyncratic. This example is
also noteworthy in showing that a bare root preverb (*yaarl-*, as evidenced by the
lack of final consonant), can attach to a complex verb which has a preverb as an
initial element.

34.4 CONCLUSION

Every language needs ways of forming new words, but it is not always clear where
the boundary lies between a phrase and a word, or between a word formed by

derivation and one formed by compounding. New nominals can be created in Warlpiri through joining free nominals with free nominals, deverbal nominals, or bound nominals. Nominals formed by joining a bound nominal with a free nominal are difficult to distinguish from nominals formed with derivational suffixes, since both the bound nominal and the derivational suffixes appear on the right. Of the processes that could most naturally be called compounding, namely the joining of free nominals to another free nominal or to a deverbal nominal, both have the same order as corresponding phrases. The entity–attribute internal order of nominals created from free nominals is the same as the unmarked order inside noun phrases, and the major syntactic difference is the possibility, but not necessity, for all the parts of a noun phrase to be case-marked. Nominals formed by joining a free nominal with a verb suffixed with the Nomic or Agentive suffix resemble in structure non-finite clauses with objects; both have the verb to the right, and non-finite clauses generally resist material intervening between the object and the verb.

New verbs can be created through joining free verbs with preverbs, nominals, or bound infinitives, or through joining nominals with bound verbs. If we exclude the bound verb and bound infinitive, the joining of preverbs or nouns and free verbs could most naturally be called compounding. However, preverbs, while a productive open class, include many forms which do not fit the template for a minimal phonological word, either because they are monosyllabic, or because they are consonant-final. On the other hand, while the preverbs themselves are restricted as to how far they can move from the verb, they may, if in the form of a minimal phonological word, take other clitics, thus forming a structure which is looser than a word.

Thus, some major word-formation processes in Warlpiri are hard to label because, while they resemble compounding, they differ from classic compounding because one element is not syntactically free, or because it does not have the shape of a minimal phonological word, or because there is no categorical way of distinguishing between a complex word and a phrase.

References

Achmanova, O. S. (1958). 'Lexical and syntactic collocation in contemporary English', *Zeitschrift für Anglistik und Amerikanistik* 1: 14–21.

Ackema, P. (1995). *Syntax below Zero*. PhD dissertation, Utrecht University.

—— (1999). *Issues in Morphosyntax*. Amsterdam: John Benjamins Publishing Company.

—— and A. Neeleman (2004). *Beyond Morphology*. Oxford: Oxford University Press.

Adams, V. (1973). *An Introduction to Modern English Word Formation*. London: Longman.

—— (2001). *Complex Words in English*. Harlow: Longman.

Adger, D. (2003). *Stress and Phrasal Syntax*. GLOW abstract.

Agathopoulou, E. (2003). 'On functional features in second language acquisition of nominal compounds: Evidence from the Greek–English Interlanguage', in J. M. Liceras (ed.) *Proceedings of the 6th Generative Approaches to Second Language Acquisition Conference*. (GASLA 2002). Somerville, MA: Cascadilla Press, 1–8.

Aikhenvald, A. Y. (1998). 'Warekena', in D. C. Derbyshire and G. K. Pullum (eds.) *Handbook of Amazonian Languages* 4. Berlin and New York: Mouton de Gruyter, 225–439.

—— (2003). *A Grammar of Tariana, from Northwest Amazonia*. Cambridge: Cambridge University Press.

Aitchison, J. (1996). *The Seeds of Speech. Language Origin and Evolution*. Cambridge: Cambridge University Press.

—— (2003). *Words in the Mind*. Oxford: Blackwell.

Alegre, M. A. and P. Gordon (1996). 'Red rats eater exposes recursion in children's word formation', *Cognition* 60: 65–82.

Alinei, M. (1995). 'Theoretical aspects of lexical motivation', *Svenska Landsmål och Svenskt Folkliv* 118/321: 1–10.

—— (1997). 'Principi di teoria motivazionale (*iconomia*) e di lessicologia motivazionale (*iconomastica*)', in L. Mucciante and T. Telmon (eds.) *Lessicologia e Lessicografia: Atti del Convegno della Società Italiana di Glottologia*. Roma: Il Calamo, 11–36.

Allan, K. (1977). 'Classifiers', *Language* 53: 285–311.

Allan, R., P. Holmes, and T. Lundskær-Nielsen (1995). *Danish: A Comprehensive Grammar*. London and New York: Routledge.

Allen, M. R. (1978). 'Morphological investigations.' PhD dissertation, University of Connecticut, Storrs, CT.

Alpher, B. (2004). 'Appendix 5.1 Proto-Pama-Nyungan etyma', in C. Bowern and H. Koch (eds.) *Australian Languages: Classification and the Comparative Method*. Philadelphia/ Amsterdam: John Benjamins, 387–570.

Anderson, S. R. (1982). 'Where's morphology?' *Linguistic Inquiry* 13: 571–612.

—— (1985). 'Typological distinctions in word formation', in S. Timothy (ed.) *Language Typology and Syntactic Description* 3. Cambridge: Cambridge University Press, 150–201.

—— (1992). *A-Morphous Morphology*. Cambridge: Cambridge University Press.

ANDREWS, S. (1986). 'Morphological influences on lexical access: Lexical or nonlexical effects?' *Journal of Memory and Language* 25: 726–40.

—— B. MILLER, and K. RAYNER (2004). 'Eye movements and morphological segmentation of compound words: There is a mouse in mousetrap', *European Journal of Cognitive Psychology* 16: 285–311.

ANGENOT-DE LIMA, G. (2001). 'Description phonologique, grammaticale et lexicale du Moré, langue amazonienne de Bolivie et du Brésil.' PhD dissertation, University of Leiden.

ANGLIN, J. M. (1993). 'Vocabulary development: A morphological analysis', *Monographs of the Society for Research in Child Development* 58: 1–165.

ANICHKOV, I. E. (1992). 'Idiomatika i semantika: zametki, predstavlennye A. Meye, 1927', *Voprosy jazykoznanija* 41(1): 136–50.

ARNOLD, I. V. (1966). *Lexikologija sovremennogo anglijskogo jazyka.* Moscow/Leningrad: Vyssaja Škola.

ARONOFF, M. (1976). *Word Formation in Generative Grammar.* Cambridge, MA: MIT Press.

—— (1994). *Morphology by Itself.* Cambridge, MA: MIT Press.

ASSINK, E. M. H. and D. SANDRA (2003). *Reading Complex Words: Cross-Language Studies.* New York, NY: Kluwer Academic.

AUGST, GERHARD (1975). 'Über das Fugenmorphem bei Zusammensetzungen', in G. Augst (ed.) *Untersuchungen zum Morpheminventar der deutschen Gegenwartssprache.* Tübingen: Narr, 71–155.

AUGUSTA, F. J. de (1903). *Gramática Araucana.* Valdivia: Imprenta Central, J. Lampert.

BAAYEN, H. R., T. DIJKSTRA, and R. SCHREUDER (1997). 'Singulars and plurals in Dutch: Evidence for a parallel dual-route model', *Journal of Memory and Language* 37: 94–117.

—— L. B. FELDMAN, and R. SCHREUDER (2006). 'Morphological influences on the recognition of monosyllabic monomorphemic words', *Journal of Memory and Language* 55: 290–313.

—— R. PIEPENBROCK, and H. VAN RIJN (1995). *The CELEX Lexical Database* (CD-Rom). University of Pennsylvania, Philadelphia, PA.

—— and R. Schreuder (2003). *Morphological Structure in Language Processing.* Berlin: Mouton.

—— R., F. J. TWEEDIE, and R. SCHREUDER (2002). 'The subjects as a simple random effect fallacy: subject variability and morphological family effects in the mental lexicon', *Brain and Language* 81: 55–65.

BADER, F. (1962). *La formation des composes nominaux du latin.* Paris: Annales Littéraires de l'Université de Besançon.

BAHNS, J. (1993). Lexical collocations: A contrastive view. *English Language Teacher Journal* 47(1): 56–63.

BAKER, B. (2006). 'Compounds, names, and nominal phrases in Australian languages.' Paper presented at Australian Languages Workshop, Blackwood-by-the-beach, Pearl Beach, NSW.

BAKER, M. C. (1988). *Incorporation.* Chicago and London: Chicago University Press.

—— (1996). *The Polysynthesis Parameter.* New York: Oxford University Press.

—— (1999). 'External possession in Mohawk', in D. Payne and I. Barshi (eds.) *External Possession.* Amsterdam / Philadelphia: John Benjamins, 293–324.

—— (2003). *Lexical Categories: Verbs, Nouns, and Adjectives.* Cambridge: Cambridge University Press.

—— (2006). 'On zero-agreement and polysynthesis', in P. Ackema, P. Brandt, M. Schoorlemmer and F. Weerman (eds.) *Arguments and Agreement.* Oxford: Oxford University Press, 289–320.

—— R. Aranovich, and L. A. Golluscio (2005). 'Two types of syntactic noun incorporation', *Language* 81: 138–76.

Bally, C. (1950). *Linguistique générale et linguistique française*, 2nd edn. Berne: Francke.

Bar-Ilan, L. and R. A. Berman (2007). 'Developing register differentiation: The Latinate–Germanic divide in English', *Linguistics* 45(1): 1–36.

Baroni, M., E. Guevara, and V. Pirrelli (2007). 'Sulla tipologia dei composti N+N in italiano', in *Atti del 40esimo Congresso della SLI*. Rome: Bulzoni.

Barz, I. (2005). 'Die Wortbildung', in *Duden: Die Grammatik*, 7th edn. Mannheim etc.: Dudenverlag, 641–772.

Basbøll, H. (2005). *The Phonology of Danish*. Oxford: Oxford University Press.

Bassac, C. (2006). 'A compositional treatment for English compounds', *Research in Language* 4: 133–53.

Bat-El, O. (1993). 'Parasitic metrification in the Modern Hebrew stress system', *The Linguistic Review* 10: 189–210.

Bates, E., S. D'Amico, T. Jacobsen, et al. (2003). 'Timed picture naming in seven languages', *Psychonomic Bulletin & Review* 10: 344–80.

Bauer, B. (2007). 'Nominal apposition in Indo-European: Development and function.' Paper presented at the 40th Annual Meeting of the Societas Linguistica Europaea, University of Joensuu, Finland, 30 August – 1 September 2007.

Bauer, L. (1978). *The Grammar of Nominal Compounding*. Odense: Odense University Press.

—— (1980) 'Deux problèmes au sujet des noms composés comprenant un premier élément verbal en français moderne', *Le Français moderne* 3: 219–24.

—— (1983). *English Word-formation*. Cambridge: Cambridge University Press.

—— (1988). *Introducing Linguistic Morphology*. Edinburgh: Edinburgh University Press.

—— (1998a). Is there a class of neoclassical compounds, and if so is it productive?' *Linguistics* 36(3): 403–22.

—— (1998b). 'When is a sequence of noun+noun a compound in English?' *English Language and Linguistics* 2: 65–86.

—— (2001a). *Morphological Productivity*. Cambridge: Cambridge University Press.

—— (2001b). 'Compounding', in M. Haspelmath, E. König, W. Oesterreicher, and W. Raible (eds.) *Language Typology and Language Universals*. Berlin and New York: de Gruyter, 695–707.

—— (2003). *Introducing Linguistic Morphology*, 2nd edn. Washington, DC: Georgetown University Press.

—— (2008a). 'Les composés exocentriques de l'anglais', in D. Amiot (ed.) *La composition dans une perspective typologique*. Arras: Artois Presses Université, 35–47.

—— (2008b). 'Dvandva', *Word Structure* 1: 1–20.

—— and A. Renouf (2001). 'A corpus-based study of compounding in English', *Journal of English Linguistics* 29: 101–23.

—— and R. Huddleston (2002). 'Lexical Word-Formation', in R. Huddleston and J. K. Pullum (eds.) *The Cambridge Grammar of the English Language*. Cambridge: Cambridge University Press, 1621–722.

Baynes, K. and M. S. Gazzaniga (2005). 'Lateralization of language: Toward a biologically based model of language', *The Linguistic Review* 22: 303–26.

Beard, R. (1981). *The Indo-European Lexicon: A Full Synchronic Theory*. North-Holland Linguistic Series 44. Amsterdam: North-Holland.

—— (1995). *Lexeme-Morpheme Base Morphology. A General Theory of Inflection and Word Formation.* SUNY Series in Linguistics. State University of New York Press.

—— (1998). 'Derivation', in A. Spencer and A. M. Zwicky (eds.) *The Handbook of Morphology.* Oxford: Blackwell, 44–65.

BECKER, J. A. (1994). '"Sneak-shoes", "sworders", and "nose-beards": A case study of lexical innovation', *First Language* 14: 195–211.

BECKER, T. (1992). 'Compounding in German', *Rivista di Linguistica* 4: 5–36.

—— (1994). 'Back-formation, cross-formation, and "Bracketing Paradoxes" in Paradigmatic Morphology', in G. Booij and J. van Marle (eds.) *Yearbook of Morphology 1993.* Dordrecht: Kluwer, 1–26.

BENCZES, R. (2006). *Creative Compounding in English.* Amsterdam / Philadelphia: John Benjamins.

BENMAMOUN, E. (2000). 'Agreement asymmetries and the PF interface', in J. Lecarme, J. Loewenstam, and U. Shlonsky (eds.) *Studies in Afroasiatic Grammar 2.* Amsterdam: John Benjamins.

BENTIN, S. and L. B. Feldman (1990). 'The contribution of morphological and semantic relatedness to repetition priming at short and long lags: Evidence from Hebrew', *Quarterly Journal of Experimental Psychology: Human Experimental Psychology* 42: 693–711.

BENVENISTE, É. (1966). 'Formes nouvelles de la composition nominale', *Bulletin de la Société Linguistique de Paris* 61: 82–95.

BERG, H. VAN DEN (2004). 'Hunzib (North-East Caucasian)', in G. Booij, Ch. Lehmann, J. Mugdan, and S. Skopeteas (eds.) *Morphologie/Morphology 2.* Berlin / New York: de Gruyter, 1367–75.

BERMAN, R. A. (1985). 'Acquisition of Hebrew', in D. I. Slobin (ed.) *The Crosslinguistic Study of Language Acquisiton 1.* Hillsdale, NJ: Lawrence Erlbaum, 255–371.

—— (1986). 'The acquisition of morphology/syntax: A crosslinguistic perspective', in P. Fletcher and M. Garman (eds.) *Language Acquisition,* 2nd edn. Cambridge: Cambridge University Press, 429–47.

—— (1987). 'A developmental route: Learning about the form and use of complex nominals', *Linguistics* 27: 1057–85.

—— (1988). 'Language knowledge and language use: Binomial constructions in Modern Hebrew', *General Linguistics* 28: 261–85.

—— (1993a). 'Developmental perspectives on transitivity: A confluence of cues', in Y. Levy (ed.) *Other Children, Other Languages: Issues in the Theory of Acquisition.* Hillsdale, NJ: Lawrence Erlbaum, 189–241.

—— (1993b). 'Crosslinguistic perspectives on native language acquisition', in K. Hyltenstam and A. Viberg (eds.) *Progression and Regression in Language: Sociocultural, Neuro-psychological, and Linguistic Perspectives.* Cambridge: Cambridge University Press, 245–66.

—— (2000). 'Children's innovative verbs vs nouns: Structured elicitations and spontaneous coinages', in L. Menn and N. Bernstein-Ratner (eds.) *Methods for Studying Language Production.* Mahwah, NJ: Erlbaum, 69–93.

—— (2003). 'Children's lexical innovations: Developmental perspectives on Hebrew verb-structure', in J. Shimron (ed.) *Language Processing and Language Acquisition in a Root-Based Morphology.* Amsterdam: John Benjamins, 243–91.

—— (2004). 'Between emergence and mastery: The long developmental route of language acquisition', in R. A. Berman (ed.) *Language Development across Childhood and Adolescence.* Amsterdam: John Benjamins, 9–34.

—— and E. V. CLARK (1989). 'Learning to use compounds for contrast', *First Language* 9: 247–70.

—— and B. NIR-SAGIV (2004). 'Linguistic indicators of inter-genre differentiation in later language development', *Journal of Child Language* 31: 339–80.

—— (2007). 'Comparing narrative and expository text construction across adolescence: A developmental paradox', *Discourse Processes* 43(2): 79–120.

—— (in press). 'Clause-packaging in narratives: A crosslinguistic developmental study', in J. Guo, et al. (eds.) *Crosslinguistic Approaches to the Psychology of Language: Research in the Tradition of Dan I. Slobin*. Mahwah, NJ: Lawrence Erlbaum, Chapter 11.

—— and D. Ravid (1986). 'Lexicalization of noun compounds', *Hebrew Linguistics* 24: 5–22. [in Hebrew]

—— and Y. SAGI (1981). 'Children's word-formation and lexical innovations', *Hebrew Computational Linguistics Bulletin* 18: 1–62. [in Hebrew]

—— and D. I. SLOBIN (1994). *Relating Events in Narrative: A Crosslinguistic Developmental Study*. Hillsdale, NJ: Lawrence Erlbaum.

BERTRAM, R., R. H. BAAYEN, and R. SCHREUDER (2000). 'Effects of family size for complex words', *Journal of Memory and Language* 42: 390–405.

BERTRAM, R. and J. HYÖNÄ (2003). 'The length of a complex word modifies the role of morphological structure: Evidence from eye movements when reading short and long Finnish compounds', *Journal of Memory and Language* 43(3): 615–34.

BETZ, W. (1949). *Deutsch und Lateinisch: Die Lehnbildungen der althochdeutschen Benediktinerregel*. Bonn: Bouvier.

BICKERTON, D. (1990). *Language and Species*. Chicago: University of Chicago Press.

BIERWISCH, M. and K. E. HEIDOLPH (eds.) (1970). *Progress in Linguistics*. The Hague: Mouton.

BILEV, R. (1985). 'Development in Use of Noun Compounds by Hebrew-Speaking Children.' Tel Aviv University: Unpublished Master's thesis. [in Hebrew]

BILLINGS, L. A. (1998). 'Morphology and syntax: Delimiting stump compounds in Russian', in G. Booij, A. Ralli, and S. Scalise (eds.) *Proceedings of the First Mediterranean Morphology Meeting (MMM1)* (Mytilene, 19–21 September 1997). Patras: University of Patras, 99–111.

BISETTO, A. (1994). 'Italian compounds of the "accendigas" type: a case of endocentric formations?' in P. Bouillon and D. Estival (eds.) *Proceedings of the Workshop on Compound Nouns: Multilingual Aspects of Nominal Composition*. Ginevra: ISSCO, 77–87.

—— (1999). 'Note sui composti VN dell'italiano', in P. Benincà, A. Mioni, and L. Vanelli (eds.) *Fonologia e morfologia dell'italiano e dei dialetti d'Italia*. Atti del XXXI Congresso internazionale di studi della Società di Linguistica Italiana. Roma: Bulzoni, 503–38.

—— (2001). 'Sulla nozione di composto sintetico e i composti VN', in V. Orioles (ed.) *Dal 'paradigma' alla parola. Riflessioni sul metalinguaggio della linguistica*. Roma: Il Calamo, 235–56.

—— (2003). 'Note su alcuni composti nominali dell'italiano', in A. Bisetto, C. Iacobini, and A. M. Thornton (eds.) *Scritti di morfologia in onore di Sergio Scalise in occasione del suo 60° compleanno*. Cesena: Caissa Italia, 29–46.

—— and S. Scalise (2005). 'The classification of compounds', *Lingue e Linguaggio* 4(2): 319–32.

BLANK, A. (1997a). *Prinzipien des lexikalischen Bedeutungswandels am Beispiel der romanischen Sprachen*. Tübingen: Niemeyer.

—— (1997b). 'Outlines of a cognitive approach to word-formation', in *Proceedings of the 16th International Congress of Linguists*. Oxford: Pergamon, Paper No. 0291.

BLOM, C. (2005). *Complex Predicates in Dutch. Synchrony and Diachrony*. Utrecht: LOT.

BLOOMFIELD, L. (1933). *Language*. New York: Holt.

BONAMI, O. and G. BOYÉ (2003). 'Supplétion et classes flexionnelles dans la conjugaison du français', *Language* 152: 102–26.

—— (2006). 'Subregular defaults in French conjugation.' Paper presented at 12th International Morphology Meeting, 2006 May 25–29, Budapest.

—— and F. KERLEROUX (2008). 'L'allomorphie radicale et la relation flexion-construction', in B. Fradin, F. Kerleroux, and M. Plénat (eds.) *Aperçus de morphologie du français*. Saint-Denis: Presses Universitaires de Vincennes.

BONGARTZ, C. (2002). *Noun Combination in Interlanguage*. Tübingen: Niemeyer.

BOOIJ, G. (1985). 'Coordination reduction in complex words: A case for prosodic phonology', in H. van der Hulst and N. Smith (eds.) *Advances in Non-Linear Phonology*. Dordrecht: Foris, 143–60.

—— (1988). 'The relation between inheritance and argument linking: Deverbal nouns in Dutch', in M. Everaert, A. Evers, R. Huybregts, and M. Trommelen (eds.) *Morphology and Modularity*. Dordrecht: Foris, 57–74.

—— (1990). 'The boundary between morphology and syntax: separable complex verbs in Dutch', in G. Booij and J. van Marle (eds.) *Yearbook of Morphology 1990*. Dordrecht: Foris Publications, 45–63.

—— (1992). 'Compounding in Dutch', *Rivista di Linguistica* 4(1): 37–60.

—— (1995) *The Phonology of Dutch*. Oxford: Clarendon Press.

—— (1996). 'Inherent versus contextual inflection and the Split Morphology Hypothesis', in G. E. Booij and J. van Marle (eds.) *Yearbook of Morphology 1995*. Dordrecht: Kluwer, 1–16.

—— (2002a). *The Morphology of Dutch*. Oxford: Oxford University Press.

—— (2002b). 'Constructional idioms, morphology, and the Dutch lexicon', *Journal of Germanic Linguistics* 14: 301–27.

—— (2005a). *The Grammar of Words*. Oxford: Oxford University Press.

—— (2005b). 'Compounding and derivation: Evidence for Construction Morphology', in W. U. Dressler et al. (eds.) *Morphology and Its Demarcation: Selected Papers from the 11th Morphology Meeting, Vienna, February 2004*. Amsterdam / Philadelphia: John Benjamins, 109–32.

—— (2007). *The Grammar of Words: An Introduction to Linguistic Morphology*. 2nd edition. Oxford: Oxford University Press.

—— and Jerzy Rubach (1987). 'Postcyclic vs. postlexical rules in Lexical Phonology', *Linguistic Inquiry* 18: 1–44.

—— and A. VAN SANTEN (1998). *Morfologie. De woordstructuur van het Nederlands. 2ᵉgeheel herziene en uitgebreide druk*. Amsterdam: AUP.

BORER, H. (1988). 'On the morphological parallelism between compounds and constructs', in G. Booij and J. van Marle (eds.) *Yearbook of Morphology 1988*. Dordrecht: Foris Publications, 45–65.

—— (1996). 'The Construct in review', in J. Lecarme, J. Loewenstam, and U. Shlonsky (eds.) *Studies in Afroasiatic Grammar*. Holland Academic Graphics, 30–61.

—— (1998). 'Morphology and syntax', in A. Spencer and A. F. Zwicky (eds.) *The Handbook of Morphology*. Oxford / Malden, MA: Blackwell, 151–90.

—— (1999). 'Deconstructing the Construct', in K. Johnson and I. Roberts (eds.) *Beyond Principles and Parameters*. Dordrecht: Kluwer Academic Publishers, 43–90.

—— (2003). 'Exo-skeletal vs. endo-skeletal explanations: Syntactic projections and the lexicon', in J. Moore and M. Polinsky (eds.), *The Nature of Explanation in Linguistic Theory*. Chicago: CSLI and University of Chicago Press, 31–66.

—— (2005a). *Structuring Sense*, Vol. I: *In Name Only*. Oxford: Oxford University Press.

—— (2005b). *Structuring Sense*, Vol. II: *The Normal Course of Events*. Oxford: Oxford University Press.

—— (2008). 'The morphological stratum – some considerations from Hebrew compounds.' Ms., University of Southern California.

—— (forthcoming). *Structuring Sense*, Vol. III: *Taking Form*. Oxford: Oxford University Press.

BOROWSKY, T. (1990). *Topics in the Lexical Phonology of English*. New York: Garland.

BOSQUE, I. (1990). *Las categorías gramaticales. Relaciones y diferencias*. Madrid: Síntesis.

BOTHA, R. P. (1968). *The Function of the Lexicon in Transformational Generative Grammar*. The Hague: Mouton.

—— (1980). 'Word-based morphology and synthetic compounding', *Stellenbosch Papers in Linguistics*, no. 5, University of Stellenbosch.

—— (1981) 'A base rule theory of Afrikaans synthetic compounding', in M. Moortgat and T. Hoekstra (eds.) *The Scope of Lexical Rules*. Dordrecht: Foris, 1–77.

—— (1984). *Morphological Mechanisms*. Oxford: Pergamon Press.

BOTWINIK-ROTEM, I. and A. TERZI (2008). 'Greek and Hebrew locative prepositional phrases: A unified Case-driven account', *Lingua* 118(3): 399–424.

BOUCHARD, D. (2002). *Adjectives, Number and Interfaces: Why Languages Vary*. London: Elsevier.

BOWERMAN, M. and S. CHOI (2001). 'Shaping meanings for language: Universal and language-specific in the acquisition of spatial semantic categories', in M. Bowerman and S. C. Levinson (eds.) *Language Acquisition and Conceptual Development*. Cambridge: Cambridge University Press, 475–511.

BRADLEY, D. (1980). 'Lexical representation of derivational relation', in M. Arnoff and M. L. Kean (eds.) *Juncture*. Saratoga, CA: Anma Libri, 37–55.

BREINDL, E. and M. THURMAIR (1992). 'Der Fürstbischof im Hosenrock. Eine Studie zu den nominalen Kopulativkomposita', *Deutsche Sprache* 20: 32–61.

BREKLE, H. E. (1970). *Generative Satzsemantik und transformationelle Syntax im System der Englischen Nominalkomposition*. Munich: Fink.

—— (1976). *Generative Satzsemantik im System der englischen Nominal Komposition*. Munich: Wilhelm Fink Verlag.

—— (1986). 'The production and interpretation of ad hoc nominal compounds in German: A realistic approach', *Acta Linguistica Academiae Scientiarum Hungaricae* 36: 39–52.

—— and D. KASTOVSKY (1977). 'Introduction,' in H. E. Brekle and D. Kastovsky (eds.) *Perspektiven der Wortbildungsforschung. Beiträge zum Wuppertaler Wortbildungskolloquium vom 9.-10. Juli 1975. Anläßlich des 70. Geburtstages von Hans Marchand am 1. Oktober 1977*. Wuppertaler Schriftenreihe Linguistik 1. Bonn: Bouvier, 7–19.

BRESNAN, J. and S. MCHOMBO (1995). 'The Lexical Integrity Principle: Evidence from Bantu', *Natural Language and Linguistic Theory* 13: 181–254.

BROWNING, R. (1969). *Medieval and Modern Greek*. London: Hutchinson.

BRUCART, J. M. (1987). *La elisión sintáctica en español*. Barcelona: Bellaterra.

BRUGMANN, K. (1889). *Grundriß der vergleichenden Grammatik der indogermanischen Sprachen*, Vol. 2.1: *Wortbildungslehre (Stammbildungs- und Flexionslehre)*. Strasbourg: Trübner.

—— (1900). 'Über das Wesen der sogenannten Wortzusammensetzungen. Eine sprachpsychologische Studie', *Berichte über die Verhandlungen der königlichsächsischen Gesellschaft der Wissenschaften zu Leipzig, philologischhistorische Classe* 52: 359–401.

BUNDGAARD, P. F., S. OSTERGAARD, and F. STJERNFELT (2006). 'Waterproof fire stations? Conceptual schemata and cognitive operations involved in compound constructions', *Semiotica* 8: 363–93.

BURANI, C. and A. CARAMAZZA (1987). 'Representation and processing of derived words', *Language & Cognitive Processes* 2: 217–27.

—— D. SALMASO, and A. CARAMAZZA (1984). 'Morphological structure and lexical access', *Visible Language* 18: 342–52.

BURTON-ROBERTS, N. (1997). *Analysing Sentences*, 2nd edn. Harlow: Longman.

BUSA, F. (1997). 'Compositionality and the semantics of nominals.' PhD dissertation, Dept. of Computer Science, Brandeis University.

BUTTERWORTH, B. (1983). 'Lexical representation', in B. Butterworth (ed.) *Language Production*. San Diego, CA: Academic Press, 257–94.

BUZÁSSYOVÁ, KLÁRA (1974). *Sémantická štruktúra slovenských deverbatív*. Bratislava: Veda.

BYBEE, J. (1985). *Morphology*. Amsterdam: John Benjamins.

—— (1995). 'Regular morphology and the lexicon', *Language and Cognitive Processes* 10: 425–55.

—— (2006). 'From usage to grammar: The mind's response to repetition', *Language* 82: 711–34.

CACCIARI, C. and P. TABOSSI (1988). 'The comprehension of idioms', *Journal of Memory and Language* 27: 668–83.

CAMERON-FAULKNER, T., E. V. M. LIEVEN, and M. TOMASELLO (2003). 'A construction-based analysis of child-directed speech', *Cognitive Science* 27: 843–74.

CAMPBELL, L. (1985). *The Pipil Language of El Salvador*. Berlin / New York / Amsterdam: Mouton.

CARAMAZZA, A., A. LAUDANNA, and C. ROMANI (1988). 'Lexical access and inflectional morphology', *Cognition* 28: 297–332.

—— G. MICELI, M. C. SILVERI, and A. LAUDANNA (1985). 'Reading mechanisms and the organisation of the lexicon: Evidence from acquired dyslexia', *Cognitive Neuropsychology* 2: 81–114.

CARLISLE, J. F. (2000). 'Awareness of the structure and meaning of morphologically complex words: Impact on reading', *Reading and Writing* 12: 169–90.

CARLSON, G. (2003). 'Interpretive asymmetries in major phrases', in A. M. Di Sciullo (ed.) *Asymmetry in Grammar*, Vol. 2: *Morphology, Phonology, and Acquisition*. Amsterdam/ Philadelphia: John Benjamins, 301–15.

CARNIE, A. (2000). 'On the definition of X° and XP', *Syntax* 3(2): 59–106.

CARR, C. T. (1939). *Nominal Compounds in Germanic*. London: Oxford University Press.

CARSTAIRS-MCCARTHY, A. (2002). *An Introduction to English Morphology: Words and their Structure*. Edinburgh: Edinburgh University Press.

—— (2005). 'Phrases inside compounds: A puzzle for lexicon-free morphology', *SKASE Journal of Theoretical Linguistics* 2(3): 34–42.

CECCAGNO, A. and B. BASCIANO (2007). 'Compound headedness in Chinese: An analysis of neologisms', *Morphology* 17(2): 207–31.

—— (forthcoming b). 'Complessità della morfologia del cinese', *Atti dell'XI convegno AISC*, Rome 22–24 February 2007.

—— and S. Scalise (2006). 'Classification, structure and headedness of Chinese compounds', *Lingue e Linguaggio* 2: 233–60.

—— (2007). 'Composti del cinese: analisi delle strutture e identificazione della testa', in A. Palermo (ed.) *La Cina e l'altro*. Naples: Università degli studi di Napoli 'L'Orientale', 503–43.

Chang, C. H. (1998). 'V-V compounds in Mandarin Chinese: Argument structure and semantics', in J. Packard (ed.) *New Approaches to Chinese Word Formation*. Berlin: Mouton de Gruyter, 77–101.

Chao, Y. R. (1948). *Mandarin Primer: An Intensive Course in Spoken Chinese*. Cambridge, MA: Harvard University Press.

—— (1968). *A Grammar of Spoken Chinese*. Berkeley / Los Angeles: University of California Press.

Cheng, L. L. (1997). 'Resultative compounds and lexical relational structures', *Chinese Languages and Linguistics 3: Morphology and Lexicon*: 167–97.

—— and Huang, J. C. T. (1994). 'On the argument structure of resultative compounds', in M. Y. Chenand and O. L. Tzeng (eds.) *In Honour of William S-Y. Wang: Interdisciplinary Studies on Language and Language Change*. Taipei: Pyramid Press, 187–221.

Chi, T. R. (1985). *A Lexical Analysis of Verb-Noun Compounds in Mandarin Chinese*. Taipei: Crane.

Chierchia, G. (2001). 'A puzzle about indefinites', in C. Ceccetto, G. Chierchia, and M. T. Guasti (eds.) *Semantic Interfaces: Reference, Anaphora and Aspect*. Stanford: CSLI.

Childs, T. G. (1995). *A Grammar of Kisi*. Berlin / New York: Mouton de Gruyter.

Chomsky, N. (1957). *Syntactic Structures*. Den Haag: Mouton.

—— (1965). *Aspects of the Theory of Syntax*. Cambridge, MA: MIT Press.

—— (1970). 'Remarks on nominalization', in R. A. Jacobs and P. S. Rosenbaum (eds.) *Readings in English Transformational Grammar*. Waltham, MA: Ginn, 184–221. (Reprinted in N. Chomsky (1972) *Studies in Semantics in Generative Grammar*. Den Haag: Mouton, 11–61.)

—— (1981). *Lectures on Government and Binding*. Dordrecht: Foris.

—— (1986). *Knowledge of Language: Its Nature, Origin, and Use*. New York: Praeger.

—— (1995a). *The Minimalist Program*. Cambridge, MA: MIT Press.

—— (1995b). 'Bare Phrase Structure', in G. Webelhuth (ed.) *Government and Binding Theory and the Minimalist Program*. Oxford/Cambridge, MA: Blackwell, 383–439.

—— (2000). 'Minimalist inquiries: The framework', in R. Martin, D. Michaels, and J. Uriagereka (eds.) *Step by Step: Essays on Minimalist Syntax in Honour of Howard Lasnik*. Cambridge, MA: MIT Press, 1–59.

—— (2001). 'Derivation by phase', in M. Kenstowicz (ed.) *Ken Hale: A Life in Language*. Cambridge, MA: MIT Press, 1–52.

—— (2004). 'Three factors in language design', *Linguistic Inquiry* 36(1): 1–22.

—— and M. Halle (1968). *The Sound Pattern of English*. New York: Harper & Row.

Cienki, A. (2007). 'Frames, idealized cognitive models, and domains', in D. Geeraerts and H. Cuyckens (eds.) *Handbook of Cognitive Linguistics*. Oxford: Oxford University Press, 170–87.

Cinque, G. (1999). *Adverbs and Functional Heads: A Cross-Linguistic Perspective*. New York: Oxford University Press.

—— (2000). 'On Greenberg's Universal 20 and the Semitic DP.' Handout of a paper presented at the Antisymmetry Conference, Cortona.

CLACKSON, J. (2002). 'Composition in Indo-European languages', *Transactions of the Philological Society* 100(2): 163-167.

CLAHSEN, H. and M. ALMAZAN (2001). 'Compounding and inflection in language impairment: Evidence from Williams Syndrome (and SLI)', *Lingua* 111: 729–57.

—— G. Marcus, S. Bartke, and R. Wiese (1996). 'Compounding and inflections in German child language', *Yearbook of Morphology 1995*. Dordrecht: Kluwer, 115–42.

CLARK, E. V. (1981). 'Lexical innovations: How children learn to create new words', in W. Deutsch (ed.) *The Child's Construction of Language*. New York: Academic Press, 299–328.

—— (1988). 'Lexical creativity in French-speaking children', *Cahiers de Psychologie Cognitive* 17: 513–30.

—— (1993). *The Lexicon in Acquisition*. Cambridge: Cambridge University Press.

—— and B. J. S. BARRON (1988). 'A thrower button or a button thrower? Children's judgments of grammatical and ungrammatical noun compounds', *Linguistics* 26: 3–19.

—— and R. A. BERMAN (1984). 'Structure and use in acquisition of word-formation', *Language* 60: 542–90.

—— (1987). 'Types of linguistic knowledge: Interpreting and producing compound nouns', *Journal of Child Language* 14: 547–68.

—— and H. H. CLARK (1979). 'When nouns surface as verbs', *Language* 4: 767–811.

—— S. A. GELMAN, and N. M. LANE (1985). 'Compound nouns and category structure in young children', *Child Development* 56: 84–94.

—— and B. F. HECHT (1982). 'Learning to coin agent and instrument nouns', *Cognition* 12: 1–24.

—— and R. MULFORD (1986). 'Acquiring complex compounds: Affixes and word order in English', *Linguistics* 24: 7–29.

COHEN, B. and G. L. MURPHY (1984). 'Models of concepts', *Cognitive Science* 8: 27–58.

COLLINS, C. (2002). 'Eliminating labels', in S. D. Epstein and T. D. Seely (eds.) *Derivation and Explanation in the Minimalist Program*. Oxford: Blackwell, 42–64.

CONTRERAS, H. (1985) 'Spanish exocentric compounds', in F. Nuessel (ed.) *Current Issues in Hispanic Phonology and Morphology*. Bloomington, IN: IULC, 14–26.

CORBETT, G. and N. M. FRASER (1993). 'Network morphology: A DATR account of Russian nominal inflection', *Journal of Linguistics* 29: 113–42.

CORBIN, D. (1987). *Morphologie dérivationelle et structuration du lexique*. Tübingen: Niemeyer.

—— (1992). 'Hypothèse sur les frontières de la composition nominale', *Cahiers de grammaire* 17: 25–55.

COSERIU, E. (1973). *Einführung in die strukturelle Betrachtung des Wortschatzes*. Tübingen: Niemeyer.

—— (1977). 'Inhaltliche Wortbildungslehre (am Beispiel des Typs "coupe-papier")', in H. E. Brekle and D. Kastovsky (eds.) *Perspektiven der Wortbildungsforschung. Beiträge zum Wuppertaler Wortbildungskolloquium vom 9.-10. Juli 1975. Anläßlich des 70. Geburtstages von Hans Marchand am 1. Oktober 1977*. Wuppertaler Schriftenreihe Linguistik 1. Bonn: Bouvier, 48–61.

COSTELLO, F. J. (1996). 'Noun-noun conceptual combination. The polysemy of compound phrases'. PhD dissertation, University of Dublin, Trinity College, Ireland.

—— and M. T. KEANE (1997). 'Polysemy in conceptual combination: Testing the constraint theory of combination', in M. G. Shafto and P. Langley (eds.) *Proceedings of the Nineteenth Annual Conference of the Cognitive Science Society*. Hillsdale, NJ: Erlbaum, 137–42.

—— (2000). 'Efficient creativity: Constraints on conceptual combination', *Cognitive Science* 24(2): 299–349.

—— (2001). 'Testing two theories of conceptual combination: Alignment versus diagnosticity in the comprehension and production of combined concepts', *Journal of Experimental Psychology: Learning, Memory & Cognition* 27(1): 255–71.

COULSON, S. (2001). *Semantic Leaps: Frame-Shifting and Conceptual Blending in Meaning Construction*. Cambridge: Cambridge University Press.

CREISSELS, D. (2004). 'Bambara', in P. J. L. Arnaud (ed.) *Le nom composé: données sur seize Langages*. Lyons: Presses universitaires de Lyon, 21–46.

CROFT, W. and A. CRUSE (2003). *Cognitive Linguistics*. Cambridge: Cambridge University Press.

CRYSTAL, D. (2003). *A Dictionary of Linguistics and Phonetics*, fifth edn. Oxford: Blackwell.

CULICOVER, P. W. and R. JACKENDOFF (2005). *Simpler Syntax*. Oxford: Oxford University Press.

CURTISS, S. (1977). *Genie: A Linguistic Study of a Modern-day 'Wild Child'*. New York: Academic Press.

D'ACHILLE, P. and A. M. THORNTON (2003). 'La flessione del nome dall'italiano antico all'italiano contemporaneo', in N. Maraschio and T. Poggi Salani (eds.) *Italia linguistica anno Mille–Italia linguistica anno Duemila*. Roma: Bulzoni, 211–30.

DAI, X-L. J. (1992). 'Chinese morphology and its interface with the syntax'. PhD dissertation, Ohio State University, Columbus, OH.

DALALAKIS, J. and M. GOPNIK (1995). 'Lexical representation of Greek compounds: Evidence from Greek developmentally language impaired individuals', in D. MacLaughlin and S. M. McEwen (eds.) *Proceedings of BUCLD* 19: 192–303.

DANON, G. (2001). 'Syntactic definiteness in the grammar of Modern Hebrew', *Linguistics* 39 (6): 1071–116.

—— (2008a). 'Definiteness agreement with PP modifiers', in S. Armon-Lotem, G. Danon, and S. Rothstein (eds.) *Generative Approaches to Hebrew Linguistics*. Amsterdam: John Benjamins.

—— (2008b). 'Definiteness spreading in the Hebrew Construct State', *Lingua* 118: 872–906.

DARMESTETER, A. (1894). *Traité de la formations des mots composé dans la langue française*, 2nd edn. Paris: Honoré Champion.

DAVIDSON, D. (1967). 'The Logical Form of action sentences', in N. Rescher (ed.) *The Logic of Decision and Action*. Pittsburgh: University of Pittsburgh Press, 105–22.

DAVIDSON, M. (2002). 'Studies in Southern Wakashan (Nootkan) grammar.' PhD dissertation, State University of New York at Buffalo.

DAVIS, A. R. and J-P. KOENIG (2000). 'Linking as constraint on word classes in a hierarchical lexicon', *Language* 76: 56–109.

DAYLEY, J. P. (1989). *Tümpisa (Panamint) Shoshone Grammar*. Berkeley / Los Angeles / Oxford: University of California Press.

DE JONG, N. H., L. B. FELDMAN, R. SCHREUDER, M. PASTIZZO, and H. R. BAAYEN (2002). 'The processing and representation of Dutch and English compounds: Peripheral morphological and central orthographic effects', *Brain and Language* 81: 555–67.

—— R. SCHREUDER, and H. R. BAAYEN (2000). 'The morphological family size effect and morphology', *Language and Cognitive Processes* 15: 329–65.

DEL PRADO MARTIN, M. F., A. DEUTSCH, R. FROST, R. SCHREUDER, N. H. DE JONG, and H. R. BAAYEN (2005). 'Changing places: A cross-language perspective on frequency and family size in Dutch and Hebrew', *Journal of Memory and Language* 53: 496–512.

DEMIRDACHE, H. and M. URIBE-ETXEBARRIA (1997). 'The syntax of temporal relations: A uniform approach to tense and aspect', in E. Curtis, J. Lyle, and G. Webster (eds.) *Proceedings of the Sixteenth West Coast Conference on Formal Linguistics*. Stanford, CA: CSLI Publications, 145–59.

DEN DIKKEN, M. (1995). *Particles: On the Syntax of Verb-Particle, Triadic, and Causative Constructions*. New York: Oxford University Press.

DERWING, B. L. and R. SKOUSEN (1989) . 'Morphology in the mental lexicon: A new look at analogy', in G. Booij and J. Van Marle (eds.) *Yearbook of Morphology 2*. Dordrecht: Foris Publications, 55–71.

DIDERICHSEN, P. (1972). *Essentials of Danish Grammar*. Copenhagen: Akademisk.

DIETRICH, R. (2002). *Psycholinguistik*. Stuttgart/Weimar: Metzler.

DIEZ, F. C. (1875). *Romanische Wortschöpfung. Anhang zur Grammatik der romanischen Sprachen*. Bonn.

DIMMENDAAL, G. J. (1983). *The Turkana Language*. Dordrecht and Cinnaminson, NJ: Foris.

—— and M. Noske (2004). 'Turkana (Nilotic)', in G. Booij, C. Lehmann, J. Mugdan, and S. Skopeteas (eds.) *Morphologie/Morphology 2*. Berlin / New York: de Gruyter, 1507–17.

DIRVEN, R. and M. VERSPOOR (1998). *Cognitive Exploration of Language and Linguistics*. Cognitive Linguistics in Practice 1. Amsterdam/Philadelphia: John Benjamins.

DiSCIULLO, A-M. (1992a). 'On the properties of Romance and Germanic deverbal compounds', in E. Fava (ed.) *Proceedings of the 17th Meeting of Generative Grammar*. Torino: Rosenberg and Sellier, 191–210.

—— (1992b). 'Deverbal compounds and the external argument', in I. Roca (ed.) *Thematic Structure: Its Role in Grammar*. Dordrecht: Foris, 65–78.

—— (1996). 'Modularity and X°/XP Asymmetry', *Linguistic Analysis* 23: 1–23.

—— (1997). 'Prefixed-verbs and adjunct identification', in A. M. DiSciullo (ed.) *Projections and Interface Conditions: Essays in Modularity*. New York: Oxford University Press, 52–73.

—— (1999). 'Local Asymmetry', *MIT Working Papers in Linguistics* 35: 25–49.

—— (2003a). 'The asymmetry of morphology', in P. Boucher (ed.) *Many Morphologies*. Somerville, MA: Cascadilla Press, 1–33.

—— (2003b). 'Morphological relations in Asymmetry Theory', in A. M. DiSciullo (ed.) *Asymmetry in Grammar, vol. 2: Morphology, Phonology, and Acquisition*. Amsterdam / Philadelphia: John Benjamins, 9–36.

—— (2004). 'Morphological Phases', in J. Yoon (ed.) *Generative Grammar in a Broader Perspective: The 4th GLOW in Asia 2003*. The Korean Generative Grammar Circle and Cognitive Science, Seoul National University, 113–37.

—— (2005a). *Asymmetry in Morphology*. Cambridge, MA: MIT Press.

—— (2005b). 'Decomposing compounds', *SKASE Journal of Theoretical Linguistic* 2(3): 14–33.

—— (2005c). 'Affixes at the edge', *Canadian Journal of Linguistics*. Special 50th anniversary issue, 83–117.

—— (2007a). 'On affixal scope and affix–root ordering in Italian', in S. Baauw, F. Drijkoningen, and M. Pinto (eds.) *Romance Languages and Linguistic Theory*. Amsterdam / Philadelphia: John Benjamins, 99–114.

—— (2007b). 'Decomposing compounds.' Ms. Université du Québec à Montréal.

—— and D. P. BANKSIRA (in press). 'On wh-words of Ethiopian Semitic languages', *Proceedings of the 35th North American Conference on Afroasiatic Languages (NACAL 35)*.

—— and S. FONG (2005) . 'Morpho-syntax parsing', in A. M. DiSciullo (ed.) *UG and External Systems: Language, Brain and Computation*. Amsterdam / Philadelphia: John Benjamins, 247–68.

—— and M. Landman (2007) . 'Morphological compositionality', *Revista Letras* 42: 1–18.

—— and A. Ralli (1999) . 'Theta-role saturation in Greek compounds', in A. Alexiadou et al. (eds.) *Studies in Greek Syntax*. Dordrecht: Kluwer, 185–200.

—— and N. Tomioka (2007) . 'Processing the object/adjunct asymmetry in Japanese verb compounds.' Ms. UQAM.

—— and E. Williams (1987). *On the Definition of Word*. Cambridge, MA: MIT Press.

Dixon, R. M. W. (1986). 'Noun classes and noun classification', in C. Craig (ed.) *Noun Classes and Categorization*. Amsterdam / Philadelphia: John Benjamins, 105–12.

Dobrovie-Sorin, C. (2003). 'From DPs to NPs: A bare phrase structure account of genitives', in M. Coene and Y. D'Hulst (eds.) *From NP to DP*, vol. 2: *The Expression of Possession in Noun Phrases*. Amsterdam: John Benjamins, 75–120.

Dohmes, P. P. Zwitserlood, and J. Bölte (2004) . 'The impact of semantic transparency of morphologically complex words on picture naming', *Brain and Language* 90: 203–12.

Dokulil, M. (1962). *Tvoření slov v češtině I. Teorie odvozování slov*. Prague: Nakladatelství ČAV.

—— (1968). 'Zur Theorie der Wortbildungslehre', *Wissenschaftliche Zeitschrift der Karl-Marx-Universität Leipzig* 17: 203–11.

—— (1978). 'K otázce prediktability lexikálního významu slovotvorně motivovaného slova', *Slovo a slovesnost* 39: 244–51.

—— (1997). 'The Prague School's theoretical and methodological contribution to "Word-formation" (Derivology)', in *Obsah – výraz – význam. Miloši Dokulilovi k 85. narozeninám*. Prague: FF UK, 179–210.

Donalies, E. (2004). *Grammatik des Deutschen im europäischen Vergleich: Kombinatorische Begriffsbildung*, vol. 1: *Substantivkomposition*. Mannheim: Institut für deutsche Sprache.

—— (2005). *Die Wortbildung im Deutschen*, 2nd edn. Tübingen: Narr.

Downing, P. (1977). 'On the creation and use of English compound nouns', *Language* 53: 810–42.

Dowty, D. R. (1991). 'Thematic proto-roles and argument selection', *Language* 67: 547–619.

Drachman, G. and A. Malikouti-Drachman (1994). 'Stress and Greek compounding', *Phonologica 1992*: 55–64.

Dressler, W. U. (1984). 'Zur Wertung der Interfixe in einer semiotischen Theorie der natürlichen Morphologie', *Wiener Slavistischer Almanach* 13: 35–45.

—— (2005). 'Towards a natural morphology of compounding', *Linguistics* 45: 29–39.

—— (2006). 'Compound types', in G. Libben and G. Jarema (eds) *The Representation and Processing of Compound Words*. Oxford: Oxford University Press, 23–44.

—— and M. Ladányi (2000). 'Productivity in word formation (WF): A morphological approach', *Acta Linguistica Hungarica* 47(1–2): 103–44.

—— G. Libben, J. Stark, C. Pons, and G. Jarema (2001). 'The processing of interfixed German compounds', *Yearbook of Morphology 1999*. Dordrecht: Kluwer, 185–220.

Dunabeitia, J. A., M. Perea, and M. Carreiras (2007). 'The role of the frequency of constituents in compound words: Evidence from Basque and Spanish', *Psychonomic Bulletin & Review* 14(6): 1171–6.

Dunkel, G. E. (1999). 'On the origins of nominal composition in Indo-European', in H. Eichner and H. C. Luschützky (with V. Sadovski) (eds.) *Compositiones Indogermanicae in memoriam Jochem Schindler*. Prague: Enigma, 47–68.

Eijk, Jan P. van (1997). *The Lillooet Language: Phonology, Morphology, Syntax*. Vancouver: University of British Columbia Press.

EISENBERG, P. (1998). *Grundriß der deutschen Grammatik, vol. 1: Das Wort.* Stuttgart / Weimar: Metzler.

ELSEN, H. (2005). 'Deutsche Konfixe', *Deutsche Sprache* 33: 133–40.

EMONDS, J. (1985). *A Unified Theory of Syntactic Categories.* Dordrecht: Foris.

ENGELHARDT, M. (2000). 'The projection of argument-taking nominals', *Natural Language and Linguistic Theory* 18(1): 41–88.

EVANS, N. (1995). *A Grammar of Kayardild: With Historical-Comparative Notes on Tangkic.* Berlin / New York: Mouton de Gruyter.

EVERETT, D. L. (1998). 'Wari (Amazonian)', in A. Spencer and A. M. Zwicky (eds) *The Handbook of Morphology.* Oxford / Malden, MA: Blackwell, 690–706.

EVERS, A. (1975). *The Tranformational Cycle in Dutch and German.* Bloomington, IN: Indiana University Linguistics Club.

FABB, N. (1984). 'Syntactic affixation.' PhD dissertation, MIT.

—— (1998). 'Compounding', in A. Spencer and A. M. Zwicky (eds.) *Handbook of Morphology.* Oxford: Blackwell, 66–83.

FAIß, K. (1981). 'Compound, pseudo-compound, and syntactic group especially in English', in P. Kunsmann and O. Kuhn (eds.) *Weltsprache Englisch in Forschung und Lehre: Festschrift für Kurt Wächtler.* Berlin: Erich Schmidt Verlag, 132–50.

FANSELOW, G. (1981). *Zur Syntax und Semantik der Nominalkomposition: ein Versuch praktischer Anwendung der Montague-Grammatik auf die Wortbildung im Deutschen.* Tübingen: Niemeyer.

—— (1985). 'What is a possible complex word?', in J. Toman (ed.) *Studies in German Grammar.* Dordrecht: Foris, 289–318.

FASOLD, R. W. A. (1969). 'Noun compounding in Thai.' Mimeographed abridged version of 1968 University of Chicago PhD Dissertation.

FAUCONNIER, G. (1990). 'Domains and connections', *Cognitive Linguistics* 1: 151–74.

—— (2007). 'Mental spaces', in D. Geeraerts and H. Cuyckens (eds.) *Handbook of Cognitive Linguistics.* Oxford: Oxford University Press, 351–76.

—— and M. TURNER (2002). *The Way We Think: Conceptual Blending and the Mind's Hidden Complexities.* New York: Basic Books.

FELDMAN, L. B. (1991). 'The contribution of morphology to word recognition', *Psychological Research/Psychologische Forschung* 53: 33–41.

FERNANDO, C. (1996). *Idioms and Idiomaticity.* Oxford: Oxford University Press.

FERRIS, C. (1993). *The Meaning of Syntax: A Study in the Adjectives of English.* London: Longman.

FIKKERT, P. (2001). 'Compounds triggering prosodic development', in J. Weissenborn and B. Höhle (eds.) *Approaches to Bootstrapping: Phonological, Lexical, Syntactic and Neurophysiological Aspects of Early Language Acquisition,* Vol. 2. Amsterdam: John Benjamins, 59–86.

FILLENBAUM, S. (1971). 'Psycholinguistics', *Annual Review of Psychology* 22: 251–308.

FILLMORE, C. (1968). 'The case for Case', in E. Bach and R. T. Harms (eds.) *Universals in Linguistic Theory.* New York: Holt, Rinehart & Winston, 1–90.

FIORENTINO, R. and D. POEPPEL (2007). 'Compound words and structure in the lexicon', *Language and Cognitive Processes* 12: 1–48.

FLEISCHER, W. (1969). *Wortbildung der deutschen Gegenwartssprache.* Leipzig: Bibliographisches Institut.

—— (1975). *Wortbildung der deutschen Gegenwartssprache.* 4th, revised edn. Tübingen: Niemeyer.

—— (2000). 'Die Klassifikation von Wortbildungsprozessen', in G. Booij, C. Lehmann, and J. Mugdan (eds.) *Morphologie / Morphology*. Berlin / New York: de Gruyter, 886–97.

—— and I. BARZ (1992). *Wortbildung der deutschen Gegenwartssprache*. Tübingen: Niemeyer.

FLORES D'ARCAIS, G. B. and SAITO, H. (1993). 'Lexical decomposition of complex Kanji characters in Japanese readers', *Psychological Research* 55: 52–63.

FOLEY, W. A. (1991). *The Yimas Language of New Guinea*. Stanford: Stanford University Press.

FOREMAN, V. (1974). *Grammar of Yessan-Mayo*. Santa Ana: Summer Institute of Linguistics.

FORSTER, K. I. and J. HECTOR (2002). 'Cascaded versus noncascaded models of lexical and semantic processing: The turple effect', *Memory & Cognition* 30: 1106–16.

FORTESCUE, M. (2004). 'West Greenlandic (Eskimo)', in G. Booij, C. Lehmann, J. Mugdan, and S. Skopeteas (eds.) *Morphologie /Morphology*, vol. 2. Berlin / New York: de Gruyter, 1389–99.

FRADIN, B. (2003a). *Nouvelles approches en morphologie*. Paris: Presses Universitaires de France.

—— (2003b). 'Le traitement de la suffixation en -ET', *Langage* 152: 51–77.

—— (2005). 'On a semantically grounded difference between derivation and compounding', in W. Dressler, D. Kastovsky, O. E. Pfeiffer, and F. Rainer (eds.) *Morphology and its Demarcations*. Amsterdam / Philadelphia: John Benjamins, 161–82.

FROMKIN, V. R. RODMAN, P. COLLINS, and D. BLAIR (1996). *An Introduction to Language*, 3rd edn. Sydney: Harcourt Brace.

FROST, R., J. GRAINGER, and K. RASTLE (2005a). 'Current issues in morphological processing: An introduction', *Language & Cognitive Processes* 20: 1–5.

—— T. KUGLER, A. DEUTSCH, and K. I. FORSTER (2005b). 'Orthographic structure versus morphological structure: Principles of lexical organization in a given language', *Journal of Experimental Psychology: Learning, Memory, & Cognition* 31: 1293–326.

FUHRHOP, N. (1998). *Grenzfälle morphologischer Einheiten*. Tübingen: Stauffenburg.

FUKUSHIMA, K. (2005). 'Lexical V-V compounds in Japanese: Lexicon vs. syntax', *Language* 81(3): 568–612.

FURDÍK, J. (1993). *Slovotvorná motivácia a jej jazykové funkcie*. Levoča: Modrý Peter.

GAGNÉ, C. L. (2001). 'Relation and lexical priming during the interpretation of noun-noun combinations', *Journal of Experimental Psychology: Learning, Memory, & Cognition* 1: 236–54.

—— (2002). 'Lexical and relational influences on the processing of novel compounds', *Brain and Language* 81: 723–35.

—— and E. J. SHOBEN (1997). 'Influence of thematic relations on the comprehension of modifier-noun combinations', *Journal of Experimental Psychology: Learning, Memory, & Cognition* 1: 71–87.

—— (2002). 'Priming relations in ambiguous noun-noun compounds', *Memory and Cognition* 30(4): 637–46.

—— and T. L. SPALDING (2004). 'Effect of relation availability on the interpretation and access of familiar noun-noun compounds', *Brain and Language* 90: 478–86.

—— (2006a). 'Relation availability was not confounded with familiarity or plausibility in Gagné and Shoben (1997): Comment on Wisniewski and Murphy (2005)', *Journal of Experimental Psychology: Learning, Memory, & Cognition* 32: 1431–42.

—— (2006b). 'Using conceptual combination research to better understand novel compound words', *SKASE Journal of Theoretical Linguistics* 3(2): 9–16.

—— (2007). 'Representing competition among relations during conceptual combination.' Poster presented at the 48th Annual Meeting of the Psychonomic Society, Long Beach, CA.

—— (n.d.). 'Representing competition among relations: An explanation of the CARIN theory of conceptual combination.'

—— and M. C. GORRIE (2005). 'Sentential context and the interpretation of familiar open-compounds and novel modifier-noun phrases', *Language and Speech* 48: 203–21.

GALLMANN, P. (1999). 'Fugenmorpheme als Nicht-Kasus-Suffixe', *Germanistische Linguistik* 141(2): 177–90.

GAMKRELIDZE, T. V. and V. V. IVANOV (1995). *Indo-European and the Indo-Europeans: A Reconstruction and Historical Analysis of a Proto-language and a Proto-culture*. 2 vols. Trends in Linguistics: Studies and Monographs 80. Berlin / New York: Mouton de Gruyter.

GARDNER, M. K., E. Z. ROTHKOPF, R. LAPAN, and T. LAFFERTY (1987). 'The word frequency effect in lexical decision: Finding a frequency-based component', *Memory & Cognition* 15: 24–8.

GEERAERTS, D. (2002). 'The interaction of metaphor and metonymy in composite expressions', in R. Dirven and R. Poings (eds.) *Metaphor and Metonymy in Comparison and Contrast*. Berlin: Mouton de Gruyter, 435–65.

—— and H. CUYCKENS (2007). 'Introducing Cognitive Linguistics', in D. Geeraerts and H. Cuyckens (eds.) *The Oxford Handbook of Cognitive Linguistics*. Oxford: Oxford University Press, 3–21.

GERNSBACHER, M. A. (1984). 'Resolving 20 years of inconsistent interactions between lexical familiarity and orthography, concreteness, and polysemy', *Journal of Experimental Psychology: General* 113: 256–81.

GERRIG, R. J. (1989). 'The time-course of sense creation', *Memory and Cognition* 17: 194–207.

GESENIUS, W. (1910). *Gesenius' Hebrew Grammar*, ed. E. Kautsch, rev. A. E. Cowley. Oxford: Clarendon Press.

GHOMESHI, J., R. JACKENDOFF, N. ROSEN, and K. RUSSELL (2004). 'Contrastive focus reduplication in English (the salad-salad paper)', *Natural Language and Linguistic Theory* 22: 307–57.

GIANOLLO, C., C. GUARDIANO, and G. LONGOBARDI (2008). 'Three fundamental issues in parametric linguistics', in T. Biberauer (ed.) *The Limits of Syntactic Variation*. Amsterdam: John Benjamins, 109–43.

GIEGERICH, H. J. (1999). *Lexical Strata in English: Morphological Causes, Phonological Effects*. Cambridge: Cambridge University Press.

—— (2000). 'Synonymy blocking and the Elsewhere Condition: Lexical Morphology and the speaker', *Transactions of the Philological Society* 99: 65–98.

—— (2004). 'Compound or phrase? English noun-plus-noun constructions and the stress criterion', *English Language and Linguistics* 8: 1–24.

—— (2005a). 'Associative adjectives in English and the lexicon–syntax interface', *Journal of Linguistics* 41: 571–91.

—— (2005b). 'Lexicalism and modular overlap in English', *SKASE Journal of Theoretical Linguistics* 2(2): 43–62.

GILIJ, F. S. (1780). *Saggio di storia americana; o sia, Storia naturale, civile e sacra de' regni, e delle provincie spagnuole di Terra-ferma nell'America Meridionale*, Vol. 1: *Della storia geografica, e naturale della provincia dell'Orinoco*. Rome: Luigi Perego.

—— (1781). *Saggio di storia americana; o sia, Storia naturale, civile e sacra de' regni, e delle provincie spagnuole di Terra-ferma nell'America Meridionale*, Vol. 2: *De' costumi degli Orinochesi*. Rome: Luigi Perego.

—— (1782). *Saggio di storia americana; o sia, Storia naturale, civile e sacra de' regni, e delle provincie spagnuole di Terra-ferma nell'America Meridionale*, Vol. 3: *Della religione, e delle lingue degli Orinochesi, e di altri Americani*. Rome: Luigi Perego.

GIRAUDO, H. and J. GRAINGER (2000). 'Effects of prime word frequency and cumulative root frequency in masked morphological priming', *Language & Cognitive Processes* 15: 421–44.

—— (2001). 'Priming complex words: Evidence for supralexical representation of morphology', *Psychonomic Bulletin & Review* 8: 127–31.

GLEASON, H. A. (1965). *Linguistics and English Grammar*. New York: Holt, Rinehart and Winston.

GLEITMAN, L. R. and H. GLEITMAN (1970). *Phrase and Paraphrase: Some Innovative Uses of Language*. New York: Norton.

GOLDBERG, A. (2006). *Constructions at Work*. Oxford: Oxford University Press.

GOLDIN-MEADOW, S. (2003). *The Resilience of Language*. New York: Psychology Press.

GOLLUSCIO, L. (1997). 'Notas sobre la incorporación nominal en mapudungun', in *Actas III Jornadas de Lingüística Aborigen* III: 155–67.

GONZÁLEZ ÑÁÑEZ, O. (ed.) (1996). *Léxico baniva*. Caracas: UNICEF Venezuela.

GORDON, P. (1985). 'Level-ordering in lexical development', *Cognition* 21: 73–93.

GOROG, R. DE (1981). 'The application of onomasiology to synonymy, word formation and etymology', *Word* 32: 99–108.

GRACE, G. W. (1981). *Essay on Language*. Columbia, SC: Hornbeam Press.

GRANVILLE HATCHER, A. (1960). 'An introduction to the analysis of English noun compounds', *Word* 16: 356–73.

GRIMSHAW, J. (1990). *Argument Structure*. Cambridge, MA: The MIT Press.

GRINEVALD, C. (2000). 'A morphosyntactic typology of classifiers', in G. Senft (ed.) *Systems of Nominal Classification*. Cambridge: Cambridge University Press, 50–92.

GROSS, G. (1996). *Les expressions figées en français*. Gap: Ophrys.

GRYNBERG, H. (2000). *Memorbuch*. Warsaw: Wydawnictwo W.A.B.

GRZEGA, J. (2002a). 'Some thoughts on a cognitive onomasiological approach to word-formation with special reference to English', *Onomasiology Online* 3/4.

—— (2002b). 'Some aspects of modern diachronic onomasiology', *Linguistics* 40: 1021–45.

—— (2004). *Bezeichnungswandel: Wie, Warum, Wozu? Ein Beitrag zur englischen und allgemeinen Onomasiologie*. Heidelberg: Winter.

—— and M. SCHÖNER (2007). *English and General Historical Lexicology: Materials for Onomasiology Seminars*. Eichstätt: Katholische Universität.

GRZEGORCZYKOWA, R. (1979). *Zarys słowotwórstwa polskiego: Słowotwórstwo opisowe*. Warsaw: PWN.

—— and J. PUZYNINA (1999). 'Rzeczownik', in R. Grzegorczykowa, R. Laskowski, and H. Wróbel (eds.) *Gramatyka współczesnego języka polskiego. Morfologia*. Warsaw: Wydawnictwo Naukowe PWN, 389–468.

GUEVARA, E. and S. SCALISE (2004). 'V-Compounding in Dutch and Italian', *Cuadernos de Lingüística del Instituto Universitario Ortega y Gasset* XI: 1–29.

GUMNIOR, H., J. BOLTE, and P. ZWITSERLOOD (2006). 'A chatterbox is a box: Morphology in German word production', *Language & Cognitive Processes* 21: 920–44.

GÜNTHER, H. (1981). 'N + N: Untersuchungen zur Produktivität eines deutschen Wortbildungstyps', in L. Lipka and H. Günther (eds.) *Wortbildung*. Darmstadt: Wissenschaftliche Buchgesellschaft, 258–80.

HAAS, W. DE and M. TROMMELEN (1993). *Morfologisch handboek van het Nederlands. Een overzicht van de woordvorming*. The Hague: SDU Uitgeverij.

HACKEN, P. TEN (2007). *Chomskyan Linguistics and its Competitors*. London: Equinox.

HALE, K. L. (1973). 'Person marking in Walbiri', in S. Anderson and P. Kiparsky (eds.) *A Festschrift for Morris Halle*. New York: Holt, Rinehart and Winston, Inc., 308–344

—— (1981). 'Preliminary remarks on the grammar of part–whole relations in Warlpiri', in J. Hollyman and A. Pawley (eds.) *Studies in Pacific Languages and Cultures: In Honour of Bruce Biggs*. Auckland: Linguistics Society of New Zealand, 333–44.

—— (2003). 'Navajo verb structure and noun incorporation', in A. Carnie, H. Harley, and M. Willie (eds.) *Formal Approaches to Function in Grammar: Papers in Honor of Eloise Jelinek*. Amsterdam: John Benjamins, 1–43.

—— and S. J. JOHNSON (1967). 'Lessons in Walbiri I-VII'. Mimeo. Cambridge, MA: Massachusetts Institute of Technology.

—— and S. J. KEYSER (1993). 'On argument structure and the lexical expression of syntactic relations', in K. Hale and S. J. Keyser (eds.) *The View from Building 20: Essays in Linguistics in Honor of Sylvain Bromberger*. Cambridge, MA: MIT Press, 51–109.

—— (2002). *Prolegomena to a Theory of Argument Structure*. Cambridge, MA: MIT Press.

HALLE, M. (1973). 'Prolegomena to a theory of word formation', *Linguistic Inquiry* 4: 3–16.

—— and A. MARANTZ (1993). 'Distributed Morphology and the pieces of inflection', in K. Hale and S. J. Keyser (eds.) *The View from Building 20: Essays in Linguistics in Honor of Sylvain Bromberger*. Cambridge, MA: MIT Press, 111–76.

—— and K. P. MOHANAN (1985). 'Segmental phonology of Modern English', *Linguistic Inquiry* 16: 57–116.

HAMPTON, J. A. (1983). 'A composite prototype model of conceptual conjunction.' Manuscript. The City University London.

—— (1987). 'Inheritance of attributes in natural concept conjunctions', *Memory & Cognition* 15: 55–71.

—— (1988). 'Overextension of conjunctive concepts: Evidence for a unitary model of concept typicality and class inclusion', *Journal of Experimental Psychology: Learning, Memory, and Cognition* 14: 12–32.

HANKAMER, J. and I. SAG (1976). 'Deep and surface anaphora', *Linguistic Inquiry* 7: 391–428.

HANSEN, A. (1967). *Moderne Dansk*. 3 vols. Copenhagen: Grafisk.

HANSEN, B., K. HANSEN, A. NEUBERT, and M. SCHENTKE (1982). *Englische Lexikologie: Einführung in Wortbildung und lexikalische Semantik*. Leipzig: Enzyklopädie.

HARGUS, S. (2007). *Witsuwit'en Grammar. Phonetics, Phonology, Morphology*. Vancouver: University of British Columbia Press.

HARLEY, H. (2004). 'Merge, conflation and head movement: The First Sister Principle revisited', in K. Moulton (ed.) *Proceedings of NELS 34*. U. Mass Amherst: GSLA, 239–54.

—— (2005). 'Bare Phrase Structure, acategorial roots, *one*-replacement and unaccusativity', in S. Gorbachov and A. Nevins (eds.) *Harvard Working Papers in Linguistics 11*. Cambridge, MA: Harvard Linguistics Department.

—— and R. NOYER (1999). 'Distributed Morphology', *GLOT International* 4(4): 3–9.

—— (2000). 'Licensing in the non-lexicalist lexicon', in B. Peeters (ed.) *The Lexicon/Encyclopaedia Interface*. Amsterdam: Elsevier Press, 349–74.

HASPELMATH, M. (2002). *Understanding Morphology*. London: Arnold.

HATHOUT, N., M. PLÉNAT, and L. TANGUY (2003). 'Enquête sur les dérivés en -*able*', *Cahiers de Grammaire*: 49–90.

HAUSER, M. D., D. BARNER, and T. O'DONNELL (2007). 'Evolutionary Linguistics: A new look at an old landscape', *Language Learning and Development* 3(2): 101–132.

—— N. CHOMSKY, and W. T. FITCH (2002). 'The faculty of language: What is it, who has it, and how did it evolve?' *Science* 298: 1569–79.

HAVRÁNEK, B. and A. JEDLIČKA (1981). *Česká mluvnice*. Prague: SPN.

HAZOUT, I. (1991). 'Action nominalizations and the Lexicalist Hypothesis.' PhD dissertation, University of Massachusetts, Amherst.

HEATH, J. (2005). *A Grammar of Tamashek (Tuareg of Mali)*. Berlin / New York: Mouton de Gruyter.

HEIM, I. and A. KRATZER (1998). *Semantics in Generative Grammar*. Oxford: Blackwell, Malden.

HENDERSON, L. (1985). 'Toward a psychology of morphemes', in A. W. Ellis (ed.) *Progress in the Psychology of Language*. Hillsdale, NJ: Lawrence Erlbaum, 15–72.

HERCUS, L. A., F. HODGES, and J. SIMPSON (2002). *The Land is a Map: Placenames of Indigenous Origin in Australia*. Canberra: Pacific Linguistics and Pandanus Press.

HERINGER, H. J. (1984). 'Wortbildung: Sinn aus dem Chaos', *Deutsche Sprache* 12: 1–13.

HERVÁS Y PANDURO, L. (1786). *Idea dell'Universo*, Vol. 19: *Aritmetica delle nazioni e divisione del tempo fra l'Orientali*. Cesena: Gregorio Biasini.

HETZRON, R. (ed.) (1997). *The Semitic Languages*. London: Routledge.

HEYVAERT, L. (2003). *A Cognitive-Functional Approach to Nominalization in English*. Berlin: Mouton de Gruyter.

HIGGINBOTHAM, J. (1985), 'On semantics', *Linguistic Inquiry* 16: 547–94.

HILL, A. A. (1962). 'Review of *The Grammar of English Nominalizations* by Robert B. Lees', *Language* 38: 434–44.

HIPPISLEY, A. (2001). 'Word formation rules in a default inheritance framework: A Network Morphology account of Russian personal names', in G. Booij and J. van Marle (eds.) *Yearbook of Morphology 1999*. Dordrecht: Kluwer, 221–62.

HIRAMATSU, K., W. SNYDER, T. ROEPER, S. STORRS, and M. SACCOMAN (2000). 'Of musical hand chairs and linguistic swing', in S. C. Howell, S. A. Fish, and T. Keith-Lucas (eds.) *Proceedings of the 24th Boston University Conference on Language Development*. Somerville, MA: Cascadilla Press, 409–17.

HIRT, H. (1932). *Handbuch des Urgermanischen*, vol. 2: *Stammbildungs- und Flexionslehre*. Heidelberg: Winter.

HOEKSEMA, J. (1984). 'Categorial Morphology.' PhD Dissertation. RU Groningen.

—— (1985). *Categorial Morphology*. New York: Garland Publishing, Inc.

—— (1988). 'Head-types in morpho-syntax', in G. Booij and J. van Marle (eds.) *Yearbook of Morphology* 1: 123–38.

HOEKSTRA, E. (1996). 'Iets over de eerste leden van samenstellingen', *Leuvense Bijdragen* 84: 491–504.

HOEKSTRA, J. (2002). 'Genitive compounds in Frisian as lexical phrases', *The Journal of Comparative Germanic Linguistics* 6: 227–59.

HOHENHAUS, P. (1998). 'Non-lexicalizability as a characteristic feature of nonce word-formation in English and German', *Lexicology* 4,2: 237–80.

—— (2004). 'Identical constituent compounds – a corpus-based study', *Folia Linguistica* 38,3–4: 297–331.

—— (2005). 'Lexicalization and institutionalization', in P. Štekauer and R. Lieber (eds.) *Handbook of Word-Formation*. Dordrecht: Springer, 353–74.

HOLMBERG, A. (2001). 'Expletives and agreement in Scandinavian passives', *Journal of Comparative Germanic Syntax* 4: 85–128.

HOLT, D. (1999). *Tol (Jicaque)*. Munich: Lincom Europa.

HOLTON, D., P. MACKRIDGE, and I. PHILIPPAKI-WARBURTON (1997). *Greek Grammar*. London: Routledge.

HORECKÝ, J. (1983). *Vývin a teória jazyka*. Bratislava: SPN.

—— (1994). *Semantics of Derived Words*. Prešov: Acta Facultatis Philosophicae Universitatis Šafarikanae.

—— (1999). 'Onomasiologická interpetácia tvorenia slov', *Slovo a slovesnost* 60: 6–12.

HORNOS, J. E. M. and Y. M. M. HORNOS (1993). 'Algebraic model for the evolution of the genetic code', *Physical Review Letters* 71(26): 4401–4.

HORNSTEIN, N. and D. LIGHTFOOT (1981). 'Introduction', in N. Hornstein and D. Lightfoot (eds.) *Explanation in Linguistics: The Logical Problem of Language Acquisition*. London: Longman, 9–31.

HOUSEHOLDER, F. (1962). 'Review of Robert B. Lees, *The Grammar of Nominalizations*', *Word* 18: 326–53.

HOVDHAUGEN, E. (2004). *Mochica*. Munich: Lincom Europa.

HUANG, H.-C. (2006). 'Argument realization of Chinese result and phase complements', *UTA Working Papers in Linguistics 2006–2007*, 66–89.

HUANG, J. C.-T. (1982). 'Logical relations in Chinese and the theory of grammar.' PhD dissertation, MIT.

—— (1984). 'Phrase Structure, Lexical Integrity, and Chinese compounds', *Journal of Chinese Teachers' Association* 19(2): 53–78.

—— (1992). 'Complex predicates', in R. Larson, S. Iatroudou, U. Lahiri, and J. Higginbotham (eds.) *Control and Grammar*. Boston: Kluwer Academic Publisher, 109–47.

HUANG, S. (1998). 'Chinese as a headless language', in J. Packard (ed.) *Compounding Morphology: New Approaches to Chinese Word Formation*. Berlin and New York: Mouton de Gruyter, 261–83.

HUDSON, R. (1975). 'Problems in the analysis of -*ed* adjectives', *Journal of Linguistics* 11: 69–72.

HUKE, I. (1977). *Die Wortbildungstheorie von Miloš Dokulil*. Giessen.

HULST, H. VAN DER, and N. A. RITTER (2003). 'Levels, constraints, and heads', in A. M. DiSciullo (ed.) *Asymmetry in Grammar*, Vol. 2: *Morphology, Phonology and Acquisition*. Amsterdam / Philadelphia: John Benjamins, 147–88.

HUME, R. (2002). *RSPB Complete Birds of Britain and Europe*. London: Dorling Kindersley.

INHOFF, A., D. BRIIHL, and J. SCHWARTZ (1996). 'Compound word effects differ in reading, on-line naming, and delayed naming tasks', *Memory & Cognition* 24: 466–76.

—— R. RADACH, and D. HELLER (2000). 'Complex compounds in German: Interword spaces facilitate segmentation but hinder assignment of meaning', *Journal of Memory and Language* 42(1): 23–50.

JAARSVELD, H. J. VAN and G. E. RATTINK (1988). 'Frequency effects in the processing of lexicalized and novel nominal compounds', *Journal of Psycholinguistic Research* 17: 447–73.

JACKENDOFF, R. S. (1975). 'Morphological and Semantic Regularities in the Lexicon', *Language* 51: 639–71.

—— (1977). *X-Bar Syntax: A Study of Phrase Structure*. Cambridge, MA: MIT Press.

—— (1983). *Semantics and Cognition*. Cambridge, MA: MIT Press.

—— (1990). *Semantic Structures*. Cambridge, MA: MIT Press.

—— (1997). *The Architecture of the Language Faculty*. Cambridge, MA: MIT Press.

—— (2002a). *Foundations of Language*. Oxford: Oxford University Press.

—— (2002b). 'English particle constructions, the lexicon, and the autonomy of syntax', in N. Dehé, R. Jackendoff, A. Macintyre, and S. Urban (eds.) *Verb Particle Explorations*. Berlin: Mouton de Gruyter, 67–94.

—— (2007). *Language, Consciousness, Culture*. Cambridge, MA: MIT Press.

JACOBI, H. G. (1897). *Compositum und Nebensatz: Studien über die indogermanische Sprachentwicklung*. Bonn: Cohen.

JACOBS, R. A. and P. S. ROSENBAUM (1968). *English Transformational Grammar*. London: Ginn.

JADACKA, H. (2001). *System słowotwórczy polszczyzny*. Warsaw: Wydawnictwo Naukowe PWN.

—— (2006). *Kultura języka polskiego. Fleksja, słowotwórstwo, składnia*. Warsaw: Wydawnictwo Naukowe PWN.

JAREMA, G., C. BUSSON, R. NIKOLOVA, K. TSAPKINI, and G. LIBBEN (1999). 'Processing compounds: A cross-linguistic study', *Brain and Language* 68(1–2): 362–9.

JENKINS, L. (2000). *Biolinguistics: Exploring the Biology of Language*. Cambridge: Cambridge University Press.

JESPERSEN, O. (1942). *A Modern English Grammar on Historical Principles*, vol. 6. London: Allen & Unwin.

JISA, H., J. S. REILLY, L. VERHOEVEN, E. BARUCH, and E. ROSADO (2002). 'Passive voice constructions in written texts: A crosslinguistic developmental study', *Written Language and Literacy* 5: 163–82.

JOHNSON, K. (2002). 'Towards an etiology of adjunct islands.' Ms. University of Massachusetts, Amherst. Available online at http://people.umass.edu/kbj/homepage/Content/Etiology.pdf.

JONES, D. (1969). *An Outline of English Phonetics*. Cambridge: W. Heffer & Sons Ltd.

JUHASZ, B. J., A. W. INHOFF, and K. RAYNER (2005). 'The role of interword spaces in the processing of English compound words', *Language & Cognitive Processes* 20: 291–316.

—— M. S. STARR, A. W. INHOFF, and L. PLACKE (2003). 'The effects of morphology on the processing of compound words: Evidence from naming, lexical decisions and eye fixations', *British Journal of Psychology* 94: 223–44.

KAGEYAMA, T. (1982). 'Word Formation in Japanese', *Lingua* 57: 215–58.

—— (1989). 'The place of morphology in the grammar', in G. Booij and J. van Marle (eds.) *Yearbook of Morphology 1989*. Dordrecht: Foris Publications, 73–94.

—— (1993). *Bunpoo to Gokeisei*. [Grammar and Word Formation.] Tokyo: Hituzi Syobo.

—— (1999). 'Word formation', in N. Tsujimura (ed.) *The Handbook of Japanese Linguistics*. Oxford: Blackwell, 297–325.

—— (2001a). 'Word Plus', in J. van der Weijer and T. Nishihara (eds.) *Issues in Japanese Phonology and Morphology*. Berlin: Mouton de Gruyter, 245–76.

—— (2001b). 'Polymorphism and boundedness in event/entity nominalizations', *Journal of Japanese Linguistics* 17: 29–57.

—— (2007). 'Agent incorporation and other peculiar morphological operations inducing individual-level predications.' Paper delivered at 6th Mediterranean Morphology Meeting, University of Patras, Greece.

KALLAS, K. (1999). 'Przymiotnik', in R. Grzegorczykowa, R. Laskowski, and H. Wróbel (eds.) *Gramatyka współczesnego języka polskiego: Morfologia*. Warsaw: Wydawnictwo Naukowe PWN, 469–523.

KARLSSON, F. (1999). *Finnish: An Essential Grammar*. London and New York: Routledge.

KÄRRE, K. (1915). *Nomina agentis in Old English*. I. Uppsala: Akademiska Bokhandeln.

KASTOVSKY, D. (1974). 'Introduction,' in D. Kastovsky (ed.) *Studies in Syntax and Word-Formation: Selected Articles by Hans Marchand*. Munich: Fink, 10–22.

—— (1980). 'Zero in morphology: A means of making up for phonological losses?' in J. Fisiak (ed.) *Historical Morphology*. Trends in Linguistics: Studies and Monographs 17. The Hague: Mouton, 213–50.

—— (1981). 'Interaction of lexicon and syntax: Lexical converses. Forms and functions', in J. Esser and A. Hübler (eds.) *Papers in General, English and Applied Linguistics Presented to Vilém Fried on the Occasion of his 65th Birthday*. Tübingen: Narr, 123–36.

—— (1982). 'Word-formation: A functional view', *Folia Linguistica* 16: 181–98.

—— (1992a). 'Semantics and vocabulary', in R. M. Hogg (ed.) *The Cambridge History of the English Language*, vol. 1: *The Beginnings to 1066*. Cambridge: Cambridge University Press, 290–407.

—— (1992b). 'Typological reorientation as a result of level interaction: The case of English morphology', in G. Kellermann and M. D. Morrissey (eds.) *Diachrony within Synchrony: Language History and Cognition*. Duisburger Arbeiten zur Sprach- und Kulturwissenschaft 14. Frankfurt-am-Main: Lang, 411–28.

—— (1996a). 'Verbal derivation in English: A historical survey. Or: Much Ado about Nothing', in D. Britton (ed.) *English Historical Linguistics 1994*. Current Issues in Linguistic Theory 135. Amsterdam / Philadelphia: John Benjamins, 93–117.

—— (1996b). 'The place of word-formation in grammar: A historical survey', in K. R. Jankowsky (ed.) *Multiple Perspectives on the Historical Dimensions of Language*. Münster: Nodus, 227–43.

—— (2000). 'Words and word-formation: Morphology in the *OED*', in L. Muggleston (ed.) *Lexicography and the* OED: *Pioneers in the Untrodden Forest*. Oxford: Oxford University Press, 110–25.

—— (2002). 'The "haves" and the "have-nots" in Germanic and English: From *Bahuvrihi* compounds to affixal derivation', in K. Lenz and R. Möhlig (eds.) *Of Dyuersitie and Chaunge of Language: Essays Presented to Manfred Görlach on the Occasion of his 65th Birthday*. Heidelberg: Winter, 33–46.

—— (2005). 'Hans Marchand and the Marchandeans', in P. Štekauer and R. Lieber (eds.) *Handbook of Word-Formation*. Dordrecht: Springer, 99–124.

—— (2006a). 'Historical morphology from a typological point of view: Examples from English', in T. Nevalainen, J. Klemola, and M. Laitinen (eds.) *Types of Variation: Diachronic, Dialectal and Typological Interfaces*. SLCS 76. Amsterdam: John Benjamins, 53–80.

—— (2006b). 'Vocabulary', in R. M. Hogg and D. Denison (eds.) *A History of the English Language*. Cambridge: Cambridge University Press, 199–270.

KATAMBA, F. (1994). *English Words*. London: Routledge.

KAVKA, S. (2003). *A Book on Idiomatology*. Žilina: EDIS.

KAYNE, R. (1994). *The Antisymmetry of Syntax*. Cambridge, MA: MIT Press.

—— (2000). *Parameters and Universals*. Oxford: Oxford University Press.

—— (2001). Prepositions as Probes. Ms., New York University.

—— (2004). 'Prepositions as probes,' in A. Belletti (ed.) *Structures and Beyond*. New York: Oxford University Press, 192–212.

KE, Z. (2003). 'Verb-noun compounds in Chinese', *Southwest Journal of Linguistics* 22(1): 109–29.

KELLER, R. E. (1978). *The German Language*. London / Boston: Faber and Faber.

KEMENADE, A. VAN and B. L. LOS (2003). 'Particles and prefixes in Dutch and English', *Yearbook of Morphology 2003*. Dordrecht: Kluwer, 79–117.

KEMMER, S. and M. BARLOW (1999). 'Introduction: A usage-based conception of language', in M. Barlow and S. Kemmer (eds.) *Usage-Based Models of Language*. Stanford: CSLI Publications, vii–xxviii.

KENESEI, I. (2000). 'Szavak, szófajok, toldalékok', in F. Kiefer (ed.) *Strukturális magyar nyelvtan*, 3: *Morfológia*. Budapest: Akadémiai Kiadó, 75–136.

KERN, S. (1996). 'Comment les enfants jonglent avec les contraintes communicationnelles, discursives et linguistiques dans la production d'une narrative.' PhD Dissertation. Université Lumière, Lyon 2.

KIEFER, F. (1990). 'Noun incorporation in Hungarian', *Acta Linguistica Hungarica* 40(1–2): 149–77.

—— (1992a). 'Compounding in Hungarian', *Rivista di Linguistica* 4: 61–78.

—— (1992b). 'Compounds and argument structure in Hungarian', in I. Kenesei and C. Pléh (eds.) *Approaches to Hungarian*, Vol. 4: *The Structure of Hungarian*. Szeged: The University of Szeged, 51–66.

—— (2000). 'Az összetételek' [Compounds], in F. Kiefer (ed.) *Strukturális magyar nyelvtan*, 3: *Morfológia*. Budapest: Akadémiai Kiadó, 519–67.

—— (2001). 'Productivity and compounding', in C. Schaner-Wolles, J. Rennison, and F. Neubarth (eds.) *Naturally! Linguistic Studies in Honour of Wolfgang Ulrich Dressler on the Occasion of his 60th Birthday*. Torino: Rosenberg and Sellier, 225–31.

—— (2002). 'Alaktan' [Morphology], in É. K. Kiss, F. Kiefer, and P. Siptár (eds.) *Új magyar nyelvtan*. Budapest: Osiris, 189–284.

KILANI-SCHOCH, M. and W. U. DRESSLER (1992). 'Prol-o, intell-o, gauch-o et les autres. Propriétés formelles de deux opérations du français parlé', *Romanisches Jahrbuch*: 65–86.

KINGDON, R. (1958). *The Groundwork of English Stress*. London: Longman.

—— (1966). *The Groundwork of English Intonation*. London: Longman.

KIPARSKY, P. (1973). ' "Elsewhere" in phonology', in S. A. Anderson and P. Kiparsky (eds.) *A Festschrift for Morris Halle*. New York: Holt, Rinehart and Winston, 93–106.

—— (1982). 'Lexical Phonology and Morphology', in Linguistic Society of Korea (ed.) *Linguistics in the Morning Calm: Selected Papers from SICOL-1981*. Seoul: Hanshin, 3–91.

—— (1985). 'Some consequences of lexical phonology', *Phonology Yearbook* 2: 85–138.

KLEIN, W. and C. PERDUE (1997). 'The Basic Variety (or: Couldn't natural languages be much simpler?)', *Second Language Research* 13: 301–47.

KLINGE, A. (2005). 'The Structure of English Nominals.' *Doctor linguae mercantilis* thesis. Copenhagen Business School.

KOCH, P. (2001). 'Bedeutungswandel und Bezeichnungswandel: Von der kognitiven Semasiologie zur kognitiven Onomasiologie', *Zeitschrift für Literaturwissenschaft und Linguistik* 121: 7–36.

—— (2002). 'Lexical typology from a cognitive and linguistic point of view', in D. A. Cruse et al. (eds.) *Lexicology: An International Handbook on the Nature and Structure of Words and Vocabularies / Lexikologie: Ein internationales Handbuch zur Natur und Struktur von Wörtern und Wortschätzen*, vol. 1. Berlin / New York: Walter de Gruyter, 1142–78.

KOENIG, J-P. (1999). *Lexical Relations*. Stanford: CSLI.

KOESTER, D., T. C. GUNTER, and S. WAGNER (2007). 'The morphosyntactic decomposition and semantic composition of German compound words investigated by ERPs', *Brain and Language* 203: 64–79.

KOLB, B. and I. Q. WISHAW (1990). *Fundamentals of Human Neuropsychology.* New York: Freeman.

KORNFELD, L. (2005). 'Formación de palabras en la sintaxis desde la perspectiva de la Morfología Distribuida.' PhD dissertation, Universidad de Buenos Aires.

—— and A. SAAB (2003). 'Morphology and syntax: The case of prepositional prefixes in Spanish', in G. Booij, J. DeCesaris, A. Ralli, and S. Scalise (eds.) *Topics in Morphology: Selected Papers from the Third Mediterranean Morphology Meeting (Barcelona, September 20–22, 2001).* Barcelona: IULA, 227–40.

—— (2005). 'Hacia una tipología de las anáforas nominales en español.' paper presented at *III Encuentro de Gramática Generativa,* Universidad Nacional del Comahue (Neuquén), 18–20 August 2005.

KÖRTVÉLYESSY, L. (2008). 'Vplyv sociolingvistických faktorov na produktivitu v slovot-vorbe.' PhD dissertation, Presov.

KOZIOL, H. (1937). *Handbuch der englischen Wortbildungslehre.* Heidelberg: Carl Winter's Universitätsbuchhandlung.

KRAHE, H. and W. MEID (1967). *Germanische Sprachwissenschaft.* III. *Wortbildungslehre.* Göschen 1218. Berlin: de Gruyter.

KRAUSS, M. and J. LEER (1981). *Athabaskan, Eyak, and Tlingit Sonorants.* Alaska Native Language Center Research Papers (No. 5). Fairbanks, AK: University of Alaska, Alaska Native Language Center.

KRIEGER, H.-U. and J. NERBONNE (1993). 'Feature-based inheritance networks for computational lexicons', in T. Briscoe, A. Copestake, and V. de Paiva (eds.) *Inheritance, Defaults and the Lexicon.* Cambridge: Cambridge University Press, 90–136.

KROTT, A. (2001). 'Analogy in morphology. The selection of linking elements in Dutch compounds.' PhD dissertation, University of Nijmegen.

—— H. R. BAAYEN, and R. SCHREUDER (2001). 'Analogy in morphology: Modelling the choice of linking morphemes in Dutch', *Linguistics* 39: 51–93.

—— and E. NICOLADIS (2005). 'Large constituent families help children parse compounds', *Journal of Child Language* 32: 139–58.

—— R. SCHREUDER, H. R. BAAYEN, and W. U. DRESSLER (2007) 'Analogical effects on linking elements in German compounds', *Language and Cognitive Processes* 22: 25–57.

KUIPER, K. (1999). 'Compounding by adjunction and its empirical consequences', *Language Sciences* 21: 407–22.

KÜRSCHNER, W. (1974). *Zur syntaktischen Beschreibung deutscher Nominalkomposita auf der Grundlage generativer Transformationsgrammatiken.* Tübingen: Narr.

—— (1977). 'Generative Transformationsgrammatik und die Wortbildungstheorie von Hans Marchand', in H. Brekle and D. Kastovsky (eds.) *Perspektiven der Wortbildungs-forschung.* Wuppertaler Schriftenseihe Linguistics 1. Bonn: Bouvier, 129–139.

KURYØOWICZ, J. (1964). *The Inflectional Categories of Indo-European.* Heidelberg: Winter.

—— (1968). *Indogermanische Grammatik,* vol. 2: *Akzent, Ablaut.* Heidelberg: Winter.

KURZOWA, Z. (1976). *Złożenia imienne we współczesnym języku polskim.* Warsaw: Państwowe Wydawnictwo Naukowe.

LABOV, W. (1973). 'The boundaries of words and their meaning', in C.-J. N. Bailey and R. W. Shuy (eds.) *New Ways of Analyzing Variation in English.* Washington, D C: Georgetown University Press, 340–73.

LACZKÓ, T. (2000). 'Az argumentumszerkezetet megőrző főnévképzés' [Deverbal nouns preserving the argument structure of the base], in F. Kiefer (ed.) *Strukturális magyar nyelvtan*, 3: *Morfológia*. Budapest: Akadémiai Kiadó, 293–407.

LADD, R. D. (1984). 'English Compound Stress', in D. Gibbon and H. Richter (eds.) *Intonation, Accent and Rhythm: Studies in Discourse Phonology*. Berlin/New York: Walter de Gruyter, 253–66.

LAKOFF, G. (1987). *Women, Fire, and Dangerous Things: What Categories Reveal about the Mind*. Chicago: The University of Chicago Press.

—— and M. JOHNSON (1980). *Metaphors We Live By*. Chicago, IL: The University of Chicago Press.

LANGACKER, R. (1987). *Foundations of Cognitive Grammar*, vol. 1. Stanford: Stanford University Press.

—— (1988). 'A usage-based model', in B. Rudzka-Ostyn (ed.) *Topics in Cognitive Linguistics*. Amsterdam / Philadelphia: John Benjamins, 127–61.

—— (1991). *Foundations of Cognitive Grammar*, vol. 2: *Descriptive Application*. Stanford: Stanford University Press.

—— (1998a). 'Conceptualization, symbolization, and grammar', in M. Tomasello (ed.) *The New Psychology of Language: Cognitive and Functional Approaches to Language Structure*. Mahwah, NJ / London: Lawrence Erlbaum Associates, 1–39.

—— (1998b). 'Linguistic evidence and mental representations', *Cognitive Linguistics* 9: 151–73.

—— (1999). *Grammar and Conceptualization*. Berlin: Mouton de Gruyter.

LANGEWEG, S. J. (1988). 'The Stress System of Dutch.' PhD Dissertation, University of Leiden.

LAPOINTE, S. (1980). 'The Theory of Grammatical Agreement.' PhD Dissertation, University of Massachusetts, Amherst.

LARDIERE, D. (1995a). 'L2 acquisition of English synthetic compounding is not constrained by level-ordering (and neither, probably, is L1)', *Second Language Research* 11: 20–56.

—— (1995b). 'Differential treatment of regular versus irregular inflection in compounds as nonevidence for level-ordering', *Second Language Research* 11: 267–9.

LARSON, R. and H. YAMAKIDO (2006). 'Zazaki "double ezafe" as double case-marking.' Paper presented at the Linguistics Society of America annual meeting, Albuquerque, NM, 8 January 2006. Available online at http://semlab5.sbs.sunysb.edu/%7Erlarson/larson-papers.html.

LAUGHREN, M. (2007). 'Deriving new verbs in Warlpiri.' Australian Linguistics Society Annual Conference, Adelaide.

—— (in prep.). *Warlpiri Dictionary*. Brisbane: University of Queensland.

LAUNEY, M. (2004). 'Nahuatl (Uto-Aztecan)', in G. Booij, C. Lehmann, J. Mugdan, and S. Skopeteas (eds.) *Morphologie/Morphology*, vol 2. Berlin / New York: de Gruyter, 1433–53.

LEECH, G. (1974). *Semantics*. Penguin Books.

LEES, R. B. (1960). *The Grammar of English Nominalizations*. Bloomington: Indiana University Press/The Hague: Mouton.

—— (1966). 'On a transformational analysis of compounds: A reply to Hans Marchand', *Indogermanische Forschungen* 71: 1–13.

—— (1970). 'Problems in the grammatical analysis of English nominal compounds', in M. Bierwisch and K. E. Heidolph (eds.) *Progress in Linguistics*. The Hague: Mouton, 174–86.

LEFEBVRE, C. and A.-M. BROUSSEAU (2002). *A Grammar of Fongbe*. Berlin / New York: Mouton de Gruyter.

LEGATE, J. A. (2002). 'Warlpiri: Theoretical Implications.' PhD Dissertation, MIT, Cambridge.

—— (2003). 'Some interface properties of the phase', *Linguistic Inquiry* 34: 506–16.

LEITZKE, E. (1989). *(De)nominale Adjektive im heutigen Englisch: Untersuchungen zur Morphologie, Syntax, Semantik und Pragmatik von Adjektiv-Nomen-Kombinationen vom Typ* atomic energy *und* criminal lawyer. Tübingen: Max Niemeyer Verlag.

LESER, M. (1990). *Das Problem der 'Zusammenbildungen'.* Trier: WVT.

LEVI, J. N. (1976). 'A semantic analysis of Hebrew compound nominals', in P. Cole (ed.) *Studies in Modern Hebrew Syntax and Semantics*. Amsterdam: North-Holland, 9–56.

—— (1978). *The Syntax and Semantics of Complex Nominals*. New York: Academic Press.

—— (1983). 'Complex nominals: New discoveries, new questions', in S. Hattori and K. Inoue (eds.) *Proceedings of the XIIIth International Congress of Linguists = Actes du XIIIe congrès international des linguistes*, 29 August–4 September 1982. Tokyo: Proceedings Publishing Committee, 183–97.

LEVIN, B. and M. RAPPAPORT HOVAV (1999). 'Two structures for compositionally derived events', *Proceedings of Semantics and Linguistic Theory 9*. Ithaca: CLC Publications, 199–223.

LI, C. N. and S. A. THOMPSON (1978). 'An exploration of Mandarin Chinese', in W. P. Lehmann (ed.) *Syntactic Typology: Studies in the Phenomenology of Language*. Austin: University of Texas Press: 233–66.

—— (1981). *A Grammar of Spoken Chinese: A Functional Reference Grammar*. Berkeley: University of California Press.

LI, Y. (1990). 'On V-V compounds in Chinese', *Natural Language and Linguistic Theory* 8: 177–207.

—— (1993). 'Structural head and aspectuality', *Language* 69(3): 480–504.

—— (1995). 'The thematic hierarchy and causativity', *Natural Language and Linguistic Theory* 13: 255–82.

—— (2005). °*Theory of the Morphology–Syntax Interface*. Cambridge, MA: MIT Press.

LIBBEN, G. (1998). 'Semantic transparency in the processing of compounds: Consequences for representation, processing, and impairment', *Brain and Language* 61(1): 30–44.

—— (2005). 'Everything is psycholinguistics: Material and methodological considerations in the study of compound processing', *Canadian Journal of Linguistics* 50: 267–83.

—— (2006). 'Why study compound processing? An overview of the issues', in G. Libben and G. Jarema (eds.) *The Representation and Processing of Compound Words*. Oxford: Oxford University Press, 1–22.

—— B. L. DERWING, and R. G. ALMEIDA (1999). 'Ambiguous novel compounds and models of morphological parsing', *Brain and Language* 68: 378–86.

—— M. GIBSON, Y. B. YOON, and D. SANDRA (2003). 'Compound fracture: The role of semantic transparency and morphological headedness', *Brain and Language* 84: 50–64.

—— and G. Jarema (2006). *The Representation and Processing of Compounds*. Oxford: Oxford University Press.

LIBERMAN, M. and A. PRINCE (1977). 'On stress and linguistic rhythm', *Linguistic Inquiry* 8: 249–336.

—— and R. SPROAT (1992). 'The stress and structure of modified noun phrases in English', in I. A. Sag and A. Scabolcsi (eds.) *Lexical Matters*. Stanford: Center for the Study of Language and Information, 131–81.

LIEBER, R. (1981). *On the Organization of the Lexicon*. Bloomington, IN: Indiana University Linguistics Club. Reprinted (1990) New York: Garland.

—— (1983). 'Argument linking and compounds in English', *Linguistic Inquiry* 14: 251–85.

—— (1988). 'Phrasal compounds in English and the morphology–syntax interface', in D. Brentari, G. Larson, and L. MacLeod (eds.) *CLS-24-II, Papers from the Parasession on Agreement in Grammatical Theory*. Chicago: Chicago Linguistic Society, 202–22.

—— (1992a). *Deconstructing Morphology*. Chicago/London: The University of Chicago Press.

—— (1992b). 'Compounding in English', *Rivista di Linguistica* 4(1): 79–96.

—— (2004). *Morphology and Lexical Semantics*. Cambridge: Cambridge University Press.

—— (2005). 'English word-formation processes', in P. Stekauer and R. Lieber (eds.) *Handbook of Word-Formation*. Dordrecht: Springer, 375–428.

—— (2007). 'The category of roots and the roots of categories: What we learn from selection in derivation', *Morphology* 16(2): 247–72.

—— and H. BAAYEN (1997). 'A semantic principle of auxiliary selection in Dutch', *Natural Language and Linguistic Theory* 15(4): 789–845.

—— and S. SCALISE (2006). 'The Lexical Integrity Hypothesis in a new theoretical universe', *Lingue e Linguaggio* 5(1): 7–32.

LIMA, S. and A. POLLATSEK (1983). 'Lexical access via an orthographic code? The Basic Orthographic Syllabic Structure (BOSS) reconsidered', *Journal of Verbal Learning and Verbal Behavior* 22(3): 310–32.

LIN, F.-W. (1990). 'The verb-complement (V-R) compounds in Mandarin'. M.A. Thesis, National Tsing Hua University.

LIN, H.-L. (1996). 'A lexical syntactic analysis of resultative compounds in Mandarin Chinese', *Studies in the Linguistic Sciences* 26(1–2): 193–204.

LING, Y. (2000). 现代汉语缩略语 *Xiandai Hangyu Suolüeyu* [Abbreviations in Contemporary Chinese]. Beijing: Yuwen chubanshe.

LINT, T. van (1982). 'The interpretation of compound nouns', in S. Daalder and M. Gerritsen (eds.) *Linguistics in the Netherlands 1982*. Amsterdam / Oxford: North-Holland, 135–45.

LIPKA, L. (2005). 'Lexicalization and institutionalization: Revisited and extended', *SKASE Journal of Theoretical Linguistics* 2(2): 40–2.

LJUNG, M. (1976). '-*ed* adjectives revisited', *Journal of Linguistics* 12(1): 159–68.

LOJENGA, C. K. (1994). *Ngiti*. Cologne: Köppe.

LONCON ANTILEO, E. (2005). 'Morfología y aspectos del Mapudungun.' PhD dissertation, Universidad Autónoma Metropolitana.

LONGOBARDI, G. (2003). 'La linguistica parametrica: un nuovo programma di ricerca tra presente futuro delle scienze del linguaggio', *Lingue e Linguaggio* 1: 3–30.

LU, Z. (1964). 汉语的构词法 *Hanyu de goucifa* [Chinese Morphology]. Beijing: Kexue Chubanshe.

LUCE, R. D. (1959). *Individual Choice Behaviour*. New York: Wiley.

LÜDELING, A. (2001). *On Particle Verbs and Similar Constructions in German*. Stanford: CSLI Publications.

LUKATELA, G., B. GLIGORIJEVIC, A. KOSTIC, and M. T. TURVEY (1980). 'Representation of inflected nouns in the internal lexicon', *Memory & Cognition* 8: 415–23.

LYONS, J. (1977). *Semantics*, 2 vols. Cambridge: Cambridge University Press.

—— (1983). *Language, Meaning and Context*. London: Fontana Paperbacks.

MACWHINNEY, B. (2004). 'A multiple process solution to the logical problem of language acquisition', *Journal of Child Language* 31: 883–914.

MAIDEN, M. and C. ROBUSTELLI (2000). *A Reference Grammar of Modern Italian*. London: Arnold.

MALIKOUTI-DRACHMAN, A. (1997). 'Prosodic domains in Greek compounding', in G. Drachman et al. (eds.) *Proceedings of the 2nd International Conference of Greek Linguistics*. Graz: Neugebauer Verlag, 87–96.

MANELIS, L. and D. A. THARP (1977). 'The processing of affixed words', *Memory & Cognition* 5: 690–5.

MANGOLD-ALLWINN, R. et al. (1995). *Wörter für Dinge: Von flexiblen Konzepten zu Benennungen*. Opladen: Westdeutscher Verlag.

MARANTZ, A. (1996). 'Cat as a phrasal idiom.' Ms. MIT.

—— (1997). 'No escape from syntax: Don't try morphological analysis in the privacy of your own lexicon', in A. Dimitriadis, L. Siegel, C. Surek-Clark, and A. Williams (eds.) *Proceedings of the 21st Penn Linguistics Colloquium*. Philadelphia: UPenn Working Papers in Linguistics, 201–25.

—— (2000). 'Roots: The universality of root and pattern morphology.' Paper presented at the Conference on Afro-Asiatic Languages, University of Paris VII.

—— (2001). 'Words.' Paper presented at the West Coast Conference on Formal Linguistics, University of Southern California Los Angeles, 24 February 2001. Available online at http://web.mit.edu/marantz/Public/EALING/WordsWCCFL.pdf.

—— (2003). 'Pulling words up by the Root.' Handout of talk presented at McGill University.

MARCHAND, H. (1960). *The Categories and Types of Present-Day English Word-Formation*. Wiesbaden: Otto Harrassowitz.

—— (1965a). 'The analysis of verbal nexus substantives', *Indogermanische Forschungen* 70: 57–71, repr. in D. Kastovsky (ed.) (1974). *H. Marchand: Studies in Syntax and Word-Formation*. Munich: Fink, 276–91.

—— (1965b). 'On the analysis of substantive compounds and suffixal derivatives not containing a verbal element', *Indogermanische Forschungen* 70: 117–45, repr. in D. Kastovsky (ed.) (1974). *H. Marchand: Studies in Syntax and Word-Formation*. Munich: Fink, 292–322.

—— (1967). 'Expansion, transposition, and derivation', *La Linguistique* 1: 13–26.

—— (1969). *The Categories and Types of Present-Day English Word-Formation: A Synchronic–Diachronic Approach*, 2nd edn. Munich: Beck.

MARKMAN, E. M., J. L. WASOW, and M. B. HANSEN (2003). 'Use of the mutual exclusivity assumption by young word learners', *Cognitive Psychology* 47: 241–75.

MARSLEN-WILSON, W., L. KOMISARJEVSKY TYLER, R. WAKSLER, and L. OLDER (1994). 'Morphology and meaning in the English mental lexicon', *Psychological Review* 101: 3–33.

MASSAM, D. (2001). 'Pseudo noun incorporation in Niuean', *Natural Language & Linguistic Theory* 19: 153–97.

MASSON, M. and C. MACLEOD (1992). 'Re-enacting the route to interpretation: Enhanced perceptual identification without prior perception', *Journal of Experimental Psychology: General* 121: 145–76.

MASULLO, P. J. (1996). 'Los sintagmas nominales sin determinante: una propuesta incorporacionista', in I. Bosque (ed.) *El sustantivo sin determinación*. Madrid: Visor, 169–200.

MATHIEU-COLAS, M. (1996). 'Essai de typologie des noms composés français', *Cahiers de lexicologie*: 71–125.

MATSUMOTO, Y. (1996). *Complex Predicates in Japanese*. Stanford: CSLI.

MATTENS, M. W. H. (1970). *De Indifferentialis. Een Onderzoek naar het anumerieke Gebruik van het Substantief in het algemeen bruikbaar Nederlands*. Assen: Van Gorcum & Comp.

—— (1984). 'De voorspelbaarheid van tussenklanken in nominale samenstellingen', *De Nieuwe Taalgids* 77: 333–43.

—— (1987). 'Tussenklanken in substantivische en adjectivische samenstellingen', *Forum der Letteren* 28: 108–14.

MATTHEWS, P. H. (1961). 'Transformational Grammar', *Archivum Linguisticum* 13: 196–209.

MATUSHANSKY, O. (2003). 'Going through a phase', in M. McGinnis and N. Richards (eds.) *Perspectives on Phase*. MIT Working Papers in Linguistics 49, 157–81.

—— (2006). 'Head-movement in linguistic theory', *Linguistic Inquiry* 37(1): 69–109.

McCAWLEY, J. D. (1968). 'Lexical insertion in a transformational grammar without deep structure', in *Papers from the Fourth Regional Meeting. Chicago Linguistic Society*, 71–80. Repr. in J. D. McCawley (1976). *Grammar and Meaning: Papers on Syntactic and Semantic Topics*. New York: Academic Press, 155–66.

—— (1978). 'Foreword', in J. Levi (1978) *The Syntax and Semantics of Complex Nominals*. New York: Academic Press, xi–xiii.

MCHOMBO, S. A. (1998). 'Chichewa (Bantu)', in A. Spencer and A. M. Zwicky (eds.) *The Handbook of Morphology*. Oxford / Malden, MA: Blackwell, 500–20.

MEIBAUER, J. (2001). 'Lexikon und Morphologie', in J. Meibauer et al. (eds.) *Einführung in die germanistische Linguistik*. Stuttgart / Weimar: Metzler, 15–69.

—— (2003). 'Phrasenkomposita zwischen Wortsyntax und Lexikon', *Zeitschrift für Sprachwissenschaft* 22: 153–88.

MEIER-BRÜGGER, M. (2002). *Indogermanische Sprachwissenschaft*. Berlin: de Gruyter.

MEISSNER, T. and O. TRIBULATO (2002). 'Nominal composition in Mycenaean Greek', *Transactions of the Philological Society* 100(3): 289–330.

MEL'ČUK, I. (1982). *Towards a Language of Linguistics*. Munich: Fink.

—— (1993) *Cours de morphologie générale. Première partie: le mot*. Montréal: Presses de l'Université de Montréal – CNRS Editions.

MELLENIUS, I. (1997). *The Acquisition of Nominal Compounding in Swedish*. Lund: Lund University Press.

—— (2003). 'Word formation', in G. Josefsson, C. Platzack, and G. Håkansson (eds.) *The Acquisition of Swedish Grammar*. Amsterdam / Philadelphia: John Benjamins, 75–93.

MELLONI, C. and A. BISETTO (2007). 'Parasynthetic compounding'. Paper delivered at 6th Mediterranean Morphology Meeting, Ithaca, Greece.

MEYER, R. (1993). *Compound Comprehension in Isolation and in Context: The Contribution of Conceptual and Discourse Knowledge to the Comprehension of German Novel Noun-Noun Compounds*. Tübingen: Niemeyer.

MICHAELIS, L. A. and K. LAMBRECHT (1996). 'Toward a construction-based theory of language function: The case of nominal extraposition', *Language* 72: 215–47.

MILLER, G. A. and P. N. JOHNSON-LAIRD (1976). *Language and Perception*. Cambridge, MA: Harvard University Press.

MILLIKAN, R. (1984). *Language, Thought, and Other Biological Categories*. Cambridge, MA: MIT Press.

MINKOVA, D. (2007). 'Stress-shifting in English Prefixed Words: Continuity or Re-invention.' Paper presented at the 5th SHEL Conference, Athens, Georgia, 4–6 October 2007.

MITCHELL, T. F. (1975). 'Linguistic "goings-on": collocations and other lexical matters arising on the syntagmatic record', in *Principles of Firthian Linguistics*. London: Longman, 99–136.

MITHUN, M. (1984). 'The evolution of noun incorporation', *Language* 60: 847–94.

—— (1986a). 'The convergence of noun classification systems', in C. Craig (ed.) *Noun Classes and Categorization*. Amsterdam / Philadelphia: John Benjamins, 379–97.

—— (1986b). 'On the nature of noun incorporation', *Language* 62: 32–37.

—— (1996). 'Multiple reflections of inalienability in Mohawk', in H. Chappell and W. McGregor (eds.) *The Grammar of Inalienability*. Berlin: Mouton de Gruyter, 633–49.

—— (1999). *The Languages of Native North America*. Cambridge: Cambridge University Press.

—— (2001a). 'Lexical forces shaping the evolution of grammar', in L. Brinton (ed.) *Historical Linguistics 1999*. Amsterdam / Philadelphia: John Benjamins, 241–52.

—— (2001b). 'Actualization patterns in grammaticalization: From clause to locative morphology', in H. Andersen (ed.) *Actualization: Linguistic Change in Progess*. Amsterdam / Philadelphia: John Benjamins, 143–68.

—— (2001c). 'The difference a category makes in the expression of possession and inalienability', in M. Herslund, F. Sørensen, and I. Baron (eds.) *Dimensions of Possession*. Amsterdam / Philadelphia: John Benjamins, 285–310.

MOHANAN, K. P. (1986). *The Theory of Lexical Phonology*. Dordrecht: D. Reidel.

MOLINSKY, S. J. (1973). *Patterns of Ellipsis in Russian Compound Noun Formations*. The Hague: Mouton.

MONSELL, S. (1985). 'Repetition and the Lexicon', in A. W. Ellis (ed.) *Progress in the Psychology of Language*. Hillsdale, NJ: Lawrence Erlbaum, 147–95.

MONTAGUE, R. (1973). 'The proper treatment of quantification in ordinary English', in J. Hintikka, J. Moravcsik, and P. Suppes (eds.) *Approaches to Natural Language*. Dordrecht: D. Reidel, 221–42.

MONUS, V. and S. ISAIAH (n.d.). *Slavey Topical Dictionary*. Summer Institute of Linguistics.

MORO, A. (2000). *Dynamic Antisymmetry*. Cambridge, MA: MIT Press.

MOSONYI, E. E. (2002). 'La fonología suprasegmental y otras particularidades del baniva de Maroa, idioma tonal arawak del Río Negro, Venezuela', in M. Crevels et al. (eds.) *Current Studies on South American Languages*. Leiden: University of Leiden, 127–36.

—— and H. CAMICO (1996). 'Introducción al análisis del idioma baniva', in O. González Ñáñez (ed.) *Gramática baniva*. Caracas: UNICEF Venezuela, 9–41.

—— and J. C. MOSONYI (2000). *Manual de lenguas indígenas de Venezuela*. Caracas: Fundación Bigott.

MOSONYI, J. C. (1987). 'El idioma yavitero: ensayo de gramática y diccionario.' PhD dissertation, Universidad Central de Venezuela, Caracas.

MOTSCH, W. (1970). 'Analyse von Komposita mit zwei nominalen Elementen', in M. Bierwisch and K. E. Heidolph (eds.) *Progress in Linguistics*. The Hague: Mouton, 208–23.

MULFORD, R. (1983). 'On the acquisition of Derivational Morphology in Icelandic: Learning about –ari', *Islenski Mál og Almenn Málfraeði* 5: 105–25.

MUNN, A. (1992). 'Topics in the syntax and semantics of coordination structures.' PhD dissertation, University of Maryland.

—— (1995). 'The possessor that stayed close to home', in V. Samiian and J. Schaeffer (eds.) *Proceedings of the Western Conference on Linguistics (WECOL 24)*, 181–95.

MURPHY, G. L. (1988). 'Comprehending complex concepts', *Cognitive Science* 12: 529–62.

—— (1990). 'Noun phrase interpretation and conceptual combination', *Journal of Memory and Language* 29: 259–88.

—— (2002). 'Conceptual approaches I: An overview', in D. A. Cruse, F. Hundsnurscher, M. Job, and P. R. Lutzeier (eds.) *Lexicology: An International Handbook on the Nature and Structure of Words and Vocabularies*, vol. 1. Berlin: Walter de Gruyter, 269–77.

Murphy, V. A. and E. Nicoladis (2006). 'When *answer-phone* makes a difference in children's acquisition of English compounds', *Journal of Child Language* 33: 677–91.

Murrell, G. A. and J. Morton (1974). 'Word recognition and morphemic structure', *Journal of Experimental Psychology* 102: 963–8.

Nagórko, A. (1998). *Zarys gramatyki polskiej (ze słowotwórstwem)*. Warsaw: Wydawnictwo Naukowe PWN.

Nagy, W. E. and R. C. Anderson (1984). 'How many words are there in printed school English', *Reading Research Quarterly* 19: 304–30.

—— M. Schommer, J. A. Scott, and A. C. Stallman (1989). 'Morphological families in the internal lexicon', *Reading Research Quarterly* 24: 262–82.

—— and P. A. Herman (1987). 'Breadth and depth of vocabulary knowledge: Implications for acquisition and instruction', in M. McKeown and M. E. Curtis (eds.) *The Nature of Vocabulary Acquisition*. Hillsdale, NJ: Lawrence Erlbaum, 19–59.

Namiki, T. (2001). 'Further evidence in support of the Righthand Head Rule in Japanese', in J. van der Weijer and T. Nishihara (eds.) *Issues in Japanese Phonology and Morphology*. Berlin: Mouton de Gruyter, 277–97.

Napps, S. E. (1989). 'Morphemic relationships in the lexicon: Are they distinct from semantic and formal relationships?' *Memory & Cognition* 17: 729–39.

Nash, D. (1982). 'Warlpiri preverbs and verb roots', in S. Swartz (ed.) *Papers in Warlpiri Grammar: In Memory of Lothar Jagst*. Berrimah, Australia: Summer Institute of Linguistics, 165–216.

—— (1986). *Topics in Warlpiri Grammar*. New York / London: Garland.

Nattinger, J. R. and J. S. DeCarrico (1992). *Lexical Phrases and Language Teaching*. Oxford: Oxford University Press.

Naumann, R. and T. Gamerschlag (2003). 'Constraining the combinatorial patterns of Japanese V-V compounds: An analysis in dynamic event semantics', *Journal of Semantics* 20(3): 275–96.

Nayak, N. P. and R. W. Gibbs (1990). 'Conceptual knowledge in the interpretation of idioms', *Journal of Experimental Psychology: General* 119: 315–30.

Ndiaye, M. D. (2004). *Éléments de morphologie du wolof*. Munich: Lincom Europa.

Nedjalkov, I. (1997). *Evenki*. London / New York: Routledge.

Neeleman, A. (1994). 'Complex Predicates.' Led PhD dissertation, University of Utrecht.

Neijt, A., L. Krebbers, and P. Fikkert (2002). 'Rhythm and semantics in the selection of linking elements', in H. Broekhuis and P Fikkert (eds.) *Linguistics in the Netherlands 2002*. Amsterdam: John Benjamins, 117–27.

Neščimenko, G. P. (1963). 'Zakonomernosti slovoobrazovanija, semantiki i upotreblenija suščestvitel'nyx s suffiksami subjektivnoj ocenki v sovremennom českom jazyke', in *Issledovanija po češskomu jazyku: Voprosy slovoobrazovanija i gramatiki*. Moscow, 105–58.

—— (1968). *Istorija imennogo slovoobrazovanija v češskom literaturnom jazyke konca XVIII– XX vekov*. Moscow.

Nespor, M. and A. Ralli (1996). 'Morphology–phonology interface: Phonological domains in Greek compounds', *The Linguistic Review* 13: 357–82.

Newman, P. (2000). *The Hausa Language*. New Haven, CT: Yale University Press.

Newmeyer, F. J. (1986). *Linguistic Theory in America*, 2nd edn. New York: Academic Press.

—— (1996). *Generative Linguistics: A Historical Perspective*. London: Routledge.

NICOLADIS, E. (1999). 'Where is my brush-teeth? Acquisition of compound nouns in a French-English bilingual child', *Bilingualism, Language and Cognition* 2: 245–56.

—— (2002). 'What's the difference between "toilet paper" and "paper toilet"? French-English bilingual children's crosslinguistic transfer in compound nouns', *Journal of Child Language* 29: 843–63.

—— (2003). 'Cross-linguistic transfer in deverbal compounds of preschool bilingual children', *Bilingualism, Language and Cognition* 6: 17–31.

—— (2005). 'When level-ordering is not used in the formation of English compounds', *First Language* 25: 331–46.

—— (2007). 'Preschool children's acquisition of compounds', in G. Libben and G. Jarema (eds.) *The Representation and Processing of Compounds*. Oxford: Oxford University Press, 96–124.

—— and H. YIN (2002). 'The role of frequency in acquistion of English and Chinese compounds by bilingual children', in B. Skarabela et al. (eds.) *Proceedings of BUCLD* 26. Somerville, MA: Cascadilla Press, 192–303.

NIKOLAEVA, I. and M. TOLSKAYA (2001). *A Grammar of Udihe*. Berlin / New York: Mouton de Gruyter.

NISHIYAMA, K. (1998). 'V-V compounds as serialization', *Journal of East Asian Linguistics* 7: 175–217.

NISSENBAUM, J. (2000). 'Covert movement and parasitic gaps', in M. Hirotani, A. Coetzee, N. Hall, and J-Y Kim (eds.) *Proceedings of the North East Linguistics Society (NELS 30)*. Amherst, MA: GLSA.

NOAILLY, M. (1990). *Le substantif épithète*. Paris: PUF.

NOSKE, M. (2000). '[ATR] harmony in Turkana: A case of Faith Suffix » Faith Root', *Natural Language and Linguistic Theory* 18: 771–812.

OGLOBLIN, A. K. (2005). 'Javanese', in A. Adelaar and N. P. Himmelmann (eds.), *Austronesian Languages of Asia and Madagascar*. London and New York: Routledge, 590–624.

OLSCHANSKY, H. (1996). *Volksetymologie*. Tübingen: Niemeyer.

OLSEN, B. A. (2002). 'Thoughts on Indo-European compounds – Inspired by a look at Armenian', *Transactions of the Philological Society* 100(2): 233–57.

OLSEN, S. (1986). *Wortbildung im Deutschen. Eine Einführung in die Theorie der Wortstruktur*. Stuttgart: Kröner.

—— (2000a). 'Composition', in G. Booij, C. Lehmann, and J. Mugdan (eds.) *Morphologie / Morphology*. Berlin / New York: de Gruyter, 897–916.

—— (2000b). 'Compounding and stress in English: A closer look at the boundary between morphology and syntax', *Linguistische Berichte* 181: 55–69.

—— (2001). 'Copulative compounds: A closer look at the interface between morphology and syntax', *Yearbook of Morphology 2000*. Dordrecht: Kluwer, 279–320.

ORTNER, L. and E. MÜLLER-BOLLHAGEN (1991). *Deutsche Wortbildung. Vierter Hauptteil: Substantivkomposita*. Berlin / New York: de Gruyter.

OSGOOD, C. E. and R. HOOSAIN (1974). 'Salience of the word as a unit in the perception of language', *Perception & Psychophysics* 1: 168–92.

OSHITA, H. (1995). 'Compounds: A view from suffixation and A-structure alteration', *Yearbook of Morphology 1994*. Dordrecht: Kluwer, 179–205.

OSTER, U. (2004). 'From relational schemas to subject-specific semantic relations: A two-step classification of compound terms', *Annual Review of Cognitive Linguistics* 2: 235–59.

OSTHOFF, H. (1878). *Das Verbum in der Nominalcomposition im Deutschen, Griechischen, Romanischen, und Slavischen.* Jena: Naumburg a/S.

PACKARD, J. (1998). 'Introduction', in J. Packard (ed.) *New Approaches to Chinese Word Formation.* Berlin: Mouton de Gruyter, 3–34.

—— (2000). *The Morphology of Chinese.* Cambridge: Cambridge University Press.

PAN, W., B. YE, and Y. HAN (2004). 汉语的构词法研究 *Hanyu de goucifa yanjiu* [Research on Word Formation in Chinese]. Shanghai: Huadong Shifan Daxue Chubanshe.

PAUL, H. (1920 [1960]). *Prinzipien der Sprachgeschichte,* 5th edn. Darmstadt: Wissenschaftliche Buchgesellschaft.

PAYNE, D. (1986). 'Noun classification in Yagua', in C. Craig (ed.) *Noun Classes and Categorization.* Amsterdam / Philadelphia: John Benjamins, 113–31.

—— (1991). 'A classification of Maipuran (Arawakan) languages based on shared lexical retentions', in D. C. Derbyshire and G. K. Pullum (eds.) *Handbook of Amazonian Languages,* vol. 3. Berlin / New York: Mouton de Gruyter, 355–499.

PAYNE, J. and R. HUDDLESTON (2002). 'Nouns and Noun Phrases', in R. Huddleston and G. K. Pullum. *The Cambridge Grammar of the English Language.* Cambridge: Cambridge University Press, 323–524.

PENNANEN, E. (1996). *Contributions to the study of back-formation in English.* Tampere: Acta Academiae Socialis Ser. A. Vol 4. Julkaisija Yhteiskunnallinen Korkeakoulu.

—— (1980). 'On the function and behaviour of stress in English noun compounds', *English Studies* 61: 252–63.

PETERSEN, W. (1914/15). 'Über den Ursprung der Exozentrika', *Indogermanische Forschungen* 30: 58–64.

PHILLIPS, C. (2003). 'Linear order and constituency', *Linguistic Inquiry* 34(1): 37–90.

PIMENOVA, N. (2004). 'Nominale Stammbildungssuffixe als Derivationsmittel im (Gemein) Germanischen', in J. Clackson and B. A. Olsen (eds.) *Indo-European Word-Formation. Proceedings of the Conference Held at the University Of Copenhagen, October 20th – 22nd 2000.* University of Copenhagen: Museum Tusculanum Press, 249–68.

PITT, D. and J. J. KATZ (2000). 'Compositional idioms', *Language* 76: 409–32.

PLAG, I. (2003). *Word-Formation in English.* Cambridge: Cambridge University Press.

—— (2006a). 'Morphology in pidgins and creoles', in K. Brown (ed.) *Encyclopedia of Language and Linguistics,* 2nd edn. Oxford: Elsevier. Vol 8: 304–8.

—— (2006b). 'The variability of compound stress in English: Structural, semantic and analogical factors', *English Language and Linguistics* 10/1: 143–72

PLÉNAT, M. (1998). 'De quelques paramétres intervenant dans l'oralisation des sigles en français', *Cahiers d'Etudes Romanes:* 27–52.

—— (1999). 'Prolégomènes à une étude variationniste des hypocoristiques à redoublement en français', *Cahiers de Grammaire:* 183–219.

—— (2008). 'Les contraintes de taille', in B. Fradin, F. Kerleroux, and M. Plénat (eds.) *Aperçus de morphologie du français.* Saint-Denis: Presses Universitaires de Vincennes.

POHL, D. (1977). *Die Nominalkomposition im Alt- und Gemeinslavischen. Ein Beitrag zur slavischen, indogermanischen und allgemeinen Wortbildung.* Klagenfurter Beiträge zur Sprachwissenschaft Beiheft 1. Klagenfurt: Klagenfurter Sprachwissenschaftliche Gesellschaft.

POLENZ, P. VON (1973). 'Synpleremik I. Wortbildung', in H. Althaus et al. (eds.) *Lexikon der germanistischen Linguistik.* Tübingen: Niemeyer, 145–63.

POLLATSEK, A. and J. HYÖNÄ (2005). 'The role of semantic transparency in the processing of Finnish compound words', *Language & Cognitive Processes* 20: 261–90.

POLLATSEK, A. and R. BERTRAM (2000). 'The role of morphological constituents in reading Finnish compound words', *Journal of Experimental Psychology: Human Perception & Performance* 26: 820–33.

PORTNER, P. and B. H. PARTEE (eds.) (2002). *Formal Semantics: The Essential Readings.* Oxford: Blackwell.

POSTAL, P. M. (1969). 'Anaphoric Islands', *Chicago Linguistic Society* 5: 205–39.

PULLUM, G. K. and R. HUDDLESTON (2002). 'Adjectives and Adverbs', in R. Huddleston and G. K. Pullum. *The Cambridge Grammar of the English Language.* Cambridge: Cambridge University Press, 525–96.

PÜMPEL-MADER, M. et al. (1992). *Deutsche Wortbildung. Fünfter Hauptteil: Adjektivkomposita und Partizipialbildungen.* Berlin / New York: de Gruyter.

PUSTEJOVSKY, J. (1995). *The Generative Lexicon.* Cambridge, MA: MIT Press.

PUZYNINA, J. (1969). *Nazwy czynności we współczesnym języku polskim (slowotwórstwo, semantyka, skladnia)*, vol. 1. Rozprawy Uniwesytetu Warszawskiego Nr. 40. Warsaw: Wydawnictwo UW.

RADDEN, G. and R. DIRVEN (2007). *Cognitive English Grammar.* Amsterdam / Philadelphia: John Benjamins.

[RAE] Real Academia Española (1931). *Gramática de la lengua española.* Madrid: Espasa Calpe.

RAIMY, E. (2000). 'Remarks on Backcopying', *Linguistic Inquiry* 31: 541–52.

RAINER, F. and S. VARELA (1992). 'Compounding in Spanish', *Rivista di Linguistica* 4: 117–42.

RALLI, A. (1992). 'Compounds in Modern Greek', *Rivista di Linguistica* 4(1): 143–74.

—— (2000). 'A feature-based analysis of Greek nominal inflection', *Glossolojia* 11–12: 201–28.

—— (2002). 'The role of morphology in gender determination: Evidence from Modern Greek', *Linguistics* 40(3): 519–51.

—— (2004). 'Stem-based vs. word-based morphological configurations: The case of Modern Greek preverbs', *Lingue e Linguaggio* 3(2): 241–75.

—— (2005). *Morfologia.* [Morphology.] Athens: Patakis.

—— (2007). *I Sinthesi Lekseon: Diaglossiki prosengisi.* [Compounding: A cross-linguistic approach.] Athens: Patakis.

—— (2008a). 'Compound markers and parametric variation', *Language Typology and Universals* 61(1): 19–38.

—— (2008b). 'Composés déverbaux grecs à radicaux liés', in D. Amiot (ed.) *La Composition dans une Perspective Typologique.* Arras: Artois Presses Université, 189–210.

—— and A. KARASIMOS (2007). 'Compound constituency and compound-internal derivation.' Paper delivered at 8th International Conference of Greek Linguistics, Ioannina: 30 August – 1 September 2007.

—— and M. STAVROU (1998). 'Morphology–syntax interface: A-N compounds vs. A-N constructs in modern Greek', in G. Booij and J. van Marle (eds.) *Yearbook of Morphology 1997.* Dordrecht: Kluwer, 243–64.

RAMERS, K. H. (1997). 'Die Kunst der Fuge: Zum morphologischen Status von Verbindungselementen in Nominalkomposita', in C. Dürscheid, M. Schwarz, and K. H. Ramers (eds.) *Sprache im Fokus. Festschrift für Heinz Vater zum 65. Geburtstag.* Tübingen: Niemeyer, 33–46.

RAPPAPORT HOVAV, M. and B. LEVIN (1992). '-er Nominals: Implications for a theory of argument structure', in T. Stowell and E. Wehrli (eds.) *Syntax and Semantics 26: Syntax and the Lexicon.* New York, NY: Academic Press, 127–53.

RASTLE, K., M. H. DAVIS, W. D. MARSLEN-WILSON, and L. K. TYLER (2000). 'Morphological and semantic effects in visual word recognition: A time-course study', *Language & Cognitive Processes* 15: 507–37.

RAVID, D. D. (1990). 'Internal structure constraints on new-word formation devices in Modern Hebrew', *Folia Linguistica* 24: 289–346.

—— (1997). 'Between syntax and the lexicon: The parallel between N-N compounds and N-A strings in acquisition', in A. Sorace, C. Heycock, and R. Shillcock (eds.) *Proceedings of the GALA 1997 Conference on Language Acquisition*. Edinburgh: University of Edinburgh, 138–41.

—— (2006). 'Word-level morphology: A psycholinguistic perspective on linear formation in Hebrew nominals', *Morphology* 16: 127–48.

—— and A. AVIDOR (1998). 'Acquisition of derived nominals in Hebrew: Developmental and linguistic principles', *Journal of Child Language* 25: 229–66.

—— and R. A. Berman (in press). 'Developing linguistic register in different text types: The case of Hebrew.' *Pragmatics and Cognition.*

—— and Y. SHLESINGER (1987). 'On the classification and structure of–suffixed adjectives', *Hebrew Linguistics* 25: 59–70. [In Hebrew.]

—— (1995). 'Factors in the selection of compound-type in spoken and written Hebrew', *Language Sciences* 17: 147–79.

—— and S. ZILBERBUCH (2003a). 'Morpho-syntactic constructs in the development of spoken and written Hebrew text production', *Journal of Child Language* 30: 395–418.

—— (2003b). 'The development of complex nominals in expert and non-expert writing: A comparative study', *Pragmatics and Cognition* 11: 267–97.

REFSING, K. (1986). *The Ainu Language.* Aarhus: Aarhus University Press.

REICHSTEIN, A. D. (1984). *Nemeckie ustojčivye frazy i ustojčivye oredikativnye edinicy.* Moscow.

REINHART, T. (1983). *Anaphora and Semantic Interpretation.* London: Croom Helm.

—— and T. SILONI. (2005). 'The lexicon–syntax parameter: Reflexivization and other arity operations', *Linguistic Inquiry* 36: 389–436.

RENOUF, A. and L. Bauer (2000). 'Contextual clues to word-meaning', *International Journal of Corpus Linguistics* 2: 231–58.

REUSE, W. J. DE. (1994). 'Noun incorporation in Lakota (Siouan)', *International Journal of American Linguistics* 60(3): 199–260.

—— (2006). *A Practical Grammar of the San Carlos Apache Language.* Munich: Lincom Europa.

RICE, K. (1988). 'Continuant voicing in Slave (Northern Athapaskan): The cyclic application of default rules', in M. Hammond and M. Noonan (eds.) *Theoretical Morphology. Approaches in Modern Linguistics.* San Diego: Academic Press, 371–88.

—— (1989). *A Grammar of Slave.* Berlin: Mouton de Gruyter.

—— (2003). 'Doubling of agreement in Slave (Northern Athapaskan)', in A. Carnie and H. Harley (eds.) *Form and Function: Essays in Honor of Eloise Jelinek.* Amsterdam/Philadelphia: John Benjamins, 51–78.

RIEGEL, M., J.-C. PELLAT, and R. RIOUL (1994). *Grammaire méthodique du français.* Paris: PUF.

RIEHEMANN, S. (1998). 'Type-based derivational morphology', *The Journal of Comparative Germanic Linguistics* 2: 49–77.

RIESE, T. (2001). *Vogul.* Munich: Lincom Europa.

RITTER, E. (1988). 'A Head-Movement approach to Construct-State NPs', *Linguistics* 26(6): 909–29.

RIVERO, M. L. (1992). 'Adverb incorporation and the syntax of adverbs in Modern Greek', *Linguistics and Philosophy* 15: 289–331.

RIVET, A. (1999). 'Rektionskomposita und Inkorporationstheorie', *Linguistische Berichte* 179: 307–42.

ROACH, P. (1983). *English Phonetics and Phonology: A Practical Course*. Cambridge: Cambridge University Press.

ROBINS, R. H. (1958). *The Yurok Language: Grammar, Texts, Lexicon*. Berkeley and Los Angeles: University of California Press.

ROELOFS, A. and R. H. BAAYEN (2002). 'Morphology by itself in planning the production of spoken words', *Psychonomic Bulletin & Review* 9: 132–8.

ROEPER, T. (1988). 'Compound syntax and head movement', in G. Booij and J. van Marle (eds.) *Yearbook of Morphology 1988*. Dordrecht: Foris Publications, 187–228.

—— (1999). 'Leftward movement in morphology.' Ms. UMASS.

—— and M. E. A. SIEGEL (1978). 'A lexical transformation for verbal compounds', *Linguistic Inquiry* 9: 199–260.

—— W. SNYDER, and K. HIRAMATSU (2002). 'Learnability in a minimalist framework: Root compounds, merger, and the syntax–morphology interface', in I. Lasser (ed.) *The Process of Language Acquisition*. Frankfurt: Peter Lang Verlag, 25–37.

ROHRER, C. (1966). Review of R. B. Lees, *The Grammar of English Nominalizations* 2nd printing. *Indogermanische Forschungen* 71: 161–70.

ROSEN, E. (2003). 'Systematic irregularity in Japanese rendaku', *Canadian Journal of Linguistics* 48: 1–37.

ROSEN, S. T. (1989). 'Two types of noun incorporation', *Language* 65: 294–317.

ROSS, J. R. (1968). 'Constraints on variables in syntax.' PhD. dissertation, MIT.

ROUDET, L. (1921). 'Sur la classification psychologique des changements sémantiques', *Journal de Psychologie* 18: 676–92.

RUBENSTEIN, H. and I. POLLACK (1963). 'Word predictability and intelligibility', *Journal of Verbal Learning and Verbal Behavior* 2: 147–58.

RUBIN, G. S., C. A. BECKER, and R. H. FREEMAN (1979). 'Morphological structure and its effect on visual word recognition', *Journal of Verbal Learning & Verbal Behavior* 18: 757–67.

RYDER, M. E. (1990). 'Ordered Chaos: A cognitive model for the interpretation of English Noun-Noun compounds.' PhD dissertation. LaJolla: University of California at San Diego.

—— (1994). *Ordered Chaos: The Interpretation of English Noun-Noun Compounds*. Berkeley: University of California Press.

SADLER, L. and A. SPENCER (1998). 'Morphology and argument structure', in A. Spencer and A. Zwicky (eds.) *The Handbook of Morphology*. Oxford: Blackwell, 206–36.

SADOCK, J. (1991). *Autolexical Syntax*. Chicago: University of Chicago Press.

—— (1998). 'On the autonomy of compounding morphology', in S. G. Lapointe, D. K. Brentari, and P. M. Farrell (eds.) *Morphology and its Relation to Phonology and Syntax*. Stanford: CSLI Publications, 161–87.

SALAS, A. (1992). *El mapuche o araucano*. Madrid: Editorial MAPFRE.

SAMBOR, J. (1976). 'Kompozycje rzeczownikowe dwunominalne i nominalno-werbalne w tekstach współczesnego języka polskiego', in M. R. Mayenowa (ed.) *Semantyka tekstu i języka*. Wrocław: Zakład Narodowy Imienia Ossolińskich, 239–56.

SAMPSON, R. (1980). 'Stress in English N + N phrases: A further complicating factor', *English Studies: A Journal of English Language and Literature* 3: 264–70.

SANDRA, D. (1990). 'On the representation and processing of compound words: Automatic access to constituent morphemes does not occur', *The Quarterly Journal of Experimental Psychology* 42A: 529–67.

—— (1994). 'The morphology of the mental lexicon: Internal word structure viewed from a psycholinguistic perspective', *Language & Cognitive Processes* 9: 227–69.

SANTEN, A. VAN (1979). 'Een nieuw voorstel voor een transformationele behandeling van composita en bepaalde adjectief-substantief kombinaties', *Spectator* 9: 240–62.

SATO, Y. (2007). 'Phrasal compounding and the Lexicalist Hypothesis: A multiple Spell-Out account.' Paper presented at the 2007 International Conference on Linguistics in Korea, Chung-Ang University, Seoul, Korea, 20 January 2007.

SAVINI, M. (1983). 'Phrasal compounds in Afrikaans.' M.A. thesis, University of Stellenbosch, South Africa.

SCALISE, S. (1984). *Generative Morphology.* Dordrecht: Foris.

—— (1992). 'Compounding in Italian', in S. Scalise (ed.) *The Morphology of Compounding.* Special issue of *Rivista di Linguistica* 4(1): 175–200.

SCALISE, S., A. BISETTO, and E. GUEVARA (2005). 'Selection in compounding and derivation', in W. U. Dressler, D. Kastovsky, O. E. Pfeiffer, and F. Rainer (eds.) *Morphology and its Demarcation.* Amsterdam / Philadelphia: John Benjamins, 133–50.

SCALISE, S. and E. GUEVARA (2005). 'The Lexicalist approach to word-formation', in P. Štekauer and R. Lieber (eds.) *Handbook of Word-Formation.* Dordrecht: Springer, 147–87.

—— (2007). 'Searching for universals in compounding.' Ms. University of Bologna.

SCARBOROUGH, D. L., C. CORTESE, and H. S. SCARBOROUGH (1977). 'Frequency and repetition effects in lexical memory', *Journal of Experimental Psychology: Human Perception & Performance* 3: 1–17.

SCHACHTER, P. (1962). 'Review of *The Grammar of English Nominalizations* by Robert B. Lees', *International Journal of American Linguistics* 28: 134–46.

SCHEBECK, B. (1974). *Texts on the Social System of the Atʸnʸamaṭaŋa People with Grammatical Notes.* Canberra: The Australian National University.

SCHINDLER, J. (1997). 'Zur internen Syntax der indogermanischen Nominalkomposition', in E. Crespo and J. L. García-Ramón (eds.) *Berthold Delbrück y la sintaxis indoeuropea hoy. Actas del Coloquio de la Indogermanische Gesellschaft, Madrid, 21–24 septiembre de 1994.* Madrid/Wiesbaden: Ediciones de la Universidad Autónoma de Madrid/Reichert, 537–40.

SCHMERLING, SUSAN (1976). *Aspects of English Sentence Stress.* Austin: University of Texas Press.

SCHMID, H.-J. (2007). 'Entrenchment, salience and basic levels', in D. Geeraerts and H. Cuyckens (eds.) *Handbook of Cognitive Linguistics.* Oxford: Oxford University Press, 169–203.

SCHREUDER, R. and R. H. BAAYEN (1995). *Modeling Morphological Processing.* Hillsdale, NJ: Lawrence Erlbaum Associates, Inc.

—— (1997). 'How complex simple words can be', *Journal of Memory and Language* 37: 118–39.

SCHRIEFERS, H., P. ZWITSERLOOD, and A. ROELOFS (1991). 'The identification of morphologically complex spoken words: Continuous processing or decomposition?' *Journal of Memory and Language* 30: 26–47.

SCHU, J. (2005). 'Zwischen Grundmorphem und Affix', *Deutsche Sprache* 33: 258–86.

SCHWARZE, C. (2005). 'Grammatical and para-grammatical word formation', *Lingue e Linguaggio* 2: 137–62.

—— (2007). 'La notion de règle morphologique et les mots complexes non construits', in N. Hathout and F. Montermini (eds.) *Morphologie à Toulouse. Actes du colloque international de morphologie 4èmes Décembrettes.* Munich: Lincom Europa, 221–43.

SELKIRK, E. O. (1982). *The Syntax of Words.* Cambridge, MA: MIT Press.

SEMENZA, C. and S. MONDINI (2006). 'The neuropsychology of compound words', in
  G. Libben and G. Jarema (eds.) *The Representation and Processing of Compound Words*.
  New York, NY: Oxford University Press, 71–95.

SEROUSSI, B. (2004). 'Hebrew derived nouns in context: A developmental perspective',
  Phoniatrica et Logopaedica 56: 273–90.

SHIBATANI, M. (1990). *The Languages of Japan*. Cambridge: Cambridge University Press.

—— and T. KAGEYAMA (1988). 'Word formation in a modular theory of grammar',
  Language 64: 451–84.

SHILLCOCK, R. (1990). *Lexical Hypotheses in Continuous Speech*. Cambridge, MA: MIT Press.

SHIMRON, J. (ed.) (2003). *Language Processing and Language Acquisition in a Root-Based
  Morphology*. Amsterdam: John Benjamins.

SHLESINGER, Y. and D. D. RAVID (1998) 'The double compound in Modern Hebrew:
  Redundancy or an independent existence?' *Hebrew Linguistics* 43: 85–97. [In Hebrew.]

SHLONSKY, U. (1990). 'Construct State nominals and Universal Grammar'. Ms. University
  of Haifa.

—— (2000). 'The form of Noun Phrases.' Ms. University of Geneva.

SICHEL, I. (2000). 'Remnant and phrasal movement in Hebrew adjectives and possessives.'
  Ms. CUNY Graduate Center.

SIDDIQI, D. A. (2006). 'Minimize exponence: Economy effects on a model of the morphosyntactic component of the grammar.' PhD dissertation, University of Arizona.

SIEGEL, D. (1974). 'Topics in English Morphology.' PhD Dissertation, MIT.

SIEGEL, M. E. A. (1980). *Capturing the Adjective*. New York: Garland.

SILONI, T. (1997). *Noun Phrases and Nominalizations: The Syntax of DPs*. Dordrecht: Kluwer
  Academic Publishers.

—— (2001). 'Construct states at the PF interface', in P. Pica and J. Rooryck (eds.) *Linguistic
  Variations Yearbook*, vol. 1. Amsterdam: John Benjamins, 321–33.

SIMPSON, J. (1991). *Warlpiri Morphosyntax: A Lexicalist Approach*. Dordrecht: Kluwer.

—— (2001). 'Preferred word order, argument structure and the grammaticalisation of
  associated path', in M. Butt and T. H. King (eds.) *Time over Matter: Diachronic Perspectives on Morphosyntax*. Stanford: CSLI, 173–208.

SKAUTRUP, P. (1944). *Det Danske Sprogs Historie*. 5 vols. Copenhagen: Nordisk.

SKOUSEN, R. (1989). *Analogical Modelling of Language*. Dordrecht: Kluwer.

SLOBIN, D. (1985). 'Crosslinguistic evidence for the language-making capacity', in D. Slobin
  (ed.) *The Crosslinguistic Study of Language Acquisition*, Vol. 2: *Theoretical Issues*. Hillsdale,
  NJ: Lawrence Erlbaum, 1157–26.

—— (1996). 'From "thought and language" to "thinking for speaking" ', in J. J. Gumperz
  and S. C. Levinson (eds.) *Rethinking Linguistic Relativity*. Cambridge: Cambridge University Press, 70–86.

—— (2004). 'The many ways to search for a frog: Linguistic typology and the expression of
  motion events', in S. Strömqvist and L. Verhoeven (eds.) *Relating Events in Narrative:
  Typological and Contextual Perspectives*. Mahwah, NJ: Lawrence Erlbaum, 219–58.

SMEETS, I. (1989). *A Mapuche Grammar*. PhD dissertation, University of Leiden.

SMITH, E. E. and D. N. OSHERSON (1984). 'Conceptual combination with prototype
  concepts', *Cognitive Science* 8: 337–61.

—— L. J. RIPS, and M. KEANE (1988). 'Combining prototypes: A selective modification
  model', *Cognitive Science* 12: 485–527.

SNYDER, W. and D. CHEN (1997). 'On the syntax–morphology interface in the acquisition of French and English', in K. Kusumoto (ed.) *Proceedings of NELS 27*. Amherst: GLSA, 413–23.

SØGAARD, A. (2005). 'Compounding theories and linguistic diversity', in Z. Frajzyngier, A. Hodges, and D. S. Rood (eds.) *Linguistic Diversity and Language Theories*. Amsterdam/ Philadelphia: John Benjamins, 319–37.

SONOMURA, M. O. (1996). *Idiomaticity in the Basic Writing of American English*. New York: Peter Lang.

SPENCER, A. (1988). 'Bracketing paradoxes and the English lexicon', *Language* 64: 663–82.

—— (1991). *Morphological Theory: An Introduction to Word Structure in Generative Grammar*. Oxford: Blackwell.

—— (1995). 'Incorporation in Chukchi', *Language* 71: 439–89.

—— (1998). 'Morphonological operations', in A. Spencer and A. M. Zwicky (eds.) *The Handbook of Morphology*. Oxford: Blackwell, 123–43.

—— (2003). 'Does English have productive compounding', in G. Booij, J. DeCesaris, A. Ralli, and S. Scalise (eds.) *Topics in Morphology: Selected Papers from the Third Mediterranean Morphology Meeting* (Barcelona, 20–22 September 2001). Barcelona: Institut Universitari de Lingüística Applicada, Universtitat Pompeu Fabra, 329–41.

—— and M. D. ZARETSKAYA (1998). 'Verb prefixation in Russian as lexical subordination', *Linguistics* 36: 1–40.

SPORE, P. (1965). *La langue danoise*. Copenhagen: Akademisk.

SPORTICHE, D. (1999). *Reconstruction, Constituency and Morphology*. Berlin: GLOW.

SPROAT, R. (1985). 'On deriving the lexicon.' PhD Dissertation, MIT.

STANNERS, R. F., J. J. NEISER, W. P. HERNON, and R. HALL (1979). 'Memory representation for morphologically related words', *Journal of Verbal Learning & Verbal Behavior* 18: 399–412.

STAROSTA, S., K. KUIPER, Z. WU, and S. A. NG (1998). 'On defining the Chinese compound word: Headedness in Chinese compounding and Chinese VR compounds', in J. Packard (ed.) *New Approaches to Chinese Word Formation*. Berlin and New York: Mouton de Gruyter, 346–69.

STEIN, G. (2000). 'The function of word-formation and the case of English -cum-', in C. Dalton-Puffer and N. Ritt (eds.) *Words: Structure, Meaning, Function. A Festschrift for Dieter Kastovsky*. Trends in Linguistics: Studies and Monographs 130. Berlin: Mouton de Gruyter, 277–88.

ŠTEKAUER, P. (1996). *A Theory of Conversion in English*. Frankfurt am Main: Peter Lang.

—— (1997a). 'On the semiotics of proper names and their conversion', *AAA – Arbeiten aus Anglistik und Amerikanistik* 22(1): 27–36.

—— (1997b). 'On some issues of blending in English word formation', *Linguistica Pragensia* 7: 26–35.

—— (1998). *An Onomasiological Theory of English Word-Formation*. Amsterdam / Philadelphia: John Benjamins.

—— (2000). *English Word-Formation: A History of Research (1960–1995)*. Tübingen: Narr.

—— (2001). 'Fundamental principles of an onomasiological theory of English word-formation', *Onomasiology Online* 2: 1–42.

—— (2002). 'On the theory of neologisms and nonce-formations', *Australian Journal of Linguistics* 1: 97–112.

—— (2005a). *Meaning Predictability in Word Formation*. Amsterdam/Philadelphia: John Benjamins.

—— (2005b). 'Onomasiological approach to word-formation', in P. Štekauer and R. Lieber (eds.) *Handbook of Word-formation*. Dordrecht: Springer, 207–32.

—— D. Chapman, S. Tomaščíková, and Š. Franko (2005). 'Word-formation as creativity within productivity constraints: Sociolinguistic evidence', *Onomasiology Online* 6: 1–55.

—— and R. Lieber (eds.) (2005). *Handbook of Word-Formation*. Dordrecht: Springer.

—— S. Valera, and L. Kőrtvélyessy (2007). 'Universals, tendencies and typology in word-formation. Cross-linguistic research.' Ms.

—— S. Valera, and A. Diaz (2007). 'Meaning predictability and conversion.' Ms.

—— J. Zimmermann, and R. Gregová. (2007). 'Stress in compounds: An experimental research', *Acta Linguistica Hungarica* 54: 193–215.

Stirling, L. and R. Huddleston (2002). 'Deixis and anaphora', in R. Huddleston and G. K. Pullum. *The Cambridge Grammar of the English Language*. Cambridge: Cambridge University Press, 1449–564.

Sugioka, Y. (2005). 'Multiple mechanisms underlying morphological productivity', in S. Mufwene, E. Francis, and R. Wheeler (eds.) *Polymorphous Linguistics*. Cambridge, MA: MIT Press, 203–23.

Sullivan, T. D. (1998) [1976]. *Compendio de la gramática náhuatl*. Mexico: Universidad Nacional Autónoma de México.

Sun, C. (2006). *Chinese: A Linguistic Introduction*. Cambridge: Cambridge University Press.

Sweetser, E. (1999). 'Compositionality and blending: Semantic composition in a cognitively realistic framework', in T. Janssen and G. Redeker (eds.) *Cognitive Linguistics: Foundations, Scope, and Methodology*. Berlin: Mouton de Gruyter, 129–62.

Swinney, D. A. and A. Cutler (1979). 'The access and processing of idiomatic expressions', *Journal of Verbal Learning and Verbal Behavior* 18: 523–34.

Szymanek, B. (1988). *Categories and Categorization in Morphology*. Lublin: Katolicki Uniwersytet Lubelski.

—— (1996). 'Parametric dimensions in morphology: On inalienable possession in English and Polish', *Acta Linguistica Hungarica* 43(1–2): 255–75.

—— (1998). *Introduction to Morphological Analysis*. Warsaw: Wydawnictwo Naukowe PWN.

Tabossi, P. and F. Zardon (1993). 'The activation of idiomatic meaning in spoken language comprehension', in C. Cacciari and P. Tabossi (eds.). *Idioms: Structure, Processing and Interpretation*. Hillsdale, NJ: Lawrence Erlbaum Associates, 145–62.

Taft, M. (1979). 'Lexical access via an orthographic code: The basic orthographic syllabic structure (BOSS)', *Journal of Verbal Learning & Verbal Behavior* 18: 21–39.

—— (1985). 'Lexical access codes in visual and auditory word recognition', *Language and Cognitive Processes* 1: 297–308.

—— (1991). *Reading and the Mental Lexicon*. Hillsdale, NJ/England: Lawrence Erlbaum Associates, Inc.

—— (1994). 'Interactive-activation as a framework for understanding morphological processing', *Language & Cognitive Processes* 9: 271–94.

—— (2004). 'Morphological decomposition and the reverse base frequency effect', *Quarterly Journal of Experimental Psychology* 57: 745–65.

—— and K. I. Forster (1975). 'Lexical storage and retrieval of prefixed words', *Journal of Verbal Learning & Verbal Behavior* 14: 638–47.

—— (1976). 'Lexical storage and retrieval of polymorphemic and polysyllabic words', *Journal of Verbal Learning and Verbal Behavior* 15: 607–20.

—— and P. Kougious (2004). 'The processing of morpheme-like units in monomorphemic words', *Brain and Language* 90: 9–16.

TAI, J. H-Y. (2003). 'Cognitive relativism: Resultative construction in Chinese', *Language and Linguistics* 4(2): 301–16.

TAMURA, S. (2000). *The Ainu Language*. Tokyo: Sanseido.

TANG, T-C. (1989). *Studies on Chinese Morphology and Syntax: 2*. Taipei: Student Book Co.

TAYLOR, J. R. (1996). *Possessives in English*. Oxford: Oxford University Press.

—— (2002). *Cognitive Grammar*. Oxford: Oxford University Press.

TERRACE, H. (1979). *Nim*. New York: Knopf.

THIERSCH, C. (1993). 'On the formal properties of constituent coordination.' Paper presented at the 16th *GLOW* Colloquium. *GLOW Newsletter* 30: 70–71.

THOMPSON, D. W. (1992). *On Growth and Form*. New York: Dover.

THOMPSON, L. C. and M. T. THOMPSON (1992). *The Thompson Language*. Missoula: University of Montana.

THRÁINSSON, H., H. P. PETERSEN, J í Lon JACOBSEN, and Z. S. HANSEN (2004). *Faroese*. Tórshavn: Føroya Fróðskaparfelag.

TOLCHINSKY, L. and E. ROSADO (2005). 'Literacy, text type, and modality in use of grammatical means for agency alternation in Spanish', *Journal of Pragmatics* 37: 209–38.

TOLLEMACHE, F. (1945). *Le parole composte nella lingua italiana*. Rome: Rores.

TOMAN, J. (1983). *Wortsyntax*. Tübingen: Max Niemeyer Verlag.

TOMASELLO, M. (2000). 'Do young children have adult syntactic competence?' *Cognition* 74: 209–53.

—— (2003). *Constructing a Language: A Usage-based Theory of Language Acquisition*. Cambridge, MA / London: Harvard University Press.

TOORN, M. C. VAN DEN (1981). 'De tussenklank in samenstellingen waarvan het eerste lid systematisch uitheems is', *De Nieuwe Taalgids* 74: 197–205 and 547–52.

—— (1982). 'Tendenzen bij de beregeling van de verbindingsklank in nominale samenstellingen', *De Nieuwe Taalgids* 75: 24–33 and 153–60.

TRIANTAPHYLLIDIS, M. (1941). *Neoelliniki Grammatiki* [Modern Greek Grammar]. Athens: OEDB.

TROMMELEN, M. and W. ZONNEVELD (1986). 'Dutch morphology: Evidence for the right-hand head rule', *Linguistic Inquiry* 17: 147–69.

TSEREPIS, G. (1902). *Ta Sintheta tis Ellinikis Glossis* [Compounds of the Greek Language]. Athens: Sakellariou.

TUGGY, D. (2007). 'Schematicity', in D. Geeraerts and H. Cuyckens (eds.) *The Oxford Handbook of Cognitive Linguistics*. Oxford: Oxford University Press, 82–116.

UHLICH, J. (2002). 'Verbal governing compounds (synthetics) in early Irish and other Celtic languages', *Transactions of the Philological Society* 100(3): 403–33.

UNGERER, F. (2002). 'The conceptual function of derivational word-formation in English', *Anglia* 120: 534–67.

—— (2007). 'Word-formation', in D. Geeraerts and H. Cuyckens (eds.) *The Oxford Handbook of Cognitive Linguistics*. Oxford: Oxford University Press, 650–75.

—— and H-J. SCHMID (1998). 'Englische Komposita und Kategorisierung', *Rostocker Beiträge zur Sprachwissenschaft* 5: 77–98.

—— (2006). *An Introduction to Cognitive Linguistics*, 2nd edn. Harlow: Pearson Longman.

URIAGEREKA, J. (1999). 'Multiple Spell-Out', in S. D. Epstein and M. Hornstein (eds.) *Working Minimalism*. Cambridge, MA: MIT Press, 251–83.

—— (2003). 'Pure adjuncts.' Ms. University of Maryland.

VACHEK, J. (1975). *A Functional Analysis of Present Day English on a General Linguistic Basis.* Prague: Czechoslovak Academy of Sciences.

VAL ALVARO, J. F. (1999). 'La composición', in I. Bosque and V. Demonte (eds.) *Gramática Descriptiva de la Lengua Española*, vol. 3. Madrid: Espasa, 4757–841.

VALLÈS, T. (2003). 'Lexical creativity and the organization of the lexicon', *Annual Review of Cognitive Linguistics* 1: 137–60.

VAN VALIN, R. and R. LAPOLLA (1997). *Syntax: Structure, Meaning and Function.* Cambridge: Cambridge University Press.

VARELA, S. (1990). *Fundamentos de morfología.* Madrid: Sintesis.

—— (2005). *Morfología léxica: la formación de palabras.* Madrid: Gredos.

—— and J. GARCÍA (1999). 'La prefijación', in I. Bosque and V. Demonte (eds.) *Gramática descriptiva de la lengua española*, vol. 3. Madrid: Espasa, 4992–5039.

VILLOING, F. (2002). 'Les mots composés [V N]N/A du français: réflexions épistémologiques et propositions d'analyse.' Doctoral thesis, Département de Linguistique, Université de Paris X.

—— (2003). 'Les mots composés VN du français: arguments en faveur d'une construction morphologique', *Cahiers de Grammaire* 28: 183–96.

—— (2008). 'Les mots composés VN', in B. Fradin, F. Kerleroux, and M. Plénat (eds.) *Aperçus de morphologie du français.* Saint-Denis: Presses Universitaires de Vincennes.

VINTERBERG, H. and C. A. BODELSEN (1966). *Dansk-Engelsk ordbog.* Andet oplag med tillæg. Copenhagen: Gyldendal.

VISCH, E. A. M. (1989). *A Metrical Theory of Rhythmic Stress Phenomena.* Dordrecht: Foris.

VOGEL, I. and E. RAIMY (2002). 'The acquisition of compound vs. phrasal stress: The role of prosodic constituents', *Journal of Child Language* 29: 225–50.

VOORT, M. E. C. VAN DE and W. VONK (1995). 'You don't die immediately when you kick an empty bucket: A processing view on semantic and syntactic characteristics of idioms', in M. Everaerts et al. (eds.) *Idioms: Structural and Psychological Perspectives.* Hillsdale, NJ: Lawrence Erlbaum Associates.

WÄLCHLI, B. (2005). *Co-compounds and Natural Coordination.* Oxford: Oxford University Press.

WALI, K. and O. N. Koul (1997). *Kashmiri.* London / New York: Routledge.

WANG JUN and ZHENG GUOQIAO (1993). *An Outline Grammar of Mulao.* Canberra: National Thai Studies Centre, The Australian National University.

WARD, D. (1965). *The Russian Language Today.* London: Hutchinson.

WARLPIRI LEXICOGRAPHY GROUP (1986). *Warlpiri–English Dictionary: Body-part section.* Cambridge, MA: Lexicon Project, Center for Cognitive Science.

WARREN, B. (1978). *Semantic Patterns of Noun-Noun Compounds.* Gothenburg: Gothenburg University Press.

WASZAKOWA, K. (1994). *Słowotwórstwo współczesnego języka polskiego – rzeczowniki sufiksalne obce.* Warsaw: Wydawnictwa Uniwersytetu Warszawskiego.

—— (2004). 'Czy w słowotwórstwie pojęcie *hybryda* jest przydatne?', in A. Moroz and M. Wiśniewski (eds.) *Studia z gramatyki i semantyki języka polskiego.* Toruń: Wydawnictwo Uniwersytetu Mikołaja Kopernika, 111–19.

—— (2005). *Przejawy internacjonalizacji w słowotwórstwie współczesnej polszczyzny.* Warsaw: Wydawnictwa Uniwersytetu Warszawskiego.

WEERMAN, F. P. (1989). 'The V2 Conspiracy.' PhD dissertation, University of Utrecht.

WEGENER, H. (2003). 'Entstehung und Funktion der Fugenelemente im Deutschen, oder: Warum wir keine *Autosbahn haben', *Linguistische Berichte* 196: 425–57.

WELDON, M. S. (1991). 'Mechanisms underlying priming on perceptual tests', *Journal of Experimental Psychology: Learning, Memory, and Cognition* 17: 526–41.

WERNER, H. (1998). *Probleme der Wortbildung in den Jenissej-Sprachen.* Lincom Studies in Asian Linguistics. Munich/Newcastle: Lincom Europa.

WHEELER, D. D. (1970). 'Processes in word recognition', *Cognitive Psychology* 1: 59–85.

WHITEHEAD, C. R. (2004). *A reference grammar of Menya, an Angan language of Papua New Guinea.* PhD dissertation, Winnipeg, University of Manitoba.

WHITNEY, W. D. (1875). *The Life and Growth of Language*, 6th edn. London: Kegan Paul, Trench & Co.

—— (1889). *Sanskrit Grammar.* Leipzig: Breitkopf and Härtel.

WHORF, B. L. (1956). *Language, Thought, and Reality.* Cambridge, MA: MIT Press.

WIESE, R. (1996a). 'Phrasal compounds and the theory of word syntax', *Linguistic Inquiry* 27: 183–93.

—— (1996b). *The Phonology of German.* Oxford: Clarendon.

WILHELM, A. and L. SAXON (2007). 'The syntax of numerals in two Dene languages', in the *Proceedings of the Workshop on Structure and Constituency in the Languages of the Americas* (WSCLA).

WILLIAMS, E. (1981). 'On the notions *Lexically related* and *Head of a Word*', *Linguistic Inquiry* 12: 245–74.

—— (1994). *Thematic Structure in Syntax.* Cambridge, MA: MIT Press.

WINDSOR, J. (1993). 'The function of novel word compounds', *Journal of Child Language* 20: 119–38.

WISNIEWSKI, E. J. (1996). 'Construal and similarity in conceptual combination', *Journal of Memory and Language* 35: 434–53.

—— and B. C. LOVE (1998). 'Relations versus properties in conceptual combination', *Journal of Memory and Language* 38: 177–202.

—— and G. L. MURPHY (2005). 'Frequency of relation type as a determinant of conceptual combination: A reanalysis', *Journal of Experimental Psychology: Learning, Memory, and Cognition* 31: 169–74.

WURMBRAND, S. (2003a). *Infinitives: Restructuring and Clause Structure.* Berlin: Mouton de Gruyter.

—— (2003b). 'Syntactic vs. post-syntactic movement.' Ms. University of Connecticut.

XIA, M. (1946). *Methods of Composing Two-character Words* [Cited in Pan, Ye, and Han 2004].

XING, J. Z. (2006). *Teaching and Learning Chinese As a Foreign Language: A Pedagogical Grammar.* Hong Kong: Hong Kong University Press.

YUMOTO, Y. (2005). *Hukugoo-dooshi Hasei-dooshi no Imi to Toogo [Semantics and Syntax of Compound Verbs and Derived Verbs].* Tokyo: Hituzi Syobo.

ZAGONA, K. (1988). *Verb Phrase Syntax: A Parametric Study of English and Spanish.* Dordrecht: Kluwer Academic Publishers.

ZAMPONI, R. (2003). *Maipure.* Munich: Lincom Europa.

—— (2005). 'Sull'enclitico relativizzatore -*li* in maipure-yavitero', *Thule* 14/15: 163–93.

ŽEPIĆ, S. (1970). *Morphologie und Semantik der deutschen Nominalkomposita.* Zagreb: Philosophische Fakultät der Universität Zagreb.

ZHOU, X., W. MARSLEN-WILSON, M. TAFT, and H. SHU (1999). 'Morphology, orthography, and phonology in reading Chinese compound words', *Language & Cognitive Processes* 14: 525–65.

ZHU, D. (1982). 语法讲义 *Yufa jiangyi* [Lectures on grammar]. Beijing: Commercial Press.

ZIMMER, K. E. (1971). 'Some general observations about nominal compounds', *Working Papers on Language Universals* [Stanford University] 5: 1–21.

—— (1972). 'Appropriateness conditions for nominal compounds', *Working Papers on Language Universals* [Stanford University] 8: 3–20.

ZUR, B. (1983). 'On the acquisition of definiteness by Hebrew-speaking children. MA thesis, Tel Aviv University. [In Hebrew.]

—— (2004). 'Reference marking in narrative development.' PhD Dissertation, Bar Ilan University. [In Hebrew.]

ZWANENBURG, W. (1992). 'La composition dans les langues romanes et germaniques: essui-glace/windshield-wiper.' Paper presented at the 'Congrès des Romanistes'.

ZWICKY, A. (1985). 'Heads', *Journal of Linguistics* 21: 1–29.

ZWITSERLOOD, P. (1994). 'The role of semantic transparency in the processing and representation of Dutch compounds', *Language and Cognitive Processes* 9: 341–68.

—— J. BÖLTE, and P. DOHMES (2000). 'Morphological effects on speech production: Evidence from picture naming', *Language and Cognitive Processes* 15: 563–91.

—— A. BOLWIENDER, and E. DREWS (2005). 'Priming morphologically complex verbs by sentence contexts: Effects of semantic transparency and ambiguity', *Language and Cognitive Processes* 20: 395–415.

INDEX

Ackema, P 383–4, 385
  and Parallel Representation 526
action modality, and compound
    meaning 119–20
Adams, V, and verbal compounds 6 n1
  Adjacency Condition 182
adjectival compounds:
  in Danish 411–12
  in Dutch 375–7
  in German 388
  in Hungarian 528
  in Mapudungun 606–7
  in Polish 474–7
    colour terms 477
    context of 477
    coordinate compounds 477
    linking elements 474–5
    structural range 477
    suffixes 475–6
    verbal heads 476–7
adjectives:
  and absence from Mohawk 572
  and ascriptive attribution 187–8
  and associative attribution 188–90
affixes:
  and Asymmetry Theory 156–9
  and compounds 327–8
  and distinguishing from bound roots 5–6
  and distinguishing from roots 5–6
  in Dutch 371
  in Maipure-Yavitero 586–7
  in Mapudungun 597–8, 601, 604–5
  and meaning 79
  and origins of 327
  and semantic skeleton 81–2
  and semantics 327–8
  and semi-affixes 327
  and theoretical status of 327
  and typology of 156–8
affixoid 208, 209
agnation 254
agrammatic aphasia 110, 112
agreement morpheme 131

Aikhenvald, A Y, and Baniva 585, 586, 590
Ainu, and compounds 344–5
Aitchison, J 20
Allan, K, and noun classification 84
Allan, R 407
Allen, M R 278, 357
  and 'IS A Principle' 366, 497
  and lexical stratification 180
  and lexicalist compounding rules 72–3
  and plural markers 13 n8
  and 'Variable R' 353
  and verbal compounds 76
allomorphy 179
ambiguity:
  and compounds 59, 64, 116
  and scope ambiguity 150
analogy 235–6
  and analogy-based model 278
analysability 237
anaphoras, in Spanish 448–50, 451
anaphoric island constraint 520
Anderson, S R 485
Andrews, S, and processing of compound
    words 267
Antisymmetry framework 151
appositive compounds, and classification
    of compounds 42, 51, 52
appropriately classificatory (AC)
    relationship 277
Aranovich, R 596
Araucanian, see Mapudungun
Arawakan, and limited use of compounding 586
  see also Maipure-Yavitero
argument relations 148
  in Dutch 373
  in German 397–8
  in Hungarian 529–30, 531–3, 535
  in Japanese 516–18
  and subordinate compounds 88
argument selection, and Distributed
    Morphology 134
Aronoff, M 323
ascriptive attribution 186–8

Verspoor, M:
 and cline of transparency/analysability 244
 and word formation 227 n12
Vietnamese, and order of elements 349
Villoing, F 428
Vogel, I, and children's acquisition of
  compound constructions 311

Wagner, S, and processing of compound
  words 268–9
Wakashan languages 592
Wälchli, B, and coordinative compounds 352, 515
Warlpiri 354, 621–2
 and nominal compounds 610–15
  body parts 611
  compound-phrase distinction 611–12
  endocentric compounds 612–13
  entity attributes 610–11
  headedness 614–15
  suffixes 613–14
  words for new things 615–16
 and place-names 612
 and preverbs 618–21
 and verbs:
  complex verbs 620
  creation of 616–18, 619–20
 and word-classes:
  nominals 609
  preverbs 609–10
Weldon, M S, and processing of compound
  words 263
Whorf, B L, and overt/covert categories 83 n4
Wiese, R, and coordination 193
Williams, E 423
 and French compounds 425
 and headedness 210
 and syntactic word 446
Wisniewski, E J 278
Witsuwit'en 544, 545, 546
Word and Paradigm approach 507
word families 205
 and processing of compound words 262–3
word formation 201
 and categories of 4
 as construction 202
 and endocentric compounds 201–2
 and problematic nature of term 323–4
 and word-formation schemas in hierarchical
  lexicon 203–9

see also onomasiology and word
  formation
Word Plus compounds, in Japanese 519–20
word recognition, and representation of
  complex words 256–7
 Augmented Addressed Morphology
  model 258
 decomposition 257–8
 Morphological Race model 258
 morphology 258–60
word-forms, and definition of 324
word-processing:
 and psycholinguistic approaches 260, 266,
  270–1
  constituent frequency 261–2
  frequency of related words 262–3
  influence of semantics 266–7
  integration 268–9
  meaning construction 269–70
  processing issues 267–8
  recent exposure to related items 263–5
  word family size 263
  word frequency 261
 and representation of complex words
  256–7
 Augmented Addressed Morphology
  model 258
 decomposition 257–8
 Morphological Race model 258
 morphology 258–60
words:
 and definition of 326
  problems with 345
 and nature of 180

X-bar theory 74–5
XP (maximal phrase for arbitrary category), and
  phrasal compounds 143–4

Yaruro 586
Yavitero, see Maipure-Yavitero
Yimas, and internal inflection 346–7
Yup'ik 5

Zamponi, R, and Maipure 585
Zimmer, K E 277, 576
Zwitserlood, P:
 and processing of compound words 261,
  264–5

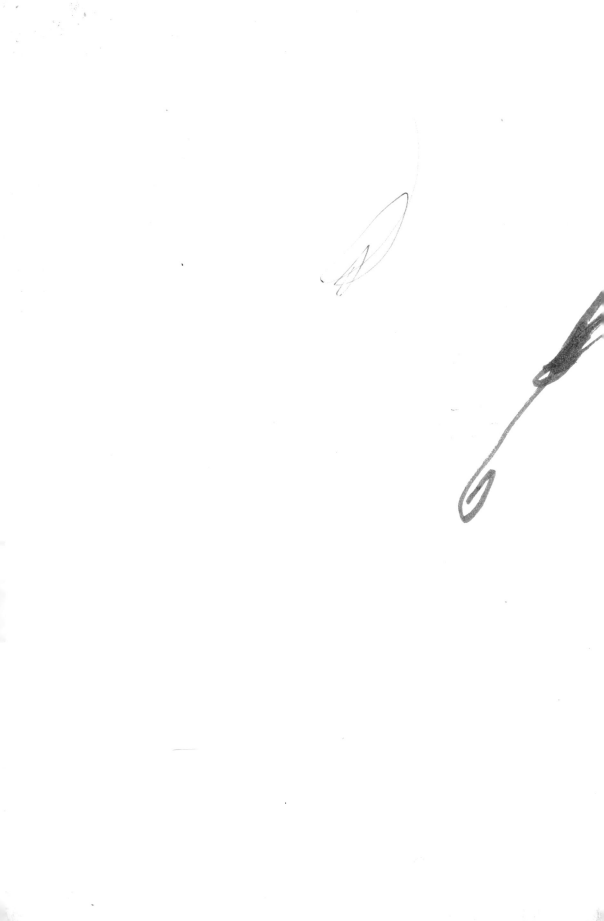